PERGAMON INTERNATIONAL LIBRARY
of Science, Technology, Engineering and Social

The 1000-volume original paperback library in
industrial training and the enjoyment of leisure
Publisher: Robert Maxwell, M.C.

China's Road to Development
SECOND EDITION

THE PERGAMON TEXTBOOK
INSPECTION COPY SERVICE

An inspection copy of any book published in the Pergamon International Library will gladly be sent
to academic staff without obligation for their consideration for course adoption or recommendation. Copies may be retained for a period of 60 days from receipt and returned if not suitable. When
a particular title is adopted or recommended for adoption for class use and the recommendation
results in a sale of 12 or more copies, the inspection copy may be retained with our compliments.
The Publishers will be pleased to receive suggestions for revised editions and new titles to be
published in this important International Library.

Other titles of interest

DJERASSI, N.
Glimpses of China from a Galloping Horse

ISLAM, N.
Development Strategy of Bangladesh

LALL, S.
Conflict and Bargaining

RODZINSKI, W.
A History of China, Volume 1

STREETEN, P.
The Limits of Development Research

WEST, J.
Alternatives in Development: Is Europe Responding to Third World Needs?

ZEMAN, Z. A. B. and ZOUBEK, J.
East–West Trade: The International Year Book

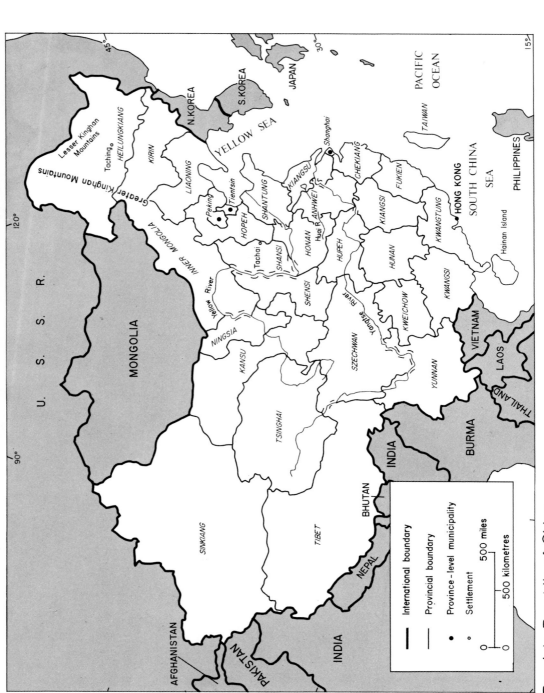

People's Republic of China

China's Road to Development

EDITED BY

NEVILLE MAXWELL

SECOND EDITION

PERGAMON PRESS

OXFORD · NEW YORK · TORONTO · SYDNEY · PARIS · FRANKFURT

U.K.	Pergamon Press Ltd., Headington Hill Hall, Oxford OX3 0BW, England
U.S.A.	Pergamon Press Inc., Maxwell House, Fairview Park, Elmsford, New York 10523, U.S.A.
CANADA	Pergamon of Canada, Suite 104, 150 Consumers Road, Willowdale, Ontario M2J 1P9 Canada
AUSTRALIA	Pergamon Press (Aust.) Pty. Ltd., PO Box 544, Potts Point, N.S.W. 2011, Australia
FRANCE	Pergamon Press SARL, 24 rue des Ecoles, 75240 Paris, Cedex 05, France
FEDERAL REPUBLIC OF GERMANY	Pergamon Press GmbH, 6242 Kronberg-Taunus, Pferdstrasse 1, Federal Republic of Germany

First edition 1976 (Special Issue of the Journal World Development, Volume 3; Nos. 7 and 8)

This edition 1979

British Library Cataloguing in Publication Data

China's Road to Development. —2nd ed.
—(Pergamon international library).
1. China—Social conditions
I. Maxwell, Neville II. 'World development'
309.2'3'0951   HN733.5   78-40343

ISBN 0-08-023140-3 (Hardcover)
ISBN 0-08-023139-X (Flexicover)

Printed in Great Britain by William Clowes & Sons Limited Beccles and London

GIFT
Other copies?
  Same ed?
    No
    Yes - how many? Location? Usage?

Diff ed?
  No
  Yes - how many? Location? Usage?

16

1984

Contents

Contributors

STEPHEN P. ANDORS, author of *China's Industrial Revolution: Politics, Planning, and Management, 1949 to the Present*, is associate professor of politics, Bard College, New York.

MARTIN BAILEY, author of *Freedom Railway*, is a free-lance journalist specializing in African affairs.

ROLAND BERGER, a writer on economic development and planning in China, is consultant to the 48 Group of British Traders with China.

DELIA DAVIN, author of *Womanwork: Women and the Party in Revolutionary China*, worked in Peking 1963-65 and 1975-76 as teacher and translator, and is a lecturer in economic and social history at the University of York.

JOHN G. GURLEY, author of *China's Economy and the Maoist Strategy*, is a professor of economics at Stanford University.

K. WILLIAM KAPP, author of *The Social Cost of Private Enterprise* (1950) and (with Lore Kapp) *Hindu Culture, Economic Development and Economic Planning in India*. Professor Kapp died in 1976, and the Kapp Foundation has been established in Geneva to continue his work.

YING-MAO KAU, author of *The People's Liberation Army and China's Nation-Building*, is a professor of politics at Brown University.

NEVILLE MAXWELL, author of *India's China War*, is a senior research officer at the Institute of Commonwealth Studies, Oxford University.

LEO A. ORLEANS, author of *Every Fifth Child*, is a China specialist with the US Library of Congress.

RUTH SIDEL, author of *Women and Child Care in China: A First-Hand Report*, teaches at the State University of New York at Purchase and the Bank Street College of Education, New York.

VICTOR W. SIDEL, co-author (with Ruth Sidel) of *Serve the People: Observations of Medicine in the People's Republic of China*, is professor of medicine and chairman of the department of social medicine at Montefiore Hospital.

JON SIGURDSON, author of *Rural Industrialization in China*, is a member of the Scandinavian Institute of Asian Studies, Copenhagen.

VACLAV SMIL, author of *China's Energy Sources*, is associate professor of geography at the University of Manitoba.

ROBIN THOMPSON, contributor to *Planning and Urbanism in China*, is a planning specialist with the London Borough of Greenwich.

PERCY TIMBERLAKE is editor of *China Trade and Economic Newsletter*.

JACK C. WESTOBY has published numerous papers on forestry subjects and was formerly with FAO.

Introduction*

NEVILLE MAXWELL

China has been a unique and striking exemplar of rapid economic development ever since the establishment of the People's Republic, but it is only quite recently that it has been widely noted as such. During the early 1950s, when the victors in China's long revolutionary civil war were labouring to lay the foundations of a new society in the rubble of the old, their successes were generally discounted. Sinologists explained the huge public works projects launched by the new government to control floods, which were characterized by the multitudinous use of human labour, as being typical of newly established dynasties, a new expression of the old "hydraulic despotism": the more openly political interpretations saw those vast popular efforts as signs of the grim efficiency of modern totalitarianism in organizing forced labour on a mass scale. The later 1950s began to indicate that China had passed out of its age of famines, but the reporting of China in the West depicted it as stricken still with endemic famine—and suggested indeed that those imagined disasters were something new, the result of Stalinism applied ruthlessly to a hitherto prosperous peasantry. By the 1960s China's progress in development was becoming undeniable, and a new theme became assertive in Western comment: that the material accomplishments of the Chinese Communists had been bought at a high cost in freedom and human dignity. Now that China is open to increasingly extensive travel by foreigners and intensive enquiry—often by specialists—the immensity of the achievements there is coming to be recognized, and the reservations about the "human cost" of the progress are being reappraised.

For those familiar with the profound human degradation experienced by the great bulk of the populations of the underdeveloped world, an experience of China is deeply encouraging: the squalor and misery of urban and rural slums, which can look so hopelessly unalterable, appear in the perspective of the changes wrought in a generation in China, circumstantial and temporary. As Jack Westoby writes in his paper on forestry, the Chinese have:

> challenged the very notion of a "point of no return". They have shown that rivers can be tamed, wind and water erosion halted, land rehabilitated, deserts made to bloom again. Moreover, they have shown that all this can be done without multi-million dollar loans, without battalions of professional foresters, without vast arrays of earth-moving equipment. The essential ingredients are few: human will-power, human muscle-power, and human ingenuity—plus a form of social/political organization which makes it possible for those human resources to be mobilized.

This collection is enlarged by seven additional papers from that published as a special issue of *World Development* for July/August 1975. Contributors to the original collection (except the late Professor Kapp) have updated and often extended their papers. The new papers are on industry (Andors), the new phase of the Tachai movement (Maxwell), women's impact on development (Davin), science (Orleans), forestry (Westoby), energy technology (Smil) and the army's role in China's deveopment (Kau). A further addition is a comprehensive bibliography on development in China compiled by Patricia Blair.

Against the evidence of China in the mass, peasantry and proletariat, lifted by their own efforts into economic sufficiency and confident consciousness of themselves as the "makers of history", it becomes more difficult to empathise with the tiny few of the old order, the élite deprived of status, the élite *manqué*. There are such people in China, who feel themselves deprived of status and frustrated of opportunity, and some of them are young—refugees to Hong Kong prove this. But what these miss, the vast mass of their compatriots never had; and what the great mass of the Chinese now have, all in China can have—material sufficiency and a conscious, creative and valued role to play in the consolidation and development of the new society.

The question now prompted by China's successes in development is whether those results can be achieved by roads other than that of revolution. It can first be noted that there is nothing miraculous, and little unexpected, in China's development techniques. The theory and intended structure of India's community development programme of the 1950s, for example, runs often in close parallel with the course taken by China's rural development, and if India's programme had been capable of implementation the Indian rural scene would, like China's, have been transformed into a linked network of autonomous cooperative villages. The idea of utilizing the unemployed and under-employed rural population in massive labour-intensive public works schemes, such as those China has used to tame and train her rivers, has often enough been mooted in South Asia; but the nearest approach found practicable has been the sterile, pauperiz-ing labour of famine-relief work. Cooperative farming, of course, has been tried again and again, but nowhere else, it seems, has it been as successful in increasing productivity and stabilizing rural society as it has in China.

John Gurley's paper on rural development traces the course of the "cooperativiza-tion" of the Chinese peasantry from tiny beginnings in the mutual aid teams into the very large groupings of cooperative villages that are the people's communes of today; and moves into close focus in examining a particular county in Hopei. A following paper narrows the focus still further and examines one small village in Shansi, Tachai—certainly the most famous village in the world, since it is familiar to every Chinese. Tachai is literally a show village, but it is argued in this paper that while its achievements have been exceptional in their extent, they have been typical of the kind of transformation achieved in varying degrees throughout rural China. And the exam-ple of Tachai is stimulating other villages to emulate and seek to outstrip its achieve-ments: this paper describes such emulation efforts in other villages in the same county. The second paper of the pair entitled "The Tachai Way" traces the enlargement of the "learn from Tachai" movement into its current scale, in which it has become a vast national effort to achieve the basic modernization of agriculture.

Jon Sigurdson's paper on rural industrialization deals with perhaps the fundamen-tal aspect of China's development strategy, the attempt to narrow the gap between country and city, peasant and worker, by taking industry into the countryside rather than bringing labour from the countryside into urban industry. Vaclav Smil shows how much of that rural industry is being powered by small, local plants, drawing on small hydrel sources or coal deposits, and notes the rapid spread of biogas in south China as a domestic fuel supply. Complementary to these is Robin Thompson's paper on city planning, on which the Chinese can proceed only because the drain from countryside into city which bedevils most governments in the underdeveloped world has been stemmed by the stabilization of rural society. The Sidels' paper on public health traces the means by which China has "made more rapid progress in health than any other society in a comparable period of time". As the Sidels say, the Chinese people appear to every observer now to be healthy, well-nourished and vigorous, while it is only twenty-five years since the country was "riddled with almost every known form of nutritional and infectious disease, with sickness and death visible on the streets". The expected consequence of such dramatic improvement in health standards, and therefore in life expectancy, would be a drastic up-surge in the rate of population increase; but what the Chinese call their "limited births planning programme" is now beginning to bite into the birth rate, and Leo Orleans concludes his paper on population control with the prediction that China "is likely to be the first developing nation of any size to reduce the growth of her population to below 1 per cent per year". Another paper by Orleans surveys China's approach to science.

Roland Berger's paper on the planning process in China, and on the "mass line" which engages the workers and peasants in the actual process of planning, illuminates some of the principles and practices which help to orchestrate the whole huge social effort. An addition to this substantially expanded paper deals with some of the chief features of China's financial policy and indicates how those promote economic and political objectives.

Percy Timberlake's paper analyses the principles by which the Chinese government directs its foreign trade; and Martin Bailey uses the Tanzania–Zambia railway project as a case study of China's style and declared purpose as a donor of development aid (this paper is updated only to early 1977).

There is a deliberate bias in this collection towards China's rural development, reflecting the primacy placed on agriculture as "the key link" in all China's development efforts. Stephen Andors' survey of China's approach to industrialization helps balance the emphasis on agriculture; and K. William Kapp's paper describes the lively Chinese concern for the environmental and polluting possibilities of industrial development, and traces the approach by which the Chinese seek to achieve "economic development and growth which includes the protection and improvement of her natural and social environment".

Delia Davin shows how the greatly increased demand for labour that has both expressed and engendered China's development at all stages was answered by, and encouraged, the entry of women into the workforce; and notes that social liberation has up to a point kept pace with the engagement of women as workers.

Ying-mao Kau deals, in his article on the People's Liberation Army, with one subject in which, on the face of it, it would seem that China has much to teach the Third World—the way to make a military establishment a positive factor, assisting development, rather than a drain upon it. But the catch is, of course, that the PLA is, at least in origin, a revolutionary army, while most Third World military forces may be politically closer to those of the Kuomintang, which were the Communists' enemy.

Professor Gurley asks the essential question in his paper: "What possible relevance has China's attempts at rural development for other underdeveloped countries?", and his own answer is, "probably ... very little". China, after all, is a revolutionary society, while revolution is precisely the fate which other underdeveloped countries are striving to avert through their development. China, furthermore, is not just attempting to develop her economy: she is consciously attempting to evolve a new pattern of human society, communitarian, socialist, drawing its vitality from the countryside rather than from the cities, and using what Marx called the "inexhaustible productive powers of modern industry" to create, ultimately, abundance for all. Such a social order requires a changed social ethic, and it appears that the change is being accomplished in China: the one commandment of the new ethic is "Serve the people", its complementary maxims are "Self-reliance" and "Mutual aid".

It is for that reason that, as Leo Orleans concludes in his paper, China cannot serve entirely as a model for developing countries: some techniques and emphases of Chinese development may be applied in different social systems, but the experience is not transferable as a whole because China's road to development began in revolutionary guerrilla warfare, and is evolving in a changed human environment. That does not mean, however, that any development specialist—or, indeed, anyone—can ignore China. If China cannot be taken as a model for development by the peasant societies of the underdeveloped world, then it is the more likely that she will be taken as a model for revolution.

Prefatory Note to Second Edition

A Bend in the Road: Right Turn or U-turn?

NEVILLE MAXWELL

China's road to development has followed a zigzag course. The alternate stretches can be signposted "right" or "left" in terms of the priority given to economic over political goals. On rightward stretches, under the direction of the group in the Chinese Communist Party whom Western observers call "moderates", priority is given to economic growth, and the implementation of socialist values is made a long-range objective. On the leftward stretches, when "radicals" are in control, economic development and progress towards socialism are seen as inseparable and mutually reinforcing. The differences between the two schools are more than tactical, since the radicals hold that policies which fail to consolidate and advance socialism for that reason undermine it—that policies which encourage the reassertion of individualism and its offspring, privilege and hierarchy, in effect work towards restoration and the emergence in China of a class society on Soviet lines. A fundamental ideological divide thus underlies differences over development strategy. This means that the changes of course, the angles in the zigzag, are abrupt and politically convulsive; while the current ideological expression will always repudiate that of the previous phase, and denigrate its economic achievements.

The phases of the People's Republic's first 30 years are well defined. The first, 1950–7, with economic planning formed by Soviet influence, carried China "rightward"; in the next, shaped by the Great Leap Forward, Mao and his supporters swung the whole Chinese economic system sharply to the left, under the principle that development was the task not of a technological elite but of the entire population. The Great Leap shattered ancient social forms and norms, and thrust China forward; but it ended in a stumble, and the "moderates" used the subsequent—and partly consequent—economic disruption to justify a veer back to the right. The changes introduced in January 1961 at the Chinese Communist Party's ninth plenum amounted to a "New Economic Policy", closely analogous to the Soviet NEP. In place of the Great Leap's egalitarianism and reliance upon popular initiative and commitment, the new policies emphasized market mechanisms, the importance of profits, the necessity of material incentives, the leadership of intellectuals and technologists, and the contribution to be made even by the remnant elite of the old order. "Egalitarianism" became a pejorative, and the continuance of inequality in the society not only tolerated, but the widening of differentials encouraged under echoes of Bukharin's "Enrich yourselfs!". One marked difference between this "NEP" and Lenin's was that it was not introduced as an expedient meant to be temporary, but rather charted as China's permanent way.

1

The "Great Proletarian Cultural Revolution" that broke out in 1966 was many things, but at bottom it was a struggle over development strategies by then perceived not as mere alternatives, but as contraries. The "NEP" line of 1961–5 was denounced by its opponents—the Maoists—as revisionist, serving the interest of a small minority composed of bureaucrats, technocrats, intellectuals and Party members, and working to separate and consolidate those groups into a new ruling class, a state bourgeoisie. The immense social convulsion of the Cultural Revolution, under the maxim that politics must be kept in command, swung China back onto the course pioneered in the phase of the Great Leap. The "NEP-men" in the leadership, Liu Shiao-chi and Teng Hsiao-ping at the summit, were anathematised and purged—but in the Maoist, not the Stalinist sense. Those with the longevity to survive waited, and their opportunity came with the decline and death of Mao Tse-tung in the middle-1970s.

No great social convulsion accompanied the reversal of course that followed the death of Mao. Gradually at first and then, over the turn of 1978–9, with astonishing confidence and speed, the line of the 1961–5 NEP phase was reasserted and consolidated. With a methodical thoroughness that left no aspect of life in China, no corner of the economy, unaffected, the principles of the Great Leap/Cultural Revolution phases were erased, and the institutions which were to have entrenched them, dismantled. At the heart of the change has been the overriding emphasis now placed on production, and the primacy given to material incentives as the key to human motivation. The spreading and sharpening inequalities that are the ineluctable consequence of such policies are not only accepted, but welcomed: the phrase equivalent to "Enrich yourself!" is, "Go first in achieving prosperity".[1] Prosperity is presented now not as the goal of socialism but as the reward for individual effort, and the private sector in agriculture which had been discouraged in the hope of making it vestigial and inert, is now encouraged and supported. The basic strategy for agricultural development is now that of the West's "green revolution"—"backing the best". Rather than seeking an across-the-board development of agriculture, at an accepted cost in pace, the new strategy is to concentrate available modern inputs in zones chosen for their potential responsiveness in expectation of quick pay-off. The accepted cost now is the widening of regional disparities that such a funnelling of resources inevitably entails.

How fundamental the change is in agricultural policy, and how far-reaching the extent of its political implications, are powerfully illustrated in the repudiation of the exemplary role of the model village of Tachai. It is not a matter only of Tachai no longer being held up as a positive example—Tachai is now being held up as a negative example, as the vehicle for a "gross violation of the Chinese Communist Party's current rural policies".[2] The village's leaders are critized for arrogance (pointing to the probable purging of Vice-Premier Chen Yung-kuei), their practice is repudiated as ultra-left; and the sole positive element found in the Tachai example is the virtue of "self-reliance and hard work". This, by ignoring the political context of Tachai's achievements, distorts the meaning of Mao's injunction, "In agriculture, learn from Tachai". Tachai stood for increased productivity achieved through the heightened social consciousness of a community—in a phrase, for "Politics in command"—and its repudiation is another expression of the primacy now given to production in the name of "modernization". It is as if the impulse towards community and equality—once again condemned as "egalitarianism"—is seen as an impediment to productivity.

The primacy given to material incentives is expressed in a rigorous implementation of reward according to labour in the countryside; while in industry the elaborate structure of bonuses and prizes, fines and penalties that was swept away in the Cultural Revolution has been reconstituted. So far as industrial organization is concerned, the favoured model is Yugoslavia, with management given independence to go all out for higher productivity and greater profitability.

All of this means that the papers in this collection have to some extent been out-dated—or at least they are now out of phase. China is now on a "road to development" sharply changed from what is described in this volume, and some of the contributors might feel they erred—as the Editor certainly did in his writing on the Tachai model—in treating as stable and consolidated policies that now appear to have been temporary. Most contributors were able to take account before publication of the changes that began to appear after the death of Mao; but the full sweep of those changes, amounting in many areas to reversal, emerged only after the deadline for revisions had passed. Even if it turns out that this volume is—and remains—"out of date", however, it will retain its value as an account and analysis of a development strategy which evolved new forms for social action, and which achieved remarkable advances in most sectors of the economy of the most populous of the world's peasant societies. The possibility remains, moreover, that China will change its "road to development" once again, with another "Cultural Revolution" that will bring about a reassertion of the social and political principles which formed the strategy in the 1966-76 phase which is, basically, the subject of this volume.
indeed, are the premises of the Chinese revolution itself.

Whether another such reversal is to be expected—or to be hoped for—must depend upon what exactly it was that happened in China upon the decline and death of Mao. There are many interpretations, of course, but they can be grouped into two main schools. One, including the main stream of the Western China-watching community of specialists, sees in post-Mao China's "about-face in economic policies" the casting-off of "ideological rigidity" in favour of "a vigorous, growth-oriented pragmatism"—the phrases are the American CIA's.[3] In that view, the Teng Hsiao-ping leadership in its emphasis on production, its toleration of re-emergent status and privilege, is casting China in the familiar, relatively safe, and potentially profitable form of an aspirant consumerism.

The other main group describes the same symptoms in political terms, diagnosing the entry of the Chinese revolution into its Thermidore: or, as some Marxists put it, the capture of power, through *coup d'état,* by "revisionists" whose role it will be to structure a Chinese version of the Soviet Union—industrially powerful, technologically developed, but financially dependent and socially polarized between an elite that has become a ruling class and a relatively backward mass of population neglected and exploited. Since that interpretation was first elaborated[4] the evidence upon which it was based has, if anything, strengthened. The repudiation of the Cultural Revolution is complete, and has become almost open. The cipher in which attacks on Mao Tse-tung are formulated becomes progressively more transparent,[5] suggesting that "Lin Piao and the Gang of Four", the declared target, are surrogates for Mao. Most tellingly, perhaps, and most reminiscent of political development in the Soviet Union, the key concept of "class struggle" is being steadily watered down. Mao's injunction, "Never forget class struggle", was the essence of his ideological bequest, coupled with the warning that those who would undo the Chinese revolution were still—or again—within the Communist leadership. And the qualifications now being attached to that concept are tantamount to its cancellation: "Never forget class struggle—but we should not go in for it artificially" is the new formulation.[6]

If that interpretation of post-Mao China is confirmed by continuing developments, then the "right-turn" will have become a U-turn. Foreseeing just such events, Mao predicted that the vast, politicized majority of the Chinese people would inevitably reassert themselves, insisting again upon their interests, and not those of a small minority, being the object of development. But whether such reassertion will be possible in the absence of his own towering leadership, must be questionable.

NOTES

1   Hsinhua News Agency, in *People's Daily*, February 19, 1978, described "the newly-adopted policy of encouraging those peasants who are more efficient or who have better conditions to go first in achieving prosperity. The policy represents a further move to eliminate egalitarianism . . ." Hsinhua, London, February 19, 1979.
2   The Party committees of Shansi and of Hsiyang county reported in Hsinhua, London, March 8, 1978.
3   *China: In Pursuit of Economic Modernization,* a research paper of the Central Intelligence Agency's National Foreign Assessment Center, December 1978.
4   Its most powerful formulation is Charles Bettelheim's in *China Since Mao,* by Neil Burton and Charles Bettelheim, New York and London, Monthly Review Press, 1978.
5   The nearest approach so far to open criticism of Mao lay in the repudiation of a critique of a play of the early 1960s, *Hai Rui Dismissed from Office,* and the play's rehabilitation and re-staging. The play was an aesopian attack on Mao, the critique, by Yao Wen-yuan, was a counter-attack written at Mao's instigation and with his close editing—and has long been seen both in China and in the West as the opening gun of the Cultural Revolution. See *People's Daily* articles January 26, February 22, 1978, reported in Hsinhua, London, same dates; and *Peking Review,* No. 10, 1979.
6   For example, articles in *People's Daily* warning against "over-estimating the gravity of the class struggle in the socialist period" (February 22, 1979); and "we should not go in artificially for class struggle . . ." (March 9, 1979), Hsinhua, London, February 23 and March 9, 1979.

Rural Development in China 1949–75, and the Lessons to be Learned from it

JOHN G. GURLEY

The precarious position of the Chinese peasants down through the ages and the oppressive conditions under which they laboured are too well known to require much comment from me. One can read at length about their diseases, their illiteracy, their superstitions and fatalistic attitudes, the natural disasters and periodic famines that all but wiped them out, in Han (206 B.C.–A.D. 220), T'ang (A.D. 618–906), or Sung (A.D. 906–1279) records, and indeed right down to yesterday.

Nevertheless, the records also reveal, if one examines them closely, an ingenious peasantry producing a substantial surplus during most of this long period, not of course for itself, but mostly for the sustenance and pleasures of a few people who made up the ruling classes—the Emperor and his family and retainers, bureaucrats, landlords, money-lenders, and military officers. This small but powerful ruling group pumped the surplus out of the countryside through taxes, rents, interest, corvée labour, enslavement, extortion, and by other means fair and foul. It may well be that, on the average over these many centuries, one third of what this peasantry produced was taken away from it for the enjoyment and support of less than two per cent of the population. What was left to the peasants was usually just enough for their survival, but from time to time not enough even for that. Undernourishment was common, starvation not unusual.

Let R. H. Tawney, who with much acumen observed the Chinese peasants in the early 1930s, have the last word:

> Exaggeration is easy. Privation is one thing, poverty to the point of wretchedness—*la misère*—another. A sturdy and self-reliant stock may grow in a stony soil. But, when due allowance has been made for the inevitable misconceptions, it is difficult to resist the conclusion that a large proportion of Chinese peasants are constantly on the brink of actual destitution. They are, so to say, a propertied proletariat, which is saved—when it is saved—partly by its own admirable ingenuity and fortitude, partly by the communism of the Chinese family, partly by reducing its consumption of necessaries and thus using up its physical capital ...
>
> It is true, however, that, over a large area of China, the rural population suffers horribly through the insecurity of life and property. It is taxed by one ruffian who calls himself a general, by another, by a third, and, when it has bought them off, still owes taxes to the government; in some places actually more than twenty years' taxation has been paid in advance. It is squeezed by dishonest officials. It must cut its crops at the point of the bayonet, and hand them over without payment to the local garrison, though it will starve without them. It is forced to grow opium in defiance of the law, because its military tyrants can squeeze heavier taxation from

5

opium than from rice or wheat, and make money, in addition, out of the dens where it is smoked. It pays blackmail to the professional bandits in its neighbourhood; or it resists, and, a year later, when the bandits have assumed uniform, sees its villages burned to the ground ...

There are districts in which the position of the rural population is that of a man standing permanently up to the neck in water, so that even a ripple is sufficient to drown him. The loss of life caused by the major disasters is less significant than the light which they throw on the conditions prevailing even in normal times over considerable regions.[1]

I. EXPLANATIONS OF PERSISTENT POVERTY BEFORE 1949

There were of course reasons for the persistence of this deprivation and misery. The conventional explanation is that, even with the highest efficiency in carrying out the best-intentioned policies to alleviate rural poverty, the job would have been a most difficult one for any government. During the past century, for example, successive governments had to contend with several rebellions, civil wars, the Japanese invasions, and the continued encroachment of other foreign imperialist powers on the economy. The argument continues that, when one considers all of this turmoil within the context of how widespread and deeply embedded poverty was in the society, it is no wonder that very little was accomplished.

While this argument has some validity, it represents a very narrow view of the social forces at work in this period. For the disruptive events themselves emanated partly from the failure of the Chinese authorities to alleviate the poverty. It was a two-way street. The battles that went on were fed by the rural misery, but these struggles in turn contributed to further political disintegration and so to a growing inability of governments to shore up the crumbling base.

However, even with this reformulation, the foregoing is only a part of the total story. Most of the rest of it has to do with the "best intentions" assumed above. Social scientists these days usually suppose that all governments really want economic development, and, if they do not achieve it, then it must be because the problems are unusually difficult to solve, or that solutions take a rather long time to work themselves out. Persistence and technical knowledge are what is required for success. This supposition, however, does not adequately take account of the class structures of societies, the often conflicting aims that exist among the various classes, and the class nature of "success" and "failure". When poverty is looked at from the standpoint of the ruling classes, it may not be a failure of the system at all but rather a prerequisite for the continuation of their accumulation of wealth, their privileges, and their social, political, and economic domination of the society.

This is partly because poverty is often the carcass left from wealth acquisition; or, at best, it is the stagnant backwaters of society, not yet touched by a development process that stresses private profit-making and hence efficiency and "building on the best". But poverty persists also because it is closely associated with peasant characteristics which are highly supportive of the existing class structures and hence of the privileges and wealth of the dominant classes. I refer to the peasants' illiteracy, passivity, obedience, fatalism; to their lack of awareness of the world around them and therefore to their propensity for mythical and spiritual explanations of personal hardships and disasters;

to their lack of organization, their willingness to work hard for very little; to their being easy set-ups for all sorts of manipulation by their "superiors".

A thorough-going programme of economic development, which is spread widely and reaches deeply into the structure of society, is a dangerous thing to ruling classes, for it tends to undermine the very attributes of the masses of people that nourish the wealthy and powerful. Such a programme awakens people, and it is often best that they doze; it mobilizes people for gigantic economic efforts, and such organization can be turned into political subversion; it sweeps away illusions, but may open their eyes to the causes of their own oppression.

Furthermore, any serious economic development programme that involves industrialization within an agrarian and commercial society threatens existing class structures by creating new economic bases from which arise new social classes, and weakens the economic foundations which support the present dominant classes. Economic development stirs up the society, establishing new classes that compete with the old order, socially, politically, and economically.

These considerations were applicable to China prior to 1949. The peasant misery of that country during the century preceding the Communist victory was due not only to the inherent difficulty, during a century of violence, of raising millions of people out of abject poverty, but, more important, to the almost complete lack of interest by the Chinese governments and foreign investors in doing any such thing. The peasants remained poor in large part because poverty served a purpose; or, at best, because it did not interfere with the wealthier classes extracting the economic surplus from the countryside.

II. CHANGES IN THE COUNTRYSIDE SINCE 1949

That degrading and humiliating sort of peasant misery is now gone from China, which is not to say, of course, that a rural paradise has miraculously arisen. Chinese peasants are still very poor, especially by the standards of industrial countries; the struggle against nature goes on, and some Chinese peasants every now and then find themselves on the losing end; and there are still plenty of problems to overcome and small areas of severe poverty to eliminate.

However, the overriding economic fact about people in China today is that for over twenty years, for the first time in their lives, almost all have had a decent standard of living in the basic necessities—food, clothing, housing, health care, education, culture, and recreation. There is no longer starvation; no longer infanticide, cannibalism, selling children into virtual slavery; no longer blank ignorance. The Chinese now have what is in effect an insurance policy against pestilence, famine, and other disasters. They have all risen together; it is difficult to see that anyone has been left far behind. And the rural areas are alive with water-control projects, small industries, transportation and communication networks, and plans for everything else that promise fuller lives for the peasants, who, while not prosperous, are prospering, awake, and optimistic. Some of the gains of the Chinese economy since 1952 are shown in Table 1.

How did this happen? I shall first present some social and political, as well as economic, reasons for this rural transformation, reasons which I believe to be basic to any understanding of what has happened in China. After that, I shall turn to a closer look at the economic policies that have changed the countryside.

TABLE 1. *Some output data of the People's Republic of China:*
selected years, 1952–75
(in million metric tons unless otherwise specified)

	Grain	Steel	Crude oil	Chemical fertilizer	Cotton	Industrial production index 1957=100	Cement	Coal	Electric power (m kwh)
1952	154	1.4	0.4	0.2	1.3	48	2.9	66	7.3
1957	185	5.4	1.5	0.8	1.6	100	6.9	131	19.3
1959	165	13.4	3.7	1.9	1.2	173	12.3	300	42.0
1965	210	12.5	11.0	7.6	1.9	199	15.3	220	42.0
1969	220	16.0	20.4	11.3	1.8	266	18.9	258	60.0
1975	270	26.0	74.5	27.9	2.3	502	40.0	427	121.0

Sources: CIA, *People's Republic of China: Handbook of Economic Indicators*, August 1976. The grain figure for 1975 is from US Department of Agriculture, *People's Republic of China Agricultural Situation*, May 1977, p.3.

III. PREREQUISITES FOR THE TRANSITION

The Chinese peasants have been able to improve their lives over the past two decades because they carried out a revolution of blood and fire, the only way which enabled them to break the bonds that retarded their economic progress. This violent revolution was necessary but not sufficient to transform an agrarian society into an industrial one. The following five developments, however, established a political-social-economic framework for such a transition.

1. After 1949 the Chinese Communist Party fashioned itself and a government into organs that represented the masses and *wanted* thorough-going and penetrating economic development for the purpose of improving the lives of almost everyone. This, perhaps, is the most important thing that one can say in this regard. The Communist Party did not represent and work on behalf of a small group of merchants and traders, or a class of landed proprietors and money-lenders, or foreign interests allied with domestic entrepreneurs; instead it gained victory through a nation-wide revolution of peasants against domestic oppression and foreign imperialism, and it continued to be a party representing the interests of these masses of poor people. That may not be exactly an *economic* determinant of peasant prosperity, but there is nothing more important.

2. The government and party proved to be efficient, honest, and well organized in carrying out its development programmes. Some inefficiencies occurred, some bribes were taken, and some confusion sown, but on the whole the party and its cadres performed remarkably well in translating plans into actions.

3. The party demonstrated its ability to mobilize the enthusiasm and energy of the masses with worthy and inspiring goals; to educate and give good health and improved nutrition to the people, enabling them to pursue these goals. It liberated women and youth from their previous oppression, and liberated most people from debilitating beliefs in "ghosts and monsters".

4. Through land reform, nationalization of industry, and cooperativization in the countryside, along with good use of monetary and fiscal powers, the government and

party generated a high savings rate, and with a fair amount of efficiency used the savings for investment across the board, in heavy industry, light industry, and agriculture.

5. The USSR aided China substantially during the 1950s. The bulk of this "aid" was Soviet exports for Chinese goods (rather than Chinese securities), but the Soviet goods consisted of over 150 complete industrial plants accompanied by thousands of Soviet technicians. Soviet aid was designed to establish, in a short period of time, the industrial base for a full-scale economic development effort. It remains, despite the subsequent rancour between the two countries, as an outstanding example of how one country can help another, if it really wants to.

IV. SPECIFIC POLICIES IN RURAL AREAS: 1949–75

The developments just described established the general environment in which specific economic policies were fashioned and carried out for rural improvement. These economic policies, however, were not neatly laid out in the early 1950s, all ready for sequential implementation later on. Instead, they have had at times an *ad hoc* nature; they have been fought over at the leadership level; and some have not worked well and have had to be replaced. But, even allowing for this, the policies in general have achieved a remarkable transformation in the rural areas.

These policies can be grouped into four categories: land reform (1949–52), collectivization-communization (1955–9), capital formation for agriculture (1960–75), and the alteration of terms of trade between agriculture and industry in favour of agriculture and the peasants (1953–75). The first set of policies redistributed wealth and income from the rich to the poor, eliminated the former ruling classes and, by so doing, raised both peasant consumption and rural savings. The second set of policies raised output in the rural areas mainly by encouraging better utilization of the labour supply. The third set further boosted agricultural output by increasing capital goods and other inputs available to this sector and by establishing small industries almost everywhere in the countryside. Finally, throughout most of the period, the terms of trade were steadily turned in favour of the peasants by the raising of prices paid by the state for agricultural products and the lowering of prices of many goods purchased by the peasants. In addition, the tax burden on the peasants was steadily reduced. Thus, the masses of peasants initially gained control; their labour was then better utilized; increasing agricultural inputs were next acquired by them; and they gradually gained throughout the period by more favourable terms of trade.

The following four sections consider, without much detail, these four sets of agricultural policies. Section IX illustrates, as an example of some of the above policies, the transformation of one rural county in China, Tsunhua, located about 100 miles from Peking. Finally, the possible relevance of all this for other poor countries is taken up in the last section.

V. THE NATURE AND IMPACT OF LAND REFORM: 1949–52

The primary objectives of the Agrarian Reform Law of 1950 were to eliminate the feudal landlord system in the countryside, improve the lives of the poor, and develop agricultural production as a precondition for the country's industrialization. Land reform took not only land from landlords and some rich peasants, but also their draft animals, farm implements, houses, and grain—and redistributed them all to middle and poor peasants. Altogether, 300 million peasants received 700 million *mou* of land[2] (about 45 per cent of total arable land) formerly owned by perhaps 10–12 million persons; of all land redistributed, two-thirds was taken from landlords and one-third from rich peasants; two-thirds of this land was given to poor peasants and one-third to middle peasants. Many rich peasants retained much of their land and other assets (but not their hired labourers) and so, even after the reform, were on the whole still better off than the middle and poor peasants. Further, since the land reform regulations did not forbid the resale or the renting of land afterwards, some of the redistributed land gravitated back to the rich peasants. Landlords, on the other hand, as a class, were wiped out by mass peasant struggles against them, confiscation, and sometimes execution.

It is important to stress that land reform was not simply legislation passed and carried out from above, for it was much more than that. It was a revolutionary movement involving millions of peasants struggling against their former oppressors, gaining confidence and understanding in the process, and taking actions themselves against the landlords which committed them to new lives and new ways, and which made the entire movement quite irreversible. Keith Buchanan quotes Liu Shao-ch'i on this as follows:

> In carrying out the land reform our Party did not take the simple and easy way of merely relying on administrative decrees and of "bestowing" land on the peasants. For three solid years after the establishment of the People's Republic of China, we applied ourselves to awakening the class consciousness of the peasants ... We consider the time spent was absolutely necessary. Because we had used such a method the peasant masses stood up on their own feet, got themselves organized, closely followed the lead of the Communist Party and the People's Government, and took the reins of government and the armed forces in the villages firmly into their hands. ... The broad masses of the awakened peasants held that exploitation, whether by landlords or by rich peasants, was a shameful thing. Conditions were thus created which were favourable to the subsequent socialist transformation of agriculture and helped shorten to a great extent the time needed to bring about agricultural cooperation.[3]

A few results of the land reform are shown in Table 2, which also contains definitions of terms used above.

The land reform, through its redistribution of rural assets, not only broke the domination of the landlord–gentry class and transferred power for the first time to poor and middle peasants, but it also immediately raised the consumption level of most peasants and at the same time increased rural savings available for investment. These were results principally of wealth redistribution and not of gains in total output flowing from land reform, for such gains were not substantial, though there were output gains that came from the cessation of civil strife and the reconstruction and repair of dikes, irrigation canals, and equipment. Much of the increase in rural savings was captured by the state for investment purposes. Thus, land reform contributed in a major way to the higher investment ratios of these earlier years.

The ratio of net investment to national income rose rapidly from perhaps 1–2 per cent in 1949 to around 20 per cent in 1953. After that, despite the cooperativization

TABLE 2. *Some results of land reform in China: 1949–52*

	Percentage of households	Share of crop area owned		Average crop area owned	
		Before reform %	After reform %	Before reform *mou*	After reform *mou*
Landlords	2.6	28.7	2.1	116.10	11.98
Rich peasants	3.6	17.7	6.4	35.75	26.30
Middle peasants	35.8	30.2	44.8	15.81	18.53
Poor peasants and farm labourers	57.1	23.5	46.8	6.25	12.14
Other	0.9	0.0	0.0		

Source. Peter Schran, *The Development of Chinese Agriculture, 1950-1959* (University of Illinois Press, 1969) pp. 21, 22, and 25.

Households were classified by amounts of income and wealth, sources of income, and size of household.

Landlords: Owners of land not engaged in labour, who depend on exploitation for their livelihood—that is, land rent, money-lending, hiring of labour, etc.

Rich peasants: Similar to landlords, except that exploitation chiefly took the form of hiring long-term labourers and it constituted somewhat lesser shares of their total incomes.

Middle peasants: Owned all or a portion of the land they worked, or perhaps none at all. They depended for a living wholly or mainly on their own labour.

Poor peasants: Rented land for cultivation and were exploited by others through rent and interest.

Farm labourers: Owned neither land nor farm implements; depended wholly or mainly on the sale of their labour for their living.

1 *mou* of land=one-sixth of an acre or one-fifteenth of a hectare.

drive in the countryside during 1955–6, the ratio rose very little more until 1958–9, when communes were introduced. Thus, the initial rapid increase in saving and investment came in the very early years of the period 1949–57.

Land reform had much to do with this, for it redistributed wealth and hence income from the rich to the poor, and much of what was redistributed was captured by the state in savings, through taxation, profits of state enterprises, differential pricing, and private savings. The land reform eliminated the luxury consumption of the rich, raised by lesser amounts the basic consumption of the poor, and made much of the rest available to the state for investment.

Victor Lippit has computed that the income flow to the rural propertied classes, in rent, interest, and farm business profits, plus net taxes to the state, were as much as 19 per cent of national income, just a decade before land reform.[4] This income flow, which was almost entirely consumed, was redirected downward, after land reform, by rural-asset redistribution to middle and poor peasants. From there it found its way into investment via several channels: self-financed investment in agriculture; increased tax payments to the state; increased profits of government and private enterprises, which wholly or partly reverted to the state budget; increased profits of state purchasing agencies (mostly grain purchases); and increased financial asset holdings of peasants, which released real resources for investment, financed by borrowed funds from the banking system. Land reform probably contributed over one-third of the total savings in 1952 (and, presumably, in later years, too) to the investment programme.

It bears repeating: the Chinese land reform did not *give* land to the poor peasants. It encouraged them to organize themselves to *take* it, and in the process to crush their former oppressors. This was the prerequisite for later socialist development in the countryside, for, without it, the old class structures and wealth ownership patterns would have been regenerated by the persistence of old attitudes and of institutions favourable to the rich.[5]

VI. RURAL COLLECTIVIZATION AND LABOUR MOBILIZATION: 1952–9

After land reform, the Chinese leaders, in four stages, transformed small private holdings into large-scale communes. The first step was the encouragement of mutual aid teams, which were units of several households, the function of which was to pool privately-owned resources in order to compensate for shortages of labour and other inputs during the rush seasons of planting and harvesting. This was at first done on a temporary, seasonal basis, the teams being dissolved at the end of the planting or harvesting period, but later some of the teams were organized on a permanent, year-round basis. These permanent teams were somewhat larger than the others and often held some capital goods and animals as common property. By 1954 almost 10 million mutual aid teams, about half of them seasonal and half permanent, were in operation, and they comprised 58 per cent of all peasant households.

The second stage was the formation of elementary agricultural producers' cooperatives (APCs), some of which were organized as early as 1950 but most of which were formed in the second half of 1955. They comprised several mutual aid teams of around 30 to 40 households, that is, a village. Land and other capital goods continued to be privately owned, but these assets were now pooled in the APCs for use according to annual plans prepared by central management. Peasants were compensated according to their labour and their contributions of land, implements, animals, etc., labour however, usually claiming most of the output. By early 1956, almost all peasant families were in these APCs.

The third stage, in 1956–7, saw the consolidation of elementary APCs into advanced APCs, each comprising several small villages or perhaps one large village, varying in size from 100 to 300 households. In the advanced APCs, peasants held title to a share in the collective equity, and they no longer had any private claim on their former holdings of land and other capital goods. Accordingly, net earnings were distributed to the peasants only on the basis of work done, and the earnings withheld, including those contributed by capital goods, were collectively owned. The advanced APCs, owing to their large size, were able to withhold larger percentages of income for collective purposes. Similarly, the payment of the agricultural tax became a collective obligation, whereas it had been an individual responsibility in the elementary APCs.

In the final step, during 1958–9, people's communes were established. The commune, as the Chinese have stated, "is the basic unit of the social structure of our country, combining industry, agriculture, trade, education and the military. At the same time, it is the basic organization of social power". Filling this out somewhat more, the communes were organized to provide larger, more efficient units for carrying out large-scale water-control projects and the building of native-type factories and workshops throughout the countryside. They were organized, moreover, to provide additional labour through the establishment of communal mess halls and other communal services which released many women from household tasks. The communes also became the basic governmental unit; they ran factories, schools, banks, controlled their own militia; and they served to weaken the patriarchal family unit and, in general, peasants' identification only with very small groups. Further, a half-wage, half-supply system was set up, which provided free supplies of many of the necessities to peasants quite aside from whether they worked or not, the remainder of income being distributed according to work done.

The communes were quickly organized during the Great Leap Forward, which was an all-out effort by the Chinese to industrialize rural areas, to build a large iron and steel industry, to grow record agricultural crops, to raise the education, health, and cultural levels of the peasants, and to catch up within 15 years to the leading industrial nations of the world.

The objective is to build China in the shortest possible time into a great socialist country with modern industry, modern agriculture, and modern science and culture. ... To carry out our socialist construction at a high speed naturally requires constant readjustment to the relations of production and constant adaptation of the superstructure to the developing economic base. The fundamental thing, however, is to develop the productive forces rapidly. ... The objectives are to abolish exploitation of man by man, and to build a classless society in which the difference between city and countryside, between mental and manual work will disappear and the ideal of "from each according to his ability, to each according to his needs," will become the order of the day.[6]

Within a short time, over 26,000 communes were organized, each containing around 5,000 households on the average, but the range was from 1,500 to 10,000. The former advanced APCs became 500,000 production brigades within the communes, and the former elementary APCs became 3 million production teams.

To summarize, during the 1950s the basic organizational unit in the countryside was enlarged from individual peasant households, to mutual aid teams (at first temporary and later permanent), to production teams (former elementary APCs), to production brigades (former advanced APCs), and finally to communes. The basis for the distribution of income also changed from distribution according to work and asset ownership, to distribution according to work only, to distribution according to work and needs; and, at the same time, the value of a peasant's work points was based on the work done by increasingly larger groups.

Some of these advances, however, were reversed in the early 1960s, during the downturn of economic activity, when Maoist ideology waned. Communes were greatly increased in number and so reduced in size of population; decision-making authority was moved down to lower units; income distribution by need was de-emphasized; communal services were greatly reduced; and private incentives in several forms were restored.

The enlargement of rural units and the collectivization which accompanied it during the 1950s no doubt, on balance, raised the standard of living of the masses of peasants, but the policies probably did not increase by much the economic surplus from agriculture until the Great Leap Forward in 1958–9. There were both positive and negative features of this series of rural programmes, but I shall concentrate only on the principal advantage gained by the economy from the rural policies just described, namely the fuller and more efficient use of the rural labour force.

Throughout the 1950s, the percentage of the rural population comprising the labour force tended to decline sharply owing to the rapid absorption of children of school age by the school system. However, since children did not work the long hours of adults or as effectively, this downward tendency was less in actual output than it was in sheer numbers of workers. In any case, it remained simply a tendency, for it was more than offset by the rapid growth of women in the labour force during the 1950s as rural collectivization and communization proceeded.

These rural policies also induced increases in the total number of days worked each year by greatly raising the number of labour-days for each employed peasant in general and for each female in particular. The total expansion effect, coming from the increased employment of women and the greater number of days worked for each employed person, was extremely large, as can be seen in Table 3. In fact, under normal circumstances, total annual labour-days would have risen by no more than 2–3 billion from 1950 to 1959. Instead, the rise was 29 billion. Furthermore, Peter Schran believes that even this might well understate the full impact of communization in this regard.

TABLE 3. *Rural population, employment, and labour-days:*
1950, 1955, 1957 and 1959

	(1) Peasant population	(2) Total employed peasants	(3) Average annual labour-days	(4) Total annual labour-days	(5) Index of col. (4) 1952=100
1950	479.7m	22.6m	119.0	26.5b	97.5
1955	523.8	243.3	121.0	29.4	108.4
1957	541.3	260.3	159.5	41.5	152.8
1959	539.6	309.1	189.0	58.4	215.0
Collectivization, 1955–7	+17.5	+17.0	+38.5	+12.1	+44.4
Communization, 1957–9	−1.7	+48.8*	+29.5	+16.9	+62.2

Source. Peter Schran, *The Development of Chinese Agriculture, 1950–1959,* Chapter 3
*Increase owing largely to increased mobilization of women and the part-time employment of school children.

TABLE 4, *Indices of the structure of rural employment by labour-days:*
1950, 1955, 1957 and 1959
(Total labour-days in 1952=100)

	Total labour-days	Farm work	Subsidiary work*	Corvée, basic construction	Other†
1950	97.5	75.2	19.2	3.1	0
1955	108.4	83.0	21.0	3.9	0.4
1957	152.8	113.4	25.8	9.7	3.8
1959	215.0	151.7	29.5	12.3	21.4

Source. Peter Schran, op. cit., p.75.
*Includes gathering activities, domestic handicrafts, administration, professional services, care of private plots and livestock.
†Includes collective affairs, communal services, and communal industry.

The increased labour was employed not only in basic farm work and in subsidiary occupations, but increasing amounts of it were set to work on large-scale water-control projects, basic construction, and rural industrial efforts; and much labour was increasingly used for communal services—administration, cultural activities, medical care, education, etc. These data are in Table 4. Consequently, this mobilization of additional labour-days served to raise not only agricultural input but also capital formation in the countryside, and it also increased the communal services offered to the peasants. Instead of fiddling away their time individually during off-seasons, the peasants were mobilized into large units for community and area projects.

The gains in total labour-days worked, however, did not result in commensurate increases in total output, for other inputs did not keep pace with labour inputs, and so resulted in diminishing marginal returns to labour, the additional labour was sometimes employed inefficiently and at tasks with quite low returns, and there was some loss of incentives to work hard during 1958–9. Nevertheless, total production in the rural areas did increase considerably throughout most of the 1950s, and capital formation made some impressive gains toward the end of the period. A few indicators of rural activity during the 1950s are recorded in Table 5.

TABLE 5. *Some indicators of rural activity: 1952–9*

	Grain output (millions of metric tons)	Area of irrigation (millions of *mou*)	Gross value of agricultural output (billions of yuan)
1952	154	320	48.3†
1953	157	330	49.9
1954	161	350	51.6
1955	175	370	55.5
1956	183	480	58.3
1957	186	520	60.4
1958	250(200)*	1,000	67.1‡
1959	270(170)*	1,070	78.3‡

Source. Nai-Ruenn Chen, *Chinese Economic Statistics* (Aldine, 1967), pp. 338–9, 289, 364.
*These are Western estimates, which are probably fairly accurate.
†Figures in this column are in 1952 prices.
‡Figures in 1957 prices.

VII. INDUSTRIALIZATION OF THE RURAL AREAS: 1960–75

Adverse weather conditions which lasted for three years ("the worst in a century"), the pull-out of the Soviet advisers, and disincentives of peasants arising out of the extremes to which some Great Leap policies were pushed—all of these combined in 1959–60, first to reduce agricultural output, including the commercial crops which fed light industry, then to hit heavy industry as the Soviet advisers withdrew with their blueprints and expertise. By late 1960 and early 1961, the economy had been damaged so severely that the Chinese leadership (probably no longer dominated by Mao), in the face of a decline of national output of around 20–5 per cent, altered its economic priorities to place agriculture first, light industry second, and heavy industry last. This officially changed the priorities that had been established under Soviet-type planning during the 1950s, in which heavy industry was the centrepiece and agriculture was relatively neglected so far as state investment funds were concerned.[7]

These new rankings, however, did not reflect any diminished interest in industrialization. Rather they served notice that the top priority would go to those industrial pursuits that directly served agriculture, either by producing modern inputs for that sector or by processing output coming from it. Industries farther out would be emphasized to the extent that they directly served these inner firms, and so on. Increasingly, as the 1960s proceeded, the countryside was expected to establish not only the small industries that directly served agriculture but also, whenever possible small basic industries such as iron and steel making, cement making, coal-mining, etc. By the end of the decade, the economy was better able than it had been to support agriculture both with the output of large-scale industry in the urban areas and with tens of thousands of small, indigenous industries throughout the countryside. Thus, the effort was redirected from the mobilization of traditional inputs (labour, natural fertilizers, draft animals, traditional tools) to the production of modern inputs such as chemical fertilizers, insecticides and pesticides, small hydroelectric plants, electric motors, rice transplanters, tractors, trucks, other machinery, and seed-improvement stations. The agricultural task of the 1960s and 1970s was, in short, to industrialize and modernize the rural areas.

Some of the results of these policies are recorded in Table 6, where it may be seen that chemical fertilizers, tractors, and powered irrigation equipment all rose very rapidly in the 1960s and 1970s. The table also shows fairly good growth for a few of the output series that are available.

TABLE 6. *Some agricultural inputs and outputs: Selected years, 1952, 1965, 1975*

	Chinese production of inputs			Chinese production of outputs			
	Chemical fertilizers (million metric tons)	Tractors (thousand standard units)	Inventory of powered irrigation equipment (million HP)	Grain (million metric tons)	Processed sugar (million metric tons)	Soybeans (million metric tons)	Cotton yield (kg per hectare)
1952	0.2	2.0	0.1	154	0.5	9.5	234
1965	7.6	23.9	8.5	210	1.5	NA	346
1975	27.9	180.0	43.0	270	2.3	17.0	495

Sources: Same publications as for Table 1.

However, we do not have enough information to make a confident assessment regarding the impact of these increasing dosages of modern inputs on agricultural output. We do not have, for example, data on some kinds of inputs, such as threshers, harvesters, and trucks. Further, we do not know the distribution of the various inputs among the several crops (wheat, rice, cotton, etc.), nor the changes in land area devoted to each type of crop during the period. Moreover, the grain output estimates at the beginning of this period are uncertain. Consequently, the most that can be said on a general level is that grain output rose fairly rapidly during the 1960s, apparently responding to modern inputs in this decade to about the same degree as it responded to traditional inputs in the previous decade.[8] It is probably true that, if further institutional changes and dosages of traditional inputs had been heavily relied upon throughout the 1960s as they were in the previous decade, agricultural output would have fared much less well than it actually did.

Somewhat more detail, however, can be supplied for chemical fertilizers, which seem to have been the most important of the modern inputs during the 1960s. The Chinese leadership did not neglect chemical fertilizers during the 1950s, though after the downturn of 1959–61 they placed much more emphasis on them. The USSR constructed several complete plants for China in the initial decade, and China imported machinery to modernize two plants inherited from the pre-1949 period. There was an increase in the production of these fertilizers from 1952 to 1959. In the next decade, China purchased four complete nitrogenous fertilizer plants from the Netherlands, Britain, and Italy, which were installed in 1966. She began building her own plants in 1964, and around this time set a goal of one large-scale plant for each of the 180–190 special districts and one smaller plant for each of the 2,200-odd counties in the country. In fact, as things turned out, much of the increase of chemical fertilizers during the 1960s came from the medium- and small-scale plants that were constructed throughout the countryside during this decade. Moreover, China began to import chemical fertilizers in increasingly larger volume, mostly from Japan and Western Europe. By 1970 available chemical fertilizers from both domestic and foreign sources totalled more than 18 million metric tons, which was six times the level of 1959.

It is possible to relate only in an approximate way the 15 million ton increase in the supply of chemical fertilizers to the 70 million ton increase in grain output during the period 1959–70. Considering the information available on this relationship, it may be roughly accurate to say that, during this period, chemical fertilizers contributed between 40 per cent and 55 per cent of the increase in grain output.[9] While this is not very exact, it probably does suggest accurately that chemical fertilizers had a substantial marginal impact on grain output in the 1960s, probably more than that of any other input. This impact, however, was most likely centred on rice output which is grown in areas where water is generally available. The impact on wheat and cotton output, grown mostly in the north where water supplies are unreliable, was undoubtedly less strong.

As I noted previously, the countryside had been industrialized to some extent during the past decade by the establishment of thousands of small industries under local authority.[10] These industries produce and repair farm implements and machinery; they produce fertilizers, consumer goods, insecticides, building materials, rural transportation equipment; they process agricultural products and develop power sources. Such industries have been encouraged by the central government to be as self-reliant as possible by developing new sources of raw materials from their own areas, utilizing waste materials and older machinery from the larger central industries, and using relatively labour-intensive, indigenous methods of production. These rural endeavours have been fashioned into more or less integrated industrial structures in each locality for the prime purpose of serving that area's agricultural needs.

The advantages claimed for these local industries are: (1) they have the ability to utilize dispersed deposits of material resources; (2) they lower average capital–output ratios and shorten the gestation periods; (3) they have the ability to undertake repairing, maintenance, and processing activities, freeing large-scale capacity for jobs which the modern sector alone could do; (4) they lower the costs of urbanization and social overhead capital in general; (5) they have a capacity to create industrial consciousness among the peasantry; (6) they contribute to national defence; and (7) they ameliorate the contradictions between cities and countryside.

More generally, this rural industrialization effort has certainly had some measure of success in expanding employment opportunities in the countryside, in balancing production geographically, and in raising agricultural productivity generally.

VIII. IMPROVEMENT IN AGRICULTURE'S TERMS OF TRADE

The fourth and final programme that has raised living standards in the rural areas is the change in terms of trade between agricultural and industrial products in favour of the former. This improvement for agriculture has apparently been fairly constant throughout the period, as shown in Table 7. By 1957, a given amount of agricultural produce was purchasing about a third more industrial goods than at the beginning of the decade. By the early 1970s, this had risen to over a half.

Over the past two decades, the government has several times raised the price at which it purchases grain from the peasants. At the present time, this purchase price is above the level at which grain is sold by the state in urban areas and in rural areas devoted mostly to industrial crops. The difference in the prices is a subsidy from the state to the cultivators of grain. Other agricultural goods have also been purchased at higher prices. On the other hand, prices of industrial products bought by the peasants rose very little for a decade after 1952, and the increases in more recent years have been relatively modest. Indeed, the prices of many industrial products, some of which are not in this index, have declined markedly. For example, the general price level of medicines is 80 per cent lower now than in 1950, and most of this drop occurred in the last few years. "For the same amount of wheat, a peasant can get 70 per cent more salt than at

TABLE 7. *Indicators of agricultural welfare gains, 1950–74*

	(1) Agricultural purchase price index (1952=100)	(2) Industrial retail prices in rural areas index (1952=100)	(3) Ratio of (1) to (2)	(4) Agricultural tax as percent of agricultural crop output
1950	82.2	91.2	90.1	NA
1952	100.0	100.0	100.0	13.2
1957	122.4	101.6	120.5	11.5
1963	154.7	114.3	135.3	NA
1971	156.2	114.0	137.0	6.0
1973	160.0+	NA	NA	5.0+a

Sources: Dwight H. Perkins, Constraints Influencing China's Agricultural Performance, in Joint Economic Committee, *China: A Reassessment of the Economy,* July 10, 1975, pp. 362–3.
   a Figure is for 1974.

the time of the birth of the People's Republic, and for the same amount of cotton, he receives 2.4 times as much kerosene."[11] Prices of fertilizers, fuel, livestock feed, electricity, and various types of equipment have been lowered.

The last column of Table 7 shows a sharp reduction over the full period of the tax burden on peasants, which is another indicator of shifting terms of trade in favor of agriculture.

IX. RURAL DEVELOPMENT IN TSUNHUA COUNTY

Some of the agricultural policies which I have discussed up to this point will perhaps have more meaning if they are shown in actual operation in one rural locality. I attempt this as follows.

Tsunhua county is one of six counties within the special district of T'angshan, which is located in the north-eastern part of Hopei Province, about 100 miles east and a bit north of Peking. The county, the size of which is about 1,640 square kilometres, has a population of over half a million, though it has only one town, Tsunhua, the county seat. The land is mostly hilly, with three mountain ranges and two valleys or plains. The economic activities of the population are largely agricultural—that is, growing wheat, kaoliang, millet, other grains, fruit orchards, chestnut trees, vegetables—but there are increasing numbers of small industries in the county, and of course some people engage in various sideline occupations. Table 8 records some of the basic economic facts about the county.

The heart of the county's economy is agriculture, mostly food-grains. Since 1949, the output of food-grains per hectare has risen more than threefold, or at an average annual rate of 6 per cent. However, since 1958 the rate has been only 2 per cent; it was rather stagnant between 1958 and 1969, but recorded substantial increases during 1970 and 1971. The Revolutionary Committee of the county attributed the stagnant period

TABLE 8. *Some economic statistics of Tsunhua county: 1970–1*

Total area	164,000 hectares (or 1,640 sq km)
Cultivated area	64,000 hectares
Irrigated area	18,700 hectares
Population	550,000
Households	116,000
Labour force	about 200,000
Communes	43 (av. of 12,800 per commune)
Production brigades	691 (av. of 800 per brigade)
Production teams	2,664 (av. of 200 per team)
Grain production	3.8 tons per hectare
Value of grain production	about 50 million yuan
Value of industrial production	18 million yuan
Income from sideline occupations	22.7 million yuan

Sources. Jon Sigurdson, Rural industry— a traveller's view, *The China Quarterly* (July–September 1972); *Collective Notes* of visiting economists to China during August 1972, mimeographed by Thomas Weisskopf, Department of Economics, University of Michigan.

to the revisionist policies of Liu Shao-ch'i and his followers, who discouraged self-reliant policies in the county, the building of small industries, and the full use of local resources. Since 1968 or 1969, however, the leaders of the county have "organized mass activities to change the backwardness of agriculture, make substantial use of local resources and rapidly develop local industry".[12]

The county has attempted to promote agricultural development by producing its own cement, chemical fertilizers, and iron and steel for the manufacture of agricultural machinery and implements, and it has supported these heavy industries, especially iron and steel, with profits from light industry and sideline activities. That is, the county has attempted to industrialize mainly on its own initiative and using its own resources for the purpose of raising agricultural productivity and the living standards of the people.

In order to produce chemical fertilizers, cement, and iron and steel, the people of the county first had to locate the necessary ores and minerals. "Initially, we were aware only of the presence of gold and iron in the hills, but now local people have discovered 23 kinds of ore, helped by the geological team."[13] They then set up the iron and steel plant—first the small blast furnace, then a converter, after that a rolling mill. The iron and steel aided in establishing the cement factory, and the latter was used largely to expand water conservancy projects.

The iron and steel plant, however, ran at a loss. So light industry and sideline activities were developed which made more than enough profits to subsidize iron and steel. The county planted tens of thousands of fruit trees, for example, then constructed a small fruit bottling factory with an annual capacity of 250 tons of bottled fruit—apples, apricots, pears, grapes, peaches, etc. This factory required sugar, so some peasants began growing sugar beets, and turned out 10 tons of sugar per year. The factory also needed glass for the bottles and so a small glass manufacturing plant was set up. The glass, of course, required pure soda, hence, this called for the establishment of a 32-ton per year soda factory. And so on and on. The result is that the county is now able to produce a complete set of machinery, such as crushers, threshers, oil presses, and machinery for digging drainage and irrigation systems, for the development of agricultural and sideline activities.

Local industries are run not only by the county but also by the communes and production brigades. At the county level, the aim of national policy is for every county to have the "Five Small Industries": iron and steel, cement, chemical fertilizer, energy (coal, electricity), and machinery. Such complete sets were established in one-half of the 2,200 counties by 1971. Tsunhua was engaged in all of these activities, except that its electricity was produced outside of the county. In addition, the county runs a sulphuric acid plant, an electromechanic factory, a plastics factory, a paper-making plant, engages in mining operations, has a textile mill, does major repairs on agricultural machinery, processes agricultural and sideline products—e.g., flour-milling and cotton-ginning.

The communes and the production brigades are also involved in small industries. For example, there is a three-level agricultural machinery repair and manufacturing network, which 90 per cent of the counties, including Tsunhua, had established by 1971, in which the county does the manufacturing and major repairs in seven plants, the communes in 37 plants do lesser repairs and assembly, and production brigades do minor repairs in their 407 shops. The three-levels also engage in processing agricultural and sideline products. Further "Three-level county, commune, and brigade agricultural scientific networks have been rapidly expanded all over the country [including Tsunhua] in recent years. One important objective of this is to achieve a rapid seed-selection process which together with modern inputs to agriculture may quickly increase the yield per unit."[14] Sideline occupations are engaged in by households, brigades, and communes, and they include such things as raising silkworms and bees, quarrying stones and mining ores, making mat bags, growing fruit.

In all of these enterprises, there were 12,000–15,000 of the 200,000 labour force employed. In the 39 county-run industries, employment was 5,500 in 1971; it was 2,500 in the 71 plants managed by communes; and 5,000 in the industrial units of the production brigades.[15] These are not large figures relative to the total labour force, but there are many other workers who are in the industrial sector indirectly. In any case, employment creation is probably not the main purpose of rural industrialization. For given the increased school enrolment of children, the fact that it is unnecessary any longer for older people to remain in the labour force and work, the continuation of large-scale labour projects in water control and reforestation, the increasing numbers of people engaged in sideline occupations (in cultural activities, medical services, education, and party work), the movement of millions of people to the north-west and west and to other relatively virgin areas of the country, and the continued rising demands for just about every kind of agricultural product—given all these things, there would seem to be no significant surplus of labour in the rural areas. This, of course, is especially true during the seasonal peaks of planting and harvesting. Instead, rural industrialization is for the principal purpose of achieving mechanization in agriculture and hence greater agricultural productivity. It is also meant to narrow the differences between town and country, workers and peasants, and to widen the horizons and the abilities of the peasants.

X. MAOIST DEVELOPMENT STRATEGY AND ITS RELEVANCE FOR OTHER COUNTRIES

What possible relevance has China's attempts at rural development for other underdeveloped countries? To begin to answer this, it is first necessary to specify exactly what the Maoist strategy for economic development is, within which rural development is contained. Since this strategy is an evolving one and has already taken several twists and turns, one cannot be certain of getting it right. But as of now the over-all development strategy appears to consist of the following steps.

1. Destroy the feudal-landlord-bureaucrat class structure, and redistribute land, other assets, income, and power to the peasants and workers.

2. Establish socialist relations of production as soon as possible, and use the party to educate peasants and workers in socialist values and ideals. That is, nationalize industry as soon as feasible and bring about cooperativization in the countryside without waiting for agricultural mechanization; begin transforming the superstructure into a socialist one.[16]

3. Establish a full planning mechanism to take the place of market-price-determined allocation of resources and distribution of incomes, and go all out for industrialization, but emphasize those industries having direct links to agriculture.

4. Achieve high rates of capital formation by encouraging savings at all levels and the use of the savings at each level for self-financed investment. Encourage rural areas,

in particular, to produce whatever can be produced by small-scale, indigenous methods, to finance these investments from their own savings, and to manage these industries themselves. Capital goods that can be produced only by large-scale, modern methods should be financed and managed at higher political levels.

5. Develop and release human energy and creativity by promoting socialist values ("serve the people", selflessness, collective incentives) over bourgeois values (individualism, selfishness, materialism), by providing health-care facilities everywhere, educating as many people as possible, providing worthy goals that inspire people to work hard, and encouraging basic decision-making at the lowest possible level.

6. Carry out a continuing revolution at all levels of society, and maintain the dictatorship of the proletariat.

It seems to me that the Maoist strategy, *considered as a whole,* probably has very little relevance to governments of most underdeveloped countries today, for it involves breaking the power of ruling classes and their foreign supporters, opting for socialism and eventually communism over capitalism, for full-scale industrialization over trade, commerce, and agrarianism, for continuing revolutionary activity over orderly procedures. Since most Third World countries today play more or less subordinate and dependent roles in the international capitalist system, serving the wealthier countries of that system with raw materials, oil, cheap labour, or additional markets, for them to follow China's path would mean first breaking out of this global system and then taking their chances on an all-out development effort with their own resources plus whatever aid can be obtained from socialist countries.[17]. This may be a programme favoured by some classes in these poor countries, but it is hardly a prescription that would be appealing to their governments and propertied classes. Furthermore, such thoughts are anathema to the United States, as the leader of global capitalism, the duty of which is to try to prevent such break-aways through some combination of economic aid, military aid, counterinsurgency, cultivation of domestic élites, or force. The alliance between the US, on the one hand, and the propertied classes and élites in the poor countries, on the other, is a powerful one.

That is the over-all picture. It stresses that one thing *does* depend on another in Maoist strategy, and indeed this is so in any development strategy. To make any substantial headway, the problem of underdevelopment often has to be tackled as a whole, not piecemeal. For example, in the Chinese experience, rural industrialization depended on the general acceptance of goals other than profits and efficiency. This general acceptance in turn was based on the prior inculcation of socialist values throughout the society, which were reinforced daily by the prior establishment of socialist institutions, including a full planning mechanism. These socialist relations of production could be developed only by the prior break-up of the old class structures of society. And so on.

I have emphasized the holistic view, the Maoist way. I now wish to ask whether other underdeveloped countries can benefit, to some extent at least, from separate parts of China's total experience. Some socialist policies should be adaptable to capitalist developmental programmes.

It is well to recognize at the beginning that many Chinese policies for development are universally known and in fact have been acquired by China from the theoretical and practical work of bourgeois economists and other development experts, as well as from the experience of the Soviet Union. To this extent, China has learned from others, and there are, of course, no reasons why other countries cannot take advantage of the same information. I refer to policies of raising capital formation relative to consumption to attain higher growth rates, of encouraging saving for this purpose through taxation, financial institutions, and in other ways, of using relative factor supplies to good advantage, of aiming for developmental government budgets and moderate growth rates of the money supply, of utilizing aid and trade efficiently, and so on. Much of China's over-all performance can be explained "simply" in terms of the very high investment and saving ratios that were attained by 1953–4 and were more or less maintained thereafter. (Recall, however, that to attain *these* the old class structures were overthrown by revolution. That is what lies behind "simply".) And larger shares of this total capital formation were applied to agriculture in the 1960s and 1970s, which goes a long way in explaining China's recent gains in rural development. Thus, much of the story is standard fare, known to everyone.

But, while China has learned much from others, she may also be able to teach a few things. First, China has demonstrated the importance of industrialization to economic development; that the large resources initially devoted to iron and steel, machine-building, non-ferrous metals, oil, electric power, and chemicals were indispensable in establishing a base for later advances in agriculture, transportation, consumer goods, and military weapons, and in freeing the economy from its dependency on foreign direction and influence. The initial stress on heavy industry, rather than on infrastructure and consumer goods, was made possible only by socialist aid and trade. Despite the growing bitterness between the USSR and China, no other country has ever received so much help toward full-scale industrialization as China did during the 1950s. This is something of a lesson in itself.

Second, China has shown, especially during the 1960s, *how* to industrialize without generating social problems that threaten eventually to blow the society sky high. China has involved increasing numbers of people, especially in the rural areas, in industrial activities in order to break down the potentially antagonistic relations between city and country and between workers and peasants; to spread knowledge of industrial processes as widely as possible so as to promote talent, ingenuity, confidence, and the scientific attitude among masses of workers and peasants; and to transform rural areas into self-reliant agrarian-industrial-cultural local economies, which are attractive places to live in and which can, at least partly, break their dependent relationships with higher political units, including the state. This is relevant for other poor countries because it demonstrates a pattern of industrialization that does not generate severe imbalances between urban and rural areas, between rich and poor, between employed and unemployed or between one region and another. The lesson that many developing countries are learning from their own experience is that high output growth rates are often the "good face" on an increasingly diseased body. Thus, a recent annual report of the World Bank, after noting the respectable growth rates of many underdeveloped countries, went on to say: "Statistics conceal the gravity of the underlying economic and social prblems, which are typified by severely skewed income distribution, excessive levels of unemployment, high rates of infant mortality, low rates of literacy, serious malnutrition, and widespread ill-health." The statistics also conceal the growing urban problems, foreign debt difficulties, social unrest, and much else in many of these countries. Perhaps the most important message that China can send to other poor people is that not one item in the above list applies to her.

The third lesson is the importance of raising work motivation and how to do it. Capitalist economists have concentrated far too much on how to reallocate economic resources to attain higher levels of national output and far too little on how to get people really interested in their work and so willing to exert great efforts to achieve their goals. I think that China has shown that the latter is much more important than the former; that people who really want to work completely eclipse the effects of nice adjustments toward more competitive markets and fine calculations regarding factor inputs.

The Maoists believe that they have inspired and enabled people to work hard by altering their work environments, changing their incentives, and providing them with education, good health, and technical training. The first point is that, in capitalist development, to raise growth rates of national output, it is necessary to do it in such a way as to reinforce the existing class structures of society and the values which support such structures. The pursuit of higher growth rates, therefore, has generally reduced many human beings to unthinking, specialized, manipulated inputs in the production process, in which hierarchical structures of capitalists and workers, bosses and "hands", mental experts and manual workers, face each other in more or less antagonistic relationships. Such alienated work environments lower the general intelligence, initiative, and willingness to work hard of broad masses of workers, which are the obvious costs of pursuing growth in the context of such sharp class alignments. the Maoists feel that the development of people as full human beings, working in a warm, egalitarian, and cooperative atmosphere, leads to the rapid development of material output; that the former is possible only in the absence of capitalist or feudal class structures; and that the latter is desirable only within the context of the former.

Thus, the Chinese lesson, in this regard, is that it is possible to increase greatly the over-all productivity of peasants and workers by establishing less alienated work environments. In the absence of full-scale revolution, underdeveloped countries might benefit from China's experience by questioning their own organizations of work both in the countryside and in the cities, and by experimenting with other forms. Are existing organizations efficient from a factor productivity point of view, or are they mainly efficient in channelling part of the economic surplus to a landed aristocracy or to a capitalist class? Do work organizations exist to maintain discipline and order or do they promote energy and initiative? And, if the former, why? Are they designed to set off one group of workers against another to the benefit of the dominant class and to the detriment of factor productivity? China may have much to teach us in this regard.

Work motivation in China has also risen, according to the Maoists, because of an increase in socialist consciousness among the masses of workers and peasants, which means that collective incentives—the willingness to work hard for increasingly larger groups of people without expectation of personal gain—have gained over individual ones. Maoists believe that people are inspired and can see real meaning in their lives only if they are working for goals worthy of human beings and not merely for their own selfish, material welfare. Indeed, people throughout China *do* seem inspired in this way, for whatever reason, and seem not only completely involved in their present accomplishments but in achieving the plans for the future: "In two years, we'll have this and have a good start on that, and then .... " Just about everyone talks this way.

Further, with regard to work motivation, it is necessary to repeat that increasing numbers of people are able to work hard and more effectively by being more literate, having better health and improved nutrition, and having more technical training.

Finally, the Chinese Communist Party has developed high motivation among its own cadres to "serve the people" in honest and incorruptible ways. The work motivation and collective incentives engendered within this large group have been of vital importance in getting policies translated into proper actions at all levels, in ways that do not dissipate the intentions of policy-makers. The CPC has for several decades now demonstrated the importance of having such cadres for the actual realization, as contrasted to the verbalization, of national goals.

China offers other lessons, too, which there is space only to mention: how to adapt education to the needs of an industrializing society; that it is not necessary for economic development to invite foreign capital into the country; the desirability of maintaining rather stable prices of important commodities over long periods of time; and so on.

The principal lesson, however, is the necessity of breaking out of all dependency relationships with advanced industrial countries and pursuing the course of self-reliance, both at the national and the local levels.

NOTES.

1 R. H. Tawney, *Land and Labor in China*, Beacon Press, 1966 (originally published, 1932), pp. 72–3, 76–7.
2 1 *mou* equals one-sixth of an acre or one-fifteenth of a hectare.
3 Keith Buchanan, *The Transformation of the Chinese Earth*, Praeger, 1970, p. 123.
4 Victor Lippit, *Land Reform in China: The Contribution of Institutional Change to Financing Economic Development* (unpublished manuscript, 1972). [See bibliography, entry 20, *Ed.*]
5 See, for example, William Hinton, *Fanshen: A Documentary of Revolution in a Chinese Village* (Monthly Review Press, 1966).
6 *Peking Review*, 9 September 1958.
7 However, the agricultural sector generated a substantial amount of internal saving that was used for investment.
8 The average annual percentage growth rates of grain output for several periods are as follows:

1952–7	3.7	1959–75	3.1
1952–8	4.5	1961–75	3.8
1952–9	1.0	1965–75	2.5

9 This is based on Jung-Chao Liu, *China's Fertilizer Economy*, Aldine, 1970, pp. 96, 106, 110–12; Kang Chao, *Agricultural Production in Communist China*, op. cit., pp. 150–1, 236; Leslie T. C. Kuo, *The Transformation of Agriculture in Communist China*, Praeger, 1972, p. 102; and JEC. op. cit., pp. 140, 348.
10 See Carl Riskin, Small industry and the Chinese model of development, *The China Quarterly*, April–June 1971, pp. 245–73.
11 *China Reconstructs*, November 1970, p. 4. See also the issue for January 1973, p. 40.
12 *Collective Notes*, op. cit., p. 63.
13 ibid.
14 Sigurdson, op. cit., p. 320.
15 In these plants, there are three types of workers: permanent, temporary, and contract. The permanent workers are employed within the regular 8-grade wage system, ranging from Y28 to about Y100 per month. Temporary workers are part peasants and part workers, who rotate regularly between agriculture and industry, and who turn over half their wages to their production teams, and then at the end of the year receive income from the teams based on their agricultural work. Contract workers are hired on a 1-, 2-, or 3-year basis, and are in general treated the same way as permanent workers; they are mostly from the city, not from production teams.
16 This is because, if mechanization is introduced in an essentially individualistic, private-enterprise framework, the fruits of the new technology will be captured by only a few, leaving the majority of peasants resentful and ready to "break the machines". Also, capitalist development creates capitalist people. Under certain circumstances, according to Mao, it is necessary to change the superstructure in order to release the productive forces of society. See point 5.
17 This is also true for the ruling classes of the major oil-producing countries, who may gain some advantages over the industrial capitalist countries but who are so greatly dependent on international-monopoly capital that they (or most of them) would not dream of breaking out of this global system.

China's Industrialization in Historical Perspective

STEPHEN P. ANDORS

INTRODUCTION

In many ways, industrialization in China is part of the global industrial revolution that began in Europe well over a century ago.[1] It is based on many of the same premises, faces many of the same problems, and in some respects is defined in much the same way. It was, after all, a process that began partially in response to Western domination. Like the countries of the Third World today, China's industrialization was an integral part of a Chinese nationalist reaction against Western imperialism which was itself made possible by the economic, technological, and organizational evolution of capitalism.

As such, industrialization in China has meant increasing exploitation of natural resources and energy harnessed to more technology. It has meant a drive to exert more extensive control over nature and intensive use of the land to raise agricultural yields. It has meant building factories, extending roads and rail networks, and constructing more mines. It has meant mechanization of the work process, automation where possible, and a constant transformation of the substance and organization of the division of labour in society. It has meant the transformation of education to reflect new social class configurations and a technologically more sophisticated society.[2] As it did in the market economies of the West, the planned economy of the USSR, or the government-supported capitalist economies of Japan and Germany, industrialization in China is in the process of profoundly transforming the lives of a rural agricultural population living in a poor and technologically backward society. There is little in contemporary Chinese attitudes toward industrialization that carries the same kind of philosophical or economic concern with problems of economic growth that there is in already indus-trialized societies.[3]

The implications of the economic and social changes occurring in China also bear similarities to the experience of other countries. The division of labour is becoming more complex, making obsolete the activity of lone craftsmen. It increasingly fosters collective and cooperative relationships even while it allocates different kinds of hard-ship and different levels of privilege and authority to people doing different kinds of work. Those who do the physically toughest and most dangerous jobs do not control and plan production to the same extent as those who work in offices. Work and life in rural China, even for those who work in offices, is harder than in the more developed urban centers. Women work within the home far more frequently than men who dominate the skilled and higher paying jobs in society.

Even within the industrial sector, work in an office within a big steel mill does not compare to the heat, noise, and danger of work near the big blast furnaces or foundry shops where molten steel flows within yards of fast moving men. Work in a government

27

office does not compare to the noise and danger of work in an auto assembly plant. Work in a mechanized machine tool plant does not compare to the backbreaking manual labour of the farmer who has no machinery to break or move the earth. Serious health risks exist in some industries such as those which use petroleum derivatives like polyvinyl chloride to make plastics, or in those manufacturing asbestos fibres. All of these realities threaten to be a part of China's industrialization and working class life as they were and still are for other countries. As it has elsewhere, industrialization creates costs which some people bear more than others.

Yet, everything has not been the same in China in spite of these similarities. Over the years, and largely under Mao Tse-tung's influence and leadership, the Chinese developed a rather unique approach to industrialization. This approach resulted from years of careful observation and bold experimentation. Two massive political upheavals, the Great Leap Forward of 1958–60 and the Great Proletarian Cultural Revolution of 1966–9 left behind a China that could never be the same. Yet still much of the old China remained and many stubborn problems persisted.

INDUSTRIALIZATION AND POLITICS

Industrialization shapes politics in three ways. By creating patterns of hierarchy and defining spheres of autonomy, daily life in a factory gives concrete meaning to political abstractions like freedom and democracy. Secondly, wage policies, incentive systems, and property ownership shape the distribution of wealth in society. Moreover, the legal and institutional arrangements that flow from basic concepts of property rights help to delimit the spheres of private life and public responsibility. Industrialization increasingly makes this dividing line a crucial issue of political life both philosophically and institutionally.

Thirdly, decisions concerning industrial development are intimately connected with the quality of life in human communities. Questions of land use, patterns of human settlement and daily life are all subjected to enormous pressures from the industrialization process. Relationships between urban and rural life, or industrial and agricultural labour are only two of the more obvious ways that industrialization transforms politics by transforming communities.

In all of these crucial areas of politics, China's industrial revolution has not been the same as the "model" which grew from the Western capitalist experience and the liberal political ideology which accompanied it. Both that experience and that ideology dominated the notion of industrialization even for those, like the Bolsheviks or the Japanese, who otherwise might have been expected to develop quite differently. Yet for the Chinese, products of a proud and independent civilization and heirs to a history of their own as well as the experiences of others who industrialized and tried to rebel against the West before them, things were different.

RELATIONSHIPS AT WORK: BASIC PRINCIPLES OF FACTORY MANAGEMENT IN CHINA

The two most basic principles of factory management in China while Mao lived were called "the two participations". These were: (1) workers' participation in management; and (2) management ("cadres" in Chinese terminology) participation in labour. Moreover, the Chinese gained an insight that these "two participations" were related both to the system of motivation or incentives used within the whole industrial system as well as to the institutional and organizational framework of planning and coordination within which each enterprise functioned.

It is a very frequent and very erroneous view, made popular largely by Western journalists and academics, that the Maoist approach to management rejected material incentives in favour of moral incentives and political exhortation. Thence it is argued that Mao cared less about modernization and industrialization than for abstract revolutionary principle. Such views are based on a fundamental misunderstanding.

The word for incentive in Chinese has the connotation of inciting or provoking action. It further implies that "incentive" acts on a pre-existing and underlying morality that is part of an individual's character. The "incentive" is simply a stimulus, triggering action to which a person is already predisposed. It is in this sense that the Maoist theory of factory management is first of all premised *not* on a theory of moral incentives as opposed to material incentives, but rather on people with the proper socialist character, i.e., those whose ethics *reject the principle of self aggrandizement*.

For workers, incentives based on the morality of self aggrandizement meant that they could not participate for long or very meaningfully in management. Work in a factory required discipline and was often hard and monotonous. If workers either looked to shirk these tasks, violate this discipline, or increase their own income without exerting their full efforts at production, while simultaneously participating in decisions which affected output and production operations, the result would be inefficiency at best, chaos at worst. To the extent that self aggrandizement was a moral basis of incentives, it was therefore a contradiction to participation. The two acted in dialectical opposition. Completely self aggrandizing workers required complete supervision to get the job done. In practical terms it meant that workers could not participate in management if they only worked to get high bonuses to maximize income or if they worked for personal privileges, in short, if they were not "responsible" and imbued with a sense of collective obligation.

In much the same way, morality was basic to the practice of cadre participation in labour. The division of labour in industry, given contemporary patterns of distribution of knowledge and technical development as well as the realities of human inequality and difference, was such that power and privilege was distributed unequally in a factory. Cadre participation in labour, as worker participation in management, was conceived as an antidote to what the Chinese saw as the elitist, technocratic, and fundamentally undemocratic, implications of factory organization in other industrial societies. But if cadres were to participate in labour, given the realities of hard, dirty manual work in comparison to office work, they too could not have a morality of self-aggrandizement; for if they did seek privilege, they would certainly not be happy about working on the shop floor.

The incentive system in China's factories thus rejected the morality of self-aggrandizement, but it did not rest secure on abstract moral exhortation to be selfless and hard working. Nor was "character", the basic element in incentives, seen as an inborn trait of human beings, as it was in the old Confucian notion of inborn virtues and vices. Instead, Mao, as a Marxist, viewed "character" as the historical product of social relations. For workers, their willingness to abandon the morality of self aggrandizement and hence their capacity for meaningful and effective participation, was therefore dependent on an appropriate material reality. Part of that reality was to be cadres participating in labour. The reality of everyone doing a fair share, working hard, and gaining *just rewards* for their work with none unduly privileged was a potent antidote to self aggrandizement in this system. Moreover, participation in the plant had to be accompanied by a relatively equal distribution of income and living standards outside it, for without tangible evidence of equality both within the plant and in society, rhetoric about equality could easily become meaningless or counterproductive. In committing oneself to equality, one was, therefore, not making only a moral statement, but, said the Chinese, one had to perceive that same commitment in the *actions and ways of life* of others. Otherwise the result was an injury to self esteem, and such injury could be fatal to the morality that left individuals frequently vulnerable to such injury. In the realization that nobody likes to look the fool, the egalitarian theory of incentive paradoxically tapped a major source of ego incentive. It is in this sense that "material incentives" which stressed self aggrandizement were attacked as undermining the "two participations" while "material incentives" which reflected notions of distributive justice were not. Thus, wage grades and income differentials were an integral part of Mao's approach to management, but policies which aggravated a perception of privilege or which encouraged people to be concerned more about their personal income than their personal contributions were not.[4]

The incentive system was, therefore, shaped to reinforce the basic organizational principles of two participations. This had an impact on the division of labour within a factory also, though here the inherited inequalities of the past in education and knowledge, as well as technical realities embodied in production sequences or engineering requirements, put constraints on the extent of structural transformation that was rationally possible. In general, the Chinese approach tried to minimize the size of separate control and supervision departments at middle levels of management and to make these functions an integral part of the production units. Essential control departments, like accounting, quality control, research, and others were often retained, but the question of power balance and distribution between departments and production units had to be determined according to technological and human circumstances which varied widely from place to place or industry to industry.

Communications, control, and supervision in this approach to management tended to be based on personal contact rather than mechanical or written procedures. Some workers participated in the making of quite important decisions concerning the quantity, quality and intensity of production on a fairly long term basis. They served on revolutionary committees at the workshop or factory levels. Still other workers were on what were called "triple combination teams" made up of technicians, administrators, and workers. These teams managed technical innovations and quality supervision or drafted rules and regulations for safety and maintenance schedules. The factory level of authority made up of a revolutionary committee and a core of Communist Party members could rotate assignments in the office with those on the shop floor. This approach to management was summed up in what the Chinese called the "Anshan Constitution", a series of five broad principles concerning participation and leadership in factory management enunciated by Mao in the early 1960s.

In addition to managing and coordinating the factory's overall production operations, while promoting the "two participations", factory level authorities provided the key links between the factory and the wider society. As such they were constrained in their ability to manage in a Maoist way by two crucial relationships. One was the society's approach to education and its links to the world of work. This link provided manpower to make worker participation in management both rational and effective. The other was the factory's relationship to planning authorities because this provided the context which shaped demands put on cadres and determined if there would be time to make participation in labour possible.

Just as the distribution of wealth and income outside the plant affected incentives and participation within it, education had an even more direct impact on the distribution of power within the factories. Factories were both physically and morally linked with the system of technical and non-technical education. They ran their own technical schools, or established close relationships for specific courses of instruction with middle schools and colleges in localities. Workers served both as students and teachers and regular teachers also taught in these schools. The industrial enterprise's activity and working class history became a central aspect of socialization, shaping the values and self images of individuals. The factory was not defined *simply* in terms of short term cost efficiency, profit and production, though those were very important, but also as an institution that made labour the moral basis of the educational experience.

In addition to education, factory level authorities were also responsible for other things: cooperation with other enterprises even if this cut down on profits; the development of sports, recreation, and welfare facilities; provision of day care and medical care; or meeting local consumer needs and providing housing or local services, technical advice or equipment for local small scale factories or other development projects. The industrial enterprise was an integral part of the local society's system of education and welfare.

PLANNING AND CONCEPTS OF COMMUNITY

The role of factory level management in fitting the factory into the local society was complemented by the need to fit it also into national planning priorities. This was where the theory of economic planning and coordination became so important. Indeed, the relationship between factory management and economic planning and coordination in forging a new concept of political community is perhaps the most unique aspect of the Chinese approach to industrialization. Aside from re-defining the general role of the industrial enterprise as far wider than production for profit, two other aspects of planning and coordination stand out: decentralization and despecialization.

These approaches to planning and coordination had been developed with no little controversy and struggle over the years. Even since the Great Leap Forward had dismantled the machinery of Soviet style, vertically integrated planning, which was implemented widely but unevenly during the First Five Year Plan, the role of economic "trusts" and central ministries *vis-à-vis* local political authorities had been a core element of debate among the Chinese leadership. After the Cultural Revolution this debate was, at least temporarily, settled in favour of a distinctly Chinese approach to planning.

Characteristic of this approach was a balance between centralized planning and decentralized operations. Central planning was to allocate major items and targets strictly but allow local authorities enormous latitude in coordinating operations. The central plan dealt with major enterprises and products needed for national development requiring supplies from all parts of the country and having a national market for production. The plan set specific targets for quantity, quality, profit and wages, and these targets were communicated to enterprises directly by way of local authorities, or were communicated to local authorities who then had the responsibility of assigning targets to specific enterprises of their own choosing. Local political or planning authorities had to make sure these targets were met, but once proper arrangements were made and assignments handed out, the local authorities could develop their own plans to meet local needs not covered in the central plans. Moreover, local authorities working closely with enterprises within their jurisdiction had the power to re-arrange supply relationships and other operational matters if unforeseen bottlenecks arose in inter-enterprise relationships. The principle to be followed was to give different levels of local authority the power to make plans for the local areas, *providing* central plans were fulfilled and local plans did not take resources from other areas. In general, local authorities would serve as the basis for a horizontally integrated system that depended on a strong personal knowledge of local conditions. Such knowledge was to be obtained more through personal observation than on written information originating in the control and supervision departments of various factories. In this way the function of these supervisory departments decreased in importance in the daily work of the plant.

This decentralization was reinforced by the despecialization and self reliance of the Chinese system of economic coordination. Despecialization and self-reliance aimed to mobilize marginal undeveloped sources of raw materials and human talent and develop all aspects of producer and consumer goods industry in poor and technologically undeveloped areas. It based investment decisions on a concept of "rationality" that went beyond nationally or centrally calculated concepts of cost efficiency and profit, thus opening up locations and opportunities for industrialization that would not be considered otherwise. The purpose of despecialization was to enhance the capacity of local authorities to meet local needs and raise local income and living standards without undermining the local authorities' commitment to contribute to national construction. Despecialization was to act as an incentive for local people, demanding their individual creativity, and contributing to collective welfare. Attempts at self-reliance, even if at first a failure, were to be a positive education for future development projects. Despecialization could and did apply to single factories which in addition to a major product also made spare parts or subsidiary products from waste solids, liquids, or gases. Factories could also establish relationships with nearby agricultural areas to provide fertilizer from factory wastes or machinery or advice for mechanization. Despecialization also applied not only to factories, but more usually to geographic regions of various sizes, especially to cities. Within cities, or localities, specialization and division of labour would be encouraged among plants as appropriate.

Despecialization thus was more than a method of industrial coordination and planning. It embraced relationships between industry and agriculture as well. Rural industry was developed in formerly completely agricultural areas, and was linked directly and closely to the technical needs and rhythms of agricultural production as well as the consumer needs of the rural population. Urban centers were increasingly provided with food grown on nearby agricultural communes, while providing rural areas with machinery, technical advice, or technically trained manpower to develop rural industry.[5] Some factories also grew their own food, or more frequently, arranged for family dependents, usually women, to undertake agricultural production to meet local needs.

This pattern of industrialization cut down greatly on the need for long distance, mechanical communications and an overly complex pattern of resource allocation over huge geographic areas. As such, it limited the functional necessity of a nationally-based administrative bureaucracy with roots in such coordinative activity. It also made local government more likely to take on programmes against air and water pollution, and gave local authorities a rational way to link these pollution control efforts to subsidiary industrial development or to agriculture. Local governmental authorities in cities or rural counties thus had to concern themselves with a host of *local* problems and relationships in addition to the supremely important, but relatively clear cut and few, central responsibilities. Local officials were to spend a large portion of their time looking for, deciding on, and summing up the positive attributes of "model" enterprises or units under their jurisdiction. These models and their performance statistics then provided concrete targets and incentives for other units because of the widespread publicity and social approval they received. They provided planners with performance standards also to measure the efficiency of other units and the feasibility of future plans. The process of finding a model often meant detailed on-the-spot investigation into morale as well as an examination of technical variables in many different places. Models offered realistic guides as to how performance might be improved by altering these variables. Models embodied not just economic or production performance standards, but political and social ones also.

The concept of "administration by model" required that officials directly participate in and often share directly the problems and routines of workers. It also fostered a close relationship between government officials, production units and intellectuals who wrote about the meaning and the specifics of the model's technical and political characteristics. Such relationships became an important part of conflict in local politics and often were linked to factions at the national level through the Communist Party.

Administration by model, when combined with the investment criteria contained in the policy of despecialization, limited the role of "profit" largely to the measurement of efficiency within enterprises. It eliminated the profit criteria as a source of reward for management in the form of bonuses and as the major criteria for new state investment to provide for the growth of an enterprise. Despecialization and administration by models helped to diminish privilege seeking and to encourage planners to calculate their costs by taking social and political factors into account. Both planners above the enterprise and factory level authorities spent less time on paper work and were encouraged and better able to investigate local conditions and periodically participate in production. Local leaders had a direct stake in the collective performance of their area or enterprise because it could be chosen as a model. They became model citizens and were not the wealthy individuals in a community, nor were they necessarily linked for all of their tasks and rewards to far-away planners or to a seemingly impersonal market. Instead, they embodied models of behaviour and values which emphasized egalitarianism and participation in local production problems. In this way despecialization could influence the over-all class structure and the politics of the whole society, as well as help create communities that practised industry and agriculture and within which production was a central core of education and socialization.

The model for such a pattern of industrialization, both in terms of management and in terms of economic coordination, was the Taching Oilfield in Liaoning Province.

Management at Taching was called the "division of labour responsibility system under the collective leadership of the Party Committee". Managers at the oilfield complex were divided into two groups, one of which was the Party's leading nucleus and the other of which was the administrative and technical leadership of the field. Together these two groups made up the Oilfield Revolutionary Committee. The Party Committee and the administrative-technical leadership divided up work as follows. The Party was the main channel of communication with planning authorities who determined the oilfield's production targets. The Party supervised relationships between people in the oilfield, made sure that the "two participations" were being implemented and its members were responsible for providing opportunities and mechanisms for educating workers both technically and politically so as to improve the workers' ability to solve production problems. One third of the Party Committee would remain in the office at the oilfield level; one third would travel from one production site to another to investigate problems, and one third would "squat" at a production site to take part in production. From the information about technical and morale factors so gained, the Party would formulate plans for the oil field to be sent to higher authority for consideration.

The administrative and technical leadership worked very closely with the Party, but their responsibilities were limited to production and technical problems that arose in the course of daily operations. These leaders were to supply members of the Party Committee with information, and like the Party Committee, they were divided into three groups of office-workers, roving trouble-shooters, and daily production leaders. These leaders were responsible for dividing up work in consultation with workers. Rules and regulations concerning safety, repair and maintenance were strict and enforced by these leaders, but were drawn up in consultation with workers. Workers also participated in accounting, electing their own team leaders, and were formally able to criticize leaders at worker's congresses.

Incentives for working at Taching came from the knowledge that everyone there was involved in a major national development project, and from the improvements in collective living standards that had become so obvious since Taching began operation. Cadre participation in labour and egalitarian standards of dress and living conditions also added to the sense of solidarity that made people willing to work hard.

On a macro-level, Taching was a fairly unique development area in regard to industrialization.[6] Consciously rejecting the idea that industrialization had to be accompanied by the development of large urban centres, Taching embodied a number of small but varying sized urban units called "residence points." Taching was therefore conceived as both a unit of production and a unit of residence and local government, and this principle applied in all the sub-units of the complex. Thus, the Party Committee of the oilfield was the same as the Party Committee of the Taching Government.

Within Taching, industry (the production of oil) was combined with agriculture. Agricultural production and some small-scale consumer goods or other kinds of industry was undertaken usually by wives or dependents of workers, but women, usually unmarried ones, were also active in various phases of oil production. Each residence unit at Taching was structured along the following lines. A "livelihood base" was the largest sub-unit, and contained a more or less integrated system of public transportation, agricultural production, and service industries all linked closely to an oil production sequence, refining processes, or drilling areas. Within each livelihood base would be a fairly large town called a "central residence point" which contained small industries for consumer goods, banks, higher level schools, commercial establishments (department stores) and fairly sophisticated medical facilities. This central residence point would be linked to four or five "residence points". A central residence point would contain 300 or 400 households, in comparison to a residence point which usually contained somewhere around 100 to 200 households. In each residence point, agricultural production would be organized to provide food for the local population if possible and services and small scale production provided carpenters, tailors, barbers, and so on. Lower level schools also functioned here.

This model of industrial management, summed up in the "Anshan Constitution", and the Taching model of industrialization in general had been at least theoretically clarified and presented by 1970. Many experiments with worker participation in management and cadre participation in labour had occurred, and the concepts of decentralized operations, centralized planning, despecialization, and local self-reliance had all become integral parts of the general approach to planning and economic development. Yet there were enormous problems remaining, and even before Mao's death these were clearly visible and no small cause of controversy within Chinese society and the Chinese Communist Party.

First of all, the degree to which the principles of Chinese industrial management as developed since the Great Leap and through the Cultural Revolution actually were implemented, was very uneven; moreover, once implemented, the degree to which the theory worked to spur production was also uneven. In some cases it worked splendidly, while in others, it created confusion or waste. Much depended on the levels of skill and education of workers, the values and political commitments of cadres, and the complex distribution of widely varying attitudes of people in a society with a powerful tradition but which had undergone years of rapid social change. In general, the theory was by 1970 a much varied part of reality, although different industries with different technical sequences, engineering requirements, and enterprises in the same industry with different labour forces, or in different parts of the country had very different specific ways in which it was experienced.

The Taching model of industrialization was, in some ways, not easily transferable to older, larger, and established urban centres where the bulk of industry was located. It was simply not realistic to discuss building industrial-agricultural residence units like Taching's where concentrated urbanization had already taken place. Thus, the role of local and municipal governments became very important in fostering the self-reliance, despecialization, and links with agriculture to support the Chinese view of community in industrial society. At times the increased role of local governments could lead to the aggravation of inequalities between regions or localities, or to the disruption of national planning as municipal authorities concentrated too much on local development and forgot about national targets. There is no doubt that tension between local and central authorities would be important early in the development of this industrialization strategy before more or less stable relationships could be established for many different factories under municipal authority, and when low levels of economic and technical development made inequalities that much more obvious. Taching after all had just one responsibility to the centre: the delivery of oil; municipal authorities in urban centres trying to develop into comprehensive communities of industrial and agricultural production and residence had a more complex and perhaps more delicate task to perform, and it would take time to establish rational relationships in this regard.

Even within China's factories, the participatory model of management created problems or contradictions to be solved. What kinds of financial controls were compatible both with efficient production and large scale use of material and machinery for experimentation in technical innovation to eliminate hard, repetitive or dangerous work? What kind of rules and regulations were necessary to assure safety and efficiency and quality in production but which also reflected a commitment to transfer power out of the hands of a small élite of privileged experts and into the hands of workers, many of whom still had only low levels of education and skill? How could profit be used to measure costs and efficiency without it turning into a determinant of an enterprise's overall activity, especially in regard to utilization of waste products or in meeting local, but costly, needs of the community or nearby factories? How would the incentive system reflect a commitment to fight privilege and increase equality, yet still reflect a sense of justice, especially where poverty made demands for higher living standards by no means equal to a demand for luxury, and where unequal ability, skill or dedication were realities that made one person produce much more than another? How did one prevent the emergence of new inequalities that resulted precisely from experiments to eliminate the old ones? Not all workers participated in management equally, and many participated not at all except for attendance at a periodic meeting. How was one to prevent the feeling, for example, that workers on triple combination teams or in management committees were part of a new élite? How much time and effort could be sacrificed on experiments in the "two participations" or in technical innovation before production began to suffer, and, conversely, how much emphasis could be placed on current production before the continuous revolutionary transformation of production relations was neglected?

By 1975, when both Mao and Chou En-lai were nearing death, these and the related problems of education and scientific research had become the central problems of Chinese politics. There can be no mistaking the fact that the system of participatory industrial management described above and the trends in economic planning and coordination, land use, and human community embodied in the efforts of local government to build up relatively comprehensive and self reliant industrial systems and industrial agricultural communities were the essence of Mao's legacy to industrialization in China. Taken together, they constituted an unprecedented contribution to what people could perceive as not only possible but also distinctly workable in a complex and interdependent industrial society. In embodying a concept of production-centred communities where the relationships between industry and agriculture, work and administration, work and residence, urban and rural are increasingly close, Chinese development up until Mao's death was in many ways the reverse of how the concentration of population and the division of social labour had proceeded in other industrialized societies.

But if these trends were very much a part of Chinese developments when Mao died in September 1976, so too were the very real problems and contradictions that remained unsolved. What has happened in China since then? Has the victorious political coalition which defeated the so-called "gang of four" abandoned the revolutionary approach to industrialization that had evolved through years of economic development and political struggle and turned China's development into a repetition of the industrial revolution elsewhere?

It would be premature and foolish to make definitive judgements about this matter, especially in light of the rapidity with which policy direction has changed in the past. But whatever else the purge of the "gang of four" may reveal about them or about Chinese politics, it does seem that the new leadership is attempting to significantly modify, and in some areas to qualitatively transform, previous policy. The contemporary situation is, as it always has been, complex and ambiguous, however, with central policy directives and theoretical pronouncements in some cases implemented and others sabotaged by local practice—which itself differs enormously according to technological and historical factors. Nevertheless, there can be no mistake that a powerful state and party apparatus at the centre has, on the level of theory, abandoned Mao's insistence that revolution in production relations and the development of the economy are mutually reinforcing. In spite of rhetoric upholding this idea, the terribly difficult and at times destabilizing task of putting the revolution in production relations into dialectical balance with the development of the productive forces, has been abandoned in favour of the development of production. It is now proposed that what are perceived to be time-tested capitalist methods and patterns of industrialization will be the most efficient and rapid way to make China a powerful and modern socialist country.[7]

Yet the situation is still mixed. In the over-all approach to development and industrialization official statements stress the importance of local industry meeting local needs[8] but also have stressed even more the need for centralization, standardization and specialization, with a consequent reduction of local autonomy in planning and resource utilization.[9] Light and heavy industry, consumer goods and basic producer goods are all to be developed within localities, but this kind of despecialization is now discussed in terms of much larger geographic markets and "economic zones" rather than as part of the development planning activities of local governments using local, even if marginal, sources of raw material.[10] Agriculture and industry are to develop in close cooperation and proximity to each other, with industry providing agriculture with income and technology and agriculture providing industry with food and some raw materials without major transport costs rising. The renewed stress on the profit target for individual enterprises is not to be an excuse for local industrial enterprises squeezing the peasants with high prices or slipshod work for products that are much in demand.[11]

Many of these changes have given rise to political conflict as local leaders find themselves losing power to officials who command larger geographic regions of economic activity and as relationships among enterprises are transformed. Nevertheless, the increased amount of centralization and the emphasis on allocational efficiency as the basis for planning cannot help but increase the demand for quantitative data, and this will have an effect all the way down to the enterprise level where the departments involved with supervision and statistics will be strengthened at the expense of worker participation.[12] The approach to factory management, therefore, is influenced by changes in the wider economy. There has clearly been a retrenchment in the amount of worker participation in management. Visitors to China report that the triple-combination teams, which were such an important part of worker involvement with technical decision-making, have been abolished. Revolutionary committees have also been abolished, and articles now stress the importance of strict division of labour and managerial authority rather than the far more flexible system of "two participations". The imperatives of discipline and a specialized division of labour, it is now argued, are inevitable consequences of modern technology.[13] Yet there are clearly forces working against the trend toward increased stratification and supervision. Even though official policy toward incentives has stressed the use of bonuses and piece wages because these are more compatible with reduced amounts of worker participation, such bonuses and piece wages are usually distributed collectively, then allocated to individuals by decisions of the relevant work group. Recent visitors report that some factories have still not been able to arrive at an acceptable means of distributing bonuses or interpreting their political implications. One visitor's report from the model Taching Oil Field noted that the workers there refused to accept the reinstatement of bonuses, though this facet of the Taching model has been ignored in the Chinese press.[14] A recent wage reform actually served to narrow income differentials by raising the pay of the lower six grades of workers. In spite of the unmistakable official emphasis on supervision, control, discipline and a strict division of labour backed up by a suitable system of economic and administrative rewards and punishments, there is some evidence that there has been significant worker opposition to this incentive system (and by implication to the management structure which it was to support), and that official policy toward incentives may be re-adjusted as a result.[15] The Chinese approach to industrialization that evolved while Mao lived was a unity. Participatory factory management was reinforced by a system of incentives within the factory and was dependent on the kinds of demands made on the factory by development priorities and the planning and coordinative systems in the wider economy.

While the system that evolved under Mao's leadership was not without serious problems, it did indicate that micro and macro patterns of industrialization that had evolved with the capitalist mode of production need not be universal ones. China's industrialization has been impressive, and it showed that revolutionary industrialization in line with the classic concerns of socialism was a distinct possibility. But since Mao's death it has become clear that China has not been able to escape completely from the constraints imposed on its revolutionary transformation; constraints imposed by poverty, technological backwardness, and military vulnerability—not to mention the historical proximity and only recently challenged hegemony of a capitalist civilization which had always defined the meaning of the future for technologically backward and poor countries.

NOTES

1   This paper is an enlarged and revised version of the concluding chapter of my book, *China's Industrial Revolution: Politics, Planning and Management, 1949 to the Present*, New York: Pantheon, 1977.
2   For a good analysis of how this relationship evolved in the US, see Sam Bowles and Herb Gintis, *Schooling in Capitalist America*, New York: Basic Books, 1976.
3   This does not mean that there is no concern with problems of environmental or ecological balance in China. For a discussion of these problems in the West, especially the US, see Barry Commoner, *The Closing Circle*, New York: Alfred A. Knopf, 1972. Also, William Leiss, *The Limits of Satisfaction: An Essay on the Problem of Needs and Commodities*, Toronto: University of Toronto Press, 1976.
4   Mao's comments on material incentives are most succinctly phrased in "Reading Notes on the Soviet Union's Political Economy", *JPRS*, 61269-2, Washington, DC, February 20, 1974.
5   See S. Andors, "Urbanization and Urban Administration in China's Development: Toward a Political Economy of Urban Community", In *Economic Development and Cultural Change* (forthcoming).
6   The discussion on the division of labour in society by Engels, in parts of "Anti-Duhring" is remarkably similar to Chinese industrialization strategy as embodied in the Taching development model. For brief but illuminating excerpts, see F. Engels, "On the Division of Labour in Production". In Robert Tucker (Ed.), *The Marx–Engels Reader*, New York: W. W. Norton & Co., 1972, pp. 321-327.

7 *"Kwangming Daily* Calls for Learning Foreign Management Experience", *Kuang-ming Jih-pao,* August 26, 1978 in *FBIS,* September 7, 1978.
8 See *"People's Daily* Condemns Gang Criticisms of Regulations", *NCNA,* July 16, 1977, in *FBIS,* July 18, 1977, especially pp. E8–E9. Also, CCP Kiangsu Provincial Committee, "The Only Way to Speed Up the Pace of Socialist Construction", *Hung Ch'i,* No. 2, February 3, 1977, in *SPRCM*, No. 913–14, Also, "Support the Peasants, Do Not Defraud Them", *Jen-min Jih-pao,* August 4, 1978, in *FBIS,* August 18, 1978.
9 "Bring About the Industrialization and Modernization of Building Construction in a Quickened Tempo", *Kuang-ming Jih-pao,* August 24, 1978 in *FBIS,* September 6, 1978. Also, see "It Is Absolutely Impermissible to Privately Divide or Conduct Illicit Sales of Products Turned Out Under the State Plan", *Jen-min Jih-pao,* July 27, 1978 in *FBIS,* August 4, 1978. See also Wu Chia-pei, "Economic Results and Economic Management", *Kuang-ming Jih-pao,* August 12, 1978 in *FBIS,* August 22, 1978. The banks are to play an increasing role in controlling activities of local enterprises.
10 "Organize the Flow of Commodities According to Economic Zones", *NCNA,* August 12, 1978 in *FBIS,* August 21, 1978.
11 See "Support the Peasants", note 8 above.
12 Li Kung-hui, "Persistently Manage the Economy with Economic Methods", *Kuang-ming Jih-pao,* July 11, 1978 in *FBIS,* July 20, 1978.
13 See notes 7, 9, 12 above.
14 Personal communication to the author, July 1978.
15 See *Peking Review,* No. 34, July 1978 for an indication of this.

The Tachai Way
Part I: Learning from Tachai

NEVILLE MAXWELL

Tachai, the village which all China's peasant farmers are exhorted to emulate, lies in the Taihang Mountains in the northern province of Shansi. It is a small village, with only 88 households and a population of 440 making a work-force of 157,[1] which collectively owns and farms 56.7 hectares of loess land. The fall of the village's land, lying across seven gullies and the ridges between, with three broader slopes, is steep, and only intensive terracing has made it suitable for crops. In the thirty years since revolution reached the village and its people set out on their new road the terracing has more than once been built and re-built, consolidating what was originally a multitude of scattered plots, some tiny and all small, into progressively broader fields. By 1971[2] the terraces covered the slopes and reached well up the hill-sides, with orchards growing above the terraces and conifer plantations established on the hill-tops; but many of the biggest fields lay in the gullies. These had been broadened by cutting out the soil from the sides, making those sheer, and with that soil building up and levelling the bottom. These fields were terraced too, their walls up to three metres high and with another metre or more beneath the ground in the foundations, massively built with stones morticed with lime; they were arched, the curve pointing up-gully to resist the often deluging run-off in the short but heavy rainy season. A small canal had brought water to the village and, pumped into a hill-top master reservoir which in turn fed smaller tanks at lower levels, irrigated four-fifths of the fields, all but those high on the hills. Five cable-lifts, erected after the state electricity grid was extended to the village in 1965, cross-laced the terraces—these save great amounts of labour, something like 10,000 workdays a year, bringing down rock from high quarries for the terrace walls, and carrying manure and fertilizer up. The village's land looked fully developed except for the hill-tops, awaiting further afforestation, and it looked permanent. But three years later the landscape had markedly changed, in detail and in character.

By the beginning of the 1970s the villagers were finding that they were approaching a ceiling of production, set by the general contours of their land's topography. While the subsidiary agricultural processes had been mechanized the basic mechanization of fieldwork—plowing, sowing and reaping—remained to be introduced, and the still relatively narrow confines of the terraces made them impracticable for tractor cultivation.[3] The way out of this impasse lay in the villagers' experience in making a new threshing-ground a year or two before. They had dynamited and levelled a hillock, using its debris to fill in small gullies and thus creating a broad flat area to be surfaced as the threshing ground: the village leadership proposed that the same technique be applied, on an immensely larger scale, to level the main ridges themselves, merging the gullies and creating broad sweeps of arable ground. Manual labour-power, with which the Tachai villagers had already transformed their environment once with their new terracing, could now be supplemented by the bull-dozers available on hire from the commune of which Tachai is a member-village. Some villagers pointed out that the rich prized topsoil which had been build up over the years on the gully terraces would be buried and lost in this process, which would leave them to grow crops on what had been sub-soil; but that reservation was answered with the point that with heavy manuring the new soil could be improved over several seasons, and the village decided to take up the project.

By 1974 Tachai had created 5.3 hectares of new land in this way, making a net addition to the village's arable of 3.3 hectares; and all of this was in micro-plains, or what the villagers call "man-made plains", relatively huge fields which will make for the efficient use of the village's tractors. Just over 20 per cent of the village's land was made up of such fields by the autumn of 1974, and more "man-made plains" have been created in the winter 1974–5. The initial yields from the new fields were about 4.5 tons/ha, well down on the average of nearly 8.2 tons/ha achieved on the terraces in 1971; but with intense manuring it is confidently expected that the new, big fields will soon produce yields higher than previously achieved in the village.

Thus Tachai began to forge on again from what had appeared to be a plateau of production, and maintained its role as "pace-setter" for China's villages. Tachai is exceptional, but exceptional only in the degree of its achievements: in the kind of transformations it has worked on its own circumstances it is typical of the majority of China's villages.

Tachai's initial physical problems were essentially two: land (not enough of it, and of poor quality); and water (not enough of that for ten months of the year, and then, often, far too much, with frequent flash-flooding and severe erosion). The land problem has been solved by reclamation and consolidation (the 4,700 plots into which the village land was fragmented in 1945 had been reduced by 1972 to 1,800,[4] and that has since been further reduced); and the water problem was basically solved in 50 days of the winter of 1967, when the villagers, helped by a company of the Army,[5] laid a small canal to Tachai, only about a metre across and 1.5 metres deep, but stone-lined and 7 km long. From the terminal of this canal water is pumped to the hill-top reservoir, 30 metres in diameter and 3 metres deep, and in recent years subsidiary reservoirs have been built; run-off in the rainy season (much reduced, of course, by the extensive contour-terracing) is drained and channelled into subterranean flask-shaped tanks, to be pumped up at need. Each year from 1972 to 1974 was sharply deficient in rainfall,[6] but agricultural production increased every year nevertheless—showing that the village is now immune to the ill effects of drought, even of successive droughts, once precursors of ineluctable famine.

Maize is Tachai's main crop, occupying half the cultivated land, with millet next (30 per cent) and then wheat (10 per cent) and sorghum and other crops, including a little rice, a recent innovation and an achievement at this latitude and 1,000 metres altitude. The total output of grain in 1973 was 385 metric tons, representing an average yield on the village land sown to grain of 7.7 tons per hectare. At the time of the writer's visit the village's record average grain yield was 8.18 tons, achieved in 1971. In 1972 drought reduced grain production. In the following year total grain production increased to a new record but yield fell off slightly because additional land had been brought under grain, and its new soil was still relatively poor. By 1977 these fields had been brought to high standard, and the average grain yield set a clear new record of 9.8 tons/ha.

Tachai's figures are, of course, outstanding. The grain-yield target for Tachai's agricultural zone (north of the Yellow River) is 3 tons/ha; for the next zone south (between the Yellow and Huai Rivers), 3.75 tons; and for the fertile zone of south China, 6 tons[7]—thus, as the Chinese put it, Tachai has "crossed two rivers". Other areas, however, are well ahead of Tachai. Chekiang was the first to become a "thousand jin province" achieving in 1971 a province-wide average grain-yield of over 1,000 jin/mou,[8] or 7.5 tons/ha, and in 1974 it registered 8.25 tons. The intensively farmed areas under the Shanghai municipality averaged 10.5 tons/ha in 1974. Extensive areas in Kwangtung and in the rich island province of Hainan registered 22.5 tons/ha in 1974—and these were production areas, not experimental plots.

TABLE 1. Grain output in Tachai, 1953–77

	1953	1958	1964	1969	1971	1972	1973	1976	1977
Total grain production (tons)	101.64	208.52	285.45	330.02	382.50	332.94	385.00	412.00	482.00
Grain yield (tons/ha):	1.80	4.07	6.06	7.12	8.18	7.10	7.70	8.25	9.80

Source for 1976 figures: FAO Circular Wk 6874, Information Gathered on a Private Visit to China; for 1977 figures, *Peking Review*, No. 50, December 9, 1977.

Of the 385 tons of grain Tachai harvested in 1974, 150 tons were sold to the state: 80 tons of that represented Tachai's quota under the state's plan, and the additional 70 tons brought a price 20 per cent higher than the rate for quota grain.[9] Distribution to the villagers, for their consumption and family stores, accounted for another 114.5 tons (an average of 260 kg per head). The balance, 120.5 tons, went to increase the village's collective grain store, and as seed for the next crops. Figures for grain output by the village in some previous years were as given in Table 1. The average grain yield in Tachai at the time the revolution reached the village, 1945, was 0.75 tons/ha. In 1974 Tachai exceeded its 1971 record for grain production—although 1974 was the third consecutive year of severe drought—and in 1977 an increase of 17 per cent in production brought output for the year to 482 tons, and the yield noted above, 9.8 tons/ha. These increases reflected not only the improvement of soil in the new "man-made plains" but also inter-cropping of soyabean, wheat and maize.[10]

Tachai's total income in 1973 was Y182,421 (yuan), of which only just under half, Y86,416 came from its main agricultural activities: the proportion of income from agriculture is decreasing, as the "sideline" sector of its economy expands. Thus even in a bad year for the major agricultural crops, such as 1971 when grain production fell back sharply, the village's total income can rise— in 1971 it rose by 10 per cent.

A tractor and transport unit, with two tractors and two trucks, makes the biggest non-agricultural contribution to the village's income. In addition to working for the village itself, this unit contracts out to the people's commune of which Tachai is one of 21 collective villages or groups of villages (called production brigades), and to the state. A grain-processing plant, also making bean noodles, serves Tachai and other villages, as does a brick and tile kiln; pig-breeding (in 1974 280 pigs were kept in the village)[11] adds to income, as does a smithy. "Forestry" (in this case mainly fruit-growing) and "animal husbandry" (a horse stud-farm and cattle) make more substantial incomes for the village (Table 2). As everywhere in rural China, Tachai's tax was low—indeed, at Y1,610, extremely low.[12]

The proportions of income distributed to consumption and saving are decided in full meetings of the village membership. Over the past three years the accounts (as shown in Table 3) have shown a decline in the proportion of gross income distributed to members, in favour of larger allocations to the public accumulation fund which provides the capital for the village's development; and the writer was told that that trend had been in effect since 1967. The members had then decided that since all families had savings and their income in grain and cash was sufficient, they could devote more of their income in the next few years to development: the value of a full work-day has been steady at about Y1.50 since 1967. At an annual distributed income of Y180[13] *per capita* the Tachai village is prosperous by average Chinese rural standards, and it is true that the villagers' standard of living may be improved by means other than increasing direct distribution to them—for example, by the collective taking on more, or all, of such charges as those for health insurance, schooling and the processing of families' grain allotments into edible forms. Nevertheless, Tachai is in this regard most unusual.

TABLE 2. *Tachai income sources*

Agriculture		86,416
Side-lines		69,960
of which:		
Transport unit	55,148	
Grain processing	4,679	
Kiln	4,505	
Pigs	1,373	
Smithy	1.300	
Miscellaneous	2,955	
Forestry		12,043
Animal husbandry		14,000
Total		182,419

It has always been a basic and emphatic injunction of Mao Tse-tung's that every increase in production should be reflected promptly in an improvement in the peasants' living standards, and an increase in their income is the most direct means of achieving that. The balance, of course, is a delicate one, a matter of politics, even of "the two lines", socialism and capitalism. To stint accumulation in favour of income is to sacrifice development to consumption: on the other hand, for members of a collective, perhaps over-influenced by their activist leaders, to pinch themselves in order to hasten their unit's development might be to sour their commitment to the socialist path. In the view

TABLE 3. *Tachai accounts*

Year	Gross income (yuan)	Production cost & tax (yuan)	Percentage of gross income	Net income (yuan)	To public accumulation fund (yuan)	Percentage of gross income	Distributed to members (yuan)	Percentage of gross income
1971	147,407	31,692	21.50	115,715	33,314	22.60	82,400	55.90
1972	168,630	53,953	32.00	114,677	38,785	23.00	76,473	45.00
1973	182,421	59,141	32.42	123,280	43,854	24.00	79,426	43.54
1976	208,937	61,944	33.73	146,993	54,887	26.27	83,574	40.00

Note: The sharp increase in production costs in and after 1972 reflects drought conditions, greater use of electricity for irrigation, etc. Figures for 1976 from M. Yahuda, London School of Economics.

from the centre, a well-run village will, after a good year, take advantage of its increased production to increase both the sum allotted to accumulation and the amount distributed to members. Peking's guide-lines for the countryside indicate that in an average year a village should aim to put 10–12 per cent of income into the accumulation fund: that compares to Tachai's 22–4 per cent. In the writer's experience, a village will use the balance between accumulation fund and distribution to even out between the good years and the poor ones (in a bad year, of course, everything may be reduced and nothing paid into accumulation); thus, in a good year, distribution will be held beneath what it could be, while in a poor one the allotment to accumulation will be reduced—and thus often a steady rate of increase in the villagers' income will be achieved.

In recent years Tachai has not needed to make provision from income for its public welfare fund, from which families can be helped by grants when, for reasons of sickness or accident (or because they are chronically "labour-poor") their income falls beneath sufficiency level. The welfare fund is sufficient for emergencies, it is banked at interest with the commune's credit cooperative, and it is several years since any of its families had to be assisted.

Tachai's heavy rate of investment is another expression of its members' highly developed political (or, as we might say, social) consciousness. It has been that, all along and under remarkable local leadership, which has kept the village moving ahead; and no doubt since in 1964 Mao issued the slogan, "In agriculture, learn from Tachai", the awareness of being the cynosure and exemplar for all China has helped keep the villagers' political consciousness at high mettle.

For any collective or cooperative operating under the socialist principle of "to each according to his work", the translation of labour performed into entitlement to reward is a critical, often vexed and potentially divisive function. The work in a farming year is so varied, that inherent variety is multiplied as a village develops and diversifies its agriculture and complements it with side-line and industrial activities, and the range of individual variations in labour capacity, skill and diligence are almost infinite. After a generation of experimentation and modification, in line with their own changing social sense as members of a cooperative community, the Tachai villagers have evolved a system which is both extremely simple and highly sophisticated; and which, with countless local variations, came into general use in China (The fact that the Tachai system of work-point calculation was, in one form or another, in such widespread use, did not mean, however, that in each case Tachai's method had been copied. Other villages, facing the same essential problems, had found their own way to the same answers as Tachai evolved.)

During the course of the year, the Tachai villagers draw grain, vegetables and other commodities produced by their own collective, according to their need. At the end of the farm year (after the autumn harvest is brought in and processed), in a general meeting of the collective, each household declares its assessment of the grain it will need in the coming year, in the light of its previous consumption; and the numbers of adult workers, children and elderly in it (young children and the old need less, full-strength manual workers need more). Such family self-assessment is subject to the comment and ratification of the other members; and then, after modification when necessary in the light of the comments of the other members (now very rare in Tachai's experience), it is registered as the family's entitlement in the coming year.

This Tachai practice is, again, unusual in China in its degree: as can be seen, it represents a move, so far as distribution of the staples of life are concerned, beyond socialism's labour-demanding maxim of "to each according to his work" towards communism's morally-demanding "to each according to his need". It is now general practice in rural China for a proportion of food staples to be distributed on the basis of need: the proportion varies from village to village, sometimes 40 per cent of grain consumed will be distributed according to need, 60 per cent according to work done; more commonly 60:40 the other way around; sometimes 80:20. Tachai was the first village in the writer's experience where all grain consumed is distributed according to need; but this practice is now apparently common in Hsiyang. The methods of assessment of need vary widely. Some villages distribute grain on a *per capita* basis, according to the numbers in a family; others use complicated point-systems to differentiate between the dietetic needs of individuals of different ages and occupations (in essence, the Tachai system merely leaves that differential calculation to the families themselves). As will be seen, this is in no sense a free distribution; grain and other staples thus distributed are counted as part of a household's basic income entitlement according to its labour contribution. But it means that even a labour-poor family will not have to go hungry; such a family will, at the end of a year, find itself with a very low cash entitlement in the collective's distribution, or possibly even with a debt—in which case the family would as a rule be helped with a grant from the public welfare fund.

Tachai does its basic accounting only once a year, at the end of December, whereas a monthly or at least seasonal incidence is the general rule. With tax paid and the decision taken on the amount to be credited to the accumulation fund, the balance (there being no allocation at present to public welfare) remains for distribution according to the criterion of the amount of work the individual member has done in the previous twelve months—and, more important, how he has done it.

The first, and usually definitive, step in the process is self-assessment. The working members of the village divide into two groups, one for men and one for women, and then, in these separate meetings, each member assesses his or her own labour capacity as a norm on a numerical scale with 11 work-points the maximum for a full day's labour by a strong, skilled man, and 8.5 work-points the maximum for a woman. (There is in almost all villages a disparity between the maxima for men and for women, reflecting the differences in physical strength and therefore capacity in heavy manual labour between the sexes; but Tachai's difference of 2.5 work-points is unusually marked. Two points is common, and some villages have reduced the gap to one point. As a rule allowance is made, on the principle of equal work, equal pay, when women's work is as productive as men's—or more productive as is often the case in cotton-picking for example.)

The norms which members assess for themselves are then discussed by those with whom they have been closely working, and at this point the social content of the work done—or, as the Chinese would have it, the political element—is put into the scales. Strength, skill, diligence are perhaps the main components; but what of the member who is not only hard-working but is also gifted with lively humour and kindliness, whose good cheer can enliven and encourage a squad working long hours in arduous conditions? Or the man or woman past the prime so far as physical work is concerned, but who is an activist attentive to the needs of others and of the community, taking on the chores, helping with the office and committee work? And what, on the other hand, of the strong, skilled, and hard-working member who is a trouble-maker, able with a few asides to disrupt the harmony of a work-squad; or a pessimistic wet-blanket, always managing to make hard work seem like fruitless toil? The opinion of their fellows will mark members up or down the scale in accordance with such qualities.

The cadres set a special problem, since their managerial responsibilities can keep them away from the productive labour which is the source of work-points. The Tachai answer is that cadres should be awarded work-points for their office work, but that in no case can a cadre earn more than does an equivalent member, with the same norm, who is not a cadre. In the Chinese perception, manual labour is the source not only of work-points but of practical knowledge and of political rectitude. Since the Cultural Revolution there has been strong emphasis on the need for cadres, at all levels, to participate regularly in manual labour, and it is the practice in rural cooperative units to post the cadres' tally of days spent in labour, so that any tendency to "separate from the masses" and spend too much time at the desk will promptly be noted. These figures were given for cadres in Hsiyang county, giving the average number of days spent at manual labour in 1972: at county level, 115 days; at commune level, 215 days; at brigade level, 310 days; at production team level, 322 days.

The very process of self-assessment and mass comment would seem to make for a sorting-out of problems and conflicts in the community, as well as producing a faithful and comprehensive translation of work into reward. Chen Yung-kuei, the leader of the village during its long years of struggle out of poverty (he is now a Central Committee member and a Vice-Premier), described the process and its role in 1966:

Personal reporting and public assessment (of work norms) is itself an important piece of political work. It is in effect a process of self-examination, self-education, struggle between two ideologies and two roads. ... It increases the self-respect of commune members, gradually fostering in them the habit of truthfulness. Moreover, it is a kind of self-discipline. As for public assessment, it consists of public commendation and criticism. ...

On making a personal report or claim, a member is required to determine reasonably how many work-points he should get in accordance with the amount of labour done and the quality of his work. Thus everyone cannot but consider what attitude he should take. If he is selfish, considers only his own interest, and reports or claims more work-points than he deserves, he may be in danger of being called selfish and backward by other commune members. Thus he has to wage a mental struggle with himself and compare his work with that done by others. ... What is assessed is not only how much work a certain man has done, whether the work is done well or poorly, and how much skill is required for the job. The basic thing is assessment of his thought and his attitude to labour.[14]

After each member has appraised his or her own norm, and that has been commented upon by his or her work-mates, the brigade leadership considers the self-appraised norms and the comments that have been made upon them; and then reports back "to the masses" (i.e., to the general meeting of all members) with a recommendation on each norm. There is at this stage opportunity for further comment, protest or criticism, and discussion; and members' norms are thereupon confirmed.

Once members' norms have been established, calculation of their entitlement is mathematical and straightforward. In Tachai, during the year each working villager has been responsible for reporting his work daily to his squad tallykeeper: the record is kept only of time worked, not the type of labour performed, and that in terms only of days or half days—an hourly count being too complex and cumbersome, considering the seasonal variation of the working day. The tally-keeper tots up time worked for the information of individual villagers every month: some villagers keep their own tally, in specially printed booklets, as a check—but fewer and fewer bother. Multiplication of the number of days worked in the year by the villager's norm yields his/her work-point entitlement for that period: for example, if a villager with a norm of 9 has worked for 308 days in the year his entitlement will be 308 x 9 = 2772 work-points. The total amount remaining for distribution to members (after payment of tax, allocation to accumulation fund, etc.) is then divided by the total number of work-points earned in the year by all members, a calculation which gives a cash value to each work-point. Then, by multiplying an individual's total number of work-points by that value, a cash sum is reached, which is the member's share of the collective's net earnings.

A family unit, or household, will then add up its joint entitlement. From that will be deducted the cash equivalent of the grain and other commodities drawn by the household in the previous year; and the balance remains to be paid in cash. It is at this stage that families in difficulties because of illness or labour shortage will be identified and considered for assistance grants or loans.

The Tachai system's distinguishing features are, first, the very long accounting period, the full year. The advantage of this is that of course much time otherwise spent in meetings is saved; but the vast majority of villages in China still do their accounting much more frequently. Even if they make distribution only once or twice a year, most of them still have their "personal assessment, mass appraisal" sessions monthly. A longer period, village leaders have explained to the writer, means that individual work-styles and the quality of work performance tend to get forgotten. Secondly, the Tachai system, with its tallying of work done only in terms of time, removing differences in type of labour performed, tends to equalize among members' contributions and therefore rewards: most villages still record the type of work done, and make provision so that heavy labour earns more work-points than light. The Tachai system differentiates solely through the norm and although that maintains the essential differences between the fully able-bodied worker and the less capable, the difference is narrower than one which directly reflects work done.

The work-point system involves a delicate political balance. The guiding maxim of the present, socialist stage in China is "to each according to his work"; but there is also the contrary, indeed almost contradictory, effort to play down the role of material incentives. Chen Yung-kuei, in a lecture in 1966, appeared rather to glide over the contradiction: "It is necessary", he said, "to avoid absolute egalitarianism, pay more to those who do more labour, and eschew material incentives." But he went on: "We [cannot] confuse the principle of more pay for more labour with material incentives. In other words, we have to recognize some differences, but the difference must not be too great."[15] The system with which Tachai, like most Chinese village cooperatives, began related work-points to particular jobs. That method, as well as being cumbrously intricate, saw the able-bodied and strong pressing for assignment to the most work-point lucrative jobs, and a widening income gap between them and the less strong workers: this came to be seen as "putting work-points in command", and Chen Yung-kuei criticized the system as "representing the world outlook of the bourgeoisie, whose purpose in life is to make profit."[16] He described the system evolved by Tachai in

1968, in which the essentials of the present system were beginning to appear, in these terms:

> Under the new system those commune members who show a high level of political consciousness, who work most conscientiously and selflessly and do not hesitate to shoulder hard farm work, receive the greatest number of work-points. The most important criterion is devotion to the public. A man's ability may be great or small, but if he works heart and soul for the public, he is respected and ensured a secure life even if he has limited labour power.[17]

Chen also pointed to the complementary relationship between strong and weak workers in the collective economy, each benefiting from the work the other does.

Tachai's progressive evolution of its present system of translating labour performed into reward entitlement has seen a steady stretching-out in the linkages between labour and reward. Initially the connection was more or less direct: plough this field in the set time, to the set standard, and you get so many work-points. Now particular jobs, even extended periods of particular labour, are subsumed and lost within the general pattern of the year's work. At the same time, the references by which norms are established have been greatly widened, and to some extent their priority reversed. The "political" factor ("political" in the wide sense here covering the member's relationship to the community) is now considered before the factors of labour skill and strength.

Postscript, 1978. The Tachai system of work-point allocation came into wide use in rural China after the Cultural Revolution, but in the later 1970s there was a general retreat. It had been found that the connection between members' norms and the actual work they performed had become so distant as to invite distortion. A member with a high norm, allotted to him after a period of good work and in consideration of his "political" bearing, might begin to slacken off; then in the period immediately prior to the next norm-consideration session (and these were becoming increasingly infrequent) he might apply himself vigorously again—would his fellow members still insist on downgrading his norm to reflect his earlier slack work? In theory they would have done so, but in the living context of relations between members of a village community the temptation to avoid unpleasantness must tend to entrench a member's norm once that has become identified with his "political" standing, i.e. with him personally rather than with his specific, recent performance in labour. This tendency meant that the basic maxim of the present phase of China's political development, "to each according to his labour", was not being effectively applied in practice. That some members would be receiving a larger share of the collective income than their work entitled them to was seen by others as unfair, became a source of resentment, and led to a widening slackening in labour effort. In many cases decreases in production—or falling-off in the rate of its increase—were ascribed to such discontents. Ideologically, the problem came to be seen as an expression of the ultra-left error of "egalitarianism"—by which the Chinese mean premature levelling—and, with so much else, was attributed to the influence of the "gang of four". More pragmatically, it was diagnosed as springing from "mechanical" adoption of Tachai's practice by communities in which the level of political consciousness and social commitment to production was not as high as in Tachai.

The corrective movement began in 1977, and amounted to a wholesale reversion to the job-specific allocation of work-points which had been in general use before the Cultural Revolution. Only a small minority of rural units, perhaps 10–20 per cent, retained the Tachai system as a whole. Under the restored system, practically every job of work in the farming almanac will have its fixed complement of work-points, assessed, tabulated and circulated in booklets by the leadership, usually at brigade level. Work-points are allocated very much more frequently, sometimes daily, and the Tachai method of "self-assessment, mass appraisal" persists only in the process of dividing the points attached to a big job among those who have done it. The system, called "two-fixeds" (fixed job, fixed work-points), is conceded as being less advanced socially than Tachai's but is seen as more adjusted to the social realities of rural China—and its practitioners claim that its reintroduction brought tangible benifts in improved morale and increased production.

Tachai's influence works towards equalizing, the removal of differences in income which reflect not disparities of effort and commitment to the common good, but only disparities in physical strength or manual skill. But even when the "learn from Tachai" campaign was approaching its height, in the early 1970s, some units were applying the principle of "to each according to his labour" rigorously. For example, watching a joint fishing and agricultural commune on the Yellow Sea constructing a new breakwater, the writer saw that the work tallying did not merely keep count of the numbers of loaded barrows of stone which the members delivered; a weighbridge had been set up and the work was being tallied according to the weight of stone each member moved. Clearly this approximated a piece-work approach, and left the physically slight member at a disadvantage in terms of income. A powerful reminder, from Mao Tse-tung himself, was sounded in China in 1975; that socialism is a transitional stage, and that the social momentum towards communism must consciously be maintained. Industry's "eight-grade wage system, distribution to each according to his work and exchange by means of money" were singled out by the Chairman as vestiges of capitalism, "scarcely different from those in the old society".[18] Similarly, women are being encouraged by the Communist Party to demand, and are demanding, equal pay for equal work—that is, that a fully able-bodied woman worker should be able to claim a maximum norm as high as her male equivalent's. (There was a strong "woman's liberation" element in the "Criticize Confucius, Criticize Lin Piao" campaign in the early 1970s, with women pressing for removal of the remaining discriminations against them—and those, for all the huge progress women have made in China, are still not few. One highly significant and radical change has been introduced in marital customs: reversing entrenched tradition, activist young men are now making it a point to go, on marriage, to join their bride's household, a reversal of practice that sharply changes a daughter's economic potential in a household.[19] This, as it becomes more common, is likely to reinforce the growing popularity of family planning. If a daughter can be expected to bring a son-in-law into the household, rather than herself leaving it, her economic potential is as high as a son's, and a couple with one or two daughters will not feel the need to have more children in the hope of getting a boy.)

As noted above, in its 2½-point differential between norm maxima for men and women Tachai is far from being "advanced", and it will be significant to note whether, and how soon, that is changed. Tachai women are well placed to lead the way. When Chen Yung-kuei in 1974 gave up his positions as secretary of the village's party branch committee and chairman of the revolutionary committee[20] he was replaced by a young woman, Kuo Feng-lien. At the time of the writer's first visit to Tachai, Kuo Feng-lien was leader of a crack girls' work squad, which had formed to assert and demonstrate the girls' ability to take on the heaviest work. The example of this squad, whom the Tachai villagers dubbed "the iron girls", has spread. Far and wide across China "iron girl squads" have formed, a dozen or two of the most activist and physically able young women showing by their zeal and skill that work traditionally thought too heavy or dangerous for women is in fact well within their prowess. One county in central China counted among its communes 2,200 "iron girls" working as blasting specialists, 940 as stonemasons and 17 as blacksmiths in 1975.[21]

While transforming their land the Tachai villagers have also transformed their dwellings. The entire village has been newly housed, and additional houses are built every year to accommodate the new households as couples set up on their own or to provide more rooms as families expand. The Tachai housing retains the traditional cave form of villages in this area, but instead of being cut into the loess hill-sides the rooms are stone-built, in connected rows. The "houses" are in fact single rooms, but the kitchens are separate (a healthy innovation which creates, however, the need for separate heating of the living-sleeping room); and a large family will occupy two or even three adjoining rooms. Again unusually for village China, in Tachai houses are rented from the collective, not owned: the rent is about 10 yuan per room per year. This means that since (as is explained below) there are no private plots either, the "private sector" in Tachai is limited to personal belongings and personal farm-tools,[22] and of course income and savings.

Mao Tse-tung has summed up the great drive of the Chinese people in terms of three struggles: the struggle for production, class struggle (that is, the struggle to establish a new social ethic reflecting a communal rather than individualistic society), and the struggle for scientific experiment; and Tachai, a model in all three regards, strives to maintain its exemplary excellence.

This winter, 1974–5, the village's main project has been to bring more land into the "man-made plain" category, and using its own tractors and bull-dozers hired from the Tachai People's Commune its members are blasting and levelling more ridges. Top-soiling of these new fields calls for much labour, with alternating layers of organic fertilizer and good soil being spread over the previous sub-soil earth from the ridges. Tachai's land area will steadily be extended, and as more of it is made suitable for mechanical working so narrow terraces high on the hills, previously, with much labour, used for grain, are being put under fruit trees. The greatest potential for continuing to improve the yield of the land, however, is seen to be in improved farming technology. The village has its own scientific farming experimental plots, with a special group tending them, including both experienced peasants and youngsters with agro-technical education. This group is responsible for providing the village with its improved seed strains, both its own breeds and those received from the central farm extension net-work, through the commune; the latter are tested and often cross-bred again before the seeds are put into general production use. The village has recently begun inter-cropping: wheat is sown in September between the rows of ripening corn, which is planted on ridges; with the corn harvest about the end of October the wheat is left in the cleared fields, with initial growth established, for harvesting in the next summer.

At any time of the year now Tachai hums. The winters, which in north China in the old order were periods of almost total inactivity when the peasants hibernated in the effort to eke out their food and fuel until the spring, are now among the busiest seasons.

All over China the commune members turn to capital construction works as soon as the autumn harvest is processed. (By the centre's count, 900,000 projects were taken up after the 1974 harvest, and 500,000 of those had been completed by the end of the year.)[23] In the spring and summer, capital construction gives way to planting and servicing the crops; in the past three years of severe drought the Tachai villagers have had to hand-water the crops on their unirrigated fields, carrying water on shoulder poles to water each plant or cluster individually.

Tachai today is an efficiently self-managed and increasingly mechanized cooperative farm. Its productivity has increased more than ten-fold in a generation and (with the exceptions noted above) that progress has been achieved with no special help from outside. The state brought electricity to the village (if it had had a falling water source no doubt it would have generated its own, as many similar villages have done),[24] but the villagers themselves had to undertake their own wiring and distribution. The state's essential contribution, however, was to provide the social and political climate in which Tachai could evolve as a socialist community. And beyond that, the state has helped by making only scant demands upon the village. With tax from the beginning light, and becoming progressively lighter, the village's surpluses were left for its own use and so, by allocating substantial portions of income to its accumulation fund, Tachai could finance its own development. It elected its own leadership and, either within the village or in outside institutions trained its own specialists.

The Tachai villagers, beginning with nothing but their poor, scattered and scanty land and their own labour-power, have transformed the circumstances of their lives, neutralizing drought, preventing floods, and so escaping, for good and all it seems, the ancient affliction of famine. They may still live spartan and hard-working lives by the standards of the better-off classes of the developed West, but by the standards of the vast majority of Third World villagers the people of Tachai have already become rich. They have security, as individuals, as families, and as a community; they have incomes they consider adequate, and savings; they are comfortably housed and well clothed; they have good health, as a result of their full diet and high standards of hygiene, and they have good medical services available if they lose it; they have their own primary school, a secondary school nearby, and access to higher education. Their social horizon they would consider as wide as China.

Tachai epitomizes revolution in more ways than one. Up to the middle of this century Chinese agriculture, over-specialized and concentrated on the fertile plains and river valleys, was at an impasse. The population was grossly excessive to the natural resources as those were then exploited. The Tachai villagers—and the Chinese peasantry in the mass—have broken out from that dead-end and by their new, cooperative social forms enabled themselves to "turn labour into capital" and made of their vast numbers an asset rather than a handicap. They have thus brought about a reversal of flow in the influence-relationship of human and physical elements in the landscape: physical factors of land and climate had shaped Chinese civilization; now man in China is re-shaping the physical landscape, defying—and even slowly modifying—the constraits of climate. The drama of change is nowhere more evident than in hill country such as Tachai's.

TACHAI'S PAST

Like most Chinese hill villages, the old Tachai was wretchedly poor. The eroded terrain, ridges and steep gullies, increased the fragmentation caused by inheritance practice, and the village's land lay in some 4,700 separate pieces, of varying area, the smallest quilt-sized. The total farmed area was about 50 hectares, and of that 60 per cent was owned by four households, the richest classified as a landlord, the others as rich peasants. Nearly 80 per cent of the villagers were poor peasants, many of those landless, or lower-middle peasants, owning or renting some land but not enough to live on. After this region of Shansi was reached by the Communist forces in 1945 the land of the landlord and the rich peasants was confiscated and distributed, as nearly as practically equally, among all the village households.[25] With this distribution of the land, the Communists kept their pledge to the peasantry; and then faced the problem of moving them away from the smallholding rural economy towards the collectivization which Mao—like Lenin—saw as the only means of escape from mass peasant poverty. Under Mao's call, "Get organized", the Communists introduced a seed of cooperation (related to a practice traditional in some parts of China) in the "Mutual Aid Teams", groupings of six to a dozen households which pooled and exchanged labour on each other's fields.

At the time of land distribution Tachai was very deficient in labour power. In 1940, in one of their anti-guerrilla punitive sweeps, the Japanese had killed 40 men of the village; after 1945 another score left to join the Liberation Army. One mutual aid team was formed by eleven work-strong households; another was organized by Chen Yung-kuei, one among the poorest of the poor peasants, who had survived the disintegration and death of his family by begging in the years before liberation. These two mutual aid teams (MATs) epitomized divergent and conflicting trends in the nascent cooperative movement. The stronger team, calling itself "The Stalwarts", had labour power and assets (tools, animals, etc.); the other team, made up of older men and youngsters apart from Chen, was weak in such things but more cohesive because of its members' greater commitment to cooperation. While the "stronger" team broke up under the strain of its members' individualism, the other prospered. Able to rationalize labour on the scattered plots that made up its members' holdings, Chen's "Oldsters and Youngsters" team brought in higher yields than Tachai had seen before on any but the landlord's best fields. More and more households joined, convinced by results that cooperation led to a fuller livelihood.

By 1949, 49 households were in the village MAT; and in 1952 Chen and his colleagues in the leadership applied for permission to transform the organization into a cooperative, in keeping with the party's guide-lines. In this first form of coop the use of land as well as of labour was rationalized. The holdings of all members could be farmed as an entity; and members, rather than drawing their income exclusively from the yield of their own fields, would take a share of the pooled production of the whole coop. Income would be apportioned to members under two headings: 70 per cent of the coop's income (after tax and accumulation fund allotment) would be distributed according to work done, under a fairly primitive work-point system; and the remainder in the form of dividends on the capital (land, tools, animals, etc.) vested in the coop by the members.[26] The party's policy at that time was to hasten slowly; to encourage the formation of coops out of MATs, but before approving the formation of a coop to scrutinize the qualifications of the would-be cooperators: were all applications for membership truly voluntary, or were some peasants being swayed by over-eager cadres, or coerced by the majority? Was the leadership up to the challenge of managing the larger unit? Was there a good enough accountant? The party did not wish to see cooperation given a bad name by the failure and disintegration of half-baked or prematurely formed coops—"no failures allowed, successes only", was the watchword. This wariness merged into over-cautiousness, and came to be denounced by Mao Tse-tung. A few years later, sensing that the cooperative movement had caught on with the peasantry, he criticized those of his colleagues who were holding the peasants back with "excessive criticism, inappropriate complaints, endless anxiety and the erection of countless taboos". Like women with bound feet, he said, they were tottering along behind and always complaining, "You're going too fast".[27]

Tachai, a poor, expectedly backward, isolated and small community, did not appeal to the local party leadership as a likely bet for a successful cooperative. Approval came grudgingly and with qualifications, in the spring of 1953: the Tachai MAT could transform itself into an elementary coop, but one of no more than 30 families. A bigger unit than that, the upper level authorities ruled, would be too much for the village leadership to manage. Since there were already 49 households in the MAT, this meant that 19 of them would have to split off and continue as a smaller MAT while the others brought their land into common management, or even return to individual household farming. Chen Yung-kuei and his fellows here gave an early—though at first disguised—example of what has recently been declared as a principle of socialist politics: they "dared to swim against the current". They formed a 49 family coop but did not declare its real size to the higher authorities, and for a period kept false accounts to maintain the deception.

This coop included about half the village land; the rest was divided among other MATs and the go-it-aloners. After the coop's first year it registered crop yields of 1.8 tons/ha; the MATs chalked up 1.35; while the individual farmers averaged 1.2 tons. The coop thus made its point—that through cooperation, and on a widening scale, the peasants could raise their living standards. More joined, both individual households and MATs merging as groups. With cooperation successfully established in the village, the prospect-horizons of the remaining go-it-aloners became circumscribed. Their hopes of improving their conditions rested on being able to hire labour, and in the long run to buy land: with the alternative of membership in the coop before them, no villagers would be prepared to hire themselves out or sell their land. Both pull and push factors thus operated in favour of coop membership.

Tachai's next step was taken in 1955, by which time practically all the households were members of the coop: this now changed its nature, and it became fully socialist. The basic problem of the elementary coop form, the "main contradiction", lay in the fact that some members were able to live on their dividend income, or nearly so. These, either "upper middle peasants" who had come through the land distribution with their holdings untouched, or "new middle peasants" who had done especially well in the distribution, accordingly tended to do much less work than other members, a relationship which came to be seen as "disguised exploitation". This group was, however, in the minority, and open to persuasion and, no doubt, to pressure. On the side of persuasion was the fact that the coop was prospering, and that guarantees could be offered that, given an average amount of work, the income of members who agreed to vest their land in the coop—that is to relinquish ownership of land to the coop—would not be less under the exclusive work-point system of distribution than it had been under the part-work-point, part-dividend system. Members were assured the right to withdraw if the coop failed to keep that guarantee. As a further inducement, members were allotted "small plots reserved for private use" ("private plots"). These they could farm as and when they wished, and the produce from them could be consumed or sold as the family decided, and would be free of tax. In one perspective, the change from the elementary to the advanced (or socialist) form of cooperative looks like the most momentous single step in the Chinese peasantry's astonishingly swift move into collective forms: in this step they relinquished the personal landownership which most members had been given only a few years before. But it must be remembered that critical elements of ownership, the right to decide on land use and the exclusive right to the produce of the land, had been surrendered when the elementary coop was formed and the land of the members put under the unified management of the elected leadership. So the shift from elementary to advanced cooperative form entailed basically only the members' agreement to waive their entitlement to dividend income, and accept the principle that in future all income would be distributed according to work done. Since the total product was confidently expected to increase under the new form, the change should not entail reduction in income for any member household which was prepared to work.

The land was not given away. The coop bought it, with the draft animals and implements to work it, at prices set on a valuation scale worked out after discussion by the full membership. Members were to be paid off in instalments over several years; but in the case of Tachai so successful was the coop in increasing production that the debts to members were paid off at the end of the first year. (The writer came across one instance, in the Chang Chin Commune near Suchow, where in 1973 a village coop was just making the final payments to members on account of jasmine-tea bushes bought by the coop when it was formed in the early 1950s.

The Tachai coop's crop yield in 1955 reached 3.25 tons/ha. In the following winter the members launched themselves on a crash land reclamation programme, beginning with their biggest gully, Langwochang. This, about 1.5 km long, and 7 metres across on the bottom, had a steep gradient and was useless for agriculture; every rainy season saw it deepened and extended. The coop members, working only with hand-tools and wheelbarrows, and with the ground frozen in the sub-zero temperatures, tore down the gully sides and levelled the floor. To overcome the gradient they terraced, building solid, stone terraces straight across the gully, and thus creating a flight of stepped fields. The following summer the Tachai legend proper begins. Flash floods in the rainy season destroyed all the new terraces, demolishing the stone walls, washing the arduously built-up top-soil down the valley. The villagers turned to again and rebuilt the terraces, this time more strongly. The following year they were washed out again. At this point, drawing on their experience, the Tachai villagers made a major inventive leap: they applied the principle of the arch, with which they were familiar from the architecture of their traditional cave-houses, to the gully terraces. They rebuilt them curving up-gully, against the direction of the floods, reinforcing the bases of the arches with boulders. These terraces held, and were productively farmed until the villagers, out-growing them, buried them under their "man-made plains".

Tachai's grain yield continued to increase year by year, reaching 5.75 tons/ha in 1958. The village's achievements began to be noted and held up as an example of what even the poorest village could achieve on its own initiatives, and without help from outside. In 1960 Chen Yung-kuei was awarded the national status of "model peasant". In the early 1960s, after the severe set-back to Chinese agriculture consequent on the natural afflictions of the "three hard years" from 1959 through 1961 and other factors, differences in central party policy on agriculture sharpened. Those who had argued that cooperativization had been allowed to move—or had been pushed—too far and too fast, damaging production, came into the ascendancy. They now argued that a swing back towards individualism in farming, with commercial incentives to spur it, was needed; the private plots were emphasized as a growth sector and peasants were encouraged to engage in private trade with their surpluses from those plots. Tachai, however, persisted on its successful collective path, and became conspicuous and politically contentious in the new climate. As early as 1961 suspicions were voiced at county level that Tachai was exaggerating its yields by understating its cultivated area: an investigatory team was sent to the village in that year to check the figures—only to confirm them.

In 1963 calamity struck Tachai. A phenomenal deluge of rain, seven days and seven nights, destroyed more than 90 per cent of the terracing, washing away the top-soil and flattening crops. Most of the dwellings of the villagers, caves cut into the hill-sides in the traditional style, were also destroyed. The destruction seemed so comprehensive and irrevocable that some villagers voted for calling it a day and asking the state for re-settlement in a more propitious area. The legend here becomes heroic. Chen Yung-kuei and his fellows in the village leadership rallied and braced the villagers. There had been no loss of life, the draft animals were safe, most of the grain store was intact, they pointed out. What had been built up before could be built up again, and this time better and stronger: starting almost from scratch, but with eighteen years' experience in cooperation behind them, the villagers could improve their field lay-out and construct modern, stone housing—all that was needed was resolve, organization, labour and time. Tachai refused the disaster assistance the state had quickly offered, and under the watch-word of "self-reliance" began to build itself up again.

In the intense collective effort to repair the damage and start anew, significant changes in organization emerged. With everyone working long hours at unusually varied jobs (field repair and crop rescue work in the day, house construction at night) work-point tallying and calculation became a nuisance in its then complex form, and was much simplified. With the collective land in desperate need of attention or reconstruction, there was no time or effort to spare for the private plots, which had been washed out with everything else. It was decided to abolish them, adding their area to the collective. The villagers had for some time been conscious of the contradictions posed by retention of private plots. Collective resources such as irrigation water had to be used privately, and the private plots required family night-soil and other organic fertilizers from which the collective could have benefited. And as a Tachai cadre explained to the writer in 1971, there was a contradiction in labour too: "Some members would work on their private plots during the long summer lunch break, when they should have been resting, and were too tired to work properly on the collective fields afterwards". A generational divergence in attitudes had been noticed: while many of the older generation were happy to have private plots to work, many youngsters found the need to add labour on private plots to a full day on the collective land irksome, an impediment to their other activities. And—perhaps most important—it had also been noted that the yield from private plots was not as high as that from the collective fields. Ultimately these factors would probably have been enough in themselves to induce the Tachai villagers to merge their private plots with the collective fields, but the great rain having done that for them physically it must have been a much easier decision to merge them organizationally as well. The villagers would henceforth make provision in their management of the collective land to supply all households with as great a variety of vegetables as members had grown on the private plots.

Out of what must have been prodigies of labour, a new Tachai emerged: the fields had been restored after two years, all members were housed again after four, in the new stone-built houses they now rented from their collective.

As the divisions in the national leadership over agriculture and then over all policy became deeper, the case of Tachai became more clamant and more vexed. By their achievements the Tachai villagers were proving Mao's most basic teaching: that once people had changed their thinking, ridding themselves of fatalism and pessimism, they could so organize their labour as to achieve what at first looked hopeless, even impossible—that spirit can be transformed into a material force:

> The masses have boundless creative power. They can organize themselves and concentrate on places and branches of work where they can give full play to their energy; they can concentrate on production in breadth and depth, and create more and more undertakings for their own well-being.[28]

Mao then held up Tachai as a model for all China. He received Chen Yung-kuei in Peking, and issued the slogan, "In agriculture, learn from Tachai". Mao thus both publicly threw his weight behind the way of socialism and self-reliance in China's rural regeneration, and nailed his own colours to the mast of Tachai's success. If Tachai failed, or could be shown to be deceptive (a collectivist Potempkin village), both Mao's prescriptions for China and Mao's leadership could be devalued. Those opposing Mao and the course for China for which he stood consequently opposed Tachai too. Teams of investigation representing and sent by those in the party who by now were grouping with Liu Shao-chi were sent to Tachai again to check all claims. In 1964, during the campaign to rectify work styles and organization in the countryside which became known as "the four clean-ups", one investigatory team from Peking dissolved the Tachai Communist Party branch committee, thus displacing Chen and his colleagues from the leadership. Another team from Peking, representing Mao's group, followed; re-measured all Tachai's fields to check its yield claims, investigated the record of the displaced party branch committee—and, declaring Tachai an outstanding unit, reinstated the Chen Yung-kuei leadership. These manoeuvres were part of the preliminary skirmishing of the Cultural Revolution, and from that convulsion Tachai and all it stood for emerged triumphant. Tachai was accepted as the model for rural China—which is to say, for the preponderant and essential China—and became the focus of a vast and continuing lay pilgrimage. Between the beginning of 1965 and the end of 1972 more than six million travelled to Tachai to learn from its example, and they still go by hundreds of thousands each year.

The state makes itself responsible for housing and feeding these multitudes while they are at Tachai and has built guest-houses and mess-halls for them. (These are the large and extensive buildings seen in photographs of Tachai, among which the more modest rows of housing that constitute Tachai proper can be missed. Since 1964 Tachai has also been commune headquarters, and a meeting hall seating several thousand, shops, hospital, school and other commune services further enlarge the settlement at Tachai.)

The Tachai villagers appear to disregard the presence of the visitors who file along the pathways through their fields most days of the year. They are personally involved only with visiting foreigners and members of the national or provincial leadership who come to Tachai. Occasionally Tachai turns out *en fête* to greet a foreign dignitary, decorating the houses and putting on music and dances of welcome—celebrations, at the cost of production, which the members perhaps regard as their contribution to China's foreign relations.

This highly compressed and therefore oversimplified account[29] of how Tachai transformed itself in a generation may also be seen as a sketch of the basic transformation of rural China as a whole. For Tachai is typical as well as exceptional; and the stages of its transformation, its struggles and set-backs, are recognizable experience for every Chinese village. Tachai has its failings too, it would be unreal—not to say un-Marxist—for them to be denied. In 1966 Chen Yung-kuei himself exposed some "capitalist-roaders" in the village who "want to report a smaller output, exaggerate natural calamities, conceal food grain, and engage in free trade".[30] In 1970 some Tachai members were criticized for "setting unity above persisting in principles—for the sake of unity they actually covered up contradictions, avoided struggle and abandoned principles".[31] Clearly, being held up as a model for China adds its own strains and temptations for the Tachai villagers.

THE LESSONS OF TACHAI

The establishment and emulation of models, "letting key points lead the area", is central to China's development. The excelling unit—village, brigade, commune or now even a whole county—which has registered outstanding progress in crop yields, in land reclamation or water control and in all-round development, is hailed as a "model in learning from Tachai". It will usually receive a certificate or banner, to be proudly hung in unit headquarters, and its achievements, techniques and spirit are publicized and held up for the emulation of all (while the unit so honoured will be expected to remind itself of the need for modesty, and of continued advance). In 1972 there were some 10,000 such model units in China.[32]

What Tachai is for the whole of China these model units become for their counties, localities or provinces. Delegations from other villages visit them, inspect the progress and are shown the techniques, and then report to their own members. Mass discussion groups are held to popularize the lesson of the advanced units and to work out ways of local application, and an "emulation campaign" sometimes launched. Summed up in one of the character groupings so popular with the Chinese because of their mnemonic symmetry, there are five elements to such a campaign: Learn From; Compete With; Catch Up With; Give Assistance To; Surpass. A model unit is not a passive object for emulation, it is an active teacher and helper. Members and cadres from model units are sent to backward units, carrying not only techniques but also confidence and drive. Chen Yung-kuei lectures these days far and wide across China to carry the message of Tachai, and there are thousands like him on local levels, disseminating the lessons of successful development. This emulation of excellence, with its powerful emphasis on morale and esprit, on the revolutionary ethic of hard work and plain living, seems to be one of the prime sources of the dynamism that is apparent in the Chinese rural scene.

The basic lesson in Tachai lies not so much in what its villagers have done, as in the spirit in which they have done it. Tachai is Mao's thought made material, the demonstration that once "people's thinking is revolutionized" they can profoundly change their physical environment: "Changes in our thinking translate into changes in our land, our harvests and our village", as one of the Tachai cadres put it. But there are some special Tachai techniques which are part of the lesson, techniques especially valid for other hill villages: the arched terracing in gullies, broadening gullies and, most recently, running gullies one into another to create "man-made plains"; the use of cable lifts; the flask-shaped water-storage pits, etc. Recently Tachai installed experimentally a Mexican-designed focused irrigation system, which conserves water and reduces weed growth by feeding water direct to individual plants; but this seems to be something grafted on to Tachai, risking making it a show-window rather than a model, and the cadres are reported to have been divided about its adoption. It is not one of the things which visitors are normally shown.

There are some components of the Tachai model which Chinese peasant visitors are explicitly warned not to copy—for example, the absence of private plots. Decisions on the management or abolition of the private plots should be taken, they are warned, only in the light of their own local circumstances and attitudes: mechanical imitation of Tachai's 1963 decision could, in different circumstances, be a serious mistake.

The vast majority of commune households retain and farm their private plots on an individual household basis. The centre's guideline is that about 5–7 per cent of total arable may be devoted to private plots; the area of an individual private plot can vary, from not much larger than a badminton court in fertile, densely populated areas, to plots of a third of an acre and more in the north and west. Private plots as a rule add about 10 per cent to a household's income, in kind or, when surplus is sold, in cash. They can provide fodder for privately raised pigs, which can be killed for family meat or sold to the state. Vegetables are the commonest crop grown on private plots, but grain, tobacco, flax for linen, and other crops are also grown. In the pastoral brigades of communes in the grass-lands, in Inner Mongolia for example, "private plots" consist of the horses, cattle and sometimes sheep or goats, kept by a household for its own use: these are branded and run with the collective herds as a rule, the households paying the collective (by deduction from their income entitlements) to cover cost of pasturage, herding, etc.

In most villages the yards around the houses provide additional private "plotlets". These too are usually closely cultivated, sown to vegetables, even grain; or to trees, planted usually as a crop as well as for shade. [See p. 240. *Ed.*]

In the official view, private plots are a useful and at present usually necessary adjunct to the collective economy, giving commune members a flexible source of table supplies and additional income. The right to maintain private plots is affirmed in the 1978 Constitution, Article 7.

Provided that the absolute predominance of the collective economy of the people's commune is ensured, commune members may farm small plots of land for personal needs, engage in limited household sideline production, and in pastoral areas they may also keep a limited number of livestock for personal needs.

A small, but apparently slowly growing, number of villages have already done away with private plots altogether however, finding that household needs can be satisfied more effectively from the collective. Sometimes, as was the case with Tachai, some extraneous factor has come into play to push members, already uncomfortable with some of the "contradictions' of the private plots, into abolition. (In an example from the writer's experience, a large village in the bend of the Yellow River area had decided not to relocate its private plots after a state-laid canal was run through them, but to do without.) In other cases of abolition, purely "political" factors, and possibly emulation of Tachai, seem to have operated—for example, almost all units in Hsiyang County (where Tachai is situated) and a considerable proportion in Shansi, have abolished private plots.

The writer has come across other instances, however, in which private plots were abolished and then reinstated. In one instance, a commune just outside Peking, members had apparently been urged to do away with their private plots in the exuberance of the Cultural Revolution, the plots being assailed by keen cadres as "tails of capitalism". After a year without private plots the dissatisfaction of the members forced a re-examination of the whole question, as a result of which the private plots were reinstated—and the cadres who had brought about their abolition "criticized". (The writer discussed this incident with the members and cadres concerned, the latter amiably conceding their error, and coolly explaining the reasons for it—the pressures and enthusiasms of the Cultural Revolution.) Villages wishing to abolish their private plots must, according to central officials, seek approval from higher levels; but in some villages the writer's suggestion that this is the case has been vigorously contradicted, with the argument that if the members decided to do away with their plots, upper levels could hardly make them keep them. The point appears to be that the upper levels insist on an opportunity to verify that it is the members, and not just the cadres, from whom the initiative to abolish has come.

Some variations of private plot management, falling between outright abolition and individual household farming of the plots, have been evolved. Sometimes special squads are formed by the collective to work the private plots: the cost of this labour is deducted from members' entitlements to the collective income, while the produce from the plots goes direct to the individual households. This leaves the members with the advantages of having their private plot produce but frees them from the need to work the plots. In some instances of that approach, the private plots have been grouped together and merged, the separate plots themselves thus becoming notional. They continue in the form of a family's entitlement to a share of produce from that area, tax-free and not considered by the state in assessing grain quotas.

With the continued progress of the collective economy, it is expected in the national leadership that private plots will become irrelevant to the peasants' needs and then will be discarded as an anachronism, even a nuisance. This process is already evident, but officials in the Ministry of Agriculture told the writer in 1974 that it was expected to take a long time, and private plots would be retained for the foreseeable future: the timing of their abolition would be decided by the villagers, and party policy was that applications by units seeking to abolish the plots would be scrutinized by higher levels before permission was granted. This policy was reaffirmed in an interview in 1978.

Comments on the private plots made by Chou En-lai in 1971 to some American farmers are still apposite. Villages like Tachai which had abolished private plots were in a minority, he said, and were "socially advanced":

The majority still have them. But of course we are not like the Soviet Union, where agricultural production is concentrated on private plots. There people expend little energy on their collective land; most of their time is spent on their plots. As a result the state often cannot purchase enough grain for public use—yet there is plenty of grain available on the free market.

We do not follow the Soviet example in the way private plots are used, but we still need to have them. In order to stimulate the initiative and enthusiasm of the peasants we still advocate private plots, so that in addition to the collective income they can earn something on the side and also ensure some variety in their diet.[33]

Another Tachai characteristic which is not for "mechanical imitation" is its "level of account". Tachai is one of 21 brigades of a people's commune which took the name of Tachai when it was formed by the confederation of advanced coops in 1958. ("Brigade" is the advanced coop renamed as a component of a people's commune.) Tachai is a unit of account: this means that the income of the entire village is pooled for distribution to all its members, as described above: but it is the common practice in China for the *production team*, a smaller unit than the brigade (equivalent to the elementary coop of the early 1950s in size) to be an accounting unit—the unit which owns the land, makes the day-to-day decisions about its working, and decides too about the distribution of income. The accounting unit can be considered as *the unit of equalization*. Within an accounting unit, the backward benefit from association with the advanced: in the Tachai context, that means that a labour-poor family benefits from its association with a labour-strong family.

During the "high tide" period of socialization in the countryside, the mid- and latter 1950s, the level of account was very commonly raised to that of the advanced coops, which in most cases embraced several villages, and even sometimes to the level of the commune, embracing scores of villages. Thus backward villages were included in the same "unit of equalization" as the more prosperous, and benefited accordingly: the prosperous villages, perhaps more enterprising and hard-working as well as more fortunate in their land, were "levelled down". Widespread dissatisfaction with this arrangement was registered in the early 1960s. After investigation the centre laid down the guide-line that the production team, not the brigade, should as a rule be the unit of account; and on a very wide scale the communes changed their organization accordingly. Tachai, retaining its level of account at advanced coop/brigade level, was one of a small minority of such cases. (But of course Tachai, with its 88 households, is smaller than most production *teams* in communes in the rich plains areas of China; there are no component production teams in Tachai.)

The trend, and the aim, is steadily to raise the level of account again to brigade, and ultimately to commune, level; but, as with the private plots, the centre is wary that over-keen cadres should not force the pace, and therefore lays down rigorous criteria, to be applied by higher levels, for any brigade wishing to become a unit of account. First, the disparity between the levels of production (and therefore of prosperity) between the production teams should not be wide; the management and accounting skills of the brigade leadership should be developed; and the political and social consciousness of all team members should be high. When these conditions are met, permission will be given for a brigade to become a unit of account.

There are marked advantages of scale in production and management in accounting at the higher level, and successful brigade units of account tend to progress faster than others with team level accounting. An interesting half-way stage is employed at the Shah Shih Yu (Valley of Stones) Brigade (Yueh Kechuang People's Commune, Hopei). This village, with about 130 households, is in many ways another Tachai, a once desolately poor hill village which has lifted itself to prosperity by its own efforts. It became the unit of account when it became an advanced coop, merging four elementary coops; but there was dissatisfaction among the members of the better-off production teams (as the elementary coops had been re-named), who felt they were being pulled down in the equalization process. After discussion in the early 1960s it was decided to maintain leadership and management at brigade level; but that in distribution of income, allowance should be made for the differing productivity of the component teams, and equivalent differences registered in the value of the work-points for the separate teams. The Shah Shih Yu members say that this gives them the advantages of brigade level accounting without which, at their present state of economic— and political—development, would be felt as its disadvantages.

In the very long term, accounting is expected to be raised throughout to brigade level; and then even to the level of the people's communes. Beyond that lies the achievement of communism and "ownership of the whole people". Of the 52,600 people's communes in China in 1971,[34] twenty were already units of account, and by 1978 that had increased to about sixty. But for the present it is accepted that the level of account most suitable is that of production team. The Constitution spells it out in Article 7.

> The rural people's commune [s] . . . at present generally take the form of three-level ownership, that is, ownership by the commune, the production brigade and the production team, with the production team as the basic accounting unit. A production brigade may become the basic accounting unit when its conditions are ripe.

To "learn from Tachai", then, is not to adopt "mechanically" organizational forms which the Tachai people have evolved out of their particular experience; and which, while they are to be seen as an ultimate goal, may not yet be apt or even attainable for other units in different circumstances. It is "the spirit of Tachai" which is to be learned; and the essential lesson of Tachai, manifested in its wide, new fields and in the material prosperity of its members, is that the spirit, translated into organized, committed and persevering labour, will transform man's physical environment, making him, in Marx's term, sovereign of his circumstances. The impulse is Promethean: "Dare to think, dare to act", is the heart of Tachai's message.

LEARNING FROM TACHAI

The Tachai spirit has lately been focused on land reclamation and river control, under the slogan, "Reshape the mountains, harness the rivers", proclaimed by Chen Yung-kuei in 1970. All over China cooperative units of every size have bent themselves to that enterprise, but nowhere, perhaps, with greater intensity and more striking effect than in Tachai's own Hsiyang County, which has now itself been declared, as a county, a "national standard-bearer in agriculture".

Proximity to Tachai did not entail a readiness to learn from it. For years, while Tachai's fame spread through China, many of the units in Hsiyang progressed sluggishly, if at all. Conditions were very hard, the narrow field-terraces suffering alternately from drought and deluge, almost equally destructive. The deep-rooted, fatalistic belief that destiny was against the people, that "heaven decides everything", died hard. Some units not only failed to follow the Tachai example but questioned it: the charges that Tachai was falsifying its accounts originated in a neighbouring village. But during and immediately after the Cultural Revolution the Tachai example caught on. The twenty people's communes in the county, comprising 400 production brigades like Tachai (most of them bigger in numbers) threw themselves into a long-term plan for land reclamation, irrigation and flood control. This is how the Chinese described developments:

> The county Communist Party committee [in autumn 1974] worked out a long-range programme for farmland improvement on the basis of detailed investigations. Cadres and [commune] members in the county, who had heightened their consciousness of class struggle and the struggle between the two lines ... made fuller use of the superiority of the socialist collective economy and their own strength in transforming nature. The heightened consciousness is reflected in the plans which were set into motion while they were rushing the autumn harvest [in 1974]. One group after another set out for the construction sites to start huge projects previously regarded [as] beyond their capability. A number of hill-tops were levelled and big dams thrown up quickly.[35]

The phrasing, almost jargon, blurs the meaning and tempts the foreign reader to dismiss this, but visits to some of the Hsiyang units concerned in construction efforts strongly indicate that what sounds like propaganda is in fact quite a factual description.

Nan Nao village is another brigade in the same commune as Tachai, as the crow flies across the steep and crumpled hills known as the Taihang Mountains a few miles, but by road more than an hour's distance. It used to be known as among the most backward villages in the whole county, reflecting the conditions which had led the villagers' ancestors to the hill-tops where the land was so bad that no one else was prepared to try farming it. Many of them were famine refugees from other areas.

The village used to consist of some fifteen hamlets, clusters of unlined cave-houses cut into the hill-sides, scattered over a distance of about 1.5 km from end to end. Starting in 1969 and finishing in the winter of 1971, the village, 65 households with a population of 300, rehoused itself in rows of "cave-houses", solidly built of stone, and in one settlement. The members rent these from their collective, as in Tachai, at Y10 per room per year. Water, which until 1966 had to be carried in buckets from a spring 2.5 km away, is now brought to the village in a small canal, pumped into a reservoir, and thence piped to two taps in the village.

The village now has 40 hectares of land under the plough—in 1966 its arable area was only 33.3 ha. Then the village was connected with the outside world only by a difficult footpath: its first enterprise, fired by the Cultural Revolution, was to cut 2.5 km of vehicle road across the hills, making it at last accessible to wheeled traffic. The state brought in a power-line in 1968, and now all houses have electricity; the basic agricultural processes after harvest are now mechanized, as is irrigation. Over the years since it became an elementary coop, Nan Nao village had progressively stepped its fields in terraces up the hill-sides, making the terrace walls progressively higher and the terraces consequently wider. In the autumn of 1974, when the writer visited the village, its members had looked beyond terrace-building and widening, and had seen the potential of levelling hill-tops—projects made feasible now because they had the use of bull-dozers run by the commune.

The village's land lay essentially on the sides of two high ridges, L-shaped, with hillocks on either side of the junction of the two ridges. One of those had already been levelled at the time of the visit, in October 1974; on the other, deep shafts were being dug for the placing of charges, carefully sited so that their detonation would throw the valley sides down into the angle of the L. By thus levelling-off the hillocks and filling in the valley a "man-made plain" of 6.7 ha would be created. This would represent a net gain of about 2.7 ha for the village. The project entailed the destruction of many terraces, laboriously built in the past few years; but being in a single very big field the new land was expected to yield a much greater than proportional increase in production when farmed by the tractor that was planned to be bought that spring. That a little temple to the mountain gods, lately used as a store-house, was demolished in the course of the project neatly symbolized the new attitudes that it reflected.

The productivity of Nan Nao production brigade has increased rapidly and fairly steadily over the past decade (see Table 4).

The village's state grain quota is 30 tons a year; it holds a collective grain reserve of 60 tons, sufficient for eight months' normal consumption, and each household holds domestic reserves. The average income per head in 1973 was given as Y130—compared to Tachai's Y180. Private plots were abolished in 1967; in 1968 the three production teams in the brigade raised their accounting to brigade level.

TABLE 4. *Grain production of Nan Nao brigade*

Year	Total grain production (tons)	Yield (tons/ha)	Quantity sold to state (tons)
1966	55	1.275	
1967	110	2.700	70
1968	175	4.125	75
1969	200	4.950	80
1970	205	5.175	50
1971	270	6.772	135
1972	177	4.050	50
1973	281	7.125	90

Shih Ping production brigade, of a neighbouring commune, is much bigger—460 households with a population of 1,900. The community was land-poor; even after decades of reclamation its arable area now totals only 213 ha. Accepting the poor land-population ratio as a permanent barrier to progress through agriculture, the brigade made a practice of sending members to construction work for the county and in cities. It was not until 1967 that the members began to draw the lesson from Tachai, and began reclaiming and improving land in earnest. The characteristic of the Shih Ping brigade's land was that while it lay on gentler ridges than Tachai or Nan Nao (both of which are much higher in the hills) the land was cut by wide river-beds. The streams filled the valley floors only briefly, during the rainy season, but the spate then left the valley floors useless, sandy and boulder-strewn. In 1970, having carried vigorous terracing as far as it would go, the brigade conceived a new approach to the problem of its valley land. The members first straightened-out the line of the stream's main channel in a valley; and then built a tunnel over that channel, by arching stonework across the river-bed. (They had first consulted the county hydrological institute on maximum flows, from which they calculated the necessary dimensions of their tunnels.) Their biggest project of this kind, completed in the two winters 1970–1 and 1971–2, involved construction of a tunnel 4.3 km long. While this was built down the valley, other team members, using commune bull-dozers as well as hand-carts, shoulder-baskets and picks and shovels, brought down soil from the valley sides and built it up to cover the tunnel to a depth of one metre and the valley floor in general to a depth of 3–5 metres. This project alone added 21 ha to the brigade's arable. Since 1970 the brigade has built 6.1 km of tunnel, adding a total of just under 27 ha to its land in this way, and all of that in wide fields.

Grain production has quadrupled since 1964:

	(tons)	
1964	300	
1965	325	
1966	250	
1967	550	
1968	640	
1969	830	
1970	1,000	
1971	1,200	
1972	630	
1973	1,300	Yield: 6.09 tons/ha

Over the same period the total income of the brigade increased from Y130,000 in 1964 to Y420,000. The brigade's state grain quota is 115 tons: in 1973 it sold a total of 525 tons.

All over China land has been and is being reclaimed by straightening-out the bends of rivers. The scale varies greatly. In the upper reaches of the Yangtse huge loops have been cut off in series, over distances of hundreds of kilometres; in small villages the loop of a stream may be cut by laying a new channel only 100 metres or so long. The resultant cut-off meander, after draining and top-soiling, provides an area of new arable much greater than that which may be sacrificed in digging the new, straight and narrow channel. One striking example of this kind of river-straightening project was seen in the Tao Ba Kou people's commune in Hsiyang, about two hours' drive from Tachai. This commune, consisting of 18 production brigades and with a population of about 8,000, has a substantial perennial river, the Sung Hsi, running through its land; and at one point the river makes a marked, wide loop. This the commune has straightened-out, creating 33 ha of new land.

In this case the river made its loop around a lofty, massive rock ridge; and rather than cutting a new channel and letting the river widen it by its own flow—the usual method—the members of the Tao Ba Kou people's commune had to mine a tunnel through the rock. The project had first been proposed by local villagers in 1958, during the Great Leap Forward, but the cadres of the day, the writer was told, "dared not think in terms of such a big project" and rejected the idea. After the Cultural Revolution, and taking up the "Learn from Tachai" movement, the commune in 1970 resurrected the old proposal and decided to go ahead, seeing that the new arable that could be created out of the deserted river-bed would help the commune break out of its grain deficiency. The decision to tackle the project was taken in mid-September 1970, and work began on 1 October. The state hydrological station was consulted and provided flow figures for the maximum recorded spate—1963, the year in which Tachai was washed out. A comfortable safety margin was left over that, and a special tunnelling team of 120 commune members began work from both sides of the ridge. In May 1972 the tunnel was completed: 300 metres long, 16 metres wide, and 12 metres high. The cut had been through solid rock, the commune members working with explosives (which they had mixed out of materials bought from the county), wedges and sledge-hammers. With the tunnel through, the construction team then threw up a dam to deflect the river into the tunnel, providing at the same time for irrigation of the new land on the river's old bed through a sluice gate and channel.

The new fields were still being built up at the time of the writer's visit, both by carrying soil in and by controlled flooding with the silt-laden waters of the river. The tunnel project was to be completed, beginning in the 1974–5 winter, by blasting out a spur tunnel from roughly the mid-point of the main tunnel to open out about half a kilometre downstream. With a sluice-gate controlling the water take-off this branch tunnel, also about 300 metres long, will cover a drop of some 17 metres and power a hydro-electric generator to be built at its point of issuance. Initially the power plant is to generate about 100 kw, but its ultimate capacity is planned at 400 kw. The commune, which is already electrified under the state grid, will then be able to supply all its own power requirements; and furthermore feed power into the grid for which the state will pay, making an additional income for the commune of an expected Y30,000 a year.

The labour for this commune project is delegated from the lower-level units, the commune leadership calculating its requirement and dividing that up among the brigades, the brigades further dividing it among their constituent production teams, so that on average each team would be sending only one or two members to work on the project, the team leadership selecting those to go.

The 33 ha of highest quality valley-bottom land created by this project will be farmed by the commune, and the income from its crops will go to the commune. With, ultimately, the revenue from the sale of electricity, the project will thus multiply the commune's income—and this income will not be distributed for consumption among members, but used to extend further the commune's productive capacities and the services it extends to its members. This expansion of productivity at higher level will facilitate the further raising of the level of account.[36] Most of the Tao Ba Kou commune's eighteen brigades are already themselves units of account: once production at commune level reaches a certain point, the income from it equalling, say, 30–40 per cent of the total of the separate incomes of the brigades, it should be possible to raise the level of account from brigade to commune without the income of even the most advanced and prosperous brigade being lowered in the process. The addition of the commune-level income to the total income of all the brigades would make the pool of wealth for sharing so much larger that all brigades would benefit—the "levelling up" which is central to Chinese development.

The Tao Ba Kou project is one of 48 of its kind carried out or begun in the winter of 1974–5 on the five chief rivers flowing through Hsiyang county. In total these will have created 3,000 ha of new land, an addition of about 13 per cent to the county's total arable area.[37] Such land, when it has settled into use, will be of the highest quality, arranged in big fields open to mechanized cultivation and of course irrigated—sustained high-yield fields, as the Chinese describe them.

Such projects as these in the hill villages of Hsiyang county and kindred works seen elsewhere in China suggest that, as the Chinese themselves put it, the movement to learn from Tachai has become "a great motive force pushing forward the socialist revolution and construction in ... [the] countryside".[38]

CONCLUSION

In 1948 the geographer Pierre Gourou considered what he called "China's un-used uplands" and saw in them great potential. He estimated that with improved terracing, with drains and reservoirs to catch and hold the rains, with diversification of agriculture to combine tree crops ("marvellously suited to Chinese conditions"), with livestock farming as complements to grain, the marginal land in China's hill country could sustain an additional 60 million people. But he saw too that such a transformation would demand nothing less than "a change in the material civilization, a revolution in the methods of exploiting nature"; and in turn that, he concluded, "would require a continuity of perspective and a freedom of action which are perhaps not to be found in the range of human capacities".[39] Tachai and the countless other Chinese villages which are doing, in varying degrees, what Tachai has done demonstrate that China's new social forms did provide that "continuity of perspective and freedom of action" which were needed to enable the peasantry to break out of the trap of their poverty. Tachai is the symbol and expression of a reorganization of the Chinese rural economy so profound, drastic and comprehensive that it does amount to "a change in the material civilization".

At the heart of that reorganization has been the enlargement of the farming unit. Originally this was the household, functioning internally like a miniature cooperative (though a highly undemocratic one) but competing, often ferociously, for the scanty resources available: and it was just that scattered, individual form of production which, as Mao Tse-tung saw, had kept the peasants in their perpetual poverty. The essence of the Chinese Communists' achievement was that they enabled the peasants to recognize that truth, by leading them, through "team farming", into the cooperative practices and organizations which steadily, and often rapidly, raised their standard of living. The basic farming unit is now the cooperative village. The secret of the Chinese Communist Party's success in this regard, which contrasts so sharply with Soviet experience, must lie in Mao's absolute insistence on persuasion. Believing that the "masses have a poten-tially inexhaustible enthusiasm for socialism", he still understood that only their own practical experience could arouse that enthusiasm, and that socialism imposed would be socialism aborted: "If we insisted on leading the masses to do anything against their will, we would certainly fail".[40]

Before it is anything else, Tachai is a socialist community. The sinological scholar, versed in the organizational patterns, the social attitudes and attributes that made up the traditional Chinese village, would find few familiar reference points left in Tachai. But the theory and history of socialism illuminate the village like a good guide-book. Fourier would quickly learn his way around Tachai, and find in it, with its centralized housing, its community-run school, its health service and shops, something very like the socialist community he called a phalanx. Robert Owen, hearing of the shift in Tachai's early progress from the elementary to the advanced form of cooperative, would find in that confirmation of his belief that members of a cooperative, if at first granted interest on their capital investments, would voluntarily and quickly give it up; and would note the Tachai work-point system as an elaboration of his own system of a flat rate for all "work-days". Members of the numerous Owenite and other communitarian colonies which flourished in the USA in the first half of the nineteenth century would be at one with the Tachai villagers' emphasis on the dignity of all labour, on the parity of worth between mental and physical work, the equal role and equal rights of women, the community's part in bringing up children, and the importance of manual labour in education. The great difference between Tachai and those other, short-lived socialist communities is that they were aberrational from the societies in which they existed—and often considered inimical to their society's interests—whereas Tachai's principles and practices are those of the huge society and established state of China.

The key to the process of development in rural China has been self-reliance. As foreseen in another context,[41] the emphasis on self-reliance ensured that development, in pace, direction and scale, would at all stages be geared in directly with the capacity of the people concerned; so from the modest beginnings suited to the meagreness of the peasants' capacities as the old order had left those, development expanded and grew in complexity in step with their abilities and vision. The physical transformation of Tachai village, of its land and its techniques and range of production, is thus the expression of the inner transformation that the villagers have worked in their own attitudes. Before that transformation began, this description of the typical Chinese villager by a nineteenth-century American missionary would have fitted Tachai's:

... his mind is like an open ditch, partly vacant and partly full of whatever is flowing or blowing over the surface. He is [excessively humble]. He knows that he knows nothing, that he never did, never shall, never can know anything, and also that it makes very little difference what he knows. He has a blind respect for learning but no idea of gathering any crumbs thereof for himself. The long, broad, black and hopeless shadow of practical Confucianism is over him. It means ... a lifetime of intellectual stagnation.[42]

The same observer put fatalism, superstition, mutual suspicion, the absence of public spirit, the absence of sympathy, the disregard of time, among the dominant characteristics of the Chinese as he knew them—as most foreigners in the old China would have done. Today's Tachai villagers are, in their cohesion and sense of social purpose, their confidence in themselves and in the future they are making, their pragmatism and inventiveness, the antitheses of what they were until only a generation ago.

That transformation of the "inner landscape" of Tachai challenges the dearly-held Western belief in the immutability of human nature. The steadily increasing productivity of Tachai's farming challenges another article of the West's orthodoxy: the belief that private ownership is the golden road to increased productivity, while, the ownership of all being equivalent to ownership by none, collective farming means negligence and stagnation. Tachai indicates rather that China's successful "cooperativization" is resolving what has been seen as the basic contradiction in agriculture by evolving large-scale, mechanized and diversified farms which are worked with all the zealous attention and intricate husbandry traditionally associated only with smallholdings.

More broadly, Tachai, and behind that village the whole of China's revolutionized rural society, confirms Kropotkin's perception that "whenever mankind [has] to work out a new social organization, adapted to a new phase of development, its constructive genius always [draws] the elements and the inspiration for the new departure from the ever-living tendency [to mutual aid]".[43] If other societies than China's are to learn from Tachai" this it seems must be the first lesson: "Combine—practise mutual aid! That is the surest means of giving to each and to all the greatest safety, the best guarantee of existence and progress, bodily, intellectual and moral".[44]

NOTES

1   Here, as elsewhere in rural China, the figure given for work-force is calculated—that is, two older villagers, each with a work capacity half that of a fully able-bodied adult, are counted as one.

2   This paper draws on visits to Tachai in September 1971 (a day) and November 1974 (three days). The figures used, unless otherwise stated, were given by members of the leadership (cadres) of Tachai and other villages visited, interviewed through an interpreter of the Chinese Foreign Ministry. Major figures for grain output and yield have been up-dated to 1977.

3   Another answer to this problem is being evolved by the Hsiyang county agricultural machinery plant—a 10-h.p. mini-caterpillar-tractor. In 1974 this was in trial use at Tachai and in other hill villages in the county, and was proving highly satisfactory. With integral plough-blades, it can plough 7–8 inches deep and because of its high manoeuvrability can reach and work high, narrow terraces.

4   *Tachai: Standard-bearer in China's Agriculture*, Peking: Foreign Languages Press, 1972, p. 12.

5   This, and earlier help from a PLA company in overcoming the destruction from severe flash-flooding in 1963, appear to be the only occasions on which Tachai has diverged from a rigorous self-reliance.

6   So climatically ill-favoured is this region that in 20 of the 21 years from 1953 to 1974 Tachai was hit by a "natural disaster" of one kind or another—drought, flood, hail or pest infestation. *Tachai*, op. cit., p. 3.

7   These targets, set in 1956 in an over-optimistic 12-year programme for agriculture, have still not been achieved as averages throughout the zones, but officials of the central Ministry of Agriculture informed the writer in November 1974 that in all three zones the average yield was now close to target.

8   A jin (or catty) is 0.5 of a kilogramme, and a mou is 1/15 of a hectare.

9   The state aims to set quotas for agriculture comfortably below productive capacity, with the premium price at which the state will buy all produce offered in excess of quota providing the material incentive to maximize production.

10   *Peking Review*, No. 50, December 9, 1977.

11   This is rather below par. Chinese villages now aim to keep one pig per head of population—as Mao put it, "a pig is a walking fertilizer factory", and pig manure is the key element in much of the intensive organic fertilization that underpins the increasing agricultural yields. Few villages have reached the pig-per-person target, but many are closer than Tachai. The Tachai villagers having done away with their private plots in 1963, they keep no "private pigs" (the vast majority of villagers do); and this reflects in the smaller number of pigs maintained.

12   Agricultural tax is not progressive. Set as a quantum on an area of land in the first half of the 1950s, tax has as a rule not been varied since: so with increasing production the proportion payable in tax (in cash or kind) has declined. It is now, on average, between 5 and 7 per cent of total agricultural income (side-line occupations serving agriculture are not taxed). Tachai's unusually low tax rate, under 2 per cent, reflects the extent to which its production has increased since the early 1950s.

13   The vice-chairman of the Tachai revolutionary committee who briefed the writer in November 1974 in fact stated that the *per capita* income for the village in 1973 had been Y170; but the other figures given showed it to have been Y180. The discrepancy was not noted at the time.

14   Chen Yung-kuei, A vivid lesson on bringing politics to the fore, *People's Daily*, in *Survey of the China Mainland Press (SCMP)*, No. 3675, 1966.

15   ibid.

16   New China News Agency (NCNA) 29 September 1968, In *SCMP*, No. 4272, 1968.

17   ibid.

18   *People's Daily* editorial, Study well in theory of the dictatorship of the proletariat, 9 February 1975, *Peking Review*, No. 7, 1975.

19   Dr. Mark Elvin has pointed out to the writer that uxorilocal marriage was quite common in some parts of China, such as Yunan and parts of Taiwan, in the early twentieth century.

20   These two posts are almost invariably held by the same person, linking the party branch committee and the revolutionary committee.

21   NCNA, 16 March, 1975.

22   Manual farm tools are bought or made and cared for by individuals in Tachai, as in almost all Chinese villages. Bigger implements the collective supplies and maintains.

23   NCNA, 5 February, 1975.

24   Twenty per cent of China's hydro-electric power comes from generators of less than 500 kw. *Peking Review*, 23 May, 1975.

25   The landlord and rich peasant households were left with a portion of their land equal to what other households were given. In Tachai there was no lynching—although the "flogging tree", a willow in the middle of what was the old village, stands as a reminder that the Tachai landlord was as oppressive as most. The former possessor families lived on in the village, labelled as being among the "five bad elements" (landlords, rich peasants, counter-revolutionaries, rightists, and simple "bad elements", or thugs); for years they were under "mass supervision", and most of the older generation died out. One by one, as they were judged to have genuinely turned their backs on the past and committed themselves to the community, they were "de-labelled" and admitted as full members, except that they are still, by law, barred from holding elective office. The children of those of the "five bad elements" inherit no disabilities.

26   The proportion of 60:40 was more common in mutual aid teams' distribution.

27   On the question of agricultural cooperation, In *Selected Readings from the Works of Mao Tse-tung*, Peking: Foreign Languages Press, 1971.

28   Mao Tse-tung, *Quotations* ... , 1967 edition, p. 119.

29   For a popular account see Gerald Tannebaum, The real spirit of Tachai, *Eastern Horizon*, Vol. X, No. 3 (1971). This article has been reprinted, with a 1974 addendum, by MSS Modular Publications, 655 Madison Avenue, New York 10021. See also, Dazhai: The mass line in practice, by Mitch Meisner, *Modern China*, Vol. 4, No. 1, January 1978.

30   Chen Yung-kuei, A vivid lesson ... , *SCMP*, No. 3675.

31   Radio Taiyuan, 1 April 1970, quoted in Jonathan Unger, Tachai, China's agricultural model, *Current Scene*, 7 September, 1971.

32   Chao Feng-nien, Learning from Tachai brings big changes, in *Tachai: Standard-bearer in China's Agriculture*, Peking, 1972.

33   To William Hinton and others. Interview in *New China*, Vol. 1, No. 1, Spring 1975.

34   This figure, given to the writer by officials of the central Ministry of Agriculture in 1974, sets a puzzle. The commonly given and used figure before this was about 60,000, or 64,000. The lower figure now given suggests that a process of consolidation must be in effect, with communes merging; but there is no other evidence of such a change.

35   ibid.

36   The writer's attention was drawn to this point by William Hinton. See his Awaken the mountains, let the rivers change their courses ... , *New China*, first (un-numbered) issue, 1975.

37   NCNA, 6 December, 1974.

38   *Tachai*, op. cit.

39   China's un-used uplands, *Pacific Affairs*, Vol. 21, No. 3, 1948.

40   Mao Tse-tung, *Selected Works*, Vol. IV, p. 243.

41   S. K. Dey, Community projects in action, in R. L. Park and I. Timber (Eds.), *Leadership and Political Institutions in India*, Oxford University Press, 1960, p. 349.

42   Arthur Smith, *Village Life in China*, p. 257.

43   Peter Kropotkin, *Mutual Aid*, Boston: Extending Horizons Books, 1955, pp. 224–5.

44   ibid., p. 75.

The Tachai Way
Part II: The Fourth Mobilization

INTRODUCTION

A run of bad seasons in China in the early 1970s, holding down grain outputs, obscured the sharp increase in agricultural productivity that had in fact been achieved. Breaking a silence concerning annual grain output figures which the Chinese government had maintained through the decade of the 1960s, Chou En-lai disclosed that total grain output in 1970 had exceeded 240 m tons.[1] The following year production increased by four per cent, bringing grain output to 250 m tons.[2] In 1972, the weather was very bad over extensive areas, with the worst drought the Chinese had experienced since the "three hard years" around 1960 and other "natural disasters", such as floods and infestations. Under that blow, grain production fell back—but only by four per cent to 240 m tons.[3] The magnitude of the achievement that year, when China's peasant agriculture overcame the sort of drought that in the pre-communist period there would almost ineluctably have caused widespread famine and succeeded in producing a grain output only marginally beneath the record of the previous year, can be appreciated by contrasting it with the effect of bad seasons on Soviet agriculture, which has registered declines in production of 30 per cent and more for such reasons.

The following year drought struck widely again in China. That summer the writer made an extensive tour of rural areas there, and the effect of the drought—in many areas in its second consecutive year—was obvious; sometimes streams that had never failed in living memory were dry, and the great rivers were at near-record low levels. Commune members and cadres spoke of the rain-failure as being "famine weather"—yet were confident of bringing in good crops. That year production bounced back, achieving a new record output of 257 m tons.[4]

What the achievement indicated was that the proportion of China's cultivated area which had been brought to the standard described there as "sustained high-yield" had attained a critical level. Increased output from those areas, either unaffected by drought or actually benefited by it (since sustained sunshine foster crop growth in irrigated fields, while absence of rain inhibits weeds), had compensated for the reduced production of the areas which had not yet attained that standard—while in some areas visited the cooperative structure was enabling the villages to undertake such labour-intensive crop rescue efforts as hand watering of wheat fields.

Sustained high-yield areas are those which have an ensured water supply and proper drainage and are of high-grade soil, with requisite availability of fertiliser, improved seed and labour and/or mechanical farming aids. Some extensive tracts, even zones, have been brought to that standard; but the most disadvantaged village or

71

commune will be expected to have some sustained high-yield fields, even if only of a few square metres—and to extend those steadily, season by season. No quantified definition of this category is possible since the productivity of a sustained high-yield area will vary according to the climatic conditions of its locality. Such an area in the Tibet Autonomous Region, for example, might have an annual yield of 4 tons/ha, while one on Honan Island would produce 20 tons/ha or more.

Such sustained high-yield areas are crucial in China's mode of agricultural development. The importance attached to them by the Chinese, and recognition outside China that in these areas lies the key factor in China's agricultural achievement and hope for continued development, have led some to the conclusion that China is taking a "green revolution" approach. The linkage is tempting, and the present writer has noted elsewhere that China's achievement shows that a "green revolution" is possible, although one that is subsequent to and consequent upon red revolution. But the connection is misleading because "green revolution" is now descriptive of a whole politico-economic approach to rural development, and China's approach is in fact contrary to that. The fundamental differences are:

Green revolution in practice implies accepting and using the hierarchical structure of the traditional village society, and following a course which in fact accentuates it so that "the rich get richer, the poor, poorer"; while China's whole development is the expression of a new egalitarian society built upon the levelled rubble of the traditional order.

Green revolution means "backing the best", concentrating available in-puts on those areas and sections of society whose advantages enable them to turn them immediately to productive effect; while China leaves the best (i.e. the most favoured and therefore advanced areas) to get on with their progress unassisted, or at least assisted at a secondary level of priority, and backs, not the worst, but what might be called "the erstwhile worst".

In the Chinese rural context "the worst" would be taken as a village or area, ill-favoured by nature and stuck at a low level of productivity. Such an area, a brigade, commune or perhaps a county, would of course by no means commend itself to China's planners as being a fruitful area for the priority investment of available in-puts; rather would it be a case calling for political attention—investigation, that is, of its leadership at every level to find out why the consequentiality of poor natural circumstances/low yields was being accepted, why it was stuck. What the Chinese back is rather the area or unit, environmentally ill-favoured or otherwise backward, which has *begun to progress*. Such villages or units, having begun, with their own resources of traditional technology plus organized collective labour, to transform their physical environment, will be given priority for available in-puts as they accumulate the capital to buy them, and credit or grants when their resources are still insufficient. Of course, advanced units also receive additional resources from the state, and in any case their local economies are often sufficiently advanced to have achieved autonomous momentum; but policy is to give priority in access to central support to developing backward regions and units.

One way in which a backward unit can begin to transform its environment is to create, out of a portion of its arable, a sustained high-yield area. Originally this will have to be a relatively small area but year by year it can be expanded. The achievement of even a small high-yielding plot proves to the villagers their own ability, indicating that the limits to growth lie not in nature but in their own capacities for labour and innovation, which they are exhorted to recognize as limitless.

The application of this approach means that sustained high-yield areas are not concentrated exclusively in the high-fertility zones of China's traditional agricultural heartlands, but are to be found throughout the country. In fertile areas, some communes will have attained sustained high-yield standards over their entire arable; while in disadvantaged areas sustained high-yield fields will be small and separated, even scattered—but they will be spreading and multiplying.

The Chinese approach is the strategic opposite of the green revolution's, a slower but steady and accelerating advance over the whole agricultural front being preferred to the sudden dramatic breakthrough into a narrow salient which is the strategy and result of the green revolution. Among the consequences of the Chinese approach are a process of equalization, achieved through "levelling-up"; a more durable productive base with a steadier, secular pattern of increased productivity; and wide-spread generation of demand, contrasting favourably with the green revolution's marked tendency to see spurting production over a narrow spatial and sectoral area leaving the size of the market behind.

The successive bad years of 1972 and 1973, with the marginal retreat to 240 m tons in the first and the sharp recovery to 257 m tons in the second, suggested that the rural economy was like a spring compressed by the constraints of weather. The extension of the sustained high-yield areas would minimize retreat in the worst years, and generate marginal advance in poor years; but when the run of the seasons brought even an average year productivity could be expected to jump into a new range of quantity. Just that happened in 1974. This was by no means a year of bumper harvest weather, but the Chinese counted it as an average year and, compared to the two preceding years, it was good. As a result, bigger crops were brought in from those areas which were not of sustained high-yield standard, and grain output for the year jumped to 274.9 m tons.[5]

These, then, were the figures for grain output for the first five years of the 1970s, from official Chinese sources:[6]

1970	242.9
1971	250.0
1972	240.0
1973	257.0
1974	274.9

The output figure for 1974 was well above the extrapolations that had been made by Western observers, and the inference was drawn that Peking had juggled the figures and achieved a misleading apparent jump in production by covertly adding soybeans to the package designated as "grain". The inference was fallacious; the grain package had been consistent (including soybeans) since the mid-1960s.[7]

The weather reported from China for 1975 was generally a further improvement over the previous year and the Chinese were prompt in proclaiming that another new record had been set in grain output. But in 1976 natural conditions were bad in many parts of the country, with "serious drought, water-logging, low temperatures and early frost", and in others disastrous—there were six violent earthquakes[8]—but again grain output was described as having set a new record.[9] The adverse circumstances in wide areas suggest that the margin over the previous year must have been narrow, even to maintain the previous year's production would have been a considerable achievement—the compressed-spring effect again. In 1977 extremely bad conditions were again widespread in China, making it, the Chinese said, one of the worst years experienced since 1949 and preventing any increase in grain output over the previous year. The run of bad seasons continued in 1978, again severe drought was widespread. But whereas grain output had moved narrowly, and both up and down, over the previous three years, in 1978 production increased to 295 million mt. That increase of 3.5 per cent over the previous year's total indicated that the technological foundation of China's agriculture is now sufficiently developed to enable production to be increased even against the run of the weather.

This is how production varied in the later 1970s:[10]

1975	280
1976	288
1977	285
1978	295

Thus it appears that China's progress in agriculture is being achieved in spurts separated by what can be mistaken as stagnation: a run of bad seasons holds production down but improving technology and techniques act as a ratchet preventing any but marginal declines; a year of good natural conditions sees a substantial jump in production, bringing that into a new range with a ratchet again set against relapse.

The breakthrough into a new range of production achieved in China in 1974 was reflected in a sharp reduction of grain imports the following year. "Grain imports, composed almost entirely of wheat, with small quantities of corn and rice, fell sharply in value in 1975 to less than half the 1974 level ... Total wheat imports in 1975 amounted to 3.34 million mt, worth around $530 million—down from 5.49 million mt valued at $837 million in 1974."[11] The expectation that the reducing trend would continue through 1976[12] was negated by events, however, as China negotiated larger grain purchases in 1976 and 1977. The earthquakes of 1976 will have necessitated heavy drawings on the national grain reserve for relief operations, and the bad year of 1977 will have made significant re-stocking impossible.[13] Imports thus seem bound to be increased again in the short-term. But while factors of transport convenience and exchange suggest that China may always import some grain, a return to the accelerated rate of increase in production achieved in the first half of the 1970s would promise to enable her to move into net exporting of grain in the 1980s.[14]

As a Western analyst put it, "the question of food production in China is subject to intense debate ... because there are serious problems regarding the availability, accuracy and comparability of data",[15] and, since population size and growth is a subject almost as vexed as grain production, the debates are at their sharpest when it comes to assessing grain production on a *per capita* basis. It is argued by some that production has barely kept ahead of population, with the result that by the mid-1970s China had become chronically dependent upon grain imports.[16] The unevenness of grain production, set against the linear increase in population, makes for differences in various periods, and it is clear that there have been stages since 1949 when population has out-distanced grain production, just as there have been other periods when grain production out-distanced population—from 1964 to 1967 grain production is taken to have increased by 6.0 per cent a year, for example.[17] Taking 1949 as the base, however, with a population of 500 million and grain production of 113 million tons gives a *per capita* production of 226 kg; assuming a population in 1974 of 900 million, the grain production that year of fractionally under 275 million tons gave 305 kg *per capita*, an increase of 35 per cent over 25 years. The achievement is not dramatic, but multiplier factors increase its effect. The equalization of distribution both vertically (through society) and horizontally (from surplus to deficit regions) makes the *per capita* figure for China much more indicative of nourishment availability than would be the similar figure for India, for example. Furthermore, there are what might be called "the thrift factor", the traditional drive of the Chinese peasant to avoid waste having been reinforced by the socialist social structure and sharpened by political exhortation; and the diversification of diet that has reflected the growth in pig- and fish-farming and vegetable growing. Finally, it should be noted that the production of the private plots, which comprise about 5 per cent of China's arable, is not included in the official output figures.

China has claimed to have achieved basic self-sufficiency in food since about 1971, and her grain production seems bound to continue to increase under the spreading impact of modernizing inputs. At the same time, the rate of population increase appears to be falling off in response to the vigorous promotion of family-planning and late marriage. Population growth is believed now to be between 1.5 and 2 per cent a year, on a reducing curve, and China, as one Western demographer puts it, "it is likely to be the first developing nation of any size to reduce the growth of her population to below 1 per cent per year".[18] [See p. 133 *Ed.*]

The Chinese ascribe the recent increase in their agricultural production to the "learn from Tachai" campaign. It is characteristic of the Chinese approach to development that great new efforts, concentrated leaps and heaves, are launched not to arrest decline or overcome stagnation but because a breakthrough has already been accomplished. The intensified effort is to catch and accelerate an achieved momentum. So the Chinese saw in the accelerated rate of increase in agricultural production achieved in the mid-1970s an opportunity to increase it still further. They saw also a need to do so since, striking as the increase achieved by 1974 promised to be if sustained, it would not be sufficient if China were to reach the goal of modernizing and industrializing its economy by the end of the century which Chou En-lai had set early in 1975. The Chinese leadership therefore decided to put the campaign to "Learn from Tachai" into higher gear, enlarging the scale and renewing the intensity so as to make it in effect a new movement. The Chinese say of this that it is "another great revolutionary movement in the Chinese countryside which, in significance and scale, is on a par with the movements for land reform, agricultural cooperation, and the establishment of the people's communes." Those were mass mobilizations of the peasantry to achieve new social patterns and forms, and through those increased production.[19] The new movement—the fourth mobilization—is aimed at laying the foundations for a modernized Chinese agriculture over the next five years.

The "fourth mobilization" aims at comprehensive agricultural development but there are particular thrusts which can be singled out for description and illustration:

LANDSCAPE MODIFICATION

Landscape modification has been going on in China for over three millennia, but it is proceeding now on a scale and with an intensity that is unprecedented. The current upsurge in this process originated with terrace construction and re-construction, especially in the uplands of north China leading on to the application of level-and-fill techniques on a giant scale to hill-tops, ridges and gullies, and to the dyking and "culverting" of rivers described in Part I of this paper.[20]

Earth removal is a large part of such projects, and while the village cooperatives are prepared when necessary to accomplish this slowly, with hoes, shovels and yoked baskets and hand-carts, they seek constantly for efficient short-cuts. Hydraulic power is sometimes used, by pumped water-jets or, more simply, by making a temporary reservoir on a hill-side, pumping it full and then suddenly demolishing one of the sides. At one brigade the writer visited in 1973 (Shah Shih-yu Brigade, Hopeh) the availability of soil for the new terraces being built was a critical limiting factor, it had to be carried in from several kilometres away. Plenty of soil was available immediately behind the village but only with a laborious and time-consuming climb over a high ridge, too steep even for hand-carts. The village had decided to tackle the problem by tunnelling through the ridge and work had just begun in 1973, a crack squad of the strongest—and often youngest—members of the village workforce being formed to cut the tunnel. The services of a member of a nearby commune with mining experience were borrowed initially. On a return visit one year later the writer found the tunnel completed and in use by the village's tractor, bringing in soil in trailer-loads. An unexpected bonus from the whole project had been derived from the railway authorities' purchase of the rock-fill taken out of the 300-metre tunnel, which had first been broken into size suitable for track ballast by the labour of the whole village. The proceeds of that sale had been sufficient for the purchase of a new 55 h.p. tractor.

When first conceived and implemented such projects as those described above are exceptional. But as they are publicized and made models for emulation in their locality and sometimes nationally other units will follow suit, promptly or gradually according to the energies and political awareness of their leadership and their members. Thus the exceptional progressively becomes more common, and ultimately should establish a new norm. A point must come in this spread effect when the leadership of a unit which is *not* "learning from Tachai" will become the object of criticism both from its own members and from cadres at higher levels. An upland brigade, for example, whose lands include a seasonal river, dry in summer but a raging spate during the rains, will come under pressure to apply the culverting technique which brigades in Hsiyang have shown to be practicable and conducive to greatly increased grain production. "Learning from Tachai" is creditable as well as beneficial; "Not Learning from Tachai" comes to be seen, over time, as discreditable as well as relatively injurious.

Some Western economists have been sceptical about the economic value of projects such as those mentioned above: "the short-term return on such activities has probably been low compared to the cost", one of them recently observed.[21] But the opportunity costs are minimal since the labour deployed on such projects is surplus at the time in which the work is undertaken, the winter months when, in north China, the requirements of field management are low. And of course the communities which conceive, plan and execute such projects are not calculating "short-term returns"—they would see such considerations as expressions of "capitalist thinking". The arable created by the labours of the community this winter and next will be growing crops through summers as far as human imagination will carry—the shift from an individualist to a communitarian social organization brings about an immense lengthening of the time-scale in which economic projections are commonly made. This is not to say, however, that the villagers concerned take up such projects in sudden surges of unanimous community dedication. Adoption of these projects is often preceded by intense debate, amounting sometimes to sharp divisions, between their advocates and others who argue that the expenditure of labour involved would be misinvested.

While land reclamation is most evident and dramatic in the uplands, it is going on throughout China. At the Ta Li commune outside Canton the writer noticed in 1974 that figures of the cultivated area indicated an increase of some 300 mou (20 ha) since an earlier visit two years before. The discrepancy was at first surprising, since this is an advanced and prosperous commune in a region which had been intensively farmed for centuries. The explanation lay in an area of low, scrub-covered hills previously used only for bamboo groves. These hills had been cleared and terraced and were being planted to fruit trees, with peanuts to be inter-cropped with the orchard. In the first plan for the development of this hill area (which was turned over for management and development to a special team of youngsters, graduates from the communes' schools) irrigation was to be from a low-level channel, water being pumped to a series of small hill-top reservoirs; but on another return visit, twelve months later, the writer saw that another approach had in the interim been conceived, adopted, and implemented. The water was pumped up to the summit of only one of the hills, nearest the prime water source, and from there it was carried to the summits of all the other hills by an aqueduct, in total about three kilometres in length, standing up to 13 metres above ground level, which split to ring each hill with a concrete crown around its flattened top. This being a large and advanced commune, with a population of about 60,000, everything used in the aqueduct was made on the commune. (See Plate 4.)

In other well-developed communes—around Shanghai, for example—where all wasteland has long since been reclaimed, additional arable has been created by covering irrigation channels. These are first laid with concrete pipes (made in commune cement fabrication factories) and then covered with soil. Loss of water through evaporation and seepage is thus diminished, in addition to the gain of perhaps five per cent in arable area—which in these regions of high-productivity farming makes for a significant increase in output.

Another aspect of the campaign to maximize land use and efficiency has recently been launched under the name of "Farmland Capital Construction". This entails the levelling of whole areas of farmland, not just individual fields, and their rational re-ordering into systematically rectangular plots, linked in a comprehensive plan with irrigation and drainage channels, plantations, fish ponds, access paths and roads and, often, new villages for the commune communities. With this, the Chinese peasantry are erasing the remaining marks of the traditional small-scale agriculture of their ancient past, and sculpting their landscape anew into patterns and shapes to match the agricultural requirements of their present and future. The process often brings them into collision with their past. In many regions of the south, for example, considerable areas of what could be arable have been taken up by ancient grave mounds; in the farmland capital construction campaign powerful impetus has been given to the absorption of grave areas into arable that has been progressing slowly since the establishment of the People's Republic, with grave mounds being used as soil quarries for the levelling of fields. (The old coffins are reburied in new cemeteries, sited in areas not planned for inclusion in arable.)

The creation of newly regularized and levelled fields is only the first step towards increased productivity, on the plains as it is in the uplands. The long- and medium-term plan looks to mechanization and the lay-out of the new fields is designed to that end; while the immediate and continuing task is to improve, indeed to transform, the soil quality of the new fields. Especially in the hill regions, these will be of significantly lower quality than what had been farmed in the same areas before, since sub-soil is layered onto the surface; but in the basic equation of the new Chinese peasant's farming calculus soil is another variable. There is no such thing, in that perception, as poor soil or bad soil, those are just soils that have not yet been transformed. Intensive application of organic fertilizers with regular deep-ploughing and complementary additions of chemicals, sustained over a few seasons, produces marked increases in the productivity of the fields. Soil improvement is one of the key areas of effort of Tachai itself. A recent article by that village's scientific research unit noted that the organic matter in the soil of newly levelled or created fields was 0.44 per cent; in less than three years it had been built up to 0.80 per cent, while the organic matter content of their sustained-high-yield fields is 1.5 per cent.[22]

IRRIGATION

Irrigation is functionally linked with landscape modification and farmland capital construction. The area under irrigation in China has trebled in the generation since 1949. In the year of Liberation the irrigated area was estimated at 16 million ha; by 1973 that had been extended to 44 million ha,[23] and the area is being extended at an average rate of 1.6 million ha a year.[24] In the winter of 1976–7 the total irrigated area in China should thus have been extended to over 50 million ha or about 39 per cent of the cultivated land. But extension is only a part of the picture. Simultaneously with the extension of irrigation systems goes their elaboration and improvement. A delegation of American water resources specialists who recently visited China expressed surprise at the extensive degree to which irrigation channels there were lined,[25] enormous use being made of masonry, locally quarried, in addition to the piping and covering referred to above. The lining not only saves water by preventing seepage, it cuts down weed growth and also saves arable because the lined channels can be deeper and narrower.

Irrigation involves not only the supply of water but its control, and especially the ability to get water away again when its job is done. In the redesigning of farming areas that is the key component of the farmland capital construction campaign, drainage is given as much attention as irrigation, since it is now recognized as of co-equal importance. (Here the Chinese have learned from their mistakes. Many of the water conservancy projects undertaken in the mass efforts of the late 1950s lacked adequate drainage, with consequent water-logging and salinization damaging extensive tracts of land, and similar problems were reported even in the early 1970s.) Newly introduced multi-cropping patterns of agriculture sometimes make special demands for effective and fast drainage. A village which is farming on a system of two rice crops followed by winter wheat, for example, must as quickly as possible dry out the fields which have been used successively through the summer for the rice crops so as to prepare them for the winter wheat. This demands the cutting of deep drainage channels, a slow and laborious task in the sodden soil of the paddy fields when performed with the traditional ditching implement, like a peat-spade. But progressively in the areas confronted with this problem mechanization is being applied, through the use of the mole-drainer. A simple implement with a torpedo-shaped steel blade mounted to bore a channel at an adjustable depth beneath the surface, the mole-drainer is winched across the fields by either an electric motor or the power take-off of a tractor or motor-cultivator. The advantage lies not only in the much greater speed of the operation. There is a small but, to the peasants' collectives concerned, rewarding increase in arable surface because the mole-drainer's channel is underground and the cut made by its vertical arm is narrow and anyway trodden closed by the operator, and so has no effect on sowing; drainage is more efficient than through open-cut channels; and the mole-bored drains last longer, making annual re-boring unnecessary.

FERTILIZER

After only land and water, intensifying application of fertilizer is the key factor in the acceleration of agricultural production in China. Essentially, the Chinese peasantry is continuing the approach it has sustained for forty centuries, farming in a circle, returning to the earth every scrap of waste, supplying every available or produceable element of nutrition.[26] Chemical fertilizers are in steadily increasing use (24 m tons in 1974)[27] but always as a complement to the basic dependence on organic material—and it is intended that that relationship will be permanent. The commonest components of organic manure in China are what they have always been: human waste, now pooled through the cooperatives and treated against bacterial infection; animal manure, especially pigs'; green manure; and river mud where it is available. As well as providing pork, pigs are seen, in Mao's phrase, as "walking fertilizer plants", and great efforts go to multiplying their numbers—the target for every cooperative rural unit is now "a pig per person". A grown pig produces three tons of excrement a year which, mixed with green manure and mud, can make 5–10 tons of high quality fertilizer. In China, unlike the West, pigs are not competitive with man in their food, only small quantities of coarse grain go into their fodder at the earliest stage of their growth, otherwise they flourish on a non-grain diet. In some areas cooperatives have moved into the hot-house cultivation of water hyacinth, the demand for pig fodder making sound sense of what in other parts of Asia, struggling to prevent this weed from smothering water surfaces, would seem a crazy aberration. The water hyacinth growth dies off in the winter: to ensure a flying start in the spring, plants are concentrated in dug-out ponds covered with plastic during the winter and in the spring transplanted into canal or lake areas. The hyacinth stalks are cut and mixed with other foodstuffs to make pig fodder.

The collection of river mud is an ancient labour in rural China, serving a dual purpose in providing fertilizer and dredging canals and rivers. It is labour-intensive, but a new commune-designed mud pump is being developed in south China to save on both time and labour.

The scientific-farming groups in the cooperatives are constantly experimenting in search of more effective methods of applying fertilizer. In one area of Kwangchow excellent results have been registered from pellet application. Pellets are made, by hand, from a mixture of organic fertilizer and chemical additives, and inserted in the ground in equidistance from rice clusters or other plants. There is said to be a marked improvement in growth since the nourishment period of fertilizer thus applied is longer than with surface application, while the saving in quantity of fertilizer is clear. The farm machinery repair and manufacture units of the communes concerned are working on designs for simple machinery for making the pellets and beyond that to adapting farm machines to mechanize the insertion of the pellets into the ground.

The supply and application of chemical fertilizer can be expected to accelerate as the foreign plants bought by China come on stream; and meanwhile small, local plants established at commune level are producing an increasing proportion of available chemical fertilizer.

FIELD MANAGEMENT

After those three essential elements, land, water and fertilizer, field management comes next in the drive for higher yields and increased production. Deeper ploughing (made easier as mechanization reaches the field processes), extra weedings and hoe-ings, faster transplanting and field preparation between crops, are all areas in which improvements are reflected in bigger crops. But the innovative thrust to find new techniques and applications which is such a feature of all development in China is expressed here too. The most striking example in the writer's field experience lies in the introduction and spread of wheat transplantation in north China. The advantages of this technique are much as they are in the traditional transplanting of rice. By planting wheat in nursery beds optimal conditions for initial growth can be provided, if necessary to the extent of hot-house cultivation by covering the beds with plastic; and while the wheat is establishing itself in the nursery beds the previous crop can be left to ripen fully in the fields. Transplantation of the wheat has been found to induce a stronger root growth as the plants re-establish themselves in the fields, making them more resistant to lodging when they reach full growth. This technique, introduced experimentally begin-ning about 1973, has been found to give yields up to 20 per cent higher than obtained with the same wheat varieties sown in the normal way, and is being extended to an increasing proportion of the wheat-growing area of the north.

The limitation, of course, lies in labour, the transplant operation involving what the Chinese call "the three bends", one of the most arduous passages in field work—plant-ing the seeds in the nurseries, taking them up again for transplanting, and then replanting them, all processes which are still largely done by hand. But here, as in many other aspects of China's agriculture, mechanization is in prospect. Mechanical rice-transplanters are coming into spreading use in the south. These were found to be extremely difficult appliances to perfect but over a long period of experimentation improved designs have been achieved (the fact that design and manufacture have often been carried out at the grass-roots, commune level, must have been beneficial in this process) and now commune members report good results. The basic design is expected to be adaptable to the transplantation of wheat, although the fact that wheat is transplanted into dry ground makes for more problems.

Another critical area of effort towards increasing agricultural production lies in the "green revolution" heartland of introducing improved, high-yielding crop strains. China has imported samples of the "miracle seeds" developed in Western research institutes, 5,000 tons of dwarf wheat from Mexico in 1972 and another 15,000 tons in 1973,[28] but the main thrust of the efforts in this direction lies at the commune level of rural organization, not in state research centres. Practically every commune, most brigades and many production teams run their own seed-improvement unit, within their scientific farming groups, responsible for introducing, where necessary crossbreeding and finally popularizing improved seed strains. The centrally run network of research institutes and extension services run by province and county administrations backs up the grass-roots research, but the main burden appears to rest at the lower level. This may result in slower progress, but it is likely also to be surer because new strains will be locally adapted and tested before introduction.[29] The national leadership has conceded, however, that "scientific research ... lags far behind the needs of speeding up the expansion of large-scale socialist agriculture" (confirming the impression registered by some groups of Western specialists), and has called for "big efforts to propagate, spread, purify and regenerate fine seed strains".[30]

Multiple cropping and inter-cropping are other areas of concentrated effort. The development of faster-growing grain varieties, making possible an additional crop, can of course bring about an increase in production sharper than can be obtained by incremental improvement in crop yields. No national multi-cropping index appears to have been published in Peking but it is clear from numerous Chinese statements and from field observations that much effort is directed in the communes to inserting additional crops into the traditional cycles. For example, in Tibet winter wheat has been widely introduced in the past few years, in addition to the traditional summer crop of barley, more than doubling grain production in many areas; communes in Kiangsu, traditionally an area of one rice crop plus winter wheat, have in recent years begun harvesting two rice crops between spring and autumn. Typically, the process of adding a crop will be begun on the experimental plots of a commune's or a brigade's scientific farming unit, using a newly developed fast ripening rice variety. With success on the experimental plots and consequent increased availability of the improved seed, some production brigades or teams will begin double-cropping on a trial basis, using perhaps a tenth or a fifth of their fields for the purpose. When these units have demonstrated that double-cropping is practicable on a production basis, the final step is "popularization", as the commune as a whole moves rapidly into the new practice.

Such intensification of cropping makes great demands on labour and organization. A day saved in the crucial rush period in which the first crop is harvested, the fields re-fertilized and prepared for the new planting, and then the second crop transplanted from the nursery beds, can have a larger-than-proportional effect at the end of the summer when the second crop is ripening. Some production teams have formed crack work-squads from their strongest and most energetic members to do this rush work, and these special squads are often now maintained on a year-round basis, turning their hands to other specialist work such as farmland capital construction in the rest of the year. The intensified use of the soil requires greatly increased application of fertilizer—and this again puts greater demand on labour. In the Suchow area which has recently moved into triple-cropping each crop is given 60 tons of organic fertilizer per hectare, a total of 180 tons/ha./pa. There are additional applications of chemical fertilizer.

Multi-cropping, with its intense demands on labour, acts as a spur to mechanization.

MECHANIZATION

Mechanization is crucial to all the aspects of development discussed above. In the mid-1950s Mao Tse-tung declared mechanization to be "the fundamental way out for agriculture" (while insisting that the new cooperative social structure must be firmly established in the countryside before machinery was widely introduced); and that maxim is one of the rallying slogans of the present movement. The "basic mechanization" of agriculture by 1980 was proclaimed as a national development target at the end of 1975 (confirming, in fact, the time-table Mao had set twenty years before), and it is an element of the new, intensified drive to "Learn from Tachai" in agriculture. But the mechanization campaign and the "Learn from Tachai" campaign are distinct as well as linked. That is, a "Tachai-type" unit need not have achieved basic mechanization of its agricultural processes, but simply to have registered "rapid progress and substantial results" towards that goal; while one that has achieved basic mechanization will by no means necessarily be judged "Tachai-type".

The concept of "basic mechanization" goes far beyond the introduction of tractors and motor cultivators. It looks to the introduction of machinery into 70 per cent of all agricultural and agriculture-related processes: water control, plowing, cultivation, harvesting, food processing, forestry, land reclamation and improvement, animal husbandry, fisheries, transportation, etc. The drive for this goal moves on two fronts, in a sense in two directions—up from the grass-roots, down from the centre, or state. The present movement is concentrated on the county, a large administrative unit (there are 2,200 odd in China) and the lowest in the purely state structure—beneath the county are, as a rule, the people's communes, which are essentially confederations of collective villages although they are also an element of the state structure. In the headquarters township of a go-ahead county will be found an extensive and thriving light-industrial complex, focussed on agriculture and the satisfaction of consumer needs in the surrounding rural area. Plants at this level turn out relatively—sometimes remarkably—complex machinery and parts, drawing as far as possible on raw materials produced within the county, either in state-run mines, etc., or from the many such projects operated by the communes. A county factory will contract out for elements of its product, both up and down: up to state factories at prefecture or province level for items, such as precision steel parts, tyres and belting, which are beyond its productive capacity; and down, to the communes, for items whose production is within the capacity of the commune—and sometimes brigade—factories. "Through its coordination of local [commune] units and the impetus provided by spin-off from the more sophisticated county plants, the county plays a key economic role in rural industry. It is also through the county that the state maintains overall control over the pace of mechanization."[31]

Manufacturing industry at county level has grown as a rule out of workshops set up there for the repair and then manufacture of farm tools and machinery. With time—and often quite rapidly—such plants grow in range and productive capacity, taking over machine tools which are replaced or discarded higher up in the structure and/or making their own. An example may be cited in the farm tools repair and manufacture plant established in the headquarters town of Hsiyang, the county in which Tachai is situated. At the time of the writer's first visit to this plant, in 1973, its manufactures were limited to basic farm machinery, tractor parts and attachments such as harrows and ploughs. But the plant's research and development group had turned out a prototype of a

miniature caterpillar tractor, designed to meet the requirements of an upland agriculture still predominantly confined to terrace farming. The intention was to make trial
models and distribute them to the local communes for testing; to adopt commune-
members' suggestions in design modifications, and meanwhile to tool-up the plant for
full production of the mini-caterpillar—an independent factory, adjacent to but hived
off from the original plant, was to be set up for the purpose. The 10 h.p. engine in the
prototype had been made at a centrally-run state factory but another farm repair and
manufacturing plant at the provincial capital of Taiyuan, 160 kilometres away, was
tooling up to start manufacturing the engines. On the writer's return visit to Tachai and
Hsiyang in 1974 the mini-caterpillars were quite a common sight on commune projects,
but they were still described as being on trial, not as products of a manufacturing run. By
1975, however, the factory was in full production. The engines were coming from the
Taiyuan plant. Thirty per cent of the elements of the tractors, over and above the
engines, came from outside the plant,[32] most of that from state factories at higher level
but some from commune factories. That proportion is expected to be steadily reduced,
but not to disappear entirely.

Manufacturing plants in advanced communes can also turn out quite complex
machinery: electric motors, for example, produced within the commune, from commune raw materials, except for ball-bearings, copper wire for armatures, and some
screws. The first task of these commune plants is to serve the needs of their own and
neighbouring communes' villages, but they can also undertake manufacturing on state
contract, for national distribution or even for export. The farm tools repair and
manufacturing plant in the Evergreen People's Commune near Suchow, for example,
began to manufacture small, handy-man type vises for export during the three years
over which the writer has been visiting the commune and on the most recent visit, at the
end of 1975, an output target of 10,000 units had been set for 1976. This factory was
also making a mud-pump designed by its own workers, originally for use in the
commune's own many canals and fish-ponds but then, as it proved itself and production
increased, for neighbouring communes too and then, on state contract, for wider
distribution.

Profits from commune factories are not distributed but used by the commune
leadership for further development. Extension and elaboration of the manufacturing
and service sectors at commune level is the usual area for this re-investment. But a trend
has recently developed, and been praised in China,[33] in which commune leadership uses
surpluses generated by commune-owned projects as aid-grants to the poorer
brigades—a further instance of the "levelling-up" which is inherent in the Chinese
approach to development. Thus while mechanization, proceeding from unequal natural
and material bases, must be seen as likely to accentuate regional disparities of productivity and income, within the communes the trend should be towards greater equalization. In 1959, just after the formation of the communes, Mao Tse-tung identified the
projects and services being run at commune level, which were then still usually
rudimentary, as "our great, bright hope" for steady advance through cooperation into
collectivization; and the raising of the level of account from the production team to the
brigade and even the commune is among the goals of the current movement, as one
expected consequence of the strengthening of the commune-level economy.

Much as can be done at county level and below towards achieving the goal of "basic
mechanization" by 1980, continuing dependence on the state sector at upper levels for

high grade steel and precision parts means that bottlenecks there would impede the movement. In that context the disclosure in 1977 that political disputes (now ascribed to the machinations of the "gang of four") had led in the previous year to the closing down for a time of the Wuhan Iron and Steel Plant is significant. The losses from such interruptions are much more than proportional to the actual time lost[34] and carry their effect downstream through the economy. Losses of production in 1977 through political disturbances were also experienced in industries more immediately linked with the campaign to mechanize agriculture. For example, the Kiangsi tractor plant, among several others now admitted to have been seriously affected, was practically closed down for ten months and produced only 1,500 tractors in the year, against its target of 5,000–6,000.[35]

Seeing the attainment of "basic mechanization" as equivalent to reaching modernity in agriculture some Western observers have concluded that it is "an achievement beyond the hope [in the next five years] of vast portions of China's countryside".[36] The Chinese would vigorously disagree—that Yao Wen-yuan "openly clamour [ed]" that the farm mechanization target could not be realized by 1980 is one of the indictments against "the gang of four".[37] The observer quoted above goes on to suggest, however, that "success in terms of achieving basic mechanization by 1980 is less important than the act of setting the goal and mobilizing the rural sector in pursuit of it"[38] and the quantification of the goal as mechanization of 70 per cent of agricultural processes certainly makes that true—a village which, starting from a very low level, achieved mechanization of half, or even 40 per cent of its processes in five years could hardly be said to have "failed".

Mechanization is making its speediest progress in China in the agricultural processes outside the fields—pumping, crop processing, and staple food preparation. The mechanical pumps, threshers, shellers, winnowers, grinders, mills, etc., usually made within the communes, which are everywhere being introduced and multiplied, release labour for field work which in consequence can steadily be intensified. William Hinton, who has seen the process of rural development in China at first hand over 30 years, notes that "this very liberation of labour power tends to act as a barrier to mechanization [of field work] because regardless of the operation the first mechanical steps are not likely to do the job as well as hand labour. With new supplies of willing hands available few are willing to risk the drop in yield that machine cultivation almost always brings for a season or two." Hinton sees a contradiction between inter-cropping and multi-cropping on the one hand and mechanization of field-work on the other, and a consequent barrier that is holding back mechanization of such work as planting, thinning, weeding, side dressing, spraying, harvesting. He concludes that the current campaign will achieve its goal of "basic mechanization by 1980" only in so far as irrigation, processing, capital construction, and transportation are concerned; the mechanization of field work entails so many problems that although "there will be striking progress [in this regard] by 1980, 70 per cent mechanization of field work is liable to require another decade or two".[39]

THE FOURTH MOBILIZATION

The impact of the "Learn from Tachai" campaign in Tachai's own county of

Hsiyang, described in the first part of this paper,[40] although delayed, was striking in its effect on the county's grain output:[41]

1966	40,000 tons
1969	80,000
1971	118,000
1974	119,000

The drought so widely experienced in China after 1971 was especially severe in Shansi, and severe drought conditions obtained there from 1972 through 1974—in spite of which, it is claimed, good harvests were reaped in Hsiyang.[42] The grain figures give only one aspect of the agricultural development achieved. Production in forestry, animal husbandry and sideline occupations also expanded markedly, total income from those sources nearly trebling between 1966 and 1974. Until 1966 Hsiyang was a grain-deficit county, its shortfall being made good from state supplies; in 1967 self-sufficiency was achieved and thereafter Hsiyang began producing surpluses for sale through the state's procurement mechanism. In the four-year period 1967–70 grain surpluses sold to the state from the Hsiyang communes averaged 15,890 tons a year while in the next four-year period average sales were 67 per cent higher, at 26,500 tons.[43] Between 1966 and 1974 distributed annual income per head of population rose from 47.50 yuan to 94 yuan. Hsiyang is still a poor county, but the improvement in living standards was greater than the figures for distributed income suggest. Villagers benefited during this period from the new housing they built for themselves, usually with tapped water supply and electricity; and from extended community services, such as cooperative medical systems and new schools, self-supplied by the communities. Workshops and small factories established at commune and often brigade level, consolidating and expanding the collective (as opposed to the cooperative) sector of the commune economy, provided additional sources of cash income in the form of wages.

Conferences to "sum up experience", surveying and analysing progress or the lack of it, seeking lessons from failure as well as from success, are intrinsic to Chinese Communist method and are applied to the task of development as consistently as they were to the tasks of revolution and war. In 1970 the experience and achievement of Hsiyang provided the central theme of the Northern Region Agricultural Conference, attended by cadres from county level upward from fourteen northern provinces, and held in Taiyuan, the Shansi provincial capital. The brisk acceleration in production that Hsiyang had achieved over the previous three years was seen as the consequence of "learning from Tachai"; and the success in spreading that lesson, galvanising villages which had previously ignored it, was attributed to the changed county leadership. The stimulus had come from the county, the communes and brigades had responded. The 1970 conference coined a new honorific, "Tachai-type County", and bestowed it on Hsiyang. From that conference emerged a new slogan:

LEARN FROM TACHAI, CATCH UP WITH HSIYANG!

The linking of the large administrative unit of the county with the village expressed the enlargement of the unit for emulation, and thus also the intensification of the campaign. The essential message of the original slogan, "Learn from Tachai", had been that if Tachai could do it, any village could do it; so, in the 1970 slogan, with Hsiyang county. The thrust of "Catch up with Hsiyang" was directed at county leaderships, challenging them to activate, if necessary to "rectify", themselves, so that they could stimulate lower-level leadership bodies, at commune and brigade level. The new spirit, and the action that expressed it, would then spread through the villages of the county as it had done in Hsiyang. "If Hsiyang could do it, why can't you?" was the challenge to the county leaderships implicit in the new slogan, and the *People's Daily* made it explicit in an editorial at the end of the conference. Addressing itself directly to the leaderships of the other counties in the country, all 2,200-minus-one of them, it asked: "Can't you accomplish what Hsiyang has achieved? If you can't do it in one year, or two, what about in three years? At any rate, four or five years should be quite enough!"[44]

In the following five years 317[45] more counties took off after Hsiyang and earned the title "Tachai-type County", bestowed on them, after investigation, by the leadership at province level and ratified by the Central Committee. In theory, this meant that in each case the great majority (say four-fifths) of the brigades and communes within the county concerned had themselves become "Tachai-type" units.

In September–October 1975, five years after the Northern Region Conference, another conference on agriculture was convened, opening in Hsiyang but continuing in Peking, and this time national in composition and explicitly devoted to the theme of "learning from Tachai". This National Conference on Learning from Tachai in Agriculture was described by *People's Daily* as "one of the most important meetings since the formation of the nation". It was attended by all party secretaries at county and prefectural level and by cadres from provincial governments in charge of agricultural machinery sector of industry, educated youngsters from the city working in the countryside and other concerned groups, about 3,700 people in all. Chen Yung-kuei, the Tachai leader become vice-premier, opened and closed the conference, and Hua Kuo-feng, then another vice-premier, was in the chair and delivered the key-note address. (This was his first emergence at the national level: shortly after, Hua became premier in succession to Chou En-Lai and then chairman of the Chinese Communist Party in succession to Mao Tse-tung.)

The title of Hua's key-note address became the slogan for the new phase of the movement—or rather, perhaps, for the new movement, since the scope and intensity were so much greater that a qualitative change was involved:

LET THE WHOLE PARTY MOBILIZE FOR A VAST EFFORT

TO DEVELOP AGRICULTURE AND BUILD

TACHAI-TYPE COUNTIES THROUGHOUT THE COUNTRY!

With this slogan the trend Hsiyang had pioneered and which had been injected into the original "Learn from Tachai" campaign by the 1970 conference was confirmed and made pre-eminent. The unit for emulation became the county and a new target was set: that by 1980 one-third of all counties—that is, just over 400 more—should have transformed themselves into "Tachai-type counties". Hua Kuo-feng said that becoming a "Tachai-type county" meant "to spread the fundamental experience of Tachai throughout the county, so that the leadership at all levels and in all departments in the county will work in the Tachai Brigade way, and the majority or vast majority of the county's communes and production brigades will be of the Tachai type".[46] That the last requirement is not applied strictly appears from a Hsiyang cadre's speech at the Tachai Conference. He disclosed that only about 120 of the county's 411 brigades, say 30 per cent, were advanced units by the end of 1975.[47]

Hua went on to set out six basic criteria which had to be met before a county could be awarded Tachai-type status:

1. The county Party committee should be a leading core which firmly adheres to the Party's line and policies and is united in struggle.

Since the unit for emulation and action in the new campaign is the county it follows that the county leadership is initially responsible for stimulating and organizing the implementation of the campaign. Over the seventeen years between the formation of the people's communes in 1958 and the launching of the new phase of the Tachai movement the emphasis in the Chinese countryside had been on leadership at the commune and brigade levels: the county, a very active leadership level in the years when the rural cooperative structure was taking shape, had tended to lapse more into organization than leadership. Hua said that most of the county Party committees were good or comparatively good, while only a handful had serious problems or were "even controlled by bad elements". But "quite a few leading bodies of the Party county committees ... [were] still soft, lax and lazy". A "general rectification" was needed. To start off the campaign well and thereafter every year county Party leadership groups should submit themselves to self- and mutual-criticism and to examination and criticism from levels beneath and above. Any "who cling stubbornly to bourgeois factionalism and refuse to correct their mistakes" must promptly be transferred, and "bad elements" must be "resolutely clear[ed] out", he said.

> 2. [The County Party committee] should establish the dominance of poor and lower middle peasants as a class so as to be able to wage resolute struggles against capitalist activities and exercise effective supervision over the class enemies and remould them.

Those who comprised the broad base of the social pyramid of rural China at the time of land reform have been seen by the Chinese communists as the real motive force in progress since Liberation, as they were during the struggles, political and military, for revolution. Those who were identified as "poor and lower middle" peasants in the categorizations during the land reform movement constitute a mass élite in China's rural society today—though one having none of the attributes of superiority, separateness, self-interest and self-perpetuation which characterize true élites in other developing societies. "Poor and Lower-Middle Peasant Associations" comprise, within the commune framework, bodies to supervise, assess and criticize the work of the leadership groups, both in the revolutionary committees which provide the executive leadership and in the Party committees which supply the basic political orientation. Hua enjoined the Party committees at county level to check that this class, through its associations, was everywhere alert and effective in its crucial supervisory role.

Elsewhere in his speech Hua noted the continuance in rural society of "fairly serious tendencies towards capitalism". This the Chinese see as inevitable, another expression of the fact that all social progress and change is uneven. A new social order is being built in China on the basis—or rather in the rubble—of the old, and the attitudes engendered and required by the old order are seen as persisting in patches.[48] Among expressions of such attitudes Hua cited:

> The expansion of the area allotted to private plots beyond the 5–7 per cent of a unit's arable that is laid down.

> Turning reclaimed land into private plots rather than collective fields.

> The practice of some commune members going off to work individually as hired labour in the towns or cities, rather than working with their fellow members on collective land.

> Erroneous trends in distribution, e.g. stinting accumulation by the collective in

favour of distribution for immediate consumption—"eating up everything, leaving no public accumulation".

Graft, theft, speculation and profiteering by a "handful of class enemies", who also may "commit sabotage".

These remaining "capitalist trends" are seen as co-existing at this stage of China's political development with the emerging and strengthening factors which express and confirm the new social order. They are seen as relatively minor phenomena and are believed to be in retreat; but the Party leadership points to them as potential sources of infection and calls for close surveillance of those "class enemies" who are still ready to encourage the ways of the old order.

3. Cadres at the county, commune and brigade level should, like those in Hsiyang, regularly participate in collective productive labour.

The Chinese see manual labour performed by members of upper leadership levels as the great leveller, the most effective preventive of the emergence of a new ruling élite through the transformation of the Party or the bureaucracy into a class. This levelling role is fundamental in the emphasis on manual labour; but the participation of all upper-level cadres in the productive processes is also seen as a requirement for efficient administration. The manual labour performed by upper-level cadres is not allowed to be a matter of giving an impression by occasionally joining in on the farm or the factory floor. Careful records are kept of periods spent by cadres at manual labour, and the record of the cadres is kept publicly posted. Targets for this are now set. In Chia Ting county, under the Shanghai municipality (visited by the writer in November 1975) these for example were the targets set for manual labour by cadres:

County cadres	40 days a year
Commune cadres	60 days a year
Brigade cadres	120 days a year

But Hsiyang is already well beyond those levels. There cadres in the county administration are expected to spend 100 days a year at manual labour, commune cadres 200, and brigade cadres 300. This approach demands not only physical exertions but also much harder and more efficient work from the cadres at their desks, of course: The Hsiyang county cadres must get through the year's administrative work-load in 265 days; brigade cadres are expected to so organize their year's administrative work as to accomplish it in 165 days.[49] Cadres' participation in manual labour serves also to bring senior leadership into the front line of the struggle for production and, as well as keeping cadres abreast of the problems and attitudes of those they serve as leaders, it also helps them retain the respect of the rank-and-file peasants and workers. The most popular and respected cadres appear to be those who live most closely with the commune members, implementing what the Chinese call "the three withs"—live with, eat with, work with the masses.

4. Rapid progress and substantial results should be achieved in farmland capital construction, mechanization of agriculture and scientific farming.

5. The collective economy should be steadily expanded and production and income of the poor communes and brigades should reach or surpass the present level of the average communes or brigades in the locality.

6. All-round development should be made in agriculture, forestry, animal husbandry, side occupations and fisheries, with considerable increases in output, big

contributions to the state and steady improvement in the living standards of the commune members.

Steady improvement in the living standard of the peasantry has always been at the top of the "Maoist" priorities for rural development. Mao Tse-tung insisted that every increase in production should be reflected promptly in an improvement of living standard. In practice this meant until recently that when deciding upon division of net income between accumulation for investment and distribution for consumption, a village will have used the accumulation fund as the variable. That is, in a good year more funds will be put into the accumulation fund, with the increase in distribution held back accordingly; while in a bad year accumulation will be held back so that the increase in consumption can be maintained, or at least that income distributed to members should not be reduced. A reversal of emphasis appears to be being urged on the commune members in the present movement. As Chen Yung-kuei put it to the writer in an interview at Tachai in November 1975, "The living standard should be raised steadily, while accumulation should be raised continuously". That puts the emphasis on accumulation and implies that in a poor year distribution should be held down or even cut back so that accumulation can be maintained. Chen Yung-kuei argued that prosperous rural units, such as the highly advanced communes around Shanghai, must hold down consumption lest they reverse, rather than remove, the "big difference" in income usual between worker and peasant. The members of such rural units, he pointed out, have housing of higher quality, smaller expenditure, much cheaper grain and vegetables; in Tachai the annual rent for a big living-unit was aboutY8 a year, compared to Y80–100 in the cities. So personal income in such prosperous units could not be allowed "to rise like a boat", floating up in direct proportion to increased production, but should be controlled and held back. Since the production team—or, infrequently, the brigade—has sole authority in deciding the proportions of income that go to accumulation on the one hand and distribution/consumption on the other, such control can be achieved only through exhortation and education.

Postscript, 1978. Chen Yung-kuei's suggestion verged on the policies repudiated after 1976 as the "ultra-leftism" of the "gang of four": since, it has again been emphasized that peasants should benefit tangibly and promptly from increased production—as Mao insisted.

Hua Kuo-feng used the instance of Hsiyang to indicate the prospects for China as a whole if the targets of the new campaign were achieved. Generally speaking, other counties in Shansi were no worse off in their natural conditions than Hsiyang, he said, so all should be able to achieve Hsiyang's present level of production. In 1975 Hsiyang had produced 750 kg of grain per head of population, of which 250 kg had been marketable or commercial grain, sold to the state after the cooperative units had paid their taxes and satisfied their members' requirements for consumption and seed stores. If all the Shansi counties attained Hsiyang's level, Hua pointed out, then total grain output in the province would increase by 150 per cent, while the grain available for sale to the state would increase by nearly 300 per cent. While China's more fertile and advanced provinces could not be expected to achieve increases of such magnitude as that, it is evident that the success of the new movement would further and sharply accelerate the rate of increase in agricultural production. The Chinese see such an acceleration as essential: "If we are satisfied with the present rate of development [of the national economy] ... we will not be able to realize the modernization of agriculture, nor that of industry, national defence and science and technology by the end of the century", Hua Kuo-feng warned the Tachai Conference.

The Chinese will not count the new campaign a success unless as well as sharply raising productivity it brings about political and organizational changes in rural society. Among those should be a raising of the level of account to brigade[50] (in the great majority of communes today the unit of account is the production team) and, through "levelling up", a reduction of inequalities. It is here that political problems may appear. The writer's discussion with cadres of the Chinese administration have shown a divergence of attitude on questions such as these at various levels: at county level, for example, cadres are more likely to stress the raising of the unit of account to brigade level as a necessary consequence of the Tachai campaign; while down at commune level cadres are much more cautious and tentative about the prospects for widespread raising of the level of account. Seeing this as basically a matter of peasant attitudes, they emphasize that decisions on the timing of such changes must come "from the masses"; they know from their own experience that reforms imposed are likely to be abortive. In this context, it is possible that the repudiation of the "gang of four" (now seen as false "ultra-left" radicals and real "rightists") will strengthen the position of the lower-level cadres.

Whether acceleration of the slow—but apparently steady—progress towards the abolition of the private plots is a goal of the campaign is uncertain. In November 1975 Chen Yung-kuei told the writer that private plots were not discussed at the National Conference on Learning from Tachai which had just been held. While that can hardly have been literally the case, it implied at least that no formal consideration was given to the subject; and that would accord with the observed official approach to this question, which emphasizes that the timing of abolition of private plots can be set only at the lowest level, that is, the production team. The Communists' line on this question is that the development of the cooperative and collective sectors of agriculture will in due course make the private plots an irrelevance and that they will then be done away with—but that the peasants are the best judges of the timing of such a step. On the other hand, some Chinese commentators have cited the elimination of "the soil for engendering capitalism" among the peasantry as one of the goals of the campaign[51] and the private plots must undoubtedly be considered a component of that "soil". Most likely the leadership's expectation is that the movement will give a spurt to the tendency towards abolishing private plots (or farming them collectively as a first step in that direction); but policy will continue to be to insist that all initiatives on this question must come from the grass-roots level.

The impact of the new movement was immediate and evident. Great publicity was given to the National Conference on Learning from Tachai while it was in session and thereafter to the new campaign. At all levels in the countryside, from county down to production team, meetings were held to discuss the Tachai conference and study the copious material from it that was circulated. The various levels began reconsidering their plans in the light of the demands of the new campaign. Delegates to the conference, returning to their units, reported at mass and cadre meetings.

To take one example: in Chia Ting county (under the Shanghai Municipality), the county administration held a special session on the conclusion of the Tachai conference, then convened a mass meeting of cadres right down to production team level to discuss the Conference and the means of implementing the campaign it had called for. Every production team in the county's 19 communes sent two delegates to this meeting—the team leader and the women's leader. The total attendance was just over 3,000.

At the Evergreen Commune, near Suchow, the Tachai Conference had been followed by meetings at team and brigade level, and then a commune mass meeting. After this the commune re-examined its forward planning in the light of the Tachai Conference, scrapped it as too limited, and drew up a new plan. As the first stage in this the commune had decided to re-make about a fifth of its land area, which totalled about 16 square kilometres, in a concentrated effort of "farmland capital construction". The project looked to filling-in the beds of five streams which meandered through the area, the biggest about 30 metres across, and digging four new, straight channels to carry the water: these would be 16 metres wide, 2.5 metres deep. The fields between were to be levelled and re-laid out in regular rectangles, 100 metres by 17, with access-ways between, and avenued roads servicing the field areas (these would be the first significant roads in this particular commune, where most movement and transport to date has been by boat or barge). The project would entail construction of 8 bridges (for tractors, trailers, etc.) three pumping units, and a sluice gate—the latter had been added on the recommendation of the county's hydraulic engineers, to whom the plan had been submitted for approval when it was drafted. The work was intended to be accomplished in one month, with a work force of between 3,500 and 4,000, about 40 per cent of the total work force of the commune. The cost had been calculated at Y180,000, of which the state would contribute a portion which had yet to be decided. This being a prosperous commune, with numerous industries run at commune level and therefore ample funds to finance the project itself, the state's contribution would probably be small, perhaps about 20 per cent.

On a return visit in 1978 the writer found that the plan had been implemented, and was told that the work had been accomplished in the time set. The state had not contributed to the project, which had been wholly financed by the commune. Additional areas had similarly been transformed in the "slack seasons" of subsequent years, and the commune's planned intention of having thus re-made all its land by the end of 1980 was felt by the leadership to be within reach. In the process a majority of members will be re-housed in new, centralized communities, coinciding with the brigade level—three such centres had been started in 1978. The five-year plan (1975–80) looks to doubling production.

The new Tachai movement appears to have had a similar stimulating, even galvanizing influence on units throughout the rural areas: in county and commune factories, with production being stepped up; and in the countryside itself, especially during the winters, with units everywhere at work, usually under the red banners that denote development construction rather than the routine work of the fields, levelling the land, re-shaping river-beds, reclaiming wasteland.

The National Conference on Learning from Tachai closed in 1975 with the declared intention of reconvening in 1980. But developments in 1976, especially political conflicts, made the leadership call a Second National Learn-from-Tachai Conference in Peking in December 1976. Judging from the published material much of the conference's proceedings were concerned with criticizing the "gang of four", and "crushing" them and eradicating their influence became a part of the exhortation to continue the Tachai campaign. The 5,000 delegates were told, however, that in spite of the interference of the "gang" and the often disastrous natural conditions met in 1976 a good start had been made to the campaign: another 100 counties had been adjudged to have attained Tachai standards.[52]

The second conference was reported to have given added impetus to the great farmland capital constructive drive of the previous winter and 150 million people, about 70 per cent of the rural labour force, were later said to have been engaged in the winter 1976–7. Special emphasis was laid on the importance of upper-level cadres' going down to the grass-roots, and over 1.5 million were reported to have thus "gone down" in work-teams to communes, brigades and teams.

One aspect of the campaign which does not appear from the published accounts of the conferences to have been emphasized but which has been noted in China as important is the strategic implication of the multiplication of "Tachai-type counties". Soong Ching Ling (Mme Sun Yat-sen) recalled that the Chinese revolution had triumphed by relying on the resources of the countryside at its then pre-industrial level, and went on: "How incalculably stronger will it be with each county having a substantial food surplus, its own industrial base, and a rural population not only politically inspired and informed but technically experienced and competent."[53]

CONCLUSION

Agricultural development has been seen as a four-stage progression:

STAGE I is limited to traditional rain-fall farming.

STAGE II sees the productivity of the land improved by irrigation, by soil enrichment through use of organic fertilizers, and by better timing of production through improved farm implements.

STAGE III is marked by the introduction of some mechanization and scientifically developed techniques, typically involving the cultivation of improved grain varieties on irrigated land, intensively fertilized with organic and/or chemical fertilizer.

STAGE IV is reached through the structural transformation of the rural economy, which involves the provision of all the modern inputs and the establishment of the institutions and infrastructures needed to support a fully modernized high-productivity agriculture.[54]

Completion of that process took about 1300 years in Japan.

While significant areas of rural China, perhaps most of it, can be said to be still in Stage II and patches—usually in the minority peoples' areas—still in Stage I, very considerable areas are already in Stage III. The present phase of the Learn from Tachai movement can be seen as intended to carry those Stage III areas into Stage IV, while, since the campaign is generalized and national in scope, if successful it should also achieve the promotion of Stage I areas into Stage II, and so on.

Development theory still holds conventionally to the belief that capital and technology, given the right combination of the two and proper timing, will of themselves open the lock that holds under-developed economies in stagnation. As a critic of that approach summed it up, "If you just put in enough capital, if you just introduce enough modern technology, the underdeveloped societies will be vitalized and start growing on their own".[55] When applied to the international scene, the approach produces this prescription: "The poor countries can feed themselves if their agriculture is modernized and their rural economies are restructured. That requires infusion of technology and capital from rich nations".[56] But some Western observers are coming round now to the conclusion that was Mao Tse-tung's premise, that the human factor is the third digit in the combination, so to speak, and without that no application of the first two will turn the lock. The Chinese experience is the best evidence the latter have and the Tachai emulation campaign, through all its stages, is central to that example.

Analysis of the social motivation involved in China's "fourth mobilization" is difficult for an outsider but should be attempted. Material incentives, the will to achieve a more prosperous and fuller life, are an essential part of the motivation; but what about the moral element, and the balance between the two?

The scope of the current campaign and the vocabulary in which it is articulated are suggestive of war—a people's war, it has been said, in which the enemy is a recalcitrant nature, the battle process, landscape modification.[57] Speaking of their enterprises in farmland capital construction, the Tachai villagers coined the slogan, "The more we do it, the better we like it and the greater our courage and ability to do it well", and the psychological process expressed there has been noted by a Western analyst of the movement: "The battles with nature ... engender a strong sense of accomplishment in the individual and collective spirits of the participants in such activities. The pride of completion—with its consequent elevation of village and/or brigade status—is rich fuel for a body of labour which will attack the landscape again—and again".[58] The sense of being part of the community's and the nation's vast effort to transform nature and advance the whole of society seems to produce élan and resolution—"the willingness and ability of people to work relatively hard and effectively, on a national scale, for goals that inspire them".[59]

The causality comes back to Tachai. What the Tachai villagers first had to learn themselves was that they need not continue as the victims of their adverse natural circumstances but could, unaided, begin to transform those circumstances. In coming to see that their external world was "systematically capable of productive manipulation", the Tachai villagers made the great leap from the "pre-Newtonian" to the "post-Newtonian world", in Rostow's concepts. And in now "learning from Tachai" on such a massive scale, the Chinese peasantry may be carrying their society into the take-off stage, where "the forces making for economic progress, which [previously] yielded [only] limited bursts and enclaves of modern activity, expand and come to dominate the society [and] growth becomes its normal condition".[60]

NOTES.

1   Chou made that statement to Edgar Snow, who reported it in various journals and included it in his book, *The Long Revolution*, Random House: New York 1972.
2   Originally this figure was given as 246, in *Peking Review (PR)* No. 2, 1972; In *PR* No. 1, 1974 it was reassessed at 250.
3   *PR* No. 1, 1973.
4   Foreign Broadcast Information Service, BBC, *Daily Report, PRC*, 6 September 1974, p. 8, quoted by Robert Michael Field, *China Quarterly*, No. 68.
5   Yang Li-kung, Deputy Minister for Agriculture and Forestry, confirmed the figure on November 14 at the FAO conference in Rome.
6   This figure was stated by Agriculture Ministry officials in an interview with the writer in Peking, July 1976. Previously the output for this year had been given as 240 million.

7   See Robert Michael Field, "Recent Chinese Grain Claims", *China Quarterly*, No. 66, 1976; and this writer's comment on recent Chinese grain figures, *China Quarterly*, No. 68.
8   Chou Chin, A Year of Advance Amid Storms, *PR*, 1977, No. 7.
9   ibid.
10 Output for 1977 and 1978 official Peking figures, 1975 and 1976 estimated from Chinese comments.
11 China's Foreign Trade in 1975 (Part II), the Editor, *Current Scene*, October 1976, Vol. XIV, No. 10, pp. 3-4.
12 ibid.
13 *Peoples Daily*, editorial, NCNA, February 18, 1977.
14 It is in the "policy of not over-squeezing the peasants that the main explanation lies as to why China having declared self-sufficiency in food production, has continued to purchase wheat from advanced countries of the West at great cost to her foreign exchange reserves. In 1973, for example, China spent US$840 million to import wheat for consumption in her big urban centres. Given a government less inclined to support agriculture, such an amount of import, totalling 7 million tons or half a kilogram per person per month, could easily have been scraped out from peasant consumption". John Wong, Some Aspects of China's Agricultural Development Experience, *World Development*, June 1976 (Vol. 4 No. 6), p. 490. Also, Dwight Perkins: "Grain imports ... backstop government guarantees that grain tax and purchase quotas will not be raised frequently or by large amounts". Constraints Influencing China's Agricultural Performance, in *China: A Reassessment of the Economy*, Joint Economic Committee of US Congress, 1975.
15 Benedict Stavis, *Making Green Revolution*: Ithaca, New York: Cornell Centre for International Studies, 1974, p. 10.
16 Kenneth R. Walker, China and Grain: A Matter of Import, *Problems of Communism*, July/August 1976.
17 Stavis, op. cit., p. 8.
18 Leo A. Orleans, China's Experience in Population Control: The Elusive Model, *World Development*, July/August 1975, p. 525.
19 See W. Haque, N. Mehta, A . Rahman and P. Wignaraja *Towards a Theory of Rural Development*, UN Asian Development Institute, December 1975. *Development Dialogue*, 1977, No. 2.
20 See pp 63–5 above.
21 Dwight Perkins, A Conference on Agriculture, *China Quarterly*, No. 67, September 1967, p. 598.
22 Tachai Field—Its reconstruction and Its Fertility Characteristics, by the Scientific Research Group of the Tachai Production Brigade, *Scientia Sinica* January/February 1976, Vol. XIX, No. 1.
23 Perkins, op. cit., p. 606, quoting Chinese Official.
24 Hua Kuo-feng, *Let the Whole Party Mobilize for a Vast Effort to Develop Agriculture and Build Tachai-Type Counties Throughout the Country*, Foreign Languages Press, Peking, 1975, p. 6.
25 Quoted by Perkins, op. cit., p. 606.
26 See F. H. King's classic *Farmers of Forty Centuries*, published in 1910 and long out of print but recently republished by Rodale Press Inc., Emmaus, Pennsylvania.
27 Perkins, op. cit., p. 356. This is a production figure, of gross weight.
28 Perkins, op. cit., p. 601.
29 Indian planners have found "the limited suitability of available [high yield varieties] to local agro-climatic conditions" a retarding factor in the programme there, and noted "an urgent need for breeding the right varieties to suit local conditions." Dr. Ric Shand, quoted in the *Australian National University Reporter*, December 1976.
30 Hua Kuo-feng, op. cit., p. 24.
31 Scott S. Hallford, "Mechanization in the PRC", *Current Scene*, May 1976, Vol. XIV, No. 5. For a description of industry in a county, see John Gurley's paper, pp 19–20 above.
32 Hallford, op. cit.
33 Chou Chin, Mechanization: Fundamental Way Out for Agriculture, *PR* No. 9, 1977.
34 An integrated steel plant is extremely vulnerable to drastic changes in operating regime. Under sudden thermal shocks refractory linings of ovens and furnaces suffer, leading to reduced operating life and the need for costly and time-consuming repairs and replacement, all reducing output and increasing costs even after production is resumed. See Managing Durgapur, by Bagaram Tulpule, *Economic and Political Weekly*, December 25, 1976, p. 1998.
35 New China News Agency, February 9, 1977.
36 Hallford, op. cit.
37 Chou Chin, op. cit.
38 Hallford, op. cit.
39 William Hinton, Mechanization: Shansi Impressions, *China Towards Modernisation*, Hong Kong; Hong Kong Federation of Students, 1977, pp. 227–40.
40 Pp 41–70.
41 Figures from Wang Chin-tzu, a Hsiyang county cadre, In Hua, op, cit., p. 52.
42 ibid.

43   Wang Chin-tzu, op. cit., p. 52.
44   Quoted in *PR* No. 48, 1975, p. 8.
45   Tien Sang, *New China News*, February 23, 1977, p. 2.
46   Hua Kuo-feng, op. cit. This pamphlet also contains excerpts from speeches at the National Conference by Kuo Feng-lien, party secretary of Tachai brigade, and Wang Chin-tzu, deputy secretary of the Hsiyang county party committee.
47   Wang Chin-tzu, in Hua Kuo-feng, op. cit.
48   In Lenin's grim metaphor, "When the old society perishes its corpse cannot be nailed up in a coffin and lowered into the grave. It disintegrates in our midst; the corpse rots and infects us". Quoted in *Peking Review*, December 5, 1974.
49   A hard-working brigade leader seems, a former member of his brigade said, "to be almost a machine. All he does is work; no rest; no time with friends. These brigade cadres and the main team cadres are all like that. They don't take days off, and after work the cadres have to sit around late to discuss and arrange for the next day's production. A lot of work. It's like taking care of a big household. Why do they do it? They feel it's a question of political power. They feel, previously members of our class were like slaves or beasts of burden. Now the Party has taken power for us; so now we are the masters of our own house. If *we* won't take up the work, that's no good, is it?" The description is by an emigre member of a Kwangtung brigade, interviewed in Hong Kong: quoted by Jonathan Unger, The Organization of Collective Incentives in the Chinese Countryside: Lessons from Chen Village, *World Development*, May, 1978.
50   See first part of this paper, p 61 above.
51   e.g. Tien Sang, 700 Million Chinese Peasants Determined to Get Mechanized, *New China News*, February 23, 1977, Vol. 15, No. 6, p. 1.
52   Counties aspiring to the honorific "Tachai-type" apply to higher-level authorities, prefecture or province, and their progress is then investigated against the six criteria of the movement. If positive the decision of the province is checked and then ratified by the Central Committee.
53   Soong Ching Ling, A Great New Movement, *China Reconstructs*, March 1976.
54   From W. David Hopper, The Development of Agriculture in Developing Countries, *Scientific American*, September 1976.
55   Harry Magdoff, Capital, Technology and Development, *Monthly Review*, August 1976.
56   Hopper, op. cit. The sentences quoted are from the summary.
57   Christopher L. Salter, The Role of Landscape Modification in Revolutionary Nation-Building, *China Geographer*, No. 3, 1976. Salter's observations call to mind William James's essay in which he noted that it was war that historically had called forth "the higher range of men's spiritual energy", and suggested that man might find "the moral equivalent of war" in "the immemorial human warfare against nature"—which points back to the Tachai movement.
58   Salter, op. cit.
59   Barry Richman, *American Economic Review*, May 1975, quoted by John Wong, op. cit.
60   W. W. Rostow, *The Stages of Economic Growth*, CUP, 1960, p. 7.

China's Experience in Population Control: The Elusive Model*

LEO A. ORLEANS

INTRODUCTION

Anyone desperate for some evidence of hope in the world's population picture can perhaps get some satisfaction from the knowledge that if the awareness and concern about population could be quantified, it would undoubtedly prove to be growing at a considerably faster rate than the population itself. And widespread awareness and concern, after all, are the first steps to any possible solution. The body of opinion which uses religious or ideological ground to deny the seriousness of population growth is declining in size and influence, while more and more governments of developing countries are coming to realize that high rates of population growth not only jeopardize national goals to raise living standards, but also threaten international stability.

Changing attitudes with regard to population control, particularly on the part of the governments of developing countries, is reflected in the United Nations, which for years carefully avoided official endorsement of any programme designed to control fertility. Whereas in 1965 the General Assembly voted that the international community should not get involved in population problems, by 1969 the UN Fund for Population Activities (UNFPA) was already operational in its responsibility for funding, programming, and coordinating the rapidly growing UN activities relating to population. In 1971 the UN approved a draft resolution which urged member states not only to pay more attention to demographic objectives in general (statistics, research, planning), but also "to cooperate in achieving a substantial reduction of the rate of population growth in those countries which consider that their present rate of growth is too high." To call attention of leaders and citizens of all countries to the dangers of continued high rates of world population growth, the United Nations designated 1974 as World Population Year and scheduled an intergovernmental conference in Bucharest devoted to consideration of basic demographic problems, their relationship with economic and social development, and population policies and action programmes needed to promote human welfare and development.

Because of sensitive internal and international political considerations, the United States was also slow to take an official stand on the population question. Consequently, for many years, it was the private organizations which led the way in calling attention to the dangers of unrestricted population growth. The ever-mounting expressions of concern from both within and without the government did finally produce results through the enactment by Congress in 1967 of title X legislation which provided the

* This report was prepared for the Committee on Foreign Affairs of the U.S. House of Representatives.

Agency for International Development (AID) with additional funds to assist a variety of population and family planning programmes in developing countries. Since the enactment of title X, funding for AID's population activities has increased rapidly, with commensurate growth in the diversity and complexity of its programmes. By now it has become the chief source of foreign aid funds for world population programmes, the principal contributor to international and private family planning organizations, the foremost contributor to the United Nations Fund for Population Activities, the foremost source of bilateral assistance to family planning programmes, the principal supplier of contraceptives and other supplies, and a leading supporter of applied research aimed at developing new and improved contraceptives.[1] A most impressive list. It is primarily because of the activities of AID that now it can be said:

> Lack of adequate funding by foreign donors is no longer a principal obstacle to progress in population/family planning programs conducted in recipient countries.[2]

What has been the effect of this dramatic increase in both concern about population growth and the expenditure of funds and talent to reduce it? The range of responses to this question is as broad as the problem itself. Critics are likely to point to the fact that all the family planning programmes have barely made a dent in the world's population growth, that the world population will reach 4 billion in 1975, with still another billion in less than 15 years. They are likely to agree with Stewart L. Udall, former Secretary of the Interior, who recently announced that "We have passed the point of no return. ... I see no evidence anywhere in the world that politicians come to grips with population unless there is a crisis".[3] Or they may subscribe to a more fundamental criticism expressed by Prof. Norman Ryder of Princeton, who believes that fertility reduction is gravely impeded by conservatism:

> I have profound reservations about family planning as the focus of population policy because its ideology is essentially conservative and counter-revolutionary. Four professional roles are prominent in its ranks, and all four are oriented to the solution of problems by manipulating individual lives within an intact social structure. First are the doctors who dispense contraceptive cures to patients in clinics. Second are the social workers, our latter-day charity profession, applying Band-Aids to the body politic. Third are the men from Madison Avenue, whose surveys reveal a market for the product, and who view the problem as one of advertising and packaging. Finally there are the philanthropists behind these endeavors, the successful embodiments of a conservative system of free enterprise.[4]

Persons inclined to be more optimistic about the progress of family planning programmes inevitably remind us that the major international effort to reduce the rate of population growth was mounted only within the past 5 or 10 years and that during this short timespan there has been a remarkable transformation of world opinion on the subject. They point to the rapid learning process that is taking place, to the recent progress and continued research in contraceptive technology which may very well reveal yet unknown ways to control human fertility, and to the few developing countries which, with the help of foreign assistance, are making impressive progress in cutting down their birth rates.

It is curious, though probably not surprising, to find that the country with the world's largest population remained out of sight, even out of mind, throughout this period of rather intense, often hectic activity and impassioned argument relating to population growth. The country is, of course, the People's Republic of China, with its more than 800 million people. Isolated and yes, inscrutable, it occupied the attention of a relatively small number of people who attempted to observe it from the outside, coming to the attention of the general public only when some major event inside China's borders happened to spill over on to the front page of the local newspaper. Population and family planning people—having neither the statistical data to dissect and evaluate nor the opportunity for field trips and first-hand observation—virtually ignored China in their considerations. China's "barrack society" seemed to have little to contribute to the solution of existing population problems—already too formidable even without the handicap of China.

But recently China reversed her attitude. No longer is she quite as aloof, secret, and unapproachable. During the past few years, President Nixon visited the People's Republic of China, she entered the United Nations, she became accessible (after more than 20 years) to select and limited tourism—and the world rediscovered China. Perhaps the most dramatic turnabout came in some segments of the family planning field. After being ignored for many years, there is now a widespread impression that China may have discovered "the answer" to the innumerable problems which have plagued family planning programmes in other developing countries. There are a number of reasons for this belief. After a long period of comparative secrecy regarding anything relative to population, the Chinese are now proud of their accomplishments in the family planning field and are willing to "show and tell". The nature of the subject is such that it is of interest to specialists and non-specialists alike; almost everyone who visits China returns with stories and figures reflecting China's birth control policies and methods. Most significantly—there is valid cause for China's pride and for foreign interest.

The purpose of this report is to review, in the light of the basic problems encountered in family planning programmes in other ocuntries, what China has been thinking about population, what she has been attempting to do, how she has been doing it, and finally to comment specifically on whether and to what extent the Chinese experience may be applicable to other developing countries.

Before proceeding, however, a word of explanation. The term "family planning" to describe activities designed to reduce a country's birth rate is an admitted euphemism in the West and inappropriate for China. It is used in this report simply because it is convenient and familiar and should be accepted in its popular connotation.

Because some groups are offended by such terms as "birth control" or "control of fertility", those concerned with the consequences of rapid population growth have managed to circumvent the objections somewhat by stressing "individual rights" and "freedom of choice" and by placing major emphasis on the precept that no woman should conceive an unwanted child—that, is family planning. In fact, of course, concerned developing countries use every means of persuasion available in family planning programmes to convince the mother that she should exercise her "freedom of choice" by not having another child.

In the earlier campaigns the Chinese also used the term "birth control" (chieh-chih-shengyu). This was difficult to rationalize *vis-à-vis* Marxist population theories. The term now used is "limited births planning programme" (chi-hua-sheng-yu)—a natural counterpart, they maintain, of economic and social planning. It has nothing to do with individual rights or freedom of choice and incorporates all means of controlling fertility: contraceptives, sterilization, abortion and late marriage. Whether or not specific words have any effect on the success of a programme to limit births is a moot question, but it does seem that by emphasizing the "planning of births", the Chinese can attack the problem much more directly and honestly.

ESTABLISHMENT OF A POLICY

A commitment on the part of the leadership is, of course, the first prerequisite of a national policy to control a country's fertility. Characteristically, however, the first recognition of the need for a programme to limit family size has come from the country's economists, planners, medical personnel and other professional segments of the society, while the leadership has been much slower in mustering the necessary courage to proclaim a national policy that would do something about it. The reason for this lag is not difficult to appreciate. The basic sense of nationalism is often translated into a direct relationship between size and national strength[5] The idea that strength can come from the quality of the population rather than from numbers alone is a more sophisticated concept and difficult to accept. Also related to nationalism is the frequent resentment and sensitivity of the "coloured" nations being urged by the "white" nations to limit their population growth. Although these attitudes may be on the decline, there is still a stated or unstated suspicion among some of the leaders of the developing countries that selfishness and fear are the primary motives of the advanced nations in pushing a population policy and therefore could not be in the interest of the country being pressured.

Even a government concerned with the improvement of the people's standard of living still tends to give priorities to education, housing and job opportunities before expending limited funds and manpower on family planning programmes. This too is not surprising. Indeed, it takes a farsighted leader to see beyond the immediate economic and social problems that beset his country and to work for the long-range national benefits that are likely to accrue not to him but to his successors. For whether a country is ruled by an elected or a self-appointed government, the leaders still seek the support and popularity resulting from policies and programmes that show more immediate and apparent benefits than would be evident in family planning. The gradual reduction of fertility has a low level of visibility and it takes a generation or more for the results to be reflected in terms of the basic indexes that are normally used to measure development.

Because of these considerations, it was not until the mid-1960s that a discernible trend became evident among some of the developing countries of Asia to initiate steps for curbing population growth. There are a number of reasons why it is the Asian countries that led the way in instituting population policies. First of all, in most of them the population problem is much more immediate in terms of pressure on land and resources than it is in Africa or Latin America. Second, in most of them religious considerations have not constituted major obstacles, as was the case in Europe and the United States during the period of declining fertility or as is the case in most of Latin America. Whatever other problems were to be faced, at least there was no obstacle with regard to birth control being thought immoral or sinful. Even in the Philippines, Thailand, and Indonesia, where opposition of organized religion was anticipated, it turned out to be unexpectedly slight—greatly diluted by educational programmes for religious leaders in Indonesia and the firm support of President Marcos in the Philippines, for example.[6] But relatively speaking, the commitment to a family planning programme is an easy first step that precedes the innumerable problems of implementation.

The new leadership in China after 1949 faced most of the same problems with respect to population that other developing nations experienced a decade or two later.[7] There were, however, some notable differences. The prestige of size was, of course, not a factor for the Chinese. They knew and the world knew that they had the largest population and that nothing was likely to change this primary position. They also did not have foreign pressures to contend with; the final decision was to be entirely their own. On the other hand, China had a most difficult obstacle to overcome, one that did not confront other countries of Asia: ideology. Accepting orthodox Marxist theory, the orthodox Chinese leadership had a difficult time rationalizing population growth as a problem. After all, they said, population can only be a problem for capitalist countries where the people are denied the benefits of economic development. In a socialist country such as China, the workers who control the means of production are also the source of all wealth and the only way to increase the welfare of the masses is to increase their numbers. In a word, Peking remained faithful to this basic precept, never contradicting Mao's idea that "people are the most precious"; in deed, however, China has managed several turnabouts (which she no longer admits) with regard to the population policy—changes that came about through both action and inaction.

Four years after the creation of the People's Republic of China the new régime planned and executed a population census/registration. Although it was a relatively primitive exercise, its results are generally accepted and continue to be used as the most reliable base for all estimates and projections of Chinese population. The reported 1953 census population of 582.6 million, growing at 2 per cent a year, was most gratifying for those who accepted the idea that large numbers result in national strength and prosperity. At the same time there were a few individuals in positions of authority who raised questions and suggested the need for controls on fertility. Although some of the doubters questioned Mao's confidence in China's ability to find solutions to all problems relating to population, they nevertheless continued to attack Malthus as a bourgeois economist and Malthusianism as a theory that has validity only under an imperialist system. The whole thrust of the argument for an introduction of measures to reduce fertility was stated essentially in terms of the health of the mother and child and specifically that too many children affect the health of the mother, reduce the efficiency of the parents in their work and study, and make it more difficult for children to acquire necessary education.

Despite the creation of a research committee under the State Council in 1954 to look into the problems of family planning and even after the Ministry of Health instructed the various health units in 1956 to assist the people in limiting the size of their families, the debate continued between the proponents and opponents of family planning. The formal endorsement for planned population growth came in September 1956 in a report by Chou En-lai to the Eighth Congress of the Chinese Communist Party, and was later incorporated into the "Outline for National Agricultural Development, 1956–67". By early 1957 it became clear that China had embarked upon an active programme of family planning. The result was a vigorous but brief birth control campaign which emphasized the widespread use of the mass media, education, and the intensive use of public health facilities and personnel.

The campaign was short-lived, however, and with the initiation of the Great Leap Forward in 1958 and the transition to the commune system in rural China, the public crusade for family planning gradually ebbed, to be replaced once again by arguments against population controls, emphasizing the country's need for additional manpower to assure reconstruction, development, and internal security. Whether the reversal of the birth control campaign was ideologically motivated or whether other factors were involved is difficult to say, but it is clear that the campaign itself did not have a fair test. It probably had some effect on the urban population but as the Chinese admitted, "owing to ignorance, poor presentation, fears, superstitions, and various mental obstacles" the vast rural population, still steeped in traditional attitudes, was unprepared for family planning. Furthermore, neither the public health system nor the political organization was yet geared to undertake a programme of this magnitude and psychological and cultural complexities. It is curious, however, that although the policy reversal seemed very real at that time, Peking now takes the position that the basic policy encouraging planned births was never changed and that birth control simply became inactive. The only support for this contention is that, despite propaganda to the contrary, China never adopted a pro-natalist policy and that contraceptives, abortion, and sterilization continued to be available to those who knew about it and requested such services.

Between 1959 and 1961, when China was attempting to overcome the serious economic crisis that followed the Great Leap, her press and radio were almost completely silent about any aspect of the population question. Beginning early in 1962, however, the Chinese resumed publication of articles encouraging family limitation to protect the health of the mother and the child, with specific emphasis on the need for young people to postpone marriage. The effort of the 1960s, if judged solely by the public media, seemed far below that of the 1957 campaign. In actuality, however, there was considerable activity in the drive for family planning, but this time it was much more action-oriented, with greater participation of mass organizations and with an important commitment on the part of both the public health system and the professional medical personnel. Medical journals carried numerous articles relating to fertility control and discussed various technical problems relating to contraception, abortion, and sterilization. Conferences and meetings of medical personnel, leading political cadres, and representatives of mass organizations were held at various administrative levels to discuss not only the technical problems relating to contraceptive paraphernalia, but also many of the practical problems involved in working with the peasant population. In a 1964 interview, Premier Chou En-lai announced that "Our present target is to reduce population growth to below 2 per cent; for the future we aim at an even lower rate. ... Therefore, our emphasis on planned parenthood is entirely positive; planned parenthood, where there is an increased production of goods and services, is conducive to raising the people's standard of living."[8]

The Great Proletarian Cultural Revolution, which was initiated in 1966 and which petered out after about 3 years, once again interrupted China's family planning efforts. Citing Edgar Snow's contention that many Red Guards took advantage of the disruptions to have premarital sex and to get married without official sanction,[9] some conclude that the Cultural Revolution was a setback to the orderly progress of the family planning programme and that there was an actual jump in China's birth rate during the late 1960s. This is not likely. Although the nation was preoccupied with other priorities and the leadership made no public pronouncements regarding fertility control, birth control paraphernalia continued to be available throughout most of the country—as it was during the Great Leap and its aftermath. More important, the sometimes wild activities of the Red Guards should not be translated into Western terms of sexual promiscuity; even if conditions were conducive to such activities, and they were not, neither the Communist indoctrination nor traditional values dissolve quite so easily and quickly.

Since the Cultural Revolution, family planning has resumed with greater fervour than ever before.With the focus of public health on rural areas, with the transfer of a large number of medical personnel into the countryside, and with birth control constituting an integral responsibility of every rural clinic and health room, China has embarked on a most intensive campaign to cut significantly the national birth rate. Unlike the birth control programmes of the 1950s and 1960s, now criticized because of the then prevailing belief that "everything would be all right as long as the women cadres and the health departments grasped such work"; the present approach is much more typical of other major all-out campaigns at which the Chinese seem to excel; it is much more pervasive, much more political in content, and seems to involve literally every segment of the Chinese society.

There is a curious aspect of this thumbnail chronology of family planning in China: although the leaders have made some statements in support of population control, it is, in fact, the activity that discloses the policy. In this rather ambiguous way China was able to mount a fully-fledged birth control campaign by 1957, cease all discussion of family planning for about 4 years, initiate another programme in 1962, forget it in 1966, and resume an intensive effort in the 1970s, while maintaining that the basic policy never really changed and avoiding the embarrassment that might accompany such shifts if they had been officially proclaimed by Peking.

In any case, that Peking is currently pursuing an intensive anti-natalist policy is no longer in dispute. At the 17th session of the United Nations Population Commission on 2 November 1973, the Chinese presented their official position on the question of population.[10] Although it restates the views that "of all things in the world, people are the most precious" and "it is wrong and far from the truth to say that overpopulation is the main cause of the poverty and backwardness of the developing countries", the statement also points out that China plans its national economy and therefore it is only natural that she should also have "planned population growth". The Chinese stress the importance of this phrase, and explain that "planned population growth" does not mean just the control of population growth. They point out that medical treatment is provided for those suffering from sterility and that no effort is made to limit family size among minority populations, most of whom live in the sparsely populated areas on China's periphery. Much is made of this latter point and the casual observer is inevitably impressed, but it should be placed in a better perspective. Minorities in China constitute only a little more than 5 per cent of the total population; because of their higher rate of mortality, the natural increase among most of these groups is lower than that of the Chinese; the still high infant mortality makes it more difficult to introduce family planning measures and have them accepted; and finally, despite Peking's sincere efforts to try and improve the lot of ethnic groups, in actual fact their treatment by the Han Chinese has not always been exactly benevolent.

Despite China's de-emphasis of economic motives for planned population growth, there is great awareness of the pressure population exerts on food, natural resources and the economy in general, and the leadership fully understands that its best laid plans will be for naught if the nation does not also achieve a reduced population growth. China's insistence that there is a basic difference between her reasons for wanting to reduce the birth rate and those of "colonial" developing countries is little more than an ideological ploy. China may be more successful in implementing programmes designed to raise the general standard of living, improve the people's health and change the traditional role of women, but it is the methods that are different, not the goals.

OVERCOMING OBSTACLES OF TRADITION

A government can proclaim a policy to control fertility, establish a reasonable delivery system for family planning, recruit and train special personnel to implement the policy and supply the necessary birth control paraphernalia, but obviously it will not succeed unless the people for whom the programme is intended take advantage of the available services and resources. To reach the people, channels of communication must be established and programmes for education and persuasion must be devised. In most developing countries, although these efforts succeed in bringing increased numbers of people to family planning clinics, all too often the end result is not necessarily an adoption of new ideas and ideals, but rather an adhesion of something new to something old—a bond that is difficult to make and easy to break. Much more basic (and therefore more permanent) transformations in attitude come only as a result of changes in the country's socio-economic conditions—changes that also alter the people's mental and emotional make-up, making them receptive to the idea of small families. This is exactly what the Chinese are attempting to do and what is making China's approach to family planning so different from other less developed nations.

UNIVERSAL OBSTACLES OF TRADITION

Perhaps the most significant obstacle to the introduction of measures that would reduce family size is the inertia of tradition. New ideas are extremely difficult to introduce into mostly illiterate, agrarian, subsistence societies. No matter how sensible a particular innovation might seem, the very fact that it is new, that "people have never done it", is a major obstacle to overcome. Since in many societies sex-related subjects are taboo and difficult to surface, innovations with regard to family planning are, of course, even more difficult to introduce. The "liberation of the woman from her status as a family chattel and biological adjunct is correlated as well as any other single variable with the level of modernization", [11] and yet, in most developing countries, the resistance of males to any change in the traditional position of the woman is as strong as it ever was. Although religious considerations which impeded family planning in some countries are not generally as important in Asia and Africa, children are still often thought of as "a blessing from heaven", and religious attitudes that encourage large families are known in the West too. Economic factors are extremely important, especially in a rural setting. Not only do children represent important labour power but, boys especially, are almost the sole source of support in old age, and in countries with high infant mortality, the survival of one male child to adulthood requires, on the average, some half a dozen births.[12] Under these circumstances it is difficult for parents in traditional rural societies where short-run considerations are paramount, to think of children as a burden. If the worst comes to the worst, the kinship unit of the community is likely to provide some type of supplementary help. A large family not only may bring prestige and economic well-being, but in countries where pleasures are few, children can provide the kind of happiness and satisfaction that is difficult to obtain in any other way, so that usually couples have more children because they want them, not because they are ignorant of how to avoid having them.[13]

It is therefore quite clear that if ignorance of what can be done to limit family size were the major problem in the introduction of family planning, the task would be much more manageable.

The effort to introduce birth control to the Chinese population had to overcome virtually all the problems encountered by other developing countries: traditional values with regard to family, the desire for children, especially male children who could provide economic support and old age security, an attitude toward sex that inhibited open discussion of the subject, the traditional subservient role of the woman. The difficulty of dispelling these attitudes is apparent from the necessity even now to initiate ideological education designed to break down traditions in the rural areas as symbolized by the "three-breaking down and three-establishing" campaign. The substance of this campaign is as follows:

First, break down the outdated idea of "attaching greater importance to sons than daughters and having both sons and daughters" and establish the new idea that "times have changed, and today men and women are equal". Second, break down the old concept that "one will have more support and help if one has more sons and daughters" and establish the new idea that "fewer children means better upbringing, and one should rely on the socialist collective economy". Third, break down the old concept that "giving birth to and fostering sons and daughters is a private matter of minor importance" and establish the new idea that "family planning is something of major importance to socialist revolution and construction".[14]

Religion as it is understood in the West has never played an important role in Chinese culture, and the peasant viewed it as a practical part of everyday life, improvising both his beliefs and ceremonies to suit his needs. Nevertheless, although religion *per se* was not a major obstacle for the Chinese, the Confucian traditions that venerated ancestors and elders placed a very special premium on children. Furthermore, the dimensions of China's problem were magnified enormously by the size of the population and the area of the country. In the 1950s some 550 million people lived in the rural areas alone and translated into a staggering target population for family planning purposes.

It is therefore not surprising that the birth control campaign in the 1950s did not really penetrate the Chinese countryside. Although the new régime already had tight political and administrative controls over the population, it did not have the time to prepare the Chinese peasant, who was still the product of the old system, for the basic changes that the family planning people were attempting to institute. Furthermore, in the 1950s the level of contraceptive technology in China, as in the world at large, was not what it is today. Neither the IUD nor the pill was yet available, so that in the first decade the Chinese government could neither adequately motivate the population nor provide them with the necessary quantities of free contraceptives. The conditions that are now making the planning of births in China a viable programme did not start to materialize until the mid-1960s.

Official Chinese statements persistently stress that the reduction of population growth cannot take place in an "environment of exploitation" and conversely can be achieved only when the livelihood of the people is improved and when they are assured of food, clothing and employment. This has long been recognized by proponents of family planning. But in the stereotyped Western models, development or "moderniza- tion"—which implies urbanization, education, increased female employment outside of agriculture and a general rise in the socio-economic level of the population—may take several generations to achieve. The problem, then, is to shortcut this process and somehow reach the people in their present setting. This is what the Chinese have been able to accomplish more successfully than anyone else. The new social, cultural and economic environment—an environment much more conducive to the acceptance of family planning by the population—has come about in China without "modernization" as we generally define the term. To understand the family planning programme in China, it is imperative to appreciate the changes that have taken place in the life of the Chinese people.

URBANIZATION

Modernization is usually considered to be almost synonymous with urbanization. China is still overwhelmingly rural. The 1953 census of China reported an urban population of 77.3 million; more than 20 years later it is estimated at between 130 and 140 million. Although a significant numerical growth, the proportion of the population that is urban has grown from 13.3 per cent to only perhaps 16 or 17 per cent of the total population. In other words, there are probably close to 700 million people now living in the Chinese countryside.[15]

Since the natural pull of the cities and the push of the countryside have been just as strong in China as in all other countries, how has China managed to control urban growth? For the purposes of this paper it is unnecessary to detail the trends and fluctuations of China's urban growth. Merely recognize that the push-pull factors have caused what the Chinese refer to as "blind infiltration" of peasants into cities; but through controls on urban migration (both at the source and point of destination) and periodic deportations of excess people, urban population has been maintained pretty much at a level consistent with the growth (or decline) of China's urban economy. This has meant that the greatest part of China's population growth (currently estimated at about 14 million per year) has had to be absorbed by the rural economy. To absorb this excess manpower, China placed primary emphasis on agriculture—a post-Great Leap policy, reiterated after the Cultural Revolution—and established a net-work of small supportive industries based essentially on local resources but also drawing on talent and equipment from major urban industries. These small industries provide the rural population with many of the daily necessities and at the same time support the rural economy by producing an ever-increasing share of China's chemical fertilizers and cement, farm machinery and implements, generators and transformers, and, perhaps most important, spare parts, the supply of which has always presented a major obstacle to even limited mechanization of the countryside. Thus, the proportion of China's rural population that is involved in non-agricultural activities is constantly increasing and gradually changing the character of the countryside.

EDUCATION

Another factor that has been changing the characteristics of the rural population is related to education. Once again, it is a subject that need only be summarized here. The level of educational attainment of the rural youth has a direct bearing on potential success of the family planning programme. Over the years China's educational policies have undergone many changes, but the primary goal of providing every child in China with 4 to 6 years of primary education has not basically changed over the past quarter of a centry. China still has not attained universal primary education, but she has done better than any other developing country, and it is estimated that by now perhaps 90 per cent of primary age children enter school and probably about three-quarters of them complete the 5-year primary school, the norm in the rural areas since the Cultural Revolution. While the substantive curriculum in these schools is pretty much limited to the three R's, a large proportion of the children's time is also spent on political study and in meetings and discussion groups. Although sex education of any sort is completely absent from their study (neither is it taught in secondary schools or colleges), the young people are well indoctrinated and prepared to accept the bidding of the state with maximum cooperation on any national policy.

Numbers are not available, but perhaps as many as 20 per cent of the graduates of rural primary schools go on to middle agricultural schools to assume eventually some of the more responsible positions in agriculture, local industry, administration, health, education and so forth. The main point here is that because most of the rural youth in China are now literate and because they are supplemented by large numbers of better educated urban youth who are sent down to the countryside, the principal target population for China's birth planning effort—the rural young adult—is much better educated and more socially aware than the average peasant in other developing countries.

CHANGING ROLE OF WOMEN

The direct relationship between the success of any family planning programme and the status of woman in the society is no longer in contention. Education, employment, participation in community and national life and other non-familial activities greatly enhance the woman's ability to make decisions with regard to the number and spacing of her children and increase the likelihood that she will do so.

The priority that Mao has given the need to change the status of women may be judged from the fact that the marriage law—a basic legal document in initiating the changes—was promulgated on 1 May 1950, less than a year after the new régime came into power.[16] The new law stipulated that marriage should be arranged by the parties concerned and not by their families, that the husband and wife have equal status, responsibility and ownership of family property, and that both husband and wife have equal right to divorce; it made other points that were intended to "do away with the arbitrary and compulsory feudal marriage system". Much of what was included in the new edict was similar to the old Nationalist marriage law; but because the old law was not known to the overwhelming majority of the population and lacked any supportive political power, it was not enforced and had virtually no effect on the life of the common people.

But it takes more than a marriage law and more than a statement in the constitution granting women "equal rights with men in all spheres of political, economic, cultural and family life", to change the attitudes that are so deep-rooted in a society. It is a slow and difficult process. Much progress has been made and by now the position of the Chinese woman is, for the most part, superior to that of women in most other developing countries of Asia, Africa, and Latin America. But the Chinese themselves admit that "remnants of the old concept that 'men are superior and women are inferior' and habits and customs left over from the old society have still to be thoroughly eliminated".[17] Even today, women's congresses in China urge the delegates to struggle against the old idea of "respecting men and despising women and regarding women as slaves and vassals".[18] Over the years, one of the major obstacles to the "liberation" of women in China has been the reluctance of most of the women to be "liberated". Women in China have certainly been accustomed to performing physical labour; most of it, however, was carried on within the basic framework of the closely knit family system. The new form of "liberation", stressing equality in the performance of the same type of work by men and women and which the women first experienced during the Great Leap when scores of millions of them were sent into productive labour, seemed to take much too literally Mao's statement that "women prop up half the heavens". Most of them would probably still prefer to stay home and engage in more traditional work activities. Furthermore, even when women are involved in productive labour, they do not necessarily get equal pay for equal work, especially in the rural areas where work-points are related to physical strength.

While recognizing the continuing difficulties in gaining equality, it is important to detail both the effort exerted toward this end and the progress that has been made. A particularly intensive drive to make some fundamental changes in the status of women has been underway since the Cultural Revolution. While at the national level attacks were mounted on Liu Shao-chi—once the president of China and now the prime example of a "capitalist roader"—for pursuing policies that deliberately neglected women, at the local level women were organized into study groups to counteract complaints that women themselves "paid attention only to their household chores and ignored the line". To increase women's participation in the political and administrative life of the country, an effort was mounted to rebuild the Committee for Women's Work within the Party, to strengthen local women's organizations and to expand the Women's Federation with all its provincial and local branches. At the same time directives were issued to recruit more women into the trade unions and the Communist Youth League, and especially to increase the number of women cadres in these and all other institutions and enterprises. Thus, although the authorities believe that women can only emancipate themselves through extensive participation in productive labour, they also recognize the need to assist this process by getting more women into positions of authority. Traditional women's chores such as cooking, washing, and sewing have not yet been denied them, but in travelling around China one frequently sees men participating in activities that used to be reserved for women only. This is particularly true in the cities, where men are often seen playing with their children in parks, taking them to the health clinics, shopping for food. Men and women may not yet be equal—an admission made more often by the Chinese themselves than by visitors to China—but the trend is certainly in that direction.

Looking at the position of women in China from the family planning vantage point it is quite clear that despite the persistence of traditional thinking among a segment of both the male and the female population, the young Chinese woman of today in no way resembles her mother or grandmother, or her rural sister in other developing countries. Chances are she has at least 5 years of education. Whether urban or rural, she is productive either by working full-time or part-time, or by participating in a variety of voluntary activities relating to sanitation, health, education, family planning or some other aspect of community life. Probably she is also a member of at least one organization and is involved at least on a weekly basis in political meetings or some form of study sessions. Whether in fact or only in fancy, a woman (as everyone else in China) is given opportunity to feel that she is participating in the decision-making process that relates to her concerns and her life. In sum, the average young woman in China is both involved and motivated and therefore much more receptive to family planning.

SOCIAL WELFARE

Anyone familiar with conditions that existed in old China cannot help but be impressed by the changes that have occurred over the last 25 years. There is no starvation and the distribution of food is much more equitable throughout the country. Although cotton goods are in short supply and rationed, everyone appears to have adequate clothing. Housing is also in short supply, but much new building has taken place and continues, and there are no slums or shanty towns of the type that existed before or that are still found in many parts of the world. The general availability of health care and basic education has already been discussed. It is true that, with the exception of the housing shortage, all these factors having improved the living standard of the population could also tend to encourage larger families. But there are countervening considerations such as security, which in the past was so closely tied to having children and which now seems to be available to all segments of the population.

For 20 years now, Peking has been claiming that there is no unemployment in China. It is a striking claim to anyone familiar with conditions in other developing countries, but using Peking's definition the statement can be supported. With almost continuous efforts to control migration into the urban areas and move excess population out of the cities, urban unemployment has, in fact, been insignificant or temporary in nature. Although the rural areas, which have acted as a sponge for the manpower overflow, have had considerable underemployment, the expansion of non-agricultural activities in the countryside have no doubt reduced this statistic. Whether the jobs are real or of the "make work" variety, the important point is that almost everyone participates in some activity and receives either pay or work-points for his efforts.

Those who are unable to work because of sickness, injury, disability, maternity or old age are taken care of. In the urban areas a large proportion of the labour force is covered by comprehensive labour and social welfare legislation, but the implementation of the established rules and regulations is left pretty much to the individual enterprises. In other words, although there are laws that provide the basic guarantees for retirement and pension plans, they are essentially guidelines to be interpreted by trade unions and management of enterprises on the basis of needs of both the production units and of the individuals. Officially male workers can retire at the age of 60, women at 55, but actually, if they are skilled and healthy, they usually go on working. Because the wage scale is already low, when a worker does retire, his income is reduced by only 25–50 per cent while most of the other benefits (notably health insurance) are not affected. In the rural areas, the commune or the production brigade is usually responsible for maintaining a welfare fund, which may vary depending on the wealth of the commune. Because of the nature of the work, the aged in the rural areas are much more likely to continue to be productive in some capacity. In both the cities and the countryside, there is a financial subsidy for those unable to work and, if the income of a family drops below the minimal level, the enterprise or the commune is responsible for bringing it up to an acceptable level.

The whole subject of welfare illustrates the practical application of the régime's insistence on maximum self-reliance within the socialist framework. Although there are homes for the aged who do not have any means of support, the family unit is still very much intact and whenever possible the old people continue to live with their adult children, taking care of the grandchildren, helping with the housework and doing other chores in the home or neighbourhood. Even the new marriage law states specifically that parents have a duty and responsibility to rear and educate their children and that children have the duty and responsibility to support and assist their parents in their old age. Thus, while the traditional responsibility of the child towards the parent (which encouraged large families) persists, a change is also occurring that is increasing the parent's responsibility to the child—a change that implies greater burden on the parent and therefore tends to act as a deterrent to high fertility. In any case, the security of one form or another that China now provides the sick and the aged is undoubtedly having an effect on the attitude of people toward the need for a large family, especially numerous sons.

If one of the basic prerequisites to successful introduction of family planning is a minimum standard of living and some form of social security, then certainly China has, by now, achieved this condition. Everyone receives wages or work-points, or is on some form of retirement or old age pension; everyone receives rations of grain and cloth; everyone has free or almost free medical care.

THE HEALTH SYSTEM AND ITS ROLE IN FAMILY PLANNING

When the leadership of a country finally makes the difficult decision, formally or informally to control population growth, it is faced with the equally difficult challenge of implementation. Although it usually has some vital financial assistance and the advice of experienced professional technicians and administrators from international organizations or private foreign institutions, each country has unique problems and conditions which must be superimposed on the more universal difficulties of setting up a family planning programme. Physical facilities must be located, a viable administrative structure must be established and, most important, a large number of personnel with wide-ranging competence must be recruited and trained. In countries where the educational attainment is low, illiteracy is prevalent, and where professional and managerial staffs are not only scarce but involved in endeavours of higher priority, the recruitment of staff for family planning programmes is difficult indeed.

Because it has an affinity with public health and medicine, it is not surprising that family planning is inevitably incorporated within the existing bureaucracy of the nation's public health system which in most countries already has a nucleus of facilities and staff. In theory, the idea of subordinating the family planning programme under the public health hierarchy appears to be a reasonable shortcut, but after years of experience, the consensus seems to be that the progress of the programme is impeded by innumerable problems which stem specifically from this arrangement. Although for practical reasons birth control is not likely to be divorced from its medical ties, gradual changes have been taking place, the most important of which is a transition from what is referred to as the "clinic era", with all the disadvantages of a client having to come in for family planning assistance, to the field era, in which the field staff attempts to contact the clients in their homes and places of work. With this emphasis on field work, the problem of recruiting, training, and motivating either paid workers or volunteers from local communities to work within their towns or villages and to create a sense of community acceptance for the family planning programme is another major hurdle that has not been easy to overcome. The so-called contemporary era, which overlaps with the field era, places much more recognition on the importance of altering traditional social values and patterns and attempts to influence such factors as age at marriage and the emancipation of women—admittedly a long-term proposition for most developing countries.[19]

Another serious problem not stemming directly from the inclusion of family planning programmes under public health, but rather of a more general nature, relates to the administration and management of these programmes. Deficient management manifests itself in many ways—defective planning, lack of control, inadequate or ill-used information, unmotivated personnel, inter-institutional friction, wasteful duplication of efforts—and can be explained by a number of factors.[20] First, there is the chronic shortage of professionally trained administrators in all fields of activity. Second, family planning programmes are usually staffed by doctors, nurses, and social workers who lack managerial inclination, skills, and experience. Third, given the rapid growth of family planning programmes, even experienced administrators understandably have problems under conditions of limited resources and often hostile environment. Finally, programme implementation on a national scale often involves difficult coordination problems among numerous relatively autonomous organizations.

Typically, the Chinese have not published any detailed information on specifically how the family planning activities are organized and administered. Nevertheless, because in China, as elsewhere, the public health system is a primary conduit of such policies and programmes, it is possible to describe the top of the governmental pyramid as it relates to family planning with some confidence.

The State Council, the highest executive organ of the state, determines all national policies, including those dealing with population problems. In 1956, as the first birth control campaign picked up steam, Peking created directly under the State Council what has been variously referred to as a birth control office or a family planning commission. It is difficult to say to what extent it was a policy-making body, or an advisory or coordinating group; nevertheless it is indicative of the priority Peking was giving the family planning campaign. Because it was never referred to during the years when birth control was not publicly emphasized by Peking, it is impossible to say whether the Commission has had an uninterrupted life since 1956. It does seem that it disappeared during the Cultural Revolution along with many other government organizations. The first mention of a successor, the Birth Planning Leading Group, did not appear in the Chinese press until September of 1973[21]—probably some time after its creation.

The Birth Planning Leading Group is headed by Li Hsiu-chen, a veteran woman official of the Ministry of Health, and its creation, leadership, and position under the State Council once again indicate the priority the régime gives the planning of births. The specific decisions with regard to family planning matters are probably made by the members of the Birth Planning Leading Group, and recommendations are made to the State Council and then passed on to the Ministry of Health for implementation through the provincial health departments, their health bureaux in cities and counties, and on down to their respective health units. It is possible that the group itself may have provincial offices associated with the regional health departments or at least individual representatives in those bodies, who would coordinate various activities relating to birth control and report directly to Peking; but this is strictly speculative. As the transmitter and implementer of family planning policies, at the national level, the Ministry of Health formulates measures relating to birth control, assigns responsibilities and gives guidance to the various subordinate units, prepares and directs propaganda work and so forth. Because it controls most of the medical research facilities, it is also involved in directing and coordinating experiments on new types of contraceptives and undoubtedly plans for production and supervises the manufacture of contraceptive devices and chemicals.

China was not able to avoid altogether some of the unfortunate consequences, discussed above, when family planning is integrated with the public health system. Over the years, however, they seem to have devised uniquely Chinese ways of coping with them. Probably the most important factor in achieving a happy marriage between family planning and public health has been the gradual evolution of the public health system itself to reflect a new and much more service-oriented approach toward medical care. Before discussing how the family planning programme functions within the health system, it is very important to understand the goals and methods of operation of public health and medicine in China.[22]

CHINA'S PUBLIC HEALTH SYSTEM

Almost from its inception the People's Republic of China has given top priority to the improvement of the incredibly poor health conditions prevailing throughout China in 1949. The government's attacks on disease and poor health were multifarious, but several major principles and approaches can be identified—all of them reflecting practical considerations which match China's resources and goals.

The first decision made by Peking was that the major emphasis was to be placed on preventive rather than curative medicine. This was an essential and obvious first step. Literally hundreds of millions of people were organized and motivated to clean up the country, learn about elementary sanitation and personal habits of cleanliness, and to participate in massive innoculation drives and other health- and environment-related activities. These massive efforts were directly responsible for the rapid elimination of the most dreaded diseases such as cholera, typhoid, scarlet fever and bubonic plague, and the three most prevalent social diseases of tuberculosis, trachoma and venereal disease. Another priority area was the elimination or control of parasitic diseases that affected the health and lives of a large segment of the population. Although not completely eliminated, schistosomiasis, malaria, hook worm and other parasitic diseases no longer pose a serious threat to the population. It is important to note that the emphasis on prevention has not diminished with the improved health conditions. The slogan "prevention is predominant" is just as true now as it was 20 years ago, and every locality in China continues to have at least one general clean-up campaign every year.

Another basic factor in Chinese health is the role of Chinese traditional medicine. Over the years the régime has persisted in its efforts to raise the stature of traditional medicine, integrate it with Western medicine, and fully utilize it in the national health programme. Once again, this was a very practical position for China to take. Mao Tse-tung was well aware that the time and cost involved in providing a population of over 600 million with Western medical services and facilities would be beyond China's capabilities. On the other hand, the half-a-million or so medical practitioners and herbalists of various degrees of competence, using empirical remedies such as acupuncture, massage and abundant local herbs, could continue to serve the people as they always had and at a minimal cost to the central government. The problem was to organize these heterogeneous and scattered individuals within a viable delivery system, improve their competence and have the sceptical Western-trained physicians accept them as colleagues. To break down the resistance of the medical professionals, to add to the stature of native medicine, and to force integration, a requirement was introduced in the mid-1950s for all doctors of Western medicine to study traditional medicine. The enthusiasm with which this and other measures designed to facilitate the integration of the two medical systems was pursued fluctuated over the years, but because of the overwhelming problems the melding of Chinese and Western medicine continued to be very superficial and spotty until the Cultural Revolution further elevated the role of traditional medicine. The new graduates from medical schools are much more likely to reflect the two schools in their practice of medicine.

In order to increase health manpower as rapidly as possible, medical education was established at different academic levels and supplemented by large numbers of paramedics trained in a variety of part-time and spare-time medical courses. In this way China trained a large body of personnel capable of providing the people with primary health care. The Cultural Revolution which closed schools for almost 4 years, introduced some drastic changes in China's medical education, particularly at the university level. The duration of higher medical education was reduced to 3 years; the curriculum was changed to incorporate traditional Chinese medical practices and ensured that each student would spend a significant proportion of his time in practical work in the hospitals and clinics; students were to be enrolled from worker, peasant and soldier backgrounds and each was to have spent at least 2 years working in a factory or on a farm before being admitted to college; although initially all examinations were abolished, some form of testing has been resumed but continues on shaky ground. These changes have predictably created many problems and the Chinese are quick to point out that education is still "in a state of flux" and that it is entirely possible for it to undergo additional changes in the years to come.

Despite the impressive progress made in the health care of the Chinese population, a very significant gap continued to exist between the personnel and facilities that served the urban population and those that served the rural population. Since the Cultural Revolution the régime has made a special effort to narrow this gap and hundreds of thousands of medical personnel, from paramedic to doctor, were sent down to the countryside to improve the health care of the peasant population. As part of this emphasis on rural health, the normal teaching functions of medical colleges have been expanded to include the responsibility of training paramedical personnel in the communes and villages. Every medical college has established rural teaching centres on the communes and has sent out mobile medical teams not only as a supplement to rural health care, but also to offer short-term medical training courses. In this way good teachers are made available for the training of rural medical manpower at the same time that urban professors receive political re-education by living and working with peasants for several months every year.

As a result over the years, there has developed in China a relatively dense network of public health facilities of all types. Gradually most of the specialized units such as disease prevention stations which concentrated on specific problems were amalgamated with the more conventional public health institutions. By now, every county has a hospital, as do many of the communes; each brigade (group of villages) has a clinic; and each team (village) a health centre. The medical units are staffed by a large number of medical and paramedical personnel representing an unusually wide spectrum of competence, from doctors trained in Western medicine, to part-time health workers who have little more than a rather elementary knowledge of hygiene and sanitation.

The success of China's health system is due in a large measure to the fact that they did not graft on a foreign system and foreign standards which would have had difficulty in taking, but rather the Chinese developed their own methods and standards which seem to be ideally suitable to their society and resources. Although the basic direction comes from the top—from the Ministry of Health—the services themselves are decentralized, emphasizing local conditions and local needs. Beyond the minimal expected health standards, each administrative unit decides for itself what portion of its resources will be spent on medical care and how many and what type of workers they will have. As is evident from the reforms in their educational system, the Chinese consider practical experience more important than "book learning" and accept maximum flexibility in standards of educational institutions and credentials of their graduates. They believe that the overwhelming majority of ailments can be handled by traditional methods and have created a referral system that moves the more seriously ill individual up the line of competence which ends in the local hospital staffed by the better trained and more experienced personnel. The most important aspect of China's health system is that, despite its uneven quality, the overwhelming proportion of the population has quick access to medical attention and care.

THE HEALTH SYSTEM AS A BASE FOR FAMILY PLANNING

Although China's health system seems particularly suited to the country's health needs, there are occasional criticisms aimed at its lack of sophistication and professionalism. Whether or not this criticism is valid is not at issue here; what is important within the context of China's family planning programme is that the strengths of the health system become even more apparent, while its weaknesses tend to diminish in significance and in some cases even become assets.

The frequent complaint in other developing countries that women have to travel long distances to obtain birth control services and materials is certainly not valid in China, particularly since the Cultural Revolution. There are no special clinics that deal solely with family planning. As has already been pointed out, the present health network, at least in the person of a barefoot doctor who is trained to cater to birth control needs, reaches virtually every rural community in the country. Although there are no statistics to support the contention, this wide geographic coverage of personnel and health units would suggest that there are more medical and public health personnel in China, *per capita*, than in other developing countries. Trained in traditional medicine, Western medicine or both, obstetricians, midwives, and other personnel most directly involved in maternal and child health care and in the planning of births, are supported and assisted by millions of other full-time and part-time medics and health workers. All this is made possible, of course, because of lower educational standards and a general de-emphasis on credentialism which, if it is a problem, is much less important in family planning than in medicine.

A frequent complaint against family planning programmes incorporated into the country's health system is that the clinical atmosphere is not conducive to the needed type of service.[23] The medical personnel are accused of having little concern about providing birth control materials to the public pleasantly and conveniently—a shortcoming much less likely to develop in the Chinese system. Chances are that the people who run the clinic are local residents who were sent out to receive a certain level of medical training and then returned to practise their skills. Most of them are known personally by the people seeking their services, the atmosphere is anything but austere, and the "Serve the People" poster that is probably hanging on the wall is taken seriously by the medical staff. The common complaint that clinics are open only during limited hours or on special days is also unheard of in China where, for all practical purposes, the clinic never closes, making it extremely simple to arrange regular repeated visits as they may be required.

Problems of administration and management that are common elsewhere in the world are much less likely to occur under the Chinese system. Administrative experience is available not only within the public health system but, when necessary, among members of the Revolutionary Committees, the Communist Party, women's and youth's organizations and others who are involved in the programme. Working within a system that does not require the statistical and substantive feedback that, under Western tutelage, is considered essential in other developing countries, managerial personnel can be at a level that is much more readily available in the countryside. Since several autonomous organizations are not competing within the Chinese system, as so often seems to be the case elsewhere, there are no inter-institutional frictions or problems of coordination among segments of organizations that may not be communicating with each other.[24] As for the medical personnel themselves, since most of them are not highly trained specialists, if they are called upon to administer a family planning programme, or to train lower-level personnel, or to devote their own time to the programme, it would not occur to them to consider this additional responsibility as an imposition—not an unusual reaction among medical personnel in other developing countries.

Related to the above discussion is the much more uncomplicated approach the Chinese take toward planning and innovation, which is true in many other fields as well. In connection with health and family planning, the mother-and-child health services and the mobile medical teams illustrate this interesting contrast between China's approach and more advanced approach to identical problems.

The advantages of having the family planning programme presented in conjunction with maternal–child health services have been long recognized. Young mothers, who represent a population with the highest fertility and probably the greatest potential for receptivity of birth control information, become a captured audience for family planners when they become pregnant. Nevertheless, to justify the expenditure of funds by Western institutions supporting the integration of family planning programmes with maternal–child health services, which deliver a large proportion of the babies, requires years of study and numerous pilot projects. The Population Council, for example, has spent more than 4 years to determine "what it would take in personnel, physical facilities, transport, supplies and equipment, and funding to bring some minimal professional and para-professional attention to every pregnant woman for the double purpose of promoting maternal/child health and family planning".[25] The Chinese, on the other hand, seem to avoid expensive feasibility studies or models to make such determinations. Even in the 1950s they concentrated much of their family planning effort in the mother-and-child health care stations simply because it seemed like the most reasonable approach to the problem. They did not worry because many of these stations had substandard facilities and personnel nor did they attempt to anticipate every possible problem before it surfaced. They did the best they could with what they had and went on to improve the facilities and resolve problems only when they were faced with them. By now, although by no means the sole dispensers of birth control in China, mother-and-child health services have become effective centres for the implementation of the family planning programme.

Similarly, although the use of mobile units for public health care in the more remote areas of developing countries has been going on for some time, their use in family planning programmes is more recent and much more limited. Here too, however, the Chinese have progressed much more rapidly and with a minimum amount of preliminary investigation. The extensive utilization of mobile health units in delivering health care to the villages was initiated in the early 1960s, and by 1966 there were over 1,000 such teams operating in China. Composed of urban medical personnel who were required to spend a certain part of the year caring for the rural population, they not only provided clinical services to the peasants and trained lower medical personnel, but were also very active in publicizing planned parenthood among the rural population and in educating both the masses and the medical staffs in the use of birth control devices and in abortion and sterilization techniques and procedures. Since the Cultural Revolution, with the permanent transfer of large numbers of medical personnel to the rural areas, the number of mobile medical teams probably did not increase, but the periodic mobile service composed of urban medical personnel continues in the rural areas and still plays an important role in family planning.

This, then, is the scheme of the health system and the basic way in which family planning is integrated into the functions and responsibilities of medical personnel and health workers in China. But in China the health system is just the trunk of the family planning tree—the roots and branches give it a special character and a special vitality.

PROBLEMS OF COMMUNICATION AND MOTIVATION

The question of changing attitudes and behaviour of people to make them appreciate the need for limiting family size and therefore be more receptive to family planning programmes has been discussed. Even within a society undergoing major socio-economic changes it takes effective communication and persuasion to achieve this goal; in a rural agricultural environment the task is much more formidable.

The earliest family planning programmes in developing countries concentrated on reaching the population through the standard channels of mass media—radio, newspapers and magazines, family planning posters and pamphlets, and a variety of mailings, primarily of visual educational materials. All these continue to play an important part in the birth control persuasion effort around the world, but over the years it has been clearly demonstrated that as important as mass media are, they can be only one of the approaches to the desired goal. This form of propaganda usually is more effective in a more literate urban population which is already in the process of changing its way of life—one that includes migrants from the rural areas who are integrating into the urban society, gradually shifting their allegiance from the family to society as a whole. Mass media are much less likely to be effective in a rural population—to convince the illiterate masses they must change the traditional point of view toward children and family, or to induce a young couple to adopt contraceptives and limit the size of their family. In the rural setting (and in the urban too, for that matter) more and more effort in "selling" family planning has been concentrated on the more intimate, inter-personal form of communication that makes more use of local personnel and attempts to tailor the message to the specific audience addressed. This approach came about slowly, following lengthy experimentation with other methods of communication and still faces many difficult problems such as the recruitment of credible and trustworthy disseminators, matching the message to the local customs and proprieties, and increased costs.[26]

But even the much more effective personal approach still runs smack into the problem of motivation. In other words, the use of contraceptives or the will to be sterilized does not necessarily follow the abstract knowledge about "how" and "why", but usually requires an additional motive that is more personal and immediate. To cope with the problem of motivating people to limit their families in rural areas of developing countries that have not yet experienced any significant social and economic changes, governments and interested organizations have been experimenting with a variety of ways to compensate families or individuals who do make an effort to limit the number of children. Many of these schemes have become quite imaginative and go well beyond the payment of cash and material goods that are still widely used, especially to induce persons to accept sterilization or agree to an insertion of an IUD. More sophisticated approaches are becoming common. There is a district in Taiwan, for example, that has been experimenting with education bonds to cover tuition to parents who have no more than three children. And in South India, a savings deposit scheme has been introduced to provide old-age security for parents who agree to limit family size.[27] Theoretically, such inducements are superior to cash payments, but understandably, peasants who are not accustomed to long-range planning will be difficult to convince. In addition to compensating those who agree to accept some method to control family size, incentives have also been provided to "change agents" or "finders" of individuals willing to be sterilized or to wear an IUD, for example. Although occasionally the use of negative incentives—increased taxation, withdrawal of certain benefits, other penalties—is suggested, the idea is quickly abandoned because the people most affected by these measures are already too poor to pay taxes and so miserable that additional penalties would be counter-productive for the country and would hardly be noticed by the family. It would seem, then, that the rapidly growing art of incentives has yet to become a science.[28]

Aside from the question of political and ethical acceptability, incentives can become quite costly and, if delayed benefits are involved as in the case of educational costs and old-age security, they can also involve complicated and expensive administrative activities. Witness: almost one-quarter of India's total family planning budget for the 1969–74 five-year plan was designated for incentives.[29] Despite these high costs, however, there seems to be no other form of effective motivation available to the developing countries so that from the government's point of view the price paid for incentives is still smaller than the cost of bearing and raising a child.

During the 1950s China also undertook the standard approach to disseminating family planning information. In the first birth control campaign the mass media were fully mobilized. Information was presented on the radio, in movies, in special exhibits and slide presentations and, of course, in the thousands of articles in newspapers and magazines and millions of pamphlets, posters, lantern slides and other visual aids. A certain amount of personal testimony and persuasion was also given by opinion leaders such as local cadres, doctors, and others in influential positions. This was not enough, however. The population was not yet adequately politicized or motivated to accept this media-intense but personally remote approach. Neither were the masses ready to be influenced by intangible incentives to delay marriage and space births in order to contribute to the "Socialist construction of the fatherland".

Today, family planning communication and motivation in China is so different from that found anywhere else in the world, that a direct comparison is impossible to make. The number of articles in the Chinese printed media discussing some aspect of family planning is rather limited, yet the national objective to reduce the country's birth rate is communicated in a campaign that is as intensive and persuasive as any that the Chinese have ever launched. Although posters, pamphlets and the ever-present public loudspeakers are still widely used in family planning education, primary reliance is centred on the political and social structure of both the urban and rural communities. Even the role of the public health personnel—the role so vital in the family planning programme—is essentially related to technical aspects. It is much more the responsibility of what the Chinese refer to as grass-roots organizations, which often include friends, neighbours, and working associates, to educate the young people in the need for the postponement of marriage and, within the marriage relationship, to persuade them to seek the birth control assistance that is provided by the public health personnel—physicians, nurses, barefoot doctors, and other medically trained individuals.

As for financial incentives, it seems they are still, in this context out of the question in China, while the exhortations to serve the people and the fatherland that had minimal influence within the family planning context in the 1950s have become much more effective with the new, post-1949 generation. Sincerity in China is almost impossible to judge. The praise of the leadership and of fellow comrades (albeit often organized) may not be the greatest reward, but it is very important in the new society, where esteem is accrued through public recognition and disapprobation through public criticism. China is now reaching a point where at least part of this approval or disapproval depends on the size of a couple's family and, as will be seen, constitutes adequate motivation for the planning of births.

MOTIVATION CHINESE STYLE

No other country is able to whip up mass national campaigns the way China can, and the present effort to convince the population that the planning of births is one of their main responsibilities is a prime example of such a campaign.

First there is, of course, the Communist Party, which plays a leading role in promulgating all policies announced by the régime and whose membership are in key positions of all organizations that are involved in the birth control programme. Party members coordinate and lead the activities of labour unions, women's federations, the Young Communist League and other mass political and social organizations which play such an important role in all national campaigns and are now deeply involved in educating and persuading people to plan births. It is usually these organizations that, in conjunction with the public health organizations and personnel, convene provincial and county level birth control work conferences. The national involvement in family planning is well illustrated by the following statement from one such conference:

> Under the party's centralized leadership, the trade unions at all levels and the youth, women's, poor and lower-middle peasant and militia organizations as well as the relevant departments such as culture and education, public health, industry, commerce, civil affairs and public security—must work together closely to jointly make a success of birth control work.[30]

After a conference participants are informed of the latest policies and plans and have an opportunity to discuss the various measures and approaches and to "exchange experiences", returning to their communities to "implement the spirit of the conference" with regard to the mass movement.

Since family planning is a national policy it is also the responsibility of each local government with its authority vested in a Revolutionary Committee. As a conduit for all national policies, the Revolutionary Committee would normally consider family planning in the light of local conditions and implement the policy accordingly.[31] To assist it in this matter, most of the Revolutionary Committees have established a Committee on Planned Childbirth consisting of at least one member of the parent committee and, for the most part, women from rural production teams or urban neighbourhoods who are involved in civic activities, education, propaganda, or some function relating to the status of women in the community. They also include either a full-time or part-time health worker who is capable of providing more specific information with regard to birth control means and methods and who constitutes an important link with the public health system. At the lowest residential levels there are Sub-committees on Planned Childbirth which function in close collaboration with (or as a part of) street committees which are extremely important in the social, political and economic life of each neighbourhood. A commune in Kiangsu Province provides a good illustration of how family planning is "grasped" at the local level:

With our comprehension raised to a higher level, we grasped the family planning work as a matter of great importance and put it on the agenda of daily tasks for the Party committee ... A deputy secretary of the Party committee took command of family planning work, and a committee member took concrete charge of such work. From the commune to the production teams, organizations for leading family planning work were set up so that there were people at all levels to grasp such work and there were also people in all production teams to supervise such work. In this way, family planning was carried through even at the basic level and was under way unswervingly throughout the year.[32]

Now let us consider more specifically some of the forces within a given community that are likely to influence a young couple's decision with regard to size of family and spacing of children. One or both members of the young married couple are likely to belong to a branch of at least one of the already mentioned mass organizations such as the Youth League, Women's Federation, Trade Union—each of which plays a very prominent role in their lives. Membership depends to a great extent on compliance and conformity and on activism and participation. To belong is to support and implement national policies and as a national policy the planning of births is of concern to the total membership. Furthermore, virtually every young person, man or woman, is presently in the labour force. The involvement of the management of the institution or enterprise and of the other workers and employees or peasants in the personal lives of each individual extends considerably beyond work-related subjects. "Experience exchange" meetings and discussions go beyond production quotas and problems, and study topics related to family planning are common, particularly "on the eve of big holidays" and especially in institutions where women constitute a large proportion of the labour force. It is not unusual for the women workers in a factory, for example, to announce their joint decision as to the number of births they will collectively have during the following year, or to see a chart on the wall of a hospital or an office again indicating the planned number of births for some specified period of time.

At the residential level, the peer pressures are even more pervasive and certainly more personal. The street health centre and the village health room are the focal points of birth planning. It is here, for example, that our young married woman will probably have her name, along with the names of other women in her neighbourhood, on a wall chart that depicts the menstrual cycle of each woman, the type of contraceptive the couple uses, the presence or absence of the husband and other pertinent information.[33] It is also from these residential health centres that local women, who may be responsible for no more than 20 to 40 households, are designated to oversee the family planning programme, stay in touch with mothers and potential mothers, and personally guide and assist them in the practice of their birth control functions. These basic-level cadres or activists constitute the backbone of the birth planning programme. Residential meetings, so common in China and dealing with everything from garbage disposal to domestic problems, are also convened to study and discuss the specific problems relating to family planning, from advantages of marrying late and types of contraceptives to abortion and sterilization. The meetings are usually led by women cadres from the health services or from one of the mass organizations. They know the Party line, how to interpret it and how to communicate it to the group. With the constant reminder both at work and at home about the desirability of having few children, it would be extremely difficult for our young couple—and especially for the female—to slip up.

This special character of the pressures that motivate the Chinese family in the planning of births is aptly analysed by Professor Liu:

Since peer group pressure is extensive and intensive, reactions to pressures tend to be circular, involving not one or two individuals as in the case of intergenerational pressures, but a larger number of friendship circles, all of which are proximate, and their collective force far exceeds singular pressure.[34]

The infrequent suggestion by overly-enthusiastic cadres that a more direct approach be tried, one that would "lay down a few hard and fast regulations, so that time could be saved and quick results produced",[35] are quickly rejected with the admonition that success can only come by relying on the "consciousness of the broad masses".

Although the public (or group) discussion of sex-related subjects is in no way typical of the Chinese culture and could only be instituted gradually and with difficulty, the process was undoubtedly helped by the fact that privacy, so valued in Western societies, is virtually non-existent in China. According to Professor Hsu, " ... neighbours, friends, colleagues, teachers and students, employers and employees share in each other's lives to an extent impossible for Americans".[36] Even more so now than in the past, the community or neighbourhood will, as a matter of course, arbitrate domestic quarrels, know every detail of a person's or family's financial status, help a family with a mentally disturbed or retarded member, and so forth. It is only within this social and cultural environment that the effectiveness of peer pressures in the planning of births can be adequately understood.

Despite claims of considerable progress in breaking down traditional attitudes, the Chinese do admit that "family planning work is by no means a soft task" and occasionally report the problems encountered by persons responsible for propagandizing planned parenthood. Here is one interesting case history from Shanghai:

A woman worker in a toy factory already had two girls. Influenced by the idea that "boys are better than girls", she herself, her husband, and her mother-in-law all hoped for a boy. The neighbourhood committee cadres and propagandists went to their home to do ideological work, explained the advantages of planned parenthood, and convinced first the woman and then her husband. Finally, the cadres and propagandists and the couple worked on the mother-in-law. Birth control measures were adopted promptly.[37]

This case not only shows the perseverance of the neighbourhood planned parenthood cadres and the personal approach they are able to take, but also reflects the persistence of traditional attitudes even in the cities, and the continuing influence of the older generation in the lives of young Chinese people.

This involvement and intimacy in the current family planning programme is also well illustrated by a relatively new approach which parallels China's contention that "along with the practice of planned economy there should also be the planning of births". Apparently in some of the more advanced communes and in some urban neighbourhoods, married women of reproductive age hold meetings at which detailed plans are made as to who in the group will have children during the forthcoming years. The discussion takes into consideration such factors as the size of present family and the length of marriage; the final plan, often represented on wall charts, shows that Mrs. X will have her next child in 1975, Mrs. Y and Mrs. Z in 1976 and so on. These discussions are guided by members of birth control committees or public health workers who follow the edict that:

> In deciding on population plans, it is necessary to have the masses participate fully, send the plans to each household and work out plans for each person, so that the leadership will have definite plans and the masses will clearly understand them.[38]

Another example of the workings of this system was reported by Han Suyin. She tells of how each courtyard in Peking held meetings to debate which of the families would have a baby the following year. "The families have to agree, between them, whose turn it will be to have or not to have a baby." Apparently one woman got pregnant out of turn, which meant that her neighbour, who was scheduled to have a baby, would not be able to do so. To show her public spirit, the pregnant woman had an abortion.[39]

As bizarre as this story might appear to an American reader, it very likely did happen. The important point, however, is not the story itself but what it tells us of the system and of the spirit that exists in China. Their approach to family planning does not resemble any method to be found in any other country. It is patterned after the numerous other campaigns that have been so successful in the past. In a way, perhaps it could be likened to an amalgamation of the spring sanitation campaign which involves the whole community in clean-up activities, and the anti-Confucius/anti-Lin Piao campaign, which involves the whole community in study and discussion activities. Everyone is expected to be involved in the new ideology and habit of "practicing birth control for the revolution." And when everyone is involved there is a different feeling among the participants; perhaps a feeling of togetherness rather than one of isolation when a family as a single unit has to bear the attention and the pressure of family planning personnel. The practice of birth control in China may not yet be "a compelling demand and spontaneous action of the masses", but there does seem to be a reasonable basis for the statement made at a Kwei-chow Province conference on birth control work that "the new custom of regarding birth control as honorable is gradually forming in the towns and countryside throughout the province"[40]—and probably throughout most of the country.

THE MEANS OF FERTILITY CONTROL

The Chinese are marvellous hosts. They will dine the visitor, wine him, cater to his comforts and, if possible, arrange his itinerary in such a way as to make sure that he will spend most of his time viewing and discussing that which is his primary professional specialty. Physicians interested in acupuncture anaesthesia will see numerous operations, computer scientists will see computers, archaeologists will visit excavations, and so forth. This is natural; it is the reason for the visit. On the subject of family planning, however, the desire of Chinese officials to cater to the special interests of each visitor sometimes tends to result in the "elephant and blind man" syndrome and conclusions are based on only partial evidence. Thus, a Japanese doctor who goes to China as a consultant on abortions can report without reservations that China plans to take the abortion route to reduce the number of births. On the basis of what they saw, other visitors can, in all honesty, report that the primary emphasis is on sterilization or on oral contraception, or on IUDs, or on condoms. The Chinese, of course, do not say anything.

All these methods and others are used and improved, and no one can say which will be the most important in the future.

POSTPONEMENT OF MARRIAGE

A rise in the age of marriage would be an important factor in reducing fertility in a developing country. Since females are usually more fecund in the earlier ages, it has demographic significance; since it gives women an opportunity to obtain more education and acquire interests outside of family, it has sociological significance. The problem is, however, that a higher age of marriage cannot be legislated because it would be extremely difficult to enforce and, in most countries, would likely result in an increase of illegitimate children.

The sociological factor was primary among the considerations which prompted the Chinese to raise the minimum legal age of marriage to 18 for girls and 20 for men and to incorporate it into the marriage law of 1950. Raising the marriage age from the mid-teens would theoretically limit if not eliminate the role of the elders in arranging marriages. It was not until the first birth control campaign was initiated in the mid-1950s that age of marriage started to be mentioned as a way to control fertility. The economic and social benefits were also emphasized in the drive to postpone marriage. As in the case of the birth control campaign itself, however, it is very doubtful that either the law or the pressures to delay marriage were very effective during that early period in China. Certainly in the rural areas the law was, at best, only loosely enforced, age records of people born before 1949 were not available, and the old traditions were too deeply ingrained in the population.

In the 1960s the campaign to reduce fertility was much more forceful in emphasizing postponement of marriage, referring to early marriage as "a poisonous gas given off by the rotting corpse of capitalism" and warning the people, "Don't fall in love too early". Numerous proposals were discussed about the pros and cons of raising the legal marriage age by 5 years or more but, probably because of the régime's concern about its ability to enforce such a law, the original ages incorporated into the marriage law still stand.

During and since the Cultural Revolution the efforts to get the people to postpone marriage have been particularly intensive, urging the young people to wait until they are in their mid-twenties before they marry. The suggested age of marriage in China now seems to vary from area to area, some reports indicating 28 for men and 25 for women, some a few years earlier, others suggesting a combined age of 50 for the marrying couple. Just how effective the Chinese are in implementing this policy is difficult to say, but the inference from both published sources and from observation and talking to the Chinese is that despite some persistence of traditional customs in rural areas the average marriage age is, in fact, a few years higher than it was 10 to 15 years ago and that it is on the rise.[41] Thus, once again, certain social reforms thought to be out of the question a decade or two ago are apparently quite possible now.

The young people the régime is currently trying to influence were either born or started school since 1949. They are all well indoctrinated in the new ideology. Not only the men but also all the young women are working. In other words, both the social and economic factors have changed. The age of each individual is generally known by the local authorities. Marriages must be registered with the public security people and a permit to marry is required from the place of employment. A marriage contemplated by individuals considered to be too young would probably not result in an outright "no" from the leadership, but it would precipitate a study session. At such a session, normally led by responsible cadres and attended by friends and co-workers, the discussion would focus on the economic, health, social, and especially political considerations which would make early marriage harmful to the individuals and undesirable for the state. Marriage not only eliminates the individual's eligibility for additional education, especially access to institutions of higher learning, but early marriage might also affect job opportunities. Consequently, although age of marriage is not legislated and enforced in the traditional sense, it is indeed an unusual young person who can withstand peer pressures, overlook possible loss of economic opportunities, and invite disapproval by ignoring the chance to demonstrate political activism and patriotism—all of which would result from an insistence on early marriage.

As difficult as it may be for the Westerner to understand the nature of controls and pressures which can, and do, influence a young Chinese to postpone marriage, it is even more incomprehensible that, within this context, premarital sex is apparently not practiced. And yet, although documentation is not possible, there seems to be little doubt that this is, in fact, the case.

To appreciate the present attitudes of the Chinese toward sex, it is necessary to understand that in traditional China "sex was either completely absent or entirely subordinate to considerations of social acceptability".[42] Sexual themes, so prominent in other cultures, are virtually non-existent in Chinese literature and art. In a discussion of the four basic attributes which characterize the Chinese in their personal relations, Professor Hsu lists "asexuality" along with continuity, inclusiveness, and authority. He points out that "their attitude is not a reflection of Puritanism, which says that sex is evil and therefore must not be enjoyed under any circumstances. Rather, the Chinese believe that sex is bad only when practiced with the wrong partner (such as someone else's wife), in the wrong place (such as in a public park), and at the wrong time (such as during broad daylight)." The persistence of these traditional values may be judged by the fact that in large sections of rural China, marriage through free association and romantic love without the approval of elders is still unusual. According to some Chinese—those few who are willing to comment on the subject for questioning visitors—"it is in part because of the traditional attitude toward sex that premarital sexual restraint is not the problem to the Chinese that Westerners conceive it to be".

If asexuality is, in fact, a basic characteristic of the Chinese, it is easy to see how conditions in present-day China would reinforce it. Dress in China does nothing to accentuate sex differences. While there is no sex segregation in school or at work, once outside any institutional framework young men and women tend to congregate with their own sex, as for example, during school recesses and work breaks. Although it must exist, any visible form of courtship is almost impossible to detect in public. Hard work and numerous extracurricular activities occupy most of the time of individual youths. Seclusion, considered indispensable in Western-style courtship, is virtually non-existent in the cities of China and not easy to come by even in the rural areas. And finally, the political, social, and psychological consequences of premarital sex, if discovered, would be subject to such severe and embarrassing group criticism that it is easy to understand how self-denial would be the better part of valour. In other words, if the revolution requires late marriage and continence, the young people of China are likely to comply.

AVAILABILITY OF CONTRACEPTIVES

Virtually all contraceptives in developing countries have been manufactured in and imported from advanced countries. This presents not only the obvious problems of cost and expenditure of limited foreign exchange, but in some cases there are also legal barriers such as import licences and duties. Frequently the market is limited, the profit margins are low, and the cost of promoting ethical pharmaceutical products is high.[43] Therefore, the supply of contraceptives in the less developed nations must be subsidized either by the government or by one of the foreign or international organizations committed to such assistance.[44] Whether the contraceptives are marketed or distributed free of charge, the Western manufacturer or the sponsoring organization most likely requires sales analysis, consumer research, and other modern marketing and survey techniques which add cost and time to the primary goal of getting contraceptives to the users as quickly and cheaply as possible.

The Chinese situation with regard to contraceptives is very different from the one just described. Although neither the specific production figures nor the number and location of all the firms producing them have ever been reported, the Chinese are known to be self-sufficient in these products so that "various kinds of contraceptive methods are available and couples use them according to their age, health, and number of children".[45]

In the mid-1950s when the demand for contraceptives in China was relatively limited, China imported condoms, diaphragms, and chemical contraceptives. Oral contraception, occasionally mentioned in those years, usually fell into the domain of the traditional doctors—the herbalists. With the accelerated birth control campaign, Peking undoubtedly allocated funds to expand domestic production of contraceptives and at the same time, under the auspices of the Academy of Medical Sciences and the institutes of the Ministry of Public Health, increased research on the means of fertility control. Nevertheless, we do know that as late as 1961 the Chinese were still importing, free of customs duty, "birth control devices and birth control medicine".[46] With the normalization of China's economy and the renewed birth control campaign of the 1960s, China must have started to increase her production of contraceptives. It was specifically during the mid-1960s that Chinese reports indicated intensive IUD experimentation by departments of gynaecology and obstetrics in hospitals and medical universities. At least one visitor to China in July 1965 returned with the conviction that the IUD had become the most popular device in China, surpassing even the condom.[47] Although a questionable conclusion based on limited observation, it does indicate the increasing use of the IUDs—all of which were already produced in China. This simple and effective birth control device may or may not be most welcomed by rural women, as reported, but from personal observation it seems quite evident that IUDs, most of them stainless spring coils, are readily available at all health stations.

By far the most information on China's production of steroid contraceptives was brought back by Dr. Carl Djerassi who, with his colleagues, was responsible for the chemical synthesis of an oral contraceptive steroid. He visited the People's Republic of

China in the spring of 1973 with the primary purpose of discovering what he could about China's production of contraceptive hardware.[48] Serious work on the production of an oral contraceptive was started in 1958 in both Shanghai and Peking. By 1964 the National Medical Journal was able to report that "although the oral contraceptive drugs at present have not entirely accomplished the basic objectives of convenience, economy and dependability, they are gradually approaching the final solutions".[49] Apparently the experimental work on the pills did not cease during the Cultural Revolution and much testing of various pills and dosages was conducted during those years, finally settling on a pill that used one-quarter of the accepted dose in the United States. According to Djerassi, the last few years have seen a rapid increase in the production and use of oral contraceptives; he estimates that the 1972 production sufficed for 20 million women. Despite the earlier caveat about making quick conclusions, it does seem that since 1972 the production of oral contraceptives has increased significantly, and that by now they not only provide most of the urban needs, but are rapidly becoming an important contraceptive in the rural areas as well.

As for the distribution of contraceptives, here again we find that China does not have the problems of other developing countries. That China is self-sufficient in contraceptive devices and need not import, simplifies matters considerably. There is neither production competition nor cost to the consumer. All contraceptives, with the exception of pills, are available in drugstores. If the individual is associated with any enterprise or institution or is part of the rural cooperative medicine system—which encompasses an overwhelming proportion of the population—contraceptives are also available free of charge through the institutional or residential health clinic. Birth control pills are not sold in drugstores, but are freely distributed not only by barefoot doctors, midwives, and other public health personnel, but also by women volunteers who specifically assist with this function. Whether contraceptive means are distributed through commercial channels, such as state stores in market towns or supply and marketing cooperatives, which is true of some of the pharmaceutical goods, or distributed directly through the public health channels, is incidental. The important thing is that they are free and that there seem to be no bottlenecks in getting the contraceptives to the users, as can be seen from the following statement:

> Annual state appropriations assist individual administrative subdivisions in providing free contraceptives to couples who want to practice birth control. The process in the cities is that the health department provides contraceptives to hospitals or clinics in factories, schools, government offices and neighbourhoods and local medical workers then distribute them to individuals. In the rural areas the barefoot doctors or health workers take the contraceptives to the peasants' homes. Medical advice or treatment is provided by birth control clinics.[50]

Whatever other problems the Chinese may still be facing in getting the masses to accept the concept of family planning, there seems to be adequate evidence in support of the claim that "the problem of 'hardware' production capacity [in China] has either been solved or is on the verge of being solved".[51]

ABORTION

Abortion—the most ancient form of birth prevention—is not a substitute for contraception. Nevertheless, in countries such as Japan and the Soviet Union, where abortion was practised legally long before the development of present-day contraceptive technology, there apparently is a conscious or unconscious laxity about contraception practices.[52] In the traditional sectors of the Asian societies abortions have never been difficult to obtain, and even now when many of the countries have been liberalizing abortions, usually on medical, eugenic and juridical grounds, abortions outside the public health system continue to predominate.[53] That is the main reason why statistics on abortions as a means of birth control are almost impossible to get in most countries.

In China, although abortion never faced the moral or legal obstacles prevalent in the West, it was never prescribed by the régime as the answer to China's population problem. Abortion prerequisites imposed by the régime in the 1950s were relatively loose and could easily be met by women anxious to terminate pregnancy. But even at the height of the birth control campaign many reservations were expressed by China's medical personnel about the use and possible abuse of the abortion technique. No doubt abortions were readily available in China's cities, but it is very doubtful that China's birth control was "centred around the artifically induced abortion", as suggested by one Japanese visitor in 1965.[54] Consistent with Chinese medical practices, here too the emphasis was on prevention—that is, contraception—rather than the "cure" of abortion. Furthermore, abortions required personnel, equipment and facilities, and involved absence from production and the risk of possible health hazards—all considered to be impracticalities in the Chinese setting.

With China's present drive to reduce the number of births, with the development of the vacuum aspiration method that is readily available in the countryside, and with the expanding body of specially trained paramedical personnel, the incidence of abortion due to contraceptive failure has undoubtedly increased significantly. Indeed abortions are free, workers and employees draw full pay during the period of recuperation, and women on the communes receive their regular work points if their activities are interrupted by abortion.[55]

STERILIZATION

Male vasectomy and female tubal ligation represent the most effective birth control methods available. At the same time, because they involve surgical procedure and raise a number of psychological, sociological, demographic and medical questions, widespread sterilization continues to be essentially a long-range goal rather than a reality for many developing countries. India is the best example of a nation that has placed special stress on a mass vasectomy project. Although it is apparently generally accepted by the population and is surpassed only by the condom in popularity as a method of fertility control, there seems to be a growing opposition in India to the emphasis on sterilization,[56] which was intensified by the excesses of the "Emergency". In general, the use of sterilization in developing countries continues to be very limited.

Although sterilization was readily available at least in the cities of China in the 1950s, it was not vigorously promoted during those years. The reason for Peking's rather passive approach toward sterilization as a means of controlling fertility was undoubtedly motivated by practical considerations. Not only was there a shortage of hospital facilities and medical personnel to perform these operations, there was also the need to overcome the universal fear of surgery and the common fear of loss of sexuality and reduced working capacity. Since the early 1960s, however, there has been an apparent accelerating endorsement of sterilization in China—an increase that quite reasonably parallels the increase in health personnel and facilities. Specifics on sterilization, however, are difficult to come by. There is even disagreement as to whether vasectomy or tubal ligation is the more prevalent in the country. There have been some reports that the Chinese wife, who is usually more anxious than her husband to take the necessary measures to limit the family, will have her fallopian tubes tied; others report that vasectomies are much more common, relating tales of men who have come to realize their selfishness in letting their wives submit to the operation, rather than having the simpler vasectomy themselves.

Notwithstanding the absence of specific data, it is fairly certain that the incidence of sterilization in China is truly on the increase. Just as in the case of abortion, the sterilization operation, including gynaecological and X-ray examinations and hospitalization, is free, and both urban and rural workers continue to receive their pay or work-points during the period of recuperation. Considering the size of China's population, however, it is very doubtful if in the national scheme of priorities sterilization has reached a level of importance implied by the comments of two recent visitors: "Tubal sterilization has been used so widely that in some places its number reaches the level of IUD insertions".[57]

THE VERDICT

An objective evaluation of China's planned birth programme cannot be made. Although there is much useful documentation, there are few facts and figures on which to base conclusions. There are success stories brought back by visitors and there is the more restrained attitude of the Chinese leaders: "We have much to learn and a long way to go." Looking at what is available in the Chinese mass media, it is possible to select items that report impressive progress; it is just as easy to find problems and failures. The most careful and impartial analysts can examine the same evidence and yet come up with very different conclusions. Much of it boils down to feelings. What follows, then, are some feelings based on many years of research and study and buttressed by the 3-weeks-in-China seal of approval.

Virtually every family planning programme spends considerable time, money and effort to measure its own performance. Whether the programme is an independent national effort or one supported by a donor country or organization, each wants some feedback to determine if the appropriated funds are well invested and, if not, what improvements can be made to ensure the desired returns. Although ideally everyone would like to know specifically how many births have been averted as the result of the family planning programme, there is an understandable willingness to settle for less. But in this field of investigation even seemingly basic questions are unanswerable. It is hard enough to determine whether or not people are changing their attitudes toward large families, are becoming aware of methods to reduce family size, and are, in fact, adopting these practices; it is impossible to say with any confidence how much of the progress being made can be credited specifically to the family planning programme, as opposed to other changes in the society. Nevertheless, there is a continuing effort to improve the methods and measures for determining the effectiveness and efficiency of

family planning programmes and to make the evaluation something more than educated guesses.

The Chinese have only a very general idea of how effective is their own family
planning programme, but because they manage to run their country with only a fraction
of the statistical data that we deem indispensable, they do not consider the lack of
specifics to be a problem. As long as the régime believes that everything possible is
being done to reduce fertility, statistical measurement of accomplishments or shortcomings could have little effect on the programme being implemented. Perhaps a useful
analogy can be made with agriculture. The Chinese are attempting to achieve maximum
food production. New policies or agricultural methods are not directly dependent on
production statistics, and improvements will be introduced whenever they are likely to
increase production. Agricultural plans are no more dependent on population projections than family planning efforts are based on food production. In each case, the goal is
maximum results.

One way to judge the effectiveness of the birth control campaign is through the use
of some demographic measures—if not the changes in age-specific fertility rates, then
changes in the crude birth rate. These rates are among the many specifics the Chinese do
not have. In connection with family planning, it is useful here to take a quick look at
what they know and what they do not know about their population in general.

The Chinese know that the population is very large; they know that it is growing
too fast; they know that if the population were not growing by some 13 or 14 million
every year, it would be easier to handle some of the country's economic and social
problems. Peking does not know more than the approximate size of China's population;
it does not know its age—sex structure and other characteristics of the population; it
does not know its birth rate, its death rate, or its rate of natural increase. In other words,
much of the information that we are trying to estimate is not even available to the
Chinese government. Some of us have been saying this for many years, but more and
more frequently this suspicion is being confirmed by statements of Chinese officials to
visitors and by statements and figures in Chinese publications.[58]

The difference between the Chinese and us, however, is that we tend to become
more disturbed by the absence of population data than do the Chinese. At the national
level the desirability of having accurate and adequate population statistics is understood, but China's leaders are well aware of the overwhelming problems involved in
obtaining such data. Consequently, they are very realistic about their own requirements
and the priorities they wish to assign to the formidable task of satisfying them. We, on
the other hand, get very frustrated if we cannot present *per capita* figures or fill in all the
blanks in statistical forms. The plans and policies of the Chinese government do not
change if the estimate of rural population is 650 million or 700 million; our evaluations
of China's performance do change on the basis of these figures. China's planners do not
have to divide grain production by population, for example, to see if the people have
enough to eat—we do. If a cadre or a statistical worker must provide a population figure
in some report, there is little concern that the figure is only an approximation. It is not
difficult to find evidence regarding the casual attitude of the Chinese toward statistics. It
was so in old China; it is only slightly changed in new China.[59]

As for the country's vital rates, even if they had the denominator of the equation—the total population—the Chinese would still be lacking the numerator—the total
number of births and deaths. The vital rates published in the 1950s are of questionable

validity,[60] and no figures for the country have been reported since then—except in rounded approximations. Births and deaths are registered at the local police station or the security office, or with an official of the rural governmental unit. National vital statistics are the responsibility of the State Statistical Bureau in Peking. The channels by which data move from the poorly trained local recorder to the bureaucrat in Peking must indeed be long and circuitous. In the summer of 1973, in direct response to a question, Hsieh Hua, the responsible person at the Ministry of Public Health, stated very frankly that national figures on birth and death rates are not yet available because the State Statistical Bureau is still in a state of transition. He was implying, of course, that the Bureau has not yet recovered from the effects of the Cultural Revolution, but we have no evidence that it was capable of producing such figures prior to 1966.

Although the Chinese lack national population statistics they do, of course, have information not available to outsiders on which they can make some reasonable assessment of the progress of the family planning programme. Total population for local areas are readily quoted by official spokesmen of the city, workers' settlement or commune—albeit the larger the administrative unit, the rounder the figures tend to be and the longer they remain unchanged. Certainly the hospitals and clinics accessible to foreign visitors maintain detailed records of birth—probably a fairly common practice in most areas. It would seem reasonable to assume, then, that aggregate figures for select cities and communes should be available to determine the local birth rate and the trend in the number of births. The question is whether or not the figures published in Chinese sources and reported by visitors are in any way representative of the nation as a whole. Not likely. Birth rates of 10 or 12 per thousand and death rates of 4 or 5 per thousand are difficult to accept even for the select locations for which they are given. First of all, an important method of propaganda is encouragement through success stories which are widely reported. And second, the local cadres are not averse to a little exaggeration—a fact well appreciated by the people in Peking who tend to react with scepticism when asked about some of the sharp declines in fertility or mortality reported by a local official. The point is, however, that by selecting representative sample areas and by sending in specially trained individuals, Peking should be able to obtain some reasonable estimates of China's vital rates. There is reason to believe, however, that because the Chinese are not experienced in sample studies and because the priority for population data is not pressing, these activities are not undertaken except, perhaps, on a random and superficial basis.

But even if the Chinese are unable to produce valid demographic measures of the family planning programme, they do have one good index that is not available to anyone else. Although they probably do not have statistics on acceptors or on the proportion of women in the reproductive age who use contraception, they do know what the national production of contraceptives is. Since most of these items reach the user, Peking should have a reasonable idea of the trend in the utilization of contraceptives—a good measure of the motivational efforts that are being made in the country.

The expressed scepticism with regard to statistics does not mean that all of China's claimed and implied successes in the family planning field should be rejected. Lacking statistical documentation, a conclusion of reasonable success can be derived from more subjective factors already discussed, which relate to changes in the society and economy and from the specific nature of the family planning programme itself.

Admittedly, statistical values to measure social and economic progress creating conditions for reduced fertility are just as rare as other types of quantitative data for China. Reasonable judgements, however, can be made without specific figures. It is not necessary to have the *per capita* gross domestic product, for example, to know that the living standard of the Chinese people has improved greatly and that, some short-run setbacks notwithstanding, the trend is continuing. Despite the absence of specific figures, it is known that China is not too far from achieving universal primary level education, that illiteracy is on the decline, and that virtually all women over 15 years are contributing to the economy—at least on a part-time basis. Again, although there are no figures, the lower infant mortality and the higher life expectancy—in part a result of a rapid increase of health workers and hospital beds—are not in doubt. These and other factors all create conditions favourable to China's family planning programme and particularly in making the population more amenable to the acceptance of late marriage and the use of contraception.

TABLE 1. *Evaluating China's family planning programme*

	Criteria[1]	Avail-ability	Comment
1	Fertility reduction included in official planning policy	Yes	Particularly since 1970; some earlier periods policy not clearly defined
2	Favourable public statements by political leaders	Yes	The programme to plan births is promulgated in the name of Chairman Mao Tse-tung
3	Contraception readily and easily available, publicly and commercially throughout the country	Yes	Distributed free of charge through the health system
4	Customs and legal regulations allow importation of contraceptives not manufactured locally	NA	Although imported in earlier years, supply of Chinese-manufactured contraceptives now appears adequate for current needs
5	Vigorous efforts to provide family planning services to all married women of reproductive age	Yes	Broadly based and wide-reaching
6	Adequate family planning administration structure	Yes	Responsibility for family planning assumed by public health and by a variety of mass organizations
7	Training facilities available and utilized	Yes	Primarily through the public health system
8	Full-time home visiting field workers	Yes	Usually locally recruited and trained
9	Postpartum information, education, and service programme	Yes	Readily available to all
10	Abortion services openly and legally available to all	Yes	But not encouraged as a substitute for contraception
11	Voluntary sterilization services (male and female) openly and legally available to all	Yes	In some areas performed by specially trained paramedical personnel
12	Use of mass media on a substantial basis	Yes	Main emphasis, however, on personal approach and group study
13	Government provides substantial part of family planning budget from its own resources	Yes	Manufacture and free distribution of contraceptives, for example
14	Record-keeping systems for clients at clinic level and programme service statistics	Yes	Programme service statistics more limited
15	Serious and continuous evaluation effort	No	Probably limited to sample areas

[1]   Criteria suggested by Robert J. Lapham and W. Parker Mauldin, National family planning programs: review and evaluation, *Studies in Family Planning*, Vol. 3, No. 2, March 1972.

The criteria that are not dependent on statistical data are related directly to the nature of the family planning programme. Lapham and Mauldin have come up with 15 standards that have been found useful and important in affecting population goals and policies.[61] If the evaluation of these criteria in terms of China's family planning programme is realistic (see Table 1), then there is little doubt that in this area she has done better than any other developing country. What does not emerge clearly from this evaluation are the strongest aspects of China's family planning programme: organization and motivation. And here we come to the fundamental question which is so frequently asked by those concerned with the world's population problem: is China's experience transferable to other developing countries?

There is little in the Chinese delivery system that is new to family planning specialists. What is impressive is that they have, to a large extent, put into practice most of the current family planning tenets that have evolved only after many years of trial and error. They did this with minimal reference to Western experience—using an approach that is characteristically their own. It is now understood that successful family planning services have to be brought to the user, rather than expect the user to search it out. The Chinese have done it. It is known that these services have to be not only easily accessible, but free. The Chinese provide contraceptives, abortions, sterilizations free of charge. For years now family planning people have been urging a more important role for the paraprofessionals and the non-professionals. Once again the Chinese have done it. They have made extensive use not only of the much-advertised barefoot doctors, but of a great variety of other locally recruited personnel, specially trained to perform both medical and educational functions in the family planning programme. If China's experience can do no more than demonstrate to the world that these are indeed legitimate, practical and achievable goals, she has made an important contribution to "the cause".

Where China's approach to family planning is particularly imaginative and peculiarly Chinese is in the area of motivation and education, but it is here that the likelihood of emulation is the most improbable. It is difficult to imagine China's saturation approach to family planning attempted in any other society. Whereas most countries must rely on the public health system and specific family planning organizations, China can and does call on all the government components, on the pervasive Communist Party, on numerous national mass organizations—all of which reach out to the community and to the individual. To limit family size Peking calls on patriotism, on service to the people, on local pride and on the competitive spirit of the group. At the same time that the régime is attacking tradition through an intense anti-Confucius campaign, it is taking full advantage of some of the traditional Chinese characteristics and attributes in its efforts to control fertility. Respect for authority and loyalty that were exercised within the family, now have been shifted to the group, the community and the State. This facilitates over-all control of the population and presumes compliance with national policies, including family planning; a couple that has too many children not only rejects Mao's wishes but disgraces its own group or community. That a young person will not be able to go to college if married and is not likely to become a cadre or a Party member or reach any position of authority if he or she has more than three children are still important deterrents to the energetic and diligent Chinese with their characteristic drive toward success. The perpetual tug-of-war between serving the people, as demanded by the State, and serving oneself, as dictated by human nature, is greatly minimized in family planning, where restraint is beneficial to both masters. Conformity, realism and the positive orientation of the Chinese people, all help make Peking's problems in instituting family planning much more manageable and soluble.

All this does not mean that the People's Republic of China has come even close to reducing its birth rate to a level acceptable to Peking. But considering the starting point and the size of the overwhelmingly rural population, China has made impressive progress in a relatively short period of time. Furthermore, she is likely to be the first developing nation of any size to reduce the growth of her population to below 1 per cent per year. As for the value of China as a model for developing countries, the answer in every field of development has become almost a cliché and holds true for family planning as well: China's experience is not transferable—but there is much to be learned from it.

NOTES

1   Agency for International Development, *Population Program Assistance*, Washington, December 1972.
2   John H. Sullivan and John C. Chester, US aid to population/family planning in Asia, report to the Committee on Foreign Affairs, US House of Representatives, 25 February 1973.
3   *The New York Times*, 21 June 1974
4   Norman B. Ryder, Realistic pathways to fertility reduction in developing countries: the perspective of the sociologist: a paper presented at the annual meeting of the Population Association of America, New York, 20 April 1974.
5   For example: "Power, be it political, economic or military, does have, as one of its necessary ingredients—even though not a sufficient one—a large or a relatively large population". Statement by the Brazilian representative at the 17th Session of the United Nations Population Commission, 1973, as quoted by Bernard Berelson in *The Population Council Annual Report 1973*, p. 25.
6   S. M. Keeny, East Asia Review, 1971, *Studies in Family Planning*, Vol. 3, No. 7, July 1972, p. 160, hereafter referred to as *SFP*.
7   For a more detailed discussion of the evolution of China's population policy, see Leo A. Orleans, *Every Fifth Child: The Population of China*, Stanford: Stanford University Press, 1972.
8   *The New York Times*, 3 February 1964.
9   Edgar Snow, Population care and control, *New Republic*, 1 May 1971, pp. 20–3.
10 *Peking Review*, No. 49, 7 December 1973.
11 Ryder, Realistic pathways, op. cit.
12 The persistence of cultural inertia with regard to male children is evident from a study of 208 students of Delhi University in India. Although economic considerations would be minimal among these obviously advantaged youths, 97 per cent of the boys and 99 per cent of the girls wanted at least one son, and 54 per cent of the boys and 37 per cent of the girls said they would have one or more children above the number they wanted in order to have a son. (Thomas Poffenberger, An experimental population education program in rural India, *SFP*, Vol. 2, No. 1, November 1971, p. 233.)
13 See, for example, Ronald Freedman, The high fertility of the less developed nations, David M. Heer (Ed.), *Readings on Population*, Englewood Cliffs, N.J.: Prentice-Hall, Inc., 1968.
14 *Jen-min Jih-pao* (People's Daily), 30 July 1973, hereafter referred to as *JMJP*; translated in *Survey of China Mainland Press*, No. 5435, 14 August 1973, hereafter referred to as *SCMP*.
15 For a more detailed discussion of urbanization in China, see Orleans, *Every Fifth Child*, op. cit., Chapter 3.
16 For a good recent study on the subject of women in China, the reader is referred to: Shelah Gilbert Leader, The emancipation of Chinese women, *World Politics*, October 1973.
17 *Peking Review*, No. 10, 8 March 1974.
18 *The New York Times*, 27 May 1973.
19 A discussion of the transition from one era to the next may be found in: Everett M. Rogers, *Communication Strategies for Family Planning*, New York: The Free Press, 1973, pp. 84–98.
20 James E. Austin, The management bottleneck in family planning programs, *SFP*, Vol. 4, No. 12, December 1973.

21   *Current Scene*, Vol. 11, No. 10, October 1973, p. 27.
22   For a detailed discussion of public health, see: Leo A. Orleans, Health policies and services in China, 1974: report to the Subcommittee on Health, US Senate, March 1974.
23   John U. Farley and Harold J. Leavitt, Marketing and family planning program management, *SFP*, Vol. 4, No. 10, October 1973, p. 270.
24   Family planning activities in Thailand are a case in point. Between 1968 and 1970 the following foreign agencies supported Thailand's family planning activities: The Population Council, AID, UNICEF, IPPF, the University of North Carolina, the Rockefeller Foundation, the Ford Foundation, and World Educational Inc. Additional support was expected "from the United Nations family of agencies, including WHO, UNICEF, UNESCO, and ECAFE, in large part through the UN Fund for Population Activities" (Allan G. Rosenfield *et al*, Thailand: family planning activities 1968 to 1970, *SFP*, Vol. 2, No. 9, September 1971, p. 191).
25   Howard G. Taylor, Jr., and Robert J. Lapham, A program for family planning based on maternal-child health services, *SFP*, Vol. 5, No. 3, March 1974, p. 71.
26   See, for example, Rogers, *Communication Strategies*, op. cit.
27   Ronald Ridker, Savings accounts for family planning. An illustration from the tea estates of India, *SFP*, Vol. 2, No. 7, July 1971, p. 150.
28   See, for example, Edward Pohlman, *Incentives and Compensations in Birth Planning*, University of North Carolina, 1971.
29   Everett M. Rogers, Incentives in the diffusion of family planning innovations, *SFP*, Vol. 2, December 1971, p. 241.
30   New China News Agency, 24 December 1973, hereafter referred to as NCNA.
31   The involvement of the Revolutionary Committees in family planning and the integration of the programme with women's health and sanitation can be seen from the following report: "The hsien [county] revolutionary committee organized the medical personnel of various communes to help barefoot doctors and health workers to combine the treatment of gynecological diseases with a household-to-household publicity campaign about the significance of planned birth and the need of sanitary knowledge". (*JMJP*, 3 March 1971, translated in *SCMP*, No. 4858, 16 March 1971.)
32   *JMJP*, 30 July 1973, translated in *SCMP*, No. 5435, 14 August 1973.
33   See, for example, Medicine in China, *Medical World News*, 14 January 1972, p. 57.
34   William T. Liu, Family change and family planning in the People's Republic of China: a paper presented at the annual meeting of the Population Association of America, New York, 19 April 1974.
35   *JMJP*, 30 July 1973; translated in *SCMP*, No. 5435, 14 August 1973.
36   Francis L. K. Hsu in Eileen Hsu-Balzer, Richard J. Balzer, and Francis L. K. Hsu, *China Day by Day*, New Haven: Yale University Press, 1974, p. xii.
37   *Chieh-fang Jih-pao* (Liberation Daily) 1 February 1973.
38   NCNA, 21 December 1973.
39   *The New York Times*, 1 September 1973.
40   NCNA, 21 December 1973.
41   A good example of the resistance to change that is still evident in parts of the country was included in an article published in the Hupeh Daily that urged the people to change old habits and customs. It said, in part, that concepts of the exploiting class in slighting women and monopolizing marriage which were left from the old society still affect people's minds. For the present there still exist in nuptial affairs various evil winds such as exacting betrothal money, indulgence in expenditure, assuming the airs of being rich, inviting guests and accepting presents and what not. (*Union Research Service*, Vol. 73, No. 25, 25 December 1973.)
      Certainly by our standards these are rather mild "crimes", but they obviously represent serious deviation from Mao's revolutionary line to abolish "old thoughts, old customs, old morals, and old habits".
42   Hsu, *China Day by Day*, op. cit., p. xv.
43   See, for example, Timothy Black Rationale for the involvement of private sector marketing institutions in family planning of Africa, *SFP*, Vol. 4, No. 2, February 1973, p. 25.
44   Nirodh condoms, for example, in India sell at 2 cents or less—more than 80 per cent below market price. (Anrudh K. Jain, Marketing research in the Nirodh program, *SFP*, Vol. 4, No. 7, July 1973, p. 184.)
45   NCNA, 5 March 1973.
46   *Ta Kung Pao*, Hong Kong, 21 January 1961.
47   An unpublished report by Tameyoshi Katagiri, Secretary, Western Pacific Region, International Planned Parenthood Federation.
48   Much of the information that follows was taken from: Carl Djerassi, Some observations on current fertility control in China, *The China Quarterly*, No. 57, January/March 1974, pp. 40–62.
49   *Chung-hua i-hsueh tsa-chih* (National Medical Journal of China), Vol. 50, No. 2, February 1964; summarized in Joint Publications Research Service, No. 43,072, 24 October 1967.
50   NCNA, 5 March 1973.
51   Djerassi, Some observations, op. cit.

52 Henry P. David, Psychological studies in abortion, In James T. Fawcett (Ed.), *Psychological Perspectives on Population*, New York: Basic Books, 1973, p.263.

53 Christopher Tieteze and Deborah A. Dawson, Induced abortion: a factbook, *Reports on Population/Family Planning*, No. 14, December 1973.

54 Majima Kan, The birth control controversy in China: induced abortion is coming into the foreground, *Bungei Shunju* (Literary Magazine), February 1965.

55 NCNA, 5 March 1973.

56 Roy C. Treadway and Jacqueline E. Forrest, Family planning program in India: an evaluation, *SFP*, Vol. 4, No. 6, June 1973, p. 149.

57 Anibal Faundes and Tapani Luukkainen, Health and family planning services in the Chinese People's Republic, *SFP*, Vol. 3, No. 7, July 1972, p. 175.

58 See, for example, Leo A. Orleans, China's population: some confirmations and estimates, *Current Scene*, Vol. 12, No. 3, March 1974. The fact that in September 1973 official Chinese sources reported that the country's population "topped 700 million" (NCNA, 23 September 1973) and less than a year later the Chinese representative at the United Nations World Population Conference in Bucharest stated that the population was "nearly 800 million" (NCNA, 21 August 1974), does not imply either collusion or programmed confusion. It is simply another example of the casualness with which the Chinese treat national population figures.

59 Some of the reasons for my scepticism regarding Chinese statistics are set down in: Leo A. Orleans, Chinese statistics: the impossible dream, *The American Statistician*, Vol. 28, No. 2, May 1974.

60 The only integrated series of population figures published by the Chinese cover the period from 1949 to 1956 (*T'ung-chi Kung-tso* (Statistical Bulletin), No. 11, 14 June 1957). Even a cursory examination of these data leaves one with too many unanswered questions and too many unquestioned answers.

61 Robert J. Lapham and W. Parker Mauldin, National family planning programs: review and evaluation, *SFP Vol. 3, No. 3, March 1972.*

IV. Tea Estates

Development Study 15 (Palmer-Jones)
Carruthers and Donaldson (1971) J.A.E. 22.1.

What factors would you take into account in planning a
tea estate?

Rural Industrialization in China: Approaches and Results

JON SIGURDSON

The existence of a rapidly growing rural industrial sector which consists of a large number of small and medium-sized enterprises is characteristic of the present develop-ment strategy in China. The systematic and integrated development of this sector has hardly any parallel in other developing countries, even if many similarities can be found in other countries, particularly in India.[1]

The rural industrial sector in China, consisting of state-owned relatively large enterprises and collectively-owned smaller companies, employs approximately 18 million people—according to preliminary estimates made by the author. This would amount to 36 per cent of the total industrial labour force in China but a third of this may be transferred back to agricultural work at peak seasons. In production value terms the rural industrial sector may represent only about 14 per cent of the industrial sector—or roughly 50 billion yuan (see Table 1). Available evidence indicates that the relative importance of the sector has been sustained or even increased in the period up to early 1978.

TABLE 1. *Industrial employment and production value in rural areas (1973)*

| | Employment | | Production value | |
	(million)	(percentage)	(billion Y)	(percentage)
Rural state-owned sector	6	12	30	8
Rural collective sector	12	24	20–25	6
Subtotal	18	36	52	14
Non-rural industry	32	64	315	86
Total	50	100	367	100

There are a number of basic differences between state-owned and collectively owned rural enterprises. First, state enterprises are centrally controlled through national or provincial plans while the collective ones are under the direct control of communes and brigades—with consequences for the access to critical inputs. Second, the state-owned enterprises are generally considerably larger and have higher capi-tal/labour ratios than the collective units. Third, the level of technical development is much higher in the state-owned enterprises and the workforce hardly undergoes seasonal changes. All these factors contribute to the fact that state-owned rural enter-prises have a much higher productivity than the collectively owned units. With agricul-

137

tural production value in the region of 100 billion yuan the figures above indicate that the production of industrial activity located in rural areas is roughtly 50 per cent. However, most of this is the contribution of the state-owned enterprises located in rural areas, under the administration of counties or regions—administrative sub-units of provinces.

RURAL INDUSTRIALIZATION AND INDUSTRIAL DECENTRALIZATION

Most developing countries, particularly those in Asia with a dominant part of the population in rural villages, used to have very substantial numbers of artisans. Those are now quickly disappearing due to changing demands and inefficiency of operation. On the other hand, modernization and industrialization are, and apparently have to be, to a considerable extent, based on modern large-scale enterprises located in the cities. Consequently, employment opportunities are disappearing from rural areas proper, and activities which would otherwise serve as catalysts of modernization are being monopolized in a few major cities.

The development is different in China, where rural industries span a considerable part of the industrial spectrum between traditional village crafts and modern large-scale industry. Rural industrialization should here be seen as part of a systematic attempt to decentralize industrial activity and promote regional development.

Most developing countries are today faced with the problem that they cannot provide enough employment opportunities in rural areas for people reaching working age, which in most countries has led to an undesirable migration into cities. Agriculture is in many developing countries in the process of being modernized through the use of new high-yielding varieties, more fertilizer and improved irrigation and drainage—increasing *land* productivity. But agriculture is also in the process of being mechanized—increasing *labour* productivity—which is likely to have a considerable effect on the labour supply/demand situation. The labour force is at the same time increasing through the natural population increase. In the long run, a very large number of people will be released from agriculture, of which it is likely that the modern industrial sector can absorb only a small percentage. Consequently, it is essential to find planning mechanisms by which the released manpower from agriculture can be gainfully employed.

Almost every person in rural areas in China is a member of a people's commune, which provides him with basic security. Agricultural mechanization is, in principle, controlled and people are hindered from migrating into the cities. However, there can be no doubt that it will be impossible for China to mechanize agriculture as well as to keep a majority of an increasing labour force in agriculture, so China has to come to grips with the problem of releasing manpower from agriculture. It certainly appears that different forms of rural industry—small-scale industry in areas dominated by agricultural or stock-farming activities—will play an important role. However, during the first stages of rural industrial development, employment is not primarily created in industrial production, but in repair and maintenance, in production of industrial raw materials, in transportation and in other services and in an increasingly diversified agriculture. At the same time, industrial structures are created outside the big cities. With the simultaneous expansion of national and local enterprises in rural areas, the former can increasingly draw on the manufacturing potential of a large number of small enterprises. Before continuing the discussion, however, it is necessary to make a clear distinction between rural industrialization and industrial decentralization.

To explain the difference, it is necessary to classify population centres according to size.[2] Communities may usefully be categorized in four size ranges:

(1) Rural communities with up to 10,000–20,000 inhabitants (market towns).
(2) Small urban centres with up to about 200,000 inhabitants.
(3) Secondary urban centres with up to about 1,000,000 inhabitants.
(4) Metropolitan centres with over 1,000,000 inhabitants.

The population marks are only approximate. The basic distinguishing feature is the economic base of the community. Small urban centres are defined as those whose existence is based mainly on the services they furnish to the surrounding rural areas. In secondary urban centres other activities take precedence over agro-related activities, and agriculture in the surrounding countryside is based mainly on the demand for food created by the urban centre. Metropolitan areas are the one or few largest population centres in almost any country, in which most industry, government and commerce are concentrated.

Industrial decentralization is a generic name for moving industry out of the metropolis to any other community. The chief aim of an industrial decentralization policy is usually to achieve a shift of future industrial growth from a metropolitan area to secondary urban centres. In most countries only a minority of the new industries—mostly those which process natural resources—are decentralized down to smaller urban centres and, to a much smaller extent, to rural communities. It is suggested that such industries be termed *regional industries*. This pattern of industrial decentralization and the place of rural industry are shown in Figure 1.

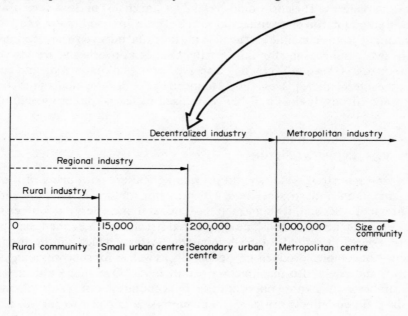

Figure 1

Industrial concentration in one or a couple of centres is commonly found in countries in the early stages of industrialization. The spreading of industrialization to secondary urban centres is found in industrially more advanced developing countries like Pakistan and India. The further spreading of industry to rural communities is found in mature industrial countries. The hypothesis has been advanced that the above order of industrial development is the optimal one. However, the experience in Japan and more recently in China indicates that an entirely different pattern involving rural communities at an early stage of development is feasible—even if the circumstances and necessary conditions are not yet fully known.

It is certainly desirable to bring industrial employment and income, and the indirect employment and income generated by industry, closer to the majority of the population living in the villages. But it does not follow that the best way to do this is to seek to locate a considerable proportion of manufacturing industry directly in the villages or even in the small urban centres (market towns). In order to achieve the objectives mentioned it is likely to be more effective to focus on the industrial development of selected towns and cities which are intermediates between villages on the one hand and secondary urban and metropolitan centres on the other hand, with a considerable emphasis on upgrading traditional village crafts serving agriculture. This would then take advantage of reasonably low costs for industrial facilities like power and transportation, and provide important external economies associated with urban locations. It would still bring industry and related services substantially closer to the majority of the population, who still live in villages.

The social and political benefits of decentralization are worth some economic cost. If decentralization were taken to mean pushing industry directly into villages, which was partly the case in China during the initial stage of the Great Leap Forward in 1958, the cost would be very great, both in terms of material and human resources required and in terms of lost efficiency. The cost would certainly be much less under a decentralization policy focused on intermediate cities and towns. There are good reasons for believing that there might be no economic cost at all in the long run, but even a net economic gain. There are two main reasons for this. Firstly, the social overheads are lower in the intermediate towns. Secondly, creating dispersed centres of innovation and economic change in the intermediate places is likely to speed up the development of the country as a whole more effectively than a highly centralized industrial pattern would do.

OBJECTIVES AND STRUCTURE

The rural industrial sector should provide agriculture with many of the needed industrial inputs and industrial services, with provision for local adaptations and changing requirements. Second, it should tap local mineral and energy resources as far as possible. Third, it should establish new industrial structures where the future potential market is. Fourth, it should establish industrial systems which can be used for the manufacture of complex products needed locally as well as for subcontracting to urban enterprises, and lately also manufacture export items. Overriding objectives are to provide rural areas with more opportunities for economic and social development and reduce the differential between cities and countryside in order to control migration, among other things.

The rural industrial sector in China consists of enterprises which vary greatly in size and in degree of technological sophistication. The total number of enterprises is very high. The largest category consists of the very small brigade-level repair and manufacture shops, of which there may be several hundred thousands. The second largest category is likely to be the small mines—or mining spots—of which there are likely to be considerably more than 100,000. There are also 50,000 small hydroelectric stations. A large number of the 50,000 communes are likely to have their own workshops for grain-milling, oil-pressing and other food processing plants, wood-working shops, etc., which are usually organized in multipurpose units. Rural heavy industry—small iron and steel plants, cement plants, chemical fertilizer plants and other chemical plants—may amount to between 5,000 and 10,000 units. The number of county-run machinery plants may amount to more than 3,000 units. Such farm machinery repair factories have been set up in 98 per cent of the 2,200 odd counties of China, employing 380,000 workers—which does not include the numerous farm machinery repair stations at commune level where peasants work part-time.[3] Then there is also a large number of light (consumer) industry enterprises in counties, communes and brigades and these may amount to more than 100,000 units.

China reports that there are 800,000 small enterprises in her rural areas, quite an impressive figure. This should be seen, however, in relation to the fact that the number of natural villages amounted to 700,000 before the establishment of the people's communes. Today China has about 750,000 production brigades and approximately 50,000 communes, so the number of small enterprises averages only one for each brigade and each commune. Furthermore, as more than 80 per cent of China's population is in the countryside, so the larger part of the new labour force, about 10,000,000 a year also appears there. Their work is arranged by their production brigades, according to the conditions of each (FE/W729/A/1). With approximately 750,000 brigades the annual increase in the labour force comes to about 13 persons to each brigade. Equally important to consider is the fact that rural industries are not evenly distributed.

When discussing national policy in China it must be borne in mind that the country is of continental size and great diversity. Consequently, it is natural to find that national policies can only be implemented with some time lag and regional differences tend to persist for some time. This is obvious from the reported figures on the road system and availability of electricity in China—both of which are important for rural industrialization programmes. Upwards of 70 per cent of the communes and half of the production brigades now have electricity, provided by small stations or by the state's power grid of medium and big power stations. Similarly, only some 83 per cent of the communes and about 50 per cent of the production brigades in China are joined by roads.[4]

The cases of Liaoning and Shanghai show that the level of productivity and technological sophistication of commune-run industries is a function of the industrial and economic development of the region where they are located.

So, total rural industrial employment is still limited. A couple of provinces have since the summer of 1973 clearly indicated that—based on local conditions and relevant instructions from higher authorities—the number of workers used by industries at county, commune and brigade levels should not exceed 5 per cent of the labour force in a county. And all other available information indicates that this may be the upper limit today.[5]

China has not released any aggregate national figures for employment in county-, commune- and brigade-level enterprises. There can be no doubt that employment in various parts of the country differs widely. Rural areas which are under the administration of big industrial cities have 20 per cent or more of the labour force in industry. Remote places in the interior of the county may hardly have any industrial activity at all. Information from a number of relatively—in terms of rural industrialization—well developed regions in Hopei Province indicates that less than 5 per cent of China's total labour force is engaged in rural industries. The labour force is estimated to be approximately 350 million which is about 70 per cent of the population between the ages of 15 and 64.

Rural industry is distributed within a county at brigade-, commune- and county-level, with the heavy industry and larger enterprises located in the county capitals. The large county capitals would usually not have a population exceeding 20,000. Most of the rural industrial enterprises are relatively small, rarely exceeding a few hundred employed. When discussing rural industry in China it is essential to realize that many of them are not small by international classification and that many of them are located in small urban centres—county seats with a population of up to 20,000—which are not considered rural areas according to international classification.

Rural industry in this article is not defined on the basis of size but as any local industry run by county, commune or brigade. The enterprise may be collectively owned, jointly financed by the state and collective units, or wholly owned by the state but under local management. Rural industry also includes units attached to middle schools, hospitals and health clinics.

Rural industry in China forms one part of the small-scale industrial sector which is basically made up of two different parts, of which the other is the urban small-scale industrial sector. The latter is not discussed in this article. The sophistication and scope of industrial activities are dependent on the level of education, economic development, natural resource endowment, nearness to ideas and new information. Consequently, it is realistic to differentiate between *rural industry in city-near locations and rural industry in rural areas proper*. The former seems to have much more in common with urban-based small-scale industry than is the case for the rest of rural industry.

The development of industries in rural areas around Shanghai, Peking and Tientsin—with a substantial amount of subcontracting—may indicate the long-term prospects for rural industry in the rest of the country. The formation of technical and organizational skills is only in the early stages of development in most parts of rural China. This and the still low level of mechanization explains why the industrial level is still comparatively low compared with more favoured rural areas around the big cities.

THE INTEGRATED APPROACH

Rural industrialization is a function of both demand and availability of local resources, where it is generally easier to influence the former than the latter. Rural industry in China can—with reference to the model for the rural industry system in Figure 2—be categorized in *backward-linkage industries* meeting a demand for agricultural inputs, and consumer goods, and *forward-linkage industries* being mainly based on locally available physical and human resources. The backward-linkage industries of course require local human resources but are initially very dependent on external technological and financial resources.

Rural industries with backward linkages to agriculture usually cannot be introduced until changes in agricultural technology create the demand for industrial inputs. And forward-linkage industries are often dependent on supplies arising from increased agricultural production. Furthermore, the demand for many industrial products will be limited until there is a general increase in the purchasing power of the locality. This is in most places, at least initially, almost totally dependent on increases in agricultural productivity. In sum, rural industrialization can progress only gradually and must be closely integrated with the over-all planning of the localities.

Figure 2 illustrates the flow chart for a county or a locality which is well endowed with natural resources including coal, iron ore and limestone. In such a locality the industrial activities can be divided into five different components. The first is the heavy small-scale industry which includes what the Chinese often term "five small industries". These supply energy, cement, chemical fertilizer, iron and steel and machinery, which directly or indirectly provide agriculture with the inputs necessary to raise productivity. These plants are usually run by the county.

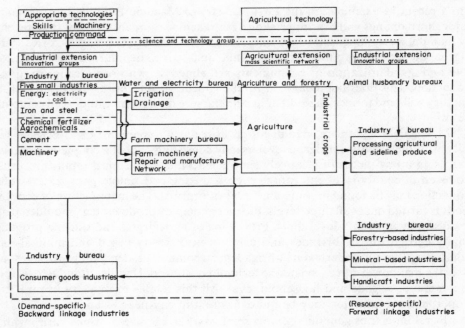

Figure 2

The second component is various resource-specific industries which may provide raw materials such as coal, iron ore, limestone and other minerals to the "five small industries" or to larger national enterprises. It is evident that the resource base—location, size and quality—decides to what extent small-scale heavy industries can be set up. Economies of scale and the development of the transportation system are other important factors.

The third and fourth components of industrial activity in a county both belong to light industry. The main responsibility of this sector is to process agricultural and sideline produce and to provide the locality with some of the needed consumer goods.

This may include flour-milling, oil-pressing, cotton-ginning, etc., as well as manufacture of textiles and shoes, household goods of porcelain and metal, canned fruit, and so on. Light industrial enterprises are found at county, commune and brigade levels.

The fifth component, the farm machinery repair and manufacture network, produces simple farm implements, tools, and also heavier equipment. The repair and maintenance of farm implements and machinery in order to sustain a high rate of machinery utilization is of primary importance. The repair and manufacture network has as a rule a three-tier structure, with each brigade and each commune within a county maintaining its own unit. Naturally, the smallest units are run by the brigades, medium-sized ones by the communes and the relatively large units by the county. The goal is to develop a clear division of labour among units at different levels: the brigade units should engage in simple repairs and manufacturing; the commune units should be able to carry out more complex repairs, and also manufacture heavier equipment; the county stations should be able to carry out the repairs of any complex farm machinery being used within the county, and also manufacture heavy equipment to be used in agriculture or in the units of the repair and manufacture network.

In a recent re-examination the First Ministry of Machine Building has recognized major shortcomings and has undertaken a far-reaching reorganization of farm machinery manufacturing. Specialized or general factories will be set up and factories will be re-grouped according to their product, while quality is to be improved. Economies of scale and standardization of components are aimed at, with some concentration of production. This does not mean that rural engineering enterprises will disappear, but that they will tend to specialize either in manufacture or in repair rather than combining the two.

Mechanical inputs are manufactured in country-, commune- and brigade-level units, with the activity at brigade level usually consisting only of a couple of metalworkers using a few pieces of relatively simple machinery. Chemical inputs are usually produced in county-level enterprises even if mixing and simple phosphate fertilizer production may be found in commune-level enterprises. The manufacture of consumer goods is carried out at all three levels, but more complex products, e.g., moulded plastic sandals, only in county-level units. Processing of agricultural and sideline produce is mainly carried out by brigades and communes. Forestry-based and mineral-based industry is generally undertaken by brigades and communes, depending on the resource base, the manpower situation and the technology utilized. Handicraft industry is found at commune, brigade and household level. All this relates to industry in rural areas proper, and the situation may be quite different in city-near locations.

Rural industries generally serve a small market, the size of which varies with the level—brigade, commune, county or region—where the enterprise is found. Through choice of enterprise size and manufacturing technology it has been possible in many industrial sectors to transfer industry into rural areas and manufacture economically to meet a local demand, if all externalities are considered. Further, size of enterprise and technology is closely related to the control-initiative level, and many localities—communes and counties—are already being drawn into subcontracting and manufacturing export items, thus also meeting an external demand. This is particularly true for rural industry in city-near locations.

It appears that the Chinese planners are now guided by a conviction that most of the facilities for economic and social activities in rural areas can be provided most effectively and economically when they are clustered in space so as to take advantage of interdependence in their functions and use.

To fully understand the financial implications of an integrated approach to agricultural development and rural industrialization it may be advantageous once more to look at the diagram (Figure 2), which shows the commodity flow between industrial components and agriculture. The figure also shows which economic units at county level control the various parts of the economic system. The county agricultural-industrial system should here be seen as one functional organization with a number of subdivisions. All the different units must not necessarily operate with a surplus. The farm machinery repair and manufacture network usually operates with little or no surplus.

The command or control of the operations of the enterprises does not lie within the single units but is vested in the *production command* of the county (left top of the figure). Under its direct control are the various economic bureaux—industry bureau, farm machinery bureau, agriculture and forestry bureau, water and electricity bureau, etc. The over-all productivity of the system depends, aside from capital accumulation, on technology improvements in agriculture and industry. So it is natural to find that both industrial and agricultural extension are under the science and technology group, which is a sub-group of the production command.

The Chinese news media have in the past few years published information on a substantial number of localities where there has existed a conflict between the development of agriculture and industry. In Tayeh County in Hupeh,[6] which may exemplify this, it was reported that efforts were made before the Cultural Revolution to change the backward features of the county's industry. However, emphasis on industry led to contention between industry and agriculture for manpower and funds with the result that agriculture was brushed aside, according to the report. In 1970 the new administration decided on a plan covering both industrial and agricultural production. It then worked out plans for the use of manpower, funds, and materials for both industrial and agricultural production and construction in order to strictly control the scope and rate of growth of the local industry within the limits permitted by agricultural production. Now the county has in the past few years spent 80 per cent of local financial expenditures for agricultural production, including investments in those local industries which serve agricultural production.

TECHNOLOGY DIFFUSION

Technology is an essential aspect of modernization knowledge in a developing country. If we now limit our discussion to the rural sector, it is obvious that there is almost everywhere need for new knowledge which must be transferred into effective demand. And it is most unlikely that technology resources will be forthcoming until the demand has been articulated through the development of a technology capability in the locality.

The justification for the locality to have its own technology capability can be summarized in the following three points. First, conditions are rapidly changing outside and inside the locality. Secondly, relevant knowledge is often not immediately available, and consequently local search (or research) must be initiated. Thirdly, there is a need to gradually train technical forces and build up a problem-solving capability for the future.

A local technology system[7] would have the following main components:

(1) *Mass scientific netword*. This is basically an extension network covering agriculture and related activities, public health and industry.

(2) *Local problem-solving capability*. Formalized groups within rural industries and other production units: (a) to articulate its demand for additional inputs; (b) to establish outward linkages into the national S & T system; (c) to extend inward linkages into the extension network serving the locality.

(3) *Local research institutes*.

The Chinese leadership has on several occasions, at least for short periods, repudiated the structural features of modernity as we know them in already industrialized countries. The Chinese seem to reason that complex mechanization and automation place increasingly rigid technical constraints on the contribution that purely practical knowledge can make to further the modernization of the country. And the Chinese leadership views mass participation as a method of incorporating distinctively native elements into the creation of a modern state.

China has used ideological education to make strong and consistent efforts to redistribute opportunities of generating technological and cultural change. This redistribution leads to a downplaying of the role of professional élites and foreign technology, and may be particularly relevant within the traditional and rural sectors. The integration of innovation and production on one hand, and of technology and labour on the other, presents an obvious contrast to the development process in modern industrial societies. Modern technological activity outside China is based upon formal scientific training, highly specialized, and carried out in specific institutions which are almost exclusively geared to technological innovaton. The Chinese approach may be highly successful as sectorial technological policy—particularly in sectors where development is relatively less science-based. But China has on two occasions tried to implement this different approach as a global technological policy—and has apparently failed.

What makes the rural sector such a challenging problem in terms of technology in developing countries is the fact that the need for new knowledge must be changed into an effective demand. This can be done in a number of ways. One is the raising of the educational level through expanded primary education, adult education, literacy campaigns, building of local technology institutions, etc., which is a slow and tedious process. In China this has at times been strongly supported by political campaigns such as those of the Great Leap Forward and the Cultural Revolution. The notion of the earlier campaign was that the peasants could master any industrial technology and that their demand for technology resources should be met without reservation from the modern sector.

No doubt, the demand exercized from the rural sector in 1958–60 was effective: some would say too effective. There are still many conflicting interpretations of the mistakes made during the Great Leap Forward. However, in terms of technology, it is true to state that the technology demand was not an articulated one. The same may partly be true during a short period of the Cultural Revolution. Economic feasibility was sometimes neglected, technical feasibility sometimes, and, on occasions, both.

A primary requirement for (rural) development in the localities is compatibility between technology and delivery system on the one hand, and potential demand on the other. This leads to the following two, secondary, requirements: first, the locality must have an efficient system for introduction/delivery of technology; secondly, there must be a good match between the costs of goods and services on one hand, and the purchasing power of the locality on the other.

Rural development and rural industrialization has required technology of two different kinds. In the early stages transfer of technology was needed to initiate any development. It is now in a consolidation stage where it is necessary to develop a local technical capacity, i.e., problem-solving capability.

Technology utilized in rural areas can be transferred in three different ways. First, part of it comes capital-embodied, i.e., incorporated in equipment and intermediate goods. This approach has been important for all of the more complex small-scale process industries in rural areas. Second, another part is human-embodied, i.e., incorporated as knowledge and experience of human resources. This approach has been very important in the initial stage of rural industrialization. Finally, another part is disembodied technology, such as handbooks, product and process specifications, etc. The latter approach is becoming increasingly important as the localities have built up a capability to demand and utilize this kind of knowledge.

However, due to unfamiliarity with industrial technology and lack of ability to interpret printed technical descriptions, it has been necessary to rely extensively on personal contacts to transmit technical knowledge. Industrial knowledge may be carried by two categories of persons. Technicians, engineers and managers from more advanced plants travel to the sites of small rural plants to assist in all stages from planning to production and distribution. At the same time people from the localities are sent for shorter or longer training periods to advanced industrial units and are given posts of responsibility for technical or managerial matters when they return. Further, people are transferred more or less permanently to work in rural areas. This formation of production and organizational skills in rural areas may be schematized as follows:

(1) *Training of personnel*
    (a) City-based, old factories train workers recruited to rural factories.
    (b) Rural factories undertake training of new workers.
(2) *Transfer of personnel*
    (a) Technical personnel are transferred from old to new factories.
    (b) Newly graduated students are allocated to new, rural factories.

A heavy reliance on person-to-person contacts in solving industrial problems indicates that the Chinese have found this to be the most effective method of technology transfer and that the problem-solving activities cannot be successfully carried out without personal contacts in the field involving responsibilities for both parties involved. Technology transfer can be initiated within the enterprise or within the local administration with responsibility for the enterprise in question. Both ways are common.

Rural industry provides a further downward transfer of technology. Agricultural workers from teams and brigades are trained in local industries, e.g., to repair pumps, electric motors and other necessary equipment for the irrigation networks. In addition, other people are trained to repair farm tools and farm machinery, and in the technique involved in the use of fertilizer. Further, most of the rural industries send repair and construction teams to assist in relevant tasks within the agricultural units. Thus, the rural industrial system serves as an important training ground for local technicians. This method of technology transfer is illustrated in the following schema, showing the activities used to build up repair and maintenance skills in a region in Honan Province.

(1) *Formal factory training*

Short-term courses are arranged in commune-level enterprises during slack farming seasons.

Principles, structure, operation and maintenance of machines are being taught.

(2) *Informal factory training*

Production teams send on their own initiative members to factories for "learning by doing".

(3) *Delivery training*

Commune-level enterprises send technicians to buying units at the time of delivery.

(4) *Mobile repair and maintenance teams training*

People are trained on the spot at the time when repair or maintenance is required.

(5) *Factory repair training*

Team members accompany machinery to the repair unit.

Source. Anyang Region Industrial Bureau (Honan), July 1973.

A number of other policies which appear now to be being systematically implemented in order to change the skill composition in rural areas should be noted. The approach suggests a strategy for future industrial growth and urbanization around the present centres of rural small scale industries.

The resettlement of educated youth which up to 1977 may have affected almost 14 million middle school graduates in the urban areas may originally have been conceived in ideological terms—to help bridge the gap between cities and countryside. At the same time there can be no doubt that one of the objectives was to deal with the lack of employment opportunities for the full increments to the labour force in the cities.

Paradoxically, the problem of finding employment for young people in the cities may not have been eased by the rapid expansion of urban collective manufacturing enterprises because these largely employ former housewives and retired industrial workers—they are now stated to employ about 6 million. The relatively low retirement age (55 for women, 60 for men) provides a large pool of active workers for this kind of enterprise. A further consequence—and an important consideration—is that the ratio between dependents and those economically active in Chinese cities is today lower than it would otherwise have been.

Even if this policy is undergoing changes in order to lessen the tensions sometimes reported between villagers and educated youth and to lessen the dissatisfaction and frustration experienced by some of the resettled youngsters, there is no indication that the resettlement programme will be discontinued. There appears to exist two major reasons, aside from the ideological objective of reducing urban-rural differences and changing the attitudes of urbanites, for resettling a considerable portion of the urban educated youth in rural areas. First, given the level and rate of economic development in urban-based activities the planners will apparently be facing great difficulties providing employment to the full increments to the labour force accruing to the cities. Second, the resettled youngsters are increasingly seen as an asset for local development which is obvious from a number of comments from Chinese news media in 1976.

And here we may venture to suggest that the various aspects of rural modernization

tion already discussed, together with the infusion of large numbers of trained manpower may provide the basis for a different pattern of rural development. The infusion of modernizing manpower in rural areas in China is made up of five more or less permanently settled groups:

First, around 14 million school-leavers have been transferred from the cities to the countryside for more or less permanent settlement.[8]

Second, the build-up of small scale industries at brigade, commune and county level has meant that approximately 18 million rural people have been trained in industrial production skills. They are now manning rural industries which are increasing in size and technological sophistication and thus providing a strong support for the development of market towns and other small urban centres.

Third, the agricultural extension system is based on the training and participation of locally recruited people who form what in the Chinese press is called "a mass scientific netword"—which in 1976 numbered approximately 13 million people.

Fourth, the demobilization of young men and women on completion of their 3–4 year service in the armed forces means that the rural areas, where they are encouraged to settle, receive an annual infusion of perhaps a million people trained in technical and organizational skills relevant to the modernization of the rural economy. (If the armed forces number about 4 million, the great majority serving four-year periods, the annual demobilization would be about a million.)

Fifth, the rural public health system has 1.5 million bare-foot doctors, 3.9 million other (local) medical personnel in addition to the large numbers of urban professionals like doctors and administrators who serve for short periods in the Chinese countryside, in rotation.[9]

CONSOLIDATION OF THE COLLECTIVE ECONOMY

Rural industries also play an important role in the realm of political economy since they are considered to be one of the tools for raising the level of collectivization in rural areas—that is, in agriculture. According to a *Red Flag* article, 90 per cent of cereals and industrial crops are produced within the collective economy.[10] Similarly, fixed assets such as machinery for soil preparation and irrigation, tractors and draft animals are mainly owned by the collectives. (The situation in industry is quite different with 14 per cent of the gross output value generated in the collective sector of the economy with only 3 per cent of the fixed assets.)

A number of observers have in recent years pointed out the problem of increasing regional differences reflecting the fact that production units can retain the bulk of the increments in income from increased productivity in agriculture. As wealthier units invest more they can obviously become wealthier. This would suggest a general pattern of increasing inequality in the Chinese countryside, since the central government does not use its power of taxation to distribute income from wealthier to poorer rural regions.

The issue of increasing commune/brigade team differences, which are an inevitable aspect of development, tends to become more difficult to handle when the rate of economic growth in agriculture is slow. In the years immediately after the creation of the communes it was evident that the leadership did not expect the commune/brigade/team inter-differences to pose any serious problems, because it was expected that the growth rate of agriculture would be 10 per cent or more, and with a high growth rate prosperous units are more likely to be willing to share their surplus for the benefit of backward units.

The approach in developing the backward units includes a number of elements of which the following ones are the more important ones.[11] First, priority is given to backward brigades in distributing machinery and equipment the state allocates for agriculture. Second, the benefits of backward brigades are first taken into consideration whenever the county and communes plan to build large and medium-sized farmland water conservation and capital construction projects. Third, for joint projects more money is to come from the county and commune while more manpower is to be provided by the backward brigades. Fourth, for sideline occupations which the county- and commune-run enterprises with backward brigades—within the latter's capability, capital is to be provided by the county or communes and manpower by backward brigades, with equal division of profits. Fifth, whenever possible, some funds are to be set aside from the reserves of commune-run enterprises to assist backward brigades.

The capital accumulation and income generation associated with mechanization of agriculture and rural industrialization is very important as it takes place at brigade and commune level. It promotes the development of a higher degree of collectivization which counteracts any tendency which might appear to develop a capitalist agriculture based on the smallest collective units—the production teams. Thus, the decentralization of economic control which China has previously experienced is today coupled with a centralization of economic activities at the the lower levels—which is illustrated in Figure 3.

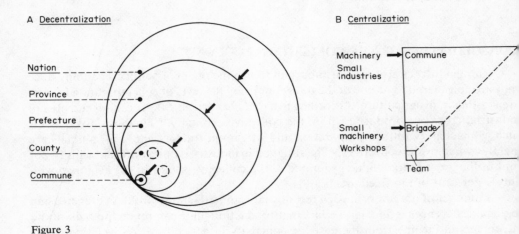

Figure 3

CONCLUSIONS

The encouragement of small-scale industries in rural areas in China is today a essential element of regional development programmes which focus on agricultura development and diversification, local raw material utilization, resource mobilizatio and long-term employment impact.

However, rural industry in China is not a homogeneous concept, as it is the consequence of two different strategy approaches. First, it is the logical outcome of *sector strategy* involving technology choices in a number of industrial sectors, most of which were initiated during the Great Leap Forward. This has required the *scaling down* of modern large-scale technology through a product and/or quality choice combined with design changes in the manufacturing process.[12] In any analysis comparing China with other countries it is important to keep in view the differences in the pattern of rural industrialization following from the differences in the economic and political systems. A case in point is the set of industries discussed earlier and usually referred to as the "five small industries". Given the system in China, it is possible to pool at various levels of aggregation requirements for specific goods and directly translate the same into demand for output of specific suppliers, i.e. the local industry. Such aggregation and direction of demand may be much more difficult or even impossible in other countries. However, in the case of certain types of industries and scales of operations, this factor may be much less of a constraint. Second, rural industry is part of an *integrated rural development* strategy where a number of activities are integrated within or closely related to the commune system. They are then often rooted in the traditional sector of the economy and have often been preceded by a long tradition of village crafts. Such industries are often based on the *scaling up* of village crafts. The scaling up of cottage industries in China is not based on improvement of technology alone, but the cottage industries have been converted into modern small-scale industries through cooperativization, electrification and access to low-cost simple machinery. The assumption for both categories is that, in the main, they should be using local resources and be meeting a local demand for producer goods and industrial services.

Industrialization in rural areas proper appears to have been successful only when the local character has been stressed. In other words, those activities, which have high coefficients for backward linkages to agriculture and for forward linkages to final users in the localities have been successful. A distinct difference between rural industrialization in the late fifties and since the Cultural Revolution is that the latter approach appears to have much higher coefficients for forward and backward linkages in the locality.

It seems that the greatest merit of small enterprises as experienced in China lies not in the superiority of their capital–labour or capital–output ratios, but, in the over-all savings in resources they make possible.[13]

The diseconomies of small-scale production are such for certain process industries that local enterprises can only operate under very favourable conditions, or for limited periods until economic development removes constraints such as transportation bottlenecks, foreign exchange limitations, etc.

Rural industry is also part of a communication network where an important task is to spread innovations as quickly as possible within a local technology system. New things and ideas often look complicated to an outsider and therefore people have to be able to ask questions, test things and try ideas, and to get a feeling for them in order fully to understand and accept them. A tightly meshed network is then a consequence of the fact that the links of personal communications are heavily restricted by distance for most individuals. And it is a fact that personal communication between pairs of individuals and direct observation are still the basic instruments for the diffusion of innovations.

Further, small-scale industries serve as an important training ground for peasants who are learning manufacturing skills and adapting to an industrial environment and thus to conditions found in larger enterprises. This training is part of a general process of breaking down the barriers to a transition from a traditional to a modern economy. Consequently, rural industrialization has positive implications for the social development of the country. This is one of the major reasons why the leadership has attempted to make rural industries reach almost every corner of the country, and thus contribute to the local formation of technical and organization skills.

Even if rural industrialization has a limited impact on the employment pattern, in relative terms, it must not be forgotten that the sector engages approximately 3 per cent of the total number of people of working age. At least another 6 per cent belong to the new skill groups in rural areas. Consequently almost 10 per cent of the working age population are in rural areas, actively engaged in activities which are likely to have a strong impact not only on productivity but also on the mental outlook in rural areas.

However, China's rural industrialization programmes have in the past undergone sharp oscillations between acceptance and rejection of major portions of a development strategy. These oscillations reflect a political struggle and changing internal and external conditions. The struggle involves contention over the most fundamental questions of social-economic goals and it affects every aspect of economic policy.

It has taken time to develop the necessary institutions and attitudes towards a development strategy which emphasizes the use of large numbers of small-scale industries in rural areas. In the meantime, a slower pace of industrial development has sometimes been accepted so that social and political objectives can be furthered first.

The encouragement of efficient and productive small-scale industries in rural as well as in urban areas has never been presented as an alternative to the development of medium- and large-scale enterprises, but they have always been seen as complementary elements in the industrialization processes. The experience of already developed countries suggests that a balanced industrial structure requires a considerable scale span of enterprises. The provision of a strong and viable development basis in China for small-scale industries is then likely to have significant long-term economic as well as social advantages.

NOTES

1 It should be noted that the Indian government in the early 1960s launched a massive programme of rural industrialization. The aim of the programme was to transform the existing lop-sided agricultural economy into a balanced "agro-industrial" economy. And it was also stressed that rural industrialization was to be based primarily on local resources and local needs. See, e.g., P. M. Mathai, Rural industrialization and the maximization of employment opportunities in India, *Small Industry Bulletin for Asia and the Far East*, No. 9, 1972. The Indian programme has had only a very limited impact, however.

2 The discussion is partly based on Rural industrialization in Mexico: a case study, prepared for the UN Expert Group Meeting on Rural Industrialization in Bucharest, 24–28 September 1973, Document ESA/SD/AC.5/9, 27 February 1973.

3 New China News Agency, May 28, 1977, as reported in BBC Summary of World Broadcasts, The Far East, Weekly Economic Report, BBC FE/W932/A/2.

4 BBC Summary of World Broadcasts, The Far East, Weekly Economic Report, FE/W893, Peking Radio, August 26, 1976; and Hsinhua News Agency, London, Special Issue, October 10, p. 34.

5 The industrial employment in rural areas is seasonally adjusted and may vary considerably to accommodate the changes in demand for agricultural manpower and some enterprises may even be closed during the busy harvest seasons. This is particularly true for many of the commune- and brigade-level enter-

prises which are generally much less capital intensive than the larger and more complex county-level enterprises.

6 New China News Agency, as reported in BBC Summary of World Broadcasts, The Far East, *Weekly Economic Report*, FE/W713, 28 February 1973.

7 It was reported in 1974 that over 10 million people took part in scientific experiments in rural areas, which approximately corresponds to 1.25 per cent of the country's population. And there are also experimental stations and groups in most rural people's communes and production brigades. (China develops science and technology independently and self-reliantly, *Peking Review*, No. 46 (1974) p. 14.) For a fuller discussion of local technology systems in China, see Jon Sigurdson, China's autonomous development of technology and science, Seminar Paper, OECD Seminar on Science, Technology and Development in a Changing World, Paris, April 1975.

8 There is another interesting consequence to be observed that the ratio between urban and rural population is likely to change in a direction which is contrary to what is happening in other developing countries. The resettlement of 14 million young people in rural areas together with a lower rate of population growth in cities than in rural areas no doubt leads to a situation where a decreasing share of the Chinese population lives in urban areas—even if the absolute figure is not decreasing. Another development which cannot yet be clearly seen is the increasing importance of smaller cities and towns as regional development and local industrialization progresses.

9 BBC FE/W920.

10 Chang Chun-chiao: On Exercising All-Round Dictatorship over the Bourgeoisie, *Red Flag*, April 1975 (Translated in *Survey of People's Republic of China Press*, CMP-SPRCP-75-16).

11 As presented in Do a Good Job in Transforming Brigades that lag Behind, by Hsiyang County CCP Committee, *Red Flag*, 1975, No. 10 (translated in *Selections from People's Republic of China Magazines*, CMP-SPRCM-75-32).

12 The best-known examples are small-scale production of nitrogen chemical fertilizer, cement and iron, all of which are discussed at length in Jon Sigurdson, ibid. For a theoretical discussion of the issues involved, see Shigeru Ishikawa. A note on the choice of technology in China, *The Journal Of Development Studies*, Vol. 9, No. 1, 1972, pp. 161–86.

13 Watanabe argues that "small enterprises seem to contribute most to the economic development of countries with surplus labour and shortage of capital (which applies to China at her present stage of development) under the following conditions:
(1) where they can be set up without heavy overhead capital expenditure on buildings, land and infrastructure;
(2) where the diseconomies of small enterprises are compensated by the use of idle capital, labour and raw materials;
(3) where division of labour between enterprises in different size groups, e.g., in the form of subcontracting, enhances the over-all efficiency of the industry." Susum Watanabe, Reflections on current policies for promoting small enterprises and subcontracting, *International Labour Review*, Vol. 110, No. 5, November 1974.

REFERENCES

Larsen, Kjeld, China's regional industry [Danish], Institute of Development Research, Copenhagen (forthcoming).

Mathai, P. M., Rural industrialization in India: a case study, prepared for the Expert Group Meeting on Rural Industrialization, Bucharest, 24–28 September 1973.

Neilson, Alexander and the UN Secretariat, Rural industrialization in developing countries, prepared for the Expert Group meeting on Rural Industrialization, Bucharest, 24–28 September 1973.

Perkins, Dwight (Ed.), Rural Small Scale Industry in the People's Republic of China. Stanford University Press, 1977.

Report of the Expert Group Meeting on Rural Industrialization, Bucharest, 24–28 September 1973, *Rural Industrialization*, Department of Economic and Social Affairs, New York; United Nations, 1974.

Riskin, Carl, Intermediate Technology in China's Rural Industries Paper presented at a Conference on Economic Choice of Technologies for Developing Countries, Organized by the International Economic Association in Teheran, September 18–23, 1976.

Sigurdson, Jon, Rural Industrialization and skill formation in Rural Areas—A Comparison of Development Planning in India and China. *World Development* special issue on Chinese Rural Institutions. Vol. 6, No. 5 (May 1978), pp. 667–80.

Sigurdson, Jon, *Rural Industrialization in China,* Cambridge: Harvard University Press, 1977.

Riskin, Carl, *Local Industry and the Choice of Techniques in the Planning of Industrial Development in Mainland China: Planning for Advanced Skills and Technologies*, UNIDO Industrial Planning and Programming Series No. 3, New York: United Nations, 1969, pp. 171–80.

—, Small industry and the Chinese model of development, *The China Quarterly*, No. 46, 1971, pp. 245–73.

Wong, Y. Lang, Establishment of industrial estates in a rural setting, In *Industrial Estates in Asia and the Far East*, New York: United Nations, 1962.

Health Care Services as Part of China's Revolution and Development

VICTOR W. SIDEL and RUTH SIDEL

The leaders of many technologically-poor countries feel that because of their limited resources a choice must be made between the expansion of industrial production and the improvement of health services. Even in countries in which the leaders' goals include just and equitable distribution of resources and priority for improvement in quality of life for those who now have least, the choice is often difficult. It is possible—even probable—that technological improvements can, by improving the quality of life of the population, lead to improvements in health status greater than those produced by medical care services. Conversely, maximizing production requires healthy workers, and it is possible—even probable—that investment in certain types of health services can be useful in increasing productivity. Furthermore, medical care services (in contrast to health services), even if they do not materially improve productivity or health status, are increasingly demanded by people as themselves an important component of quality of life.

Which to do first—industrialize or improve health services—or, more practically, since both must be done, how to allocate the scarce resources between them, is a pressing and difficult question in poor countries. Because of the methods used by China and the results, her choices and her allocation of resources are of widespread interest in both technologically-developed and less-developed countries. In brief, China has chosen to do both, but has husbanded her resources—and almost certainly improved her results—by limiting her health care investment in "high-level" technology (such as speciality hospitals or highly-trained doctors) and insisting instead in services carried out by the people themselves through what is now being called "intermediate" or "appropriate" technology.

China's choices of methods and her allocation of priority are of interest too because she has, in twenty-five short years, made startling progress in improving the health of her people. While comparisons with other societies are hard to make because of differing disease patterns and different social, economic, cultural, and historical circumstances, a case can be made for China's having made more rapid progress in health than any other society in a comparable period of time. China has moved from a society which was riddled with almost every known form of nutritional and infectious disease, with sickness and death visible in the streets, to a society whose people appear to every observer to he healthy, well-nourished and vigorous. It is a society in which there is not only no visible evidence of gross ill-health but even no evidence of the drug abuse, alcoholism, or ambulatory psychosis that one sees on the streets of large cities of other countries.[1]

155

Although statistics are still hard to obtain, there is good evidence that over the past twenty years China has eliminated smallpox, cholera, and plague, essentially eliminated venereal disease and drug addiction, and effected a major reduction in the prevalence of parasitic illness like schistosomiasis. In Shanghai and Peking, which are certainly atypical but whose health indices are now becoming available, current infant mortality rates are reported to be lower than those of New York City (Table 1) and indeed lower than those of most of the world's cities. The leading causes of death in Shanghai are now cancer, stroke and heart disease (Table 2), an ironic testimonial to the improvement of health in a city in which twenty years ago the leading causes of death were said to be complications of malnutrition and infectious disease. Health statistics from China's rural areas are more difficult to obtain but those which have been made available show remarkable improvement; for example, Jutung County of Kiangsu Province has shown a fall in infant mortality rate from over 200 per thousand live births before 1949 to 33.9 per thousand in 1973. This figure compares favourably with those of rural areas in countries far wealthier than China.[2]

TABLE 1. *Infant mortality rates in Shanghai and Peking*
(Deaths in the first year of life per thousand live births)

Year	Shanghai City proper	Peking City proper
1948	150.0	
1949		117.6
1959	38.9	
1972	8.7	
1973		11.6
1976		10.4

TABLE 2. *Causes of Death in Shanghai City proper and in New York City*

	Shanghai*	New York City† White	New York City† Non-white
Cancer	25	23	18
Stroke	19	7	8
Heart disease	12	45	28
All others	44	25	46
Total	100	100	100

*Data for January through June 1972.
†Data for 1970.

The change in health status reflected by the observations of visitors and the limited statistics are all the more remarkable when one considers the size of China's population. Not only is it by far the world's largest—only that of India even approaches it— but the population is distributed very unevenly. The population is shifted very much toward the East, with very dense concentrations in the basins of the three great river systems of eastern China. Much of the mountain and desert regions of western China are almost uninhabited. The four least densely-populated provinces—Inner Mongolia, Sinkiang,

Tsinghai, and Tibet—include just over half of the area of the country but less than 4 per cent of the population. Both the resulting sparseness and denseness of the population lead to problems in health care delivery. Even more important from the point of view of health care, some 80 per cent of China's people live in its countryside; four out of every five people are required to grow food, from a very limited amount of cultivatable land, using labour-intensive methods.

Finally, China remains a poor society. The concept of "gross national product *per capita*" of course has limitations in the description of a country's wealth or even of the income of its people but is one of the few measures available. China's GNP in 1975 has been estimated at about $350 *per capita*. An understanding of how this relatively poor country, with its enormous, unevenly distributed population, has organized its health care system and indeed its entire society in order to arrive at its current health picture may in our view provide some valuable insights into the whole of China's developmental experience over the last two decades, and may provide some lessons for other countries in comparable stages of development.

HEALTH SERVICES IN PRE-LIBERATION CHINA

The characterization of China in the first half of this century as the "Sick Man of Asia" was largely used metaphorically. It referred to China's technological backwardness, its inability to feed its people or provide them with other necessities of life, and its defencelessness in the face of economic and military onslaughts from the technologically-developed nations. In a literal sense, too, China's sickness was very deep and very extensive indeed. The country was plagued with almost every known form of nutritional and infectious disease. Although accurate data on incidence and prevalence are unavailable, the list of diseases caused by China's bacterial invaders included cholera, leprosy, meningococcal meningitis, plague, typhoid fever and typhus. Viral illnesses included Japanese B encephalitis, smallpox, and trachoma. Diseases due to parasitic onslaught included ancylostomiasis (hookworm disease), clonorchiasis, filariasis, kala-azar, malaria, paragonimiasis, and schistosomiasis. Venereal disease was widespread. Nutritional illness included most known forms of total calorie, protein, and specific vitamin deficiencies, including beriberi, osteomalacia, pellagra, and scurvy; "malnutrition" was often a euphemism for gross starvation.

Not only are reliable data on morbidity rates unavailable, which is not surprising, but the few available data on mortality rates are also grossly unreliable. One estimate of the crude death rate in China, made in 1943, was 25 deaths per thousand annually, more than double the crude death rate of the technologically-developed countries at that time. The infant mortality rate, as we have already noted, was estimated to be as high as 200 deaths in the first year of life per thousand live births; in other words, in most of China one baby in five died during its first year of life.

One of the roots of the sickness, of course, was the poverty in which the vast bulk of China's people lived. Under such circumstances of poverty, medical care might have made relatively little difference in health conditions even if medical resources had been adequate. But compounding these overwhelming needs was the gross inadequacy and unavailability of modern health workers and medical facilities prior to 1949.

China did have a large number of practitioners of traditional Chinese medicine (which in China is called *zhongyi*, "Chinese medicine") whose progenitors were practising herb medicine centuries before the beginning of the Christian era. The practitioners varied greatly in their training and skills, and the absence of any well-defined national qualifications for them prior to 1949 makes it very difficult to estimate their number precisely. When qualifications for doctors of Chinese medicine were formally defined by the government in 1955 and a survey was made, the total number for the entire nation was given as 486,700. It is therefore not unreasonable to estimate the number of traditional doctors in 1949 at about 500,000 or about one for every 1,100 of the estimated 540 million population at that time.

Although the definition of a doctor of modern or scientific medicine (which in China is called *xiyi*. "Western medicine") is considerably simpler, estimates of their number in 1949 are almost as varied as those of traditional doctors. A reasonable guess is about 20,000 or about one doctor for every 27,000 of China's people. Technologically developed countries at that time had one doctor for every 1,000 to 2,000 people.

Hospital facilities with Western-style equipment were similarly limited. The range of estimates of the number of hospital beds in 1949 is wide; one relatively high guess, provided by a group of Chinese physicians visiting Canada in 1971, was 90,000, or one bed for every 6,000 people. Rich countries had one bed for every 200 to 500 people.

Even worse, as in most countries, but especially so for China, the minimal resources for Western medicine, both doctors and hospitals, were concentrated in the cities. In short, the only medical care available to the vast bulk of China's population in the rural areas, and vast majority of the poor urban population, was that provided by traditional practitioners and herbalists, many of them inadequately trained even in traditional Chinese medicine. Preventive medicine was almost non-existent, and the cycle of poverty, disease, and disability seemed to many to be endless and immutable.

FROM LIBERATION TO CULTURAL REVOLUTION

It therefore comes as no surprise that a revolutionary like Mao Tse-tung, from both principle and pragmatism, should as early as the 1930s have placed health care high on the priority list of the Chinese Communist Party and People's Liberation Army. As each village was wrested from the control of the Kuomintang or the Japanese, the first objectives of the liberating forces included land reform, mobilization of the peasants, and health care. The pattern was seen in Kiangsi in the early 1930s, during the Long March, and in Yenan during the late 1930s and early 1940s.

With the success of the revolution and assumption of state power by the Chinese Communist Party in 1949, health care retained its high priority and visibility. A combination of directives from Chairman Mao and principles adopted at a National Health Congress in Peking in the early 1950s resulted in a set of precepts which to this day form the widely-quoted ideological basis for the development of health services in China:

1. Medicine must serve the working people in the Chinese idiom, *gong-nong-bing*, "workers, peasants, and soldiers".

2. Preventive medicine must be given first priority.

3. Practitioners of Chinese medicine must be "united" with practitioners of Western medicine.

4. Health work must be integrated with mass movements.

Implementation of these principles in the 1950s and early 1960s in part followed patterns now "classical" for many developing countries. The development was in large measure influenced, and in part diverted, by the rapid influx of consultants, technology, and methods of organization from the Soviet Union. Medical education was largely remoulded into the Soviet system of separate "faculties" for adult medicine, pediatrics, public health, stomatology, and pharmaceutics, with students differentiated early into the separate streams. Urban polyclinics followed Soviet organizational models, with separate departments, for example, of medicine, surgery, and obstetrics-gynecology. Also adopted was the Soviet system of incentive rewards, including membership in a prestigious Academy of Medical Sciences and considerably higher pay for professors and chiefs. Even preventive medicine, in a society with vastly different disease problems and different cultural and societal characteristics, followed the Soviet organizational model of the "sanepid" (sanitation-epidemiology) stations, separated organizationally, conceptually, and attitudinally from the medical care components of the system.

Categories of medical personnel ranged from "assistant doctors" (following a long-existing model, called a *feldsher*, in the USSR) and nurses trained for three years in "middle" or "secondary" medical schools to highly-specialized physicians trained at the site of the Peking Union Medical College. Health care personnel were trained at an astonishing rate. Although data on the total number vary, some official figures were issued for the years 1949 to 1958: in 1957 one Western visitor was given the estimate of 70,000 doctors. Since then, data have been less easily available. Leo Orleans, an American analyst, has estimated that by the end of 1966 there were about 150,000 doctors of Western medicine in China—an increase of over 100,000 doctors in less than twenty years.[3] If we take Orleans' figure and assume a 1966 population of 725 million, the ratio of 1:5,000 would still be grossly inadequate judged by Western standards of medical care needs. Furthermore, although efforts were being made to shift this new manpower into the countryside, these doctors were still concentrated in the cities.

TABLE 3. *Estimated number of medical personnel in the People's Republic of China, 1966*

		Ratios*	
Type of personnel	Number	Health workers: 100,000 population	Population: health worker
Graduates of schools of "Western" medicine			
"Higher-level" schools			
Doctors	150,000	21	4,800
Stomatologists	30,000	4	24,000
Pharmacists	20,000	3	36,000
"Middle-level" schools			
Assistant doctors	170,000	23	4,300
Nurses	185,000	26	3,900
Midwives	40,000	6	18,000
Dispensers	100,000	14	7,300
Practitioners of "Chinese medicine"	500,000	69	1,500

*Based on an estimated population of 725 million.

Large numbers of assistant doctors, nurses, midwives, pharmacists, and radiology and laboratory technicians were trained in China's secondary medical schools, Orleans estimates that by the end of 1966 there were in China approximately 172,000 assistant doctors, 186,000 nurses, 42,000 midwives, and 100,000 pharmacists.[4] In addition, forerunners of what during the Cultural Revolution were to become known as "barefoot doctors" were trained, in part under the impetus of the Great Leap Forward, in the late 1950s and early 1960s in the rural areas surrounding Shanghai.

Over-all, then, Table 3 would appear to present a reasonably informed estimate, based on limited Chinese sources as interpreted by Western observers, of medical manpower in China at the time the Cultural Revolution began in 1966. These ratios were still low compared to Western or Soviet ratios, but represented an extraordinary increase in fifteen years.

Health facilities had also been constructed with equally amazing rapidity. Another Western visitor in 1957 reported that "between 1949 and 1957, 860 new hospitals were built, averaging 350 beds".[5] This works out to one new hospital completed somewhere in China every three-and-a-half days, a total of some 300,000 beds in eight years. The Chinese physicians visiting Canada in 1971 stated that from 1949 to 1965 "the number of hospital beds was increased eightfold", implying that some 400,000 additional beds were built in the eight years from 1957 to 1965. By June 1965 a Ministry of Health official could proudly state that every county in China had at least one hospital.[6] The "classical" strategy of building "centres of excellence" still, however, determined some of the placement and equipment of hospitals and other institutions.

While technology was still grossly under-developed compared to that of European countries, Japan, or the USSR, it was expanding rapidly and from all evidence the newly-organized pharmaceutical industries far surpassed their troubled Soviet counterparts. There were reports of success in special areas of technological medicine such as the reimplantation of severed limbs and the salvage of patients with extensive burns. Basic research was limited, but appeared to be active and successful in the laboratories of the Chinese Academy of Sciences (Academia Sinica) and of the Chinese Academy of Medical Sciences. Considerable clinical research was also being done, particularly under the auspices of the Academy of Medical Sciences.

While these classical strategies of rapid manpower development and building of centres of excellence were being followed—on a scale which dwarfed similar attempts in other countries—the Chinese were also following health care development strategies which were in many ways unique to China. One technique was the effort to integrate doctors of traditional Chinese medicine with doctors of Western medicine. It was hoped in this way to make effective use of the large number of traditional practitioners, to cull useful techniques from what Mao called the "treasurehouse of Chinese medicine", and to convince those, particularly in the rural areas, who mistrusted Western medicine that it could work together in an integrated way with the medicine which they knew and trusted. These efforts indeed led to some successful integration, perhaps more than in any other country, but the marriage was apparently still a shaky one.

The other technique largely unique to China was that of organizing the great mass of people in campaigns to protect their own health. Through the Great Patriotic Health Movements, the people were mobilized against the "four pests" (at first, flies, mosquitoes, rats, and grain-eating sparrows, with the sparrows later being replaced in the list of public enemies by bed-bugs, when it was found that destruction of sparrows caused undesirable ecologic consequences). Vast immunization, sanitation, and health education campaigns were carried out. As the process was described in 1971, "old customs and habits of the people were changed", "society was remoulded", and "a new social attitude of 'regarding hygiene as an honour' took root among the mass of our people".

Over-all by the mid-1960s China seemed to have developed a socially-oriented, prevention-oriented, and reasonably well-rounded health care system that had a long way to go to meet China's needs, but that had made enormous progress in the distribution and quality of its services and in the health of the population it served. In the space of the fifteen years from 1950 to 1965, incredible changes were accomplished in the delivery of health services to, and in the health of, 600 million people—changes that were apparently unprecedented in extent and rapidity in the history of the world. Cholera, plague, smallpox, and most nutritional illnesses quickly disappeared: opium addiction was eliminated, largely through community-based efforts; venereal disease took somewhat longer, but by a combinaton of social and medical techniques was reportedly almost completely wiped out in most of China by the early 1960s.

THE CULTURAL REVOLUTION

In short, it appeared to outside observers—and seems to have appeared to many Chinese leaders at the time—that the Ministry of Health had done the job assigned to it reasonably well considering the point from which it started and the paucity of its resources in relation to the job to be done. Yet in 1965 the Ministry was considered by some in China to have failed to accomplish its goals in several key areas: urban health services still received a disproportionately large share of the still limited resources and, with 80 per cent of the population living in the countryside, the disproportion was a glaring one; curative medicine was still receiving more attention in research, teaching and service than preventive medicine; traditional medicine still received relatively short shrift and was accorded low status compared to scientific medicine; in spite of efforts to the contrary, a hierarchical managerial structure had developed which was said to be relatively unresponsive to criticisms or suggestions from below; and despite recognition of the importance of speedily assuring access of medical care to everyone in the society, there was said to be increasing concern with "raising of standards" rather than with "popularization" of what was already available.

Mao singled out the Ministry of Health for criticism in a statement made on 26 June 1965. He said that "the Health Ministry renders service to only 15 per cent of the nation's population", and that it "should better be renamed the Urban Health Ministry or the 'Lords' ' Health Ministry". The final sentence of the statement—"In medical and health work, put the stress on the rural areas!"—was widely published and became known as the "June 26th Directive". In his statement Mao presented several prescriptions for action:

On Medical Education: Three years in medical school after primary school are enough; after completion of medical school the students should continue the "improvement of their skill through unceasing practice".

On Medical Research: Less men and materials should be devoted to the "peak" problems—the highly complex and hard-to-cure diseases—and more should be devoted to "the prevention and improved treatment of common diseases ... the masses' greatest needs".

On Medical Service: All doctors, except those who "are not extremely proficient", should "go to the rural villages" to practise.

During the Cultural Revolution the Chinese medical care system underwent the "struggle, criticism and transformation" which characterized every facet of Chinese life. The two central strains or "roads" of Chinese communist revolutionary thought were in conflict: the "expert" philosophy urged centralized organization and national hierarchy to achieve the desired goals; the "Red" philosophy encouraged belief in and reliance on the aroused masses. As Mao's philosophy, a belief in the primacy of the masses, gained ground over the technological, hierarchical approach, Chinese medicine reflected the change.

During the Cultural Revolution medical schools admitted no new classes; students already in school were given accelerated programmes of practical training and assigned to work in the countryside. Medical school faculty members, researchers in the institutes of the Academy of Medical Sciences, and other urban health workers spent periods in the rural areas performing manual labour and carrying out medical work such as training barefoot doctors, providing consultation and continuing education for medical workers, offering direct medical and preventive services, and mobilizing the peasants to play a major role in their own health care.

By 1970 medical schools had begun to admit new classes, resumed teaching, and initiated significant experimentation with the traditional model of medical education. The medical curriculum has been considerably shortened from the six to eight years before the Cultural Revolution. The three-year curriculum suggested by Mao now appears to be the norm, on an "experimental" basis, but a half year is added at the beginning for science and language courses.

The selection process for admission to medical school has also been drastically changed. Prior to the Cultural Revolution urban sons and daughters of professionals and cadres had a far greater chance of admission to medical school than children of other classes. The admission procedures have since been reformed to enable far more peasants and workers to enter medicine. In addition barefoot doctors and middle-medical workers have priority. Students are currently selected by their peers with whom they are working on the basis of three criteria—ideological commitment, academic ability and physical fitness. Thus the effort is being made to recruit those who will be motivated by a desire to be of service rather than those motivated primarily by self-interest.

Although there were precedents for the development of what in the West would be called "auxiliaries" prior to 1965, and even prior to 1949, the Cultural Revolution brought a rapid addition of new forms of health manpower very different from the regular doctors and the secondary medical personnel. These new types of health workers are not counted in the statistics as medical workers. They are counted as, and apparently consider themselves to be, primarily agricultural workers (barefoot doctors and health aides), production workers (worker doctors), or housewives (Red Medical Workers).

Further changes have taken place in the organization of medical care—and of all institutions in Chinese society—in the wake of the Cultural Revolution. One of the issues underlying this upheaval was said to be the development since 1949 of a managerial and intellectual élite—a counter-revolutionary trend in the view of Mao and his supporters and of the substantial group to his left. During the Cultural Revolution, the direction and leadership of every organization or "unit", and in some cases the function and even the existence of the unit, were reexamined. By the fall of 1971 the administrative leadership of all important institutions, including those dealing with health, was in the hands of "revolutionary committees".

The Cultural Revolution also led to the reduction of salary, status, and role differences among medical personnel with different levels of expertise. Efforts had already been made prior to 1965 to improve interaction among health workers but after 1965 greater efforts were made to break down the hierarchical structure that persisted in health care institutions and to provide a setting in which all the personnel can work together more effectively for the benefit of the patients.

HEALTH CARE IN THE CITIES

Health care in the urban areas has been decentralized to the lowest administrative levels capable of providing the services. By utilizing neighbourhood organizations, the place of work and indigenous paraprofessionals, health care is now within easy access of the consumer and is often provided by health workers with whom the patients live and work.

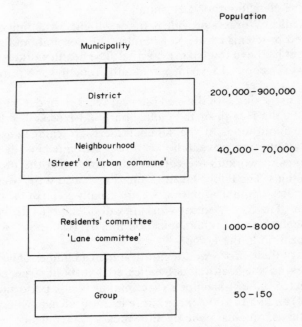

Figure 1

The city of Peking, for example, is divided into nine districts, each with a population ranging around 400,000. Among the medical services provided at the district level are hospitals, sanitation facilities and "prevention stations" for illnesses such as tuberculosis and mental illness. Within each district there are "neighbourhoods" consisting of approximately 50,000 people (see Figure 1), The West District of Peking has nine neighbourhoods, of which the Fengsheng Neighbourhood, one of the older neighbour-hoods of Peking with a population of 53,000 is one. Within the Fengsheng Neigh-hood's jurisdiction are factories, shops, primary schools, and a neighbourhood hospital.[7]

The people of Fengsheng are grouped into twenty-five residents' committees, each of which encompasses about 2,000 people. The residents' committees usually provide a health station and other social services. The health workers at the residents' committee level are local housewives called "Red Medical Workers". Three of them serve the Wu Ting Residents' Committee, located in the western part of the Fengsheng Neighbour-hood. Wu Ting houses 400 families, approximately 1,500 people. In Wu Ting the residents' committee health station is located in a single room off one of the courtyards. The major function of the health station is preventive medicine, although treatment of some minor illnesses is performed there.

The Red Medical Workers received one month of training at the Fengsheng Neighbourhood Hospital where they learned history-taking and simple physical exami-nation techniques such as blood pressure determination, the uses of a number of Western and herb medicines and techniques of acupuncture and of intramuscular and subcutaneous injection. Preventive measures, such as sanitation, immunization, and birth control techniques were an important part of the curriculum. After their original training, the health workers received continuous in-service training both at their health stations and at the Neighbourhood Hospital.

The Red Medical Workers provide care for patients with "minor illnesses", refer more complicated problems to the Neighbourhood Hospital, and provide follow-up care after a patient has been treated in a hospital. The health workers are paid a modest sum for their work, about 15 yuan per month, roughly one-third the wages of a beginning factory worker.

A large part of the duties of the Red Medical Worker, under the supervision of the Department of Public Health of the Neighbourhood Hospital, relates to sanitation work in the neighbourhood. In the summer there are campaigns against flies and mosquitoes and attempts to prevent the spread of gastrointestinal disease; in the winter and spring the health workers are concerned mainly with the prevention of upper respiratory infections. The Public Health Department also supervises the Red Medical Workers in providing immunizations, which are usually given in the residents' commit-tee health station. The Red Medical Workers will often go to the homes to bring the children to the health station for immunization and, if it is necessary for any reason, may give the immunization in the home.

The success of their efforts was demonstrated in a number of ways. An immuniza-tion chart in a Peking lane health station indicated that about 80 per cent of the children had been protected against smallpox (vaccination is not performed if there is any contraindication) and 95 to 100 per cent were immunized against tuberculosis (BCG), diphtheria, pertussis, tetanus, poliomyelitis, measles, meningococcal meningitis, and Japanese B encephalitis.

The Red Medical Workers also have as their responsibility the provision of birth control information. The Red Medical Workers make periodic visits to all of the women of the residents' committee area encouraging the use of contraception. An example of the work of the Red Medical Worker in the area of birth control was observed in a residents' committee or lane in Hangchow. Careful records are kept of the contraceptives used by each woman of childbearing age, which is defined as being from the time of marriage to menopause. We were told that pregnancy among unmarried women was exceedingly rare. Abortions are free and easily available, but are almost never requested by single women; out-of-wedlock births are essentially unheard of. This is true despite the fact that the ideal marriage age for men is now from twenty-six to twenty-nine and for women, from twenty-four to twenty-nine. Late marriage is, of course, itself a powerful method of population control. The crude birth rate for this neighbourhood is an almost unbelievably low 7 per thousand per year, but confidence in the figure is bolstered by other reports, for example, that the crude birth rate for the entire Shanghai City Proper was 6.4 per thousand for the year 1972.

In the factories of the Fengsheng Neighbourhood there are also health stations, whose size depends on the size of the factory. Health stations in moderate-size factories are presided over by "worker doctors", workers in the factory who have had one to two months of medical training and who continue to spend most of their time in factory work. Like the Red Medical Workers their tasks are largely preventive and educational, but they also care for "minor and common illnesses". In the larger factories there are large medical units run by regular doctors with the assistance of "middle medical workers" and worker doctors.

HEALTH SERVICES IN THE COUNTRYSIDE

Health services in China's rural areas are decentralized in a fashion similar to health care in the cities. The basic unit of a commune is the production team; a number of production teams form a production brigade; communes taken together form counties. One county near Shanghai, for example, has eighteen communes, with a population of 500,000.

Over-all, the ten Shanghai counties, with a population of four million, include two hundred communes divided into 2,727 production brigades and 28,710 production teams. This population is served by 7,702 barefoot doctors and 28,979 health workers. The Sing Sing Production Brigade of the Horse Bridge Commune outside of Shanghai, for example, has 1,850 people, divided into twelve production teams. The Sing Sing Brigade has four barefoot doctors and one midwife in its health station and each production team has one to three health workers.

Barefoot doctors generally have a three- to six-month training period followed by on-the-job supervision and periods of continuing education. As seems true of most job requirements in present-day China, there appears to be little emphasis on a particular type or duration of training, and even less on earning a specific credential or degree; rather it is on the skills an individual demonstrates in a particular job.

While the duties of the barefoot doctor vary from area to area, they are usually responsible for environmental sanitation, health education, immunizations and first aid. These medical workers spend approximately half of their time working as peasants and half of their time doing medical work. They are paid as peasants, receiving, as do other commune members, an equal share of the produce distribution and a share of the cash income based on the number of work points they acrrue. In 1976 there were said to be 1.5 million barefoot doctors in China, one for each 450 of the roughly 700 million people in rural China.[8]

Health aides, volunteers who work primarily on environmental sanitation during their spare time, function under the supervision of the barefoot doctors. They are members of the "mass" who have been mobilized to work in the health sector thereby involving people in their own health care and providing a learning experience for the worker. They work full-time, doing agricultural work, and are not paid for the medical work they perform.

Health problems which cannot be managed by rural paraprofessionals are referred to the commune hospital which is staffed by fully-trained medical personnel.

THE ROLE OF MASS PARTICIPATION

The basic Maoist belief in learning through doing has been a significant thread which has run through all phases of Chinese development since 1949 and particularly since the Cultural Revolution. The classic example of the use of mass organization in health has been the campaign against schistosomiasis. According to Joshua Horn, this campaign was based on the concept of the "mass line"—the conviction that ordinary people possess great strength and wisdom and that when their initiative is given full play they can accomplish miracles.[9] Before the peasants were organized to fight the snails they were thoroughly educated in the nature of schistosomiasis and were then mobilized twice a year, along with voluntary labour from the People's Liberation Army, students, teachers and office workers: they drained the rivers and ditches, buried the banks of the rivers, and smoothed down the buried dirt. Horn points out that in the anti-schistosomiasis programme the concept was not only to recruit the mass to do the work, but to mobilize their enthusiasm and initiative so that they would fight the disease. It must be noted, however, that the Chinese have not been entirely successful in the efforts to wipe out schistosomiasis and are still working on the problem.

USE OF HEALTH CARE RESOURCES

The pattern of use of health care resources in China may best be summarized through what appear to be some key underlying principles.

Distribution. A central question raised in China since 1949, but particularly emphasized since the onset of the Cultural Revolution, has been "for whom?"—in this case, "medical care for whom?" Since Liberation attempts have been made to provide basic medical care to all segments of the population, particularly that segment which received the least medical care prior to 1949, the rural areas. This effort has been greatly intensified since the Cultural Revolution. Through the use of barefoot doctors, mobile medical teams, the building of additional facilities and encouragement of urban doctors to resettle in the countryside, the imbalance between urban and rural medical care is being gradually redressed. Economic and social barriers to access to medical care—once very strong in China—have now essentially been eliminated.

Decentralization. Medical services are provided at every level of rural and urban organization utilizing professional, paraprofessional and non-professional manpower. An attempt is being made to decentralize services to the lowest level at which they can be performed. The services are thus brought closer—physically, culturally and emotionally—to the people they are meant to serve. Health problems which cannot be adequately dealt with at the lower level are referred to the next higher level by means of clear referral pathways.

Deprofessionalization. Local health care is provided, in large measure, by barefoot doctors, worker doctors, and Red Medical Workers with short periods of formal training, people trained to just the level needed to give simple medical care and health education. Great efforts have been made to demystify medicine through the recruitment of personnel with little formal education and enabling them to participate in health care.

Mass participation. "Mobilizing the mass" is a central principle in the organization of current Chinese society and of the health care system. It is felt that great transformations can be made through mass participation and it is further felt that the individual will simultaneously be educated—himself transformed through active participation in society.

Continuity with the past. Part of Mao's genius has been his ability to adapt socialist principles to China's needs and, even more important, to China's traditions. Much of what we now see in China has its roots firmly implanted in the past. This is true not only of the obvious—the continued and integrated use of traditional Chinese medicine—but in the continuation of selected traditional forms of community organization. The past is interwoven with the present but remoulded to lead to new goals. It is therefore extremely difficult to determine which of the methods of the Chinese are successfully transferable to other societies and which are so culture-bound that they are unique to China.

HEALTH CARE SERVICES AS PART OF A REVOLUTION

It should be noted in conclusion that improvements in health care services are only one part—and probably not the most important part—of the effort to change the health status of a people. Improvements in nutrition and in living conditions are, for example, almost certainly much more important than are services for therapeutic medical care.[10] Furthermore, health care services are in every country an expression of the political structure and political struggles of the society. This fact is clearly recognized in China and criticism or advocacy of specific health care policies is closely linked to criticism or advocacy of broader political, economic, and social policies and to the protection and expansion of revolutionary changes in the redistribution of wealth and power. In China, in short, health care is part of a revolution. In this China differs from most countries, technologically-developed or developing, in which health care is often one of the methods used to attempt to delay a more fundamental redistribution of the resources of the society and thus—in some ways—acts as a barrier to better health for all of its people. Whether China will be able to retain this revolutionary orientation in its health services in the face of current demands for more rapid "modernization" of technology, for more academically-structured education, and for dissolution of "revolutionary committee" management, with a return to more hierarchical structures, is far from clear. The struggle to find the appropriate balance between "red" and "expert" continues.

Summing up, through a combination of improvements in nutrition, in living conditions, in sanitation, in preventive medicine, in health education, and in medical care—built on the base of a revolution which changed the control of resources and therefore the priorities of the society—the health of the Chinese people has improved markedly over the past twenty-five years. This change has been one of the factors in the development of a vigorous, confident, productive population whose rapid further developmental progress seems assured.

NOTES

1   More complete descriptions of the changes in health status of China's people and the development of its health services may be found in Joshua S. Horn, *Away With All Pests ... An English Surgeon in People's China*, New York: Monthly Review Press, 1971; Joseph R. Quinn (ed), *Medicine and Public Health in the People's Republic of China*, Washington: US Dept of Health, Education and Welfare Publication No. (NIH) 72–67, 1972; Myron B. Wegman, Tsung-yi Lin, and Elizabeth F. Purcell (Eds), *Public Health in the People's Republic of China*, New York: Josiah Macy, Jr. Foundation, 1973; Joseph R. Quinn (Ed), *China Medicine As We Saw It*, Washington: US Dept of Health, Education and Welfare Publication No. (NIH) 75–684, 1974; and Victor W. Sidel and Ruth Sidel, *Serve the People: Observations on Medicine in the People's Republic of China*, Boston: Beacon Press, 1974.

2   Chinese Medical Association, Child health care in New China, reprinted in *The American Journal of Chinese Medicine*, Vol. 2, No. 2, 1974, pp. 149–58; China achieves initial success in planned population growth, Hsinhua News Agency, Peking (News Release No. 082302) 23 August 1974; Mu Cheng, Women's and Children's Health Work, *China Reconstructs*, Vol. 27, No. 7, July 1978, pp. 29–31; and data given the authors by the Department of Public Health, Shanghai. Comparisons with other cities are presented in Sidel and Sidel, op. cit.

3   Leo Orleans, Medical education and manpower in Communist China, In C. T. Hu (ed.), *Aspects of Chinese Education*, New York: Teachers College Press, Columbia University, 1969, pp. 27–8.

4   ibid., p. 37.

5   F. Avery Jones, A visit to China, *British Medical Journal*, Vol. 2, November 1975, pp. 1105–7.

6   Chang Tze-k'uan, The development of hospital services in China, *Chinese Medical Journal*, Vol. 84, 1965, pp. 412–16.

7   The Fengsheng Neighbourhood is described in greater detail in Ruth Sidel, *Families of Fengsheng: Urban Life in China*, Baltimore, Maryland: Penguin Books, 1974.

8   One and a Half Million Barefoot Doctors in China, *Peking Review*, August 20, 1976, pp. 14–16.

9   Horn, op. cit., p. 96.

10 Virginia Li Wang, Food Distribution as a Gurantee for Nutrition and Health: China's Experience, *Milbank Memorial Fund Quarterly–Health and Society*, Spring 1976, pp. 145–65.

Economic Planning in China

ROLAND BERGER

When the Chinese communists took over the country in 1949 they had behind them many years of experience of rural organization, land reform and of agriculture in north-west China but little knowledge of industry, the running of cities and over-all economic planning. Five years earlier Mao Tse-tung was already advising his comrades to "learn how to administer the industry, commerce and communications of big cities, or otherwise we shall not know what to do when the time comes".[1]

When the time did come, and after eliminating the hyper-inflation, unstable prices and corruption inherited from the Kuomintang, the Chinese turned their attention to planning the economy, looking chiefly to the Soviet model, with its emphasis on heavy industry.

In the area more familiar to them, however, they continued on their own path carrying through a steady, step-by-step process from land reform to agricultural collectivization which generally had the support of the poor peasants and a majority of the middle peasants. Most of the upheavals and set-backs which characterized collectivization in the Soviet Union were avoided.

In carrying through the First Five-year Plan, which started in 1953, the two contrasting trends—the stress on heavy industry and the successful agrarian reform and collectivization policies—could hardly fail to pose problems if not actually to conflict. Among the "mistaken ideas" attacked by Mao Tse-tung in 1955 was the notion that industrialization could advance rapidly but that the developments in the agricultural sector could be slowed down. He observed: "We must on no account regard industry and agriculture, socialist industrialization and the socialist transformation of agriculture as two separate and isolated things, and on no account must we emphasize the one and play down the other."[2] A considerable part of the large funds needed to accomplish both, Mao explained, had to be accumulated through agriculture. Many years earlier, Lenin had also warned of the consequences arising from the disproportionate development of the two sectors:

Agriculture lags behind industry in development. This is a feature of *all* capitalist countries constituting one of the most profound causes of disproportion between the various branches of the economy, of crises and of soaring prices.[3]

At the Chengtu Conference in March 1958, Mao Tse-tung cast his mind back to the problems of the years immediately after Liberation:

In the period following the liberation of the whole country (from 1950 to 1957), dogmatism made its appearance both in economic and in cultural and education work. ... In economic work dogmatism primarily manifested itself in heavy industry, planning, banking and statistics, especially in heavy industry and planning.

Since we didn't understand these things and had absolutely no experience, all we could do in our ignorance was to import foreign methods. ... In commerce it was less so, because there was more control and exchange of documents with the Centre. There was also less dogmatism in light industry. The socialist revolution and the cooperativization of agriculture was not influenced by dogmatism because the Centre had a direct grasp of them.[4]

The Chengtu speech serves to explain the considerations which were in the fore-front of Mao's thinking when in 1956, within a year of the 1955 pronouncement, he returned to the question of the relationships between the various sectors. China had, he said, put comparatively more emphasis on light industry and agriculture and had not committed "mistakes of principle" which in the Soviet Union and a number of East European countries had resulted in a shortage of goods on the market and an unstable currency. But, said Mao, we must make adjustments in "the ratio between heavy industry on the one hand and in agriculture and light industry on the other, in order to bring about a greater development of the latter".[5]

These observations formed part of a major policy statement by Mao Tse-tung on 25th April, 1956, in which he applied the law of contradiction to the main aspects of China's economic and political situation. Throughout, Mao's statement is a criticism of the disproportionate and one-sided methods of economic development which charac-terized the Soviet approach. "It was by drawing lessons from their experience that we were able to avoid certain detours in the past, and there is all the more reason for us to do so now".[6]

Mao's statement was made after a two months' examination by the Political Bureau of the Central Committee of the Communist Party of reports on the work of thirty-four industrial, agricultural, transport, commercial, financial and other depart-ments under the central authorities. These reports identified a number of problems. "In all", said Mao Tse-tung, "they boil down to ten problems, or ten major relationships". Since the principles enunciated have been of cardinal importance in shaping China's economic policies and in evolving effective planning methods to ensure the proportion-ate growth of all sectors of the economy, several of the points in the statement merit a closer look. It is significant that the "Ten Major Relationships" was the first of Mao Tse-tung's unpublished speeches to be made publicly available after the arrest in October, 1976, of the "Gang of Four".

THE TEN MAJOR RELATIONSHIPS

1. THE RELATIONSHIP BETWEEN HEAVY INDUSTRY ON THE ONE HAND AND LIGHT INDUSTRY AND AGRICUL-TURE ON THE OTHER

To put proportionately more investment into light industry and agriculture, Mao explained, did not mean that the priorities had been changed. "The emphasis in our country's construction is on heavy industry. The production of the means of production must be given priority, that's settled. But it definitely does not follow that the produc-tion of the means of subsistence, especially grain, can be neglected. Without enough food and other daily necessities, it would be impossible to provide for the workers in the first place, and then what sense would it make to talk about developing heavy industry? Therefore, the relationship between heavy industry on the one hand and light industry and agriculture on the other must be properly handled ... . Does this mean that heavy industry is no longer primary? It still is, it still claims the emphasis in our investment. But the proportion for agriculture and light industry must be somewhat increased".[7]

By increasing the proportion of investment devoted to agriculture and light industry, Mao Tse-tung argued "the daily needs of the people will be better satisfied, the accumulation of capital will be speeded up." Given China's economic conditions, said Mao, light industry and agriculture can accumulate more quickly than heavy industry.

In the long run, he said, this increase in the proportion of investment going to light industry and agriculture will have the effect of speeding up the development of heavy industry, not slowing it down. "Is your desire to develop heavy industry genuine or feigned, strong or weak? If your desire is feigned or weak, then you will hit agriculture and light industry and invest less in them. If your desire is genuine or strong, then you will attach importance to agriculture and light industry so that there will be more grain and more raw materials for light industry and a greater accumulation of capital. And there will be more funds in the future to invest in heavy industry."[8]

2.   THE RELATIONSHIP BETWEEN COASTAL INDUSTRY AND INDUSTRY IN THE INTERIOR

During the period of foreign occupation, industrial development, such as it was, had been concentrated in the coastal regions and the north-east.[9] In redressing the balance and introducing industry into the hinterland, particularly during the period of the war in Korea when the question of the vulnerability of coastal industries was posed, in Mao's opinion the swing had gone too far with the result that too little attention had been given to building on the already-established industrial base in the coastal regions. "In recent years we have underestimated coastal industry to some extent and have not given great enough attention to its development."[10]

Mao advocated a more dialectical approach: "Making good use of and developing the capacities of the old industries in the coastal regions will put us in a stronger position to promote and support industry in the interior".[11] However, said Mao, "the greater part of the new industry should be located in the interior so that industry may gradually become evenly distributed;[12] moreover, this will help our preparations against war. But a number of new factories and mines, even some large ones, may also be built in the coastal regions."[13]

3.   THE RELATIONSHIP BETWEEN ECONOMIC CONSTRUCTION AND DEFENCE CONSTRUCTION

It has been argued that, by engaging in costly atomic developments, China has distorted and slowed down her economic progress. Leaving aside the strategic importance of nuclear power for China and the rest of the Third World in the face of pressures from the two superpowers, the economic rationale presented here by Mao Tse-tung is, to say the least, of more than passing interest.

Military and administrative expenses accounted for 30 per cent of all expenditure in the State budget in the period of the First Five-year Plan. "This proportion", stated Mao, "is much too high", and should be reduced in the period of the Second Five-year Plan to around 20 per cent "so that more funds can be released for building more factories and turning out more machines".

For the handling of this relationship Mao Tse-tung's prescription was that "only with the faster growth of economic construction can there be more progress in defence construction". He remarked: "If your desire (for the atom bomb) is genuine and very keen, then you will reduce the proportion of military and administrative expenditures and spend more on economic construction".[14]

4. THE RELATIONSHIP BETWEEN THE STATE, THE UNITS OF PRODUCTION AND THE PRODUCERS

The fine tuning between the needs of the State, the collective and the individual touches directly on the politics of democratic centralism. "The relationship between the State on the one hand, and factories and agricultural cooperatives on the other, and the relationship between factories and agricultural cooperatives on the one hand, and the producers on the other, should both be handled well. To this end we should consider not just one side but must consider all three, the State, the collective and the individual ... . In view of the experience of the Soviet Union as well as our own, we must see to it that from now on this problem is solved much better."[5]

In this section Mao Tse-tung also addresses himself to the question of the conditions of industrial workers, remarking that, "as their labour productivity rises, there should be a gradual improvement in their working conditions and collective welfare ... . We have recently decided to increase wages to some extent, mainly the wages of those at the lower levels ... in order to narrow the wage gap between them and the upper levels."[16]

Mao argues against placing everything "in the hands of the central or the provincial and municipal authorities without leaving the factories any power of their own, any room for independent action, any benefits".[17] Experience on sharing power among the central authorities, provincial and municipal authorities and the factories, stated Mao, was limited and called for further study.

Our relations with the peasants, said Mao Tse-tung, had always been good, although mistakes had been made, particularly in increasing State purchases of grain in 1954 when production was reduced owing to floods. "A decrease in production and an increase in purchasing—this made grain the topic on almost everyone's lips in many places last spring .... . The peasants were disgruntled, and there were a lot of complaints both inside and outside the party."[18]

"The Soviet Union has taken measures which squeeze the peasants very hard. It takes away too much from the peasants at too low a price through its system of so-called obligatory sales and other measures. This method of capital accumulation has seriously dampened the peasants' enthusiasm for production ... ."

"Our policies towards the peasants differ from those of the Soviet Union and take into account the interests of both the State and the peasants. Our agricultural tax has always been relatively low. In the exchange of industrial and agricultural products we follow a policy of narrowing the price scissors, a policy of exchanging equal or roughly equal values. The State buys agricultural products at standard prices while the peasants suffer no loss, and, what is more, our purchase prices are gradually being raised. In supplying the peasants with manufactured goods we follow a policy of larger sales at a small profit and of stabilizing or appropriately reducing their prices; in supplying grain to the peasants in grain-deficient areas we generally subsidize such sales to a certain extent ... .

"Similarly, the relationship between the cooperative and the peasants should be well handled. What proportion of the earnings of a cooperative should go to the State, to the cooperative and to the peasants respectively and in what form should be determined properly ... .

"Except in case of extraordinary natural disasters, we must see to it that, given increased agricultural production, 90 per cent of the cooperative members get some increase in their income and the other 10 per cent break even each year, and if the latter's income should fall, ways must be found to solve the problem in good time."[19]

The effective application of these principles has contributed in large measure to China's successes in the agricultural sector since 1962, expressed in a steady rise in outputs of staple crops and sidelines and in accumulation at the commune and production brigade levels which has provided investment funds for income-generating projects in the form of small and medium industry and processing units. At the same time sales to the State by the communes have risen year by year.

5.   THE RELATIONSHIP BETWEEN THE CENTRAL AUTHORITIES AND THE LOCAL AUTHORITIES

Here Mao argues for an extension of regional power within a unified central plan: "Our territory is so vast, our population is so large and the conditions are so complex that it is far better to have the initiative come from both the central and the local authorities than from one source alone. We must not follow the example of the Soviet Union in concentrating everything in the hands of the central authorities, shackling the local authorities and denying them the right of independent action ... .

"We want both unity and particularity. To build a powerful socialist country it is imperative to have a strong and unified central leadership and unified planning and discipline throughout the country; disruption of this indispensable unity is impermissible. At the same time, it is essential to bring the initiative of the local authorities into full play and let each locality enjoy the particularity suited to its local conditions".[20]

Mao comments that in the handling of the relationship between the central and local authorities and that between different local authorities "our experience is still insufficient and immature".

Whilst, as we shall see, the principles enunciated by Mao Tse-tung in this section have provided the guide lines in determining the relative functions and responsibilities at the various levels, his specific proposals were at this time on the whole tentative, certainly in comparison with the decentralisation of later years.

6. THE RELATIONSHIP BETWEEN THE HAN NATIONALITY AND THE MINORITY NATIONALITIES

In dealing with this relationship, the main emphasis, stated Mao Tse-tung, is put on opposing Han chauvinism. If the Han people who comprise 94 per cent of the population practised Han chauvinism and discriminated against the minority peoples that would be very bad. "We say China is a country vast in territory, rich in resources and large in population; as a matter of fact it is the Han nationality whose population is large and the minority nationalities whose territory is vast and whose resources are rich, or at least in all probability their resources under the soil are rich."[21]

The relationship between the Han nationality and the minority nationalities should be frequently reviewed, stated Mao. "We need to make a thorough study of what systems of economic management and finance will best suit the minority nationality areas."

Since 1956 support for the systematic development of both industry and agriculture in the minority nationality areas has been built into China's economic planning policies. Some indications of such assistance, through State subventions and preferential tax systems, are given later when dealing with financial policy.

7.   THE RELATIONSHIP BETWEEN PARTY AND NON-PARTY

8.   THE RELATIONSHIP BETWEEN REVOLUTION AND COUNTER-REVOLUTION

9. THE RELATIONSHIP BETWEEN RIGHT AND WRONG

These do not touch directly on economic and planning issues although in 7 Mao states that bureaucracy and a cumbersome apparatus must be opposed and proposes that "the Party and government organs should be thoroughly streamlined and cut by two-thirds". This injunction remained, in effect, a dead letter until ten years later, when during the Cultural Revolution, over-staffed administrations were criticized and simpler and more direct methods introduced, thus reducing the number of non-productive personnel.[22]

10.   THE RELATIONSHIP BETWEEN CHINA AND OTHER COUNTRIES

The policy enunciated here is clear eough: to study the strong points of all countries and to learn "all that is genuinely good" in the economic, scientific and technological fields. But, stated Mao Tse-tung, this must be done "with an analytical and critical eye, not blindly, and we mustn't copy everything indiscriminately and transplant mechanically".[23]

The policy as Mao defined it and that of self-reliance, which we will examine later, clearly stand in contradiction and the Chinese experience has shown that to achieve a correct balance between the two is no easy task, necessitating the pursuit of a course between the extremes of excessive, even slavish, reliance on and worship of things foreign in technology and industry, and a "leftist" position advocating "self-sufficiency", the closed-door outlook, which despises and rejects even useful and advanced techniques solely because they are not Chinese.

MAO AND ECONOMIC PROBLEMS

Although Mao Tse-tung's "Ten Major Relationships" are a striking demonstration of his capacity to analyse broad economic categories within a global political framework, he was at pains to explain a few years later that he had devoted little time to economic problems, since before August 1958 his main energies were concentrated on revolution.

At no time have Mao and his associates pretended that China had found the answers to all the economic problems. Thus, in February 1957, Mao Tse-tung observed:

With barely seven years of economic construction behind us, we still lack experience and need to get more. We had no experience to start with in revolutionary work either, and it was only after we had taken a number of tumbles and learned our lesson that we won nation-wide victory. What we must now do is to cut the time we take to gain experience in economic construction to less than it took us to get experience in revolutionary work and not pay such a high price for it. We'll have to pay some sort of price, but we hope that it will not be as high as that paid during the revolutionary period. We must realize that a contradiction is involved in this question between the objective laws of development of socialist economy and our subjective understanding, a contradiction which needs to be resolved in practice.[24]

In his talk with Edgar Snow in 1964, Chou En-lai was equally modest in his approach:

The laws governing economic development are extremely complicated. We have gained some experience, but we have to acquire much more experience. We have understood some of the laws, but there are many more laws governing economic development which remain to be understood. We have done quite a few things right in the past fifteen years, but we have also done some wrong things.[25]

But however tentative, imperfect or incomplete may have been the economic principles which Mao Tse-tung and those close to him were fashioning from their practical experience, they consistently fought against tendencies to put production rather than politics in command. "Political work is the lifeblood of all economic work", declared Mao in 1955, when the movement for agricultural collectivization was rising to its peak. Here Mao was clearly in line with Lenin who came into conflict with Trotsky and Bukharin on the same issue in 1921 when they accused him of taking a "political" approach, whilst theirs was an "economic" one. "Politics", Lenin said, "must take precedence over economics. To argue otherwise is to forget the ABC of Marxism." Later in the same speech Lenin observed:

Trotsky and Bukharin make as though they are concerned for the growth of production whereas we have nothing but formal democracy in mind. This picture is wrong, because the *only* formulation of the issue (which the Marxist's standpoint *allows*) is: without a correct political approach to the matter the given class will be unable to stay on top, and *consequently* will be incapable of solving its *production problems either.*[26]

This divergence between the economic or "economist" and the political approach is no abstract or academic issue, nor is it just a theoretical disputation between people doing the same thing by different methods. Principles of planning, the character of economic development and, indeed, the totality of social and political progress in socialist construction all depend upon which of the two policies is followed.

PRODUCTIVE FORCES; PRODUCTION RELATIONS

As early as 1937 Mao Tse-tung was rejecting the mechanical, deterministic approach to the relationship between productive forces and production relations[27] and between the economic base and the superstructure, whilst accepting that *generally* the productive forces and the economic base play the principal and decisive role. No situation is static and, said Mao, "the principal and non-principal aspects of a contradiction transform themselves into each other and the nature of things changes accordingly".[28]

Some people think that this is not true of certain contradictions. For instance, in the contradiction between the productive forces and the relations of production, the productive forces are the principal aspect . . . in the contradiction between the economic base and the superstructure, the economic base is the principal aspect, and there is no change in their respective positions. This is mechanical materialist conception, not the dialectical materialist conception. True the productive forces . . . and the economic base generally play the principal and decisive role; whoever denies this is not a materialist. But it must also be admitted that in certain conditions, such aspects as the relations of production . . . and the superstructure in turn manifest themselves in the principal and decisive role. When it is impossible for the productive forces to develop without a change in the relations of production, then the change in the relations of production plays the principal and decisive role . . . . When the superstructure (politics, culture, etc.) obstructs the development of the economic base, political and cultural changes become principal and decisive. Are we going against materialism when we say this? No. The reason is that while we recognize that in the general development of history the material determines the mental and social being determines social consciousness, we also—and indeed must— recognize the reaction of mental on material things, of social consciousness on social being and of the superstructure on the economic base. This does not go against materialism; on the contrary, it avoids mechanical materialism and firmly upholds dialectical materialism.[29]

Later, in a critical analysis of a Soviet theoretical work on political economy, Mao Tse-tung referred to the interaction between the forces of production and production relations, mentioning in particular the impetus which changes in production relations can impart to the speed with which the forces of production are developed.[30] Conversely, he explained that at times imperfections in socialist relations of production stand in contradiction to and therefore obstruct the growth of the productive forces.[31]

Mao concludes:

We should make the balance and imbalance between productive forces and production relations, and the balance and imbalance betwen production relations and the superstructure, serve as the key to the study of the economic problems of socialism . . . to make a study of production relations clearly, we have to link it with the study of productive forces on the one hand, and on the other hand link it with the positive and negative roles the superstructure plays in production relations.[32]

An example of the application of this thesis is in the relationship between industrialization (a change in the forces of production) and the collectivization of agriculture (a change in the relations of production). In their text books on political economy, the Soviet theorists propounded the principle that the collectivization of agriculture was only possible after socialist industrialization had been accomplished. As Mao explained, this interpretation does not accord with the Soviet Union's own experience since collectivization took place between 1930 and 1932 and at that time mechanized farming constituted only one-fifth of the total cultivated area.

The view that socialist industrialization was a pre-requisite of the collectivization of agriculture was also advanced by Liu Shao-chi, to be rejected by Mao (July 1955): "In agriculture, with conditions as they are in our country, co-operation must precede the use of big machinery".[33] Mao makes it crystal clear that this in no way denies the importance of raising the level of production forces in the agricultural sector by mechanization. Whilst rejecting the notion that mechanization is a necessary precondition of collectivization, he stresses its importance in consolidating the collective organization, thus:

> We are now carrying out a revolution not only in the social system, the change from private to public ownership, but also in technology, the change from handicraft to large-scale modern machine production, and the two revolutions are interconnected. In agriculture, with conditions as they are in our country, co-operation must precede the use of big machinery (in capitalist countries agriculture develops in a capitalist way). Therefore we must on no account regard industry and agriculture, socialist industrialization and the socialist transformation of agriculture as two separate and isolated things, and on no account must we emphasize the one and play down the other.[34]

One of the underlying assumptions which distinguishes the Soviet from the Chinese pattern of development is to equate the productive forces with the material means of production. Once such an assumption becomes part of political and economic thinking, it follows that in socialist construction the decisive role is attributed to the accumulation of new means of production and the role played in economic development by the political understanding, the initiatives and the drive of the workers and peasants is diminished. As we shall see, in Soviet economic strategy and planning the economistic tendency has been accentuated in recent years. By contrast, the Chinese in their political and economic approach are constantly reminding themselves of Marx's dictum that "of all the instruments of production, the greatest productive force is the revolutionary class itself.[35]

The basic divergence in the paths which the two countries have followed in agricultural development, rural organization and the relationship between town and country, between mental and manual labour, worker and peasant—all, in Marx's view, cardinal factors in socialist development— may be explained, at least in part, by the differing interpretations of the role of productive forces. Where economic progress hinges on the slogan that "technique decides everything", the relationship in the factory between the technicians and the workers (i.e. between mental and manual labour) must necessarily be hierarchical.

The Soviet approach has led to a situation in which the workers and peasants have little say in the management of their own affairs.

THE THEORY OF PRODUCTIVE FORCES

In China, conflict between the two lines of policy was in evidence even before Liberation and, since 1949, two Congresses of the Chinese Communist Party have seen battle joined on this issue. The political resolution passed at the Eighth Congress in September 1956 included the following:

In view of the fact that a socialist system has already been established in our country, the major contradiction, in essence, is between the advanced socialist system and the backward productive forces of society.[36]

According to Chou En-lai, this "theory of productive forces" was "smuggled into the resolution . . . by Liu Shao-chi and Chen Po-ta".[37] A few months later, when he delivered his speech "On the Correct Handling of Contradictions Among the People", Mao presented a totally different viewpoint:

The basic contradictions in socialist society are still those between the relations of production and the productive forces and between the superstructure and the economic base.[38]

In his Report to the Tenth National Congress, Chou En-lai referred to a second attempt to introduce the "theory of productive forces" into the counsels of the Chinese Communist Party, on this occasion in a draft political report produced in 1969 by Lin Piao in collaboration with Chen Po-ta. "They were opposed", Chou stated, "to continuing the revolution under the dictatorship of the proletariat, contending that the main task after the Ninth Congress was to develop production". In the event, Lin Piao's draft political report was rejected and another, drawn up, according to Chou En-lai, "under Chairman Mao's personal guidance", presented to the congress. This made reference to "the evil counter-revolutionary wind of economism".[39]

These attempts in China to promote a policy of "production first" certainly correspond with the Soviet approach. Thus, as two Soviet administrators put it:

The raising of the efficiency of production depends first and foremost on the production of new equipment, the improvement of technological processes and the organization of production and management.[40]

And:

Scientific and technological progress is the most important and inexhaustible basis for our economic successes.[41]

In both statements not only are the productive forces emphasized to the exclusion of the relations of production, but those are deemed to be solely the material means of production, techniques and organization of management—to the exclusion of the vital element in the productive forces, the working people.

Playing down the role of production relations and playing up the importance of productive forces means in effect boosting the bureaucracy, the administrators of the economy and the technocrats, and failing to mobilize the people. The Chinese refer to this as planning by "the typewriter, the computer and the telephone". The trend in this direction in the Soviet Union seems unmistakable. A decree of 1966 established "a State network of computer centres for the collection and processing of information and the solution of problems of planning and control of the economy".[42] According to a report submitted to the Joint Economic Committee of the US Congress (June 1973):

The manning for long-range forecasting is providing many new opportunities for bureaucratic aggrandizement, particularly for the government organs concerned with the glamorous subjects of science and technology and for the numerous scientific and technical research institutes scattered throughout the economy . . . .
Resources and people have been allocated to launching the grandiose projects to establish nationwide, uniform information systems, data banks, computer net-

works and the like and to computerize everything that seems susceptible of computerization.[43]

Quoting a Soviet source, the statement concludes that "the innovations also help to swell the administrative bureaucracy, which has increased nearly one third since 1965 (to 1971)".[44]

The motive force in the making of world history, said Mao Tse-tung in 1945, is "the people and the people alone"[45]—definitely not the material forces of production to the exclusion of the working people who are by far the most important single productive force.[46]

The group in the Chinese leadership denounced in 1976 as the "Gang of Four" had exaggerated one aspect of the key contradiction. In effect, they had so emphasized the necessary primacy of politics that production was not only relegated but became suspect; and they conveyed the impression that endeavours to raise the level of productive forces were in themselves equivalent to putting political factors out of consideration. They attacked those who were concerned with raising the level of production as adherents of the "theory of productive forces"—with the implication that they were subversively concerned with the policy of "production first".

The Gang of Four made the "revolution in the superstructure" their focus and denigrated production. They exaggerated the impact of the superstructure as decisive in pushing society forward, whereas in fact the productive forces and the relations of production determine the state of social development and its advance.[47]

In their advocacy of this one-sided, undialectical policy, the "Gang of Four" were clearly departing from one of the Central Committee's directives for the carrying through of the Cultural Revolution, the Sixteen Points:

The aim of the great proletarian cultural revolution is to revolutionize people's ideology and as a consequence to achieve greater, faster, better and more economical results in all fields of work. If the masses are fully aroused and proper arrangements are made, it is possible to carry out both the cultural revolution and production without one hampering the other, while guaranteeing high quality in all our work. *The great proletarian cultural revolution is a powerful motive force for the development of the productive forces in our country.* Any idea of counterposing the great cultural revolution against the development of production is incorrect. (Point 14.)[48]

In virtually denying the role of the productive forces, the Four were implicitly identifying the productive forces with the material means of production, thus negating the role of the people as the major productive force. It is not surprising, therefore, that a major criticism of the Four, linked with Lin Piao in 1975 by Hua Kuo-feng, Teng Hsiao-ping and other leaders was their failure to apply the mass line, and their reliance rather on cliques and "rebel factions".[49]

Mao Tse-tung, whilst always insisting on keeping politics in command, was equally insistent—to the point in 1933 of being accused of being a "Right deviationist"—that specific attention must be given to economic construction, which could not be left to take care of itself as an automatic by-product of politics. He made this point explicitly in numerous articles and speeches over the years. In setting out the six standards for evaluating the Socialist Education Movement in June 1964, Mao included, "We must see whether production is increasing or decreasing". Later, in the Twenty-three Points, issued by the Central Committee in January 1965, this was spelled out:

In the course of the movement, from start to finish, we must grasp production. At the same time we must pay attention to grasping each year's distribution (the question of livelihood). If we do not grasp production and distribution, we will become divorced from the masses and will bring grievous harm to our cause.[50]

The leadership in China, following the arrest of the "Gang of Four", has certainly adopted measures to raise the levels of production in industry and agriculture and to bring science and technology up to advanced world standards. But in so doing, Hua Kuo-feng and other leaders have been careful to centre their policies on the dialectical relationship between the productive forces and the relations of production, as Mao Tse-tung defined it. Thus Hua Kuo-feng:

The productive forces are the most revolutionary factor. In the final analysis, the expansion of the productive forces demands the continuation of the revolution in the realms of the superstructure and the relations of production under the dictatorship of the proletariat. Changes in the superstructure and the relations of production will, in turn, open the way to the development of the productive forces.[51]

Charles Bettelheim writing in May 1978 charges that the new leadership has in practice abandoned the recognition of the differences between changing the juridical ownership of enterprises and changing the relations of production and distribution—i.e. is now ignoring that an enterprise can be socialist in form but capitalist in content.[52] The record shows, however, that far from discarding the notion that social ownership of an enterprise is no guarantee that it operates in a manner significantly different from a capitalist one, the leadership emphasizes just this point. Thus Vice-premier Yu Chiu-li, responsible for the State Planning Commission, explicitly reiterated before a conference of 7,000 the formulation enunciated earlier by Mao:

Historical experience has proved to the hilt that it is not enough only to carry out revolution in the ownership of the means of production; it is also necessary to continue to carry out a thoroughgoing socialist revolution on the political and ideological fronts and ceaselessly transform that part of the relations of production not in harmony with the productive forces and that portion of the superstructure not in harmony with the economic base.[53]

POLITICS IN COMMAND

From this starting point, putting "Politics in Command" means not only ensuring that economic strategy subserves the broad political objectives, but that, in any branch of economic activity, the greatest impetus will derive from the understanding of the people, through regular discussions and study, of the central political issues. This perception, by people at every level, of what the country is striving to achieve will, the Chinese maintain, provide a framework and an approach, as well as give a sense of perspective and a goal, that will make for effective solutions to the everyday problems in the factory and the commune; and will establish the co-ordinates for longer-term planning in which, as we shall see, the workers and the peasants at the grass roots are involved. In the Chinese view, it is increasingly political understanding and social principle and decreasingly the influence of the pay packet that provide the main motivation in industry and agriculture.

PLATES 1 & 2   Medium scale irrigation projects like the Leap Forward Canal in Honan, shown here, are of special importance to rural development in China since they can be implemented by local units, with minimal state assistance, and brief gestation period. Typically they are undertaken by one or a group of neighbouring communes, and they often involve striking feats of engineering.

PLATES 3 & 4 Two ways of constructing an aqueduct. The commune in Shantung (above) has access to cranes, and the design of its aqueduct relies upon them; the Kwantung unit (below), which built its aqueduct to irrigate a small area of former wasteland (see p. 77) makes do with scaffolding.

PLATE 5   The first step towards mechanization of agriculture usually looks to the speeding up of crop processing after harvest. In south China (above) threshing of rice is done in the fields and portable pedal-operated threshers like this are now practically universal there — the next stage in mechanization sees them operated by electric motors.

PLATE 6   Rice transplanting — taking up the seedlings, transporting them to the fields, and replanting — is one of the most strenuous passages of the agricultural year, and concentrated efforts are being made to develop mechanical transplanters. Effective designs having been evolved such transplanters as this are coming into increasing use.

PLATES 7 & 8   The "man-made plains" created by blasting hills and levelling with bulldozers, pioneered by the model village of Tachai (above), are now to be found throughout the loess hill country of north China. The extensive fields thus constructed, replacing narrow terraces, are suitable for mechanized field-work, and small caterpillar tractors have been produced specially for upland agriculture. (Pages 41–42.)

PLATE 9   The maxim for the period of socialism, "from each according to his ability, to each according to his labour", is rigorously applied in China. The labour of this commune member, carting stone for a new breakwater on the Yellow Sea, is assessed not just by the number of loads, the commune had built a small weigh-bridge to count the quantity of rock moved. (Page 50.)

PLATES 10 & 11   The "farmland capital construction" that is now the subject of a mass campaign looks to the comprehensive re-ordering of rural China, with its fields laid out in equal rectangles designed for mechanized farming, roads and irrigation channels planted with trees.

PLATE 12   Aquaculture, traditional in China, is being greatly extended often as an adjunct of new irrigation works, and intensified. Methods of "scientific farming" are applied, as in the induced spawning technique being practised here in a Kiangsu commune.

PLATE 13 "Desertification" had long been a problem in parts of China, but now the spread of the sands is being checked, and sometimes reversed, by labour-intensive planting of shelter-belts of trees (page 233). Projects like this are undertaken during the agricultural slack season, when the full labour force can be devoted to them.

Almost all visitors to China seek to find an explanation of the enthusiasm and sense of direction that are so impressive and so markedly in contrast with the situation in other countries. It is not simply that the Chinese people are hard-working, though they are certainly that. Their prodigious endeavours have a purposeful aspect because the ordinary worker at the bench and the peasant on the farm understands and identifies himself with the political goals, both as they are being worked through in his own unit and in their wider aspect. He can see for himself the practical results in higher and better quality output, less burdensome working conditions and a year-by-year improvement in his standard of living.

Essential in the Chinese approach is an acceptance that there are contradictions among the people, although, unless wrongly handled, these are non-antagonistic. Mao Tse-tung mentions contradictions within the working class, contradictions within the peasantry, contradictions between the working class and the peasants, and so forth.[54] Thus in deciding on the spatial and sectoral allocation of investment and other resources, there are a variety of competing interests that have to be reconciled, whilst the balance between immediate and long-term benefits also requires careful determination.

In their planning policies the Chinese start from the assumption that without a central and over-all national plan it is impossible to organize the economy to serve the interests of the whole working people; the industrial workers and the peasants. "By over-all planning", said Mao in 1957, "we mean planning which takes into consideration the interests of the 600 million people of our country".[55]

The theoretical journal *Hongqi (Red Flag)* examined the place of "centralism" in a socialist economy, in 1970:

There is only one master of the multitudes of enterprises under socialist ownership by the whole people— the state of the dictatorship of the proletariat led by our Party. Only this state can represent the fundamental interests of the working class and the masses of labouring people and determine the principles and policies to be followed by enterprises, the orientation of their development, the production and distribution of their products and the disposal of their assets. In dealing with enterprises, the state practises democratic centralism, that is, centralized power on major issues and decentralized power on minor issues, centralized leadership and level-to-level administration. This is necessary for consolidating ownership by the whole people and for consolidating the dictatorship of the proletariat.[56]

In the application of the central plan the Chinese refer to "Five Unifiers" which give direction and effective co-ordination, provide safeguards against the danger that an over-emphasis on local interests might jeopardize the wider needs of the province or the State and ensure that the plan as a whole and the process of its implementation have the maximum popular support. (i) Unified *understanding,* that is ideological and general political understanding through continuous study which is universal, and through which the level of political and social consciousness is rising from year to year; (ii) unified *policy*—the application of this general political line at each phase and to each specific problem; (iii) unified *plan*—co-ordination and reconciliation of the various interests in carrying through the policy; (iv) unified *direction*—leadership for each economic and social unit coming from the next level above; (v) unified *action*—mobilization of the working people at each level.

In a speech in January 1962, first published for general circulation in July 1978,

Mao Tse-tung explained his conception of centralism:

What is meant by centralism? First, there must be concentration of correct ideas. Unity of understanding, of policy, plan, command and action is attained on the basis of concentrating correct ideas. This is unity through centralism.[57]

These are the centralizing factors in economic planning, but in the Chinese view they are only one side of the coin; the other is the application of the "mass line", the ongoing process from the grass-roots to the centre and down again:

Within the ranks of the people, democracy is correlative with centralism and freedom with discipline. They are the two opposites of a single entity, contradictory as well as united, and we should not one-sidedly emphasize one to the denial of the other. Within the ranks of the people, we cannot do without freedom, nor can we do without discipline; we cannot do without democracy, nor can we do without centralism.[58]

Before going on to describe the operation of the mass line in economic planning, it is necessary to explain the forms of ownership which in China fall into two broad categories: (i) *State*, or all-people's ownership, and (ii) *collective* ownership. In the first is virtually all industry—State industry—including the small and medium factories at county level. There are certain small neighbourhood factories, usually started by local housewives, which are collectively owned. When these reach a certain size and fulfil certain other conditions, they may pass into State ownership. In the second category is the agricultural sector, excluding State farms, organized in 50,000-odd communes. Tractors, threshers and other farm equipment, animals, fisheries, any commune factories and processing shops are collectively owned by the commune members organized at three levels: commune, production brigade, production team.

So far as the planning process is concerned there is little differentiation in method between one type of ownership and the other. Outside of the plan are the private plots, individually farmed, the produce from which can either be consumed or sold to the supply and marketing cooperative or at local markets—but these latter are strictly regulated as to types of goods traded, quantities and price, and are now coming under collective supervision as poor peasants' associations are taking over from state inspectors. In time both the private plots and the markets are likely to pass from the economic scene. However, in an interview with the Ministry of Agriculture in April, 1976, I was informed that the private plots were still serving a useful, if limited, purpose and that they were likely to continue for a "fairly long period". It follows that as long as there are private plots, there will be local markets.[59]

There is no evidence to suggest that there exists in China any "unofficial economy" with "fixers", sideline operators and private contractors such as that which in the Soviet Union is said to amount to anything between 10 and 25 per cent of the official economy—though clearly any such estimates can only be conjectural.[60]

THE MASS LINE IN THE PLANNING PROCESS

The principle of the mass line was enunciated by Mao Tse-tung in 1943:

In all the practical work of our Party, all correct leadership is necessarily "from the masses, to the masses". This means: take the ideas of the masses (scattered and unsystematic ideas) and concentrate them (through study turn them into concentrated and systematic ideas), then go to the masses and propagate and explain these ideas until the masses embrace them as their own, hold fast to them and translate them into action, and test the correctness of these ideas in such action. Then once again go to the masses so that the ideas are perservered in and carried through. And so on, over and over again in an endless spiral, with the ideas becoming more correct, more vital and richer each time.[61]

This broad policy has its specific application to economic planning. In this, the system of levels coupled with a policy of devolution is all-important in making for the success of planning procedures and in providing organizational channels through which the mass line can be applied, from bottom to top and from top to bottom. The units of political, social and economic activity at the different levels which enjoy a considerable measure of autonomy form a pyramid from base to centre. At each level the interests, the most valuable ideas and the initiatives coming from the unit below can be reconciled and adjusted to the interests of the larger area and then transmitted to the level above and so on up to the centre. Of great importance in this method is the limited span of responsibility at each stage of the pyramid, the next higher level being familiar with the problems of its area through regular and constant contact in day-to-day operations. The organizational structure of the province of Shensi illustrates the series of levels involved in the planning process as in Figure 1 below.

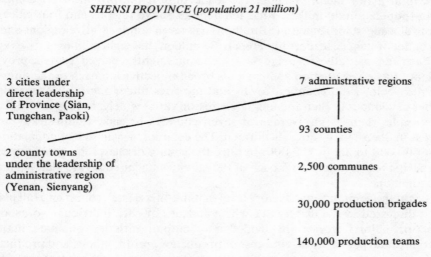

SHENSI PROVINCE (population 21 million)

3 cities under direct leadership of Province (Sian, Tungchan, Paoki)

2 county towns under the leadership of administrative region (Yenan, Sienyang)

7 administrative regions

93 counties

2,500 communes

30,000 production brigades

140,000 production teams

Figure 1

China's Five-year Plans have set forth broad targets for the major sectors of industry and agriculture but have not attempted to lay down rigid and detailed quotas. By the Constitution adopted by the National People's Congress in January 1975, the State Council will in future prepare a long-range Ten-year Plan, Five-year Plans and Annual Plan. [This provision is replicated in the 1978 Constitution.–Ed.] It is the working of the annual and more detailed plans which I shall deal with here.

In late September or early October of each year the State Planning Commission, under the State Council, sends projected requirements and broad planning objectives for the next year to the 21 provinces, the five autonomous regions (Tibet, Sinkiang, Inner Mongolia, Ninghsia and Kwangsi) and the three municipalities (Peking, Tientsin and Shanghai). These take account of the actual results of the first three-quarters of the current year's plan and an assessment of the fourth quarter's results. Each of the provinces, autonomous regions and municipalities then produces a provisional plan divided into nine main categories: (1) industrial production, (2) agricultural production, (3) main capital construction projects, (4) raw materials, supplies, (5) finance, (6) communications and transport, (7) commerce, (8) wages and manpower, (9) social services.

The province, autonomous region and municipality also receive suggested quotas of those items for export which they are expected to produce. The procedures followed are broadly the same for provinces, municipalities and autonomous regions. Here we shall deal with methods as applied to provinces.

The province, with these indications before it, makes its own review of the situation within the province as a whole, taking account of past performance and the specific needs of the area for the next year. They then make their broad proposals to each of the units at the next lower level—the administrative region or prefecture and any towns and factories under the direct leadership of the province. Thus, in the case of Shensi, economic indicators are sent to each of the seven administrative regions, three towns and several major factories under the leadership of the province. By comparison, Honan (population 50 millions) has ten administrative regions and four cities under provincial leadership; Kiangsu (52 million) has seven administrative regions and seven cities under provincial leadership; Hupeh (38 million) has eight administrative regions.

Each administrative region reviews the requirements received from the province in the light of its own situation and presents broad objectives to each of the units at the level next below, the counties, towns and factories under regional leadership. The number of counties in each administrative region varies widely. In Hupeh and Kiangsu, for example, there is an average of seven counties to each administrative region, whereas in Shensi the average is thirteen. The counties vary in size of population from about 400,000 to about 750,000. In turn, the county discusses the general principles and specific requirements with each of the factories under county leadership and with each commune.

It is at the commune and factory level that the "mass line" comes into full play. The plan is discussed by the factory as a whole and also by each individual workshop. The targets of major factories are divided into: output, varieties, qualities, major raw materials, fuel, power costs, etc., cost of production, profit, labour and productivity.

In the case of the communes a further process of division takes place since they are organized in three tiers: commune, production brigade and production team. The commune divides its plan into smaller plans for each brigade which, in turn, divides the plan again for each production team. Whilst the communes and brigades include in their planning proposals factories and enterprises administered at their own level, the team is regarded as the basic planning unit in the rural areas since it is, with few exceptions, the team which is directly concerned with the production of grains, cotton and oilseeds as well as sideline occupations—fish, silkworm breeding, orchards and so forth—and is the "accounting unit". The size of teams varies enormously depending on the local situation. Most range from 50 to 250 people but there are some as large as 700. At the team level the whole working population is involved in discussing the plan. In so doing they are enjoined to take into account the interests of the State, the collective and the individual and to ensure that, in normal years, the income of individual peasants will be increased. As a collective the production team is responsible for its own gains and losses and, in considering the plan, it has to find a balance between State requirements, its own plans for investment and expansion, and the income of its members. Approached purely in terms of increasing their individual incomes it could, for example, be advantageous to extend sideline occupations and put less emphasis on cotton, grains and oilseeds. The balancing of the interests of the State and the wider collective (the brigade and commune) with those of the individual, therefore, is a crucial question, the solution of which turns very largely on the social and political consciousness of the peasants involved.

As a result of the continuing study of political and social issues and of the working people progressively taking into their own hands the management of their own affairs, the political, social and cultural consciousness of the people is rising constantly, although across the length and breadth of a vast country, political understanding and class consciousness will obviously vary considerably.

From these grass-roots discussions a provisional plan starts on its way back up to the Centre, from team to brigade, from brigade to commune, from commune to county, and from workshop to factory level and on to the county. The county proposals, which bring together the agricultural and industrial elements at this level, go on to the administrative region, from there to the province, and up to the Centre. A similar process applies to the five autonomous regions and the three municipalities.

Each level will consider the proposals of the several lower units and how these, put together, satisfy the total possibilities and requirements of the area as a whole. Thus, modifications may be considered at every stage: the next higher level may consider the proposals from a lower level unit as too ambitious in terms of availabilities of raw materials, finance or manpower, or take the view that the lower level has failed to rise to its full potential in applying the famous directive for "Going all out, aiming high and achieving more, better, faster and more economical results in building socialism".

At every stage, therefore, an exchange back and forth takes place between the upper and lower levels before the plan is passed upward to the next level. It must be understood that such discussions on economic questions do not take place solely once a year, but that the two levels are in continuous dialogue throughout the year in the actual working of the plan and as a built-in feature of all economic, political and social activity. In this sense the plans provide an opportunity to bring together for review the successes and failures of the previous year and would normally lead to new increases in production, whilst making it possible to apply to backward sectors any corrective, stimulation or readjustments which may be necessary.

The provisional plans, from the 21 provinces, three municipalities and five autonomous regions, are then sent to the Central Planning Commission in Peking where they are coordinated and centralized. These proposals from the "areas" are at this stage brought into relation with the requirements and interests of the industrial ministries, such as those of Machine Building, Transport, Mining, Light Industry, Telecommunications, and so forth, which the Chinese describe as the "line". The Planning Commission has the task of coordinating the proposals of "area" and "line" into one plan.

The question of the correct relationship between "area" and "line" has evoked much debate and has been the subject of a struggle between the two conflicting policies identified respectively with Mao Tse-tung—the revolutionary line—and with Liu Shao-chi—the "capitalist road". In advocating emphasis on the "line" at the expense of the "area" Liu Shao-chi was arguing for tighter centralization and, in fact, placing the accent on the productive forces. The question was argued during the Cultural Revolution. As a result there is today a much stronger emphasis on the "area" as against the "line" and a larger degree of decentralization.

The plan produced by the Planning Commission is considered by a conference held usually in December which is attended by representatives of both "area" (each province, autonomous region and municipality) and the "line" (each industrial Ministry). From this conference emerges a plan, further modified, which then goes down again through the same process to each successive level. This up-and-down process is said to take about two months.

Thus the system of levels, forming a pyramid of relationships and responsibilities, serves the policy of devolution. The object, the Chinese say, is to give the greatest possible encouragement and scope for the exercise of "two initiatives"—one from below and one from above, or "two ups and two downs."

By this method the most valuable ideas coming from below can be incorporated into the plan and the reconciliation of interests at each level ensured. The limited span of responsibility at a given level of the pyramidal structure presents the upper-level unit with problems, applications of policy and leadership functions well within its grasp, since the scope is comprehensible and defined and the issues requiring decision familiar as a result of day-to-day operations with the lower level units.

At the same time statistical reporting is greatly simplified in a system of aggregation from the smallest to the next largest unit and so on up to the summit of the pyramid.

Thus a production brigade on a commune has little difficulty in keeping effective statistics for the several production teams at the level below. Moreover, the administration of the agricultural and other taxes, of quota systems for agricultural output and the planned allocation of raw materials which depend on accurate reporting, all seem to function quite effectively.

For the lowest-level units, the centralizing factor does not come from a far-off, faceless authority, but from the commune, an organ of "people's power" with which there is a continuous give-and-take relationship arising from mutual support, mutual interests and mutual benefit. Contradictions there will certainly be but these, in the Chinese context, can be resolved by discussion and persuasion and not by the exercise of "authority" or "commandism". Mao Tse-tung explained the correct approach:

Without democracy you have no understanding of what is happening down below; the situation will be unclear; you will be unable to collect sufficient opinions from all sides; there can be no communication between top and bottom; top-level organs of leadership will depend on one-sided and incorrect material to decide issues, thus you find it difficult to avoid being subjectivist; it will be impossible to achieve unity of understanding and unity of action, and impossible to achieve true centralism.[62]

The structural relationships are one thing, the common purpose deriving from understanding of policy is another and more important feature. The "Five Unifiers" have already been mentioned. There are other unifying factors which, through discussion at every level, provide coordinates with which the working people approach the problems of planning and production.

There is, of course, the general political line which, as it changes from period to period, is under constant discussion in the factories, the communes, the universities and the schools.

There is the broad acceptance of the need, as defined in Mao's "Ten Major Relationships", to reconcile the interests of the State, the collective and the individual. There are also aspects of policy of particular relevance to the country's economy which are well known and the practical applications of which are regularly discussed and elaborated. One such is the principle, which also derives from the "Ten Major Relationships", that "agriculture is the foundation and industry the leading factor" in the economy. At the grass roots targets will be discussed in terms of whether or not they serve this principle. This attempt at a proportionate development of agriculture and industry, and within industry between the heavy and light sectors, distinguishes the Chinese from the Soviet model.

In discussing their plans every factory and commune will also take into consideration the directive: "In industry take steel as the key link and in agriculture take grain".

As the Chinese conceive it, a global balance involving all sectors of the economy at any given moment can only be provisional or accidental, not the norm. The constant feature, they maintain, is imbalance, the periods when across-the-board balance is achieved being temporary phases no sooner reached than they begin to be modified into imbalance. The process is described as "balance—imbalance—new balance". Insistence on equilibrium at each and every phase would only result in holding back the dynamic elements in the infrastructure. At the heart of this notion lies the dialectical principle of "uninterrupted development" (or as the Chinese say, "One is always dividing into two"). Its practical effect is first to accept a certain flexibility by acknowledging the fact that imbalances will arise and then to ensure that when one sector runs ahead of the others and is the cause of the imbalance, the emphasis is placed on bringing up the laggard rather than restraining the faster sector in order to achieve a formal balance.

"It is incorrect", Mao Tse-tung has remarked, "to claim that our annual plan and five year plans can meet all the requirements of economic law ... . Whether or not we succeed will be proved through objective practice!"[63]

Practice has shown that insistence on rigid quotas runs counter to the "balance—imbalance—new balance" concept, is likely to inhibit grass-roots initiatives and frustrate the execution of the plan when unforeseen situations arise. Thus, says Mao:

A constant process of readjustment through State planning is needed to deal with the contradiction between production and the needs of society, which will long remain as an objective reality. Every year our country draws up an economic plan in order to establish a proper ratio between accumulation and consumption, and achieve a balance between production and needs. Balance is nothing but a temporary, relative unity of opposites. By the end of each year, this balance, taken as a whole, is upset by the struggle of opposites; the unity undergoes a change, balance becomes imbalance, unity becomes disunity, and once again it is necessary to work out a balance and unity for the next year. Herein lies the superiority of our planned economy. As a matter of fact, this balance, this unity, is partially upset every month or every quarter, and partial readjustments are called for. Sometimes, contradictions arise and the balance is upset because our subjective arrangements do not correspond to objective reality; this is what is called making a mistake. The ceaseless emergence and ceaseless resolution of contradictions is the dialectical law of the development of things.[64]

Plan fulfilment is therefore reviewed and adjustments made at the level of the province, administrative region and county quarterly and monthly. At the commune and factory levels the targets are checked weekly. These adjustments are facilitated by two main factors—the system of levels and the practice of "leaving a leeway".

The system of levels, each with its span of responsibility, makes it possible to carry through adjustments arising from shortfalls or surpluses at the level below with the minimum of dislocation of the plan as a whole, and often without recourse to help from the higher echelons. For example, a commune in difficulties can call for assistance from the county which, in many cases, can find the solution in terms of equipment, supplies or even manpower from another commune in its area. In other words, problems are solved at the lowest level possible, thus strengthening self-reliance and reducing bureaucracy.

The practice of "leaving a leeway" (*liu you yu ti*)[65] makes for flexibility and allows modifications to be made as the plan is implemented. At the provincial, administrative region, and county levels the plan includes a margin of finance, raw materials and manpower which can be deployed to deal with emergency situations, or shortfalls, or to meet requirements arising from overfulfilment by any unit.

Of interest, too, is the method applied on the economic front of "the war of annihilation"—drawn from the military technique, "concentrate a superior force to destroy the enemy forces one by one."[66] This method is applied to major works of capital construction or the building of large factories of key importance for which materials, manpower and capital are all concentrated in a short, sharp attack on the project. The giant petro-chemical complex built in 1969 some thirty kilometres from Peking was constructed and commissioned by workers drawn from Peking factories, peasants from neighbouring communes, and soldiers. In Hupeh province a large tractor plant was built and commissioned within the space of a year by using this method.

Mao Tse-tung has described how the Great Hall of the People in Tien An Men Square was built in only ten months:

Twelve thousand people brought from all over the country, representing the force, the technical capacity, the human capacity, of all the provinces in the country, taking no Sundays off at all, working three shifts a day, and not working on any piecework wages system; many of them began working eight hours a day, and ended up working twelve hours without a stop. Did they want to be paid for the extra four hours? They didn't.[67]

SELF-RELIANCE

China's policy of self-reliance was born in the Red Areas of Kiangsi in the early 1930s when Chiang Kai-shek, by his "encirclement and suppression" campaigns, was attempting to impose an economic blockade.[68] Later (August 1945), Mao Tse-tung was to use the phrase "*tse li gen sen*"—literally "regeneration through our own efforts" —as maxim for a policy which rests on his confidence that "the masses have boundless creative power". This approach, which should not be confused with "self-sufficiency", depends essentially on the initiative of a politically and socially motivated people. At the grass-roots and, indeed, at every level the economic unit is encouraged to utilise its resources, whether human or material, for accumulation and expansion. In the countryside, by using labour as capital and with a minimum of mechanical equipment, works of capital construction, road and bridge building, canal digging and so forth, have been developed on a vast scale by the local people without recourse to aid from the State. The same principle has played a large part in the creation of local, small and medium industry at the county, commune and production brigade levels. The encouragement of a sense of responsibility of the grass roots economic units without undue dependence on the State and the central administration, clashed with the approach of Liu Shao-chi and his apparatus men. The shake-up and the criticisms of bureaucracy during the Cultural Revolution gave an enormous fillip to the self-reliance principle, as can be seen on both a small and large scale wherever a visitor travels in China.

When planning new developments, such as water conservancy systems, soil improvement schemes, road, bridge and even local railway construction, small and medium factories and mines, the commune or county, as indeed the higher levels for large-scale projects, have to make a choice between asking for State aid or relying on local material and human resources coupled with mass initiative and enthusiasm. So ingrained is the notion of self-reliance that it has become a matter of pride to do without State support to the greatest possible extent and to make use of public accumulation funds of the county or commune for local projects.

The Red Flag Canal, to take one example, in Lin County, north-west Honan, with its 200 miles of canals and side-channels, aqueducts, hydropower stations, and reservoirs, was built over a period of ten years from 1958 at a cost of 4,760,000 yuan, including the cost of manpower. Eighty per cent of this fund was provided by the thirteen communes and their production brigades, the State finding twenty per cent. The Tachai (Shansi) and Shahshiyu (Hopei) brigades are other examples of quite small units overcoming the most daunting natural and other difficulties whilst raising the standard of living of their members year by year, all without outside assistance.

Across the length and breadth of China grass-roots units with a minimum of mechanical equipment and by using labour as capital have carried through such projects without recourse to aid from the State. Individual communes undertake the smaller schemes whilst larger works of capital construction are planned and built jointly by several communes or a group of counties working together or even by neighbouring provinces for major projects—a flexible system bringing together without too much red tape the appropriate grouping of units suited to the scale of each project.

Following the same policy of self-reliance small and medium industry has been developed at the county and commune level throughout the country, based upon locally available manpower and materials. Modern sophisticated and large industrial undertakings are being commissioned, but not at the expense of the small and indigenous-type factories which the Chinese refer to as "the five smalls".[69]

Since labour and most of the materials are found locally, the medium and small factories can be set up speedily and at low capital cost. Even if the quality of the product does not reach the national standard in the initial stages, it will certainly be tailored to local needs. The savings on transport and other infrastructural costs are obvious.

Some indication of the contribution which small-scale industry is making to the national economy may be drawn from figures published in 1977 which show that, of total national output, 70 per cent of chemical fertilizer, 66 per cent of cement, 33 per cent of coal, 11 per cent of steel, 27 per cent of iron and 33 per cent of hydro-power is supplied by these units. This investment and accumulation on the basis of self-reliance accelerates over-all economic growth and clearly relieves the State of a considerable burden, leaving it free to direct investment into the expansion of major industries.

The Chinese stress the importance of the growth of small and medium industry in the countryside as an important factor in breaking down the gap between town and country. They seem to have set their faces against the creation of huge industrial conurbations in favour of balanced growth and a dispersal of industry. In Mao Tse-tung's view:

> The cities of the future cannot be so big. We should disperse the residents of the big cities in the countryside and build many small cities.[70]

Local industry and the capital construction projects take up the slack of underemployment of rural labour which was such a negative feature of pre-1949 China. (Tawney, writing in 1931, refers to some districts where only one hundred days a year were spent on farm employment.) However, this is not the principal purpose, as Mao Tse-tung has explained:

> The question does not rest with old-type technology, a large population, or with increasing employment. We are developing a large number of medium and small-sized enterprises under the guide of big enterprises and adopting extensively indigenous methods under the guide of foreign methods mainly for the sake of achieving a high rate of industrialization.[71]

The bulk of the rural population remains and will remain in the countryside and will not drift into urban industry. In fact the trend is in the other direction, since possibly threequarters of town students at the end of their middle school education go down to work on the communes. Many of those who enter universities after a minimum of two years' manual labour return to the countryside again after graduation.

FINANCIAL POLICY

"Financial considerations are subordinate to economic considerations which are, in turn, determined by politics", stated members of the Budget Bureau of the Ministry of Finance in an interview in 1973. China's financial policy, they said,

> "is framed to help consolidate the dictatorship of the proletariat. Finance must play an active role in bringing about the socialist transformation of the economy by mobilizing funds and correctly handling the balance between consumption and accumulation."

As we shall see, China's deployment of her finances has played a cardinal role in the operation of an economic policy based upon the Ten Major Relationships, particularly in dealing with the contradictions between town and country, between the Han people and minority nationalities and between the relatively industrialized coastal areas and the less-developed provinces of the interior: in a word, in providing the financial back-up to a policy of proportionate economic growth. In the Chinese view the economy determines financial policies, although whether these policies are good or bad can influence the economy.[72]

Budgetary policy, therefore, rests squarely on the actual output of agriculture and industry. Increases in the sources of finance are to be found by expanding the production of agriculture and industry and accumulation will be realized by "reliance on one's own efforts". Planned expenditure must be balanced in relation to national production which determines budget income. In fact, the plan provides for a marginal surplus of income over expenditure, allowing some leeway (*yü ti*) for contingencies. If a shortfall in income larger than this margin should arise from unforeseen circumstances such as adverse climatic conditions the solution would be sought in a special appeal to the people to practise economy and increase output. "We do not adopt the practice of printing money to solve our economic problems" as the Budget Bureau members put it. The financial plan provides for some relocation of funds to assist the poorer regions (for example, in the interior and the autonomous regions of the minority nationalities) by drawing on the richer. Each provincial plan includes items of income and expenditure but these are treated separately and a province or municipality cannot apply all its income to its local requirements. Control is exercised by agreeing a figure for expenditure for each province, autonomous region and municipality in the plan. Whether this is in excess of, or less than, the unit's income, will determine whether the surplus passes to the centre or the deficiency is made up by the centre.

The planned expenditure for the municipality of Shanghai, for example, is 10 per cent of its income. For the comparatively better-off provinces of Liaoning and Kiangsu, expenditure is 18 and 30 per cent of income, respectively. In contrast, for the province of Yunnan, whose population includes a large proportion (one-third) of minority nationalities, revenue, at the time of my visit in 1975, was only 85 per cent of expenditure. The autonomous region of Singkiang has, since it was established in 1955, kept all local revenue for its own use and received in addition (to 1974) subsidies amounting to 53 per cent of its local revenue. Another autonomous region, Ninghsia, from 1958 to 1974 received subsidies equivalent to 110 per cent of the region's revenue in this period. The principle of divorcing income and expenditure applies equally at the level below the province, the administrative region or prefecture. The income of the administrative region of Suchow (Kiangsu), to take one example, was in 1973 75 per cent more than its expenditure. The evening-out process applies, therefore, both at the national level and within each province.[73]

The shift in the sectoral origins of budget revenue as China has industrialized and with the socialization of the economy, illustrates the application of financial policy to assist in adjusting the town/country relationship.

In 1950, State industry and the cooperatives accounted for 34.3 per cent of State revenue, capitalist industry and commerce 32.9 per cent, and individual peasants 29.6 per cent.[74] By 1960, the last year for which we have a sectional breakdown, the progressively increased, and as the *amount* to be provided has not been changed (except to effect a one-time reduction of 30 per cent in 1962 after the "three difficult form of agricultural tax and taxes on rural industry and commerce, 5.9 per cent. In 1973, the Budget Bureau informed me, more than 90 per cent of budget revenue was derived from the State sector.

Within the broad lines of policy already described, the Budget is directed to giving support in five main areas: capital construction, the countryside, social services, minority nationalities and foreign aid.

CAPITAL CONSTRUCTION

A major part of the Budget (60 per cent in 1972) is devoted to support production and capital construction. (This compares with an average of 49.5 per cent for the years 1953–7 when the level of total expenditure provided in the State budget was obviously considerably lower). Investment funds for major projects of capital construction, such as the Wuhan Iron and Steel Complex or major river-control projects are totally provided by the State. Medium-sized construction works may be funded by both the State and Province in agreed proportions. A significant part of China's capital accumulation, however, is not pecuniarily quantifiable.

Edgar Snow in 1971 reported an interview with Chou En-lai:
The Premier put agricultural product value for 1970 at about 25 per cent of total combined output value of industry, transportation and agriculture. Calculated on that basis, China's industrial-transportation-agricultural output value in 1970 was around 120 billion American dollars. There is, however, no reliable index for converting "output value" in China in terms of gross national product systems used in the West. "Out-put value" omits or minimizes important "service values" such as rents, privately owned rural homes—now rising by the millions, built with mutual labour—as well as major and small water conservancy projects constructed by army and volunteer labour. Or consider China's nationwide urban and rural air-raid shelter systems, built largely by unpaid neighbourhood mutual labour teams. It would elsewhere cost billions of dollars. Finally, how is one to fit into the GNP formula the value of some 30 million acres of marginal land added during the past ten years to the cultivable area by peasant labour—with unbelievable toil—at a cost of little more than peasant food consumption.[75]

In the allocation of state funds for capital construction works and major industrial enterprises the autonomous regions and provinces with a large percentage of minority peoples, such as Yunnan, receive proportionately more of the total investment funds than the Han areas, an approach radically different from that of the Soviet Union.[76]

SUPPORT FOR THE RURAL POPULATION

Perhaps in no area of the economy have China's achievements been so strikingly successful as in the handling of agricultural collectivization and, with special emphasis since the Cultural Revolution, in raising the standard of living in the countryside to bring economic and social conditions in the rural areas closer to those of the towns.

Over the years, the weight of the agricultural tax on the rural economy has been consistently reduced. Levied originally on the output of basic grains, oil-bearing seeds and cotton (or on livestock in the case of communes on the grasslands)[77] of each basic agricultural unit, the tax in 1952 averaged 13.2 per cent of total national production of these items from the collective sector (i.e. excluding state farms). As production has progressively increased, and as the *amount* to be provided has not been changed, (except to affect a one-time reduction of 30 per cent in 1962 after the "three difficult years"), the average for China as a whole has dropped year by year, so that today it is in the region of five per cent. In minority and poor areas the tax can be as low as 1½ to 2 per cent.

The agricultural tax is collected by the county which retains five per cent for its own use and passes the rest to the state.

Another feature of financial benefit to the rural areas is the fixing of a supply-quota system on a five-yearly basis. This provides for the supply by the commune of a stated quantity of grain, oil-bearing seeds and/or cotton at prices fixed by the State. Any surplus over this level is bought by the State at a price which can be anything up to 30 per cent higher than the quota price. The last quotas were fixed in 1971 and since, in the majority of cases, commune production is rising year by year, the operation of this system is a sizeable factor in increasing the income of the rural population. In the ten years from 1964, State allocations for water conservancy schemes, soil improvement, tree planting, seed selection and agricultural mechanization, amounted to 80 per cent, more than the revenue from agricultural tax for the same period.

PRICE SCISSORS

Of major benefit to the peasant population has been a systematic policy of closing the gap between the prices paid to the communes for agricultural supplies and those charged for industrial products needed in the rural areas. A significant cut in prices of industrial goods took effect in July 1971. Prices of tractors and diesel engines, petrol and lubricating oil were then reduced by 20 per cent; fertilizers and insecticides, plastic sheeting and piping by 16 per cent. Over the years prices paid to the communes for sugar cane, oil-bearing seeds, tea, some fibre products and various sideline items have been raised. The price paid to the growers for cotton was raised in 1955 and again in 1964. Together, these amounted to a 25 per cent rise. The purchase price of grains has been increased several times since 1949 without changing the sale price to the consumer and all seasonal differentials in grain prices have been eliminated. In fact, in the case of some items—even major ones—the prices paid to the communes are greater than those at which the items are sold in the towns. Thus, rice is bought at 16 cents a catty and sold at 14 cents. Taking account of the cost of transport the State loses 2.8 cents per catty. Rape seed which is bought at 81 cents is sold at 78 cents involving a loss of 3 cents, the State absorbing the cost of handling and transport. The imbalance between the purchase and sale prices of these and other items, plus costs of transportation and handling, is covered by the State to the tune of about Yuan 2,000 million a year.

These price adjustments reflect one aspect of a policy which the Chinese describe as "exchange on the basis of equal value", although in some cases industrial goods are actually sold to the communes below cost. Members of the Budget Bureau gave me examples of how these adjustments in price relations had affected the peasants' sales and purchases. In the early period after Liberation one catty of salt was exchanged for several dozen catties of grain. Today, one catty of salt could be exchanged for one catty of grain. One tael of gasoline twenty years ago cost the equivalent of three eggs—today the ratio is two taels for one egg. One injection of penicillin, which cost 50 catties of flour, is now the equivalent of one catty.

BANK LOANS

The People's Bank offers facilities to the communes to borrow at low rates of interest. For the purchase of farm machinery interest is charged at 0.18 per cent a month (2.16 per cent per annum) and for farm production (seeds, fertilizers, and so forth) at 0.36 per cent a month (4.32 per cent per annum). Since these loans are mostly for seasonal requirements it is customary in China to quote interest rates on a monthly basis.

For poorer production brigades and teams or those facing temporary difficulties due to weather or other adversities, special low-interest or interest-free loans may be granted.

The effect of assistance in these various forms has resulted in a notable change in the standard of living in the countryside in recent years, despite the rise in population. This is reflected in the level of savings by both the communes (and brigades and teams) and individual families. According to Chinese reports, commune savings in 1971 were double those of 1965 and private savings in the same period rose by 30 per cent. This trend has continued in recent years.

To take a grass-roots example, albeit one above the average, the total savings of the Pin Chou commune, Nan Hai county, in Kwangtung at the time of my visit in 1975 were 3,390,000 yuan, having risen from 580,000 in 1965. During another visit in May, 1977, I was informed that the figure for 1976 had risen to 4,090,000 yuan. Another indication of the rising prosperity of this commune could be expressed in terms of its pig population:

1963	27,000
1972	86,000
1974	90,000
1976	107,000

There are clearly wide differences in the natural conditions—fertility of soil, water supply, character of the terrain—from one area of China to another, which might make for wide disparities in the relative prosperity of the 50,000-odd people's communes. To avoid a situation in which the rich communes get richer whilst the poorer remain poor a policy is operated to preserve a nice balance between local self-reliance and assistance from the State. There are production brigades—Tachai and Shashiyu are the outstanding but not the only examples—where peasants have succeeded by their own efforts in the most adverse conditions without calling for State assistance. Generally, the adjustments in the application of the agricultural tax and quota system make allowance for communes which have special difficulties, but where assistance in this form is not adequate direct financial support is provided by the State. Substantial amounts were granted after the formation of the communes in 1958 to give the poorer units a flying start.

PROVINCIAL BUDGETS

In drawing up its budget each province, autonomous region and municipality will deploy its finances to support the overall policy—agriculture the foundation, industry the leading factor—with application to the area's specific conditions. For example, the province of Shensi, with a population of 21 million people (at the time of my visit in November, 1972), is a drought-stricken area and the budget allocation for the province reflects an attempt to deal with this problem. Thirty per cent of the province's total investment is applied to agriculture, including irrigation and water conservancy, and most of the investment in industry is directed to those sectors which support agriculture. Each of the 93 counties has an agricultural machinery factory, and steel used in agriculture absorbs 40 per cent of the total steel used in the province. In the programme of mechanization of agriculture for this province water conservancy and land improvement is the top priority.

SOCIAL SERVICES

On the basis of expanding production the Budget can allocate increasing amounts to improve and expand provisions for health, education, science, technology and cultural services. Here again, the Chinese strive to maintain a balance between state aid and local self-reliance, with its concomitant of grass-roots democracy. The number of pupils in primary and middle schools in 1972, according to Budget Bureau figures, increased by 30 per cent over 1965. Much of this increase would be accounted for by additional places in rural schools as a result of the campaign to provide at least five years' primary school education for children in the countryside. These schools are under the supervision of the peasants, and the production brigades receive 120 yuan a year for each teacher from the State, the balance of salary coming from brigade funds.

Each of China's 2,200 counties has a hospital and every commune at least a clinic (many advanced, populous communes also have hospitals), with 60 per cent of the salaries of doctors in commune clinics paid by the State (through the county). The rest is provided through the cooperative medical service for which peasants contribute one yuan a year per head. All social services for industrial workers—health, pensions, crêches, kindergartens—are provided free of charge through the factory welfare fund, 11 per cent of the total wage bill of which is provided by the State. Family members of workers pay half the cost of medical treatment, although in cases of special need funds can be made available from the factory welfare fund. This fund is also used to make adjustments in the wages of individual workers where, as in the case of workers with large families or other difficult domestic circumstances, the strict application of the policy of "payment according to work" might result in hardship.

SUPPORT FOR THE MINORITY NATIONALITIES

Financial assistance to the minority areas, the Budget Bureau explained, is provided within the context of the Party's policy of "unity, mutual help and love". This support takes a number of forms: (a) subsidies to cover the deficit between the area's expenditure and its income (see earlier page 27) (b) financing of capital construction schemes and large industrial enterprises; (c) lower incidence of tax; (d) special subsidies for "cold, mountainous and border" areas. The last three are considered as contingency funds, outside the planned revenue and expenditure included in the annual budget but, even here, special concessions are made to the minority nationalities who are allowed to retain part of any over-fulfilment of revenue and all savings on planned expenditure.

These provisions operate within a system described as "budgetary autonomy", which applies to the autonomous regions as well as to the levels of prefecture and county within these regions. State investments for railway and road development have gone a long way to bring the areas inhabited by the minority nationalities into the national network. The length of railways in Inner Mongolia, for instance, has increased five times compared with 1950. The Kweiyang (Kweichow)–Kunming and, more recently, the Chengtu–Kunming railways and the building of an extensive road system have transformed communications for the province of Yunnan which, before the building of the Burma road, was described as having no road on which any wheeled vehicle could pass.

State investment in water conservancy and land reclamation schemes have played a major part in strengthening agricultural growth in the minority regions. From 1949 to 1975 Inner Mongolia received 8,500 million yuan for capital construction works and Yunnan 500 million yuan for water conservancy alone. With State aid, the Kwangsi Chuang Autonomous Region has been able to allocate 100 million yuan a year for material and equipment for water-control projects. Such financial support from the State has buttressed the policy of self-reliance in these regions. In Yunnan, for example, no fewer than four million people were mobilized during the winter of 1974 and spring of 1975 for works of agricultural capital construction. Large tracts of the Gobi desert (Sinkiang) have been reclaimed and are now producing substantial quantities of grains, cotton and sugar beet.

The State has also invested in major industrial projects in the minority areas such as the Karamai oilfield in Sinkiang, the Paotou Iron and Steel Complex, one of China's largest, in Inner Mongolia, the Heavy Machinery factory and, more recently, the Natural Gas Enterprise in Yunnan. In 1974 alone, with special funds, raw materials and equipment allocated by the State, 120 new factories were set up in the minority regions. As a consequence of this State aid, coupled with local self-reliance, new industrial cities have been created in all these regions.

SUPPORT FOR DEVELOPING COUNTRIES

"Each year when we prepare the Budget", said members of the Budget Bureau, "we have to think of our obligation to those countries which are not yet liberated in order to assist them in their just struggles. China is herself a developing country and we are conscious of the fact that the aid which we are able to provide at this stage is still quite limited."

Despite the modesty of the Budget Bureau's statement, China's economic aid commitment to the developing countries in the years 1970–4 increased to $2.4 billion, more than double the $1.1 billion extended in the previous 14 years.[78]

The typical Chinese agreement of the sixties was interest-free and allowed repayment over 10 years after 10 years grace. Now, larger grace periods are allowed, ranging up to 20 or 30 years, and amortization periods often are larger than before. These terms make Chinese aid ever more attractive, particularly to the poorer LDCs.[79]

TAXES

Taxation in China is operated through a unified system, the State deciding on forms of taxes to be levied, rates and methods of collection. Only in this way can the principle of politics in command be effectively implemented to ensure both the overall interests of the country as a whole and the equitable distribution of the tax burden on the various sectors and geographical areas. Local governments have no power to levy taxes other than those laid down by the State nor to apportion levies from the people. Accumulation by State or all-people's enterprises provides the major part of revenue and these enterprises pay the bulk of the taxes. Thus, production of the petroleum industry which increased sevenfold from 1965 to 1975 resulted in a sixfold increase in taxes received by the State. Levels of tax are set in accordance with the principle that taxation should assist economic growth. Steel billets and ingots are tax free. Low rates are paid on iron, copper, chemical fertilisers, machinery and other means of production, as well as on daily necessities such as grains and some textiles. In order to assist agriculture, diesel fuel, insecticides, certain farm implements and a number of other products required for farm use are tax free. On the other hand, higher taxes are paid on cigarettes, wines and spirits and certain consumer goods.

There is no personal income tax in China. State-owned industry provides revenue in two forms—profit and tax. Commerce pays a tax based on turnover and the communes are responsible for the agricultural tax.

Industrial enterprises pay tax on ex-factory prices, commercial departments pay a "business tax"—usually about 3 per cent on the volume of business, and services—such as hotels and laundries—pay a tax of from 3 to 15 per cent on the basis of income.

The profit of an industrial enterprise, in the context of China's economic and financial policies, is used primarily as a yardstick whereby economical methods, productivity and factory management generally may be judged. The enterprise is enjoined to "improve business-accounting, increase production and reduce production costs and, while fulfilling the State production plan, achieve the quota of profit set by the State and thus provide the State with funds for construction."

Profit is not in any way determinative in planning and production policies, where use not profit is the crucial factor. How this works at the enterprise level was explained to me at the Nanking Petroleum Plant in November, 1975. Gasoline carries a large profit (the difference between 300 and 560 yuan a ton) whereas heavy oil involves a loss (the difference between 70–80 yuan and 50 yuan). But heavy oil is a vital necessity for industry and the plant had been asked by the Ministry to increase its heavy oil output, even if this meant a slower growth in the production of gasoline. The key factor, I was told, was to ensure that quotas were fulfilled, profits were secondary. The factory's welfare fund which covers costs of crèches, nurseries, assistance to workers in special need and educational services within the factory, is provided by the State (normally 11 per cent of the total wages fund) and is in no way affected by the level of profits.

PRICES

Prices of all major items, including most of the "daily necessities", are fixed centrally with marginal differences depending on quality and with some small regional variations—which are gradually being eliminated—reflecting costs of transportation Prices of some small items—towels, slippers, leather shoes, pots and pans—are decided at the provincial or administrative region level where they are produced and consumed. These arrangements do not exclude some flexibility to avoid waste. When, for example, there is a glut in one area or another of fish, fruit or vegetables which cannot all be processed or stored prices are temporarily reduced and the items are sold at a loss to the State, although the prices paid to the communes which produce them remain stable.

Special financial provision is made to ensure that those living in remote areas do not have to pay higher prices for essential goods on account of transport costs. This benefits especially the minority nationalities. What is described as a preferential or protective price policy brings other benefits to the minority peoples. The herdsmen of Inner Mongolia, for example, prefer brick tea from Southern China. Whilst the purchasing price to the producers has more than doubled in the last twenty years, the retail price to the herdsmen has not changed. For this one item the State subsidy to the regional commerce department amounts to 3,800,000 yuan a year.

Many visitors to China have remarked favourably on the price, quality, range and design of consumer goods offered in the large urban department stores as in well stocked village shops run by production brigades. Professor J. K. Galbraith, who visited China towards the end of 1972, had this to say:

> The Chinese seem to have developed a plain but remarkably efficient system for the distribution of consumer goods. The markets and stores we examined were handling a dense traffic at markups that are most miniscule by our standards—4.4 per cent on fresh produce and meats, 13 per cent in a big Peking department store. The department store is helped by having no packaging, no high- and slow-moving times, no advertising, no style-goods, no fitting, few returns, no shop-lifting.

THE ROLE OF THE PEOPLE'S BANK

In the implementation of China's financial policy, a major role is played by the People's Bank, established in 1948, prior to the formation of the People's Republic. In 1950 the Bank of China was placed under the direction of the People's Bank, to be responsible for overseas financial transactions.

As China's only autonomous financial institute the People's Bank is concurrently the issuing body, the state bank, credit establishment for industry and agriculture, an organization for financial compensation, and an agency for financial and economic control.[80]

The State, through the bank, "absorbs temporarily idle funds from enterprises in the form of deposits and uses them to provide credits for other enterprises for use as temporary working funds . . . in accordance with the principle of 'making banking deposit on a voluntary basis' and 'freedom to withdraw deposits', the State absorbs and uses the savings of the people to speed up the turnover of funds and thus increase its financial strength. This also helps to promote among the people the practice of 'running one's household industriously and frugally' ".[81]

Financial relations between China and the commercial world outside are channelled through the Bank of China. Correspondent relationships have been established by the Bank of China with 600 foreign banks and their 1,700 branch offices in 130 countries. The rising activity in foreign trade transactions and financing of the Bank of China is reflected in its increased assets which rose substantially from 1973 to 1974 and again by 23 per cent to $7,900 million in 1975. Total capital funds at the end of 1975 at $384 million were 2½ times the level of the previous year. The Bank of America analysts report that the Bank of China's balance sheet for 1975 reveals "a strong financial condition, with adequate liquidity and satisfactory profitability".

The Bank of China has branches in Hong Kong, Singapore and London, the London branch dealing mostly with European transactions. Traders and bankers hold the Bank of China in high esteem for its punctiliousness in transactions, efficiency and the friendly assistance offered by its staff. The London branch maintains normal banking relationships with the clearing and merchant banks, although as one British banker remarked, "the Bank of China never borrows, you place deposits with them". This is all short-term financing, never exceeding one year. The same banker commented, "the Bank of China has never been to the medium-term market. Were it to do so there's little doubt that there would be a long queue of people anxious to talk to them". Similarly, in Eurocurrency operations the Bank of China's activities are confined to reciprocal and short-term/normal banking business.

EXTERNAL FINANCIAL POLICY

China, whilst giving aid, has not, until recently, relied on foreign loans for investment funds. Loans received from the Soviet Union to help reconstruct the economy after Liberation and to back China's aid to the Democratic People's Republic of Korea represented no more than 2 per cent of State revenue for the years 1950 to 1959. These loans, said to be of the order of 1,406 million roubles, were all repaid by the beginning of 1965, one year ahead of time. Alexander Eckstein wrote in 1966:

China is in a unique situation, for it is perhaps the only country today that has no long-term credits or foreign aid to draw upon. On the contrary, since 1955 it has been a net exporter of capital.[82]

China is unique in another respect, it is alone among the centrally-planned economies "both in utilizing its own currency in international trade and allowing Western entities to hold accounts in RMB (renminbi or people's currency). The RMB is an untraded, inconvertible currency in most important respects."[83] The rate of RMB—the Yuan—to other currencies as they fluctuate is determined by the Bank of China.

INFLATION AVOIDED

By planning for an effective balance and to ensure the proportionate development of heavy and light industry and agriculture, by maintaining a supply of consumer goods to correspond with the purchasing power of the community and operating a price policy to serve the interest of the workers and peasants, China has successfully avoided inflation.

There is clearly no place in this scheme of things for the Keynesian remedy of gradual and eventually cumulative inflation or devices such as bank rate manipulations, stop-and-go techniques, price controls (which at best are only temporarily effective) and other nostrums to which other countries have resorted, albeit without much confidence that they will succeed in halting inflation for any length of time.

This is not to say that conditions in China automatically excluded the threat of inflation on a number of occasions since 1949. In the three difficult years, 1959–61, floods, typhoons and drought played havoc with agriculture, drastically reducing the output of foodstuffs and the supply of industrial crops for light industry which, at the same time, had an unfavourable effect on Government receipts and expenditure. Faced with these problems, there were those in China, such as Liu Shao-chi, who advocated recourse to deficit budgeting, allowing the currency to "find its level"—which would have resulted in a huge increase of money in circulation and the probability of serious inflation. But Liu Shao-chi's notions did not find acceptance. Instead, the Chinese adopted a masterly policy of self-reliance and just and equitable distribution and, thanks to the commune system, scarcity was fairly shared and starvation averted. On the purely technical level, the avoidance of inflation in these circumstances was an historic achievement which the majority of economists in the West seem to have ignored.

Later, a decision of the Central Committee to raise the wages of many of the workers in the lowest three grades of the eight-step scale clearly increased monetary income and could have contributed to a degree of inflation unless compensatory action was taken on the supply front. The ruling was made in August 1971 and factories were given time to effect the changes but the increments had to be back-dated to July 1971.

By the time the enterprises came to put the ruling into effect workers received nine or ten months' increased pay. The injection of such a sizable sum of purchasing power into the economy (in some factories 30 per cent of the workers benefited) could obviously have caused a run on consumer goods with dangers of inflation. In fact, the problem had been foreseen and supplies of consumer goods were increased to meet the additional demand.

In so far as the disruptive effects on the economy ascribed to the "Gang of Four" resulted in temporary or local shortages of supplies and a fall in State revenue from Shanghai and other industrial centres, one may assume that in 1975 and early 1976 some inflationary tendencies were set in motion. However, whilst hard information on this aspect of the economy is not available, there is little to suggest that inflation on any significant scale was generated, presumably because overall financial policy was kept in safe hands.

CONCLUSION

The picture of China's economic and financial policy presented here may have conveyed the impression of a perfectly tuned, smooth-running system in which all the answers to the problems of planning and economic growth have been discovered. The Chinese would be the first to disclaim any such conclusion, which runs counter to their philosophy of uninterrupted change and development ("one is always dividing into two"). Those successes which have been achieved, and they are considerable, are the result of a hard struggle between two lines of policy and much inevitable trial and error.

Looked at in the broad, however, China has achieved much success in creating a harmonious relationship between industry and agriculture and in the proportionate development of heavy and light industry. She has considerably reduced the gap in the standard of living between town and country. She has devised, or is well on the way to devising, planning methods which avoid an inhibiting rigidity and eschew over-centralization. Above all, she is pursuing a policy in which workers and peasants increasingly play an active and meaningful part. "It cannot be argued", said Mao Tse-tung, "that history is being created by the planners and not by the masses." This seems to provide the clue to China's economic success—that she has found a way, not perfected as yet, of tapping the productive power of the hundreds of millions of her workers and peasants.

NOTES

1 Mao Tse-tung, Our study and the current situation, 12 April 1944, *Selected Works*, Vol. III, p. 1973.
2 Mao Tse-tung, On the question of agricultural cooperation, 31 July 1955, *Selected Readings from Mao Tse-tung*, Peking: Foreign Languages Publishing House, 1967, p. 330.
3 V. I. Lenin, New data on the Laws governing the development of capitalism in agriculture. *Collected Works*, Moscow: Progress Publishers, 1964, Vol. XXII, p. 94.
4 *Mao Tse-tung Unrehearsed,* edited by Stuart Schram, Penguin Books, 1974, p. 98.
5 On the Ten Major Relationships, Mao Tse-tung, Foreign Languages Press, Peking, Dec. 1976, p. 3.
6 ibid, p. 1.
7 ibid., pp. 2 and 3.
8 ibid., p. 3.
9 Mao Tse-tung defined the coastal regions as Liaoning, Hopei, Peking, Tientsin, Honan, Shantung, Anhwei, Kiangsu, Shanghai, Chekiang, Fukien, Kwangtung and Kwangsi.

10   ibid., p. 5.
11   ibid., p. 6.
12   In 1956, 70 per cent of all China's industry, light and heavy, was located in the coastal regions.
13   ibid., p. 5.
14   ibid., p. 7.
15   ibid., p. 8.
16   ibid., p. 9.
17   ibid., p. 9.
18   ibid., p. 10.
19   ibid., p. 12.
20   ibid., p. 15.
21   ibid., p. 17.
22   At the Learn from Taching Conference, April–May, 1977, Yu Chiu-li, Vice-premier, stated "The number of non-productive personnel in general should not exceed 18 per cent of the total payroll in an enterprise".
23   ibid., p. 28.
24   Mao Tse-tung, On the correct handling of contradictions among the people, speech at Eleventh Session of Supreme State Conference, 27 February 1957, Peking: Foreign Languages Press, 1960, p. 68.
25   Edgar Snow, *The Long Revolution*, Random House, 1972, p. 224.
26   V. I. Lenin, *Collected Works*, vol. XXXII, pp. 83–4.
27   The Chinese define relations of production as having three aspects: (a) the ownership of the means of production, i.e. private, collective, or all-people's/State; (b) people's place in the process of production and their mutual relations; (c) the pattern of distribution. Of these the most important, in fact the basis of the relations of production, is taken to be the ownership pattern of the means of production.
28   On contradiction, *Selected Works of Mao Tse-tung*, Vol. I, p. 333.
29   ibid., pp. 335–6.
30   *Miscellany of Mao Tse-tung Thought*—a selection of items from Mao Tse-tung Ssu-hsiang Wan-sui—speeches and articles attributed to Mao Tse-tung and published in English translation by the US Joint Publication Research Service. The authenticity of this material cannot be verified until the later volumes of Mao's *Selected Works* are published. On the same theme Marx observed: "What is operative here is not merely an increase of individual productive power by co-operation, but also the creation of new productive power, the productive power of the masses". *Capital*, Co-operation, Vol. 1, Part IV, Chapter II.
31   Mao Tse-tung, On the correct handling of contradictions among the people, *Selected Readings*, Peking: Foreign Languages Press, 1956.
32   *Miscellany of Mao Tse-tung Thought*, op. cit., p. 280.
33   Mao Tse-tung, On the question of agriculture co-operation, *Selected Readings*, Foreign Languages Press, Peking, 1967, p. 329.
34   ibid. p. 329. See also Berger, The mechanization of Chinese agriculture, *Eastern Horizon*, Vol. XI, No. 3, 1972, p. 7.
35   Marx, *Poverty of Philosophy*, Chapter II, Section 5.
36   Resolution on the Political Report of the Central Committee, Eighth Congress of the Communist Party of China, Peking: Foreign Languages Press, 1956.
37   Tenth National Congress of the Communist Party of China (documents), Peking: Foreign Languages Press, 1973, p. 5.
38   Mao Tse-tung, *Selected Readings*, p. 359.
39   Tenth National Congress of the Communist Party of China, op. cit., p. 5.
40   N. Brogochinsky, Chief of Department for the Application of New Methods of Planning and Economic Incentives, *Ekonomicheskaya Gazeta* (translation in *Soviet News*, 10 December 1968).
41   Mikhail Suslow, Member of the Political Bureau and Secretary of the Central Committee of the CPSU, 13 July 1973 (translated in *Soviet News*, 24 July, 1973, p. 324).
42   *Ekonomicheskaya Gazeta*, No. 13, 1966, p. 25.
43   Compendium of Papers, 27 June 1973, US Government Printing Office, 1973, p. 36.
44   ibid., p. 38, quoting *Narodnoe SSSR*, Vol. 1971, p. 347. Although not defining his categories, M. Rutkevich, Corresponding Member, USSR Academy of Sciences, states, "An especially rapid increase is registered by the group of specialists employed in the national economy, whose number increased from 8.8 million in 1960 to 21.4 million in 1974". He gives figures for the increase in the numbers of the working class for the same years as 45.9 million and 70.2 million respectively. This would suggest an increase in the number of workers of 53 per cent and of "specialists" of 143 per cent in the fifteen-year period. Social Structure of Developed Socialist Society, *Pravda*, 4 July 1975
45   Mao Tse-tung, On coalition government, *Selected Works*, Vol. III, p. 257.
46   "The masses have boundless creative power. They can organize themselves and concentrate on places and branches of work where they can give full play to their energy, they can concentrate on produc-

tion . . . ." In introductory note to Surplus labour has found a way out, 1955, *The Socialist Upsurge in China's Countryside,* Chinese Ed, Vol. II.

47 *People's Daily,* September 1977.

48 Decision of the Central Committee of the CCP. Concerning the Great Proletarian Cultural Revolution. Adopted 8 August 1966.

49 See *The Case of the Gang of Four,* by Chi Hsin. Cosmos Books: Hong Kong, p. 245.

50 *Ssu-Ch'ing: The Socialist Education Movement of 1962–1966,* Richard Baum and Frederick C. Teiwes, University of California, Berkeley, 1968.

51 Political Report to 11th Party Congress, August 1977.

52 *China Since Mao,* Charles Bettelheim, New York: Monthly Review Press, p. 41.

53 National Conference on Learning from Taching in Industry, 4 May 1977, Selected documents. Foreign Languages Press, Peking, p. 65.

54 Mao Tse-tung, On the correct handling of contradictions among the people, op. cit.

55 ibid.

56 Class Struggle in the Field of Socialist Construction and Economics by Writing Group of the Kirin Provincial Revolutionary Committee, *Hongqi,* No. 2, 1970.

57 Talk at an Enlarged Working Conference convened by the Central Committee of the CCP, 30 January 1962. Translation in *Peking Review,* No. 27, 1978, p. 9.

58 Mao Tse-tung, On the correct handling of contradictions among the people, op. cit., p. 355.

59 The Constitution of 1975, article 7 states: "Provided that the development and absolute predominance of the collective economy of the people's commune are assured, people's commune members may farm small plots for their personal needs, engage in limited household sideline production, and in pastoral areas keep a small number of livestock for their personal needs".

60 It seems that in 1975 and 1976, as a result of interference with the regular supply of consumer and other goods to the communes, commune members, in some areas, were trading, by means of various forms of barter, outside the State plan.
    In his report to the second Taching Conference Vice-premier Yu Chiu-li observed: "As a result of interference and sabotage by the "gang of four", a small number of enterprises over a long period of time violated state plans, broke supply and marketing contracts and went their own way in production, exchange and fixing prices, thus opening the floodgates to illicit activities by old and new bourgeois elements. We must take firm steps to end this."

61 Mao Tse-tung, Some questions concerning methods of leadership, *Selected Works,* Peking: Foreign Languages Press, 1965, Vol. III, p. 119.

62 Mao Tse-tung, Talk at an Enlarged Work Conference, 30 January 1962, *Mao Tse-tung Unrehearsed,* op. cit., p. 164.

63 *Miscellany of Mao Tse-tung Thought,* op. cit., p. 193.

64 Mao Tse-tung, On the correct handling of contradictions among the people, op. cit., p. 361.

65 "In drawing up plans, it is necessary to mobilize the masses and see that there is enough leeway." Mao Tse-tung, quoted in *Peking Review,* No. 9, 1969, p. 2.

66 Title of an article by Mao Tse-tung, 16 September 1946, *Selected Works,* Peking: Foreign Languages Press, 1961, Vol. IV, p. 103.

67 *Mao Tse-tung Unrehearsed,* op. cit., p. 156. The same approach was followed in the building of his own mausoleum in Peking, which was another prodigy of concentrated, rapid construction.

68 See Berger, Self-reliance, past and present, *Eastern Horizon,* Vol. IX, No. 3, 1970, p. 8.

69 "The five smalls": small steel works; small coal mines; small cement works; small fertilizer factories; and small farm implement shops.

70 *Miscellany of Mao Tse-tung Thought,* op. cit., p. 295.

71 ibid, p. 271.

72 "Many of our comrades place one-sided stress on public finance and do not understand the importance of the economy as a whole; engrossed in matters of revenue and expenditure as such, they cannot find solutions to any problem hard as they try. The reason is that an outmoded and conservative notion is doing mischief in their minds. They do not know that while a good or bad financial policy affects the economy, it is the economy that determines finance. Without a well-based economy it is impossible to solve financial difficulties, and without a growing economy it is impossible to attain financial sufficiency." Mao Tse-tung, Economic and financial problems in the Anti-Japanese War, December, 1942, *Selected Works,* Vol. III, p. 111.

73 From an analysis of an earlier period, Nicholas Lardy concludes that in 1959, the revenues of fifteen provincial-level administration units were in excess of approved expenditures, the balance being remitted to the central government, whilst the other fourteen had revenues less than their approved expenditures, the difference being made up by subsidies from the centre. *Compendium of Papers submitted to the Joint Economic Committee of Congress of the United States,* July 10, 1975, p. 106.

74 A somewhat different breakdown is provided in the State budget for 1950, the first year after Liberation.

<table>
<tr><td colspan="2" align="center">STATE BUDGET, 1950</td></tr>
<tr><td>*Revenue*</td><td>%</td></tr>
<tr><td>Agricultural tax</td><td>41.4</td></tr>
<tr><td>Other taxes</td><td>38.9</td></tr>
<tr><td>State owned enterprises</td><td>17.1</td></tr>
<tr><td>Revenue from clearance of State warehouses and granaries</td><td>2.4</td></tr>
<tr><td>Other sources</td><td>0.2</td></tr>
<tr><td>*Expenditure*</td><td></td></tr>
<tr><td>Military</td><td>38.8</td></tr>
<tr><td>Administrative expenses</td><td>21.4</td></tr>
<tr><td>Investment in State-owned enterprises and services</td><td>23.9</td></tr>
<tr><td>Cultural, education and public health</td><td>4.1</td></tr>
<tr><td>Subsidies to regional governments</td><td>2.3</td></tr>
<tr><td>Payment and interest on Government Bonds floated in North-east</td><td>0.1</td></tr>
<tr><td>Total Reserve fund</td><td>9.4</td></tr>
</table>

75 Edgar Snow, *The Long Revolution*, 1971, p. 155.
76 In the *Compendium of Papers of the Joint Economic Committee of US Congress*, June, 1973, which deals with the incidence of industrial development in the different areas of the USSR, it is suggested that:
> industrial development of the Central Asian Republics and the economic regions east of the Urals will continue to focus primarily on the extraction and processing of natural resources, particularly fuels and non-ferrous metals, while development in the European regions and Republics will concentrate chiefly on increasing capacity (p. 223).

The Report adds:
> If industrial growth ... must depend primarily on increases in factory productivity, regional differences in *per capita* industrial output probably will continue to increase, with the less developed Republics falling still further behind the rest of the country (p. 224).

77 A production brigade in Siziwang Banner Inner Mongolia, which I visited in spring, 1976, paid agricultural tax of 2 per cent, all in sheep.
78 Carol H. Fogarty, *China's Economic Relations with the Third World, Compendium of Papers—Joint Economic Committee of US Congress*, July 10, 1975, p. 730.
79 Carol Fogarty, op. cit., p. 734.

She adds:
> China has provided more than half a billion dollars of its aid in the form of grants. Grant aid recently has averaged about $40 million annually. In addition, China has provided the equivalent of about $1 billion of grant aid in the form of free technical services to development projects. China does not include the value of these services in estimates of its aid undertakings. ...
> Generous payment terms and rapid delivery of Chinese aid combine to make it an attractive form of assistance. High ratios of Chinese inputs of labour, cash and commodities have helped keep projects moving. At present, China's annual gross aid outlays are not reduced significantly by reflows for debt servicing. This contrasts with other Communist aid programmes under which some LDCs already are experiencing a zero net aid flow. No interest is collected on the LDC aid debt to China and only small payments on principal have begun. The People's Republic usually accepts repayment in goods rather than hard currency. In many cases this arrangement helps ease the LDCs repayment burden, especially where non-traditional exports, not easily sold in world markets, are used.

80 Pierre-Henri Casson, Le Système monétaire Chinois, *Le Bulletin de l'Economie et des Finances*, October–December, 1973.
81 How China raises funds for national construction, *Peking Review*, 1 January, 1966, p. 22.
82 *Communist China's Economic Growth and Foreign Trade*, McGraw-Hill, p. 246. By contrast, banking and other financial circles have been showing increasing unease at the scale of East Europe's debt to the West, which has risen from an estimated $8.3 billion at the end of 1970 to an estimated $45.3 billion at the end of 1976. David Ashby, Senior Economist of Bankers Trust, has stated that total Comecon indebtedness could reach a level between $55 billion and $60 billion by 1980. Based on the level of debt at the end of 1976 it is estimated that annual interest obligations alone are approaching some $3 billion. From articles by Richard Portes, in *Foreign Affairs*, July, 1977, p. 751 and *International Herald Tribune*, 22 July, 1977.
83 David L. Denny, International Finance with the People's Republic of China, *Compendium of Papers submitted to the Joint Economic Committee of US Congress*, July, 1975, US Government Printing Office, p. 659.

Women's Impact on China's Development*

DELIA DAVIN

If women are excluded from economic activity, the whole pace of development is thereby slowed. In countries where their work has been limited to household tasks and children, their labour represents a tremendous productive potential capable of making a real impact when the proper social and political conditions exist to unleash and make good use of it. In China, a many-sided campaign has destroyed many of the traditional constraints which used to prevent women working outside the home. Since the growth in the female workforce which has taken place since 1949 has had repercussions on the size of the workforce as a whole and on the movement of the birth-rate, it has important implications for development and development strategy.

A full description of the ways in which women contribute to development would involve the whole sphere of economic activity, for women in China farm, work in factories, mines and offices, drive buses and trains, treat and nurse the sick, teach and administer. In this paper I have tried to concentrate on the difference that their participation has made to China's development. It is an irony intrinsic to the subject that the more equal women become, the less distinctive their role and the less there is to write about. For the moment, however, because women's participation in the workforce started from a low baseline in 1949, the changes which their entry into it has made can be clearly distinguished. Moreover, in some spheres at least, because of difficulties in assimilating them into the economy, their contribution is still a distinct one.

The relationship between women's status and development is complex. It is a commonly-held belief that the greater the degree of modernization, the higher the position of women and the fuller their participation in economic activity. This view, derived from the recent history of the West, would lead us to expect women's economic contribution to increase automatically in any third world country in the course of development. But it has been shown that many different patterns exist.

Economic development does always entail a change in the division of labour between the sexes, but this may increase or reduce women's economic functions.

In parts of Africa where women were once the chief cultivators, the managers of large-scale, mechanized farms, following European-derived preconceptions, tend to employ male labour while women remain in less prestigious subsistence agriculture.[1] Similarly, even where women once dominated traditional trading and handicrafts, men are preferred for employment in modern commerce and industry.[2] Only a society which, like China, is committed to allowing all its people, regardless of sex, to play their full part in development, is making full use of its human resources. And even a society such as China's at times, because of lingering prejudice, conservatism or practical difficulties, fails in the full realization of this goal.

* This paper draws on my experience during a year spent in China (1975–6). Except where I give other sources in the notes, figures and other specific information were gathered in that period.

205

PRE-LIBERATION CHINA

Although the orthodox ideal of the seclusion of women within the household could only be practised by those wealthy enough to be able to afford servants to fetch water, wash clothes and do other outdoor tasks, the work roles of all females in traditional Chinese society were strictly limited. The proportion of farm work performed by women in pre-liberation China varied considerably. In the double rice cropping areas it could be as high as 29 per cent while it was only 5 per cent in areas where cultivation was less intensive. Nationally the average was put at 13 per cent.³ Besides this regional variation there was a class variation. Poor peasant women, driven by extreme need, were far more likely to do farm work than women in better-off households. As Chinese agriculture was based on small family farms this would not normally have been wage labour, but rather work in fields belonging to husbands or fathers. Land passed from father to son. A woman could not normally inherit, own or rent land. The boy who helped in his father's fields might one day expect to farm them. The girl who helped out at her father's in the busy seasons would afterwards do the same, in her married home. She would never become a fully-fledged farmer. Women often worked in traditional handicraft production for the market, but here again they were most often part of a family enterprise. In imperial China women were completely excluded from the bureaucracy and teaching. Such employment as was open to them was in despised spheres like domestic service and prostitution. In the villages some might also earn money as midwives or marriage go-betweens, jobs seen as particularly appropriate for women. The early twentieth century development of modern industry, especially the textile industries, in the treaty ports brought the recruitment of large numbers of young female workers who obtained financial independence from their families at the cost of long hours in factories where appalling conditions were a threat to health and even life. At this time too, educated women began to enter the professions, though their numbers remained very small.

BRINGING WOMEN INTO THE WORKFORCE

The Chinese Communist Party (CCP), in keeping with Marxist analysis, was committed to enabling women to enter productive labour as the key to assisting them to achieve equality, and since 1949 there has been a huge increase in the work performed outside the home by women. It has not been achieved without effort—the CCP has had to overcome considerable difficulties, among them traditional prejudice and the fact that much additional labour had to be integrated into the economy. This phenomenon is most often discussed in relation to the improvement it has brought about in women's status, and the ending of oppressive practices like arranged marriages, child betrothals, the sale of female children and the binding of girls' feet. Here I wish to consider mainly its implications for development, although the one to some extent involves the other. Since the difference between countryside and town is basic to the subject, it seems best to write about them separately.

RURAL WOMEN

The prejudice against women doing agricultural work which existed in many parts of China has almost disappeared; indeed peasant women now have many incentives to enter the agricultural workforce. Propaganda campaigns to bring them into it were carried out throughout the 1950s and 1960s. The new idea that a woman could and should contribute to socialist construction gradually superseded the tradition that her place was in the home. Women's image and self-image changed as new paths to status and respect replaced the old one of bearing numerous male children.

When in the mid-1950s the great mass of the Chinese peasantry joined socialist cooperatives household income ceased to depend on the individual ownership of land, livestock and tools, becoming instead a function of the amount and quality of the labour contributed by members of the household to the collective. This meant that those families which had the most labour power would also have the highest incomes, and thus the incentive to work became as strong for all women as it had previously been for the poorest. Moreover, men now had a greater incentive to encourage the female members of their family to work in the cooperatives.

Given that increasing numbers of women began to wish to do more agricultural work, the problem of absorbing additional labour had to be solved. Traditional Chinese agriculture was certainly labour intensive, but not so much so that more labour could not be used. In pursuit of their twin goals of socialist agriculture and agricultural growth, the Chinese have taken collectivization as their organizational strategy, while their technological strategy relied on the increased use first of traditional inputs, and then of modern ones.

Collectivization of course facilitated the mobilization of enormous numbers of peasants for large-scale irrigation and flood control projects, which reduced under-employment in slack seasons. The technological strategies for growth employed by the Chinese also had important implications for rural employment. Since in the 1950s most investment was channelled into industry, leaving agriculture relatively deprived, agricultural growth in that period depended mainly on the intensified use of traditional techniques and inputs. The terracing and remodelling of the land which Tachai has made famous is easier where machinery is available, but many teams and brigades carried out these sorts of projects with picks and shovels. Double and treble cropping were extended into areas where they had been unknown or little employed. This type of cultivation requires enormous amounts of labour, since it doubles or trebles the busy planting and harvest seasons. Furthermore the busy seasons overlap, giving rise to sharp peaks in the demand for labour. As the Chinese economist Ma Yin-ch'u wrote in the 1950s:

> The big problem in the rural areas is that of uneven busy and slack periods, as in south China where the double rice crop is being extended. In the 15 days which witness the cutting of early rice and the planting of the late rice, peasants have more work than can be accomplished. The future key to rich increases in rural production is in mechanical assistance during the excessively busy period.[4]

In fact, the investment for large-scale mechanization was not available in this period, and the demand for labour generated by the extension of double-cropping was met by the mobilization of women. More intensive cultivation also created the need for better irrigation, met at this stage by canals dug with picks and spades rather than bulldozers. Water was propelled along them, or raised from one level to another, by electric pumps where these were obtainable, otherwise traditional hand or foot powered devices were used.

Finally, the growing demand for fertilizer had to be satisfied from natural materials at a period when little chemical fertilizer could be supplied. Since the obvious sources, latrines, pig-sties, and household waste, were already being fully exploited, it was necessary to go further afield. Cliffs were scoured for bird-dung, vegetation was brought down from remote hillsides, while lakes and ponds were dredged for green manure. Thus the need for better irrigation and more fertilizer entailed yet another increase in the demand for labour. Traditional technology had its limitations, however, eventually a ceiling would be reached. The need to invest more heavily in agriculture was recognized and China embarked on what has been dubbed her "green revolution".[5] The basis of the programme under which new technology was introduced was the Eight Character Charter for Agriculture, in effect a condensation of the National Programme for Agricultural Development.[6] The eight points so economically expressed in Chinese characters were:

1. soil improvement
2. fertilization
3. soil conservation
4. seed selection
5. close planting
6. plant protection
7. tool improvement
8. field management

The use of the improved seeds for which the charter called was conditional on abundant fertilizer, good irrigation, and frequent, meticulous hoeing. These also made possible the further extension of multi-cropping, since they produced fast-ripening crops. The demand for labour therefore continued to grow. Though the developing chemical industry could now meet much of the new demand for fertilizer, irrigation could be powered by electric pumps, and tractors were gradually becoming available for earth-shifting and cultivation, the demand for traditional labour-intensive inputs also continued to grow.

Thus the more intensive use of labour, including hitherto under-utilized female labour, enabled the Chinese to increase the productivity of their rare factor—that is the land itself—while postponing the use of modern inputs at a time when investment funds were very short. When the potential for agricultural growth using these methods was reaching exhaustion and modern inputs were introduced, the availability of female labour meant that the labour requirements of the new growth strategy could be easily met.

The primary significance of the entry of great numbers of peasant women into the agricultural workforce was that it allowed China to substitute labour for the capital of which she was so short. Once it had occurred, this massive increase in female employment naturally had many side-effects of importance to the economy.

China, like other underdeveloped countries, is handicapped by a very high dependency ratio, that is the number of mouths which have to be fed by each food producer. It was doubtless aggravated in the 1950s by the success of the health system in bringing down the infant mortality rate while enabling more people to survive to old age. In this context female labour has been of fundamental importance, for it has made possible the recruitment of labour from already existing farming communities, thus lowering the dependency ratio.

Still more important than this immediate effect on the dependency ratio are the longer-term repercussions on the birth-rate of the entry of women into the workforce. As women's labour increased in value the population at large became more receptive to birth control, recognising that each pregnancy, and the subsequent birth and rearing of the child, inevitably meant a loss of earnings. In most societies, young women of child-bearing age are comparatively easily persuaded of the advantages of family planning—after all, it is their health which is threatened by frequent pregnancies, and it is on them that the main burden of caring for the children falls. In the traditional Chinese family, however, it was in just this age-group that women lacked power. Young women were unlikely to attempt the control of their fertility in the face of the united opposition of their husbands and mothers-in-law, particularly since the bearing of sons was their surest way of obtaining the respect and influence which they lacked. But when they began to work, young women could gain respect not only for their fecundity, but for hard work and the income that produced, for special skills, or for unselfish devotion to collective interests.

Finally, once women could be bread-winners, their parents were less anxious to marry them off. Late marriage has been an important plank in the birth control campaign in China. It is a difficult reform for which to win general support as it flies in the face of tradition, but the transformation of young women from economic burdens into bread-winners has doubtless assisted in its implementation. Again this has obvious implications for the birth-rate. A further development has been the increasing practice of men joining their bride's family on marriage.[7] Though still very much a minority trend this is being officially encouraged and a few such matches have probably taken place in most communes.[8] They are particularly advocated as the solution in cases where a couple has only daughters. Such parents can count on at least one daughter staying in the household when she reaches working age, and then of a son-in-law joining it when she marries, thus ensuring that the parents can rely on family support in old age. If this becomes a generally accepted practice, it will eliminate one cause of big families, the tendency of parents who have only daughters to "go on trying" until they have a son, and thus contribute to the birth control movement.

The higher household incomes which resulted from the entry of more peasant women into the work-force, also had an impact on the economy by increasing savings and stimulating demand for light industrial goods. Pressure on women's time and energy, together with greater prosperity, gave peasants both the incentive and the means to purchase more goods and services, drawing them ever further from subsistence. Households, lifted above subsistence level by the addition of women's income, were enabled for the first time to purchase labour-saving products such as detergents, thermos-flasks, bicycles and machine-made cloth, or items for pleasure, convenience and comfort such as radios, clocks and toothbrushes. The demand for complex industrial products had its main effects in the urban areas where they were manufactured, but the new spending power of the peasants, coinciding with the movement to develop rural industries, also fostered the growth of many local enterprises supplying simple consumer products such as cooking pans, pottery and plastic household goods.

Obviously women who have begun to go to the fields, or have greatly increased the hours they spend in them, were not idle before. On the contrary, they worked hard and long, preparing food for their families, fetching fuel and water, cleaning their houses, making, washing and mending clothes and tending their children. The pressure to relieve them at least partially of their doubled burden has led to some of the work formerly performed at home being taken over by team or brigade-run enterprises and by coops, a change which has itself made a significant contribution to the economic development of the villages and small manufacturing centres. Although in this situation such work is often still done by women, they earn workpoints or wages for doing it and thus what was formerly unpaid domestic work gains a socially acknowledged value.

Crêches and nurseries have eased the problem of childcare, while production teams run canteens, at least in the busy season. Chinese childcare institutions have attracted a lot of attention in the West, reflecting perhaps the fact that children are a working mother's greatest single problem there. But though the nurseries are quite popular, care of children in China's countryside at least is rather easier. Children, once they can toddle, are less at risk and require far less concentrated attention than in our congested cities. Moreover, in China grandparents or older children are usually available to give them the care they need. From the point of view of women in rural China, the fact that processing of staple foods has been taken over by the community has usually been of much greater importance than the establishment of crêches and kindergardens.

It is seldom realized how time-consuming the crude processing of basic foodstuffs can be. In some parts of Africa women spend an hour preparing the staple food before they start to cook a meal, while in Mexico 4–6 hours a day per family are spent in grinding grain.[9] The biggest daily time-saver for Chinese women has probably been the mechanization of the processing of staples. Here is a glimpse of the economies gained by using a mill in Liu Ling, northern Shensi:

Li Yangqing's household consisted of 7 persons. They consumed about 1,500 kilos of grain a year. Formerly she used to grind all this herself, by hand. Now it was being ground for her in the brigade mill. The brigade charges at cost for this service. The prices vary slightly for different sorts of grain. On average it is 0.66 yuan per 100 kilos of grain. Last year Li Yangqing paid about 10 yuan. This is deducted from the money she gets for her work. But since the mill has freed her—as it has the other women—from the hardest and most time-consuming part of her household work and this has given her more time for agriculture so has her working income risen.[10]

In areas where rice is the main staple, women can get it husked mechanically. Flour can be taken to noodle-making shops to be exchanged for machine-made noodles, whereas previously the housewife had to cut them from the dough which she had mixed and rolled. Beancurd, a laboriously made bean product which is an important item in the Chinese diet, is also on sale in many brigades. Clothes can be ordered at sewing stations, where workers using treadle machines can finish in an hour jobs which would take a housewife many evenings of hand-stitching.

Women's employment thus fosters rural industries and they in turn foster women's employment, partly simply because they increase the general employment level in the countryside, partly also because in many cases they involve what are traditionally women's skills. This is clearly so with local industries such as tailoring and food processing, which have taken over tasks previously performed by the housewife for her family. However, the same will apply where local industries are based on old handicrafts in which women have always worked. The products of some of these reach a national and even an international market. Processed tea, embroidery, baskets and fans are only a few examples of items which may originate in a brigade or commune factory and go on to earn China foreign exchange for the purchase of capital goods.

Although the idea that women have a role to play in agriculture is now very generally accepted in China, there is still not complete agreement on what that role should be. In some communes, women really have the chance to work on equal terms with men and equal pay-rates give them the incentive to do so, while in others female labour is regarded very much as an auxiliary force, and women are poorly paid and tend to spend less time in the fields.

The official line, reiterated many times, is one of equal pay for equal work. Unfortunately, of course, the interpretation of this ruling is difficult. According to *Hung-ch'i* (Red Flag) the theoretical journal of the Party,

Physically, some people are stong while others are weak. There is some heavy manual farmwork which it is appropriate that strong men should do. Such a division of labour based on the physical differences between the sexes is quite proper. We must not force male and female commune members to do the same work, ignoring women's physiological characteristics and physical strength. On the other hand, differences in physical strength must certainly not be used to justify paying men and women unequally for equal work. Our principle for distribution is: "from each according to his ability, to each according to his labour". Therefore, the criterion in assessing remuneration should be the quantity and quality of each commune member's work, that is the amount he has contributed to socialist production. It should not be based on the degree of physical strength or on sexual differences.[11]

Discussion of remuneration in the Chinese countryside is always complicated by the fact that every commune operates its own system. Basically, each peasant is awarded work points for the work that he or she does, and a record is kept of them. When the harvest is in and the accounting has been done, each team or brigade having made certain deductions for investment, new seed, welfare fund, etc., divides the rest amongst its members on the basis of the number of work points each has earned. Some communes award a fixed number of points to eacn job on the basis of the skill and energy it requires. Others assess the capacity of each individual, valuing a full day's work from one peasant at ten points, and from another at five. Others again—and from the visits I have made I would judge this system to be the most frequently operated—divide members into categories, usually based on sex and age, allocating a work point value to each category. The most typical pattern seems now to be ten points for a man and eight for a woman, with 3–4 points less for adolescents or old people.[12] Some communes however practise refinements of this system to make it more equitable, giving especially strong men and women valuation higher than the norm for their categories. Presumably this produces results closer to those of the system under which each individual's work is evaluated.

Another complicating factor is that where women get fewer work points for a working day, they also sometimes do fewer hours for them. Tachai, where women are not expected to go to the fields before breakfast in order "to leave them time to do their housework and prepare a meal for the family" is a case in point.[13] In the Lukouchiao commune near Peking where strong women earn as much as men, there is no such automatic attribution of household tasks to the women. They seem rather to be shared by all members of the family as they return from work.

Different as the systems are, they all involve the difficulty of calculating the comparative value of different jobs within a collective unit. The tendency under all three systems is to give heavy or highly skilled work the highest remuneration. Physiological factors often exclude women from the first, and social conservatism from the second. To quote once more from *Hung-ch'i*:

> There are even some areas where the distinction inherited from the old society between "men's farm work" and "women's farm work" is still retained. Jobs requiring more skill, like the sowing of rice or wheat, the making of paddy fields or the application of fertilizers, are the so-called "men's jobs". Women are not allowed to do them or to learn to do them.[14]

Furthermore, the definition of what *is* heavy or skilled work is very much a cultural matter. The traditional belief that women are inferior, too easily influences judgement even today, leading to the dismissal of jobs which they do as "light" or "unskilled".

Obviously a key point here is the division of labour. Some production teams organize men and women into separate work groups. The explanation for this segregation is that it facilitates the allocation of women to tasks appropriate to their physiques, but of course it presupposes uniformity of physique among them, and often results in all women being allocated work associated with low work point evaluations. The "Iron Girls' teams", set up by young unmarried women who wished to show that they could work as well as men, were a reaction against the idea that a woman could not do the heaviest work. Such teams are useful as standard-bearers, serving to break down preconceptions about women's capabilities. However, membership of such teams is only a stage in a woman's life, since their members usually transfer to other teams on marriage or on becoming pregnant. In Tachai, I was told that Kuo Feng-lien, now chairwoman of its brigade revolutionary committee, was the only one of the original Iron Girls to have remained in the village.[15] Obviously such a turnover precludes these teams from offering a permanent solution for women.

In the long-run, I believe that women's best hope for more equitable treatment lies in the mixed work groups found in the most developed areas, especially those on the outskirts of towns. In them, men and women work together at the same tasks. The speed and quality of their work is easily assessed, and judgement of the value of the work done by one team on one job compared to that by another doing something else, is no longer coloured by prejudice against women.

The importance attached by the Party to the implementation of the principle of equal pay for equal work is beyond doubt. Cadres who make light of this problem have often been condemned.

> While admitting the irrationality of "giving men ten points and women eight points for a day of work", some comrades do not seriously seek a solution to this problem. They hold that since every household consists of men and women, no household will thereby suffer economic loss, nor will this affect the enthusiasm of women. ... This view is wrong ...
> Observance of the principle of equal pay for equal work for men and women is not only an economic problem, but first of all a political problem, of line. ... To regard it as inconsequential is essentially to regard women's status as inconsequential, a feudal idea, that belittles women.[16]

It is interesting that mixed work groups, shared responsibility for household tasks and a work point system under which a woman can obtain a rating as high as a man's seem often to go together. Typically this occurs in communes on the outskirts of towns, as in the Lukouchiao commune mentioned earlier. The influence of the city leading to a readier acceptance of the equality of women may be one factor in this, but economic factors are probably vital. Cash incomes in such communes are high because they produce vegetables for the nearby city. Nightsoil from the city gives a steady and plentiful source of fertilizer, assuring high productivity. These favourable economic factors have produced *rapid* growth in such communes. Thus because the marginal value of each additional unit of labour has been maintained at a high level, the mobilization of more labour has never threatened the value of the work-point as can happen in more backward communes. Where this occurs, the team leadership may be tempted to maintain the work-point's value, and thus the earnings of established (male) workers by keeping down the number of work-points which its new (female) workers are able to earn. Wealth has also enabled suburban communes to mechanize the heaviest work, thus eliminating the justification for the sexual segregation of the workforce. The social and economic advancement of such communities makes birth control more acceptable to them, and the consequent lower birth-rate has also reduced women's physical handicaps. In many ways in fact, suburban communes may be said to bridge the great difference in conditions which still exists between cities and the countryside.

WOMEN IN THE URBAN WORKFORCE

Although women were recruited into industry on a large scale during the 1950s and the media campaigned vigorously to encourage them to take jobs outside the home, this support was by no means unwavering. Urban unemployment was a widespread problem in the first years after liberation and the industrial development strategy of that time, based primarily on heavy industry and capital-intensive projects, could not relieve it. The peak periods of unemployment saw the publication of articles and reportage emphasizing the value of women as wives and mothers, whose contribution should lie in servicing those members of their families with jobs outside the home.[17] This trend reached its height in 1957 before it was swept away by the development strategy of the Great Leap Forward whose attempt to substitute labour for capital demanded mass participation in economic activity. The mood swung back briefly in the early 1960s to a greater emphasis on women's domestic role, although this time the tendency was less marked. During the Cultural Revolution these attempts to glorify the wife-mother image were condemned, being identified as the revisionist trend in the two-line struggle in the women's movement.[18] Since then, the press has sustained the image of women contributing like men to their country's development as industrial workers, shop assistants, service workers, teachers, cadres, medical personnel and so on. Other family members, and husbands in particular, are urged to regard housework as a shared responsibility rather than a wife's natural duty.

In many ways the contribution made to development by urban women are similar to those which rural women have made. The entry of more women into the workforce has increased its size, lowered the dependency ratio, and stimulated the demand for labour-saving devices and services. It has also helped to make the urban population more receptive to family planning and even to the official ideal of the one- or two-child family. However, some features of these trends have particular significance in the urban setting.

In the early years after liberation, China, like many underdeveloped countries, was bedevilled by rapidly growing cities with a high dependency ratio. The cost of providing an adequate infrastructure of housing, educational and leisure facilities, public utilities, roads, etc., for cities like this can be very high. Many Third World countries have ignored such needs, simply allowing shanty towns to grow and failing to provide educational and municipal services. This is clearly not a way out which the Chinese government could adopt.

Another pattern which occurs in some developing countries where women support themselves wholly or partially in agriculture, is based on male migration to the towns.[19] This produces a lower dependency ratio in the cities since the migrants leave their families in the villages. But it also gives rise to immeasurable human misery, as well as other side-effects such as prostitution, drunkeness, crime and deserted families, which may be hard to cost but are clearly undesirable both economically and socially.[20]

A third way to lower the dependency ratio within towns is by lowering it within families. This has been achieved in China by encouraging women to enter and to remain in the workforce, and by promoting birth control. The social overhead costs of urban development have thus been kept down, because cities have been able to increase their workforce to meet the needs of industrial growth, without a proportionate increase in the urban population.

The assumption that both husband and wife will work has affected city planning. When residential accommodation, schools, nurseries, shops and other support services are all to be found in the environs of the work-place, the logistical problems of the morning and evening which so frequently torture the working couple in the West do not arise. Commuting is necessary at most only for one of the parents, nearby schools ease the problems of delivering the children or enable them to go by themselves, and shopping for the evening meal can be done by the children or by their parents on their way home from work. This pattern, at least in the case of large enterprises, produces a community in which much of the social life of its members is contained. Not surprisingly therefore, young people quite frequently pick their spouses from among the workforce of their own enterprise, a phenomenon which again eases the problems of working couples.

The effect on the demand for manufactured goods and the household's dependency on the market induced by higher family incomes and the pressure on women's time, have gone further in the towns than in the rural areas. Grain is obtained already processed and nearly all food is purchased, though some families grow vegetables and hens or more rarely a goat may be kept. In Peking though, all livestock, even hens, have now been banished from residential areas for reasons of hygiene. Canteens are used by most workers at midday and by substantial numbers in the evening. Even those who prefer to eat at home frequently buy a meal or part of one to take home with them. Clothes are most often obtained ready-made, while hand-spinning and weaving, which linger on in remote rural areas, are unknown in the towns. Only knitwear is still more usually made by hand, because wool is expensive and, if hand-knitted, worn or out-grown garments can be unravelled, and the yarn re-used.

In some cities families may aspire to own a gas-stove, otherwise few products which we would recognize as labour-saving are available besides those already mentioned for the countryside. The production of consumer durables on a large scale would divert much-needed resources from the production of capital goods and would thus retard development.[21]

On the whole in China, transfers of labour from the household to the public sector have to be effected in a capital-saving, labour-intensive way. Thus, though fridges, washing-machines and vacuum cleaners are almost unknown, canteens, nurseries and sewing-shops are very general. Sometimes they are supplied by sub-units of industrial or administrative organizations. Every large urban enterprise has its own canteen and its own nursery. But street committees also include the provision of such services among their many activities. In doing so they not only free some women for work outside the home, they also provide employment which utilizes female skills. There is a residue of women not in employment who cannot obtain regular jobs because their household responsibilities are too heavy, their health is poor, or they lack the required education or confidence. These women, along with a minority of men, mostly above retiring age, have found in the street committees another chance to work for the development of their society.

The industrial enterprises run by street committees produce small, usually rather labour-intensive goods, very cheaply. As they have little capital equipment their product can be comparatively easily switched in response to changes in demand. This flexibility makes them very useful for the supply of cheap consumer goods, spare parts for industry and even the production of export items such as fashions and toys. Inevitably with a low investment level, their productivity is also low. Their pay, which is a division of the profits, is therefore lower than that of workers in state industry and they do not receive the same fringe benefits as the latter. There is some danger that the existence of this two-tier system of industry could lead to a situation in which women get relegated to the least capitalized, least productive sector of industry. Up to now, however, street industries have on balance been beneficial, employing women whose energies could not otherwise have been mobilized for production.

Other street committee activities, also staffed in the main by women, contribute towards healthy urban development. For example, they are responsible for welfare, street cleansing, home-nursing and liaison between residents and schools, shops and hospitals. They run clinics in which basic medical treatment can be given and which have special responsibility for family planning, immunization and infant welfare. The committee members who run the street committee are unpaid, although its staff, of doctors, nurses, teachers, etc., receive a salary. Whether professional or voluntary, all the work of the street committee may be seen as a vehicle through which women contribute to development.

TACHING

Taching, the cradle of one of the proudest achievements of China's industry, has been turned by women into an agricultural area. The role played by women in the oilfields is an interesting one because although it must be seen as a special case, outside the normal pattern of development in China, it does point up, in an extreme form, the problems for women of the two-tier system already discussed in connection with street industry.

When the oil-workers' wives and families first arrived at Taching in the early 1960s, they were truly "dependants". They lived in tents with their husbands and shifted with them from one site to another. As the oilfields developed, the question of permanent settlement came up. The idea of a big, modern city was rejected, instead the settlements took a village-like form and women began to cultivate the wastes around them. This proved very hard work, but they persevered and managed in the space of a few years to satisfy half the grain requirements of the oilfield's population as well as supplying it with vegetables and pork.

Later, women began to set up small workshops to serve both the needs of the industry and the local population. They produce nuts and bolts, chemicals, clothes, and repair bicycles, watches and radios and recycle worn clothing. The agricultural, industrial and service enterprises all function on a cooperative basis, that is their workers share the profits on the basis of the workpoints they have earned. They are thus quite distinct from the oilfield workers who are wage-earners in a state-owned industry.

Perhaps conscious of undesirable implications in a situation in which women were segregated in separate fields of labour, in 1970 the local leadership organized the first women's oil drilling team. It remains, however, that 90 per cent of Taching's female population is engaged in agriculture.

Bearing in mind that Taching is in a remote and previously sparsely populated area, and that one of the most severe constraints on its development is one of transportation and supplies, it is clear that the measure of self-sufficiency the work of these women has conferred on it must have been very beneficial. On the other hand it resulted in a situation where men were employed in an advanced, modern industry while women worked for work-points at far more mundane tasks. Thus there is a paradox in the achievements of the women of Taching. By undertaking the full range of agricultural work—indeed more than the usual full range, in that they brought a wilderness under the plough—they provided an exemplary rebuttal of the persisting traditional male attitudes that elsewhere in China still generally restrict women to auxiliary roles in agriculture. So, in the national context, the women of Taching have clearly advanced the cause of women's equality. But when their role is examined in the specific context of Taching, it can be seen that the agricultural work done by the women is still auxiliary to the prime economic activity of producing oil.

CONCLUSION

In China today, participation in socialist construction, the chosen path of national development, is the means to public esteem and self-respect. Some women contribute to socialist construction much as men do, others have to be differently mobilized for tasks appropriate to their particular situation. There seems to be some awareness of the dangers of highly segregated participation and attempts are being made to avoid them. However, even the present role of women, though it falls short of complete equality, is one whose primary and secondary effects have had an enormous impact on the pace and quality of Chinese development.

NOTES

1   Ester Boserup, *Women's Role in Economic Development*, London: Allen and Unwin, 1970, Chap. 3.
2   Op. cit., Chap. 10.

3   Figures from J. L. Buck, *Land Utilization in China*, Nanking: University of Nanking, 1937, p. 293. I do not think these figures should be taken as anything more than a rough indication of women's participation. For a much fuller discussion of their significance see Delia Davin, *Woman-work: Women and the Party in Revolutionary China*, Oxford: Clarendon Press, 1976, pp. 117–21.

4   Ma Yin-ch'u, "My Philosophical Thoughts and Economic Theory" quoted in Kenneth Walker, Ma Yin-ch'u: A Chinese Discussion on Planning for Balanced Growth, p. 182, In C. D. Cowan (Ed.), *The Economic Growth of China and Japan*, London: Allen and Unwin, 1972.

5   See Benedict Stavis, *China's Green Revolution*, Cornell University East Asia Papers, No. 2, 1974.

6   *National Programme of Economic Development, 1956–1957*, Peking 1960, and Wu Yi-cheng, Eight Measures for Higher Yields, *Peking Review*, 23 June, 1959.

7   See Neville Maxwell's paper above, p. 41.

8   Among the 20-odd communes on which I gathered information during a year's residence in China (1975–6) only two were wholly without such matches. On a visit to Lukouchiao commune, just outside Peking, in May 1975, I was told that the man had joined his wife's family in 5 of the 11 marriages which had been registered in the preceding month. This was considered unusually high, and the practice is rarer in backward areas.

9   Ester Boserup, op. cit., p. 164.

10 Jan Myrdal and Gun Kessle, *China: the Revolution Continued*, Harmondsworth: Penguin, 1973, pp. 10–12.

11 Chin Chi-tsu and Hung Sung, Nan nu t'ung kung yao t'ung ch'ou (Equal Pay for Equal Work for Men and Women), *Hung-ch'i*, No. 2, Feb. 1, 1972, p. 59.

12 This at least represents some progress from the 1950s when 10 points for men and 5 for women was quite common.

13 I was told this on a visit to Tachai in November 1975.

14 *Hung-ch'i*, Feb. 1972, p. 90.

15 Asked why all the others had joined their husbands' families on marriage our guide, an oldish man, who appeared to find the question comical, replied that their husbands would have been missed by their parents had they joined their wives. He could find no answer when asked if the girls had not been similarly "missed".

16 *Hung-ch'i*, Feb. 1, 1972, pp. 61–2.

17 The worst example of the articles, An Tze-wen, A correct approach to the problem of retirement of women cadres, *Women of China*, February 1958, actually urged women to withdraw from their jobs. For details of these policy fluctuations see: Delia Davin, The Implications of Some Aspects of CCP Policy Towards Urban Women in the 1950s, *Modern China*, Vol. 1, No. 4, October 1975 and Phyllis Andors, Politics of Chinese Deveopment: The Case of Women, 1960–1966, *Signs*, Autumn 1976, Vol. 2, No. 1.

18 Hung-se fu-nu, *Red Women–A Women's Red Guard Paper*, 19th May 1967.

19 The pre-liberation male migration from parts of Kwangtung where women customarily worked in the fields, to South-East Asia, followed this pattern.

20 China, because of its emphasis on the equal importance of the jobs of both husband and wife, does have a share of families split, for a time at least, by separate job assignments. This is obviously rather a different phenomenon, and affects only a small minority of the population, mostly skilled and professional workers.

21 It is often supposed that time spent on housework decreases with the availability of domestic appliances and higher general standards of living. Ann Oakley has shown that it tends to remain constant or even increase, as housewives raise their standards and elaborate their routines. [Ann Oakley, *Housewife*, Harmondsworth: Pelican, 1976, pp. 6–8.] From my observations in China, I believe that up to the point at which certain basics such as tapped water, drainage, and labour-saving methods of heating and lighting are assured, prosperity can cut down enormously on housework; after that, the correlation may become negative—obviously it takes less time to sweep a cement floor than to set up a vacuum cleaner and go over a fitted carpet.

Science in China

LEO A. ORLEANS

During the brief history of the People's Republic the Chinese leadership's attitudes and policies towards economic development, education and science have followed a course marked by repeated major, and often sudden, changes of direction. Since the death of Mao Tse-tung and the downfall of the group now repudiated as the "gang of four" there has been another such sharp change, and China is now on a tack which only a few years ago the Chinese would have termed "revisionist". The emphasis is on rapid economic development, and science and technology have been designated the "leading factors" in the projected "four modernizations"—of agriculture, industry, national defence, and science and technology. Intellectuals in general and scientists in particular have been not only cleared of the suspicion that they are innately "bourgeois" and therefore politically unreliable, but elevated to an elite position within the society—from being "stinking intellectuals" they have become "fragrant". In order fully to appreciate the implications for the goals and values of science and technology of the new directions so clearly proclaimed to 6,000 delegates who attended the National Science Conference in Peking in the spring of 1978, these drastic changes must be silhouetted against the recent past.

The prime factor behind the veerings in course has been the degree to which the Maoist principle "Politics in Command" has been adhered to during given years. There were basically two periods in which the role of politics was overwhelming and the related concepts of the "mass line" and mass initiative dominated the Chinese scene: those of the Great Leap Forward (1958–9) and of the Great Proletarian Cultural Revolution (1966–9). Although the domination of science by politics during both these periods had an adverse effect on scientific development and on the economy in general, there was also a growing body of opinion that these massive campaigns were a necessary prerequisite to generating political will for Mao-style development; that even occasional visits to the countryside by scientists, to work and mingle with the peasants, may not seriously have affected their performance—and in some cases may have enhanced it. While the case for this point of view—which may have a certain validity—is still espoused outside China, the present Chinese leadership, and certainly the scientists, appear to be hard pressed to find any redeeming values in the policies pursued during the Cultural Revolution.

During the less volatile periods somewhat more practical considerations tended to play a greater role in decision-making and policy formulation. But even then it was only a question of degree, because for the highly politicized Chinese population politics is never entirely absent. The political cycles from pragmatic to radical (convenient if only approximate designations), with their concomitant variations in development strategy, reflect an almost perpetual tug-of-war between Mao's revolutionary values, stressing mass mobilization and participation even in science and technology, and the forces that would attempt to achieve economic development and modernization by making fuller use of foreign technological models and foreign know-how. None of the developmental cycles through which China has passed has in any sense bypassed science and technology, although, for better or worse, politics have throughout been in command.

What can be missed is that China moved in and out of these periods of extremes over periods of time—leaning either towards rapid economic development through the acquisition of modern science and high technology, or towards installing "the love of science" among the masses and complete integration of science with production. Furthermore, since the mid-1950s there has never been a time when the influence of the school or faction temporarily out of favour or power was not making itself heard or felt through the "two-line struggle"—a polemic which Mao considered inevitable and valuable in achieving the wise consensus. Undoubtedly this cyclical alternation has worked to slow development at times; but what is surprising is that in spite of the policy shifts China has made significant progress in both areas.

SCIENTIFIC GOALS

In the most general sense the demands that China has been making on science have not changed in 30 years. Science must make China a competitive world power, and science must pull the hundreds of millions of Chinese people into the second half of the twentieth century—indeed, in the formulation of the new campaign of the "four modernizations", push them to the threshold of the twenty-first. China needs science—and therefore China must depend upon scientists. But from the beginning this presented a dilemma or, as Mao put it, a contradiction. Most of China's scientific élite had been trained either in the West or by Western-trained professors. They valued academic training, foreign experience and contacts, and independent, pure research. Such scientists, as well as those trained in the Soviet Union in the 1950s, found it difficult to sympathize with the value Mao placed on the native intelligence and initiative of the masses, or to accept that the primary function of science was in the service of production. Nevertheless, in the early years of its "march on science" China had no choice but to rely on these scientists, who, in close but not necessarily friendly cooperation with their Soviet counterparts, were in the process of producing the Twelve Year Science Plan, with its twelve priority categories, designed to place the country on a par with the advanced world.[1] Gradually, however, first by creating the Science Planning Commission in 1956 and later by strengthening it and expanding its functions as the State Scientific and Technological Commission, the regime began wresting primary control over science from the Academy of Sciences which, until then, had been the chief policy-maker and performer in the science area. During the 1960s and certainly during the Cultural Revolution, Peking's control over the scientific community was such that scientists were not very likely to stray from goal-oriented research related to the state's economic plans. In order to further ensure goal-oriented science, the authorities managed to shift many scientific activities from the universities and academically oriented institutes of the Academy of Sciences to the practical environment of the plants, factories and farms. As a result, the number of institutes under the Academy's jurisdiction was drastically reduced by the time the Cultural Revolution died down. The emphasis on local needs and production led to most of the institutes that remained open being placed under regional control.

Within the real scientific establishment the most persistent and heated debate has centred around the conceptual problem of basic versus applied research. Looking in from the outside it is difficult to see why this argument should have persisted over two decades. Given China's level of development, it seems quite reasonable that most of the country's scientific, human and capital resources should go into applied research, development, and the adaptation of existing scientific knowledge and technology to China's needs. Occasional departures into basic research by individual scientists should not have disturbed those broad priorities. Unfortunately, during periods of radical control, reasonable policies tended to be carried to unreasonable extremes. During the Cultural Revolution scientists, by definition, became suspect and, with little discrimination, were accused of being élitist, of "living in ivory towers", seeking "personal fame and gain", of persisting with theoretical research unrelated to production needs. Re-education was prescribed for them all. But, such extreme attacks notwithstanding, there were always people in the leadership who knew all too well the extent to which the achievement of China's goals depended on those very scientists who were being denounced. They also appreciated that while the older generation of scientists had been prone to élitism (inevitably, in the communist view, considering their training under the old or a foreign social system), élitism is relative: changes had occurred in the attitudes of the older scientists, while the new generation of scientists was even more amenable to some of the policies promulgated during the Cultural Revolution.

An early sign of the reassertion of pragmatism may be seen in the progressive re-opening, beginning in the 1970s, of many of the research institutions; by mid-1976 seventy had been identified as functioning again under the Academy of Sciences—now there are ninety, and their number is still growing. A similar trend has been evident in the number of institutes under the Academy of Agricultural Sciences (now the Academy of Agriculture and Forestry Sciences) and the Academy of Medical Sciences (see Appendix). Now it can be seen that, after vacillation—or, more likely, hidden struggle—during the early 1970s, the basic responsibility for research in science and technology is reverting to the academies and to the most qualified scientists. This represents a shift of advantage in the strife between the science professionals and Communist Party administrators for control of the scientific institutions and programmes that has been almost perennial since 1949. In principle, Chinese scientists have learned to accept, perhaps even to understand, the ultimate authority of the Party in establishing the general direction of scientific research. They have tended to react strongly, however, on occasions when politics came to dominate science and Party administrators attempted to extend their role as "facilitators of research" to becoming in effect research directors.

That was one of the areas most affected in the great change instituted in China after the arraignment of the "gang of four"—a change that for the intellectuals amounted to a "Thaw". The attacks on their political probity made during the Cultural Revolution and sustained as a persistent under-current through the first half of the 1970s were vigorously disavowed, and those who had orchestrated the attacks were themselves cast into odium and oblivion. In a speech to the National Science Conference Teng Hsiao-ping carefully circumscribed the role of the Party in science. He said that for research institutes, scientific results were the only criteria by which the work of the responsible Party committee should be judged, and that "putting politics in command" without showing scientific results "will remain empty talk". The Party leadership must ensure the correct political orientation, they must guarantee supporting services and supplies, and they should even "get acquainted with the work of the scientists"; but the scientific leadership of the research institutes should have a "free hand in the work of science and technology".

It is characteristic that in China the nub of the argument about basic versus applied research has been couched in political terms, as an argument over the interpretation of Mao's maxim that: "Class struggle, the struggle for production, and scientific experiment are the three great revolutionary struggles for building a great, modern socialist country." The "radicals", or the "gang of four", contended that Mao meant class struggle to have priority over the other two "struggles": they denounced their opponents as adherents of the "reactionary policy that science decides everything", and upheld the primacy of class struggle as "a locomotive pulling history forward". The present leadership repudiates that as a misinterpretation of Mao, arguing that he meant the "three struggles" to be co-equal in importance. Mao, they say, fully appreciated the role of science in the revolution, appreciating that without "the struggle for production and scientific experiment" China would not be able to improve the well-being of the people and consolidate the power of the proletariat. This argument is now even pushed to the extent of claiming that scientific research must lead not only production and construction, but even class struggle.

In his address to the National Science Conference Teng Hsiao-ping translated such philosophical wranglings into a concrete new line: "The crux of the four modernizations", he said, "is the mastery of modern science and technology." He went on to point out the close relationship between the laboratory (basic research) and production, arguing that although there are many theoretical research projects which have no practical application in plain sight, "a host of historical facts have proved that once a major breakthrough is scored in theoretical research, it means tremendous progress for production and technology sooner or later". "Backwardness must be perceived before it can be changed", said Teng, and the new goals of science and technology must not be politically determined. What this seems to mean is that at least for the time being China will attempt to maintain a balanced approach to scientific goals and that while applied research will undoubtedly continue to dominate the scientific establishment, basic research will no longer have to be disguised.

Undoubtedly the dominant theme in the National Science Conference was conveyed in Teng's speech, but Hua Kuo-feng, Mao's successor as chairman, interjected a balancing warning that the modernization of science and technology should not be "left to a few people in research institutes or universities". Some may read that as no more than a still-necessary show of reverence for Mao's principles; but it might be more prudent, against the background of past developments in China, to note Hua's words as a reminder that "science for the masses" is still a part of China's policies.

While both Peking and the outside world emphasize the changes in China's policies since the death of Mao, the continuity which is evident upon closer examination tends to be lost in the rhetoric of the Chinese media, which was first controlled by the "gang" and which is now exaggerating its influence by ascribing to the "gang" all the adversities suffered by China in the past decade. In fact, even during periods when Communist Party direction of scientific research was most emphatic, basic, non-directed research was not entirely neglected and members of the Academy of Sciences were being credited by international science with a number of scientific accomplishments—such as the synthesis of insulin, work in high energy physics, in plasma physics, in high polymer chemistry, in laser research. Even when the need for rigorous self-reliance in science as in all fields was being most stridently proclaimed, countervailing voices expressed themselves with the argument that "self-reliance in no way means shutting one's doors to sincere and effective international aid". China never shut the doors. The volume of imports fluctuated but the purchase of significant quantities of technology from Western Europe and Japan and, after 1972, from the USA never completely stopped—this included scientific instruments, machinery, transportation equipment and scores of whole plants.[2] While emphasizing development of her own technology, China has throughout, when necessary, imported more sophisticated technology for immediate use and adaptation to her specific needs. Except briefly at the very height of the Cultural Revolution, China's scientists also continued to receive all the latest scientific and technical publications and reports, keeping them informed of advances in the outside world. In other words, practical considerations prevailed; China received the critical technology she required, but frugality combined with the push for self-sufficiency controlled the flow of that imported technology to carefully selected priority areas.

"WALKING ON TWO LEGS"

In a sense, the slogan "walking on two legs" expresses and allows for a compromise which can accommodate all of the contradictions inherent in the constant political tug-of-war between advocates of "redness" (political purity) and "expertness" (technical proficiency). China's fundamental policy is to encourage simultaneously science for technological advancement and science for the people—and to assure maximum flexibility in the development of both. Now, in the intense campaign to achieve "the four modernizations", that "leg" represented in the will to provide the Chinese scientists and engineers with all necessary facilities, equipment and foreign know-how is foremost; but the equally important effort that has been made at the mass level to transform the basic but somewhat abstract national virtue, "love of science", into a more practical economic asset continues, especially in the progressive introduction of simple technology into the rural areas. The two-leg image's inherent alternation links with the dialectic emphasized by Mao. He urged that China "should learn from the strong points of all nations", but warned that she must not "copy everything indiscriminately and transplant mechanically". Mao's formulation for resolving that dichotomy was: "Rely mainly on our own efforts while making external assistance subsidiary."

It is easy to see how the opposing factions in the Chinese leadership would use those maxims, the "gang of four" demanding self-sufficiency rather than self-reliance in science and technology, and branding their opponents as subscribing to the "philosophy of servility to things foreign"; and the moderates and modernizers insisting that obtaining scientific help and advanced technology from abroad was nothing more than "making foreign things serve China"—just what Dr. Mao ordered. Now, after the period in which "self-reliance", often distorted into "self-sufficiency", was the foremost "leg", all the emphasis is on maximizing scientific and technological intercourse with the technologically advanced nations. As Teng Hsiao-ping put it to the National Science Conference, "a person must learn from the advanced before he can catch up and surpass them". The determination of the Chinese to learn was evidenced in the 1978 invitation to the American scientific delegation led by Dr. Frank Press, the US President's Science and Technology Adviser, and China's approach was spelled out by Fang Yi, vice-premier and minister in charge of science and technology, at the farewell to that delegation: while still "relying on our own efforts", he said, "we will take an active attitude toward strengthening international scientific and technical exchanges and cooperation and developing both governmental and non-governmental contacts in these fields, on the principle of equality and equal benefit". In other words, China feels she can now continue with her basic self-reliance without isolating herself from the world of foreign science and technology—and the experience of more emphasized self-reliance in the recent past has left her with confidence that scientific exchanges with the outside world will not be entirely one-way.

EDUCATION AND SCIENTIFIC MANPOWER

The alternation of emphasis is very apparent in China's approach to scientific and technological education. Before the Cultural Revolution China maintained a two-track system in education. Recognizing that the nation could neither provide quality education for the whole school-age population nor absorb into a developing economy unlimited numbers of highly trained specialists, the educational system produced graduates at many different levels of competence, from low-grade technicians to highly trained scientists. By the mid-1960s Mao was charging that the system was too élitist and discriminatory against the children of workers and peasants. The Cultural Revolution had a drastic effect on education. All schools were closed, for from at least two years at the primary level to four years or more at the college level. When the institutions reopened the curricula at all educational levels were shortened, all study was integrated with productive labour, most examinations were abolished and many more students from worker and peasant families were admitted into both secondary and higher education. The Chinese now admit that those changes went too far—indeed, injury to the educational system is one of the most severe charges against the "gang" and those they influenced. Well aware that the goals envisaged by "the four modernizations" are directly related to the availability of a highly trained manpower pool, educational reforms are receiving top priority in China. College entrance examinations conducted throughout the country are selecting the most able youth as students in the 88 "key" universities which are presumably receiving priority funding, support and attention. Many of the universities and institutes of the Chinese Academy of Sciences are once again providing graduate education to Chinese students. At the same time, the July 21 Workers' Universities and innumerable other educational institutions are providing education for the more production-oriented worker and peasant. There is no doubt that China is reverting to a two-track system—"walking on two legs" again.

The damage done by the excesses of the Cultural Revolution will take time to correct, however. Teng Hsiao-ping has conceded that an age-gap had been left in the scientific and technological force "which makes the training of a younger generation of scientific and technical personnel all the more pressing". The "National Plan for Development of Science and Technology" presented at the Conference includes the goal to "increase the number of scientific researchers to 800,000 by 1985". Clearly that target is not to be reached solely through new graduates from the educational system—it will take time to rev that up and therefore, as the Chinese stress, great effort will be made in training and raising the level of the existing contingent of scientific and technical workers to "bring their role into full play". The urgency with which China is embarking on her crash programme of modernization is most startlingly evident in the intended dispatch of some 10,000 Chinese students to study in the technologically advanced nations—an experiment that must involve ideological risk, both that the "foreign-trained" may become an élite on return to China (as in so many developing countries) and that the students will imbibe some politics with their Western technology.

PROSPECTS

How successful China will be in her present drive for modernization must depend on the availability of funds to purchase foreign technology and know-how and on the quantitative and qualitative adequacy of her scientific and technological manpower to absorb, adapt and manage the world's most advanced knowledge to the country's advantage. Certainly the current reforms in the educational system and the planned dispatch abroad of massive numbers of Chinese students are essentially of long-term significance, and will have only limited effect on China's immediate problems. Plans to permit senior scientists and engineers to spend extended periods studying and doing research abroad would obviously have more direct benefits, but the question of numbers versus goals remains.

China's changing road to development, the almost rhythmic exchange of priority between the "two legs" have been so apparent in her approach to science and education since 1949 that the permanency of Peking's current direction cannot go unquestioned. Will the all-out drive for the "four modernizations" falter with the death of the 75-year-old Teng Hsiao-ping, the policy's most ardent and effective implementer? Does the different tone set by Hua Kuo-feng's public proclamations indicate that the "struggle of the two lines" may become a serious dispute within the leadership, or should they be taken as mere gestures towards the values that only recently were uppermost in China's policies? Can we anticipate yet another cycle which will shift China's priorities from the pragmatic to the ideological? Experience leaves all those questions open. Nevertheless, since China without Mao can never be what China was when Mao was alive, it seems unlikely that shifts in policy could ever be as drastic as they have been in the past. And probably as China gains momentum in her economic development and security in her relations with the outside world, it will become more difficult for the residual forces of radicalism to force a major turnaround in her policies.

In the West the dominant reaction to the latest change in China's course, understandably, has been one of gratification. Yet it is possible to feel some regret that her drastic veering did not settle this time on some more middle course. Mao's dedication to the creation of an egalitarian society, his "serve the people" ethic, the sense of idealism he attempted to instill in the people, captured imaginations outside China as well as within, and some of those who disagreed with China's politics and policies could still identify with Mao's utopian ideals—unrealistic though those might have been, still they set China apart from every other nation. Like, surely, many Chinese, such observers will be watching to see whether, in their impatient and turbulent drive towards modernization, the current Chinese leaders will be tempted to entomb Maoism with Mao.

NOTES

1   The specific priority areas identified by the twelve-year plan were: (1) peaceful uses of atomic energy; (2) radio electronics; (3) jet propulsion; (4) automation and remote control; (5) petroleum and scarce mineral exploration; (6) metallurgy; (7) fuel technology; (8) power equipment and heavy machinery; (9) problems relating to harnessing the Yellow and Yangtse rivers; (10) chemical fertilizers and mechanization of agriculture; (11) prevention and eradication of detrimental diseases; (12) problems of basic theory in natural science.
2   Even before the recent great surge in China's technology purchases abroad, the number and types of high technology sold to the Chinese by US firms was wide and growing. In addition to the well-publicized sale of ten Boeing aircraft and eight ammonia plants sold by M. W. Kellogg, a general appreciation of the nature of China's purchases, even then, can be obtained from a partial list from the testimony of Christopher H. Phillips, President of the National Council for US–China Trade, before the Subcommittee on Investigations of the Committee on International Relations, US House of Representatives (8 December 1975):

>   RCA Global Communications, Western Union International, and Comtech Laboratories, Inc., have sold China satellite communications equipment. Clarke Equipment and International Harvester have sold China towing tractors for use at airports. Bucyrus-Frie has sold China $20 million worth of blast hole bits and power shovels. Caterpillar has sold China $3·8 million worth of medium-size pipe-laying equipment. Rucker has sold blow-out preventor stacks to control oil well pressure. Glenson Works—automobile gear and axle producing machines: Picket Corporation—a scanning system for the detection of radioactive pharmaceuticals.

APPENDIX

RESEARCH INSTITUTES OF THE CHINESE ACADEMY OF SCIENCES

Applied Chemistry Institute of Kirin, Changchun
Astronomical Observatory, Peking
Astronomical Observatory, Purple Mountain, Nanking
Astronomical Observatory, Shanghai
Atmospheric Physics Institute, Peking
Atomic Energy Institute, Peking
Automation Energy Institute, Peking
Biochemistry Institute, Peking
Biophysics Institute, Peking
Botany Institute of Kwangtung, Canton
Botany Institute, Peking
Chemical Engineering and Metallurgy Institute, Peking
Chemical Physics Institute, Lanchow
Chemical Physics Institute, Luta
Chemistry Institute, Peking
Chemistry Institute, Tsinan
Chemistry Institute South Central, Canton
Computer Technology Institute, Shanghai
Computer Technology Institute, Shenyang
Electrical Engineering Institute, Peking
Electron Optics Institute, Shanghai
Engineering Mechanics Institute, Harbin
Entomology Institute of Kwangtung, Canton
Entomology Institute, Shanghai

Environmental Chemistry Institute, Peking
Experimental Biology Institute, Shanghai
Genetics Institute, Peking
Geochemistry Institute, Kweiyang
Geography Institute, Peking
Geology Institute, Peking
Geology Paleontology Institute, Nanking
Geophysics Institute, Peking
Glaciology, Permafrost and Deserts Institute, Lanchow
High Energy Physics Institute, Peking
Hydrobiology Institute, Wuhan
Materia Medica Institute, Shanghai
Mathematics Institute, Peking
Mechanics Institute, Peking
Metallurgy Institute, Shanghai
Metrology Institute, Peking
Nuclear Physics Institute, Shanghai
Oceanography of the South Seas Institute, Canton
Oceanography Institute, Tsingtao
Optics and Precision Instruments Institute, Changchun
Optics and Precision Instruments Institute, Shanghai
Organic Chemistry Institute, Shanghai
Pedology Institute, Nanking
Physics Institute, Peking
Physiology Institute, Peking
Physiology Institute, Shanghai
Plant Physiology Institute, Shanghai
Plateau Atmospheric Physics Institute, Lanchow
Radio Engineering and Electronics Institute, Peking
Rock Soil Mechanics Institute, Wuhan
Saline Lakes Research Institute, Sining
Scientific and Technical Information Institute, Peking
Semiconductors Institute, Peking
Silicate Chemistry Technology Institute, Shanghai
Structure of Matter Institute of Fukien, Foochow
Technical Physics Institute, Shanghai
Vertebrate Paleontology and Paleo-Anthropology Institute, Peking
Zoology Institute, Peking

RESEARCH INSTITUTES OF THE CHINESE ACADEMY OF AGRICULTURE AND FORESTRY SCIENCES

Agricultural Mechanization Institute, Peking
Agriculture Institute, Peking
Atomic Energy Utilization in Agriculture Research Institute, Peking
Bee Institute of Kiangsi, Nanchang
Citrus Fruit Research Institute, Chungking

Cotton Institute, Peking
Crop Breeding and Cultivation Institute, Peking
Olericulture Institute, Tientsin
Plant Protection Institute, Peking
Sericulture Institute of Kiangsu, Chenchiang
Soil Fertilizer Institute, Techow
Tea Institute, Hangchow
Tobacco Institute, Tsinan
Vegetable Institute, Peking

RESEARCH INSTITUTE OF THE ACADEMY OF MEDICAL SCIENCES

Antibiotics Institute, Peking
Cardiovascular Diseases Institute, Peking
Dermatology Venerology Institute, Peking
Epidemiology Institute, Peking
Experimental Medicine Institute, Peking
Hermatology Institute, Tientsin
Hypertension Institute, Shanghai
Materia Medica Institute, Peking
Oncology Research Institute, Peking
Parasitology Institute, Shanghai
Traumatology Institute, Shanghai
Tuberculosis Research Institute, Peking

RESEARCH INSTITUTES OF THE ACADEMY OF CHINESE TRADITIONAL MEDICINE

Acupuncture and Moxibustion Institute, Peking
Chinese Medicine Research Institute, Peking

RESEARCH INSTITUTES OF THE CHINESE ACADEMY OF SOCIAL SCIENCES

Agricultural Economics
Archeology
Chinese History
Chinese Literature
Economics
Foreign Literature
Industrial Economics
Information
Journalism
Law
Modern Chinese History (after 1840)

Nationalities
Philology
Philosophy
Trade and Commerce
World Economy
World History
World Religions

Note: Except for the social sciences, the institutes represent a slightly revised listing from *Current Scene,* Vol. XIV, No. 6 (June 1976), pp. 17–21. The list of institutes of the Chinese Academy of Social Sciences was given to Mary Brown Bullock (Staff Director, Committee on Scholarly Communication with the PRC, National Academy of Sciences) when she visited the Academy of Social Sciences on 1 August, 1978. She also was told by an official of the Chinese Academy of Sciences that "at present there are about 90 research institutes under the CAS". No listing of these has yet been published by Peking.

"Making Green the Motherland": Forestry in China

JACK C. WESTOBY

China is engaged in the mightiest afforestation effort the world has ever seen. There has been nothing like it before, anywhere, and its like will not be seen again, because no other country will ever face a forestry problem of the magnitude which China faced on Liberation. There are many other countries in dire need of an intense afforestation effort. But their problems, though acute, cannot be measured on the same scale as those China faced.

Deforestation had been going on in China through at least four millennia. There is evidence to show that at one time most of China had tree cover. A great forest belt extended from central and southeastern coastal China all the way up to the Kinghan mountains in the northeast, while much of the mountainous interior was also forested. When, in later Neolithic times, some of the hunters and gatherers of the north China plain started to practice agriculture, there must have been considerable areas of forest and woodland in this predominantly grassland region. Rainfall dictated the differentiation between the sown and the steppe, the settled farmer and the nomadic pastoralist. It was here that Chinese civilization was born, and from here that it spread. It was here, too, that forest clearance started, first for hunting, later for farming. The likelihood is that the north China plain was already virtually treeless by the establishment of the Han dynasties. In the course of the five centuries that preceded the unification of China under Chin Shih Huang—a period that encompassed the transition from slave to feudal society—the destruction of the forests of the Yellow River basin was completed.

With the Han dynasties—the four centuries straddling the birth of Christ—started the push south: to the warmer, wetter, heavily forested lands of the Yangtze basin and beyond, lands occupied sparsely by diverse indigenous non-Han peoples, practising hunting, fishing and slash-and-burn agriculture. In the ensuing centuries the clearance of forest for farming accelerated. Such islands of forests as were left by the farmers' advance—for example, on hills too steep to terrace and till—suffered progressive degradation down the centuries as they were razed for timber and firewood.

It is true all over the world, of course, that the forests today stand on land that the farmer cannot use, does not want, or has not yet claimed. But in few countries has the farmer's appetite for forest land been as voracious and as sustained as it has been in China. One consequence is that the only substantial areas of natural forest left in China lie in the inhospitable northeast provinces and in the mountainous areas, difficult of access, of the south and southwest. Vestiges of the original natural forest survive elsewhere, but they have been badly depleted down the years—small temple forests, left intact, bear eloquent witness to the former rich forest cover. By 1949, the forests had dwindled to only five per cent of China's total land area. Another consequence of deforestation has been soil erosion by wind and water on a gigantic scale, with floods of disastrous proportions an almost annual occurrence for centuries past. And a third consequence has been a chronic shortage of both industrial timber and fuelwood over most of China, with timber consumption levels close to the world's lowest.

In 1949 this inherited forestry situation had been exasperated by over a decade of reckless forest depletion under the Japanese occupation and by the damage and dislocation of civil war. As Chinese resistance to Japan mounted, the Japanese army sought to crush guerrilla activity and support for guerrillas by applying the policy of "Kill all, burn all, loot all", and sizeable areas of forest suffered in consequence. China's richest forest resource, that in the northeast, had in fact been ruthlessly creamed since the beginning of the century—Japanese concessionaires were operating there long before the formal annexation of Manchuria by Japan in 1931.

Thus the government and people of China in 1949 confronted a whole range of forestry problems of the utmost gravity. Any hope of long term economic development was dependent upon their solution.

The Chinese Communist Party had long been aware of at least some of these problems. Indeed, afforestation efforts were undertaken well before 1949 in the "liberated areas". An example is the mass movement to realize the Programme of Ten Small Points in every community of the Border Region in 1944. This urged each family to dig one well; to plant so many trees; to keep more pigs; and to build one new latrine: each administrative village unit was to have a "mutual aid granary", a producers' and consumers' cooperative, one midwife, a blacksmith's shop, a school run by the people, and a folk-dance group. Gunther Stein reported sitting in on a representative meeting in Greater Yenan in 1944 at which an official concerned with a tree-planting movement was criticized for his bureaucratic attitude.[1]

Article 34 of the Common Programme of the Chinese People's Political Consultative Assembly, the first and most important document of the new government, laid down that "Forests shall be protected, and afforestation shall be developed according to plan". Responsibility for developing this program rested with the Ministry of Forestry and Land Reclamation.

Thus, immediately on Liberation both government and Party threw themselves into a campaign to mobilize mass participation in tree-planting activities. The first decade of the People's Republic saw the basic social transformation of the Chinese countryside: from mutual aid teams, through elementary and advanced producers' cooperatives, to the establishment of peoples communes in 1958–9. This decade also saw the first decisive steps towards "making green the motherland". But even though early visitors to the new China had reported on the scale and ubiquity of tree-planting efforts, the claims as to areas newly afforested which began to be advanced were such as to strain the credulity of most foreign commentators. Scepticism mounted as successive press releases provided figures which were clearly inconsistent with those which had been released earlier. These inconsistencies, allied to the fact that all the claims were of a magnitude to seem megalomaniac to Western minds, caused some commentators to dismiss the claims altogether. In this they were wrong. Perhaps if they had been aware of some of the pitfalls inherent in forestry statistics they might have had some sympathy with those Chinese foresters in Peking who over the years sought to draw up a realistic balance sheet of what had actually been achieved.

Hu Ku-yueh, writing in *Peking Review* in the spring of 1958,[2] endeavoured to sum up the achievements of the first five-year plan, 1953–7, even though final figures for 1957 were not available to him. He reported that in that period China had afforested an area greater than all the forests of Britain, Belgium, the Netherlands, Greece and Italy combined, and presented the following figures:

Area afforested, 1953–7	Million hectares
Forests for timber	5.16
Forests of industrial crop-yielding trees[a]	2.16
Shelter belts	1.47
Forests for water and soil conservation	1.40
Miscellaneous forests[b]	1.10
Total	11.29

a. e.g. tung oil, tea-oil, camphor, rubber, palm, coconut, coffee.
b. e.g. fuelwood, wood for charcoal.

If the above figures were anywhere near correct, it would mean that roughly a hundred trees had been planted during the quinquennium for every Chinese.

What are some of the pitfalls concerning afforestation statistics? When an area of forest is felled, one may rely on nature to restock and bring forth the second crop, or one may resort to planting the felled area with saplings—natural or artificial regeneration. But in neither case, strictly speaking, should this be called afforestation, since there is no net addition to the forested area. Again, within an area of land classified as forest, there may be bare patches. These may be planted up so as to give adequate tree cover—again, such plantings do not represent a net addition to the forested area. The fact is that the world's leading forestry statisticians have over the last decades spent a good deal of time trying to hammer out satisfactory definition of afforestation, reforestation, etc.; and even though there are now some internationally agreed definitions, there are as yet few national forestry administrations which have succeeded in consistently conforming to those definitions.[3]

There is another pitfall. In the early years in communist China tree-planting targets were often set and achievements reported, particularly at the local level, in terms of the number of trees planted rather than the area covered. How to convert to area? A million trees planted at a 2 × 2 metre spacing represent 400 hectares, while planted at 1 × 1 metre they represent only 100 hectares. Spacing in fact varied with location and according to species. It also changed with time, since the Chinese found that in many of the early plantations the spacing had been too close. But somebody had to make guesses about conversion factors as reported planting performances were aggregated at successive levels. Now China started out with very little in the way of professional forestry expertise. Her small corps of professional foresters included few forest economists and statisticians. And in any case the new authorities concentrated most of such forestry expertise as was available in the traditional forestry zones, in particular the northeast, seeking quickly to reestablish the flow of timber so sorely needed for China's reconstruction programme.

A good deal of the planting in those early years was carried out by workers, peasants, students and men and women of the People's Liberation Army who had been mobilized to help in State planting schemes. But even then a substantial proportion of the planting was carried out by the peasants in the cooperatives on their own land. In either case, professional and technical guidance was often minimal, with consequences that are discussed below. In these circumstances, there is small wonder that, even if the plan fulfilment reports coming from below were accurate as to number of trees planted, the areas reported may often have become exaggerated as the figures were successively inflated, and certainly substantial areas were classified as having been afforested when in fact they had simply been reforested. Thus one can justly have reservations about the areas claimed to have been afforested without in any way disparaging the magnitude of the tree planting effort. In fact the Chinese did not know then—and probably do not know even now with any great accuracy—the total area of forest they possess. A rapid reconnaissance survey was carried out with the aid of Soviet specialists in 1954. This could have given only a rough indication of forest area, with little or no detail concerning composition, quality and accessibility. It did, however, reveal somewhat larger reserves than had been suspected. This is no doubt why Hu Ku-yueh, in the article quoted above, spoke of the call to raise the forest area from 10 to 20 per cent of the land surface within the ensuing ten years, i.e. from the then 100 million hectares to 200 million hectares.[4]

Quite apart from the pitfalls of forest statistics, it appears, however, that with the launching of the Great Leap Forward, afforestation reporting, like reporting in so many branches of the Chinese economy, entered into the numbers game. Li Fang, writing in *Peking Review* in May 1959, reported that 27 million hectares had been afforested in 1958, and that 1959 plantings were running considerably ahead of the 1958 rate.

The aftermath of the Great Leap was a period of sober reflection in forestry as in other sectors. Chinese foresters had much more to worry about than the validity of the afforestation statistics. The quality of the afforestation effort was disappointing—in many instances survival rates in the new plantations were abysmally low. This was tacitly conceded by Li Fang, in *Peking Review* in July, 1961:[5]

Summing up past experience and particularly that gained in the past few years, six basic measures have been popularized by forestry experts to get the best results in afforestation. These call for (1) selection of the most suitable variety of trees for the location in question; (2) meticulous cultivation; (3) the use of good strains of seeds and hardy saplings; (4) rational close planting; (5) the adoption of the best methods of tree care and forest protection; and (6) the reform and improvement of tools and machines used in afforestation.

Li Fang went on to claim that "it is thanks to these measures that some 85 per cent of the saplings planted in recent years have survived and thrive"—a claim which, however, time was to prove premature.

Throughout the 1950s and even into the early 1960s much of the afforestation effort was misdirected, and there were many failures. S.D. Richardson, an experienced professional and an extremely acute observer who travelled widely in China in 1963, noted that planting had indeed been carried out on an enormous scale, but pointed out that a good deal of planting had taken place in unsuitable habitats and that, even where conditions were more favourable, survival rates were often low.[6]

In general, the success rate of those early plantings was very much higher in those areas which already had a strong forestry tradition. In these traditional forestry areas afforestation posed fewer technical problems since there was already a good store of knowledge about what species were suitable, how to organize seed collection and nurseries, and what planting techniques were appropriate. Elsewhere, expertise was very thinly spread. But a high proportion of the new planting, then as now, was undertaken outside the traditional forestry areas, on a wide range of difficult sites, often on locations that had not seen trees for centuries past. This meant a whole variety of new problems, with little technical experience to go on.

The technical reasons for the early failures are, in retrospect, fairly obvious, and Chinese foresters and forest workers today discuss these frankly: seeds of poor quality; species chosen that were ill-adapted to the particular site conditions; shortcomings in nursery practice; badly organized transfer from nursery to planting site; poor planting techniques; failure to recognize and counter pest invasions and so on. But most important of all, perhaps, was that all emphasis was placed on getting trees into the ground, while the subsequent tending necessary to ensure their survival was neglected. In the course of the 1960s, and particularly after the cultural revolution, most of these errors were corrected. Forest workers met in many areas of China today affirm: "We learned our lesson the hard way. Now 30 per cent of our effort goes into planting, 70 per cent into tending."

This is why professional foresters who have visited China in recent years tell a very different story from that of Richardson in 1963. Areas which were badly stocked have been replanted and survival rates in both the replanted areas and in new plantings are everywhere satisfactory. New planting continues at a prodigious rate. Travelling through China now, one frequently comes across hills carpeted with green and new plantations with a uniformly high "take", established within the last decade or so. Projecting above the green carpet will be isolated stems or clumps of trees, the survivors of earlier plantings. Similarly, many rail- and road-side plantings display two distinct generations, the casualties of an earlier campaign having been made good in recent years.

An example will serve to illustrate some of the difficulties encountered in the early afforestation efforts. In 1952, following Peking's decision that year to create shelter belts and start afforestation in the western parts of northeast China and the south of Inner Mongolia, a Dune Fixation and Shelter Belt Experimental Station was set up in Chang Wu county, Liaoning province, in what later became Chang Ku Tai people's commune. The station started out with one trained engineer, five young learners, and seven local workers. It was situated in lands which three generations before had been rich pastures. But from the turn of the century land-hungry peasants, moving up from the south, had started to plough. The thin, poor soils, exposed to wind erosion, yielded only one crop, and the peasants then had to move on. At the same time, over-grazing reduced ground vegetation, and the invasion of the sands accelerated. One village had had to move and rebuild itself three times within living memory, as successive sites were engulfed by drifting sands.

The small team which arrived in 1952 had little to go on: no experience of dune fixation, no equipment, no literature. The only member with professional training, the forester, knew much about nursery techniques but nothing about sand dunes. In these parts the sand starts to drift when the wind speed exceeds 5 metres per second, which on average occurs 240 times a year. It took several years of trial and error before appropriate techniques were devised. It was found that four kinds of local shrub, planted part way up the dunes to windward and leeward, would fix the sands, permitting subsequent tree planting.[7]

By 1974, when the writer visited this area, the moving sands had been replaced by forest, the earliest plantings having reached an average of 8 metres. There were bare patches here and there within the forest, but the forest was firmly established and there was already ample natural regeneraton. The desert had been halted once and for all. Behind the defensive forest belt, agricultural land, much of it reclaimed, was criss-crossed by a networkof shelterbelts,[8] countering wind erosion, building up soil quality, and permitting continuous cultivation with steadily increasing yields.

The station's efforts are concentrated now on helping neighbouring communes to apply its findings. It has established a seed orchard to provide improved seed to its tree nursery, which now delivers over four million saplings a year. This station also experimented with fruit trees—never seen in this area before—and, after trying out 89 varieties, now has an orchard where 300 vines, 200 pears and 500 apple trees are thriving. With the help of the station staff, most of the nearby communes have established their own orchards. The station staff has increased to 42, of whom 19 are technicians.

The Chang Ku Tai example illustrates the essentially bootstrap nature of much of China's early afforestation effort, undertaken with a bare minimum of expertise and little or no relevant experience. It also points to the intimacy of the relationship between forestry and agriculture—an intimacy without parallel elsewhere in the world—and the very catholic interpretation in China of the responsibilities of the forester—again without parallel elsewhere.

The years 1960 and 1961 brought about an agonizing reappraisal of all forestry activities. This was not simply the consequence of evident shortcomings in afforestation work—the recall of the Soviet experts in 1959 caused the Chinese to call in question some of the advice they had been receiving and acting upon. Doubts and reservations which Chinese foresters had held for some time came into the open and were freely discussed.

Chinese foresters in the northeast acknowledge gratefully the help received from the Soviet Union in the first years after Liberation. Without Soviet experts and Soviet equipment it would have taken very much longer to get the essential supplies of timber flowing again. But Russian forests are very different from the forests of Heilungkiang, and Soviet equipment and Soviet methods were not always the most appropriate for Chinese conditions. Thus the Soviet KT-12 wood-burning tractors could not operate on slopes greater than 12 degrees—in the Soviet Union they did not need to—and consequently were liable to over-turn in the Kinghan Mountains. Most of the Soviet experts came from logging enterprises, at that time quite separate in the USSR from forest management authorities,[9] and their customary aim was to extract the maximum quantities of commercial-sized logs as economically as possible, making use of clear-felling and relying on natural regeneration. But China is not a forest-rich country like the Soviet Union, and there timber wastage cannot be countenanced. Every cubic metre counts. Moreover, it was becoming clear that natural regeneration could not be relied upon to restock clear-felled areas.

The essence of Chinese forestry re-thinking was expressed in a 7,000 word article which appeared in *Red Flag* at the beginning of December, 1961, over the signature of

Chin Hsueh.[10] This article surveyed the whole forestry field and was a masterpiece of reasoned argument, cogent thinking, and wise analysis of past experience. Without dwelling excessively on past errors, it set forth a whole array of valid guidelines for the future. It emphasized such matters as prompt regeneration of all forests exploited, with recourse to artificial regeneration where necessary; closer combination of agriculture and forestry; better technical support for the forestry efforts of the communes; greater emphasis on fast-growing species; attention to the great potential of the secondary forests; more effective extraction of small-dimensioned timber; timber price differentials to encourage rational use of large dimensions and better qualities; raising the degree of mechanization; revised labour quotas to encourage waste elimination; revised measures for providing fuelwood needs, thereby releasing greater quantities of timber for industrial use; and so on.

This article—which was evidently the fruit of long discussions to which many had contributed—marked a turning point in the Chinese forestry effort; henceforth there would be a greater attention to quality as against quantity. It foreshadowed the basic regulations for the protection of forests promulgated by the State Council on 27 May 1963, the seven chapters and 43 articles of which still govern forestry activities in China, the amendments since incorporated having simply registered certain institutional changes which have taken place since then.[11]

An article of this kind in a journal like *Red Flag* is no ephemeral magazine article. At once a text and an action programme, it is matter for unremitting study and vigorous discussion by party cadres and forest workers at all levels. The nation-wide discussion this article evoked began steadily to show results in practice, and the shifts in emphasis in forestry were greatly helped by the changes brought about by the Cultural Revolution.

Two of the general effects of the Cultural Revolution were a systematic devolution of responsibilities from centre to province, province to county, county to district, and so on, and the emergence of new organs of management (revolutionary committees) at every level. In forestry, the Academy of Forest Science was relocated from Peking to Harbin, capital of Heilungkiang, China's foremost forestry province. Two forest research institutes were also moved from Peking, one to Nanking, the other to Ichun in Heilungkiang. The well-known Peking Forestry College was moved, lock, stock and barrel, to Yunnan province.

Alongside those shifts went a severe thinning of the ranks of administrators, scientists and technicians at the centre and at provincial levels, and their redistribution to counties and districts. Every administrator, scientist and technician is now obliged to spend at least one-fourth of his time each year working on the "production" front, engaging in practical forestry tasks in the districts, in the communes, on forest farms. In addition, most have attended the May 7th Cadre Schools, where political education is combined with manual work.

Forestry education, like all other higher education, was radically transformed in the course of the Cultural Revolution.[12] Courses were shortened, from 5 to 3½ years; curricula were overhauled, with greater emphasis being given to topics of more direct relevance to the problems faced in the communes; more time was accorded to practical work, mostly undertaken in cooperation with the communes; staff rotated between teaching duties, direct on-the-spot advice to the communes, and research. Most importantly, the new generations of students, who began to take their places in the field in

1972, have already had two to three years production experience (since all middle school graduates must work "on the production front"—at the factory bench, on the farm or in the forest—before proceeding to tertiary education) and have each been nominated by their fellow workers, whose nomination will have taken into account the candidate's political consciousness and attitude to work, as well as his or her academic attainments. It follows that the new forestry students are older, more mature, and more highly motivated than their predecessors.

One aspect of Chinese forestry that is often not appreciated outside China is that nine-tenths of the forestry effort comes, not from the state sector—that is from the forests, forest farms, etc., managed by the county and district forestry bureaux—but from the collective sector, that is from the people's communes. This goes some way towards explaining the tremendous impact which the changes which came about in the wake of the Cultural Revolution had on the afforestation programme: the quantitative impetus, and the leap in quality to which reference was made above. This impact was two-sided. It radiated the available expertise into the countryside, making the special knowledge of forestry science more directly the property of the masses. And it helped and encouraged the peasants to analyse their own experience: to become forestry scientists themselves. It was not simply that more of the available professional resources were located where they were really needed, and that their efforts were concentrated on problems that mattered. Certainly of equal, and probably of greater importance, was the fact that science was no longer the monopoly of the few. The scientific attitude, the scientific approach to problem-solving, is steadily gripping the workers and peasants. The Western forester visiting China today soon comes to understand that no dialogue, be it with a man from the Ministry, an academician, a machine operator, a skidder-driver, or a simple worker in a tree nursery, is complete without a passage starting: "Summing up our experience to date . . .". As a rule this is followed by a listing of open and unresolved questions, together with indications of the intended lines of attack.

Millions of peasants have taken to heart, and are vigorously applying, words of a famous article *"Where do Correct Ideas Come From?"*, by Mao Tse-tung published in May, 1963, urging them "to become good at investigation and study and at summing up experience." The struggle for scientific experiment, along with the class struggle and the struggle for production, is one of the "three great revolutionary movements" set out in the new constitution of the Communist Party of China adopted in August, 1975. The struggle for scientific experiment is thus not something that concerns "scientific circles" only. It concerns everybody.[13]

What exactly happens when the forestry scientist leaves his laboratory to go to work on a forest farm in the commune? Of course, he acquires an enhanced respect for manual labour, an appreciation of the peasant's hardihood, resource and common-sense, and this is a factor breaking down the barrier between intellectual and manual labour. But he is not expected to spend all his time mixing compost, levelling ground, picking out tree seedlings. He starts to exercise his mind on the technical problems that are actually giving concern to the peasants. Moreover, his very presence gives the impetus to releasing the latent talent, energy and imagination of the peasants engaged in forestry work. This is why thousands of peasants engaged today in forestry work are conducting grafting experiments, germination tests, spacing trials, fertilizer trials, testing out exotic species, and so on—steadily "becoming good at investigation and study and at summing up experience".

To some extent the process of bringing science to the people in this way has temporarily handicapped certain centrally conducted research, including lines of long-term and fundamental research without prospect of immediate application—and this has lately been conceded by the Chinese. But this seems a small price to pay compared with the enormous potential opened at the grass-roots by the spread of scientific consciousness and a scientific approach to problem-solving.

Many Western observers of the old China cited the ruthless profligacy with which forests, over centuries, had been destroyed as one of the most conspicuous expressions of the total absence of any feeling of responsibility for the community or for posterity which such outsiders believed to be an innate characteristic of the Chinese. Yet today, after less than three decades, the Chinese have become the most forest-conscious people in the world. There is nothing whimsical or romantic about their attachment to trees. It is based on a solid understanding of the role of trees as industrial raw material and fuel, as a shield against flood, erosion and desiccating wind, and as a key factor in the quality of both the urban and rural environment.

The building of forest-consciousness starts in the schools. The basic facts about the Chinese economy and the orientation of Chinese development are taught in all schools throughout China. Thus every schoolchild is aware that China takes "agriculture as the foundation and industry as the leading factor" in developing her national economy. These notions will have been presented in simple terms to the younger age-groups, but in the middle schools they are elaborated to impart an understanding of the interdependence of industry and agriculture, of the various ways in which they mutually support and promote each other. Moreover, every schoolchild learns that, in agriculture, the policy is to take food grains as the key link and to ensure an all-round development of animal husbandry and forestry. These slogans serve as texts for political—and economic—education. The consequence is that many middle school students in China show a firmer and clearer grasp of the essential problems of underdevelopment than do some academic economists in the West.

Thus no child leaves school in China without having acquired some notions of the significance of forestry, notions which will have been reinforced by visits to people's communes, forest farms, forest industry establishments. And each will probably, in the course of his or her school life, have made a personal contribution towards "making green the motherland" by tree-planting and tree-tending around the school, on vacant city lots, or in the commune. Needless to say, in China as elsewhere, these school-derived notions take root in the family.

And education does not stop with school. Nowhere is the idea of education as a continuing, lifelong process more widely accepted than in China. Every factory, every commune, has its own programme of continuing education, with organized adult education facilities. These classes consist in part of political study groups, newspaper reading groups, and literacy classes. In all these the orientation and aims of Chinese development are studied and discussed—which means that rather precise notions about the role of forestry are acquired. But classes in a wide range of technical and cultural subjects are also organized, and these include courses in forestry wherever forestry is a significant activity.

But if the foundation of forest-consciousness is laid in the school and amplified by widespread continuing education, it is also important to remember that tens of millions of Chinese—literally, not figuratively—are engaged part-time in forestry activities, mainly, at this stage, planting and tending. In the countryside, forestry is an integral part of the total activity of the communes. That part of the key slogan—"ensure an all-round development of forestry"—is interpreted by each commune in accordance with its own needs and possibilities. Thus the forestry activity may be relatively minor, confined to planting along the roads and field borders, with the odd small woodlot, aimed at producing locally some of the industrial timber needed in the commune, especially poles for construction and transmission poles. This is the case, for example, with most of the agricultural communes in the plain around Peking, though even there the aggregate amount of planting in the commune is usually sufficient to warrant the commune establishing its own tree nursery. Elsewhere the forestry activity may be a vital element in the agricultural programme, as in the case of dune fixation, shelter belts, and the protection of water conservancy works. Or it may form part of a larger programme aimed at valorizing land unsuitable for agriculture and thereby laying the foundation for future forest industries, thus diversifying the economy of the communes. The Hunan Chinese fir programme is a good example of this last.[14]

How is it that the Chinese peasant has become committed to forestry in this wholesale way? Two particular aspects of the forestry programme have helped to fasten in the mind of the Chinese peasant the importance of forestry. One is the emphasis given to tree planting around individual houses in the commune. These are usually quick-growing species, with a realizable harvest date within sight. Since these trees remain the property of the individual householder he can see future income, from sale to the commune, accumulating under his eye, so that the trees in his yard are as palpable a supplement to his income as are the pigs he has raised behind his house for eventual sale to the State purchasing organization. The other is that, throughout China, forestry is taken as encompassing not only timber trees but also orchard trees and so-called "economic" crops.[15] Thus all kind of plantation crops—tea oil, tung oil, nut trees, fruit orchards, as well as bamboo groves—will each have a place, if soil and climate conditions are appropriate, in the afforestation programme. This undoubtedly influences the way in which the peasant in the commune looks upon forestry activities. There is no sharp categorization between fairly quick-yielding plantation crops and slower maturing timber crops. The importance attached to fast-growing species blurs any difference there may be in the time taken for the crop to mature. The commune may be taking its first harvest, in the form of thinnings, from its timber plantations before some of its "economic" plantation crops have reached their peak yield. Thus the peasant has come to look upon tree-growing as a fruitful economic activity, no less important than field or plantation crops. And this has come to be as true of protection forestry as of production forestry, since he can measure the increased yield behind the shelterbelts, see the new land under cultivation after dune fixation, and can recognize the diminished incidence of flood and erosion following on protective afforestation.

The Hunan Chinese fir programme mentioned above is a good example of the more ordered planning that came into afforestation in the 1960s. The counties in Hunan were invited to prepare plans and proposals for submission to, and discussion with, the provincial authorities. After approval, the province was to give a subsidy, at the rate of about 105 yuan per hectare afforested, these funds coming from the provincial afforestation fund, derived from a 5 yuan levy on every cubic metre of timber felled in the province. The communes and their constituent production brigades were urged to set up forest farms. By 1974, 2,300 forest farms had come into existence, staffed by workers and technicians, most of the technicians being peasants from the brigades who had received short-course training. The programme has passed the half-way mark, thinnings have already been taken from the first plantations, and by the 1990s this programme will provide an annual supply of between 10 and 15 million cubic metres, which is about four times as much timber as all the forests in the UK provide today. A significant feature of this programme was joint planning by neighbouring communes—of forest roads, for example—which grouped themselves together to establish a "forest base", looking forward to the day when their joint output would permit the establishment of a major forest industry. This was fully in line with the forestry re-thinking of the early 1960s.

China has succeeded in something which very few other countries have achieved: in establishing a truly effective and fruitful integration between agriculture and forestry. The structure reflects this, although this is not the decisive factor—an appropriate structure can hamper or facilitate such integrations, it cannot of itself compel. At the national level, forestry affairs are dealt with in the Ministry of Agriculture and Forestry,[16] and are conducted under the leadership of one of the seven Vice-Ministers. There is no state forest service such as is common in most other countries, i.e. an independent or semi-autonomous forest service with a hierarchical chain of command running down through forest regions and forest conservancies. Instead, agriculture and forestry are integrated at all levels, from the Ministry down, usually in the agricultural and forestry bureaux of the provinces, administrative districts, counties, etc. These bureaux are under the political control of the revolutionary committees at the respective levels, and the bureaux at each level deal with agricultural and forestry matters alike, along with the interrelations between agriculture and forestry. Naturally, the forestry members of these bureaux have very frequent contacts with their counterparts at the immediately higher and lower levels.

These bureaux, at the appropriate levels, have direct responsibility for the state-owned (as distinct from the collective) sector—state forests, state-owned forest industry enterprise, research institutes.[17] Their other important function is to give guidance and technical advice to the collectively owned sector—in essence, the communes, production brigades and teams—as well as to other organs and institutions conducting forestry activities: these include municipalities, railways, mines, factories, and so on.

The services which the forestry bureaux (and the state-owned enterprises for which they have responsibility) provide are not confined to professional advice and technical assistance; they go far beyond what is normally encompassed by a forestry extension service. Most important perhaps are the education and training activities, which take many forms: short training courses; one-day or one-week technical consultations for cadres, technicians or model workers, arranged at provincial, county or district level; the promotion of exchange visits; on-the-job training in sawmills, timber yards, forest farms, research institutes; preparation of information sheets and instructional pamphlets; and so forth. In addition, each state enterprise has a demonstration function. Also important is the on-the-spot advice offered to the communes, brigades and teams by the staff of the forestry bureaux, state forest farms and research institutes. These staff now constantly visit, and for sustained periods work alongside members of, the communes. Any new problem coming up, therefore, is promptly spotted, and steps taken to cope with it. Staff in the state sector give advice on management, and in some cases actually provide management services until the collective has acquired its own nucleus of trained and experienced people. They act as animators, persuading the communes to undertake various kinds of forestry activities, providing the know-how and even lending executive staff to get things moving. They supply seed and planting stock. They organize experiments and trials. The living and fecund relationship between the state and collective sectors has contributed greatly to the effective integration of forestry and agriculture. In fact, the overwhelming majority of forestry activities in China today are, directly or indirectly, agricultural-supportive.

This varied range of services provided by foresters in the state sector to the collective sector goes some way to explaining how an afforestation campaign of the magnitude of China's can be sustained by what is still a relatively small corps of highly-trained foresters. The organization and frequency of contacts are such that news of successful innovations, relevant new research findings, promising experiments, is disseminated with extraordinary speed. The singling out and publicizing of specific achievements and the establishment of models for general emulation is central to China's mode of development—"let key points lead the area" is the maxim. Forestry has its "Tachai-type models" too, and these, like Tachai itself and Tachai-type models in agriculture, have become centres of "lay pilgrimage".[18] Thus Chuting county, in Hunan province, includes several production brigades which have recorded noteworthy achievements in the Chinese fir campaign, so that the county became a diffusion point for the organization and techniques of afforestation. In 1973 it had no less that 60,000 visitors, and, expecting this stream to continue, in 1974 the county government built a guest house to help accommodate some of these. At the same time, while happy thus to impart its own experience, it was not above learning from others. A Chuting delegation returned from Tachai and set the local communes planning to enlarge their rice fields by increasing the height of their terraces and thus to facilitate mechanization and the introduction of machine irrigation. Another delegation had visited another model county, Kweitung, in southeast Hunan, and their report gave an impetus to intercropping in the young fir plantations with a wide variety of crops, including melons, beans, and ground nuts.

More timber forests, more protection forests: no nation has had greater need of these than China. Yet even so the Chinese have found time and energy to create or develop amenity and recreation forests, and to carry out urban forestry on an unprecedented scale. By now thousands of tourists and members of diplomatic, cultural and commercial delegations have reported with enthusiasm on the magnificent tree-lined avenue that leads from Peking airport to Peking city. Yet this scarcely calls for comment. There are few countries today, great or small, rich or poor, that have not attempted some kind of cosmetic verdure on the approach to their capital cities. It is only when one leaves the main tourist centres, travelling between the provincial capitals and penetrating into the depths of the countryside, that one understands that in China today no road, be it a trunk route between major cities or simply a local road linking out-or-the-way communes, is considered complete until the saplings which line it have become firmly established. Meanwhile railside planting proceeds at an astonishing pace. And there are few factories that have not made some effort to plant up waste ground and line their service roads with trees. But it is in the cities, in the huge urban afforestation programme, that Chinese genius has found one of its highest expressions. Informed visitors[19] have been deeply impressed not only by the scale of the achievements but even more by the thought, care and skill with which they have planned. The central concept has been not only to give aesthetic satisfaction, but also to effect a qualitative improvement in the urban environment, by improving the quality of air, controlling pollution, reducing noise, and providing summer shade. Furthermore, wherever possible a proportion of trees are planted which have some commercial value. Thus in the streets of Peking walnut and persimmon trees are prominent. Nanning, in the Kwangsi Chuang Autonomous Region, harvests 20 tons of mangoes and jackfruit from its street trees, while several cities have planted the palm, *Trachycarpus fortunei*, the fibre of which is used for basket weaving. The urban planting programmes concentrate on trees which are reasonably fast growing, which are capable of being planted at an advanced stage (4 to 8 metres in height), which are not subject to serious attack by pests or diseases, and which are known to survive in an urban environment. While city landscaping departments take care of parks, tree nurseries and trees along the streets, factories and other work units organize their own people to plant trees in their compounds, while trees in residential areas are planted by the residents under the leadership of the neighbourhood committees.

How much forest has China today? The probability is, as was suggested above, that no one in China knows the answer, or is likely to know for some time yet.[20] Senior forestry officials conceded in 1974 that the 20 per cent forest cover, representing roughly 200 million hectares, the target rashly set for 1968 at the time of the Great Leap, was as yet far from achievement, but remained only the long term target. It is conceivable that if successive annual afforestation claims were cumulatively added, and some area allowance made for street, field, rail- and road-side planting, one might begin to approach that figure. But such a figure would include much replanting of failed areas and much reforestation, and therefore double counting. In any case, such a numbers game is irrelevant. There is no magic about a 20 per cent forest cover, nor about 200 million hectares. What matters is that there should be sufficient trees of the right kind, in the right place, to provide existing industries and those yet to be established with raw material, to protect and serve agriculture, and to contribute to the quality of urban and rural life. This last goal is well within sight. Marked progress has been made towards the first: traditional forest areas have been brought under effective management, and some important new resources have been created. There is still, however, great scope for creating new industrial forests, while the task of opening up and managing the subtropical forests of the south has only just begun.

It is in protecting and serving agriculture that most remains to be done. Many, probably most, communes have already taken significant strides towards meeting their own needs of fuel and industrial timber. Trees protect the major and minor water conservation schemes which have already been executed, but the task of taming China's rivers is as yet by no means complete. But perhaps the most gigantic task still facing Chinese forestry lies in the arid north and northwest, the completion of the Great Green Wall. Deserts cover 100 million hectares in China, over a tenth of the land surface. It has been estimated[21] that over 13 million hectares of this could be reclaimed and turned into farm land. Though a number of important successes have already been recorded in making the desert bloom, in Liaoning, Kansu, and Sinkiang, there is hard work here for the Chinese people and Chinese foresters for generations ahead.

China's afforestation achievements mean that the balance between man and nature, lost through centuries of reckless forest destruction, is steadily being restored. This is being done without foreign experts—the few Soviet experts in the early years scarcely count since they were virtually all concerned with timber extraction—and without foreign loans.[22] Also it is being achieved with a remarkably small force of professional foresters. The fundamental lesson to be drawn from this is that there is no man/resource situation, no matter how extreme, how hopeless-seeming, that is not recuperable—given the political will and the social organization. There are vast areas within the underdeveloped world which are today considered by both ecologists and development economists as having passed, or as ineluctably approaching, the "point of no return". But the Chinese have challenged the very notion of a "point of no return". They have shown that rivers can be tamed, wind and water erosion halted, land rehabilitated, deserts made to bloom again. Moreover, they have shown that all this can be done without multi-million dollar loans, without battalions of professional foresters, without vast arrays of earth-moving equipment. The essential ingredients are few: human will-power, human muscle-power, and human ingenuity—plus a form of social/political organization which makes it possible for those human resources to be mobilized.

China's successful afforestation campaign is a remarkable technical achievement. But, much more fundamentally, it is a political achievement.

NOTES

1   Gunther Stein, *The Challenge of Red China,* McGraw-Hill, 1945.
2   Turning the Whole Country Green: Hu Ku-yueh, *Peking Review,* Vol. 1, No. 8, 22/4/58.
3   It is illuminating to study Appendix I of the report of the first World Symposium on Man-Made Forests, reported in *Unasylva,* Vol. 21, Nos. 86–7, 1967.
4   The figure usually accepted for the forested area at the time of Liberation is 5 per cent of the land area, or 48 million ha. With claimed afforestation up to and including 1958 of about 40 million ha, plus some additional reserves revealed by the 1954 air reconnaissance inventory, this would make up the new base figure of 100 million ha.
5   State Forest Plantations, Li Fang, *Peking Review,* Vol. 14, No. 30, 28/7/61.
6   S. D. Richardson, *Forestry in Communist China,* Johns Hopkins Press, 1966.
7   The four shrubs are: *Artemisia halodendron, Caragana microphylla, Lespedeza bicolor,* and *Salix flavida.* Thirty-four tree species were experimented with, the station eventually fixing on *Pinus sylvestris var. mongolicia* and *Pinus tabulaeformis.*
8   Each consisting of 7 rows of *Populus simonii* with 4 rows of shrubs on the windward side.
9   A separation which was subsequently to generate a good deal of controversy in Russian forestry journals.
10 Energetically develop the work of forest regeneration, make rational use of the forest resources, by Chin Hsueh, *Hung-ch'i* (Red Flag), No. 23, December 1, 1961. In translation in *Communist China Yearbook, 1962,* Harvard University Press.
11 Reference to the "people's councils" of provinces, autonomous regions and municipalities, and to the "management committees" of people's communes, have been replaced by reference to "revolutionary committees" at these several levels, while the references to the Ministry of Forestry has been replaced by reference to the Ministry of Agriculture and Forests, within which the Ministry of Forests has now been absorbed.
12 Changes more fully described in "How the Chinese Learn about Forestry", Jack C. Westoby, *American Forests,* July 1975.
13 *Physical* property relations having been revolutionized, a sustained effort is being made to socialize *intellectual* property, to bring scientific knowledge under collective control. Perhaps this is what distinguishes the Chinese experience.
14 A programme launched in 1964 by the Hunan provincial authorities to plant up the bare hills, too steep for terraced rice cultivation, mainly with Chinese fir (*Cunninghamia lanceolata*), but also with other species, including various plantation crops. Over much of Hunan, land suitable only for forestry accounts for 80 per cent of the land area. By 1974, many communes had already completed their share of the million-hectare target. For a full description of this programme, see Growth Industry from Chinese Firs, Jack C. Westoby, *Geographical Magazine,* June 1975.

15 This is not the case in most countries. Elsewhere, forestry is still usually regarded, especially by foresters, as a separate activity, carried out within a separate forestry domain, requiring its own special skills and preserving its own mystery.

16 Central responsibility has changed several times since 1949. At the outset a Ministry of Forestry and Land Reclamation was set up. In November 1951 land reclamation was transferred and combined with state farms in another ministry. In May 1958 the Ministry of Timber Industries was merged into the Ministry of Forestry. In the course of 1971 a consolidated Ministry of Agriculture and Forestry was set up, combining the former Ministries of Agriculture, State Farms and Land Reclamation, Forestry and the Water Conservation section of the Ministry of Water Conservation and Electric Power.

17 Not, however, for forestry education institutes, which ultimately depend, through the education departments or bureaux, on the Ministry of Education.

18 See the papers on the "Learning from Tachai" campaign by Neville Maxwell, in this volume.

19 For example, a six man Australian delegation in 1975, led by Professor J. D. Ovington, which reported on Gardens, Parks and Open Spaces in China, in 1976 (unpublished).

20 China's detailed forest inventory is not yet complete; it is proceeding at different rates in the several provinces, depending on the urgency with which the information is needed and the resources available to conduct it.

21 Geography of China: Deserts, *China Reconstructs,* October, 1974.

22 Costed conventionally, China's afforestation programme to date would have needed a loan of the order of $5 billion. By 1976, after 23 years of existence, the World Bank, for example, had financed 17 forestry projects to a total loan value of $170 million. The bulk of these loans were for export industries or for industrial plantations destined to feed export industries.

Development and Environmental Protection in China*

K. WILLIAM KAPP

I. INTRODUCTION

As compared with prerevolutionary conditions, contemporary China offers a number of striking contrasts. It is no longer a country of abject misery with periodic famines and epidemics, with recurrent natural catastrophes resulting either from drought or the flooding of its major river systems and without medical care in rural areas. Chinese policies seem to have been successful in protecting and even improving the natural and social environment and in maintaining a connection between economic development and the satisfaction of essential human needs. This is no small achievement, particularly if we compare China's performance with conditions in other less developed countries, including those which at the UN Conference on Human Environment (Stockholm, 1972) voiced their concern about suggestions that greater attention be paid to the disruption of their environment. Some countries were outspoken in their refusal to sacrifice rapid industrial growth to environmental protection, apparently in the belief that their natural environment was still able to absorb considerable amounts of pollutants. These countries insisted on giving priority to rapid industrialization without paying attention to the ecological consequences and health hazards of development policies.

China seems to have chosen a different road. The Chinese leadership is aware of the fact that the development of productive forces in many industrial countries has gone hand in hand with the emergence of social costs and cumulatively destructive forces. For this reason, they seem to be determined not to repeat the "mistakes" which the industrial countries have committed in the past and which would sooner or later call for costly clean-up operations of land, air and water resources. As a result, China offers the picture of a country which attempts to pursue simultaneously a policy of economic development and environmental protection and improvement.

I am not suggesting that China is an environmental paradise or that it has solved its environmental problems. Nor am I arguing that she has avoided all social costs of economic development. However, the Chinese leadership is not only conscious of the environmental hazards of expanding production indiscriminately but has taken positive steps to cope with the possibly harmful effects of economic growth; moreover, they seem to have developed specific strategies and, above all, succeeded in mobilizing grass-root participation on a scale which goes far beyond anything existing in other developing and developed countries. Of course, China is only at the beginning of its industrialization, and what the future holds is still uncertain. However, and this seems to

* First published as "Recycling in Contemporary China", *Kyklos*, Vol. XXVII (1974).

me the crux of the matter, Communist China has taken positive steps to cope with the environmental disruption not only during the last three years but almost from the very beginning of its systematic efforts to plan its agricultural and industrial future. For this and other reasons, which cannot be discussed here in greater detail, I am prepared to argue that China's environmental prospects are better than those of most developing and even of industrialized countries some of which are just beginning to realize the short-sightedness of their past neglect of social costs and are forced today—partly by public opinion and partly out of economic necessity—to start, however reluctantly, costly "clean-up" operations of their physical and social environment.[1]

II. TRADITIONAL AGRICULTURE AS A "RECYCLING" AND AN ENERGY-PRODUCING ECONOMY

Traditional agriculture in China has always been a "recycling" economy in the wider sense of the term. Poverty has forced China's population to frugality out of necessity, and the "reuse" of waste and sewage materials is not an altogether new phenomenon. As a predominantly agricultural economy the country has always practised the principle of the "comprehensive" re-use of materials and human waste which has made it possible to provide the necessary food for the oldest and greatest agglomeration of people within a unified and relatively stable civilization which history has ever known. The role of this systematic recovery of organic waste in China's agriculture has a long history; it was well known to Western observers during the nineteenth century as can be seen from the following quotation of Victor Hugo's *Les Misérables*: "No Chinese peasant goes to the city without carrying back, at the ends of his bamboo, two buckets of what we call filth". Human excrements were not free goods in China and apparently no prejudice, as in other countries, stands in the way of the systematic re-use of human excreta. Even today it is estimated that "about 80 per cent of all fertilizer used is organic—either animal or human wastes, mulches or green manure crops".[2] Figure 1 provides a highly simplified visual presentation of this process of re-utilizing organic waste materials.[3]

In view of the current critical energy problem in the west, I may point out that Chinese wet-rice agriculture is a highly efficient producer of energy—indeed, much more efficient per unit of (human) energy put into the system in the form of calories (of food consumed by the farmer) than our Western systems of *"farming with petroleum"*. In fact, one calorie (of food) yields about 40 cal. in rice which, incidentally, accounts for the relatively small amount of land needed by the average Chinese farmer living in fertile regions and practising wet-rice agriculture.[4] In contrast modern agriculture far from being an energy producing sector has become a major consumer of energy using today more petroleum than any other single industry. "There have been estimates that Chinese wet-rice agriculture could produce 53.5 BTU (British Thermal Unit) of energy for each BTU of human energy expended in farming it. For each unit of energy the *Chinese* wet-rice farmer expends, *we* get about one-fifth in return. On the basis of these two ratios, Chinese wet-rice agriculture is far more efficient than our own system"[5]—that is if measured in terms of output per unit of energy instead of output per hour of farm labour or in terms of (market) value of output per dollar input.

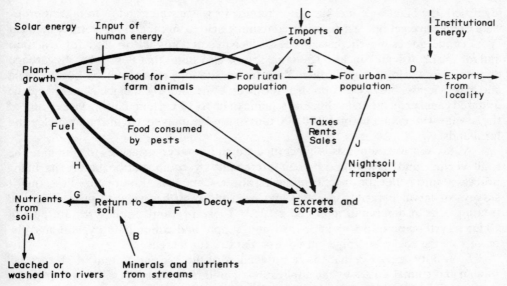

Figure 1. *The flow of plant nutrients in a traditional Chinese farming ecosystem (highly simplified)*

III. CHINA'S EFFORTS TO IMPROVE THE USE OF WASTE MATERIALS IN AGRICULTURE

Of course, Chinese policy makers are well aware of the fact that the use of untreated human excreta in agriculture has serious limitations. Human (and animal) excrements may lead to the contamination of surface and underground water and the spreading of serious parasite diseases (e.g., schistosomiasis in tropical climates);[6] moreover, excreta are inadequate to meet the rising requirements for fertilizer in Chinese agriculture. Since 1958 China has shown a highly critical attitude toward the traditional use of human excrements as manure, and of sewage water for the irrigation of rice fields. Scientific research in the epidemiological departments in 18 major cities and municipalities has been carried out since the Scientific Planning Committee of the State Council ordered such studies to be undertaken in 1958.[7] The results of these studies indicated that *"under certain responsible conditions"* the self-purification of sewage water could be greatly increased and oxygen consumption, floating matter and bacterial content in sewage water could be greatly reduced after five days; the breeding of mosquito larvae was also reduced. It should be noted that this type of research which led to the drawing up of "Health Regulations in the Utilization of Sewage Water for Irrigation"[8] goes back to the late fifties, i.e., to a time when other less developed countries were hardly concerned with the pollution of water and its purification for irrigation purposes.

Today, Peking possesses more than a dozen sewage treatment and disposal plants in which high pressure pumps deliver waste water at a rate of 3 tons per second to a 6 metre deep sedimentation basin where dirt and residue carried in the water settle to the bottom. After sterilization the water is channelled to farmlands for irrigation. These processing plants are said to carry out constant analysis with a view to identifying poisonous matter exceeding specific safety limits. If such matter *is* found and the source identified, the plant is ordered to stop draining its waste water and/or to take appropriate preventive action. Waste water containing acid from the Peking Petro-Chemical Works undergoes a bio-chemical process which makes it possible to use it for irrigation and for raising fish and ducks.[9] The same source also states that Peking has 48 garbage disposal yards using a high fermentation (compostation) process which kills bacteria and makes it possible to use rubbish as fertilizer. Other cities (Changchu and Shanghai) initiated canal projects and a pipeline scheme of up to 30 km length using 90 per cent of the sewage water and pumping 300,000 tons of sewage daily to irrigate paddy fields and farmlands.

As far as schistosomiasis is concerned China has taken measures to eliminate the snail vectors and to sterilize human excrement by compostation before its being processed into pellets prior to its use as fertilizer. China has also organized systematic surveys of larval parasites in water and particularly with a view to preventing and treating schistosomiasis in man and cattle.[10] These preventive measures are part of China's systematic effort to improve water supply and community hygiene and the quality of the social and physical environment in rural areas.

I am not suggesting that the improvement of the ancient custom of "recycling" human and animal wastes by the application of modern techniques will be adequate for meeting China's long-run requirements. Her increasing food requirements will call for considerable supplementation of organic waste products by chemical fertilizers both from internal sources and imports. China's estimated needs for chemical fertilizers (35 million tons in 1971) still far exceeds its domestic production (14 million tons in 1971).[11]

IV. "TURNING THE HARMFUL INTO THE BENEFICIAL" AS A GUIDING PRINCIPLE OF CHINA'S ANTI-POLLUTION POLICIES

Chinese experts would have no difficulties in accepting the view that man can neither create nor destroy matter or energy, i.e., the first law of thermodynamics or the principle of the conservation of energy. Indeed, the Chinese come close to accepting what has come to be known as the material balance approach and the related view that man's economic activities neither produce nor consume matter or energy. While most economists would admit that there is a qualitative difference between what goes into the economic process and what comes out of it, and some unorthodox economists today "would say that what goes into the economic process represents valuable resources and what is thrown out of it is valueless waste",[12] the Chinese seem to take the position that there is no valueless waste.

In making one product, resources are partially transformed into this product and the rest becomes "waste" ..... From the metaphysical point of view, waste cannot be got rid of. On the contrary, the materialist dialectical view holds that what is waste and what is not waste are relative terms. There is nothing in the world that is absolute waste. "Waste" under one condition may be valueless; under different ones waste material left from one product can become a good material for another product.[13]

This way of looking upon waste is one of the guiding principles for China's policy of the multipurpose use of resources; it supports and explains current campaigns in favour of recovering and re-using waste materials or, as it is called in the Chinese literature, "Turning the harmful into the beneficial".

Of course, this comprehensive use of materials may be interpreted as a carry-over of the old and persistent attitude of frugality borne out of the necessity of making the maximum use of scarce resources under conditions of poverty.[14] However, the present insistence on the recovery and re-use of waste materials goes far beyond anything China has undertaken in the past. In fact, the recovery and re-use of the "three wastes" (i.e., waste liquid, waste gas and waste slag) is being advocated as a method of transforming waste into wealth and as an important means of diversifying and increasing output. More than this: the principle of the comprehensive use of waste is in fact regarded as a necessity of socialist development; while it serves, above all, the protection of the social and physical environment and thus of human health rather than the recovery of materials which have economic value, it is also a means of changing the traditional division of labour and the specialization of work. In short, it is simultaneously an anti-pollution measure, a method of increasing production, an approach to diversifying and re-locating industry and an improvement of urban and rural sanitation. It is multipurpose in this comprehensive sense.

V. RECYCLING IN INDUSTRY

As far as the recovery and re-use of waste materials in industry is concerned China uses both labour-intensive and highly modern capital-intensive techniques. Labour-intensive methods play an important role in connection with remedial measures after pollution has occurred, such as large-scale dredging operations and the cleaning up of polluted streams, rivers and lakes affected by the discharge of untreated industrial waste materials and the collection of human and animal waste not used for fertilizing fields. In some instances, substantial quantities of waste materials have been recovered and are being re-used such as oil, chemicals, slag waste, etc. Such waste materials are said to have yielded thousands of tons of fertilizer.

In little more than a year Shanghai has recovered gases and slag, several hundred tons of dye-stuff, 8,000 tons of oils and thousands of tons of chemicals. In addition, some 10,000 tons of metal were recovered. Waste slag made 200,000 tons of cement. Paper, electroplating and leather industry wastes yielded hundreds of thousands of tons of fertilizers and the processed waste water now irrigates 6,650 acres of farmlands.[15]

In recent years, China seems to have concentrated its major efforts on the *prevention* of water and air pollution. Much attention has been given to the construction of urban sewage systems and treatment facilities for the proper disposal of human waste in the more densely populated areas.[16]

With respect to air pollution the Chinese approach calls for the installation of recovery and purification facilities in big and middle-sized factories[17] and the elaboration, imposition and enforcement of rules on emission, the location of new and the relocation of old factories "on the opposite side of the city from which the wind usually blows".

As an illustration of the use of a *modern* recycling technology we may cite the case of the Peking Petro-Chemical Works which are reported to operate a waste water treatment plant (similar to advanced systems in Europe and the US) which is said to remove almost all contaminants except nitrogen from waste water.[18] Reports from Kirin (North-western China) also support the thesis that China employs modern technology in her recycling practices. Thus, a plant (in Kirin) processes waste oil and lubricants on a large-scale basis as an economic process after it has originally been established on an *ad hoc* basis to overcome industrial bottlenecks through the collection and refining of waste oil. The Kirin Chemical Fertilizer Plant recovers a wide range of products among which are mercury, benzene, hexanol, hydrochloric acid, *et. al.*, totalling some 25 different kinds of chemicals.[19] Slag from iron plants is being used as ingredient for making cement.[20] Iron plants are reported to design and build ovens in order to collect and make use of coal tar. Wheat and rice straw (formerly used for thatching of houses and huts) are being used as raw materials for paper mills.[21]

The recovery and re-use of materials may take place either in the factory in which the waste originates or in specialized industries or in separate small-scale plants or even in home industries. In this way the traditional division of labour and the lines of demarcation between industries are said to be changed.

A factory is divided into several, one raw material is used in many ways, a piece of machinery is used for many purposes, one worker is capable of many kinds of work apart from his specialization, and a factory can produce many things while engaging mainly in [the production of] one product. All this gets better results from limited manpower, equipment and resources.[22]

From the numerous examples listed in the literature it appears that several patterns of recovering and re-using waste materials are in process of development: (1) A large plant operating its own small plant to process its waste material; (2) a large plant operating several small plants to process its waste materials (into raw material and consumer goods); (3) several large plants (e.g., in Shanghai) operating in cooperation one waste utilization plant using old, discarded, unused or rebuilt equipment turned over to them;[23] (4) neighbourhoods, cities and villages operating small-scale factories either processing scrap materials collected by retired workers, housewives and children or turning them over to other small and large-scale factories; and (5) plants specializing in acquiring waste products and making them available to specialized factories which turn them into useful products.

Of course, the available data on the recovery and re-use of materials are fragmentary and do not permit any definite conclusions as to the relative importance which the recovery of materials and recycling play in contemporary China. There are no over-all data on recycling for China as a whole just as it would be difficult to ascertain, at the present time, the relative importance of recycling in Switzerland or the United States. However, it is significant that the systematic re-use of materials has been accepted as a policy of environmental protection at a very early stage in China's planning for development and industrialization. In view of the emphasis placed upon the thesis that there is "nothing in the world that is absolute waste" as well as the continuous campaign for the comprehensive use of materials I am inclined to conclude that recycling will remain one of the guiding principles of China's environmental policies. Viewed in this fashion, recycling may be regarded as part of a persistent search for alternative technologies[24] which are ecologically speaking less disruptive than those which have evolved under the influence of the entrepreneurial calculus in terms of market costs and returns.

Economists will inevitably raise the question of how far the recovery and re-use of materials can actually be carried. That is to say, how far is it "economical" to transform waste materials into useful things? Furthermore, are there not some harmful residual materials or indisposable wastes which cannot be recycled without negative effects for the environment or only at exhorbitant costs? All these questions are being raised in the Chinese literature. The Chinese viewpoint may be summarized by the axiom "that there are no wastes but only things that are left unused; there is nothing that cannot be used".[25] Difficulties of transforming waste into its opposite are conceded to exist but are seen to be due to the comparatively backward state of techniques and of scientific know-how, lack of research, failure to apply correct methods of thinking and inadequate methods of mobilizing the grass root knowledge of worker-artisans actively engaged in production, and the diffusion of such know-how throughout society. For the Chinese "there is no limit to people's ability to know and transform the objective world. Thus, there is no limit to utilizing the "three wastes" ... there is no absolute waste which cannot be utilized. Continued scientific experiments have yielded important material from remaining wastes."[26] Evidently, the Chinese experts have not yet taken into consideration that some industrial residues cannot be recycled (e.g., radioactive materials) and have therefore failed to raise the question of how to dispose of the indisposable.

VI. THE CHINESE INTERPRETATION OF THE CAUSES OF ENVIRONMENTAL DISRUPTION

It will hardly come as a surprise that the Chinese interpretation of the causes of environmental disruption puts considerable stress on the capitalist mode of production as the main cause of the environmental crisis. By "capitalist mode of production" the Chinese understand not simply the existence of private ownership of the means of production but, above all, the resulting orientation of output and allocation, the choice of techniques and location of industries as well as distribution, all of which determine the relations between man and his social and natural environment in contemporary industrial economies. In short, it is this complex system of institutionalized economic and socio-political relationships and behaviour patterns which the Chinese marxist interpretation regards as the cause of environmental disruption.[27]

This interpretation considers it as axiomatic that man's environment is continuously being transformed through the "industrious labour" of man and the development of science and technology. However, in contrast to certain Western proposals of slowing down or even arresting economic growth, the Chinese differentiate between conditions in developed and underdeveloped countries. Whereas some highly industrialized countries have seriously polluted their own environment and frequently affected that of other countries even on a worldwide scale, "the urgent need for the developing countries at present is to develop their national economy, to build a modern industry and a modern agriculture and achieve complete economic independence and, ... to improve their environment step by step".[28] This view found expression in China's 10 principles presented at the Stockholm Conference on the Declaration of the Human Environment:

> The history of man has proved that the pace of development of production, science and technology always surpasses the rate of population growth. In the course of social progress and with the development of production, science and technology,

mankind can create an ever greater amount of wealth to meet the needs of its own subsistence and development and is entirely capable of improving its environment ever more effectively. It is wholly groundless to hold a pessimistic view in respect to the relationship between population growth and environment conservation. Of course, the natural growth of population will bring new problems to the protection of the environment. But such problems can be solved if a government truly takes the interests of its people to heart and adopts such correct principles and measures as rational planning for the distribution of urban and rural population in the course of the development of the national economy, appropriate control of the urban population, greater effort to protect and improve city environment and popularization of family planning.[29]

It may come as a surpise to Western readers that the prevention of social costs may have played a role in the theoretical and political struggle between the "two lines" advocated by the followers of Mao Tse-tung and those of Liu Shao-chi respectively. Apparently, one of the issues in this struggle centred around the method of economic planning and the formulation of environmental policies. However, this is too broad a subject to be dealt with in this context.[30]

According to the Chinese perspective the task of preventing the impairment of the environment, i.e., the elimination of the "three wastes" (i.e., waste liquid, waste gas and waste slag) presents itself within the framework of the production plan in the form of the following specific questions: Which is the primary task: to fulfil the production plan or to reduce the dangers resulting from the "three wastes"? Is the elimination of the three wastes a secondary task which can be neglected? Is the elimination of the three dangers (to people's health, to industrial production and to agriculture) to be considered as a separate problem of secondary importance? In short, what are benefits and costs? How are these to be determined? Apparently, some planners and managers considered it as their primary task to fulfil the production plan while the elimination of the three dangers of environmental pollution was regarded as an extra burden which could be neglected or even ignored. Apparently, some managers and industries allowed the dangers from the three wastes to become serious and were interested only in those preventive activities "which require little labour, are easy and yield large profits. Any waste product that is of low value is considered unprofitable and not worth recovering."[31]

This managerial way of calculating costs and benefits from the perspective of the individual production unit is now rejected as the road to continued and increasing environment disruption and to rising social costs. Some of the "three wastes" may be difficult to avoid but to consider them only within the context of the micro cost-benefit calculations of individual industrial units is said to be equivalent to ignoring the well-being of present generations and of neglecting that of future generations.[32]

The "correct" approach to the problem of measuring costs and benefits must be worked out on the basis of practical experiences, scientific research and experimentation, as well as the mobilization and encouragement of the initiative of workers to turn waste and harmful materials into useful things. In effect, this approach rejects the belief that "waste is waste" and cannot be turned into positive uses. What is called for is to follow Chairman Mao's dictum: "In observing a problem, a Marxist usually looks at the whole situation instead of only a part of it".[33] In short, the answer to the question of what are costs and benefits can be found only by discovering ways and means of improving the methods of recovering and re-using the "wastes" and of limiting, as far as possible, the environmental degradation by taking into account the situation as a whole.

In some cases, judging from appearances, the loss might be bigger than the profit to an individual factory. However, judged from the over-all situation, the profit [i.e., the over-all benefit to society] might be bigger than the loss ... If we are concerned only with petty profits and ignore the major issues, if we pay attention only to the present and not to the future, if we only take care of our own unit instead of considering the over-all situation, and if we exert efforts only in proportion to the amount of [individual] gains expected, we must have been poisoned by the Liu Shao-chi theory of putting profits in command. Instead of eliminating the dangers from the "three wastes", we may even lead our enterprise into the path of capitalism.[34]

According to the Chinese point of view the problem of the three wastes and the elimination of the "three harms" is not only technically but also economically solvable. But it cannot be solved on the basis of a system of monetary calculation in terms of market prices because losses and gains, costs and benefits thus calculated would necessarily be judged from the narrow point of view of the individual factory. The actual issues and the social dangers would be neglected or underestimated. That is to say, for the Chinese planner both the prevention and the elimination of the "three harms" caused by the "three wastes" by means of a systematic recovery and re-utilization of waste materials is at the same time "an important scientific and technical task" and "a serious political assignment".[35]

As far as priorities are concerned the Chinese seem to adopt a pragmatic approach according to which it is first necessary

to grasp the projects which are most harmful and wasteful and to gradually solve the problems of the "three wastes" in each specific trade and unit ... In developing industry, particularly in developing the agricultural chemical industry, the medium-sized and small cities and towns must attach importance to protecting farmland and water resources, so as not to affect the development of agriculture and fisheries. In places where this has already occurred, immediate action must be taken to solve this problem. To eliminate the "three wastes", it is necessary, first of all, to keep a firm grip on capital construction ... Measures for eliminating the "three wastes" must be included in all industrial projects under construction.[36]

Special emphasis must be placed on the need to absorb all available knowledge and successful experiences in the field as well as on the conduct of research.[37]

Despite the optimistic undertone of the literature on the subject the Chinese do not underestimate the difficulties of eliminating the "three wastes" and "three harms".[38] Nor is there a failure to realize the need for an economical use of manpower and the assessment of costs *and* benefits. The Chinese literature actually warns against any extravagance in the use of manpower and calls for a comparison of inputs and outputs with a view to making maximum gains with minimum expenditures.[39] However, input and output, costs and benefits of the prevention and elimination of the "three harms" are not evaluated in terms of monetary or market values but rather in socio-economic terms or social use values. Unfortunately, the concrete details of this assessment are not set forth and it is uncertain to which extent these important theoretical and practical problems have actually found a solution in China at the present time.

VII. CONCLUSION

Chinese experts are convinced that a solution of the environmental problem is possible. However, this conviction is not equivalent to a belief that industrialization, modern techniques, economic development and population growth will not change the natural and social environment of China. In any event, Chinese planners see no need to pursue a policy of "zero growth", either with regard to material output or to population. In fact, China considers it necessary to pursue a policy of economic development and growth which includes the protection and improvement of her natural and social environment. Her development policies do not aim at maximizing output regardless of environmental or social costs. Chinese development planning is guided by other priorities than a concentration on rapid industrialization and specialization. Ecological criteria and communal needs seem to play a significant role in her planning and decision-making. In other words, her notion and her criteria of economic calculation differ from those which have guided the process of industrialization and economic development in other parts of the world.

NOTES

1 For a fuller treatment of the thesis that China's environmental prospects are better than those of the industrial world and most developing countries, see the author's *Environmental Policies and Development Planning in Contemporary China and Other Essays* (Paris, La Haye: Mouton, 1974). I wish to add that this publication provides also a general background for the problems discussed in the present paper; the treatment of the general issues raised in Sections IV and VI follows closely the discussion of the earlier study.

2 Energetic Chinese, *Ecologist*, Vol. 8, No. 3, 1973, p. 290.

3 From J. B. R. Whitney, Ecology and environment control, *Academy of Political Science*, Proceeding 31 March 1973, p. 97.

4 In fact, according to official calculations (Wu Hsueh-yieu, Chinese Department of Agriculture) a family of four living on good land can support themselves on $\frac{1}{2}$ acre of cultivated land; cited by Robert Rodale, publisher of *Organic-Gardening and Farming and Environmental Action Bulletin*, quoted in Energetic Chinese, op. cit., p. 289.

5 Michael J. Perelman, Farming with petroleum, *Environment*, Vol. 14, No. 8, 1972, p. 12.

6 According to doctors at Peking's Anti-Imperialist Hostpital schistosomiasis is China's most serious health problem; this disease is taking the place of malaria as the most important parasitic disease in many countries with tropical climates. Salley Reston, Report from Red China, *The New York Times*, (Eds.) Avon, N.Y., 1972, p.311 and Schistosomiasis and leishmaniasis, *Life Science Research Report*, Vol. 3, No. 2, 1971, Stanford Research Institute, Menlo Park, Calif., quoted by Frank P. Sebastian, Waste treatment in China: ancient traditions and high technology, *Ambio*, Vol. 1, No. 6, 1972, p. 210.

7 Wang Te-p'u, *et al.*, China's major scientific and technical achievements in community hygiene in the past decade, *People's Health*, Vol. 1, No. 10. 1959, JPRS 2745, p. 25.

8 ibid., p. 26.

9 John Sigurdson, Recycling that Pays, *Lakartianingen*, Vol. 69, No. 23, 1972, pp. 2837 ff.

10 For a detailed description of some of the control techniques applied to snail control in combination with agricultural production see, Lois Wong Chi's review of *Fun Zhi Schistosomiasis Shou Chai* (Prevention and Control of Schistosomiasis, Handbook) compiled by the Revolutionary Committee of Shanghai, Schistosomiasis Research Institute, second ed., Shanghai: People's Press, 1971, in *Science*, Vol. 179, pp. 1118–19.

11 Estimates by Chou En-lai; see Frank P. Sebastian, Waste treatment in China: ancient traditions and high technology, *Ambio*, Vol. 1, No. 6, 1972, p. 212.

12 Nickolas Georgescu-Roegen, *The Entropy Law and the Economic Problem*, Dept. of Economics, University of Alabama, 1970, p. 3.

13 Multipurpose use: important policy for industrial production (by the Writing Group of the Tientsin Revolutionary Committee), *Peking Review*, No. 6, 1971, p. 7.

14 As early as 1958 (i.e., during the "Great Leap" period) and probably earlier, Mao called for a struggle against "waste" at all levels. "Every cooperative, every shop, every office, every school and every military unit must seriously conduct its own anti-wastefulness campaign and will continue to do so once every year." Jerome Ch'en (Ed.), *Mao Papers*, Oxford, 1970, p. 61.

15 Charles Snyder, Tomorrow's challenge, *Far Eastern Review*, 31 October 1970, p. 43.

16 Leo A. Orleans and Richard P. Suttmeier, The Mao ethic and environmental quality, *Science*, Vol. 170, p. 1174.

17 Wang Te-P'u *et al.*, op. cit., p. 21.

18 Sebastian, op. cit., p. 113. See also ibid., pp. 113–14 for further details of the use of modern recycling technology. This interest in utilizing modern technology in recycling is also confirmed by reports from Japan where the Nippon Steel Corporation received a request from China for technical guidance for equipment for the recovery of exhaust gases from converters enabling the recovery of carbon monoxide gas generated in the process of steel making and its re-use as fuel at steel mills. Peking requests NSC technology, *The Japan Economic Journal* (10 July 1973), p. 4.

19 Sebastian, op. cit., p. 215.

20 Sigurdson, op. cit., p. 2840.

21 ibid., pp. 2840–1.

22 Chi Wei, Turning the harmful into the beneficial, *Peking Review*, 28 January 1972, p. 7.

23 Honan's Chung-chon city operates more than 200 small plants to make full use of its waste liquid, gas, and residue, *Chung-Kuo Hsin-wen*, 9 November 1970, JPRS 52527, 3 March 1971.

24 There is considerable evidence to the effect that the systematic development of new ecologically less destructive technologies has an important place in China's environmental programme. Thus, while China's pesticides programmes have relied mainly on chemical methods, the use of biological methods of pest control are in process of development and actually in operation. Cf. Combating insects harmful to rice, *Peking Review*, No. 3, 1971.

25 Hua Ching-yuan, In multipurpose utilization of materials, it is necessary to promote what is beneficial and eliminate what is harmful, *Red Flag*, 1971, and reprinted in *People's Daily*, 7 September 1971, p. B2, Peking Domestic Service, 1971, translated.

26 Chi Wei, op. cit., p. 7.

27 "Under the capitalist system, because the capitalists seek enormous profits and because of severe anarchism in production, large quantities of waste, liquid gas and slag are allowed to pollute the air and rivers, drain into farm land, affect the people's health, damage marine resources and harm agricultural production. In the United States, Japan, in many other capitalist countries, industrial wastes have become insurmountable nuisances in society and unsolvable political problems for the ruling class, causing growing dissatisfaction and objection on the part of the working people". Hua Ching-yuan. "In multipurpose utilization of materials it is necessary to promote what is beneficial and eliminate what is harmful", *Red Flag*, and reprinted in *People's Daily*, 7 September 1971, p. B1, Peking Domestic Service, 6 September 1971, translated. At the Stockholm Conference this emphasis on the institutional causes as the main cause was further elaborated by pointing to "monopoly capitalist groups which seek super-profits under serious anarchy in production" as the real culprits who "discharge at will and in disregard of the fate of the people harmful substances that pollute and poison the environment", *Peking Review*, 27 June 1972.

28 Statement of China's Spokesman on the Draft Resolution at the Conference in Stockholm, *Peking Review*, 27 June 1972.

29 ibid.

30 For a sceptical appraisal of the position of Liu Shao-chi, see K. S. Karol, *La deuxième révolution Chinoise*, Paris: Robert Laffont, 1973, pp. 128–36 ff.

31 Hua Ching-yuan, op. cit., p. B3.

32 "Socialist production must serve proletarian politics, and the function of all socialist enterprises must be geared to the entire revolutionary situation, to the requirements of people throughout the country and the welfare of future generations". ibid., p. B2.

33 ibid., p. B4.

34 ibid., p. B4.

35 ibid., p. B5.

36 ibid., p. B5.

37 ibid., p. B5. "Leading personnel at all levels on the industrial front must maintain a firm grip on the task, strengthen their guidance, work out over-all plans, carry out investigation and study in depth, and map out effective measures".

38 "It must be conceded that we might frequently encounter problems in eliminating the "three wastes" because our lack of practical experience or scientific know-how prevents us from discovering the laws for dealing with the problems and arriving at the ideal solution". ibid., p. B4.

39 ibid., p. B5.

China as a Trading Nation

PERCY TIMBERLAKE

For three decades China's trade links with the industrialized countries were growing stronger while her technological links remained weak. Since the formation of the People's Republic a nucleus of modern technology had been created by the import of plant from abroad and intensive development—in certain branches—internally, but the main thrust had been in the area of intermediate technology. When many developing countries were paying lip-service to this, China was practising it.

The role of intermediate technology in launching the process of development is vital, but it is transitional. Several alerts since the beginning of the seventies have heralded a new approach in China to the introduction of modern technology from outside. Now change has come, and for many the rapid shift it has brought in the trade picture is more startling than the raised production targets which precipitated it. Foreign suppliers are being called on to accept assignments to plan new coal mines, install new steel-works, modernize major engineering plants, extend oil exploration, add new capacity to consumer goods industries and produce blueprints for factories to manufacture goods for export.

In a word, foreign trade is to play a role it has not played since the nineteen-fifties, the role of a leading factor in China's industrialization. In most countries this turn would cause no surprise at all, but in China, which until now has made remarkable headway with very selective use of foreign trade, it looks like a complete reversal of policy.

By the standards of any other country or system, foreign trade has appeared for the last quarter-century to occupy an excessively subordinate position in the Chinese economy. The Chinese have always explained this by pointing to the principle of self-reliance, which has been at the very heart of the development of the People's Republic, and before that of the revolutionary base areas back to the days before the Long March. They knew that unless they could in the last analysis rely on their own unaided efforts to carry through the changes and construction needed, they would risk jeopardizing their prospects of breaking with the old bondage and setting foot on the road of independent development. Self-reliance was never confused with self-sufficiency, however. The need to develop two-way trade with as many countries as possible, and to purchase technology from the most advanced, if necessary under credit arrangements, was stressed from the outset. But one strict limiting factor was applied: it was never to be done in a way that could allow any function vital to the livelihood of the people to come under outside control.

That principle has been followed and foreign trade has been developed as a subsidiary, not a main prop, of the economy. At first the Chinese were strongly confirmed in this course of action by the almost total Western embargo from 1951 to 1957 and by the Soviet Union's unilateral cancellation of hundreds of industrial contracts in 1960. Thus for years there were external constraints to the expansion of

China's foreign trade. Much has changed since then, and especially during the nineteen-seventies. There is no reluctance to trade with China today, nor is there any illusion that China can be coerced through trade, and the new Chinese leaders have finally launched the all-out plan of modernization several times hinted at by their predecessors.

Instant verdicts are apt to be wide of the mark with China, and those who see the present eruption of foreign trade as a final break with self-reliance should ponder how many times before Chinese policy has alternated from one phase to its counterpart in obedience to the tactical principle of "walking on two legs".

Of all legacies of Mao's leadership none is more potent than the understanding that a policy with bound feet fails to galvanize people. It is better to step out boldly with one foot at a time, the other following to redress the balance. Even within the sphere of foreign trade, which in terms of China's overall development has always been in a relatively subordinate position hitherto, this alternation has been clearly visible for three decades. The crash programme of intensified investment and modernization of technology now lifts the alternation to a higher plane, on which foreign trade may even for a period become a principal factor in shaping the economy. China's past trade is the foundation on which it can build.

CHINA'S TRADE IN HISTORICAL PERSPECTIVE

China before 1949 had provided one of the world's most pitiful examples of distortion of trade by plunder from without, and profligacy within. For more than a hundred years merchants from Britain and Hong Kong had effectively decided the character of the country's external trade, playing a leading role first in the lucrative commerce in silk, tea and porcelain and later in the traffic in opium from India to the South China ports. From the late 1870s the balance of trade had been consistently unfavourable to China, the deficit being met in the main by emigrant remittances from overseas Chinese. The steady drain of commercial imbalance was, however, by no means the worst feature. Western governments repeatedly came forward in support of demands by their nationals for more far-reaching concessions from the Chinese. These took a variety of semi-colonial forms, culminating in the humiliation of the unequal treaties under which China was compelled to surrender territory, spheres of influence, railway concessions, extra-territorial rights, tariff autonomy and jurisdiction over taxes, customs and debt service.

The dominating role of foreign commercial interests did not disappear from the trade with the relaxation of Britain's hold at the outbreak of the First World War, but passed into Japanese and American hands. In the final period preceding the overthrow of the Kuomintang government the United States, according to the Maritime Customs Returns, was taking between a quarter and a third of China's exports and supplying more than a half of her imports. As late as the thirties foreign banks financed over 90 per cent of Chinese foreign trade.

The massive American aid in the forties did nothing to counteract the essentially semi-colonial character of the trade, and subservience combined with corruption to make trade a burden on the economy instead of a support. The main purpose it served was to hold the door open for the import of luxuries or of goods that might otherwise have been produced at home. "One of the unforgettable impressions of Shanghai after

1945 is of streets full of Cadillacs and Buicks, of bazaars laden with California Sunkist oranges (Szechuan produces the best tangerines in the world), Max Factor cosmetics and the latest foreign gadgets".[1]

SUPPORTING INSTEAD OF WEAKENING THE ECONOMY

In the first two years after the establishment of the People's Republic of China not only most of the industry but the whole of foreign trade was brought under the direct control of the state. To some ears this may sound like the laying on of a dead hand, and certainly there have been examples in other places of the nationalization of foreign trade producing excessive rigidity. In China it was decided at a fairly early stage to go for a larger number of foreign trade enterprises or corporations and, more important, to aim at the maximum devolution of authority and initiative to provincial branches of corporations, even to specialized local corporations subordinate to the national ones. In the organization of foreign trade there has been no compromise on central control. It is a state function and has never been devolved on to local authorities or communes. Only the day-to-day conduct of trade has been decentralized. Different branches sometimes appear to act independently of each other but closer scrutiny usually suggests they have applied similar criteria in different local circumstances.

At the very beginning, however, there was only one foreign trade corporation, the China National Import and Export Corporation, though even that showed a flexibility not often associated with a nationalized system. The profits it made on its operations went into state funds, just as those of all the dozen or so foreign trade corporations[2] do today. Nationalization had brought a new discipline into trade. Simultaneously the greatly enhanced scale of transactions and opportunity to view a wider sector of trade than before developed a better knowledge and expertise. These factors began to operate in the first years after the proclamation of the People's Republic, when trade recovered rapidly from the low point of 1949 to reach $1,000 million in 1950, $2,000 million in 1951, and $3,000 million in 1953. In 1951—the first full year of stable currency conditions following the setting up in 1950 of central control over government receipts and expenditure and the currency itself—exports and imports were brought into balance for the first time in 73 years.

During the early fifties, when existing commerce was being restored, balanced and expanded and longer-term trade strategy had yet to emerge, China rapidly regained her previous eleventh place in world trade (she had sunk to twenty-second during the final years of the Kuomintang régime). It was not long before new contours appeared but at the beginning of the fifties they were only a shadow of things to come, while by the end of the decade they were already the fading outline of a policy adopted to meet a temporary need (like the USSR's New Economic Policy).

When the Chinese People's Republic proclaimed the principle of "equality and mutual benefit" as the foundation of its foreign trade it already had the advantage of long experience of trade on a different footing. But it took some years for this thought to penetrate the consciousness of the outside world. In one of the most ineffectual gestures of twentieth-century politics the NATO powers and Japan greeted the emergence of a finally unified China with the sanction of a "strategic" embargo on the sale to the People's Republic of all but a fraction of the materials and machinery needed for its industrialization. Beginning as the extension to a communist-led China of restrictions already in force against the Soviet Union at the end of the forties, the embargo was soon reinforced by a special resolution of the UN General Assembly in May 1951. This declared China to be an aggressor (her Volunteers were helping the North Koreans) and enjoined all member states of the UN to stop supplying her with "items useful in the production of arms, ammunition and implements of war". The interpretation put on "implements of war" was so wide that even life-saving drugs were embargoed.

WEST FORCES CHINA TO DEPEND ON SOVIET SUPPLIES

A nation that could not be deterred from attending to what it judged to be the demands of its security by American threats to detonate an atom bomb on its soil was scarcely likely to change course on account of a trade embargo. The full rigour of the multifarious prohibitions the UN embargo came to entail was endured by China for the greater part of the fifties, and tolerated by the exporting industries of the enforcing countries. Repeated assurances were given by the Western governments, notably those of the US and Britain, that China would not regain her former importance as a market, partly through inability to earn foreign currency for imports and partly through her crippling suspicion of the capitalists and all their works. The underlying assumption that communist China would feel at ease only in trade with the Soviet bloc was in some ways as far from the truth in the fifties as it was finally seen to be in the sixties. Nevertheless, the Soviet Union did step in with proposals to supply capital goods on credit and for the greater part of a decade China ran a substantial trade deficit with the Soviet bloc, importing about a third of the 600 or so "key projects ... laying the initial foundation for socialist industrialization".[3]

Perceptive observers inside and outside China in the 1950s realized that the Soviet Union was trying to cast the newly-formed People's Republic in its own mould, as it had done with the East European countries detached from the capitalist West at the end of the War. Trade and credits were one of the principal means employed, the more so when contracts led to the stationing of large numbers of Soviet and East European engineers and technicians in China, the training of Chinese technicians and managers in Soviet bloc countries and the integration of standards, inspection, shipping and forwarding and insurance procedures. The mistake made by many who were able to take a detached view of this process was to assume that its success was again more or less assured.

The outcome in the case of China was, of course, very different. Both the determination of the Chinese people to resist a return of subjection in any form, and the suspicion that there were differences between the two countries in political method and objective, played a part in this.

To the political causes should be added some specifically trade reasons. The Russians overplayed their hand in insisting on their own specifications of design, power sources, materials and feedstock; they increasingly held back necessary technical information; and they overcharged. Absorbing accounts have been written of this renewed experience by China of trade not based entirely on equality and mutual benefit.[4]

From the vantage-point of the mid-seventies it is not necessary to peer too closely into this period as the picture changed with China's Great Leap Forward in 1958. "During the First Five Year Plan," the Chairman of the State Economic Commission remarked to an American journalist on one occasion, "we had no experience in large-scale industry and could only copy the Soviet Union. The speed was not all we wished and there were other lacks. In 1958–60 we tried some ideas of our own under the name of Great Leap Forward. We made some big achievements, and also some errors."

One big achievement was that instead of continuing to do 70 per cent of her foreign trade with the Soviet bloc and 30 per cent with the rest of the world China began gradually to reverse these proportions. She completed the process in four years and since then has avoided being committed to any one source for a predominant part of her trade. Secondly, instead of having to earmark large quantities of frozen meat, fruit and vegetables, textile piece-goods and clothing every year for the Soviet Union the Chinese can now decide for themselves what quantities of these goods are to be exported, and to which countries.

Between 1950 and 1958 the Soviet bloc supplied 77.9 per cent of the machine tools imported by China, 91.4 per cent of her imports of diesel engines, 84.5 per cent of imported drilling machines, 92.1 per cent of imported motor vehicles, 99.5 per cent of imported locomotives, 74.7 per cent of imported precision instruments, 57 per cent of ferrous metal imports and 96.6 per cent of petroleum imports. The other side of the coin is revealed in Table 1. Up to 1956 Soviet deliveries to China regularly exceeded those from China to the Soviet Union. From then on the position was reversed, China stepped up her exports to a peak of $1 billion a year and by the beginning of 1965 she had discharged her debt.

TABLE 1. *China's trade balance with the USSR, 1950–77*
(US $ million)

	Exports to the USSR	Imports from the USSR	Balance
1950	191	389	—198
1951	331	478	—147
1952	414	554	—140
1953	475	697	—222
1954	578	759	—181
1955	644	748	—104
1956	764	733	31
1957	738	544	194
1958	881	634	247
1959	1,100	955	145
1960	848	817	31
1961	551	367	184
1962	516	223	293
1963	413	187	226
1964	314	135	179
1965	225	191	34
1966	143	175	— 32
1967	57	50	7
1968	37	60	— 23
1969	29	28	1
1970	22	25	— 3
1971	77	79	— 2
1972	124	111	13
1973	112	112	—
1974	137	141	— 4
1975	140	120	20
1976	183	245	— 62
1977	180	162	18

CHINA REVERSES PARTNERS' ROLES

The Leap Forward internally brought a spurt in trade with Britain and Western Germany, followed soon after by the beginning of largescale trade with Canada based on the purchase by China of part of the wheat surplus. Australia, too, which for some years had been an intermittent supplier of wool and steel to China, became a supplier on a much bigger scale of wheat and barley. The Chinese grain purchases were not all destined—as they are not today—for the domestic consumer market. A big part goes towards meeting commitments undertaken to other countries, and an increasing proportion towards boosting state reserves, which by 1970 stood at 40 million tons. But there is no doubt that the timing of the first wheat purchases was connected with the "three bad years" of 1959-61, when freak weather and floods frustrated agriculture for several seasons in succession while the dislocation caused by the July 1960 Soviet withdrawal of technicians and blueprints and cancellation of contracts, coinciding with the inevitable element of over-reaching in the Great Leap, upset the balance in industry.

At first the switch in Chinese buying from Eastern to Western Europe brought only increased orders in the West for machine tools, iron and steel and copper. On 26 November 1959, a statement by the Machine Tool Trades Association in London began: "The China National Machinery Import and Export Corporation has placed two exceptionally large orders with British machine tool firms. This news follows the virtual lifting of the strategic ban last August to Soviet bloc countries and China". In fact the embargo had not been lifted, but it had been scaled down, and one of the first fruits was that Asquith horizontal milling and boring machines and David Brown turbine gear hobbing machines which the Chinese had been examining could at last be supplied, and duly were, to the value of over £1 million. The Chinese had been quick to react but the extent of their reaction was not apparent at first. Early in 1960 an order for a complete cement factory was placed with F. L. Smidth of Denmark, In 1961 the first order for British airliners (six Viscount turbo-jets) for the Chinese People's Republic was received by Vickers-Armstrong. But it was another three years before a significant instalment of the type of contracts which had provided the backbone of Soviet exports to China for a decade appeared in Western order books.

One of the reasons for this delay—the hesitation of Western firms in becoming committed in a little-known area about which even the Russians evidently had their doubts—was also the explanation of the mixed results of the contracts themselves. Yet despite discouragement from both the US and the Soviet the years 1963–5 saw between fifteen and twenty contracts for complete plants signed and executed by engineering groups in Japan and the main West European countries. Beginning with a £7 million synthetic fibre plant from Japan and fertilizer plants from Stork-Werkspoor in the Netherlands, Humphreys & Glasgow in Britain and Montecatini in Italy, the series included half a dozen petrol-refining installations from firms like Snam-Progetti of Milan and the Speichim Corporation in France, a polythene factory from Simon-Carves, a polypropylene plant from Vickers-Zimmer and a polyester plant from Scott Bader. Courtaulds supplied an acrylic fibre factory, Lurgi of Western Germany a 10,000 ton per annum acrilonitrile plant, and Plessey a production line for carbon track potentiometers. The range of installations commissioned and the sources chosen for them had a twofold rationale. They represented an area of technology in which Soviet processes and design would not in any case have satisfied Chinese demands; in addition they marked the launching of a key phase of the independent industrialization of China, the extraction, processing and exploitation of fuel oil.

TABLE 2. *Re-distribution of China's foreign trade between planned-economy and free-economy areas*
(Percentage of China's total trade)

	1950	1955	1959	1965	1972
USSR	37.3	51.0	47.9	10.7	5.0
Other Eastern Europe	1.9	17.2	15.7	5.4	10.5
Non-European socialist states	0.7	4.2	6.4	14.1	5.5
	(39.9)	(72.4)	(70.0)	(30.2)	(21.0)
Western countries	60.1	27.6	30.0	69.8	79.0

The percentages used for the years up to 1965 are derived from official figures converted to an f.o.b. basis.

The years in which China was turning towards the West, which had eased its restrictions, instead of to Eastern Europe, which had in its turn imposed an embargo, coincided with a period of acute conflict in Japan over the whole question of relations with China. The industrial nations of Western Europe were the beneficiaries in the short term but by the mid-sixties the stage was set for the pattern of trade to revert to what it would have been if it had taken its natural course five years earlier. Japan succeeded the Soviet Union as China's principal trading partner and retains that position unchallenged today. The composition of China's trade with Japan has been very different, however, from that with the Soviet Union. Steel and fertilizer have bulked larger than machinery in Chinese imports while raw silk and oilseeds took the place normally occupied by textile manufactures and processed foods in Chinese exports. Another former Chinese import from the Soviet Union, fuel oil, is today a lucrative Chinese export to Japan.

Initially China's imports from Japan heavily outweighed her exports. Foreign exchange earned from countries with which she was in surplus was transferred to the Japanese account. This was not a practice easily reconciled with the principle of "equality and mutual benefit" and the Chinese resolved to dispense with it by increasing their sales to Japan. They increased them by nearly 50 per cent in 1965-7, and by nearly 300 per cent in 1970-3.

After its rapid recovery in the early fifties China's overall foreign trade settled down to an average annual rate of growth of 10 per cent. This continued until 1960, when the three years of economic stringency arrested the growth and cut back turnover to its 1955 level. By 1963, however, the same steady growth rate as before was reasserting itself and until the Cultural Revolution the annual rate of increase again averaged 10 per cent. Thus for the greater part of two decades the growth in foreign trade had been closely related to the rate of growth of industrial production. Sharp fluctuations in trade with particular partners or areas had not affected the overall trend, which was for external trade to expand at the same rate as the economy and not alter its relative position within it.

A decade has now passed since the beginning of the Cultural Revolution. Foreign trade has developed a good deal, quadrupling in value terms between 1965 and 1974 and practically trebling in terms of volume. Yet it is still true that by other countries' standards its total amount is small. If imports and exports are aggregated and their combined value compared with that of total production in China they are found to represent only about 5 per cent; in Britain the figure is nearer 40 per cent, in the United States 10 per cent.

In the sixties it became even clearer than before that other trading nations were not judging the importance of the China trade by its size. Apart from the recollection of its rather special past there was the unique fascination of its hypothetical future potential. China still represented a quarter of mankind and every year brought new revelations of the riches of her soil and seas and the ability of her people to exploit them even without foreign help. Probably the most compelling factor, however, was the realization that the whole corpus of Chinese foreign trade was scrupulously controlled and directed, none squandered and nothing done by accident. This meant that the impact of Chinese judgements and decisions, compared with many of those made in other countries, was often far out of proportion to the amount of business concluded. The People's Republic's standing as a trader, always high, had moved to the front rank.

HOW DIVERSE IS CHINA'S TRADE?

China's trade was beginning to be assessed less by its quantity than by its effectiveness. In this respect it set precedents, not only for other primary producers but for all countries which were still industrializing or beginning to industrialize and wanted to follow their own preference and not be deflected by outside pressure. The best-known example of Chinese support for another developing country in the form of direct trade in primary products is the annual rice–rubber exchange with Sri Lanka, which began with the China–Ceylon agreement of 1952 and remains in force a quarter of a century later. Quantities vary slightly from year to year but the terms have continued extremely favourable to Sri Lanka, some 200,000 tons of rice being traded against 40,000–50,000 tons of sheet rubber bought by China at a premium. There is considerable trade in other goods between the two countries but it is built on the foundation laid by the rice–rubber agreement: for example, the 1974 agreement provided for an additional quantity of rubber to be taken by China, together with coconut oil and ilmenite, to balance Sri Lanka imports of Chinese cotton textiles and newsprint.

Another example of a framework that has proved very durable and equally flexible is the Sino-Iraqi agreement, where a basis is provided by China's large regular purchases of Iraqi dates. Over the last fifteen years the emphasis in Chinese deliveries has shifted from metals and general industrial supplies to equipment needed for specific engineering projects, while Iraqi exports have been extended by the addition of sulphur and oil. The export of dates, however, has reached a new peak of 85,000 tons in a single year's contract, worth over £1½ million. Of more recent origin is the agreement between China and Bahrain under which the latter supplies 2,000 tons of aluminium a year (5,000 tons were supplied in 1974) in return for textile fibres, clothing, footwear and foodstuffs. China is now Bahrain's fifth largest supplier.

If the last ten years have seen Chinese trade and technical assistance take on a new importance in Africa and the Middle East, they have also marked a breakthrough in the leading Western commercial centres.

Until the mid-sixties Chinese orders from European suppliers had had their principal impact in the metal markets and in the machine-tool industry. It had been clear since the fifties, however, that China would soon be building all her own machine tools and her substantial buying in Western Germany, France, Italy and Britain was recognized as a stop-gap. With the turn in 1971 towards more elaborate engineering products such as Trident airliners and plant incorporating advanced steel and chemical technology Chinese trade took on a dimension that had been lacking previously. For example, in Britain, which had led the way with the unofficial "Icebreaker" Mission in 1953 and trebled its China trade in five years, the overwhelming bulk of the business at the end of the sixties still consisted of shipments of metals against imports of textiles and pig bristles. Four years later, while metals still made up about a fifth of exports, industrial machinery, aircraft and man-made fibres accounted for a quarter each; and among Chinese counter-deliveries foodstuffs and chemicals had begun to balance textiles and bristles and there was a noticeable growth in the ratio of manufactured goods to raw materials.

In Britain the main industrial machinery sent to China has been for mining, materials handling and power generation, in France for transport and the chemical industry. In Western Germany the most constant export in this category has been metal-working machinery, with textile and power generating machinery bulking larger in some years.

Chinese exports to Europe have not altered in character very much. They are greater in quantity and the manufactured goods element has become more prominent (notably categories like footwear, glass and chinaware, furniture, carpets and sports and travel goods which compete with the exports of other developing countries—and may well be blocked in the EEC markets in the future by the operation of preferential terms for associated areas). There is no striking new element, like oil in the case of exports to Japan.

There are grounds for thinking that this situation may shortly begin to change, with the extension to Western Europe of China's developing export of capital goods. This may sound somewhat long-term, as well as less welcome than other forms of trade, but the evidence is already appreciable. Chinese machine tools made their début in several West European countries in the early seventies, and later in Canada. Now they have entered the British market, where resistance is on the whole stronger. Actual shipments to Britain are at the level of £150,000 per annum (plus another £100,000 per annum for other types of industrial machinery). This is no higher than current shipments to Canada, but a much bigger potential will be uncovered if a Chinese gear-hobber becomes established in the British market. That is entirely possible, and would be a logical response to the squeeze now being put on some of the longer-established trade, e.g. the import of textiles from China.

FEATURES APPLICABLE TO OTHER DEVELOPING COUNTRIES

The Chinese economy, the stability of which is probably increased by its high degree of decentralization, stood up to the storms of the Cultural Revolution in a way the West finds incomprehensible. Expectations of a collapse in external trade as the internal political battles grew fiercer were never realized. Evidence of this may be seen in the published returns of the principal industrial nations involved at the time (Table 3).

TABLE 3. *Trade turnover with leading Western partners, 1965–70*
(Published returns, converted to £ million)

	1965		1966		1967		1968		1969		1970	
	X	M	X	M	X	M	X	M	X	M	X	M
Japan	80	87	109	112	113	120	94	135	98	163	106	238
Canada	6	42	8	70	10	35	10	68	11	51	8	59
Australia	9	59	9	30	10	70	11	33	13	44	13	48
West Germany	26	28	33	46	27	74	36	73	37	66	35	70
France	16	22	19	33	17	34	20	33	30	18	29	34
United Kingdom	30	26	34	34	30	39	34	29	38	54	34	45
Italy	14	20	20	23	25	30	29	25	27	23	26	24
TOTAL (7 countries)	181	284	232	348	232	402	234	396	254	419	251	518

Note: X=Chinese exports; M=Chinese imports.

Over the last fifteen years China has steadily increased in weight as an importer of primary products. Some of these—cotton, rubber, unwrought metals, sulphur—come from developing countries; others, notably wheat, mainly from Australia and Canada. In 1973 China imported five million tons of wheat (equivalent to about 2 per cent of her own total grain production), partly to boost reserves and facilitate the execution of commitments to supply grain to other countries. In the same period she exported three million tons of rice. The price of grain on the home market, where there is no inflation, remains fixed and the government pays a subsidy to cancel out the differential between the price of imported grain and the domestic price.

When the Chinese corporations are referred to in trade circles as discriminating buyers it is not only the bias towards self-reliance that is meant but their unusual flexibility in placing or withholding business. Other state-trading countries often switch from one supplier to another at a late stage in negotiation. The Chinese are liable to place an entirely different order from the one expected, perhaps opting to buy part of an equipment and make the rest themselves, perhaps deciding to drop the original scheme in favour of an alternative solution that incorporates a few of its features. In all cases the impression left is of wide and searching study before the decision is reached. If this is a feature of Chinese buying, however, it is probably an even more distinctive feature of the marketing activities of the export corporations, particularly in produce and other bulk commodities. It sometimes appears as if it were a matter of complete indifference to Chinese sellers whether they placed their goods in the foreign market or released them for home consumption. Lying behind this is, of course, the even wider strategic calculation perceptible in China's selling during the last decade: whether the handling of her surplus can contribute to improving the terms of trade, or preventing their deterioration, for other developing countries. Commodities in which this has certainly been a consideration are rice, oils and oilseeds and the situation in several ores and metals is closely comparable.

Withholding goods from the market on grounds arising from the terms of trade is not a course open to most other developing countries. The Chinese would not, however, concede that a policy of self-reliance is at all beyond the reach of these countries. It might be if self-reliance got confused with self-sufficiency. Self-reliance includes exchanging a country's relative surplus of one set of commodities for an equivalent quantity of other goods which are in short supply. Provided they are never manoeuvred into a situation in which they could be immobilized, or left unable to support life, by the cutting off of trade by one partner or group self-reliance leaves it open to developing countries to improve their position by their own efforts in trade just as much as in production.

The additional dimension in China's trade comes, on the export side, from having adopted an economic régime which can, when desired, reduce trade without arresting development and, on the import side, from highly coordinated buying by state agencies within a nationalized system.

China is an importer of commodities and raw materials as much as of capital equipment, in fact she is *first* an importer of commodities and only after that a larger importer of capital goods. On the other hand she is an *exporter* not only of commodities but of consumer goods, capital goods and now oil.

THE MID-SEVENTIES NEW LOOK

The growth of Chinese prestige in world commodity markets—especially in sugar, cotton, grain and non-ferrous metals—was one of the principal factors in bringing Chinese trade to public notice. The twice-yearly Export Fairs at Kwangchow (Canton) since 1957, attracting buyers from every quarter of the globe, played a significant part in this as the volume of export business concentrated into these eight weeks comprised a big segment of the country's trade.

The post-war period has seen trade fairs playing an enhanced role in many countries. In fact this served to highlight rather than to obscure the contrast between China's Commodities Fair and those held elsewhere. Canton's effect on world markets was unique not only because the business was large in bulk but because it covered a large part of the commodity spectrum and tended to set the tone in primary markets, either by taking or by refraining from initiatives that would influence prices. In some branches it is assumed that with the extension of China's commodity trade to new areas, notably to the whole American continent, the role of the Canton Fair will decline in relation to total turnover. The very rapid growth in turnover in recent years makes this unavoidable to some extent, since no fair could grow as fast. Yet a new and versatile development in China appears to be producing a family of mini-fairs to supplement Canton. These relate to individual trades, e.g. Fur and Leather Garments (Peking), Carpets (Peking), Basketware (Tientsin), Chemicals and Pharmaceuticals (Shanghai or Tientsin), and are therefore the responsibility of particular corporations and tend to be known to the people in a particular trade and not much to those outside it.

TABLE 4. *China's trade with Japan*
($ million)

	1950	1952	1958	1960	1965	1970	1973	1975	1977
Chinese exports	39.0	14.9	54.4	20.7	224.7	253.8	974.1	1531	1680
Chinese imports	20.0	00.6	50.6	2.7	245.3	568.9	1041.3	2259	2101

The development which has dominated Chinese trade with Western Europe since the beginning of the seventies, however, is not the headway made by Chinese exports but the more dramatic impact of Chinese buying. In a remarkable series of contracts, the first of which were concluded in 1972, China ensured that a quarter of her imports during this decade, and possibly through into the eighties, will come from the countries of the European Community.

Without apparently cutting back on any of their regular imports the corporations began placing substantial orders, many of them running into tens of millions of pounds, for equipment to develop the coal, steel, electric power, fertilizer, plastics and transport industries. Some of the largest were placed in Japan and a few in the USA, but the main body was with manufacturers in Western Europe, particularly within the EEC. The value of those placed by the end of 1974 in France alone was around £250 million. West German orders totalled £150 million, while those with British firms, including the successive purchases of Trident airliners, were also worth £150 million.

Engineering business on this scale naturally invited comparison with the previous capital goods bulge, that with the Soviet Union in the fifties. The volume was not as great, yet the technological content was just as substantial. There were three more important differences. The contracts were made with a large number of independent groups in more than half a dozen countries. They followed a decade of investigation and comparison by Chinese technical teams travelling in all parts of the world, and a long experience of trade with each of the countries concerned. Finally, the only accommodation needed to enable Chinese buyers to meet their obligations was reasonable payment terms, not long-term credits or loans.

In the past the Chinese have said very little about payment problems, simply making their payments on schedule, sometimes ahead of schedule, as in the case of the final payments under the Soviet and East European contracts. It is not unknown for China to ship late. It *is* unknown for her to be a late payer. The anxiety voiced in the financial columns of the Western press every now and again about an adverse trade balance and dwindling foreign exchange reserves in Peking has invariably been felt more keenly by financiers hoping to be approached for credits to China than by the Chinese, who merely repeated that they had no need of credits. When there has been imbalance, as in 1974-5, it was usually more localized than at first appeared (China has a big export trade to the Third World and parts of Eastern Europe), and there are also other ways of replenishing foreign exchange reserves. One is by the sale of gold on the European market. This has never been resorted to on a major scale but recently touched $350m in one transaction (80 tonnes on the London exchange in February, 1977).

There is no reason to think that the Ministry of Foreign Trade has abandoned its ultimate objective of balancing trade area by area. This demands the flexibility to move trade from one zone to another, but the Chinese corporations have shown themselves flexibile in the past and it would be prudent to anticipate greater flexibility in the future. To prevent imbalances being built into the trade structure with major partners they will switch their buying from one market to another, even revising decisions on what should be bought immediately and what deferred until other contracts have been worked through.

In the case of the Soviet Union China balanced her trade over a fifteen-year period, in the case of Japan over a twenty-year period. In between she met the adverse balance with one partner or area by drawing on surpluses earned in trade with other areas, notably Hong Kong, Malaya and, for a while in the early sixties, Britain.

If a large imbalance appeared in their exchange of merchandise with a major partner—or, as in the case of Japan, reappeared—the Chinese were pretty certainly not taken by surprise. Their external trade is, after all, nationalized. On the other hand, the imbalance has never for long remained a matter of indifference. This is one factor for traders to keep in mind in anticipating future switches. China has re-routed her trade several times since the fifties and is now in the process of doing so again: the element of trade management in this should not be overlooked.

Fully half the industrial countries now trading with China to the tune of more than $100m a year have entered that category since 1970. Undoubtedly this reflects increased overall volume and geographical spread, but it is also influenced by the import–export balance.

It is fifteen years since Western Europe and Japan virtually took over the place of the Soviet Union in trade with China, cutting Eastern Europe's inflated 75 per cent share to 25 per cent. Today several countries in the region (Romania, the USSR, Czechoslovakia) must be counted as important partners, but even taking all the planned-economy countries together, both in and outside Europe, they probably do not account for much more than 10 per cent of China's trade. The composition of the trade is also very different from formerly; for example, the predominant Soviet export to China is aircraft while, as regards industrial machinery, China now exports as much to the planned-economy countries as she imports from them.

One element in the remaining 90 per cent of trade with the market economies is disputable, and that is trade with Hongkong, fully $1,800 million per annum, and nearly all imports from China. The Chinese regard Hongkong as part of China and, while showing every sign of being prepared to wait a long while for its return, make a major contribution towards its regular food supply and raw material input. Whatever the status of this commerce in Chinese eyes it is certainly foreign trade in the sense that it earns foreign currency—nearly £1,000 million a year. Fully a quarter of China's annual trade turnover is with Japan, and a quarter with Western Europe and the US. In both cases the predominant Chinese imports are still capital equipment and industrial supplies (steel, non-ferrous metals, chemicals, man-made fibres, etc.) and the bulk of the Chinese exports foodstuffs, animal and vegetable produce, textiles and mineral products (in the case of Japan, crude oil).

As has already been seen, commodities bulk much larger in the remaining quarter of China's trade, particularly on the import side (rubber, wheat, cotton). The fastest-growing share is that of the developing countries, primarily in Asia but also in Africa and now Latin America, and in this area Chinese exports of industrial consumer goods are already of secondary importance to the sale of industrial equipment.

In the years 1950-5, China's imports exceeded her exports. For eighteen years after that (1956–73) the situation was reversed. There was an almost uninterrupted export surplus, right through until 1973. At that point the trade was growing very rapidly. Annual turnover, which had been around $4,000m in the sixties, rose to nearly $6,000m in 1972 and went on to reach $9,000m the following year. The increase in imports—notably from the United States and Western Germany—outstripped the growth in exports. For European banking interests this was a welcome development, as they were convinced the Chinese would have to accept credits or guarantees from foreign banks to avoid the embarrassment of asking suppliers to postpone shipment or wait for payment.

The Chinese did none of these things (though they certainly renegotiated the schedule for Japanese steel deliveries and cancelled some preliminary reservations of US grain, both at considerable cost). Instead of looking for credits to close the import-export gap they dealt with the situation by adjusting the trade flow to ensure that exports would increase faster than imports. That was achieved within a fairly steady annual turnover figure in the neithbourhood of $15,000m during the three years 1974-6, setting the stage for further expansion during the remainder of the seventies.

TABLE 5. *Trade with China*
Published 12 months' figures for 1974-7 for countries maintaining an annual trade turnover of more than $100m with China

	US $ million					
	1975		1976		1977	
	Imports	Exports	Imports	Exports	Imports	Exports
Japan	1,531	2,259	1,371	1,663	1,560	1,955
West Germany	223	523	272	622	287	502
France	174	374	195	355	194	95
Romania	215	220	202	250	272	238
USSR	140	120	179	239	180	162
Australia	86	326	103	268	124	461
USA	158	334	222	135	225	452
Singapore	288	42	260	39	280	60
Canada	55	371	90	201	78	347
United Kingdom	132	178	156	126	188	112
Italy	129	145	155	127	161	86
Malaysia	148·9	52·4	134·4	44·8	141	120
Netherlands	81	134	89	39	94	52
Czechoslovakia	55	69	56	72	90	80

The flaw in most outside comment on shifts in Chinese trade has been the excessively narrow time-scale on which it is based, often the bare year-to-year calculation common in the West. This is not of much use in China, where calculations are invariably related to longer periods. Once China's trade policy is seen in perspective its consistency becomes unmistakable. At one time it may be industrial raw materials the corporations are importing, at another fabricated products, at another fully manufactured machinery. There is no uniformity in the pattern of physical imports, but equally no deviation from the principle of harnessing foreign as well as native technology to develop the resources of China. Whether it was Russian and British in the fifties, European and Japanese in the sixties, or all these with the addition of American in the seventies, technology has been China's most consistent import (apart perhaps from one or two raw materials in which she is deficient, like rubber, timber and copper). In the last few years, despite several attempts to give the steering a twist the other way, the emphasis has been put more and more firmly on intensive study of foreign technology and its application to Chinese conditions, with no trace of a separation between technical exploration and its follow-up in technical transactions and trade. Thus, in 1976 alone, there were eight foreign technological exhibitions in Peking and Shanghai with substantial trade concluded on the spot or shortly afterwards—French (data systems and telecommunications), Yugoslav (electrical power tools), East German (optical and measuring instruments), Italian (food packaging and electrical medical instruments), Japanese (environment protection and hydraulic-pneumatic techniques), Swedish (transportation equipment), Hungarian (electrical medical instruments) and British (broadcasting, radar and instrumentation).

In the past China has done a substantial part of her trade with countries for which figures are not available (Albania, North Korea, Vietnam) and today a growing part is in transactions which are not recorded in trade returns (e.g. payments under the £100m Rolls-Royce Spey licence agreement). This results in foreign journalists repeatedly underestimating total turnover, and will increasingly lead to underestimates of the technology element in China's purchases from abroad.

In retrospect both the Great Leap Forward of 1958-60 and the Cultural Revolution of 1967-9 appear to have had a stimulating effect on China's foreign trade. Each movement released a burst of fresh ideas and caused old horizons to be swept aside as newly-realized potential suggested bolder initiatives. In 1976 the lifting of the restraints imposed by those dubbed the "Gang of Four"— who, in their bid for power, had over-ruled many of the leaders most experienced in industry and agriculture—opened the way for another upsurge. This, more abrupt and marked than any before, has already brought Chinese trade into renewed prominence

MODERNISATION GIVES TRADE A LEADING ROLE

China's foreign trade atom bomb, which in a few short months has blown away barriers maintained for at least two decades, is usually linked with the Fifth National People's Congress in February 1978. It was there that Hua Kuo-feng spelt out the main implications of the new investment plan and said that since it was geared to a greater increase in industrial production between 1978 and 1985 than had taken place in the whole period 1950–77 it would be necessary to "use advanced techniques as much as possible", "keep abreast of current developments in technology at home and abroad" and plan for "a big increase in foreign trade". But Hua's report to the National People's Congress was not the first preview of the trade explosion. The State Planning Commission's press article on the first anniversary of Mao Tse-tung's death (September 1977) in effect launched the new phase with the words:

While we rely on our own efforts to build up an independent and comprehensive economic system, this does not mean we are closing our doors to the rest of the world. We must expand our economic, technical and cultural exchange with other countries on the principle of equality, mutual benefit and one supplying what the other needs. We must learn hard from the good experience of other countries and combine this with our own originality. We learn from other countries and introduce their advanced technology to meet our needs, not to hinder but to promote our own creativeness, not to weaken but to increase our ability to develop our national economy and achieve modernization independently. Only the most decadent and reactionary ruling classes close their doors and reject any good things from other lands. Chairman Mao always opposed "total Westernization" and the dogmatism of mechanical copying and slavishness—but he also opposed the anti-foreign mentality of locking our door against the outside world and holding fast to established ideas.

Five months passed between this and Hua Kuo-feng's statement. Some of the contours of the modernization programme were becoming familiar by then: the targets of 400 million tons of grain a year, 900 million tons of coal and 60 million tons of steel, all by 1985, the programme of 120 new large-scale industrial projects (including 10 iron and steel complexes, 9 non-ferrous metal complexes, 8 coal mines, 10 oil and gas fields, 30 power stations, 6 new trunk railways and 5 harbour developments), and the development of "14 fairly strong and fairly rationally located industrial bases" spread over the existing pattern of 6 regional economic systems.

For some industries a fair amount of detail was given, but hard on the heels of each outline came announcements of specific projects, most of them in one sort of partnership or another with foreign suppliers. The pent-up pressure for further imports of technology was so great that new channels began opening up everywhere, with industrial Ministries and technical bureaux making direct approaches to foreign enterprises, public and private, on a scale amounting to stampede in comparison with that of earlier years.

As previously—e.g., in the early seventies, before the aberrations of the "Gang of Four" period—the two areas of most intense activity are Japan and Western Europe. The tempo is higher than before, and indications after the first six months of build-up are that the scale will far exceed anything previously seen in Chinese external commerce, even in the years of peak plant imports from the Soviet Union. This would still be true if China's *existing* trade with Japan, West Germany, France and Britain were left out of the reckoning and only additional trade counted. Nothing illustrates this better than the deal that launched the programme, the first non-governmental long-term trade agreement with a country already in full trade relations with China. Negotiated by the Japan-China Long-term Trade Consultation Committee, this lays out a programme of trade totalling $10,000 million in each direction stretching over a period of eight years, 1978–85. In fact, even before the first annual review, the validity of the agreement is being extended to 1990, partly on the initiative of the Japanese Government, who see its stimulating effect on business as possibly the most valuable antidote to the falling-away in other markets as a result of the rise in the Yen.

The original eight-year programme includes the export by Japan of plant and technology worth $7–8 billion and machinery and construction materials worth $2–3 billion during the first five years. The bulk of the orders for plant and technology are expected to be placed in the first three years. Counterpart deliveries by China over the first five years include 47 million tons of crude oil, about 5¼ million tons of coking coal and 3–4 million tons of steam coal.

A number of the largest plant orders in the agreement had actually been placed within a few months of its provisions becoming known. Among them were the new Paoshan Iron and Steel Works at Shanghai (Nippon Steel), an integrated circuit assembly plant (Toshiba and Hitachi), artificial leather and ethylene factories, and a pyjama factory at Shanghai to supply 300,000 pairs a year to the Japanese market (Itoman). In other instances the details of projects have become enough known for them to rank as firm transactions, e.g., a plant to produce 200,000–300,000 colour television tubes a year (Hitachi, Toshiba, Matsushita, Dainippon, Asahi).

The middle months of 1978 saw the most concentrated sequence of high-level trade and economic missions to Western countries the People's Republic has ever mounted, many of them led by Ministers or even Vice-premiers. Their object was not only to prepare the way for a heavy increase in purchases of plant and technology but to issue invitations to leading manufacturing groups to dispatch negotiators to Peking. In Britain alone several dozen invitations were immediately taken up, some in industries which had supplied China before (mining machinery, petrochemicals, electronic equipment and aerospace), some in areas in which the main British groups had previously been by-passed (steelworks plant, power generation, mineral exploration). Orders quickly began to materialize in the first category and the volume of contracts in course of execution for China increased in a few weeks by £300–400 million. The longer-term prospects, if realized, rise to much higher figures and imply a closer relationship between Chinese and British industry than any envisaged hitherto. Financial commitments would move to a new level, also the involvement of public authorities (nationalized industries in top-level dialogue with China for the first time include coal, steel, railways, shipbuilding, electricity and telecommunications).

Expectations that an invitation to a British team to design two new coal mines may lead to contracts to equip the mines, worth perhaps £200 million, have proved a foretaste of larger prospects still for West German industry. A protocol signed in Peking in September 1978 envisages a programme of German collaboration in five deep coal mines, modernization of a sixth, extension of two open-cast mines, a new mining machinery factory and modernization of seven old ones, costing in all some £2,100 million (DM 8,000 m.). Instead of a period of consolidation in West German share markets, as lately forecast, there is now a new stimulus from the prospect of larger business with China, as well as a new category of shares—those with the "China touch". In the footsteps of the Japanese, West German economists are beginning to describe China as one of the future "supports" of their economy.

France's share in this picture, the last to be made known, may yet prove to be the largest in Europe. There is little doubt that the $2,000 million order for two nuclear power plants, discussed several times by Ministers and now communicated to the Press, will form one of its firm elements. Sino-French political exchanges have consistently been conducted at the highest level, and have been the most frequent and most productive. Michel Poniatowski, received in China towards the end of 1978 as personal representative of President Giscard d'Estaing, was told by Vice-Premier Teng Hsiao-ping that China remained determined to accord France priority among West European nations in the allocation of foreign contracts. The long-term agreement which followed a few weeks later envisaged a programme of business worth nearly $14,000 million, including steel works, thermal power stations, an aluminium complex and a substantial flow of military sales. Contracts were to start in 1979 and reach their height in 1985.

Not all of the contracts discussed with foreign suppliers may in the end be signed and many will change their form in the course of negotations, but it would be surprising if the volume of additional business fell short of $30,000 million, spread over the ten years from 1978 and divided mainly between Japan and Europe. This may mean some increase in the ratio of foreign trade turnover to gross national product, but probably not much if China's plans for raising labour productivity are partially realized during the eighties.

China's trade is advancing on other fronts besides Japan and Western Europe (shipbuilding orders with Yugoslavia and Pakistan and the highest level of business for many years with Eastern Europe are two recent indicators), but in most cases this could be accounted for as part of the steady 10 per cent per annum uplift. The bulk of the *additional* business arising from the technical modernization programme is naturally enough channelled to the technologically most advanced countries.

The banks of these countries will have the responsibility of agreeing with the Chinese on the combination of methods to be used for financing the initial spate of contracts. Imports have to be paid for in the long run by exports, but it is no good looking for more than a modest expansion of Chinese exports within the delivery period of the equipment that needs to be ordered immediately. The Ministry of Foreign Trade began to spell out the long-term problem in 1977, saying that special capacity should be earmarked, where necessary created, to manufacture consumer goods for export, using buyers' designs, materials, packaging and trademarks. It is the short-term problem that now has to be looked at again.

In 1977-8 China ran a suplus in foreign trade. That position will be reversed by 1979 and for some years after that the gap will continue to grow, reaching proportions far outstripping the aggregate of foreign exchange reserves, emigrant remittances and potential earnings from gold and silver sales. Neither the foreign trade corporations themselves nor the Bank of China should have difficulty in obtaining credits or loans. The question is rather what form these are to take. Since the fifties China has been making extensive use of supplier credits, mainly in the form of payment spread-overs of 5 to 7 years. For many years the Bank of China has been accepting deposits from foreign banks to ease the burden of payments during the period preceding the commissioning of imported plant. By 1977–8 a new phase was beginning in which larger deposits, in effect lines of credit, were being opened with official support. This acquired impetus after the visit to Britain of a Chinese delegation headed by Vice-Premier Wang Chen in November 1978. A programme of trade was sketched out amounting to $8,000–$10,000 million over a five-year period. Shortly after this, an aggregate package of credit lines totalling $1,200 million was underwritten by the British Export Credits Guarantee Department. (The Midland and National Westminster Banks led the way with $400 million and $300 million respectively; Barclays followed with $150 million; Standard Chartered contributed $100 million; Lloyds and S. G. Warburg provide another $100 million, as do Kleinwort Benson and the Bank of Scotland; and a last $50 million is put up jointly by Williams and Glyn's and the Royal Bank of Scotland. Contracts, to qualify, must have a minimum value of £5 million and be placed before the middle of 1980.) Other British banks and a larger number of foreign ones have informed the Bank of China that they would like to make similar arrangements. China is entering the export credits market at the best possible moment ("Given high levels of liquidity in the international banking system and China's virtually unborrowed status, bankers are queuing for a more active role in Peking's financial activity", the *Far Eastern Economic Review* noted in its issue of 22 September 1978.)

The British banks' credit lines will now be drawn upon for the mining machinery deliveries, even though the previous round of deliveries to China was conducted on the basis of straightforward suppliers' credit. It is a safe assumption that suppliers' credits will continue to be relied on where they are available at acceptable rates (the Chinese would define these as 6 per cent or less), while a bigger proportion of the new programme of capital equipment purchases will be linked with specially opened lines of credit.

As China's foreign trade operation unfolds at the threshold of the eighties, not the least dramatic of the adjustments it will demand will be in the use made of loans. There is no reason why the Chinese should not continue to steer clear of governmental loans, or of joint ventures with foreign investors (probably making an exception here for undersea exploration for oil and possibly for tourism). But bridging loans they must have if the import of advanced technology is to be stepped up faster than exports, which for a while will be inescapable. In the same way as the balancing of trade with a major partner has sometimes required a decade or more, now the re-balancing of exports with imports in several markets simultaneously will spread over a long period.

The difference is that the operation is now on a much larger scale. One of the consequences of China's success in her present objectives would be that by the second half of the eighties she would have established herself as a crucial factor in the future of world commerce.

NOTES

1   S. Adler, *The Chinese Economy*, 1957, ch. XI, Foreign trade.
2   China National Cereals, Oils and Foodstuffs Import and Export Corporation, China National Native Produce and Animal By-products Import and Export Corporation, China National Textiles Import and Export Corporation, China National Technical Import Corporation, China National Foreign Trade Transportation Corporation, China National Chemicals Import and Export Corporation, China National Machinery Import and Export Corporation, China National Metals and Minerals Import and Export Corporation, China National Complete Plant Export Corporation, China National Machinery and Equipment Export Corporation, China National Light Industrial Products Import and Export Corporation, China National Chartering Corporation, China Ocean Shipping Company and Ocean Shipping Agency, Guozi Shudian, exporters of printed matter, China National Publications Import Corporation, China National Arts and Crafts Imports and Exports Corporation.
3   Po I–po, The socialist industrialization of China, *Peking Review*, October 1963.
4   See, e.g., F. H. Mah, *The Foreign Trade of Mainland China*, Edinburgh University Press, 1972.

Intermediate Energy
Technology in China

VACLAV SMIL

Increasing numbers of experts have been questioning the transfer of capital-intensive Western technology into the developing countries. These experts argue that adoption of a developmental model which combines both the modern and the traditional approaches is the only sensible way to modernization in populous Third World nations.

Ernst F. Schumacher, perhaps the most influential proponent of this new approach, outlined four fundamental rules required of a new technology to support an economy based on people, not on goods: (1) make things small where possible, (2) reduce the capital-intensity because labour wants to be involved, (3) make the process as simple as you can, (4) design the process to be nonviolent.[1]

China, the largest and the most populous of all the developing countries, has been forced by necessity to adopt an intermediate technology approach based on very similar principles; any effort to modernize her vast and backward countryside in any other way is hard to imagine. "Walking on two legs"—developing not only large complex enterprises but also simple projects in rural areas—has been a dictum of the Chinese economy ever since the late 1950s. Although the achievements have been mixed, the basic soundness of the approach cannot be doubted.

Adoption of intermediate technologies in China has been especially important. The energy output of large enterprises has increased dramatically since 1949, but virtually all of this production has been destined for major industries and urban areas. And the country's sparse and overloaded transportation network makes it difficult and costly to transfer fuel over long distances to the rural areas. Thus, the production of fuels and electricity by small rural enterprises has played a crucial role in the rudimentary modernization of the Chinese countryside.

Small-scale developments in the country's energy industries have been predominantly concentrated in three areas: coal mining, hydroelectricity generation and biogas production.[2]

During the years of the Great Leap Forward (1958—60), the native pits campaign for the extraction of coal from small outcrop mines, together with the erection of little backyard "iron" furnaces were central to Mao's hopes for rapid introduction of industrial technology into rural areas. Some 100,000 coal pits were in operation by the end of the first Great Leap Year (1958), engaging the incredible number of 20 million Chinese peasants.[3] Coal pit output, totalling 3·11 million tons in 1953 and 7·5 million tons in 1957, surpassed 50 million tons in 1958.[4] Extraction was supplemented by the mass construction of primitive coking batteries.

The coal output from native pits continued to increase rapidly in 1959, but further expansion was obviously unsustainable. Much of the output from the hastily expanded and badly disorganized mines was often wasted because they did not have coal preparation facilities, so the coal was burned unwashed and unsorted and contained a large proportion of incombustible matter.[5] The lifetime of many of the small mines was ephemeral, and a large part of production was consumed in an equally ephemeral iron-making campaign. In fact, it appears that in many cases the human and animal energy necessary just to open, operate and maintain the small mines surpassed actual energy yield and, at the same time, drained farm production of essential human and animal energy inputs.

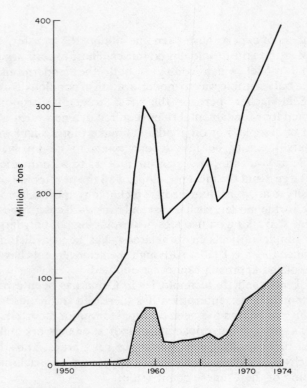

Figure 1. *Raw coal production in China, 1949–74*

After the collapse of the Great Leap in 1960, the coal industry was thrown back almost to its 1957 level; output from small mines declined by about 60 per cent (from over 66 million tons in 1960 to about 26 million tons in 1961). Production did start to climb in the mid-1960s, but most of the new small mine capacity has been added since the end of the Cultural Revolution (1969).

This new wave of expansion differed substantially from the aborted Great Leap expansion. However, the basic rationale is undoubtedly the same: small mines can be opened up and brought to their full capacity much faster than large enterprises; by supplying diverse local industries (iron, cement, fertilizer production, electricity generation, food processing), small mines can at least partially compensate for inadequate transportation; small mines can be run at a relatively low cost, relying on abundantly available labour which can be supplemented, if necessary, by simple, locally produced machinery. Consequently, these small coal mines can yield a quick and favourable return on a limited investment, enabling the accumulation of funds for farm mechanization, light rural industries, chemical fertilizer and farmland capital construction.

However, the actual execution is different. New small mines (that is, mines run by administrative regions, counties, communes and production brigades with daily output between 100 and 1,000 tons) are now opened in a more orderly manner, with some essential planning. If one accepts official claims, they are operated with much more real success—close to one-third of China's raw coal is from these small mines,[6] a higher share than at the height of the Great Leap native pits campaign.

In some southern provinces of China, small mines account for an even higher share of raw coal output, and are instrumental in lessening the costly dependence of southern China on northern coal.[7] While the total southern coal output about doubled between 1965 and 1973, local pit production increased about six times. Every province south of the Yangtze, and even Tibet, now has a large number of permanent or seasonal small mines; and it is anticipated that moderate expansion in capacity and number will continue.

Small and medium size coal mines are also very important in some northern regions. In Shansi, the country's leading coal-mining province, these mines provide 40 per cent (almost 22 million tons) of total production, and there are many small mines also in Kansu, Ningsia and Hopei.

When judged in terms of modern Western economics, it is, of course, undeniable that small mine coal extraction has many drawbacks. The quality of raw coal from small mines is usually lower than from large mines; economies of scale cannot be attained with thousands of scattered enterprises; labour productivity is rather low and the lifespan of many outcrop mines is often very short. However, these criteria are hardly appropriate when the main concern is to introduce the technology to poor peasants in rural areas.

Construction of small hydro stations has been perhaps the most meaningful application of intermediate energy technology in China, especially during the recent past.

The programme was originally initiated as part of a massive water conservation effort during the Great Leap years, when as many as 100 million people were engaged in building dykes, dredging and regulating streams, repairing reservoirs and digging new irrigation canals.[8] Thousands of small stations with a total generating capacity of 900 megawatts were begun in 1958, and very ambitious plans were made for 1,000 megawatts in 1962 and as much as 2,500 megawatts in 1967.

The reality was much less impressive. Between October 1957 and September 1958, 4,334 small stations with a generating capacity of 131.5 megawatts were put into operation, and by 1959 another 200 megawatts were on-line.[9] Then the Leap collapsed, and the massive construction of small hydro stations was abandoned. The programme was resurrected only in the latter half of the 1960s, with most of the work starting after the end of the Cultural Revolution (1969).

The general guidelines for the development of small hydro stations are quite simple—dependence on local resources, maximum thrift and construction speed. Stations are built with funds accumulated locally through agricultural production or light industry activities; central funds are released only for necessary assistance in design, manufacturing of power generating equipment or training of future operators.

Labour and construction materials are strictly local. The traditional mass methods of construction in China—large numbers of peasants marshalled to a site and performing all tasks with the aid of chisels, picks, shovels, shoulder-poles, straw or bamboo baskets and hand carts—are used in almost all cases, and the work is often accomplished in a very short time. Small dams are either rock-filled or earth-filled structures, requiring only minimum cement, steel and timber. Many provinces are now producing even their own small water turbines and generators, transformers, cement poles, aluminium wire and switches, and training new electricians and operators.

By 1973 some 50,000 small and medium hydro stations were operating and over 60,000 by September 1975, concentrated overwhelmingly in the rainy southern half of China. The Yangtze Basin has about one-third of all the stations, approximately four-fifths of the total are in the eight southernmost provinces and Kwangtung alone accounts for almost 20 per cent (Figure 2).

The typical installed capacity of a station is very small. Available figures for the southern provinces indicate that the weighted average is roughly 42 kilowatts per hydro station. This means, for example, that a typical small Chinese hydro station could hardly serve four average American kitchen ranges. (The average electric range in the United States with an oven has a power rating of 12.2 kilowatts.)

The total electric generating capacity of China's small hydro projects was around 2,000 megawatts in 1973 and about 2,500 to 3,000 megawatts in 1975, that is, about one-third to one-half of the power of the world's largest hydro stations such as Grand Coulee in the United States and Sayany and Krasnoyarsk in the Soviet Union. But although the generating capacity of the rural hydro plants is small, these tens of thousands of units built and maintained by millions of Chinese peasants have contributed immensely to the basic electrification of the Chinese countryside.

In many southern provinces the generating capacity of some of the small hydro stations is much larger than the national or regional means. However, some of the higher averages may be simply due to the inclusion of larger medium-sized stations in the county totals. A 1974 report from the New China News Agency claimed that a county in the Kwangsi-Chuang Autonomous Region was engaged in building a one-megawatt hydro station, that is, an installation 10 to 30 times larger than a project of typical size.

The Tientsin Electro-Driving Research Institute is producing seven different types of miniature hydro turbogenerators (up to 12-kilowatt capacity) suitable for isolated mountain villages with scattered water resources.[10] The smallest hydroturbine, a 0.6-kilowatt unit costing about 300 yuan (about $150), taps the power of a spring, which has an outflow of 1 kilogram per second, in Su-tsang-tzu brigade in Hopei.[11] Other remarkable installations include a series of small hydro stations in southern Kwangtung which use low head tidal power for single (ebbing) or bi-directional generation.[12] Technical details are, unfortunately, available only for one medium-sized tidal project, the 5,000-kilowatt Kan-chu-tan station.[13]

Although the load factor of the small and medium hydro stations is considerably lower than the average for large installations, these rural plants accounted for about one-third of total hydro generation in 1974 (that is, about 9 billion kilowatt hours) and produced most of the power for more than 70 per cent of the communes and about 50 per cent of the production brigades in China.

Household consumption of electricity in rural areas is still very low, usually only one or two 15 to 40 watt light bulbs are installed for each household. Power is available for small local industries, including fertilizer production, as well as for irrigation and drainage, grain threshing and milling, fodder crushing, oil extraction and timber sawing. And the use of power for these activities is often the first step toward modernization in many Chinese villages. Regulation of the water supplies for irrigation and flood control, provided by the small reservoirs of the hydro stations, is certainly no less important than power generation, however. This multipurpose nature of the small hydro projects is perhaps the best assurance of their further vigorous development.

BIOGAS PRODUCTION

Since the early 1970s the technology of producing biogas from organic matter has been spreading throughout some of China's rural areas. The procedure is, at least in principle, rather simple, and the processes involved are well known.

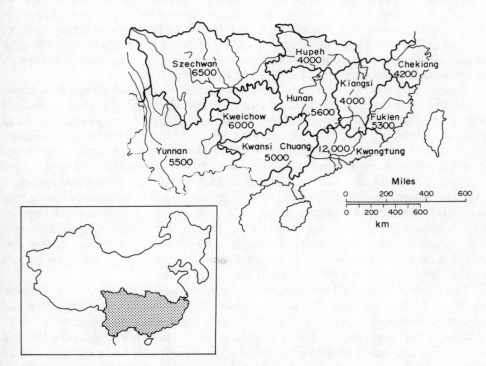

Figure 2. *Small and medium hydro stations in South China*

Animal dung, night soil, pieces of vegetation (crop stalks, straw, grass clippings, leaves), garbage and waste water are sealed up in insulated containers (digesters, pits) and left to decompose. Digestible organic materials (liquids, proteins, most starches) are broken down by acid-producing bacteria and the volatile acids are, in turn, converted by anaerobic methanogenic bacteria into a gas which is typically composed of 55 to 70 per cent methane, 30 to 45 per cent carbon dioxide and traces of hydrogen sulfide, hydrogen and nitrogen. Besides yielding the versatile low pressure medium-caloric biogas (between 5,300 and 6,300 kilocalories per cubic meter; pure methane (CH_4) has 9,345 kilocalories per cubic meter), the process yields an organic fertilizer of outstanding quality. Implementation of the technology also results in considerable improvement in sanitation in the rural areas.[14]

Small-scale non-commercial production of biogas was tested in India and in Europe in the late 1930s, but has received greater worldwide attention only during the past decade. The biogas is also called "dungas" and "gobar gas" in India. The Chinese reports use mostly the name "marsh gas".

The first attempts by the Chinese date from the Great Leap period; but a massive and apparently well organized campaign to popularize the technology started only a few years ago in Szechwan province, where the number of fermentation pits has been growing at a very fast rate.[15] More than 30,000 tanks were built throughout the province by the end of 1973; the total was 209,000 a year later (with 169,000 containers used for biogas production); and twice as many (410,000) digesters were reported to be in operation by the middle of 1975. Over 1.3 million digesters were built in the first six months of 1976, and more than 2.8 million peasant families in Szechwan were producing their own biogas by the beginning of August 1976. The leading area in the province, and in all of China, is Mienyang county where, as of July 1975, some 60,000 pits were completed and another 20,000 were under construction, with more than 60,000 peasant households using biogas for cooking and lighting.[16]

Recent reports from China stress the advantages of the method. Biogas production is undoubtedly an economical method to solve fuel problems in many rural areas, as it conserves local fuelwood or imported coal and kerosene, upgrades vegetable refuse and human and animal wastes into an excellent fertilizer and contributes to a cleaner environment.[17] With minor equipment modifications, biogas can be used to power internal combustion engines and as a substitute for diesel oil in small electric generators. And it is, of course, a clean and convenient fuel for household cooking and lighting.

Consequently, the biogas campaign continues to spread the technology throughout the country. About 50,000 containers were operating outside Szechwan in the summer of 1975, mostly in the Tung-ting Lake area in Hunan, in Kiangsu, Kiangsi, Kwangsi, Kwangtung and other regions of South China. The New China News Agency also claimed in mid-1975 that biogas pits are used not only north of the Tsinling Mountains and the Yellow River, but even north of the Great Wall.

The effort is supported through national conferences (organized by the Chinese Academy of Sciences, State Planning Commission and Ministry of Agriculture and Forestry), the training of technicians (100,000 in Szechwan alone), the manufacture of simple gas stoves and lamps, rubber or plastic pipes and pressure gauges, and through the design of differently-shaped fermentation pits. Construction of a typical 10 to 15 cubic meter digester, consisting of loading, fermentation and slag compartments is becoming simpler and cheaper (see Figure 3). For a 10 cubic meter unit, cement consumption was reduced from 400 kilograms to less than 100 kilograms and the cost dropped from 100 to 40 yuan (from about $50 to $20). (For comparison, most Chinese peasants earn 12 yuan or less per person per month from communal activity on a farm.)

When properly managed, a digester is sufficient to supply a South Chinese family of five with enough fuel for cooking and lighting. Thus, peasants are encouraged to build their own pits, using cement, rocks or bricks, and larger digesters are built collectively to produce biogas for fueling water pumps, farm processing machinery and small-scale power generation.

But biogas production is not without problems. Certainly the most important limitation is the impossibility of using it efficiently in colder regions of the country because of the thermal requirements of the fermentation process.[18]

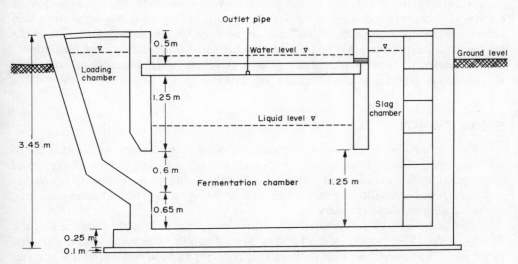

Figure 3. *Cross-section of a Szechwan-type biogas digester*

While the Szechwan Basin and the southern provinces (Fukien, Kwangtung, Kwangsi and southern half of Yunnan), which have high average ambient temperatures and less than five freezing days a year, are best suited for the fermentation of the organic matter involved, the possibilities of widespread, economic biogas generation in areas with more than 100 freezing days a year are practically nil—notwithstanding any claims of "encouraging results". (High, steady digester temperatures can be, of course, maintained even in a cold climate; but the heating may easily require more energy than is released in biogas by methanogenic bacteria.)

Even in a warm climate with concrete digesters well insulated in dry soil a considerable drop in efficiency and eventual cessation of biogas production can occur *if* the pH is not maintained near neutrality (a value of 6.8 to 7.4), *if* the materials fed into a digester do not have a proper carbon/nitrogen ratio (between 25 to 35), and *if* the sludge lacks the necessary quality and liquidity to balance the acid and the methanogenic bacteria.

According to the Chinese (the Office of Science and Technology of Mien-yang county, Szechwan), the best combinations for digester loading are 10 per cent human waste, 30 per cent animal waste, 10 per cent straw and grass, 50 per cent water; or 20 per cent human waste, 30 per cent hog manure and urine, and 50 per cent water; or 10 per cent each of human and animal waste, 30 per cent marsh grass and 50 per cent water.[19]

Other problems associated with biogas generation involve sand accumulation, scum build-up and removal, and collection and loading of human and animal waste. The contents of the digester must be stirred regularly to break the dried scum on the top of the liquid and to mix the loaded materials; the accumulated slag must be removed, and the fermenter thoroughly cleaned at least twice a year.

On the assumption that digesters can operate viably only south of the Yellow River, I have estimated the maximum potential of biogas generation in China at some 60 billion cubic meters annually, equivalent to about 50 million tons of hard coal.[20] The full realization of this potential is, of course, highly unlikely. However, as approximately three-quarters of China's rural population (at least 500 million people) live in areas where biogas production is viable, all attempts to introduce this technology into suitable regions are most desirable. And, in spite of the associated problems, well-managed biogas production offers a clean, efficient and—what is certainly most important—a non-exhaustible source of energy which can be tapped inexpensively to benefit indefinitely a large segment of China's population.

SOLAR ENERGY

The latest addition to China's intermediate energy technologies has been the use of solar energy for water heating and cooking. While effective large-scale utilization of solar radiation faces difficult obstacles, simple solar furnaces are economically viable and can be used intermittently for household cooking, space and water heating, cooling, water desalination and crop drying.

The first series of 1,000 small solar stoves was experimentally produced by the Shanghai No. 15 Radio Factory in 1974 to be used mainly by peasants on the outskirts of the city.[21] The simple device has a parabolic collector and will boil three litres of water in 20 minutes and cook a kilogram of rice in 15 minutes; these rates are comparable with those for a small coal stove.

Use of solar stoves has since spread to several provinces; no figures are available, however, except for Honan province where 2,300 stoves and eight solar water heaters had been built by the end of 1975. As for price, folding type solar stoves for boiling and cooking produced in the province of Kansu cost 15 yuan (about $7.50). Several institutions in Peking have been experimenting with large solar water heaters; the supply office of the Peking Electric Bureau has an installation with a surface area of 108 square meters and capacity of 12 tons, sufficient to provide warm water for 400 to 500 people to bathe daily.[22]

The most advantageous conditions for small solar technology exist in Tibet, where annual sunshine averages 3,000 hours and is accompanied by low air density, low humidity and low turbidity. A 280-square meter glass absorber now heats water for a public bath in Lhasa, and similar smaller units as well as solar stoves for heating and cooking are operating elsewhere in Tibet.

CONCLUSION

The advantages of intermediate energy technologies for China are indisputable. Providing fuel and electricity for development of diverse local light industries, for agricultural modernization and for household consumption, these projects while small are introducing modern technology in a way which allows for large-scale labour participation and reduces capital investment to the essential minimum.

Moreover, the benefits go even further. The part of the energy output which is for private consumption helps to raise the standard of living in China and to ease household work; many peasants acquire various basic technical skills, which are necessary for more sophisticated work to be done in the future; local production of a substitute fuel and electricity, previously produced by large enterprises, brings not only considerable savings but also greatly reduces the need for energy-intensive transportation and transmission of primary energy.

Environmental implications of small energy projects are mostly positive: the availability of coal, electricity and biogas reduces or even eliminates the need for using firewood, grasses or crop residues as fuel, which means they can be used for composting or as fodder or conserved. The role of the small dams for irrigation and flood control might be, in many instances, economically more important than power generation. The same may be true about improvement of hygienic conditions and concomitant reduction of infections and parasitic diseases due to biogas generation. Biogas fermentation also yields an excellent fertilizer, representing further savings. This is doubly important in an era of rising hydrocarbon prices, mirrored by rapidly increasing costs for chemical fertilizers.

Based on these considerations, I would not hesitate to forecast the further diffusion of small energy projects in China and elsewhere in the developing world.

NOTES

1 Ernst F. Schumacher. Economics Should Begin with People, Not goods, *The Futurist*, 8:6, Dec. 1974, p. 274; for details on Schumacher's intermediate technology, see *Small is Beautiful: Economics as if People Mattered*, New York; Harper 1973.
2 For details on the Chinese energy situation see Vaclav Smil, *China's Energy Achievements, Problems, Prospects*, New York: Praeger, 1976.
3 Yuan-li Wu with H. G. Ling, *Economic Development and the Use of Energy Resources in Communist China*, New York: Praeger, 1963, p. 44.
4 Yuan-li Wu, *Economic Development*, p. 40.
5 While the conversion rate of output of Chinese raw coal to its hard coal equivalent was 0.71 for the First Five Year Plan years, it dropped to 0·48 in the year 1958. See Yuan-li Wu, *Economic Development*, pp. 39, 108-9.
6 The source of this figure, as well as most of the figures cited in the article, are the New China News Agency releases and the Chinese provincial broadcasts monitored by the British Broadcasting Corporation, *Summary of World Broadcasts, Far East*, January 1974 through July 1976.
7 Virtually all of China's large collieries are north of the Yangtze River (in Anhwei, Shansi, Shantung, Hopei, Liaoning and Heilungkiang provinces), and the costly transfer of the northern coal to the south has been a major intractable problem. Another obvious advantage is the saving of the timber used in the mines, a commodity which is in chronically short supply in China.
8 Marion R. Larsen, China's Agriculture Under Communism, In *An Economic Profile of Mainland China*, New York; Praeger, 1968, p. 241.
9 Robert Carin, *Power Industry in Communist China*, Hong Kong: Union Research Institute, 1969, p. 144.
10 Midget Water-Turbine Generators for Mountain Villages, *Peking Review*, 18:21, May 23, 1973, 30-31.
11 Tientsin Electric Transmission Design Institute, *Ta Kung Pao*, April 4, 1975, p. 2.
12 Power Generation by Low Water Head, *K'o-hsueh Shih-yen (Scientific Experiment)*, 1 Jan, 1973, 4-5.
13 James W. Daily, Hydropower: A Mirror of Self-Reliance, *Mechanical Engineering*, 97:5, May 1976, 32.
14 For detailed description of anaerobic fermentation and methane power plants, see, for example, "Anaerobic Treatment Processes" In *Advances in Chemistry*, Series 105 (Houston: American Chemical Society, 1973); L. John Fry, *Practical Building of Methane Power Plants for Rural Energy Independence* (Santa Barbara: Standard Printing, 1974); *Proceedings of International Biomass Energy Conference* (Winnipeg: Biomass Energy Institute, 1973); Chaman Kashkari, *Energy Resources, Demand and Conservation* (New Delhi: Tata McGraw-Hill, 1975), pp. 86-94; *Energy Primer Solar, Water, Wind and Biofuels* (Menlo Park: Fortola Institute, 1975), pp. 142-7; A Makhijani and A. Poole, *Energy and Agriculture in the Third World* (Cambridge, Mass.: Ballinger, 1975), pp. 143-60.

15   Marsh Gas Used in Rural China, *Peking Review,* 16:2, Jan. 12, 1973, 22.

16   Popularizing the Use of Marsh Gas in Rural Areas, *Peking Review*, 18:30, July 25, 1975, 15.

17   Biogas generation also saves the labour involved in cutting and transporting firewood. For an interesting example of various savings effected by biogas in South China, see Mi-lo County, Hunan, Exploits Methane in a Big Way, *Jen-min Jih-pao (People's Daily)*, Jan. 19, 1976, p. 3.

18   Methanogenic bacteria, unlike their acid precursors, reproduce rather slowly and are very sensitive to environmental changes. During mesophilic fermentation—that is, fermentation of organisms which thrive best at a moderate temperature—the temperature should be optimally at 28° to 45° C, without fluctuating more than ±2 C. Thermophile fermentation—of organisms which thrive at an elevated temperature, 55–60° C—is even more temperature sensitive, while psychrophilic bacteria—which thrive at a low temperature (0–7° C)—are unsuitable for digester biogas production.

19   Native Method of Manufacturing and Utilizing Marsh Gas, *K'o-hsueh Shih-yen (Scientific Experiment)*, 5, May 1973, 33.

20   This figure must be seen as a mere order of magnitude estimate. The actual maximum potential may not be more than 35 billion cubic meters annually.

21   Solar Energy Stoves, *Peking Review*, 17:40, Oct. 4, 1974, 38.

22   City of Peking Actively Begins Work on Use of Solar Energy, *Chung-kuo Hsin-wen,* August 30, 1975, p. 2.

Chinese Aid in Action:
Building the Tanzania–Zambia Railway*

MARTIN BAILEY

China is a developing country and it might therefore appear surprising that the Chinese have emerged as one of the most important aid donors to Africa. Yet it is partly because of China's level of development that her aid has proved so effective in the Third World. Chinese aid to Africa began on a significant scale in the early 1960s and assistance has now been offered to twenty-nine countries. By 1974 aid commitments had reached $2057 million, of which over three quarters has been pledged since 1970.

China has also established extensive diplomatic and political links with Africa. Almost all African leaders who have visited Peking have been favourably impressed with the progress achieved in developing the world's most populous nation. President Julius Nyerere, during his first trip in 1965, confided to his Chinese hosts: "If it were possible for me to lift all the ten million Tanzanians and bring them to China to see what you have done since liberation. I would do so." Countries such as Tanzania have welcomed Chinese aid because of the opportunity it provides to learn from China's experience.

The last decade has witnessed a growing disillusionment with Western and Soviet aid, both among the recipients and the donors. This has aroused considerable interest in Chinese assistance as an important alternative for the Third World. The Eight Principles (see pp. 296–7) laid down by Premier Chou En-lai during his visit to Africa in 1964, have formed the theoretical basis on which China has provided aid to other developing countries. But, although the general principles of Chinese assistance are well known, until recently surprisingly little detailed information had been published on how it has actually worked in practice. This article therefore focuses on one project—the Tanzania–Zambia railway which has been built from the Tanzanian port of Dar es Salaam to the Zambian Copper Belt—to provide a picture of Chinese aid in action.

In one important respect the Tanzam railway has not been a typical Chinese-assisted scheme. The railway's cost of nearly £200 million puts it on a much larger scale than most projects financed by China. A better idea of the general scope of China's aid programme can be seen from other aid provided to Tanzania and Zambia. The Tanzanian government was offered £16 million in loans and grants in June 1964, and an additional £3 million was pledged two years later. These funds were used for the Friendship Textile Mill, a police training college, the Ubungo Farm Implements Factory, a short-wave radio transmitter to beam broadcasts to Southern Africa, medical personnel, a shoe factory, a stadium, the Upenja State Farm, a cigarette factory, and a tractor repair station. China has also become the major supplier of military equipment

* For further details on the Tanzam project see Martin Bailey, *Freedom Railway: China and the Tanzania–Zambia Link*, (London: Collings, 1976)

and training to Tanzania. Zambia received a £6 million loan in June 1967, which was used to build a radio transmitter and a road in the Western Province, and a £4 million grant was given in May 1973 to help develop emergency transport routes after Ian Smith's closure of the Rhodesian–Zambian border.

Forty per cent of China's aid to the Third World has been allocated to the transport sector and, in this sense, the Tanzam railway represents a typical Chinese project. China has undertaken to build roads in a number of African countries, including Somalia, the Sudan, Zambia, and Rwanda. In May 1968 the Chinese also agreed to help construct a rail link between Mali and Guinea but, following the Malian coup later in the year, the plan was shelved. This article does not attempt to present a global picture of Chinese aid commitments. The aim is to examine one project in detail in order to look at China's motives in providing assistance, the terms on which aid is offered, and the way in which a development scheme is implemented.

The 1,155-mile Tanzam railway is the largest aid project that China has ever undertaken. To lay the track from Dar es Salaam to the Zambian terminal of Kapiri Mposhi presented serious engineering problems, particularly on the Tanzanian section where the line rises from sea level to almost 6,000 feet. Twenty-two tunnels and three hundred bridges were built in Tanzania, while 90 million cubic yards of earth had to be moved before the first train reached the Zambian Copper Belt. The cost of this huge project, nearly £200 million, has only been exceeded by two other development schemes in Africa—the Aswan and Volta Dams.

The leaders of Zambia and Tanzania became interested in a railway linking their two countries during the early 1960s. Foreign aid was essential for a project of this size. Formal requests for financial assistance were therefore submitted to a number of countries in 1965, but Tanzania's relations with its three largest aid donors deteriorated during that year. In February, West German military assistance was cut off after East Germany had been permitted to open a consulate in Dar es Salaam. The West German government also announced that economic aid would be reconsidered; this led President Nyerere to demand the withdrawal of all West German assistance. In December the Tanzanian government, following a resolution approved by the Organization of African Unity, broke off diplomatic relations with Britain over Rhodesian UDI. Britain then froze a £7½ million loan promised for the First Five-year Development Plan. Tanzania's relations with the United States also deteriorated during the mid-1960s and the level of American aid was subsequently reduced. These incidents indicated the extent to which Western economic aid was used as a means of exerting political pressure. China, too, had also suffered from similar pressure as when Russian aid was withdrawn in 1960 because of the growing Sino-Soviet dispute.

Tanzania and Zambia approached Britain, the United States, West Germany, France, Japan, and the Soviet Union—as well as the British company of Lonhro, the World Bank, and the African Development Bank—for assistance in building the railway. Numerous reports and surveys were commissioned, but all requests for finance were rejected. The scene was set for China to embark on its most ambitious move into Africa.

Why did China—whose *per capita* income is actually less than half that of Zambia—finance and build the Tanzam railway? The primary purpose of the line was to free landlocked Zambia from its dependence on rail outlets through Rhodesia and the former Portuguese territories of Mozambique and Angola. Until recently, Zambia's freedom of action was limited, since she depended on transport routes through these white-ruled countries, and support to the liberation struggle in Southern Africa was dangerous. This was brutally demonstrated in January 1973 when Smith closed Rhodesia's border with Zambia, blocking off the main rail outlet to the port of Beira, on the grounds that guerilla fighters in Rhodesia were operating from Zambian bases. But President Kenneth Kaunda took emergency measures to make greater use of the Benguela Railway to the Angolan port of Lobito and the Great North Road to Dar es Salaam, in the knowledge that trains would be running on the Tanzam line within two years. The Zambian leader declared that it was a "golden opportunity" to make a final break with the racist régimes of Southern Africa. Half of Zambia's trade was diverted to the Benguela railway. But the outbreak of the Angolan civil war led to the closure of the line in August 1975. Two years later the Benguela route still remained closed to Zambian traffic. This emphasized the importance of a reliable rail outlet to the sea.

The Tanzam railway should also play an important role in the economic development of Tanzania and Zambia. Large areas of the two countries which had peviously suffered from poor communications are now being opened up. Agricultural production in Tanzania's fertile Kilombero Valley and Southern Highlands should increase. Mineral deposits in Southern Tanzania, not far from the Zambian border, are going to be exploited to form the basis for the development of heavy industry. The Chinese are already assisting in building rail spurs to the Chunya iron ore deposits and the Songwe-Kiwira coalfields. Plans have also been announced for a massive £150 million iron and steel plant, to be located near Mbeya, and this will represent a vital stage in the country's industrialization programme. Iron and steel production provide the basis for the creation of a whole range of ancillary industries. The establishment of efficient tranport links should also lead to an increase in trade between Tanzania and Zambia and enlarge the potential market for agricultural and industrial products.

The railway will therefore play an important role in the struggle of the two African nations to secure greater political and economic independence. In Africa the line is called the Great Uhuru (Freedom) railway, rather than by the politically neutral term of Tanzam.

The Chinese government decided to finance the project because it wanted to assist the liberation of Southern Africa and strengthen the economies of Tanzania and Zambia. In the mid 1960s China also saw the railway as a means of breaking out of its isolation and increasing its influence in the Third World. Since the United States and the Soviet Union (as well as a number of other Western countries) had refused to build the line, the Chinese offer was an effective snub to the two super-powers that appeared to demonstrate their lack of commitment to Africa.

The Chinese government first considered building the railway in 1964, but it was in February 1965, during President Nyerere's visit to Peking, that the project was seriously discussed. A few months later, a small Chinese survey team arrived in Tanzania for a brief examination of the route. The Zambian authorites were at this time suspicious of China's intentions and the survey only covered the Tanzanian section of the proposed railway. Rhodesian UDI in November 1965 made the Tanzam railway even more important for Zambia, but it soon became clear that the West was unwilling to finance the line.

President Kaunda's visit to Peking in June 1967 left a deep impression on the Zambian leader; he witnessed the developments that were taking place and became convinced of the government's positive intentions. Three months later, at the height of the Cultural Revolution, a tripartite agreement was signed which committed China to finance and build the railway. A full survey of the route was begun in May 1968 and completed by the end of the following year. The final agreement on the Tanzam railway was signed in July 1970 and work immediately began on the construction of the 1,155 miles of track from the Indian Ocean to the Copper Belt.

The cost of the railway was originally estimated at 988 million yuan (£166 million). Extra costs later increased this figure by 10 per cent to 1094 million yuan. These additional costs were financed by the Chinese as a grant.

£166 million was provided in the form of an interest-free loan, since the Chinese never charge interest on any of their aid. The loan is repayable over thirty years, after a grace period of a decade, which means that repayments will be due between the years 1983 and 2012. As the Tanzanians and Zambians have said, it is their grandsons who will pay for the railway.

One of the principles of Chinese aid is that the time limit for repayment will be extended in cases when the recipient cannot afford the payments, an automatic form of debt rescheduling. This eventuality does not appear to have been publicly mentioned in connection with the Tanzam loan, but if the Tanzanian and Zambian governments asked for a lengthening of the repayment period this would presumably be acceptable to the Chinese. There should not, however, be serious problems in meeting the repayment charges, amounting to £5.6 million a year, since the line is expected to run profitably. (An Anglo-Canadian survey of the railway suggested that initially the surplus might amount to £11 million a year.) Inflation will also eat into the repayments so that the annual figure of £5.6 million will be worth considerably less in real terms by the twenty-first century.

Repayment will be accepted in either a third-party currency or in exports. The loan could therefore be repaid in Zambian copper and Tanzanian cotton; these commodities would presumably be bought at prevailing market prices. About 70 per cent of the costs of building the railway were incurred in Tanzania, partly because the length is slightly greater, but mainly because of the more difficult terrain. Following a decision of the Tanzanian and Zambian governments, however, the loan will be repaid on an equal basis by the two countries.

One of the features of the Tanzam railway was the high proportion of locally incurred costs—for local materials and, more important, for labour charges. The local costs of development projects are usually funded by the recipient, but in this case these amounted to an estimated £87 million, or 52 per cent of the total sum, which could only have been raised by the Tanzanian and Zambian governments with great difficulty.

China is short of foreign exchange and to have paid the local costs in hard currency would have proved a heavy burden. These expenses were therefore raised by a commodity credit: Chinese goods, provided on a credit basis to Tanzania and Zambia, were sold through the state trading organizations to raise the necessary funds. Products supplied on this basis represented about 10 per cent of Tanzania's total imports and 5 per cent of Zambian imports when construction was at its height. This meant that in 1971 Tanzanian imports from China reached £33 million and replaced Britain as the largest source of imports.

When the commodity credit arrangement was first announced there were some fears that it would be difficult for the two African countries to absorb such large quantities of Chinese goods, either because they would be of inferior quality or else compete with locally made products. Some problems did develop—it was reported, for example, that Tanzania had unsold stocks of 5 million Chinese umbrellas—but difficulties have usually been due to poor management within the two African state trading corporations. The Chinese have not insisted that all local costs should be met from the commodity credit and during 1970—1, when purchases from China were not quite high enough to cover all the locally incurred expenses, Tanzania is believed to have received about £2 million in cash. The financial terms of the Chinese loan for the Tanzam railway were generous, particularly when one considers that China is also a developing country.

It could be argued that aid for the Tanzam project was "tied" because the offer was conditional on the use of Chinese labour and equipment, while the local costs were dependent on the import of Chinese goods. But this is to take a narrow view of the question. The point is that the railway was built on conditions that were acceptable to the Tanzanian and Zambian governments. The financial terms were very favourable and, as President Nyerere commented, "this is real 'aid' " with fewer strings, economic or political, than most of the assistance which Tanzania had received from the West. The Chinese "know that we would not sell our independence, even for the railway", the Tanzanian President remarked, "and they have never at any point suggested that we should change any of our policies—internal or external—because of their help with this railway".

The most striking aspect of the actual construction of the Tanzam railway was the size of the labour force involved—up to 45,000 African and 15,000 Chinese workers. Western-financed projects generally use a small number of foreign technicians, but make much greater use of expensive equipment and complex technology. The World Bank, for example, suggested that a total of only 1,500 workers would be required to build the Zambian section of the Tanzam railway. Labour-intensive methods, however, are usually more suitable for Third World countries with a shortage of capital and a large number of unemployed or under-employed people. There are also a number of important spin-off effects from the intensive use of labour, some of which should benefit Tanzania and Zambia long after the actual railway track has been laid.

Paid employment was provided to a large number of people for the first time in their lives. Forty-five thousand Tanzanians had been engaged on the project at one time and, when the track crossed into Zambia in August 1973, many of them were replaced by Zambians. The Tanzanian workers, who came from all over the country, represented about one-seventh of the nation's labour force in paid employment and one per cent of the total male population. Part of their wages were spent in the area where the line was being built, while the remainder was usually sent back to their families. The injection of this money into the economy had a multiplier effect and acted as a stimulus to economic growth.

Construction of the railway provided technical training to the huge labour force engaged on the project. The Chinese usually emphasize on-the-job training, as opposed to more formal teaching, and this covered all aspects of the running of the railway. Two hundred Africans also studied at the North China Communications University, on the outskirts of Peking, where they took courses in engineering and the financial aspects of railway administration. But the Chinese prefer to train people locally, rather than in China, and railway schools were set up in Dar es Salaam and Mpika.

When the railway was formally handed over to the Tanzanian and Zambian governments, in July 1976, only one thousand Chinese workers still remained on the project. Almost all the Chinese were involved in completing the training of their African counterparts and it was expected that by 1978 almost all of them would have returned home. Later reports suggest this may have been over-optimistic, however.

"The railway will be of tremendous value to my country and free Africa", Nyere pointed out, "but the example of hard work and selfless service which is being provided by the Chinese comrades who are acting as technicians and teachers on the railway may be of equal importance for Tanzania's future development." There is an obvious discipline required to work on such a complex and highly organized project—but much more significant is the example which the Chinese provided.

The most visible difference between a Chinese and a Western aid project is in the behaviour of the foreign expert. Westerners tend to work in a directing capacity and take little part in the actual work itself. They have a very high standard of living (usually considerably higher than they would have in their own country) and have little real contact with local conditions. Westerners working in the developing countries are often arrogant and frequently foster elitist tendencies in the society. The Tanzanians and Zambians—who have seen too many expatriates coming to "develop" their country from the comfort of an air-conditioned office and a luxurious villa—were certainly very conscious of the different style of the Chinese technicians.

The Chinese engineers took part in manual work on the railway—believing that intellectual and physical labour should not be separated—and this made a deep impression on their African colleagues. It was pointed out that the Chinese did not mix with the local people on a social level and, indeed, there appeared to be relatively little contact with the African population outside the work situation. But the Chinese lived very simply, in the same conditions as the African labourers, and they did not ask for special privileges. This point was vividly made by Premier Chou En-lai in his message to Chinese personnel working in the Third World: "If you die there, do not ask for any special treatment; just have the corpse cremated, and don't let them put up a plaque in your honour."

The railway track reached Kapiri Mposhi, the Zambian terminal, on 7 June 1975 and trial operations on the line began on 23 October. Then on 14 July 1976 the Tanzam Railway was formally handed over by the Chinese to the Tanzanian and Zambian governments. TAZARA, the Tanzania–Zambia Railway Authority, took over responsibility for the line. Completion came at a critical time for Zambia. The country's two rail outlets, through Rhodesia/Mozambique and Zaire/Angola had both been cut. The Tanzam line soon became Zambia's main artery to the coast. By the end of 1976 the railway was carrying approximately 50,000 tons of Zambian copper every month, vitually all of Zambia's exports, and a similar tonnage of imports.

The fast progress in completing the Tanzam line was inevitably compared to the American-built road to Zambia, running parallel to the railway for part of the way, which was finished more than six months after schedule. The efforts of the two countries were compared to the fabled race of the tortoise and the hare—with the technologically inferior Chinese playing the role of the victorious tortoise. The fact that the Tanzam railway was completed ahead of schedule, in just five years and eight months, suggests that Chinese methods proved suited to Africa's needs and that there was excellent cooperation between the Chinese and the Africans, both on a government level and, most importantly, between the workers.

This article has focused on the Tanzam railway as a case study of Chinese aid in action. But it is important to stress that it is an African railway—not a Chinese line. Building the Tanzam railway has not made Tanzania and Zambia more dependent on the external world, but it has increased their self-reliance.

The most important difference in the aid provided by China and other donors is the Chinese emphasis on self-reliance. The expression (a key slogan in China) was first used by President Nyerere in 1965, during Premier Chou En-lai's visit to Dar es Salaam, and the principle was enshrined in the Arusha Declaration of 1967, which drew attention to the dangers of accepting foreign aid and to the necessity for rural development.

At first sight an agreement to accept a Chinese offer to build the Tanzam, signed only a few months after the Arusha Declaration, appeared to contradict the principle of self-reliance; it meant depending on a foreign loan of £166 million (larger than the total annual development budgets of Tanzania and Zambia together) and on 15,000 foreign workers (considerably more than the total number of other expatriate foreigners employed in Tanzania), for a project whose primary impact is on the urban sector of the economy. But this is to take a short-term view of the project. In the long run it will make the two African countries more self-reliant.

During the building of the railway the African workers were exposed to Chinese attitudes to self-reliance: a good example is the way in which the technicians from China grew their own vegetables in small fields next to their camps. By the time that the line was opened most of the workers needed to operate the railway had been trained, so that very few foreign experts will be needed within a few years. Africans have also been instructed in the maintenance of trains and equipment—and even in the making of spare parts—so that Tanzania and Zambia should, at least in theory, not remain dependent on further supplies of Chinese equipment. The financial terms under which the loan was offered were very generous and repayments are unlikely to be a drain on the economies of the two African states.

The initiative to build the railway was taken by the Tanzanian and Zambian governments and the project was not "sold" to them by the Chinese. Zambia has been freed from dependence on transport routes through the white régimes of Southern Africa and the government will therefore be able to give greater support to the liberation struggle. Economically the two African states have become more self-reliant. The exploitation of coal and iron ore should form the basis of a heavy industrial sector and reduce Tanzanian and Zambian dependence on the developed countries. The establishment of cheap communications between Dar es Salaam and the Copper Belt will encourage trade and help break down the artificial barriers that Africa inherited from the colonial period.

Chinese assistance to the Tanzanian and Zambian governments in building the Great Uhuru Railway (to give the Tanzam railway its official name) illustrates how the Eight Principles of China's foreign aid have been put into practice. It represents a genuine attempt, in the words of Premier Chou En-lai, to help the newly independent countries of the Third World to "gradually develop their own national economy, free themselves from colonial control and strengthen the anti-imperialist forces in the world". Aid from China is very different from most of the assistance provided by donors in the developed countries, primarily because of the Chinese emphasis on the need for self-reliance in the Third World. This is the message that was carried when the first train from Dar es Salaam arrived at the Copper Belt.

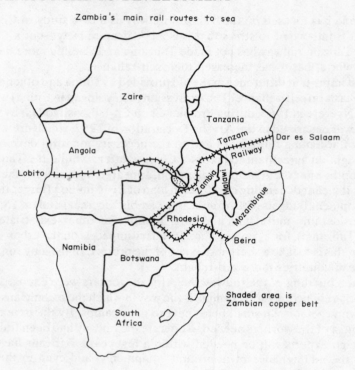

Zambia's main rail routes to sea

Figure 1

The Eight Principles of Chinese Aid: announced by Chou En-lai at Accra on 15 January 1964:

In providing economic and technical aid to other countries, the Chinese government strictly observes the following eight principles:

First, the Chinese government always bases itself on the principle of equality and mutual benefit in providing aid to other countries. It never regards such aid as a kind of unilateral alms but as something mutual. Through such aid the friendly new emerging countries gradually develop their own national economy, free themselves from colonial control and strengthen the anti-imperialist forces in the world. This is in itself a tremendous support to China.

Second, in providing aid to other countries, the Chinese government strictly respects the sovereignty of the recipient countries, and never asks for any privileges or attaches any conditions.

Third, the Chinese government provides economic aid in the form of interest-free or low-interest loans and extends the time limit for the repayment so as to lighten the burden of the recipient countries as far as possible.

Fourth, in providing aid to other countries, the purpose of the Chinese government is not to make the recipient countries dependent on China but to help them embark on the road of self-reliance step by step.

Fifth, the Chinese government tries its best to help the recipient countries build projects which require less investment while yielding quicker results, so that the recipient governments may increase their income and accumulate capital.

Sixth, the Chinese government provides the best-quality equipment and material of its own manufacture at international market prices. If the equipment and material provided by the Chinese government are not up to the agreed specifications and quality, the Chinese government undertakes to replace them.

Seventh, in giving any particular technical assistance, the Chinese government will see to it that the personnel of the recipient country fully master such technique.

Eighth, the experts dispatched by the Chinese government to help in construction in the recipient countries will have the same standard of living as the experts of the recipient country. The Chinese experts are not allowed to make any special demands or enjoy any special amenities.

REFERENCES

Bailey, Martin, *Freedom Railway: China and the Tanzania-Zambia Link,* London: Rex Collings, 1976.
Bartke, Wolfgang, *China's Economic Aid,* London: Hurst, 1975.
"China and the Tazara Railroad Project", *Current Scene, Hong Kong,* May-June 1975, pp. 14–21.
Hall, Richard and Peyman, Hugh, *The Great Uhuru Railway: China's Showpiece in Africa,* London: Gollancz, 1976.
Horvath, James, *Chinese Technology Transfer to the Third World: A Grants Economy Analysis,* New York: Praeger, 1976.
Hutchison, Alan, *China's African Revolution,* London: Hutchinson, 1975.
Larkin, Bruce D., *China and Africa 1949–70,* Berkeley: University of California Press, 1971.
Ogunsanwo, Alaba, *China's Policy in Africa 1958–71,* London: Cambridge University Press, 1974.
"The Tanzam Railway", *Jenga,* Dar es Salaam, No. 11, pp. 21–7.
Weinstein, Warren (Ed.), *Chinese and Soviet Aid to Africa,* New York: Praeger, 1975.
YU, George T., *China's African Policy: A study of Tanzania,* New York: Praeger, 1975.
Z Magazine, Luzaka, May 1973 (pp. 4–7 and 22), October 1973 (pp. 16–21), November 1975 (pp. 4–7 and 11), and June 1976 (16–21).

City Planning in China

ROBIN THOMPSON

China has developed unique answers to the problems of urban growth and rural deprivation which bedevil the developing world. Kingsley Davis predicts that "during the twentieth century the proportion of humanity housed in cities will have moved from a negligible percentage to nearly four-fifths!" A change which is increasingly "faster, more gargantuan, more impoverished, and more chaotic".[1] Planners seem doomed to search only for palliatives. A group of planners, including the present writer, visited China in October 1974[2] to find out whether China had discovered fundamental cures rather than surface remedies and their perception was that the cures China had begun to develop were indeed fundamental.

Since the death of Mao Tse-tung there have been major changes, with greater emphasis being placed upon industrial production and technological development, while steps have been taken to raise the living standards of urban workers. These must have their impact on the cities; but there is no evidence that China's basic approach to city planning, as observed in 1974, has been seriously affected.

Cities grew rapidly in the decade after the 1949 Liberation (Table 1): yet with some 85 per cent of the population still in the countryside in 1959, the potential for further massive urbanization was immense.

Indeed, during the 1950s Chinese policy seemed designed to manipulate rather than stem this tide. The First Five-year Plan (1953–7) accepted the need to develop industry and assumed that this would most efficiently be effected in the towns with their funds of existing services and skilled manpower. As Chairman Mao candidly admitted: "We had no experience in economic construction, we had no alternative but to copy the Soviet Union".[3]

The Plan's intention was to channel growth into medium-sized cities in the interior and moderate the development of the large coastal cities where foreign investment had been heaviest. "The abnormal concentration of our industry in a few areas and in the coastal cities is irrational both from the economic point of view and in respect to national defence."[4]

Inland cities certainly grew:[5] Urumchi, for example, from 140,000 to 700,000 between 1953–9. Of the 22 fastest growing municipalities over the period 1938–58, all but two are inland.[6] Fears that urban planning was out of control were quickly expressed: "At the present time (1955) there remain defects and errors in urban construction work. A number of cities, in drawing up plans, overestimated the increase in population .... Therefore when a city fixes the range of its short- and long-term population increase it must correctly calculate this in accordance with the national economic plan."[7]

Policies changed, particularly during the Great Leap Forward with its attempt to stimulate small rural industries; but there is no doubt that cities continued to expand up to the time of the Cultural Revolution in the mid-1960s. Since then, we move into the near-unknown. In the absence of official data, the US Bureau of Census and the UN published, within a year of each other, population estimates for China in 1980 which diverged by over 100 million. The only work in English on Chinese cities is an anthology by American scholars, none of whom had set foot in China.[8]

TABLE 1. *Urban and rural population of China 1949–57*
(Absolute figures, in thousands, refer to population at end of year)

Year	Total	Urban*		Rural	
		N	%	N	%
1957	656,630	92,000	14.0	534,630	86.0
1956	627,800	89,150	14.2	538,650	85.8
1955	614,650	82,850	13.5	531,800	86.5
1954	601,720	81,550	13.6	520,170	86.4
1953	587,960	77,670	13.2	510,290	86.8
1952	574,820	71,630	12.5	503,190	87.5
1951	563,000	66,320	11.8	496,680	88.2
1950	551,960	61,690	11.1	490,270	88.9
1949	541,670	57,650	10.6	484,020	89.4

Source. H. Yuan Tien, *China's Population Struggle.*
*Including population living in market places and towns in the suburbs of urban places, but excluding population living in villages of such suburbs.

My own conviction is that the growth and planning of Chinese cities are now very firmly and efficiently in control. The following are some reasons:

1. In the 1950s, the birth rate was 32 to 38 per thousand p.a. Now, the World Bank accepts 18 per thousand p.a. We were told by Changsha's Chief Planner that the national average is in fact 11 to 12 and will "soon" be down to 9 per thousand p.a.[9] His statistics were offered verbally and without differentiation of urban and rural birth rates. But the rate has at least halved since the 1950s.

2. "It takes time for a nation's demographic policy to take shape and to develop."[10] As Chairman Mao recalls: "In economic work dogmatism manifested itself ... especially in heavy industry and planning. Since we didn't understand these things and had absolutely no experience, all we could do in our ignorance was import foreign methods."[11] Recation to the failure of these methods and Russia's withdrawal of development aid help to explain the independence of recent urban policy.

Professor Gurley has shown all too well how appalling was the legacy which the Communist planners inherited. (See his paper above pp. 5–25.)

3. Chairman Mao led a peasant revolution and has always mistrusted the city. Here he expresses anger at the tendency of towns to monopolize services and facilities: "Tell the Ministry of Public Health that it only works for 15 per cent of the total population of the country, while the broad masses of the peasants do not get any medical treatment. ... Why not change its name to Ministry of Urban Gentlemen's Health?"[12]

He also perceived the vulnerability of agglomerations to nuclear attack.[13]

4. As Neville Maxwell points out,[14] the Chinese have attacked urbanization at source by improving rural conditions. Our experience was that the quality of life was

higher outside the cities and that there is an increasing variety of job opportunities in rural areas. Observers inside China suggest that there is far greater economic and political dissatisfaction inside the towns than in the countryside. Shing Ching Commune, sited about 20 miles from Central Shanghai, is in an immensely productive farming area supplying the vast needs of Shanghai, but in 1974 10 per cent of its work-force was employed in 8 workshops. From modest beginnings in tractor repairs and food processing, its local industries were now quite specialized. One, for example, made screws and another light industrial tools. The workshops already accounted for one-third of the commune's annual output by value.

5. Unease at the failure to contain urban growth resulted in a ban on individual and family migration into cities. A system of removal permits allows for exceptions. These will normally be for those with a specific job awaiting them, or university students, or those going temporarily.[15] This seems likely to be more effective than similar systems in other nations because it is administered at the local, Party-supervised level of the peoples' committees. There is presumably some "seepage", but Chinese society is too "open" for many newcomers to settle undetected.

6. Turning to empirical evidence, primate cities in developing nations tend to expand even faster than the national average, especially in South-east Asia. "In Burma, Thailand, Cambodia, South Vietnam, and the Philippines, the largest urban concentration is at least five times as large as its nearest rival."[16] The UN *Demographic Yearbook* designates Shanghai as the world's largest city with 10.8 million. However, the Chinese revised their definition of Shanghai's boundaries to include a very wide hinterland, whereas the UN includes only the urban cores of Tokyo, New York *et al*. Several observers agree that the population of central Shanghai has remained almost constant—at about 5.5 million—since Liberation.[17]

7. A long discussion with the Head of the Changsha City Planning Bureau revealed that its population had risen from 380,000 to 600,000 in the decade after Liberation—as we would expect of an inland town. However, between 1959 and 1974, Changsha grew by only 70,000. This is less than 1 per cent as compared with an average urban growth of 4·4 per cent p.a. in the Third World and even higher figures elsewhere in Asia. Changsha's city plan anticipates a continued stabilization: the target for 1980 is 700,000, i.e., an increase of 30,000 in the next six years.[18]

8. These figures were given orally by the planners without written or quantified justification. We were willing to accept their integrity, and the figures would match our observations (see next paragraph). The Wuhan Bureau had no hesitation in telling us that their city's population was still growing fast. Occupying a nodal position across the Yangtse, Wuhan is an acknowledged exception, whose population has tripled since Liberation. With a massive bridge spanning the Yangtse and China's largest steel works, Wuhan's exception is understandable.

9. Extensive, sometimes unaccompanied, journeys around six towns of varying sizes gave us the same physical picture.[19] Evidence of a core inherited from colonial occupation; an inner ring still beset by overcrowding and poor infrastructure; an outer ring of estates looking 10–20 years old, and then an intensely cultivated "green belt"; relatively little sign of new construction beyond the redevelopment efforts in the inner ring.

10. Most important of all, the Cultural Revolution reappraised city planning as it did every other aspect of life. "The really big change in the system of planning wrought

by the Cultural Revolution lies in *motivation*, not in the formal system. Not only the profit motive is rejected, but even profit as a criterion of efficiency is rejectedd."[20] "Mao does not believe in the old theory which contends that by developing heavy industry the benefits will eventually be diffused throughout the society ... He is willing to sacrifice a more rapid economic growth by building the economy from the bottom up."[21] To build a dam with human labour rather than earth-dumpers may be less efficient, but it provides people with work, it keeps them in their villages, it demonstrates the power of collective labour, it thereby relieves stress in the towns—and in the end a dam is still built.

The Chinese are now saying that the social costs of rapid industrial growth based on towns are too heavy to justify economic gains which will anyway advantage only the privileged urbanites. How does their alternative of balanced development based on collective, "moral" incentives work? It operates through a two-tiered approach to urban planning. a few general, unwavering *principles* and a pragmatic, incremental approach to achieving them.

PLANNING PRINCIPLES

"When it comes to questions of line, questions of principle, I take a firm hold and do not relax my grip" (Mao Tse-tung).

Mao and his followers emphasize the significance of contradictions between, for example, the needs of industry and agriculture, or the Centre and the regions. If understood and correctly tackled, contradictions can be a source of creative tension. "If there were no contradictions and no struggle there would be no world, no progress, no life!"[22]

Take industry and agriculture, which Mao regards as perhaps the most important "relationship". Their requirements may often conflict; each needs scarce resources. We visited the Red Flag Paper Mill which is located on the periphery of Hangzhou. Caustic waste from the factory had been emptied into surrounding waterways, killing fish and crops. The mill was obliged to pay compensation to the commune peasants. Dutifully turning to dialectics, the Red Flag workers invented a technique which combined their effluent with that of neighbouring factories. A primitive and "uneconomic" process resulted, which still only eliminates about half the offending discharge. But the total effect is a new fertilizer product, better fishing and farming, and the faith to develop ideas for utilizing the remaining effluent.

Balance and self-sufficiency are being attained by tackling conflicts or contradictions. Chinese planners are concerned with three particular contradictions which they term "the three gaps": town/countryside, industry/agriculture, mental/manual. They are interlinked.To develop poorer regions and rural areas, industry must be introduced; "urban gentlemen" need working sojourns each year with the peasants to correct any élitism. A region with good balance of manufacturing and farm produce will be more self-sufficient and thereby resilient in case of flooding or other national disasters—or of invasion—and will be less demanding of transport and bureaucratic "middlemen". Cities gain from cultivation of every available space: we saw pigs and geese running around the backstreets of Shanghai's "Old Town" and statues of Mao surrounded not by garlands, but by plots of cabbages! Professors till alongside farmers and they learn from each other.

PLANNING PRACTICE

City planning is just one means of furthering equitable distribution of resources. Its subservience to the higher political principles is reflected in the relative insignificance of the City Plan. City planning or construction bureaux do produce five-year land-use plans, but these are essentially detailed interpretations of the economic plans emanating at national and regional levels. The bureaux are lightly staffed by Western standards. Wuhan's had only forty "technical planners" for a three million population. There appear to be three reasons which go to explain this relatively scant regard for city planning as we know it in the West:

1. ASPATIAL PLANNING

Our planning traditions are spatial. Planners determine how land should be used—whether site A is more appropriate for an activity like industry or housing than site B? What is the best way to utilize site C? A plan is produced for an "area". The Chinese have almost a reverse approach, which begins with the activity, i.e., what are the needs for factory A or school B? Then ask which site will suit them best. A plan is produced for an activity.

Within the city, the key activities are the large units of production. A factory is not just a place of work, but a foundation for the local community. Take, as a very fair example, a porcelain works we visited in Changsha. Of its 1,820 employees, 80 per cent live in the flats built by (and next to) the works.[23] Their factory offers three meals per day in the canteen, a free health service, a nursery, a primary school, and excellent recreation facilities. A larger concern mounted a full-scale Peking Opera which we saw in their capacious theatre.

On average, new factories provide about two-thirds of their employees' housing.[24] If a medium- or large-sized factory is moved, therefore, the effect is virtually to move a community. Most workers will follow to the new location because the factory will be able to rent them a new flat and because alternative employment may not be easily found. Rents are almost nominal. Our porcelain workers received 50 yuan per month, and paid 1.50 yuan rent: the bill for three canteen meals per day would be 12 yuan per month.

Hence the primacy of production planning and the principle of equitable distribution over town planning. The movement of a productive unit out of a city and into a small town or village can resolve the contradictions of both. The city gains space, and loses a source of pollution, congestion, and housing demand. The rural areas gain new employment opportunities and greater facilities, which increase their self-sufficiency and reduce the impulse of youth to move to the cities.

Clearly the integration of economic and physical planning, which has never been satisfactorily resolved in the West, is facilitated by this orientation towards units of production rather than land use. Though similar models have been attempted in Eastern European countries such as Poland, the increasing correlation of economic growth with urbanization has reduced their effectiveness. China, consciously learning from these precedents, has relegated pure economic growth below increased equity of distribution.

A second advantage of "aspatial" planning is its diminution of the disruptiveness of redevelopment. "Redevelopment areas" need not exist since activities can be selectively relocated. Benefits accrue on both ends of the redevelopment. The receiving area gains an embryo community. "New-town blues" are an unlikely syndrome since most of the exported population will have been and will remain fellow-workers and, probably, neighbours. Facilities arrive at the start of the new development, not when the population threshold is high enough to entice supermarkets and cinemas. Indeed a unit of production which is about to relocate must satisfy planners that its reconstruction scheme includes not only the plant, but layouts of housing, roads and all other supporting services.

We visited a massive new residential district of 92,000 at Kuang Kiang in outer Shanghai. Though most adults work at one large factory, there were fourteen small workshops run by the Neighbourhood Committee. These add diversity: their light-bulb factory was small, but staffed by local housewives. By our standards, the physical environment is bleak. At 400 persons per acre and two to three persons per room the densities are very high. Better, nevertheless, than the housing from which these people had come in an area known as "Straw Sheds". Toilets and kitchens are shared by two to four families each, but they exist. If this seems cramped by our standards, remember two things. China is a "communal society". The street is an extension of the house and individual "possessions" are far less significant. It is also still a poor Third World country, as the Chinese readily agree. This is essential to any appraisal of their achievements.

The social environment of Kuang Kiang is as lively as the physical environment is functional and bare. A plethora of committees and shops, seven markets, and a park are shown with immense and justified pride.

At the other end, the exporting area does not necessarily lose its diversity in the way Jane Jacobs deplores in the United States.[25] Whole physical neighbourhoods are not uprooted, except for the most intolerable housing—like the Straw Sheds. These are now rare. Slums are gradually replaced and factories decentralized, but small crafts and industry remain undisturbed or move into the ground floor of new buildings.

An impressive urban renewal strategy, but not necessarily perfect. It requires undeniable constraints on choice of living and working place, and on the production unit's autonomy. Not everyone moves out if their factory leaves town: the family, still a tight-knit three-generational community, may occasionally have to split up.

Not all factories are easily persuaded that they will benefit from relocation. The Changsha Planning Bureau recalled a case in which the Revolutionary Committee of a city centre timber factory resisted the request of their Bureau and the Industry Bureau that the works be resited in a "satellite" town. Production was extremely efficient on the existing site. Planners pointed out the indirect benefits of dispersal: easier access for supply and distribution of raw materials; more room for expansion; better living conditions for the workers. They also suggested that any disruption of production would be offset by the long-term benefits for the community: the end of a noisy, traffic-intensive activity in a mainly residential area and the subsequent release of land for more suitable use. The timber works eventually agreed to move and, of course, their production has soared.

Though the Bureau admit that production does not always improve, or need to, they were vague when asked about implacably obstinate non-movers. it must be a fair assumption that they are often coerced into moving (as, indeed, they might be in British Comprehensive Development Areas). Perhaps the timber works was.

A more serious reservation concerns the ultimate capability of this policy. Firstly, many decentralization plans are operated through satellite towns. Depending on boundary definitions, "Greater Shanghai" has 60 to 70 satellites of perhaps 30,000 to 60,000 inhabitants. Certainly the "green belt" of all the cities we visited is more protected and better cultivated than their equivalents in Britain. Nevertheless, the Chinese may be in danger of containing the city at the expense of polynuclear metropolitan regions.[26] Their hopes of avoiding this fate must lie in the deceleration of the birth rate, the gradual end to slum clearance programmes and success in promoting the growth of the outer regions.[27] Shanghai's "Old Town" is picturesque, but lacking in sewage and drainage. As an amazed Edgar Snow discovered, the local committees ensure immaculate cleanliness.[28] However, these services must eventually come as standards and resources grow. With current densities of 600 persons per acre and without the technology (or tradition) for high-rise building, there is bound to be a shortfall of about 200 persons per acre to be decanted when such an area is rehabilitated. The city's planned annual overspill figure of 100,000 persons, therefore, represents no more than is necessary—a problem which is less acute for smaller towns like Changsha, whose inner "green belt" population has fallen from 340,000 to 260,000 since 1959. Changsha, nevertheless, still retains legacies from the bestial conditions of pre-Liberation China and has large tracts of poor housing to renovate or replace.

Secondly, we have yet to see whether the planners can go beyond containment of the city. Chinese policy is to move central enterprises selectively over a long period. They have yet to reach a stage at which activities conventionally regarded as essential to central areas might be moved. Is the large furniture or department store a necessity if choice is to be maintained—again, an issue especially complex in coastal cities where colonial powers built up a strong central business district. One factor which is on the Chinese side, here, is their determination to minimize service industries, especially bureaucracies, which tend increasingly to monopolize the space and employment structure of Western central areas.

As a final reflection on the aspatial nature of Chinese planning, people, as well as production units, have been relocated. Cynics argue that the de-urbanization process was given its impetus by the need to expel the Red Guards from the cities. However, as early as 1949 Chinese writers were saying: "Because no more than 3 million of the Shanghai's 6 million people actually take part in productive work, the number of people who do not participate in production amounts to more than 3 million".[29] Equal job opportunities for women and the allocation of socially useful work to the elderly has lessened the burden of dependents. It is the young people who are exhorted to emigrate to the countryside: 8 million have done so since 1968, according to Chinese sources. Millions more of the urban youth work temporarily on the farms in their vacations. Shing Ching, a small commune of 20,000 outside Shanghai, had absorbed 3,000 school children for a few weeks each in 1973.

2. INCREMENTALISM AND MONITORING

The second distinctive characteristic of Chinese urban planning is the employment of incremental means to achieve the long-term principles or goals. They have rejected the "master plan", which has been the dominant tradition of Western planning and which, through the vehicle of consultancies, has been exported to the developing nations. Arising from the profession's origins in the physical sciences, the "master plan" expounds the size, location and composition of population, employment and other land uses over a 20- to 30-year time period. Unfortunately, unlike a bridge or a house, a city cannot be built exactly to the specifications of a design. Indeed, our increasing uncertainty about the future has rendered most master plans ineffective within 20 months rather than 20 years. Even the relatively sophisticated Census of British Population has proved wildly inaccurate over 10-year, let alone 20- or 30-year, time periods as the 1971 figures show. Erratic economic cycles and the market economy, haphazard politics, climatic disasters, and more assertive community activism, are just some sources of uncertainty.

Western planning theorists are now advancing the idea of "incrementalism",[30] a methodology which seeks to achieve long-range goals by the accumulation of short-range actions, each capable of quick and definite implementation. This avoids the seemingly inevitable, built-in redundancy of the "master plan". If the actions do not seem to be helping the achievement of goals, either fresh actions can be taken, or the planners may decide that the goals need reappraisal.

Curiously, the Chinese are practising what we are beginning to preach. We have seen that firm long-term goals exist. It may surprise many to discover how undogmatic Chairman Mao was about the means of attaining them. Here he gives a perfect example of incrementalism:

> There remains a question in my mind about producing, in the course of the second five-year plan, 20 million tons of steel. Is this a good thing, or will it throw everything into confusion? I'm not sure at present, so I want to hold meetings. We'll meet four times a year, and if there are problems, we will make adjustments.

The emphasis upon activities rather than physical design, explained above, facilitates an incrementalist or, in Chinese terminology, a "step by step" approach. Factories and other units can be selectively relocated: there is no need for a grand 20-year industrial location strategy. As each activity is relocated, planners learn which are the best industries to move, the best locations to develop, the most efficient layouts.

Chinese housing policy is similarly pragmatic. In 1958, the state took over privately owned, rented houses. However, at first only the major slum landlords were "nationalized", then the smaller operators. Twenty-four per cent of Wuhan's housing stock is still under owner-occupation and, perhaps more typically, ten per cent of Changsha's. Elimination of private housing has been done gradually, since this eases the burden of compensation, of red tape, and of the suffering of small landlords.

Similarly, slum clearance has not been tackled by the mass demolition of wide areas, except in the worst cases. Much of the stock has been renewed, and Neighbourhood Committees are encouraged to plan and implement their own local redevelopment, subject to the City Planning Bureau's approval of design and siting and of availability of building materials.[31]

Incrementalism will succeed only if the planners are capable of "learning from past mistakes to prevent future ones".[32] They must know which of their short-range plans have succeeded and which have not—and why—if they are to make successful adjustments. City Planning Bureaux do have Statistics Sections and there are regular censuses. These must, at present, be of doubtful quality and Chinese planners showed little acquaintance with techniques of analysis, evaluation and forecasting, such as gravity models and linear programming—a case in which many might feel that ignorance (or disinclination) is bliss.

Far more significant is the immersion of planners in a general learning process, characterized as "from the top down and from the bottom up". With extraordinary durability, the Chinese are capable of endless rounds of negotiation and consultation. At each level of their powerfully structured hierarchy there is regular and unfettered discussion with the tiers above and below, both within and without the Party machine. This means that the allocators of resources at the higher levels are aware of the problems, needs, and expectations of the grass roots.[33]

Because of this system of consultation, public participation is our formal sense becomes relatively insignificant. The City Plans are in fact publicized and displayed for public comment in a very similar way to the British system. However, the continuous exposure of the planners to the criticism and suggestions of District, Neighbourhood, and Street Committees is a far more effective check upon potential professional arrogance or mystification.

What we would describe as monitoring and incrementalism has not come to the Chinese as a refined theoretical construct. Rather the reverse: it arises from lessons of past dogmatism, such as the "Great Leap Forward", and from Chairman Mao's distrust of theories and grand designs: "All genuine knowledge originates in direct experience".

3. DEVOLUTION OF PLANNING POWERS

A third distinctive characteristic of Chinese planning is its attempt to devolve the making of decisions down to the level at which they will be executed. It must be emphasized that we are discussing essentially technical, resource-allocating and utilizing decisions rather than fundamental political decisions. The problems of "democratic centralism" are at the root of the Cultural Revolution and the anti-Confucian campaign, which have sought to destroy the development of a bureaucratic élite. At the same time, the Communist Party remains the controlling mechanism and is centrally directed, however popular its policies may be.

For day-to-day decision-making, Mao's ideas are far less ambiguous. In 1956 he said: "I propose that the Party and government organs should be streamlined and that two-thirds of their numbers should be axed".[34] The axe fell. Since Mao's death there are signs of a new revival in the size and strength of the bureaucracy.

There is a powerfully defined hierarchical administration as Charts 1 and 2 demonstrate. Two illustrations from different levels will testify to the workings of a decentralized system.[35]

The Ma-Yi-Hsing Neighbourhood is in an old quarter of Changsha, with poor housing and cramped industries. Redevelopment is gradually taking place. Initiatives have mainly come from the Neighbourhood Committee, which has, for instance superintended the erection of three new blocks of flats. The idea emanated locally; the Committee decided which slums most urgently warranted clearance and who needed new accommodation; the flats were built by residents' labour with the help of their two full-time builders.

However, these projects are subject to discussion and control with higher tiers. Urban District and Street Committees will usually have one member responsible for planning matters who would advise and liaise at Neighbourhood level. In our Changsha example, planning permission was required from the City Planning Bureau, which operates a development control machinery reminiscent of Britain's. However, criteria used in evaluating applications include not only technical standards of design and density, but also contribution to production, minimizing of journeys to work, elimination of "wastes", and linkages with related activities. The Changsha Bureau had consulted the City Housing and Industry Bureaux at its own municipal level to check that the resources needed for the Ma-Yi-Hsing projects were compatible with general quotas. This case demonstrates how devolution of planning meshes with an aspatial, incremental methodology.

A far more ambitious, six-million yuan hydro-electric and irrigation project is being undertaken in Shen Deh County. The County Planning and Water and Electricity Bureaux control and finance the scheme. However, they are in constant consultation with their Province, for higher level clearance, and with their ten Communes who provide and pay the labour force and who will become collective owners of the electricity plant and the reclaimed land.

Equation of policy-making with implementation is a characteristic blend of socialist theory, expediency in a country of 700 million or more, and instinctive distrust of urban élites and bureaucracies. Whether it could exist without a central Party "brain" is not debated here. Suffice it to say that it operates only in a climate of critical debate and that it seems to bring people and planners far closer together. It also reduces the numbers of specialist plans, planners and their attendant trappings. When Mao says, "We must drive all actors, poets, dramatists and writers out of the cities, and pack them all off to the countryside", the suspicion lurks that he would willingly include town planners in his list.

TWO LESSONS FROM THE CHINESE URBAN PLANNING SYSTEM

Despite some reservations, this article clearly rests on the belief that out of a terrible legacy, Chinese planning has produced a successful and effective system. Towns are clean but lively; there are no traffic jams but there is plenty of bustle; conditions are still poor, but the worst excesses are over. Services and facilities do not congregate in CBDs but are relatively dispersed; districts are not monochrome, but have a multitude of activities. People participate.

The lessons we can learn are of two kinds. The first is probably accessible only to developing nations for whom a socialist model is still viable. Fully-fledged capitalism has gone too far along the road of economic incentives, individual competitiveness, specialization and professionalism. Dare one hope that countries like India can still make the difficult and initially damaging turn to moral incentives, collective effort, and encouragement of the poor, be it people, regions, or rural areas?[36]

More attainable is the Chinese approach to urban planning. Certainly they are less beset by problems of uncertainty as a uniquely "cut-off" and single-party nation. There are still complexities, however, which range from political upheavals to the ravages of flooding. The technique of pronouncing, through debate, a set of planning goals and working towards them step-by-step looks as valid for New York or Liverpool as it does for Shanghai or Changsha. Less emphasis upon spatial aspects and more upon planning of activities should be within the compass of a young profession, as should the humility and courage to shed some of its decision-making and to retain only the powers and controls necessary for guidance of more localized and personalized planning.

CHART 1

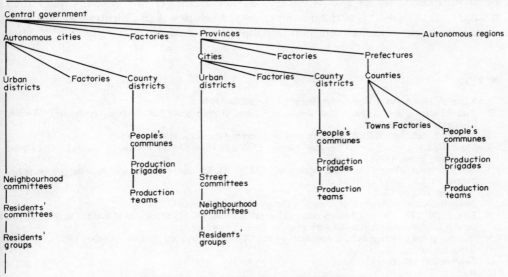

CHART 2. *Hierarchy of Chinese planning administration*

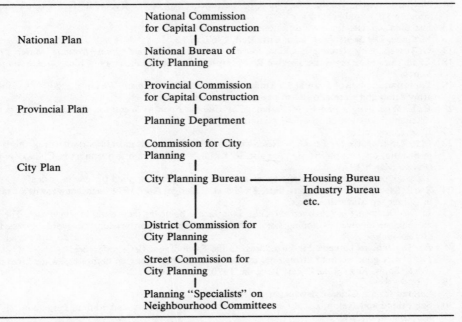

Note. Plans and information flow from "the bottom up and the top down".

To dismiss the Chinese achievements as the product of dogma and foreigners' gullibility is in itself to be guilty of dogmatism and naive complacency.

Let the final word rest with the former British Home Secretary, Roy Jenkins, on the right of the Labour Pary and a recent visitor to China and India: "one of the most disturbing questions in the minds of anyone who believes in democracy is that if one goes to Shanghai and then goes to Calcutta and then asks: in which city would the mass of its inhabitants rather live, it is very difficult to answer this in terms other than Shanghai . . . I think it is at the moment nearer a solution than Calcutta, perhaps even than New York, perhaps even than London".[37]

NOTES

1   Kingsley Davis, preface to Cities, *Scientific American*, 1965.
2   The 21-strong group spent four weeks in China, visiting Shanghai, Canton, Hangzhou, Wuhan, Changsha and Kweilin.
3   Mao in S. Schram (Ed.), *Mao Tse-tung Unrehearsed* (Penguin, 1974), p. 98
4   Quoted from China's First Five-year Plan by H. Yuan Tien, *China's Population Struggle*, Ohio State University Press, 1973.
5   See l. Orleans, *Every Fifth Child*, Methuen, 1972, p. 83, for the best treatment of demographic policy before the Cultural Revolution.
6   Tien, op. cit., p. 57.
7   From the Chinese newspaper, *People's Daily*, 23 November 1955.
8   Lewis (Ed.), *The City in China*, Stanford University Press, 1971. For reasons alluded to in the text, this cannot be recommended as an authoritative source, however.
9   Figures given to our group by members of the Changsha Planning Bureau, October 1973.
10 Tien, op. cit., p. 18.
11 Schram, op. cit., p. 98.
12 ibid., p. 232.
13 ibid., p. 197.
14 Neville Maxwell, The City in China, in the proceedings of the Exploding Cities Conference, 1974 (*Sunday Times* publication).
15 See Tien, op. cit., for a good treatment of this.
16 McGhee, *The South East Asian City*, Bell, 1967, p. 23.
17 G. Towers, City planning in China, *Journal of the Royal Town Planning Institute*, March 1973.
18 Changsha's planning is discussed in R. Thompson, Containing the city in China, *Architectural Design*, March 1974.
19 For instance, three of us walked ten miles out from Kweilin and back. We unwittingly walked into a large army camp and were allowed to pass through unattended.
20 E. L. Wheelwright and B. McFarlane, *The Chinese Road to Socialism*, Penguin, 1973, p. 145. An excellent discussion of economic planning.
21 Orleans, op. cit., p. 197.
22 Mao Tse-tung, *On the Ten Great Relationships*, 1956. One of his most important works, this is included in Schram, op. cit., pp. 61–83. See also R. Kirkby's introduction to Planning in China, *Architectural Design*, March 1974.
23 Sixty-six per cent is the average we were given for housing supplied by new factories.
24 See R. MacQueen, Housing in China, *Architectural Design*, April 1974. In fact new towns are rarely built in China; see Maxwell, op. cit.
25 In *The Decline of Great American Cities* Jane Jacobs bemoans their trend to single uses. The planning mechanism involved is zoning, i.e., industry zone, etc. Appropriately the word derives from the Greek—*pantie*!
26 As Roy Jenkins perceived in his address to the Exploding Cities Conference.
27 For a very good account of regional development, and of Shanghai before and after Liberation, see Edgar Snow, *Red China Today*, Penguin, 1970.
28 ibid.
29 Quoted from a Chinese newspaper by Tien, op. cit., p. 33.
30 See Friend and Jessop, *Local Government and Strategic Choice*, 2nd edition, Pergamon, 1977.
31 MacQueen, op. cit.
32 Schram op. cit., p. 294.

33 See Joan Robinson's excellent *Economic Management in China,* Society for Anglo-Chinese Understanding, 1973.
34 Schram, op. cit., p. 75.
35 For a well documented account of this system see N. Jeffrey, Administrative/political system in China, *Architectural Design,* March 1974.
36 The evidence of the Exploding Cities Conference suggests one dare not.
37 Jenkins, ibid.

The Role of the People's Liberation Army in China's Development: the Maoist Model of Army-building

MICHAEL Y. M. KAU

It is estimated that in 1975 a total of over 26 million men and women were under arms in the world, and each year more than $371 billion is spent in direct support of military forces. On the average, military expenditure consumes approximately 20 per cent of the national budget of every country.[1] These staggering figures raise an obvious and serious question: How can this enormous military manpower and these resources be used for the constructive purposes of nation-building and modernization? The question is of particular significance to the developing countries of the "Third World", where material and human resources available for development are scarce, while expectations and demands for modernization are high. The probe into the feasibility of harnessing and converting armed forces into a vehicle of modernization and nation-building clearly goes beyond the confines of academic interests.[2]

The practice of army-building in China under the Chinese Communist Party (CCP) and Mao Tse-tung in the last half-century seems to have successfully developed a unique model for military forces which deserves the close attention of the developing world. As conceptualized by Mao, the armed forces should be made to function not only as a "fighting force" but also as a "working force" and a "production force". Moreover, the civil-military relationship should be based on the principle that "the Party commands the gun, and the gun shall never be allowed to command the Party".[3] The Maoist model of army-building demands that the Party penetrate the army thoroughly to guarantee political control over it on the one hand, and that the armed forces be systematically used for a wide range of non-military activities on the other. Throughout the various stages of the revolutionary movement and socialist construction, the Chinese military, in addition to shouldering the main burden of military tasks and national defense, has been mobilized to organize and educate the masses, to take part in agricultural and industrial production, and to support social and political reforms. The broad extramilitary activities performed by the Chinese Red Army during the periods of protracted guerrilla movements were certainly conspicuous enough. Even after liberation, the nonmilitary role of the People's Liberation Army (PLA) has remained equally evident.

The conventional concept of the military's place in society as evolved from the Western experience emphasizes organizational separation of the military from the rest of society and the functional primacy of the military in national defense and security. Under such a system, the contributions of the military to modernization or nation-building, if any, are at most accidental or peripheral.[4] Thus, in contrast with the Western model of military institutions, which stresses a high degree of professional specialization, organizational differentiation, and political neutrality, the Chinese model, as developed by Mao, is marked by the multifunctionality, structural diffuseness, and politicization of the military.[5] Although the Maoist model of army-building experienced, at times, deviations and challenges—ranging from the phenomenon of attempts by the military to withdraw from the extramilitary activities, to the problem of the gun trying to control the Party—the Maoist leadership has managed to overcome them with reasonable success. These successes are naturally attributable to Mao's unique formula of ideological ingredients and organizational mechanism that has proved to be capable of both disciplining the military and, at the same time, tapping its resources for development.

This article is aimed at analyzing the Chinese model of army-building and its contributions to political development and socio-economic modernization in China. Special emphasis is placed on the historical roots and organizational characteristics of the model, and on the scope and function of extramilitary activities. The operational dynamics of the model within the broad context of China's changing political and social systems is also examined in light of the growing challenges to Mao's military thinking stemming from the changes and developments within the PLA in the past five decades.

THE GENESIS OF THE MAOIST MODEL

An understanding of the Maoist strategy of army-building and the current role of the PLA requires a brief analysis of the legacy the Red Army developed during the years of the revolutionary guerrilla wars. Generally speaking, strategies involved in violent political revolution tend to be of two basic types: the swift *coup d'état,* or the protracted guerrilla insurrection. As Chalmers Johnson has articulated, the former generally involves a sudden, strategic attack on the regime in power and a quick seizure of governmental power through a military coup or uprising. The latter normally involves prolonged guerrilla warfare and an organized mass movement, which systematically seek to challenge the legitimate authority of the existing regime and the effectiveness of its military and police forces.[6] This guerrilla-type insurrection requires the revolutionaries to organize a mobile and multifunctional army, to establish defensible revolutionary bases, to mobilize the population in support of the revolutionary effort, and to maintain self-sufficiency with regard to necessary supplies. Hence, the political and the military quality of the guerrillas as a multifunctional insurgent force becomes the key determinant in the outcome of any revolutionary struggle.

After the strategic shift to the guerrilla model of revolutionary insurrection in 1927, Mao tried to organize the Chinese Red Army of Workers and Peasants into a new type of politicized and multifunctional army. The Red soldiers were trained to be not only good guerrilla fighters but also dedicated political workers committed to the Communist revolution. They were inculcated with a progressive political ideology, instilled with a new class consciousness, and taught a work-style of egalitarianism and discipline. Moreover, in the course of the revolution, the Red Army did not confine itself to battles, but participated in a wide range of nonmilitary tasks as well. From the early stages, the Red Army undertook the political and social mobilization of the masses, took part in land reform, built roads, and laboured in agricultural and industrial production in the guerrilla bases.

The effectiveness of the Red Army in mobilization and in war was greatly aided by the creation of the so-called "political work system", through which Party organization was systematically superimposed on the guerrilla forces to ensure Party countrol and to lead them in nonmilitary work.[7] It is clear that initially the prototype of the political work system, which was introduced by Mao in 1927–8, was modelled after the Soviet system of political commissars. The early system of Front committees quickly gave way the next year to the slightly more complex structure of Party representatives and Party committees. During the historic Ku-t'ien Conference of 1929, the theoretical basis and organizational framework for political work were clearly articulated by Mao and laid down as key components of the revolutionary strategy.[8] From 1929 onward, the system developed an elaborate infrastructure consisting of a political commissar, a political department, a Party committee, a Party secretariat, and Party cells within the larger units of the Red Army. Under the overall leadership of the political commissar, it operated as an integrated system for political work. In turn it formed an integral part of the command system of the Red Army functioning under the overall control of the CCP. The leadership of the political work system of the Red Army was so heavily penetrated by and interlocked with the regular Party apparatus that the memberships of the two hierarchies were virtually indistinguishable.

As the system evolved through the practice of revolutionary war in the 1930s and 1940s, a division of labour was emphasized, in principle, between military and political work within the Red Army. While the commanding officer was in charge of "military matters" related to combat training and military operation, the political commissar was responsible for "political matters", including control of personnel, ideological training, political loyalty, the economic and cultural well-being of the military units, and all other matters of political significance.[9] He was also responsible for rectifying "feudal" attitudes, "backward" value orientations, and "evil habits", and for inculcating a new political outlook, eliciting activism and voluntarism among the soldiers, and developing a new style of "hard work and plain living". The political work system was also entrusted with operating schools, theatres, and libraries, organizing literacy classes and sports activities, and directing participation in manual labour, construction projects, and farm work, in order to enrich the cultural and material well-being of the rank and file of the Red Army. The leadership explicitly stressed the principle that correct ideological orientation and proper work-style were the very foundation of the solidarity, comradeship, morale, and effectiveness of the Red Army. It was during this period of guerrilla operations that the Red Army eliminated military rank, insignia, and differential pay. Officers were asked to cast off their traditional status consciousness and to practise the "four togethers", by living, working, studying, and eating together with their soldiers and the peasant masses. While cautioning against the excesses of "absolute egalitarianism", the Red Army instituted the system of "supply in kind"—providing the daily necessities equally to all—to replace the graduated pay scale, and used the red star to replace the differential insignia of rank.[10] These measures were more than symbolic, having a significant impact on the solidarity of the revolutionary forces.

Outside military barracks, the function of the political work system also quickly outgrew its initial concern with the political security and loyalty of the guerrilla army and assumed a broad range of political, social, and economic responsibilities. As the effectiveness of guerrilla activities required the cooperation of the masses, the political work organs were given responsibility to work among the masses in ideological training, political mobilization, economic production, counterinsurgency work, and a host of other noncombatant tasks. Extensive propaganda and educational campaigns were carried out among the masses to convince them of the legitimacy of the revolution and to dissipate the traditional fear and distrust of the military. The masses were mobilized to join the militia and other auxiliary forces and to give direct support to guerrilla activities. In return, the soldiers were organized to work side by side with the peasants on the farms and to teach them how to read and write.[11] During the period of guerrilla operations, military personnel were also used in organizing Soviet and Party organizations in newly occupied territories and behind enemy lines, wherever the regular Party and Soviet organizations were weak. In those instances, the distinction between the Red Army's political work system and the regular Party organizations virtually disappeared.

Throughout the thirties and the forties, a series of political campaigns was launched by the army aimed at creating a new relationship of "mutual respect and cooperation" between the army and the people. The goal was to build a new image of the army as a respectable, well-disciplined political force, different from the warlord troops, the forces of the Kuomintang (KMT), and the armies of the Imperial government. The leadership was convinced that unless the Red Army could win the genuine respect and voluntary cooperation of the people, it would be impossible to gain mass support in demolishing the traditional local power structure, carrying out land reform, and establishing local Soviets. As early as 1928, for example, the Party representatives started conducting intensive educational and disciplinary campaigns to propagate the "three main rules" and the "eight points for attention" laid down by Mao, in order to train the soldiers to treat the people with courtesy, honesty, and respect.[12] The "three-unity" movement launched after the Japanese invasion of China in 1937 was meant to create unity between officers and soldiers, between the army and the people, and among various regional troops.[13]

The period was also marked by an intensification of campaigns to mobilize the masses to support the army, as guerrilla activities extended deep into the vast regions controlled by the troops of Wang Ching-wei's "puppet government" and the Japanese occupation army. The campaigns to "support the government and cherish the people" within the army were always coupled with efforts to educate the masses to "respect the cadres and cherish the soldiers". Organizations were set up on a *hsien*-by-*hsien* basis in which local people were taught to respect and support the Red Army, to identify with the cause of resistance, and to help with intelligence and other tasks. Villagers were organized by guerrilla cadres into "Self-Defense Corps" to gather intelligence, post sentries to observe road traffic, and help take the wounded to field hospitals. In return, soldiers helped local peasants with farm work, provided armed cover for planting and harvesting, offered free medical aid, operated schools and literacy classes, and even organized village celebrations. Soldiers were instructed to respect local customs and religious practices and, where possible, cadres were assigned to work in their native places. By the late 1930s, army personnel in newly liberated areas were increasingly involved in setting up local Party organizations as well as "anti-Japanese democratic regimes" based on the "three-thirds principle" of coalition among the CCP, the KMT, and neutral elements.[14] Indeed, the political work system became a mechanism through which the army was effectively turned into a highly politicized and multifunctional force.

THE DEVELOPMENT OF THE MAOIST MODEL SINCE LIBERATION

The ability of the Red Army to serve as a multifunctional force came under its severest test during the transitional period of 1947–9, when the tide of the civil war turned in favor of the Communists. This development presented the Communist forces with many urgent and difficult problems, such as the necessity of converting a large portion of military manpower to carry out civilian tasks in the newly occupied areas and of managing the takeover of administrative control at all levels. Under Mao's call to turn the Army into a "working force", crash programs were set up to further enlarge the role of the army.[15] In the meantime, army cadres were transferred in great numbers to civilian sectors to perform nonmilitary tasks. Indeed, the activities of the Red Army in this transitional period were so extensive and diffuse on all fronts that it was virtually impossible to draw any meaningful distinction between the military and the nonmilitary. By the end of 1949, the PLA had clearly demonstrated its capability as a "working force" under the severe test of the transition.

The conclusion of the civil war moved the Chinese Communist movement from the stage of armed insurgency to a new stage of national reconstruction and socialist transformation. But the multifunctional role of the PLA as articulated in the Maoist model and developed through the practice of the Red Army continued as before. Despite the new emphasis on "institution-building" and "organizational regularization" in the government bureaucracy and economic enterprises, the PLA did not desert, either organizationally or functionally, its "glorious tradition" of the guerrilla period. The army's assignments continued to involve the employment of its manpower and skills to meet the acute need for loyal cadres and for effective organization to assist in the formidable tasks of postwar political control and construction.

During the early fifties, it was the PLA that played a key role in managing the administrative takeover of most Nationalist government organizations and public enterprises and in organizing the military control commissions, which governed in the cities. Below the national government, the regional military and administrative committees, dominated by the military, functioned as the highest local authority in the country. To reduce the army's burden on the nation's shaky postwar economy and to strengthen local leadership, large numbers of soldiers were demobilized and transferred to civilian organizations, industry, and administrative organs. Military units were also detailed on a large scale to help with agrarian reform and new industrial projects. The official emphasis on the nonmilitary roles of the PLA was clearly reflected in the formal recognition of the "political work" apparatus of the PLA in both the 1949 Common Program and the 1956 Party Constitution.[16]

After 1949, to be sure, the PLA did play the conventional military role, defending China's national security in the military confrontations in Korea and in the border conflicts with India and the Soviet Union. Yet most of the extra-military activities outside the conventional scope of the military have not received attention commensurate with their importance. The unconventional nonmilitary role of the PLA can be analyzed conceptually at two levels. At the institutional level, the army as a whole has been used systematically to promote political transformation, social mobilization, and economic development. At the individual level, the PLA has played an important role in the reshaping of the values, behavioral norms, and career patterns of the large number of Chinese who at some point in their lives have served in or have had contact with the military.

In the economic area, the PLA's efforts to channel its enormous manpower, approximately three million strong, into production and development are most noteworthy. Since 1949 the military has made significant contributions to agricultural and industrial production, both for its own consumption and to meet the general needs of society. In 1958, for instance, the PLA produced over 480,000 hogs and 460 million catties of vegetables. A large number of army units attained complete self-sufficiency in meat and vegetables. During the same year, army divisions and regiments left their barracks *en masse* to assist in a wide range of construction, engineering, and agricultural activities, contributing over 59 million man-days and turning 8,800 military trucks over to civilian use. The PLA also completed over 20,000 water conservancy projects in the countryside, produced more than 3,000 tractors for collective farms, and sent some 70,000 officers to People's Communes to participate in administrative reorganization.[17] During the recent mass campaigns in early 1976 to develop the "Tachai-type *hsien*", for instance, a certain artillery unit of the Shenyang Military Region was reported to have contributed 91,500 man-days assisting the local peasants in repairing 760 *mou* of terraced fields and 110 irrigation waterways.[18]

The contributions of the PLA in economic development were particularly significant in the underdeveloped hinterlands such as Inner Mongolia, Sinkiang, and Tibet, where manpower of any kind, and especially skilled workers, was extremely scarce. During the first decade of Communist rule in Sinkiang, the Production and Construction Corps of the PLA, for instance, set up 147 large, modern state farms covering about 1.7 million acres of virgin land, developed 23 large-scale ranches with 1.3 million cattle, established 100 irrigation projects and 343 industrial mining enterprises, and built housing with more than 800,000 square meters of floor space.[19] More important, these projects provided on-the-job training for civilian technicians, tractor drivers, and managerial cadres. By the early 1970s, it was reported that PLA production and construction corps had been established and active in at least four military regions and eight provincial military districts. In most instances, state farms are established at the battalion level.[20]

At the local level, troops are routinely mobilized to help the peasants during the busy periods of spring planting and autumn harvesting. They are also frequently called upon to provide emergency relief and carry out rescue operations at times of crisis or natural disaster. After the disastrous earthquake in the Tang-shan region in July 1976, the PLA played a major role in the rescue and reconstruction mission. Included in the aid from the PLA were 7,000 military horses to cope with the paralyzed transportation system.[21] In the late 1950s and the early 1960s, according to the General Political department of the PLA, army units on the average devoted two months each year to a wide variety of industrial production and seasonal agricultural activities.[22]

In other parts of the country, the PLA was widely acclaimed for its participation in the construction of railroads, highways, airports, bridges, and other transportation and communication facilities. The contributions of the army in major projects of national reputation, such as the Yangtze bridges at Wuhan and Nanking, the Ying-Hsia and the Li-Tsan Railroads, the Tsinghai-Tibet Highway, and the Shih-san-ling Reservoir, further attest to the breadth of the PLA's productive activities.[23] At the central level, although the seven Machine-Building Ministries are involved primarily in the production of major weapon systems and other military hardware such as missiles, nuclear weapons, jet fighters, warships, and artillery, yet they are also known to work closely with the civilian sectors in facilitating the research and development of such industries as shipbuilding, electronics, nuclear science, communications, etc.

The policy statement that "the PLA is the defender as well as the builder of the cause of socialism" reflects accurately the leadership's emphasis on using the army to promote socio-cultural change under the leadership of the Party.[24] As in the pre-1949 years, the army has continued to be instrumental in most social and political reform movements. In the 1950s the army played a role in the campaigns for land reform, the new marriage law, the suppression of counter-revolutionaries, the collectivization and communization of the countryside, and the socialist transformation of private enterprises in the cities. During these campaigns, soldiers and officers not only undertook propaganda and educational activities but also helped Party and state cadres in the actual organization and administration of the campaigns.

Periodic literacy and educational campaigns carried out by the PLA among the masses are another feature of the military's nonmilitary role. The significance of such campaigns, it should be noted, goes beyond the obvious immediate objectives of the transmission of basic literacy and technical knowledge. The army propagandists are also simultaneously engaged in promoting ideological and cultural change by attacking traditional values and norms and replacing them with new attitudes supportive of the goals and priorities set by the Communist regime. The key role played by the PLA in effecting significant change in the themes and style of contemporary literature, art, and theatre—from the traditional to the revolutionary—testifies to the subtle yet crucial cultural role of the military in China. It should also be noted that since 1965 the medical teams dispatched by the PLA have played a crucial role in the highly acclaimed successes in the training of hundreds of thousands of barefoot doctors and in the campaign to develop health and medical care in the countryside.[25]

In the political arena, the role of the PLA as the mainstay of Communist power and defender of Party leadership was most dramatically demonstrated under the leadership of Lin Piao in the 1960s.[26] After the overhauling and restrengthening of the political work system within the military was completed in 1961–2, the PLA launched a wavelike series of mass campaigns aimed at developing "correct" ideological orientation. (These included campaigns for the "four firsts", the "three-eight work style", the "four-good company", and the "five-good fighter".) The campaigns were first carried out within the army, then in society at large. Beginning in 1963, the entire nation was encouraged to espouse the political loyalty, ideological commitment, and behavioral norms of PLA heroes like Lei Feng, Wang Chieh, and Mai Hsien-te through the mass movement to "Learn from the PLA". In 1964 and 1965, political work structures modelled on those of the PLA were systematically introduced into civilian Party organizations, the state bureaucracy, school systems, and economic enterprises, and a large number of military cadres were transferred to lead the new organizations.[27]

When the turmoil of the Cultural Revolution threatened basic political stability and social order, the role of the PLA expanded still further. The PLA was called upon to intervene militarily in early 1967 to support the Maoist leadership and defend the "dictatorship of the proletariat", to impose "military control" on administrative organizations and economic enterprises, and to conduct military and political training in schools. By the late 1960s PLA officers played a leading role both in the new provisional organs of power (known as revolutionary committees) and in the reconstructed Party committee at all levels. The army's power was mobilized to support the "left", to settle factional fights, and to carry out the campaigns of "struggle-criticism-transformation".[28] It is clear that during the 1960s the military once again played an extensive political role comparable with the one it filled before 1949. The PLA was once again assigned the role of winning, defending, and consolidating a grip on power for the Party.

The impact of the extramilitary functions of the PLA is greatly augmented by its control over the vast forces of the People's Militia at the local level. Operating as an auxiliary to the regular army, the militia serves as an organizational link between the PLA and the masses of Chinese peasants. In times of war or emergency the militia can be mobilized for national defense and internal security; in times of peace it becomes a mechanism for the training and management of the enormous reservoir of manpower available in the countryside. Although the strength and effectiveness of the People's Militia waned at times, the revival of the Maoist line in military affairs in 1958 brought about a rapid and massive expansion through the "everyone-a-soldier" movement. By June 1960 the PLA claimed that over 250 million men and women had been organized into militia units and were engaged in a variety of training and learning activities on a regular basis.[29] During the first half of the 1970s the strength of the militia was further expanded to cover millions of urban workers.[30]

From the perspective of the PLA as a whole, the impact of the military's "civic action" is indeed clearly visible and statistically conspicuous. From the perspective of the individual citizen, however, the measurement of such impact is much more difficult. Nonetheless, its significance should not be overlooked. To begin with, there are probably nearly three million people currently under arms in China. Since the introduction of the conscription system in 1955, each year about 700,000 young people are drafted to serve from two to three years in the armed services, and an equal number of veterans return to civilian life.[31] During their military service, these men and women, mostly from rural backgrounds, acquire organizational and vocational skills—most recruits would now already be literate. In addition, the education and training provided constitutes an intensive socialization effort aimed at instilling the new citizenship and value orientation emphasized by China's new leaders. As Lucian S. Pye argues, the relatively successful socialization of military personnel into modern values and norms in many underdeveloped countries is due to the highly disciplined and controlled nature of the military environment.[32] If this is the case, we may infer that the PLA can work as an effective vehicle for transmitting "modern" values, impersonal and achievement orientations, and the Chinese Communist ethic of hard work and selfless dedication to a large part of the nation's youth.

The organizational setting in which this political socialization takes place is also highly conducive to the homogenization of parochial identities and the promotion of nationalism and national integration. The military forces, more than any other organization, represent a cross-section of class, ethnic, and regional backgrounds. The use of the national language in the political and military training of conscripts and cadets, for example, can provide the basis of an effective nationwide communication network, which the leadership can in turn use to facilitate the cultural and social integration of all citizens.

The impact of the military is not limited to those who have actually served in the

PLA. Skills and values are also transmitted through the vast militia system to the broad masses. The PLA's extensive extramilitary activities bring large segments of the population under the indirect influence of the army. Moreover, the demobilization process makes available roughly 700,000 people each year to be placed in relatively important leadership positions at local levels, because of the special training and skills they received during service. For instance, scattered data on cadre recruitment for Agricultural Producers' Cooperatives in selected areas in 1956 revealed that from 46–60 per cent of Party and administrative leaders at that level were deliberately recruited from among former military personnel.[33] It is estimated that since liberation, as many as 18 million trained veterans have been infused into the civilian work force. Thus, the military as a channel of social and political mobility for a wide cross-section of rural youth and as an instrument for controlled social change and class restratification is clearly a crucial factor in China's nation-building.

THE CHALLENGES TO THE MAOIST MODEL

The guerrilla legacy and post-1949 practice of the PLA as a functioning institution have crystallized two underlying concepts, namely, the multifunctionality of the army and the control of the military by the Party. These two concepts, in fact, deal with the two most intricate problems of the military as a societal institution. The former is concerned with the division of labor within the military and the differentiation of functions between the military and the nonmilitary, while the latter deals with the delicate power relationship between the civilian and the military authorities. Hence, the thrust of Mao's theoretical and functional concerns is readily evident. The model is rationally designed to serve the purpose of using the military to aid the nation's quest for modernization, while making sure that the military is kept under Party control. In the real world of practice, however, the model has run into challenges and problems which are inherent in the processes of China's quest for modernization and political transformation. These challenges and problems seem to have stemmed from two major sociological and political trends within the PLA: (1) the tendency toward institutionalization and professionalization, which leads to an increased demand for the professional autonomy of the military, priority for the development of military technology, and exclusive emphasis on the regular army; and (2) a continual expansion of the nonmilitary role, leading to military domination and intervention in virtually all areas of society.

From the perspective of the Maoist model, these two deviant trends have resulted in two different types of institutional behavior on the part of the military. Emphasis on institutionalization and professionalization promoted the separation of the PLA from the Party and hence stimulated the military's desire to withdraw from political and other nonmilitary involvement. In contrast to this, the expansion of the role of the military in extramilitary activities furthered the infusion of the military into society and the ascendence of military power, and eventually led the military to intervene in politics. Once the military became excessively involved in internal politics, it was carried away by the momentum of the political dynamics and got itself entangled in power and policy struggle. A brief examination of these challenges is essential for an understanding of the operational dynamics as well as the structural problems inherent in the Maoist model of army-building.

Military professionalism began to emerge as a major policy issue following the end of the civil war in 1949, when the new regime shifted to an emphasis on institution-building and modernization. As the government and the Party assumed more and more of the administrative and economic functions that had previously been assigned to the military control commissions and the military and administrative committees at the local level, the PLA began to withdraw from its nonmilitary activities and moved toward specialization and professionalization in military affairs. The military confrontation with the United States in the Korean War further heightened the military's sense of the need to modernize as rapidly as possible so as to be able to cope effectively with modern warfare. Moreover, the introduction into China of modern Russian military equipment and related organizational forms helped establish the "advanced experience" of the Soviet Union as a model for the Chinese.[34] The trend toward differentiation between the military and the nonmilitary sector was clearly reflected in the sweeping administrative reorganizations at the regional level in 1954. The six regional military and administrative committees (together with the six greater administrative regions) were abolished in order to centralize bureaucratic control; it was also decided that the regional and district military commanders should not concurrently hold key Party and administrative positions at the provincial level as they had in the past.[35]

By 1954 the PLA had also developed an elaborate and highly centralized command and logistics system supported by a large number of military academies offering specialized, professional training. A system of conscription was formalized in 1955 to emphasize the development of a regular professional army, thus downgrading the role of the militia. The adoption of the Regulations on the Service of Officers in February 1955 formally introduced into the PLA, as part of its movement toward regularization and professionalization, a highly stratified system of ranks with differential pay and privileges, modelled after the Soviet pattern.[36] As the newly emerged officer corps and the veteran military leaders became increasingly committed to the course of modernization, they began to attack the informality, flexibility, spontaneity, and egalitarianism that had been such central aspects of the guerrilla tradition as "organizational anarchy" and "indiscipline". Condemning the old "guerrilla mentality and habits" as obsolete and dysfunctional, they argued that "technical work" should replace political work as the "life-line" of the new military order.[37] The military leaders also began to perceive the strength of the PLA primarily in terms of its professional and technological quality rather than its ideological commitment and extramilitary capability. Thus, in the military barracks the balance of priorities in training tipped in favor of professional and technical matters. As the authority of political commissars was allowed to wane, Party organizations within the PLA also deteriorated. A mood of indifference toward political work in the military in this period was clearly reflected by the fact that by the late 1950s as many as 6,000 companies were reported to have had no functioning Party branches.[38] This was particularly evident in those units most oriented toward advanced technology, such as the air force, artillery, and armoured divisions. It was argued that, "when the army is carrying out the work of modernization, training tasks are heavy. Participation in national construction will affect training and will do more harm than good."[39]

The growing demand for modernization and professionalization within the military eventually set the stage for the open struggle between "two lines" in the late 1950s and early 1960s over the role of the military: the struggle between the Maoist line and the "revisionist" line. The major attempt to control the challenge of professionalism was launched in 1957 and 1958 through a series of mass movements such as the rectification campaigns, the movement to send "officers to the ranks", and the intensification of ideological training. But these efforts did not come to fruition until the whole nation was radicalized by Mao's push for the Great Leap Forward and the communization movement in 1958. As the Great Leap Forward gained momentum, the army was mobilized on a massive scale to take part in capital construction, perform relief work in times of flood and drought, and help organize and streamline the management of rural communes. Beginning in 1958, the militia was once again reinvigorated through the mass movement to make "everyone a soldier". All troops and military academies were involved in an intensive campaign to study Mao's thought and military writings.[40] As the individual campaigns coalesced into the nationwide push to put "politics in command of everything" in 1958 and 1959, the Maoist model seems to have regained the level of strength it had achieved in the early 1950s. It is worth noting, however, that if it were not for the fact that the massive campaigns happened to coincide with the purge of the top proponents of a modern army such as P'eng Te-huai, the Minister of Defence, and Huang K'e-cheng, the chief of staff, the triumph of the Maoist military line over the "revisionist" line in the late 1950s might not have been possible.

The appointment of Lin Piao to be in charge of the Ministry of National Defence and the Party's Military Commission in September 1959 marked a sharp return to the Maoist line. Under Lin's leadership, as indicated earlier, the political work system and the Party organizations in the army underwent a major overhaul. Political education for the rank and file, with stress on the study of Mao's thought, was restored as the central task in the day-to-day activity of the army. In 1961 five sets of important regulations—four on political work and one on management and education at the company level—were issued as guidelines for the systematic revamping of political work.[41] In March 1963 the Party reissued, with great fanfare, a comprehensive set of Political Work Regulations for the PLA in every service and at every level.[42] The Regulations reaffirmed the Maoist model as the "guidepost of both the political and the military work of the army". By the mid-1960s, the PLA had re-emerged as a vigorous multifunctional "working force", taking a leading role in every mass movement and actively participating in every aspect of national life.

However, even in the midst of this impressive success of putting the Maoist line back in command, the "sins" of professionalism continued to present a problem. As revealed during the Cultural Revolution, Lo Jui-Ch'ing, the chief of staff from 1959 to 1966, had pursued the same "revisionist" line on the development of the military as his predecessor, the purged Huang K'e-cheng, had advocated. He was accused of having sponsored the mass campaigns for "great competitions in military skills" in order to enhance the priority of military professionalism, technological superiority, and technical training. It was said that he covertly undermined the political control over the PLA, encouraged the withdrawal of the army from nonmilitary work, and sabotaged the dual-control system in the PLA. Once again, in 1966, a major purge was required to rid the military establishment of the tendency toward a "purely military viewpoint".[43] Since the death of Mao and the purge of the "gang of four" in late 1976, however, the new leadership under Hua Kuo-feng and Teng Hsiao-p'ing has proclaimed "four modernizations" to be of the highest priority for the nation.[44] It should be noted that the modernization of national defence has been designated as one of the four major goals of modernization. Evidence clearly shows that the PLA has stepped up the development of military technology, weapon systems, and professional manpower in recent years. Although the new leadership has, at the same time, reiterated the importance of adhering to the Maoist line of army-building and the principles of "people's war" by reintroducing within the PLA a series of campaigns such as "Learn from Lei Feng", "Learn from the Hard-Bone Sixth Company", and "Support Agriculture and Industry", the scale and intensity of these campaigns are definitely not up to the level of those conducted in the 1950s and 1960s.[45] Moreover, virtually all military leaders who were accused of having committed the sins of holding a "purely military viewpoint" and practising military professionalism in the 1960s are now restored to positions of power and prominence.[46] At present, the pendulum of military policy orientation is clearly swinging towards an emphasis on modernization and professionalization. In this respect, it would not be surprising to see another new wave of controversy between the Maoist model and the "revisionist" line of military development emerge in China in the years ahead.

The purges of key military leaders and the disputes between the "two lines" of army-building since the early 1950s clearly point to a serious contradiction inherent in the Maoist model. As long as the PLA functions as an autonomous institution specialized in military affairs and national security, the challenge of professionalism can, at best, only be contained, and not eliminated. Hence, the role of the PLA as a multifunctional force is bound to be subject to chronic controversy and challenge by the increasingly professionalized military élite and the increasingly modernized armed forces.

Aside from the challenge of professionalism, a second source of instability for the Maoist model stems from the multifunctionality of the PLA. An expansion of extramilitary function enables the military to play a major role in political affairs and encourages the military to assume political power. In contrast to the danger from military professionalism, which involves a contravention of Mao's military thinking, the risk of military domination or intervention results from an overly enthusiastic application of Mao's doctrine with regard to the use of the military as a "working force" and a "production force". By virtue of its organizational strength and nonmilitary activities, the military acquires influence over a wide variety of policy matters. At times of political crisis, the military further expands its extramilitary role, often by request of the civilian authorities, by taking responsibility for the maintenance of social order. A concomitant of such development is the military's assumption, first, of a dominant role in policy-making, and later, of control over political power. The dominant role played by the PLA over the Party and other sectors of society prior to and during the Cultural Revolution typifies this type of problem.

Beginning in the late 1950s, particularly during the "three hard years", the PLA, under the newly established leadership of Lin Piao, started to assume a more active role in supporting the massive campaigns for production, construction, socialist transformation, and emergency relief. By 1962, when the process of internal overhaul and reinvigoration had been completed, the army began turning outward even more, exerting a conspicuous influence on society at large. From 1964 on, army heroes were hailed as revolutionary models for the whole nation to emulate as part of the movement to "Learn from the PLA". Between 1964 and 1966, an organizational structure modelled on the army's political work system was introduced into schools, trade organizations, factories, and even Party organs throughout the nation; and army cadres were transferred to man the newly organized political work departments in all sectors of civilian life.[47]

The power and influence of the military grew still further during the Cultural Revolution. As the regular Party apparatus and state bureaucracy were paralyzed by the Red Guards' violent attempts to seize power from the "powerholders" and "capitalist-roaders", the military emerged in early 1967 as the "mainstay of the dictatorship of the proletariat". The army was finally asked by the Party to intervene to maintain order when armed conflict seriously threatened the state. Since then, the army's formidable influence and presence have been maintained in every walk of life through the nationwide "three-support" and "two-military" campaign (i.e. to mobilize the army to support the broad masses of the left, support industry, and support agriculture; and to carry out military control and military training).[48]

In April 1969, Lin Piao and his military followers even went so far as to force Mao and the by-then crippled Party to acquiesce at the Ninth Party Congress and proclaim Lin Piao the official successor to Mao in the new Party Constitution. Later, Mao complained bitterly that the fine tradition of unified leadership by the Party and the primacy of "the Party controlling the gun" had been undermined by the PLA's enhanced position of power.[49] It is no exaggeration to suggest that by 1969 the military had virtually taken over the power of the Party and had practically imposed military rule over the entire nation.

That the military's growing domination of the political system followed the outbreak of the Cultural Revolution is clearly reflected in the membership compositions of the major political organizations at the time. Strong military representation was evident at all levels from 1967 through 1971, prior to the purge of Lin Piao and his generals. For instance, in the powerful Political Bureau of the Ninth Central Committee reorganized in April 1969, 13 out of a total of 25 seats went to military leaders. At the provincial level, the generals headed nearly three quarters of all the Party committees and revolutionary committees.[50] The interlocking directorship between the Party and the military has long been a salient tradition of the Maoist model, designed for exercizing dual control over the army; however, the phenomena of the late 1960s, though similar in appearance to earlier practice, were totally different in substance. The practice in the mid-1950s called for the provincial-level secretaries to serve concurrently as political commissars of their local military regions or districts.[51] Now the direction of penetration and control was completely reversed: it was the military commanders and commissars who served concurrently as Party secretaries and revolutionary committee directors.

When the PLA changed its role from one of passively to one of actively seeking and consolidating political power, it crossed the threshold of "reactive militarism", to borrow a concept articulated by Morris Janowitz.[52] In pursuit of such aims, the military did not hesitate to create new symbols and structures to protect their new gains and satisfy their new aspirations whenever they found the old symbols and structures to be inadequate. Hence, during the Cultural Revolution they energetically promoted ideas such as the "Theory of genius" and Mao's "close comrade-in-arms", and launched campaigns like "Learn from the PLA" and "Support the Army". All this was clearly aimed at enhancing the prestige and authority of the military and its leader Lin Piao. New organizational structures such as the "political work departments" and the "three-way alliances" were also introduced in order to institutionalize and legitimize their newly-gained power and status.[53]

In the wake of Lin Piao's abortive coup in September 1971, Mao and the Party began to undertake strenuous efforts to scale down the PLA dominance and to restore Party supremacy. By the early spring of 1973, a total of 48 top provincial-level Party leaders (5 first secretaries, 3 second secretaries, and 40 secretaries or deputy secretaries) were removed; among them were 35 professional military commanders and political commissars (representing 73 per cent of those dismissed).[54] The removal of these military leaders reduced the proportion of the PLA representation in the provincial Party committees from the 60 per cent registered in August 1971 to about 46 per cent. By October 1975, this figure was reduced further to 34 per cent (66 out of 193 provincial Party secretaries).[55] Of the 195 full members and 124 alternate members of the Tenth Central Committee elected in August 1973, the PLA accounted for only 32 per cent and 29 per cent respectively, showing a reduction of over 13 per cent from its previous strength.[56] In the 25-member Politburo, the loss of military representation was even sharper between 1969 and 1973, when it fell from 52 per cent to 24 per cent. When the unprecedented large-scale reshuffle of top military commanders and political commissars in eight out of China's eleven military regions was made in December 1973, these military leaders were also relieved of all Party and administrative responsibilities. In the fall of 1975, another large-scale transfer of military personnel took place, involving 83 leaders; they too were relieved of their previous Party and administrative positions. These moves clearly demonstrated Mao's determination to weaken further the power base of the PLA and to put it under a tighter control by the Party.

While the balance between the civil and military personnel was being readjusted after the Lin Piao incident, Mao also launched a series of mass campaigns to help rectify the PLA's excessive expansion of its roles and its power. The movement to "Learn from the PLA" in the 1960s was matched by a new campaign based on the slogan, "The Army Must Learn from the People". The Three Main Rules of Discipline and the Eight Points for Attention were reissued in early 1972 in conjunction with the PLA's campaigns to study and eliminate its arrogance and disobedience. The PLA is now instructed to place equal emphasis on military and political training. In contrast with the frenzied movement to "put politics to the fore" during the Cultural Revolution, the PLA is now told that "politics must be in command of and lead military affairs, but it cannot replace military affairs". The earlier campaign for "two militaries" and "three supports" has now been replaced by an emphasis on "the Party's unified leadership".[57]

After the foiling of the military coup attempt in September 1971, actions taken by Mao to curb the military did show considerable effect, statistically at least, in readjusting the balance of power in favour of the Party. The increasing number of military leaders removed from positions of power between 1972 and 1975, the continued rehabilitation of Party veterans purged during the ascendance of military power during the Cultural Revolution and the vigorous campaigns to reassert the Maoist principles of army-building are indicative of the trend. The fact remains, however, that about one third of all the membership in key organs of power at the central and provincial levels are still controlled by professional military commanders and commissars. Developments since September 1976 suggest further uncertainties and complications. The death of Mao, the architect and guardian of the theory of "people's war" and the multifunctionality of the PLA, deprived the Maoist model of its most crucial source of strength. The establishment of the "four modernizations" as the indisputable national goals by the new leadership has clearly tipped the balance of policy orientation in favor of military professionalism and autonomy.[58] In the election of the Eleventh Central Committee in August 1977, although the military representation among the 333 members (201 full and 132 alternate members) remained at the previous level of 31 per cent, the proportion of military leaders in the powerful 26-member Political Bureau was boosted significantly, from 24 per cent to 38 per cent.[59] The excesses of military control and its monopoly of political power in the late 1960s have apparently been reduced, but the battle to restore the primacy of the Maoist formula for the ideal Party-army relationship is apparently still far from being decided.

According to the general theory of the "unity of opposites" as articulated by Mao, the PLA should be a combination of a "fighting force" and a "working force", engaging in both military work and political activities, and emphasizing both military and ideological training. The function of the "gun" and the power of the Party must also be correctly integrated. Deviation to either extreme will inevitably upset the "correct balance" of opposites and disrupt the healthy operation of the PLA in society. From the perspective of this Maoist model, therefore, P'eng Te-huai and Lo Jui-ch'ing were guilty of the "rightist" deviation of espousing a "purely military viewpoint", overemphasizing military professionalism and technology at the expense of their counterparts of nonmilitary work and political commitment. Lin Piao, in contrast, went to the opposite extreme, espousing a "leftist" deviation by overstressing political work and political power. This one-sided emphasis of Lin's eventually, according to Mao, turned the PLA into a "cultural army", and induced the army to seize political power. The PLA's enormous contributions to China's development and transformation notwithstanding, the risks and problems inherent in the Maoist model, as analyzed in the preceding paragraphs, should not be overlooked.

CONCLUSION

The Maoist model of army-building, as conceptualized in this article, involves two basic principles: that the military should function not only as a "fighting force" but also as a "working force" and a "production force"; and that "the Party commands the gun". In essence, this means that the PLA should participate in political, economic, cultural, and other work outside the barracks, but also that such work should be done only under the leadership of the Party. The military should never be allowed to dominate the Party or exercise direct control over society. Although the model was formulated originally in response to the unique historical circumstances and the harsh operational environments of the revolutionary wars, the model persisted in the postwar years and was continuously upheld by the Maoist leadership as the ideal type for nation-building.

Aside from the legacy of revolutionary experience, the continued employment of the PLA in nonmilitary work is clearly based in part on a rational, conscious decision in support of China's choice of a "mobilization" approach to national development and political transformation. The policy of mass mobilization, as David Apter points out, is based on the belief that rapid social transformation and development can only be achieved through the synchronized mobilization of the nation's human and material resources.[60] In China, the PLA has been identified by the leadership as an organization capable of mobilizing both its own resources and those of the masses for general development purposes. Indeed there is no doubt that the PLA, as a well-trained and highly organized block of nearly three million people, can, if used skilfully, carry out a wide variety of "civic action" tasks. Moreover, by coordinating its activities closely with those of the millions of demobilized veterans and the extensive militia network, the PLA can undoubtedly play an extremely significant role in mass mobilization, policy implementation, and task performance.

In the realm of political transformation, as long as the leadership continues to be committed to the goal of "uninterrupted revolution" and presses for radical change in political values, the social structure, and policy priorities, "class enemies" and political opposition are bound to emerge. This emergence would naturally entail the need for the military to shoulder the extramilitary burdens of social reform and political control in support of the Party's quest for "continuing the revolution". During times of extensive and drastic revolutionary change, the coercive power of the military is always needed to ensure internal security and to buttress political authority. The loyalty and subordination of the military to the revolutionary leadership under such circumstances becomes a prerequisite for political stability and the implementation of reform. Thus, it is likely that the PLA will remain highly politicized and active in political work.

However, as shown in this paper, a close examination of the record of the last twenty-five years reveals some serious built-in problems in the Maoist model of army-building and the role of the military. One of the powerful forces at work which will certainly strongly challenge the persistence of the model is the general trend toward institutionalization and professionalization that China has been experiencing since 1949 in every sector of society. Institutionalization and professionalization are bound to enhance the influence and authority of professionals and bureaucrats. Within the PLA the conflict between "red" and "expert", between political control and military autonomy, and between political work and military work has been evident for many years. There is no question but that the continued advancement in military technology, especially with the development of nuclear weapons and the related delivery capability, is going to push the PLA further in the direction of specialization and centralization. In a more advanced and modernized stage, the military professionals cannot but view the diversion of the PLA to nonmilitary activities as dysfunctional and counterproductive for national security.

The record of the model further shows that efforts to enlist the military for the performance of nonmilitary tasks carry considerable risks and consequences. Such efforts tend to upset the proper balance of the Party-army relationship, especially the ideal of Party supremacy and control over the military. Attempts to utilize the organizational and technical skills of the military for economic development and social modernization introduce military personnel into the arena of power and policy struggles, and eventually prompt generals to practise "reactive militarism". Calling on the armed forces to share power or form a partnership in domestic politics for the purpose of sustaining the political system in crisis inevitably leads to a military dominance over the Party and government. Worse still, the involvement of the military in power struggles and political intrigue might even undermine the unity of the military.

Although the record of the PLA as a "working force" and a "production force" fluctuated over the years, when viewed as a whole, it has proved to be rather impressive.

In spite of the tensions and crises that the Maoist approach to army-building has brought about in the course of the revolutionary movement and socialist transformation, the contributions of the Red Army and the PLA to China's nation-building over the last half a century cannot be over-emphasized. Through the skilful leadership and control he exercized, Mao was remarkably successful in tapping the strengths and resources of the PLA for both revolution and construction. If the post-Mao leadership is as committed and dedicated as Mao was to China's continued quest for uninterrupted political transformation and economic development through the strategy of mass mobilization and self-reliance, then the Maoist model of army-building will remain relevant and effective. China is a developing society with limited economic resources and professional manpower, and at the same time is a revolutionary polity aspiring for continuous political and social transformation. The PLA as a solid block of well-trained and disciplined resources has played, and should be enlisted to continue to play, an active part in this process. Naturally, the new leadership will have to be on guard, as Mao was previously, against the military's tendency to deviate either to the "leftist" extreme of military intervention or to the rightist extreme of clinging to professionalism. As history has proved, this task is not easy; yet if correctly and skilfully executed, the result will be most significant and rewarding. There is no doubt that the continued successful operation of the Maoist model will have much to offer, not only to China in its renewed quest for modernization and transformation, but also to the Third World as a tested model for emulation.

NOTES

1   US Arms Control and Disarmament Agency, *World Military Expenditures and Arms Transfers, 1966–1975,* Washington, D.C., 1976, pp. 1–15.
2   For a general discussion of the problem, see Morris Janowitz, *The Military in the Political Development of New Nations,* Chicago: University of Chicago Press, 1964.
3   See Mao Tse-tung, *Selected Works of Mao Tse-tung,* Peking: Foreign Languages Press, 1961–1965, II, p. 224, and IV, pp. 337–40.
4   For further analysis of the theme, see Wilson C. McWilliams (Ed.), *Garrisons and Government,* San Francisco: Chandler, 1967; Henry Bienen (Ed.), *The Military and Modernization,* Princeton: Princeton University Press, 1971.
5   See, for example, David B. Ralston (Ed.), *Soldiers and States,* Boston: Heath, 1966; Samuel P. Huntington, *The Soldier and the State,* Cambridge: Harvard University Press, 1957.
6   For an excellent discussion of the typology of revolutionary strategies, see Chalmers Johnson. *Revolutionary Change,* Boston: Little, Brown, 1966. Also Nathan Leites and Charles Wolf, Jr., *Rebellion and Authority: An Analytic Essay on Insurgent Conflicts,* Chicago: Markham, 1970.
7   For a fuller treatment of the Red Army's political work, see Ying-mao Kau, *et al., The Political Work System of the Chinese Communist Military,* Providence: East Asian Language & Area Center, Brown University, 1971.
8   English translation of the complete text of the Resolution may be found in my work *The People's Liberation Army and China's Nation-Building,* pp. 5–50.
9   The complete text of the three most important sets of Political Work Regulations is published in English in Kau, *et al., The Political Work System of the Chinese Communist Military.*
10 Important works on the PLA's nonmilitary activities include Davis B. Bobrow, *The Political and Economic Role of the Military in the Chinese Communist Movement, 1927–1959* (Ph. D. thesis, MIT, 1962); John Gittings, *The Role of the Chinese Army,* London: Oxford University Press, 1967; Wang Chia-hsiang *et al., Cheng-chih kung-tso lun-ts'ung* [Discussion on Political Work] (n.p.: Pa-lu-chün, 1941); Lo Jui-ch'ing, *K'ang-Jih chün-tui-chung ti cheng-chih kung-tso* [Political Work in the Anti-Japanese Military Forces] (n.p.: Chung-kuo wen-hua she, 1939); and Ching Ch'in, *Chan-shih cheng-chih kung-tso* [Wartime Political Work] (Shanghai: Shih-tai shih-liao, 1938).

11   Chǔn-tu Hsüeh and Robert C. North (trans.), The Founding of the Chinese Red Army, in E. Stuart Kirby (Ed.), *Contemporary China,* Hong Kong: University of Hong Kong Press, 1964, VI, pp. 59–83; Toa Keizai Chosakyoku, *Shina sovieto undo no kenkyu* (A Study of the Chinese Soviet Movement), Tokyo: n.d.

12   Mao Tse-tung, *Selected Works,* IV, p. 156: "In the spring of 1928 . . . Mao Tse-tung set down Three Rules of Discipline: (1) Obey orders in your actions; (2) Don't take anything from the workers and peasants; and (3) Turn in all things taken from local bullies. In the summer of 1928 he set forth Six Points for Attention: (1) Put back the doors you have taken down for bed-boards; (2) Put back the straw you have used for bedding; (3) Speak politely; (4) Pay fairly for what you buy; (5) Return everything you borrow; and (6) Pay for anything you damage. After 1929 Comrade Mao Tse-tung made the following changes: Rule 2 became 'Don't take a single needle or piece of thread from the masses', and Rule 3 was changed first to 'Turn in all money raised' and then to 'Turn in everything captured'. To the Six Points for Attention he added two more: 'Don't bathe within sight of women' and 'Don't search the pockets of captives.' This was the origin of the Three Main Rules of Discipline and the Eight Points for Attention."

13   See Note 10 above for sources discussed in this section.

14   Pa-lu-chün cheng-chih-pu, *Chung-kuo ti-hou k'ang-Jih min-chu keng-chü-ti kai-k'uang* [The Conditions of the Anti-Japanese Democratic Bases Behind Enemy Lines in China] (n.p.: Hsin-Hua, 1944); Conrad Brandt *et al., A Documentary History of Chinese Communism,* New York: Atheneum. 1967, pp. 279–315.

15   For an excellent report on the transitional period, see A. Doak Barnett, *China on the Eve of Communist Takeover,* New York: Praeger, 1961.

16   Article 21 of the Common Program provides: "The People's Liberation Army and the people's security forces shall, in accordance with the principle of unity between the officers and the rank and file and between the army and the people, set up a system of political work. . . ." Article 35 of the 1956 Party Constitution reads: "The General Political Department in the People's Liberation Army, under the direction of the Central Committee, takes charge of the ideological and organizational work of the Party in the army."

17   Fu Chung, Achievements Made by the Armed Forces in Support of Socialist Construction, *Jen-min jih-pao* [People's Daily] April 6, 1960; translated in *Current Background,* No. 624 (1960); Hsiao Hua, Participation in National Construction Is a Glorious Task of the PLA, *Hung-ch'i* [Red Flag], No. 15, August 1959; translated in *ECMM,* No. 182 (1959); and Henry Schwartz, The Chinese Communist Army in Sinkiang, *Military Review,* XLV, March 1965, 69–79.

18   *Chung-kung nien-pao* [Yearbook on Chinese Communism] (1976), Section II, p. 47.

19   A Brief Account of the Achievements of the Sinkiang Production and Construction Corps of the Army in the Last Ten Years, *China Land Reclamation,* No. 2, February 5, 1960; translated in *ECMM,* No. 204 (1960); Chang Chun-han, Production and Reconstruction Army Corps in Sinkiang, *Jen-min jih-pao* [People's Daily], July 31, 1966; translated in *SCMP,* No. 2318 (1966).

20   *Chung-kung nien-pao* [Yearbook on Chinese Communism] (1972), Section II, p. 90.

21   Ibid., 1977, Section IX, p. 25.

22   *Jen-min jih-pao* [People's Daily], February 26 and March 14, 1959.

23   See *Hsin-Hua pan-yüeh-k'an* [New China Semi-Monthly], No. 1, January 10, 1957, 98–99; No. 3, February 10, 1957, 7–8; and *Jen-min jih-pao* [People's Daily], February 19, 1958.

24   *Second Session of the Eighth National Congress of the Communist Party of China,* Peking: Foreign Languages Press, 1958, p. 54.

25   See, for example, Victor W. Sidel and Ruth Sidel, *Serve the People: Observations on Medicine in the People's Republic of China,* Boston: Beacon Press, 1974.

26   For a full study of Lin Piao and his politics, see my book *The Lin Piao Affair: Power Politics and Military Coup,* White Plains: International Arts & Sciences Press, 1975. An excellent study of his career before 1949 may be found in Thomas W. Robinson, *A Politico-Military Biography of Lin Piao, Part I, 1907–1949,* Santa Monica, California: Rand, 1971.

27   *Jen-min jih-pao* [People's Daily], June 7, September 30, 1964; *Ta-kung-pao* [Ta-kung Daily], February 28, March 22, 27, June 19, 1965; *Jen-min shou-ts'e* [People's Handbook] (1965), pp. 504–18, 537–9; Chalmers Johnson, Lin Piao's Army and Its Role in Chinese Society, *Current Scene,* IV: 13–14, July 1966; Ralph L. Powell, Commissars in the Economy, *Asian Survey,* V: 3, March 1965, pp. 125–138.

28   The growing role of the PLA in the 1960s was the central theme treated in *Chinese Law and Government,* V: 3–4, Fall-Winter 1972–73; VI:1, Spring 1973.

29   Ralph L. Powell, Everyone a Soldier: The Communist Chinese Militia, *Foreign Affairs,* XXXIX: 1, October 1960, 100–11.

30   An extensive report on the development of urban militia may be found in *Chung-kung nien-pao* [Yearbook on Chinese Communism], 1976, Section V, pp. 56–74.

31   *The Communist Bloc and the Western Alliances,* London: Institute for Strategic Studies, 1964, p. 8.

32   Lucian W. Pye, Armies in the Process of Political Modernization, *Archives Européennes de Sociologie,* No. 2, 1961, 82–92.

33 *Jen-min jih-pao* [People's Daily], January 30, 1957.
34 Ellis Joffe, *Party and Army,* Cambridge: Harvard University Press, 1965, pp. 1–45.
35 Yeh Hsiang-chih, Chinese Communist Army's Relationship with Party and Government Organizations, *Chung-kung yen-chiu* [Studies on Chinese Communism], XI: 1, January 1975, pp. 5–11.
36 For the text of the regulations, see *Jen-min jih-pao* [People's Daily], February 9, 1955.
37 See, for example, *Chieh-fang-chün pao* [Liberation Army Daily], editorials, February 13, 1957; Jan. 4, and July 1, 1958.
38 A rich collection of data of this nature may be found in the restricted military journal *Kung-tso t'ung-hsün* [Bulletin of Activities], January-August 1961; translated in J. Chester Cheng, (Ed.), *The Politics of the Chinese Red Army,* Stanford: Hoover Institution, 1965.
39 Such complaint was cited by Hsiao Hua, Participation in National Construction Is a Glorious Task of the PLA. See note 17 above.
40 Gittings, *The Role of the Chinese Army,* pp. 225–62; S.M. Chiu, The PLA and the Party, *Military Review,* XLIII:6, June 1963, pp. 58–66.
41 The text may be found in *Chung-kung nien-pao* [Yearbook on Communist China], 1967, pp. 798–804. The text of other relevant regulations may be found in *Jen-min jih-pao* [People's Daily], November 22, 1961.
42 *Jen-min jih-pao* [People's Daily], April 29 and May 10, 1963. For the text in English, see Kau, *et al. Political Work System of the Chinese Communist Military,* pp. 217–324.
43 For the purge of P'eng and related development, see Ralph L. Powell, The Party, the Government and the Gun, *Asian Survey,* X: 6, June 1970, pp. 441–71.
44 See, for example, Hua Kuo-feng's report to the Fifth National People's Congress, Unite and Strive to Build a Modern, Powerful Socialist Country, delivered on February 26, 1978, *Peking Review,* No. 10, March 10, 1978, 7–40.
45 See, for example, "Hsian Lei Feng hsüeh-hsi" [Learn from Lei Feng], *Jen-min jih-pao* [People's Daily], editorial, March 3, 1977; Chan-k'ai hsüeh-hsi ying-ku-t'ou liu-lien ch'ün-chung yün-tung [Develop 'Learn from the Hard-Bone Sixth Company' Mass Movement], *Chieh-fang-chün pao* [Liberation Army Daily], February 25, 1977.
46 During the Cultural Revolution, 102 military leaders with the rank of general and above were reported to have been purged. By October 1975 as many as 88 of those purged (accounting for 86 per cent) had reemerged. It is worth noting, for instance, that the infamous ex-Chief of Staff Lo Jui-ch'ing is now a deputy director of the National Defense Scientific and Technological Commission, while the former Director of the General Political Department, Hsiao Hua, now serves as political commissar of the Academy of Science. See Fan Chün-kuei, An Analysis of October First Celebration Activities, *Chung-kung yen-chiu* [Studies on Chinese Communism], IX: 10, October 1975, pp. 12–19.
47 See note 27 above.
48 A large collection of materials on these movements is available in *Chung-kung nien-pao* [Yearbook on Chinese Communism], 1969, Section II, pp. 33–38.
49 See Summary of Chairman Mao's Talks to Responsible Local Comrades During His Tour of Inspection, Mid-August–September 12, 1971, In Ying-mao Kau, *The Lin Piao Affair,* pp. 55–66.
50 Ting Wang, The Emergent Military Class, In William Whitson, *The Military and Political Power in China in the 1970's,* New York: Praeger, 1972, p. 118.
51 Parris H. Chang, Changing Patterns of Military Roles in Chinese Politics, ibid., pp. 47–70.
52 Morris Janowitz, *The Military in the Political Development of New Nations,* Chicago: University of Chicago Press, 1964, pp. 83–8.
53 For details of these movements, see my book, *The Lin Piao Affair.*
54 Ibid., pp. xlvi-xlvii.
55 Wang Han-min, Reorganization of the CCP Committees at the Provincial Level, *Chung-kung yen-chiu,* Studies on Chinese Communism, IX: 11, November 10, 1975, pp. 45–53.
56 Data discussed in this section are based on the author's own computation.
57 See note 53 above.
58 See, for instance, Speed Up the Modernization of National Defence, an editorial by Renmin Ribao, *Hongqi,* and Jiefangjun Bao, *Peking Review,* No. 32, August 5, 1977, 15–17.
59 Based on the author's computation.
60 David E. Apter, *The Politics of Modernization,* Chicago: University of Chicago Press, 1965, pp. 357–90.

Selected Bibliography*

Compiled by PATRICIA BLAIR

The items included in this bibliography are intended to represent the most judicious available assessments of the development experience of the People's Republic of China. The authors represented are among the most eminent China specialists writing in (or being translated into) English, and many have had an opportunity to visit the People's Republic for fairly extended periods. Their works have hitherto been addressed primarily to the community of China watchers and others concerned with international relations. The purpose of this selected bibliography is to make their insights available to a rather different audience—those interested in the socio-economic and institutional changes inherent in development, whose primary interest is in assessing China's development strategy and performance in relation to development elsewhere.

The sources have been divided into sectors and categories familiar to development specialists. Introductory notes to each section attempt to point the reader to the most comprehensive or distinctive sources in each category, and annotations have been added to items whose titles may not be self-explanatory. Inevitably, judgments have had to be made in categorizing items that could logically be included under more than one heading. Furthermore, books and journals containing several articles have been entered only under the general heading judged most appropriate. Where sections overlap, the introductory notes call attention to related items.

As the reader will discover, differences persist among China specialists as to interpretation of most aspects of the Chinese experience. Aside from the usual differences in perceptions and insights among scholars, there are a number of reasons specific to China why objective interpretation is particularly difficult: (1) first-hand observation by outsiders was rare until quite recently; (2) official statistical data for the period after 1958 have been sparse and often questionable; and (3) the Chinese themselves have paid relatively little attention to data-gathering and other impedimenta common to social science scholarship in the West.

For the most part, entries are restricted to material published between 1970 and mid–1976, although some important earlier works are included as well as some more recent. Works that involve detailed analysis of doctrinal, intra-party, or personality conflicts—fascinating to the China specialist but less useful or comprehensible to the "lay" reader—have been omitted to the extent possible, as have works that involve political rhetoric of either the right or the left.

This bibliography consists almost exclusively of books and articles about the People's Republic written by outsiders. For readers wishing to go more deeply into research on the Chinese development experience, a brief section on standard sources,

* Originally prepared for the China Round Table of the Washington Chapter of the Society for International Development and published as Overseas Development Council Occasional Paper No. 8, 1976. Additions to update the listing have been made by the Compiler and by the Editor of this volume.

reference materials, and translations of materials from the People's Republic itself has been included. Special attention should also be called to the few journals that regularly contain solid analytical work based on primary sources. The most important of these—as the frequency with which it is cited in this bibliography makes evident—is *The China Quarterly*, published by the Contemporary China Institute of London University. *Asian Survey* (University of California Press, Berkeley) and *Pacific Affairs* (University of British Columbia Press, Vancouver) also include material of development interest and *World Development* (Pergamon Press, Oxford) frequently includes papers on China. *Modern China* (Beverly Hills: Sage Publications) publishes papers on development, especially in the context of ideology. These journals offer a starting point for any research on China. It should be noted that, for journals not put out in the United States, the country of origin is indicated in parentheses.

Only a few of the works cited in the bibliography reflect changes in the Chinese leadership following the death of Chairman Mao Tse-tung or the effects on the economy of serious earthquake damage in northeast China in 1976. These events will profoundly affect the course of development in the People's Republic. Whatever happens in the future, however, Chinese development experience as of 1978 contains much that is, or should be, of interest to development specialists everywhere.

CONTENTS OF BIBLIOGRAPHY

I. DEVELOPMENT STRATEGY

I-A. GENERAL

The books and articles in this section describe the various stages of Chinese development strategy and offer varying analyses of the continuing tension between "radical" and "pragmatic" points of view.

Among the most useful analyses of these trends are the studies by Eckstein and Richman; the symposia of Oksenberg, Unger and Schram; and the analyses by government specialists writing for the Joint Economic Committee of the US Congress—the latest compendium of these papers was published in November 1978. Donnithorne deals mainly with the complex institutional side of the Chinese economy. The Sdobnikova collection provides Soviet and East European views of Chinese development.

The relevance of the Chinese experience as a development model is open to question, in view not only of the unique political system of the People's Republic but also of the long history and culture of the Chinese people. Keesing, Gurley, and Reynolds, among others, discuss this "transferability" issue, as do most of the prominent economists who have recorded impressions of their visits to the People's Republic. The Perkins collection, on the other hand, stresses the Chinese roots of recent development strategy.

Entries focusing on "Development Strategy" and on "Economic and Social Performance" comprise separate parts of this bibliography, but they are, of course, closely related. Most important works discuss both strategy *and* performance. The reader, therefore, should also consult the entries in section II-A, which includes several comparative commentaries on Indian and Chinese development experiences as well as specific analyses of the levels of Chinese performance in the areas of economic and social policy.

1 *"Revolutionary Nation-Building: The Chinese Model"*
Boyd, R. G. *International Journal* (Canada), Vol. 25 (Winter 1969–70), pp. 69–93.
2 *"Peking and the Provinces: Decentralization of Power"*
Chang, Parris. *Problems of Communism*, Vol. 21 (July–August 1972), pp. 67–75. See also *"Peking and the Provinces: Continuing Central Predominance"*, by Victor C. Falkenheim, *idem*, pp. 75–83.
3 *"Economic Fluctuations in a Planned Under-Developed Economy: A Case Study of Mainland China"*
Chen, Kuan-i. *Asian Survey*, Vol. 12 (April 1972), pp. 349–56.
4 *"Structural Changes and Sectoral Interdependence in the Chinese Economy: 1952–1980"*
————, and Tsuchigane, Robert T. *Keio Economic Studies* (Japan), Vol. 10, No. 1 (1973), pp. 11–26.
5 *The Chinese Economy under Communism*
Chen, Nai-ruenn, and Galenson, Walter. Chicago: Aldine, 1969. 250 pp.
6 *"Economic Development in Communist China"*
Clark, Colin. *Journal of Political Economy*, Vol. 84 (April 1976), pp. 239–64.
7 *China: Inside the People's Republic*
Committee of Concerned Asian Scholars. New York: Bantam, 1972. 433 pp.
8 *The People's Republic of China, 1978.*
Current History. A special issue on the People's Republic is published annually in September.
8a *"The Relevance of China's Development Experience for Other Developing Countries"*
Dernberger, Robert. *Items* (Social Science Research Council), Vol. 31, September 1977, pp. 24–34.
9 *Special Issue on China*
The Developing Economies (Japan), Vol. 9 (December 1971).
10 *China's Economic System*
Donnithorne, Audrey G. London: Allen & Unwin, 1967. 592 pp.
11 *China's Economic Development: The Interplay of Scarcity and Ideology*
Eckstein, Alexander. Ann Arbor: University of Michigan Press, 1975. 399 pp.
12 *China's Economic Revolution*
Cambridge, UK, Cambridge University Press, 1977. 340 pp.

13 China: The Impossible Dream
    Ensminger, M. E., and Ensminger, Audrey. Clovis, Calif.: Agriservices Foundation, 1973. 311 pp.
14 A China Passage
    Galbraith, John Kenneth. Boston: Houghton Mifflin, 1973. 143 pp. Photographs by Marc Riboud.
15 China's Search for Plenty: The Economics of Mao Tse-tung
    Goodstadt, Leo. New York: Weatherill, 1973. 266 pp.
16 China's Economy and the Maoist Strategy.
    Gurley, John W. New York: Monthly Review Press, 1977. 325 pp.
16a China's Economy: A Basic Guide
    Howe, Christopher. London: Elek Books, 1978. 248 pp.
17 China as a Model of Development
    Imfeld, Al. Maryknoll, N.Y.: Orbis Books, 1976. 159 pp. Translated from German.
18 "Economic Lessons from China"
    Keesing, D. B. Journal of Development Economics (Netherlands), Vol. 2 (March 1975), pp. 1–32.
19 "Socialism in China"
    Leontief, Wassily. Atlantic Monthly, Vol. 231 (March 1973), pp. 74–81.
20 Land Reform and Economic Development in China: A Study of Institutional Change and Development
    Finance
    Lippitt, V. D. White Plains, N.Y.: International Arts and Sciences Press, 1974. 183 pp. Also published
    in Chinese Economic Studies, Vol. 7 (Summer 1974), pp. 3–183.
21 "The Chinese Model: Politics in Command"
    Maxwell, Neville, M. Yahuda, E. L. Wheelwright, C. Jayawardena, Political Economy of Develop-
    ment. Sydney: Australian Broadcasting Commission, pp. 174–218.
22 China's Developmental Experience
    Oksenberg, Michel, ed. New York: Praeger, 1973. 227 pp. Fourteen contributors: Donald Munro
    (education), C. H. G. Oldham (science and technology), Dwight Perkins (agriculture), Victor Sidel
    (health), Jon Sigurdson (rural planning), Tang Tsou (ideology), J. B. R. Whitney (environment), et al.
    Previously published as Annals of the American Academy of Political Science, Vol. 31 (March 1973).
23 "China, 1974: Problems not Models"
    Padoul, G. New Left Review, No. 89 (January 1975), pp. 73–84.
24 "China's Fourth Five-Year Plan"
    Perkins, Dwight. US–China Business Review, Vol. 1 (March–April 1974), pp. 19–22.
25 "Plans and Their Implementation in the People's Republic of China"
    ————. American Economic Review, Vol. 63 (May 1973), pp. 224–31.
26 China's Modern Economy in Historical Perspective
    ————, ed. Stanford: Stanford University Press, 1975. 344 pp. Ten papers focussing on the degree to
    which China's post–1949 economy was a product of the nation's own past. Contributors: Kang Chao,
    Thomas Rawski, Carl Riskin, Stuart Schram, et al.
27 People's China: 25 Years
    Problems of Communism (special issue), Vol. 23 (September 1974), pp. 1–38. Eight articles, including
    Audrey Donnithorne on economics.
28 "Impressions of the Chinese Economy"
    Prybyla, Jan S. Virginia Quarterly Review, Vol. 51 (Winter 1975), pp. 19–35.
29 The Political Economy of Communist China
    ————, Scranton, Pa.: International Textbook Co., 1970. 605 pp.
30 "China as a Less Developed Economy"
    Reynolds, Lloyd G. American Economic Review, Vol. 60 (June 1975), pp. 418–28.
31 Industrial Society in Communist China: A Firsthand Study of Chinese Economic Development and
    Management, with Significant Comparisons with Industry in India, USSR, Japan, and the US.
    Richman, Barry M. New York: Random House, 1969. 968 pp.
32 Economic Management in China
    Robinson, Joan. Modern China Series, No. 4, rev. ed. London: Anglo-Chinese Educational Institute,
    1975.
33 China in Transition
    Robson, W. A., and Crick, Bernard, eds. Beverly Hills, Calif.: Sage Publications, 1975. 118 pp. Seven
    contributors: Derek Bryan (social ethics), Jack Gray (ideology), Christopher Howe (economic trends),
    Rudiger Machetzki (education), Michel Oksenberg (political change), et al. Previously published as a
    special issue of Political Quarterly (United Kingdom), Vol. 45 (January–March 1974).
34 In the People's Republic of China
    Schell, Orville. New York: Random House, 1977. 217 pp.
35 Authority, Participation, and Cultural Change in China: Essays by a European Study Group
    Schram, Stuart R., ed. Cambridge: Cambridge University Press, 1973. 350 pp. Contributors: Marianne

Bastid (economic decision-making), John Gardner (education), Jack Gray (development strategy), Christopher Howe (labour), Jon Sigurdson (rural industry), Andrew J. Watson (family life).

36 *Present Day China: Socio-Economic Problems*
Sdobnikova, Galina, trans. Moscow: Progress Publishers, 1975. 248 pp. Thirteen articles by Soviet and East European scholars.

37 *Strike While the Iron is Hot: A Documentary of China's Socialist Development*
Selden, Mark, ed. New York: Monthly Review Press, 1978, forthcoming (the title may be changed).

38 *China's Rural Institutions and the Question of Transferability*
Unger, Jonathan, ed. Oxford: Pergamon, 1978. Contributors: Dwight Perkins (meeting basic needs); Jack Gray (Mao and the rural economy); Benedict Stavis (research and extension services); Carl Riskin (political conflict and rural industrialization); Suzanne Paine (rural/urban bias) *et al.*

39 *China: A Reassessment of the Economy*
US Congress, Joint Economic Committee. Washington, D.C.: Government Printing Office, 1975. 737 pp. Twenty-eight contributors: Arthur Ashbrook (overview), N. R. Chen (trade), Jack Craig (telecommunications), David Denny (international finance), Robert Michael Field and Thomas Rawski (industry), Nicholas Lardy (planning), Ian MacFarlane (construction), Leo Orleans (population, environment), Dwight Perkins (agriculture), Carl Riskin (incentives), Jon Sigurdson (rural industry), et al.

39a *Chinese Economy Post-Mao*
————, 1978. 880 pp. Contributors: Robert F. Dernberger (overview), Nicholas R. Lardy (prospects), William W. Whitson (politics), Nai-Ruenn Chen (modernization), Leo A. Orleans (Soviet view), *et al.*

40 *An Economic Profile of Mainland China*
————, New York: Praeger, 1968. 684 pp. Twenty-three contributors: John S. Aird (population), L. G. Bouchard (fisheries), Charles Hoffmann (incentives), William H. Hollister (capital formation), M. Larsen (agriculture), V. D. Lippitt (transportation), S. C. Tsiang (money and banking), Yuan-li Wu (planning), *et al.* Previously issued as US document, 2 vols. Washington, D.C.: Government Printing Office, 1967. 737 pp.

41 *People's Republic of China: An Economic Assessment*
————, Washington, D.C.: Government Printing Office, 1972. 382 pp. Contributors: John Aird (population), Arthur Ashbrook (overview), Edwin Jones (overview), Alva Lewis Erisman (agriculture), R. M. Field (industry), Leo Orleans (science and technology), P. D. Reichers (electronics), Leo Tansky (aid), A. H. Usack (trade), P. W. Vetterling (transportation).

42 *The Chinese Road to Socialism: Economics of the Cultural Revolution*
Wheelwright, E. L., and McFarlane, Bruce. New York: Monthly Review Press, 1970. 256 pp.

43 *China: A Handbook*
Wu, Yuan-li, ed. New York: Praeger, 1973. 915 pp. Thirty contributors: John Aird (population), George Ecklund (banking and finance), Kung-chia Yeh (national income, agriculture), *et al.*

44 *"The Chinese Way of Industrialization: An Analysis of the Interdependence between Industry and Agriculture in China"*
Yu, C. L. *Asia Quarterly* (Belgium), No. 4 (1973), pp. 263–77.

45 *"China by Daylight"*
Zagoria, Donald. *Dissent*, Vol. 22 (Spring 1975), pp. 135–47.

I–B. MANPOWER AND MOBILIZATION

Even though there have been occasional reports of Chinese complaints about a labour shortage, China's reserves of unskilled labour are generally considered to be almost unlimited. Statistical data are rare, however. For professional manpower, the basic—although probably outdated—source remains Cheng's 1965 work. Emerson's estimates also end with 1965.

The literature cited in this section should provide the interested reader with adequate information on wages, incentives, and the standard of living of Chinese workers, as well as on their relation to management. Hoffman's book is the most comprehensive. A continuing theme in many of these sources is the mobilization of the workforce through non-wage incentives, although wage differentials do continue to exist. Whyte focuses on the role of political study and mutual criticism sessions in the mobilization of the Chinese population.

Additional information on skilled manpower and professional labour is included elsewhere in this bibliography in some of the sources listed in sections II-E on science and technology and II-F on education. Mass mobilization is a major theme of Barnett's *Chinese Communist Politics in Action* (entry 342) and of Lewis's compendium, *The City in Communist China* (67); it is also treated in many of the works cited in section I-A on development strategy, and is the subject of Cell's *Revolution at Work* (45a).

45a *Revolution at Work: Mobilization Campaigns in China*
    Cell, Charles P. New York: Academic Press, 1977.
46 *Scientific and Engineering Manpower in Communist China, 1949–1965*
    Cheng, Chu-yuan. Doc. NSF-65-14. Washington, D.C.: National Science Foundation, 1965. 588 pp.
47 *Administrative and Technical Manpower in the People's Republic of China*
    Emerson, John Philip. US Department of Commerce, International Population Reports, Series P-95, No. 72, April 1973. 137 pp. Estimates stop with 1965.
48 *"Trade Union Policy in China: Introduction to Some Afro-Asian Comparisons"*
    Fletcher, M. D. *Australian Journal of Politics and History* (Australia), Vol. 20 (April 1974), pp. 54–61.
49 *Huan-Ying: Workers' China*
    Goldwasser, Janet, and Dowty, Stuart. New York: Monthly Review Press, 1975. 404 pp.
50 *"Worker Participation in Management in Communist China"*
    Harper, Paul. *Studies in Comparative Communism*, Vol. 4 (July & October 1971), pp. 111–40.
51 *The Chinese Worker*
    Hoffmann, Charles. Albany: State University of New York Press, 1974. 252 pp.
52 *"China: Evolution of the Industrial Relations System from 1949 to 1970"*
    Howe, Christopher. *Bulletin of the International Institute of Labour Studies* (Switzerland), No. 10 (1972), pp. 48–84.
53 *Wage Patterns and Wage Policy in Modern China*
    ————. Studies in Chinese History. Cambridge, Eng.: Cambridge University Press, 1973.
54 *"Welfare and China's Industrial Workers"*
    Kallgren, Joyce K. Reprint Series No. C-10, Centre for Chinese Studies. Berkeley: University of California, 1969.
55 *"Serving the People and Continuing the Revolution"*
    Pfeffer, Richard M. *China Quarterly* (United Kingdom), No. 52 (October–December 1972), pp. 620–53.
56 *"Making a Living in China"*
    Reynolds, Lloyd G. *Yale Review*, Vol. 63 (June 1974), pp. 481–97.
57 *"Maoism and Motivation: Work Incentives in China"*
    Riskin, Carl. *Bulletin of Concerned Asian Scholars*, Vol. 5, No. 1 (July 1973), pp. 10–24.
58 *"Institutional Continuity and Motivational Change: The Chinese Industrial Wage System, 1950–1973"*
    Schran, Peter. *Asian Survey*, Vol. 14 (November 1974), pp. 1014–32.
59 *"Assignment of University Graduates in China, 1974"*
    Teiwes, Frederick C. *China Quarterly* (United Kingdom), No. 62 (April–June 1975), pp. 308–9.
60 *"Workers' Politics in Shanghai"*
    White, Lynn T., III. *Journal of Asian Studies*, Vo. 36 (November 1976), pp. 99–116. Discusses, inter alia, the equalities and inequalities of compensation among workers prior to 1970.
61 *Small Groups and Political Rituals in China*
    Whyte, Martin K. Berkeley: University of California Press, 1974. 271 pp.

I-C. URBANIZATION

The effects of various economic and social policies on the ebb and flow of China's urban population has made it extremely difficult to estimate the number of people who now live in the cities and towns. We do know, however, that the Chinese regime has been reasonably successful in controlling urban growth—not the least through "rusticating" many urban youth; every year hundreds of thousands of young people are sent to the countryside to settle, most of them permanently. The older urban centres appear to have suffered from relative neglect compared to other areas in China.

The studies cited in this section provide primarily general description rather than statistical data on the situation in China's cities and towns. The Vogel work is particularly valuable. Readers interested in the rustication movement should consult the works by Chen, Prybyla, Ivory and Lavely, and Bernstein. Those concerned about China's urban environmental problems should consult the following section on environmental issues. It should also be noted that the National Academy of Sciences (US) report on small-scale industry (entry 188) in section II-C contains previously unavailable information on the development of new towns in rural China.

62 *Up to the Mountains and Down to the Villages: The Transfer of Urban Youth to Rural China*
    Bernstein, Thomas, New Haven: Yale University Press, 1977. 371 pp.
63 *"Directions in Chinese Urban Planning"*
    Buck, David D. *Urbanism Past and Present*, No. 1 (Winter 1975–76), pp. 24–35.
64 *"Population Growth and Urbanization in China, 1953–1970"*
    Chen, C. S. *Ekistics* (Greece), Vol. 38 (September 1974), pp. 192–98.
65 *"Overurbanization, Rustication of Urban-Educated Youths, and the Politics of Rural Transformation"*
    Chen, Pi-chao. *Comparative Politics*, Vol. 4 (April 1972), pp. 361–86.
66 *"Rustication, Demographic Change and Development in Shanghai"*
    Ivory, Paul and Lavely, William. *Asian Survey*, Vol. 17 (May 1977), pp. 440–55.
66a *Planning and Urbanism in China*
    Jeffrey, N. and M. Caldwell, eds. London and New York: Pergamon Press. 86 pp. (Special issue of *Progress in Planning*.) Eleven contributors.
67 *The City in Communist China*
    Lewis, John Wilson, ed. Stanford: Stanford University Press, 1971. 449 pp. Twelve contributors.
68 *"Hsia-fang: The Economics and Politics of Rustication in China"*
    Prybyla, Jan S. *Pacific Affairs* (Canada), Vol. 48 (Summer 1975), pp. 153–72.
69 *"Bad Old Shanghai has Turned into a Showplace of New China"*
    Schechter, Jerrold. *Smithsonian Magazine* (March 1974), pp. 25–36.
70 *"Concepts behind Urban and Regional Planning in China"*
    Schenk, Hans. *Tijdschrift voor Economische en Sociale Geografie* (Netherlands), Vol. 65, No. 5 (1974).
71 *"Notes on Urban Spatial Planning and Development in China"*
    ————. *Eastern Horizon* (Hong Kong), Vol. 11, No. 3 (1972), pp. 34–41.
72 *Families of Fengsheng: Urban Life in China*
    Sidel, Ruth. Middlesex, Eng.: Penguin, 1974. 166 pp.
73 *Flowers on an Iron Tree: Five Cities of China*
    Terrill, Ross. Boston: Little, Brown, 1975. 423 pp. Descriptions of Shanghai, Dairen, Hangchow, Wuhan, and Peking.
74 *"Containing the City: Changsha, China"*
    Thompson, Robin. *Ekistics* (Greece), Vol. 38 (September 1974), pp. 199–201.
75 *"Housing and City Planning in China"*
    Towers, G. *Ekistics* (Greece), Vol. 38 (September 1974), pp. 202–8.
76 *Briefs on Selected People's Republic of China Cities*
    US Central Intelligence Agency. Reference Aid Series, November 1975. Descriptions, including maps, of 13 major cities. Available through Photoduplication Service, Library of Congress, Washington, D.C.
77 *Canton under Communism: Programs and Politics in a Provincial Capital, 1949–1968*
    Vogel, Ezra. Cambridge, Mass.: Harvard University Press, 1969. 448 pp.
78 *"China: Report on a Visit by American Architects"*
    Wagner, W. F., Jr. *Architectural Record*, Vol. 156 (September 1974), pp. 111–24.
79 *"The Integration of Town and Countryside in China"*
    Wertheim, W. F. *Cultures et Developpement* (Belgium), Vol. 6, No. 4 (1974), pp. 723–36.

I-D. ENVIRONMENTAL ISSUES

China has gained a reputation as a country concerned with problems of the environment. Although many of China's policies have in fact proven to be beneficial to the environment, their primary objectives were economic rather than explicitly environmental. In the countryside, for example, improvements in the utilization of water and land, afforestation, and other rural-conservation measures were undertaken in order to increase agricultural production. In the cities, the motivating slogan is "make treasure out of waste"; most of the effort has been focused either on extracting economic value out of various forms of pollution or on preventing economic losses from unchecked pollution. Air pollution from industry and home heaters does remain a problem, however.

Although most of the entries in this section are short and offer only a fragmentary picture of the kinds of environmental measures that have been taken in China, two of the sources cited in this listing, Kapp and Myers, do offer reasonably comprehensive coverage of the issues.

80 *"Agriculture, Environment, and Current Policy in China"*
    Broadbent, Kieran P. *Asian Survey*, Vol. 16 (May 1976), pp. 411–26.
81 *China: Recycling of Organic Wastes in Agriculture*
    F.A.D. Rome: Food and Agriculture Organization, 1977.
82 *Environmental Policies and Development Planning in Contemporary China and Other Essays*
    Kapp, K. William. Paris: Mouton, 1974. 175 pp.
83 *"'Recycling' in Contemporary China"*
    ————. *Kyklos* (Switzerland), Vol. 27, No. 2 (1974), pp. 286–303. Reprinted in this volume.
84 *"Environmental Action in China: Excerpts from an Address"*
    Liu, C. Y. *Science News*, Vol. 108, October 4, 1975, pp. 214–15.
85 *"China's Approach to Environmental Conservation"*
    Myers, Norman. *Environmental Affairs*, Vol. 5 (Winter 1976), pp. 33–63.
86 *"How is China's Wildlife Faring?"*
    ————. *International Wildlife*, Vol. 5, No. 4 (1975), pp. 4–11.
87 *"The Mao Ethic and Environmental Quality"*
    Orleans, Leo A., and Suttmeier, Richard P. *Science*, Vol. 170, December 11, 1970, pp. 1175–76.
88 *"Chinese and Indian Development: An Interdisciplinary Environmental Analysis"*
    Richman, Barry. *American Economic Review*, Vol. 65 (May 1975), pp. 345–55.
89 *"The Smog in China"*
    Rodale, Robert. *Environmental Action Bulletin*, Vol. 4, March 17, 1973, pp. 2–4, 8.
90 *"China's Way with Waste"*
    Schell, Orville. *Ekistics* (Greece), Vol. 38 (September 1974), pp. 217–19. A similar article appears in *Ecologist*, Vol. 3 (February 1973), pp. 56–59.
91 *"Waste Treatment in China: Ancient Tradition and High Technology"*
    Sebastian, F. P. *Ambio* (Sweden), Vol. 1, No. 6 (1972), pp. 209–16.
92 *"Resources and Environment in China"*
    Sigurdson, Jon. *Ambio* (Sweden), Vol. 4, No. 3 (1975), pp. 112–19.
92a *Water Conservancy and Irrigation in China*
    Vermeer, E.B. The Hague: Leiden University Press, 1977. 350 pp.

I-E. PUBLIC FINANCE

Few data are available on China's financial and monetary policies of the 1960s and 1970s, and little work has been done on the subject. Studies more recent than Hsiao's analysis of monetary policy in the 1950s are based on fragmentary data.

Among scholars writing in English, Donnithorne has attempted the most continuing coverage. For information on how China's financial and other economic institutions work and are related to one another, her *China's Economic System* (entry 10), cited in section I-A of this bibliography, remains indispensable. In the works cited below, she and Lardy reach somewhat different conclusions on the extent to which decentralization measures of the 1950s have affected investment decision making.

93 *"Financial Aspects of Chinese Planning"*
    Berger, Roland. *Bulletin of Concerned Asian Scholars*, Vol. 6 (April–August 1974), pp. 15–19.

94 "The Chinese Monetary System"
    Cassou, Pierre-Henri. *China Quarterly* (United Kingdom), No. 59 (July–September 1974), pp. 559–66. Translated from French.
95 *China's Allocation of Fixed Capital Investment, 1952–1957*
    Cheng, Chu-yuan. Ann Arbor: University of Michigan Press, 1974. 115 pp.
96 *The Budget and Plan in China: Central-Local Economic Relations*
    Donnithorne, Audrey G. Contemporary China Papers, No. 3. Canberra: Australian National University Press, 1972. 19 pp.
97 "China's Anti-Inflationary Policy"
    ————. *Three Banks Review* (United Kingdon), No. 103 (September 1974), pp. 3–25.
98 *Money and Monetary Policy in Communist China*
    Hsiao, Katherine Huang. New York: Columbia University Press, 1971. 308 pp.
99 "Centralization and Decentralization in China's Fiscal Management"
    Lardy, Nicholas R. *China Quarterly* (United Kingdom), No. 61 (January–March 1975), pp. 25–60.
100 "On the Allocation of Investment in the 1970s: A Hypothesis"
    Onoye, Etsozo. *The Developing Economies* (Japan), Vol. 9 (December 1971), pp. 475–89.
101 "A Note on Incomes and Prices in China"
    Prybyla, Jan S. *Asian Survey*, Vol. 15 (March 1975), pp. 262–78.

I-F. EXTERNAL ECONOMIC RELATIONS

The 1970s have seen a growing interest in China's international trade, aid, and finance on the part of outside observers. The relatively new journal, *US- China Business Review* (published by the National Council for US-China Trade), is devoted entirely to these issues. The most substantive articles from that journal have been cited below; but interested readers should note that each issue also contains "how to" articles that might be useful to businessmen engaged in importing from or exporting to the People's Republic.

Several other materials cited call for comment. The US Central Intelligence Agency annually publishes the most comprehensive statistics available on China's foreign trade. The Bartke and Copper selections are notable among the sparse literature on Chinese foreign aid (which, in China's case, as in that of most other aid donors, has been directed primarily to countries of particular political interest to the People's Republic); Bartke includes country-by-country data on Chinese aid and trade concessions. Several selections offer information on China's still tentative entry into the realm of international finance.

Besides the works cited in this section, the 1975 study by the Joint Economic Committee of the US Congress (entry 39) cited in section I-A contains useful analyses of various aspects of China's foreign economic relations. Also relevant are the studies of China's prospects for exporting petroleum cited in section II-D on energy and minerals.

102 *China's Economic Aid*
    Bartke, Wolfgang. New York: Holmes & Meier, 1975. 215 pp. Translated from German; issued by the Institute of Asian Affairs, Hamburg.
103 "China and the European Economic Community: The Politics of a New Trade Relationship"
    Broadbent, Kieran P. *The World Today* (United Kingdom), Vol. 32 (May 1976), pp. 190–98.
104 *China's Foreign Aid*
    Copper, John Franklin. Lexington, Mass.: Lexington Books, 1976. 197 pp.
105 "China's Foreign Financial Liabilities"
    Denny, David L. *US-China Business Review*, Vol. 2 (January–February 1975), pp. 34–38.
106 "China's Foreign Trade System Changes Gear"
    Donnithorne, Audrey G. *US-China Business Review*, Vol. 1 (January–February 1974), pp. 16–20.
107 "China's Trade Policy and Sino-American Relations"
    Eckstein, Alexander. *Foreign Affairs*, Vol. 54 (October 1975), pp. 134–54.

108   *Communist China's Economic Growth and Foreign Trade*
——————. New York: McGraw Hill, 1966. 359 pp.

109   *"China's Industrialization and Foreign Trade"*
Etienne, Gilbert. *Asia Quarterly* (Belgium), No. 2 (1975), pp. 105–20.

110   *"China's Financing Prospects"*
Fry, Richard. *Banker*, Vol. 124 (December 1974), pp. 1487+.

111   *China's Changing Role in the World Economy*
Garth, Bryant G., ed. New York: Praeger, 1975. 222 pp. Ten contributors: David Denny (international finance), Hans Heymann (technology choices), David G. Luther (lump sum settlements), H. W. Rood (trade with Japan), Kim Woodward (attitudes toward global resource distribution), *et al*. Previously published as *Stanford Journal of International Studies* (special issue), Vol. 10 (Spring 1975).

112   *"China's Merchant Marine"*
Heine, Irwin Millard. *US-China Business Review*, Vol. 3 (March–April 1976), pp. 6–18.

113   *"The Market in China for Foreign Consumer Goods"*
Kamm, John T. *US-China Business Review*, Vol. 2 (March–April 1975), pp. 4–14.

114   *China and the Third World*
Kaushik, Devendra. Mystic, Conn.: Verry Publishers, 1975. 87 pp.

115   *"Do the Chinese Have an International Marketing Strategy?"*
Landeau, Jean-Francois. *US-China Business Review*, Vol. 2 (May–June 1975), pp. 40–42.

116   *"Trade between the US and the People's Republic of China: Practice, Policy, and Law"*
Lubman, Stanley. *Law and Policy in International Business*, Vol. 8, No. 1 (1976), pp. 1–76.

117   *The Foreign Trade of Mainland China*
Mah, Feng-hua. Chicago: Aldine, 1971. 270 pp.

118   *"Forecasting China's Trade over the Long Term"*
Perkins, Dwight. *US-China Business Review*, Vol. 2 (March–April 1975), pp. 40–47.

119   *"Mainland China and Western Trade Credits"*
Reese, K. *Intereconomics* (Germany), No. 2 (1976), pp. 45–49.

120   *International Trade Handbook of the People's Republic of China*
US Central Intelligence Agency. Research Aid Series. Annual. Available from Photoduplication Service, Library of Congress, Washington, D.C.

121   *The Chinese Economy and Foreign Trade Perspectives, 1976*
US Department of Commerce. Washington, D.C.: Government Printing Office, June 1977. 57 pp.

122   *"China's Aid and Trade with the Developing Countries of the Third World"*
Weiss, Udo. *Asia Quarterly* (Belgium), No. 3 (1974), pp. 203–13 and No. 4 (1974), pp. 263–309.

123   *Doing Business with China: American Trade Opportunities in the '70s*
Whitson, W. W., ed. New York: Praeger, 1974. 593 pp. Thirty-five papers, including preliminary surveys of 14 industries; some of the papers, especially the sector surveys, are now outdated.

124   *"China Moves into International Finance"*
Wiegold, C. Frederick. *American Banker*, Vol. 140, March 10, 1975, pp. 1, 16.

125   *"The Bank of China's Expanding Role in International Finance"*
Wilson, Dick. *US-China Business Review*, Vol. 1 (November–December 1974), pp. 21–26.

126   *"China's Trade Missions: The British Experience"*
——————. *US-China Business Review*, Vol. 3 (July–August 1976), pp. 16–22.

II. ECONOMIC AND SOCIAL PERFORMANCE

II-A. GENERAL

China's development performance has been better than most—but by no means all—developing countries. Despite some setbacks, gross national product appears to have grown at an average rate of 4 to 6 per cent a year since 1953. But what is more impressive to development specialists than these statistics is the Chinese success in distributing the benefits of growth relatively broadly. The extremes of poverty and wealth that characterize many developing countries do not exist in China.

Although there is agreement on the general dimensions of Chinese performance, specific estimates of economic growth differ. Among the works cited in this section, those by the US Central Intelligence Agency and by Liu and Yeh offer relatively conservative estimates; the estimates of Eckstein and Rawski range somewhat higher. Several works in this section compare Chinese and Indian development experience, usually to the detriment of the latter. For continuing coverage of Chinese economic performance, interested readers should check the weekly *Far Eastern Economic Review*, (Hong Kong), which carries frequent, often firsthand reports on the People's Republic.

Development performance is closely related to development strategy. Readers should, therefore, also consult the entries in section I-A, which complements this section. Detailed estimates of sectoral performance are included in relevant sections throughout Part II.

127 *Freedom Railway: China and the Tanzania–Zambia Link*
Bailey, Martin. London: Rex Collings, 1976.
128 *Capital Formation in Mainland China, 1952–1965*
Chao, Kang. Berkeley: University of California Press, 1974. 178 pp. Emphasizes methodological problems outsiders face in analyzing Chinese performance.
129 *India and China: Studies in Comparative Development*
Chen, Kuan-i, and Uppal, Jaginder S., eds. New York: Free Press, 1971. 404 pp. A collection of previously published writings by specialists.
130 *Chinese Economic Statistics*
Chen, Nai-ruenn. Chicago: Aldine, 1967. 539 pp. Official PRC statistics for the 1950s. See entry 395 (p. 78) for original People's Republic publication.
131 *"Economic Growth and Change in China: A Twenty Year Perspective"*
Eckstein, Alexander. *China Quarterly* (United Kingdom), No. 54 (April–June 1973), pp. 211–41.
132 *"China 1978: Into the Mainstream"*
Far Eastern Economic Review (Hong Kong), Vol. 102, October 6, 1978, pp. 35–66. A similar special section is published annually. In addition, this weekly news magazine carries regular, often first-hand coverage of developments in the People's Republic of China.
133 *"Some Overlooked National Product Data"*
Field, Robert Michael. *China Quarterly* (United Kingdom), No. 59 (July–September 1974), pp. 583–86.
134 *"A Hypothetical Projection of the Chinese Economy: 1966 to 1981"*
Ishikawa, Shigeru. *The Developing Economies* (Japan), Vol. 8 (September 1970), pp. 249–79.
135 *"The Chinese Economy at the Present Juncture–Chinese and Other Asian Economies: A Quantitative Evaluation"*
Liu, Ta-chung, and Yeh, Kung-chia. *American Economic Review*, Vol. 63 (May 1973), pp. 215–23.
136 *Basic Data on the Economy of the People's Republic of China*
Phipps, John, and Matheson, JoNelle. US Department of Commerce, Overseas Business Reports, No. OBR 74–21, 1974. 37 pp. Also see earlier reports of the same title.
137 *"Recent Trends in the Chinese Economy"*
Rawski, Thomas. *China Quarterly* (United Kingdom), No. 53 (January–March 1973), pp. 1–33.
138 *"Economic Development in China and India: Some Conditioning Factors"*
Richman, Barry. *Pacific Affairs* (Canada), Vol. 45 (Spring 1972), pp. 75–91.
139 *"Chinese Economic Performance"*
Sinha, R. P. *World Today* (United Kingdom), Vol. 30 (January 1974), pp. 33–42.
140 *"Economic Growth in China and India, 1952–1970: A Comparative Appraisal"*
Swamy, Subramanian. *Economic Development and Cultural Change*, Vol. 21 (July 1973), Part II, pp. 1–84.
141 *"Size and Composition of the Chinese Gross National Product"*
Ullerich, Curtis. *Journal of Contemporary Asia* (United Kingdom), Vol. 2, No. 2 (1972), pp. 163–80.
142 *People's Republic of China: Handbook of Economic Indicators*
US Central Intelligence Agency. Reference Aid Series, August 1975. Available from Photoduplication Service, Library of Congress, Washington, D.C.
143 *China and India: A comparative Survey of Economic Development Performance*
Weisskopf, Thomas. Doc. No. MI 48108. Ann Arbor: University of Michigan, Centre for Research on Economic Development, October 1974. 43 pp. Similar Themes are discussed in his paper and subsequent discussion in *American Economic Review*, Vol. 65 (May 1975), pp. 345–71.

II-B. AGRICULTURE

China has been successful so far in achieving basic self-sufficiency in food production, with production increases averaging some 2 to 3 per cent a year. At present, the major emphasis is on intensive cultivation of high-yield areas, with special attention to management practices, extending irrigation, and application of such modern inputs as fertilizers, pesticides, and improved seeds. With the purchase of thirteen of the world's largest ammonia-urea fertilizer complexes to supplement domestic production, China should be able to keep agricultural production ahead of population growth for the near future, although some observers believe that continued increases in agricultural output will present problems for the long term.

Of the entries cited below, the report of the American Plant Studies Delegation is especially current and valuable. The US Department of Agriculture annually provides a comprehensive survey—including production estimates—of the agricultural situation in the People's Republic. The book by Perkins remains a basic source for a comprehensive view of China's agricultural problems and attempted solutions. Other works cited focus on specific aspects of Chinese agricultural development. The few available works on forestry are also listed below.

In addition to the works cited in this section, most of the symposia listed in section I-A of this bibliography include at least one article pertaining to agriculture in China; the 1975 study of the Joint Economic Committee of the US Congress (entry 39) includes four. Section III-C on changing values contains sociological studies of rural areas.

144   *"The Political Economy of the People's Commune in China: Changes and Continuities"*
       Ahn, Byung-joon. *Journal of Asian Studies,* Vol. 34 (May 1975), pp. 631–58.
145   *Plant Studies in the People's Republic of China: A Trip Report of the American Plant Studies Delegation*
       American Plant Studies Delegation. Washington, D.C.: National Academy of Sciences, 1975. 205 pp. Delegation leader: Sterling Wortman. Is more comprehensive than its title would suggest.
146   *Rural Development: Learning from China*
       Aziz, Sartaj. London: Macmillan, 1978, 201 pp.
147   *"Chinese and Indian Agriculture: A Broad Comparison of Recent Policy and Performance"*
       Bardhan, Pranab K. *Journal of Asian Studies*, Vol. 29 (May 1970), pp. 515–38.
148   *"The Mechanisation of Chinese Agriculture"*
       Berger, Roland. *Eastern Horizon* (Hong Kong), Vol. 11, No. 3 (1972), pp. 7–26.
149   *"How China Uses Organic Farming Methods"*
       Blobaum, R. *Organic Gardening and Farming*, Vol. 22 (July 1975), pp. 45–49.
150   *"A Note on Understanding Socialist Economic Terminology: The Case of China and the Need for a Dictionary of Agricultural Economics"*
       Broadbent, Kieran P. *Journal of Agricultural Economics* (United Kingdom), Vol. 25 (January 1974), pp. 93–95.
151   *"The Transformation of Chinese Agriculture and Its Effects on the Environment"*
       ————. *International Relations* (United Kingdom), Vol. 4 (May 1972), pp. 38–51.
152   *"Five Communes in China"*
       Champeau, Harold C. A series of articles in *Foreign Agriculture*, Vol. 13, Nos. 29–33 (July & August 1975), various pages.
153   *Agricultural Production in Communist China, 1949–1965*
       Chao, Kang. Madison: University of Wisconsin Press, 1970. 357 pp.
154   *Economic Effects of Land Reform in Taiwan, Japan, and Mainland China: A Comparative Study*
       ————. Doc. No. LTC 80. Madison: University of Wisconsin, Land Tenure centre, 1972. 35 pp.
155   *"The Production and Application of Chemical Fertilizers in China"*
       ————. *China Quarterly* (United Kingdom), No. 64 (October–December 1975), pp. 712–29.
156   *"Chinese Insect Control Integrates Old and New"*
       Chemical and Engineering News, Vol. 54, March 15, 1976, pp. 30–32.

157 *"Agricultural Productivity in a Newly Settled Region: The Case of Manchuria"*
Chen, Nai-ruenn. *Economic Development and Cultural Change*, Vol. 21 (October 1972), pp. 87–95.
158 *"Pest Management in the People's Republic of China"*
Chiang, H. C. *FAO Plant Protection Bulletin*, Vol. 25 (1977), pp. 1–8.
159 *"Collective Farms in Communist China"*
Crook, Federick W. *Monthly Labour Review*, Vol. 96 (March 1973), pp. 45–50.
160 *China: Men, Grain and Machines*
Etienne, Gilbert, ed. Studies and Documents (Switzerland), Vol. 2 (1977), 80 pp. Papers by European experts.
160a *Learning from China: A Report on Agriculture and the Chinese People's Communes*
FAO Study Mission (9 Sept–5 Oct. 1975). Bangkok: FAO, 1977. 112 pp.
161 *"'Output' v. 'Surplus' Maximization: The Conflicts between Socialized and Private Sectors in Chinese Collectivized Agriculture"*
Fung, K. K. *The Developing Economies* (Japan), Vol. 12 (March 1974), pp. 41–55.
162 *"For Water the Chinese Move Mountains"*
Gayn, Mark. *International Wildlife*, Vol. 2 (November–December 1972), pp. 20–25.
163 *Iron Oxen: A Documentary of Revolution in Chinese Farming*
Hinton, William. New York: Vintage Books, 1971. 225 pp.
164 *Agricultural Development in China*
Jacoby, Erich. Stockholm: Economic Research Institute, Stockholm School of Economics, 1974. 89 pp.
165 *"Farm Crops of China"*
Kung, Peter. Four-part article in *World Crops*, Vols. 27 and 28. Part I (March–April 1975), pp. 55–64; Part II (May–June 1975), pp. 122–32; Part III (September–October 1975), pp. 228–36; Part IV (January–February 1976), pp. 40–43.
166 *The Technical Transformation of Agriculture in Communist China*
Kuo, Leslie T. C. New York: Praeger, 1972. 266pp.
166a *Agriculture in the People's Republic of China*
———, New York: Praeger, 1977. 288 pp.
167 *"Grain Production in China, 1950–1970"*
Liden, David. *Asian Survey*, Vol. 15 (June 1975), pp. 510–29.
168 *"The Commune in Chinese Development"*
Lippitt, V. D. *Modern China*, Vol. 3 (April 1977) pp. 229–52.
169 *China's Fertilizer Economy*
Liu, Jung-chao. Chicago: Aldine, 1970. 173 pp.
170 *"Agriculture: Institutional and Technological Changes"*
Ma, L. J. C. *Focus* (United Kingdom), Vol. 25 (May 1975), pp. 1–11.
171 *Agricultural Development in China, 1368–1968*
Perkins, Dwight. Chicago: Aldine, 1969. 395 pp.
172 *Forestry in Communist China*
Richardson, S. D. Baltimore: Johns Hopkins Press, 1966. 237 pp.
173 *"The Litany of Tachai and the Foolish Old Man: Landscape Modification in Mainland China"*
Salter, Christopher L. *Professional Geographer*, Vol. 24 (May 1972), pp. 113–17.
174 *"The Role of Landscape Modification in Revolutionary Nation-Building"*
———. *The China Geographer*, Vol. 1, No. 3 (1976).
175 *"Reorganizing Rural Trade: Unified Purchase and Socialist Transformation"*
Shue, Vivienne. *Modern China*, Vol. 2 (January 1976), pp. 104–34.
176 *"Chinese Agriculture: Past Performance and Future Outlook"*
Sinha, R. P. *Journal of Agricultural Economics* (United Kingdom), Vol. 25 (January 1974), pp. 37–52.
177 *"Chinese Agriculture: A Quantitative Look"*
———. *Journal of Development Studies* (United Kingdom), Vol. 11 (April 1975), pp. 202–23.
178 *"Agriculture in China"*
Sprague, G. F. *Science*, Vol. 188, May 9, 1975, pp. 549–55.
179 *"China's Rural Local Institutions in Comparative Perspective"*
Stavis, Benedict. *Asian Survey*, Vol. 16 (April 1976), pp. 381–96.
180 *Making Green Revolution: The Politics of Agricultural Development in China*
———. Rural Development Monograph No. 1. Ithaca: Cornell University Press, 1974. 287 pp.
181 *"A Preliminary Model for Grain Production in China, 1974"*
———. *China Quarterly* (United Kingdom), No. 65 (January–March 1976), pp. 83–95. See also *"Recent Chinese Grain Claims,"* by R. M. Field, *idem*, pp. 96–97; and *"Recent Chinese Grain Figures"* by Neville Maxwell, *China Quarterly*, No. 68 (December 1976), pp. 817–18.
182 *China: Agricultural Performance in 1975*
US Central Intelligence Agency. Reference Aid Series, March 1976. 25 pp. Available from Photodup-

lication Service, Library of Congress, Washington, D.C.
183   *The Agricultural Situation in the People's Republic of China and Other Communist Asian Countries: Review of 1975 and Outlook for 1976*
US Department of Agriculture. Foreign Agricultural Economic Report, No. 124, August 1976. 65 pp. Updated version published annually.
184   *"How the Chinese Learn about Forestry"*
Westoby, Jack C. *American Forests,* Vol. 81 (June 1975), pp. 8–11 *passim.*
185   *"Growth Industry in Chinese Firs"*
———. *Geographical Magazine* (United Kingdom), Vol. 47 (June 1975), pp. 567–71.
186   *Land Reform in the People's Republic of China: Institutional Transformation in Agriculture*
Wong, John. New York: Praeger, 1973. 319 pp.
187   *"Agriculture in China"*
Wortman, Sterling. *Scientific American*, Vol. 232 (June 1975), pp. 13–21.

II-C. INDUSTRY

Overall industrial growth in the People's Republic of China appears to have averaged 10 per cent a year. Specific production indices, based on fragmentary data, can be found in Field, Lardy, and Emerson, as well as Rawski, among the entries cited below.

High-technology industry, under central control and direction, continues to be the key to China's industrial growth. A number of entries in this section focus on specific industries: chemicals (Yuan), fertilizer (CIA), textiles (Chen), machine tools (Cheng), steel (Clark and Clarke), electronics (Szuprowicz), construction (Chao), and aircraft (Heymann). Heymann's two-part study focuses specifically on the importation of technology, which has played a more important part in heavy industry than in other sectors of the Chinese economy.

Labour-intensive, small- and medium-scale industry, frequently based in rural areas, provides an increasingly important source of farm machinery and construction inputs. Riskin and the CIA, among others, offer information on this aspect of China's industrialization, but the most comprehensive report is that of the Rural Small-Scale Industries Delegation (entry 188).

Studies cited in other sections of this bibliography also will be of interest to those concerned with China's industrial development. The 1975 study by the Joint Economic Committee of the US Congress (entry 39) cited in section I-A includes a rather comprehensive series of articles on overall industrial performance, planning and management, regional development, labour incentives, rural industrialization, construction, petroleum, iron and steel, and telecommunications. The study by Richman (31) continues to be a basic source on industrial management. Labour incentives are covered in section I-B on manpower and mobilization. China's petroleum potential is treated in section II-D on energy. Some of the interesting questions surrounding the choice of industrial technology are discussed in works listed in section II-E on science and technology and in section I-A on development strategy. Those interested in industrial imports and exports should also consult section I-F on external economic relations.

188   *Rural Small-Scale Industry in the P.R.C.*
American Rural Small-Scale Industries Delegation, Berkeley, Calif.: University of California Press, 1977. 288 pp.
189   *China's Industrial Revolution: Politics, Planning and Management, 1949 to the Present*
Andors, Stephen. New York: Pantheon Books, 1977. 344 pp.
190   *Cultural Revolution and Industrial Organization in China: Changes in Management and Division of Labour*
Bettelheim, Charles. New York: Monthly Review Press, 1974. 128 pp. Translated from French.

Generalizations based on a study of a hosiery factory in Peking.

191 *"Technological Choice in Construction in Two Asian Countries: China and India"*
Bhala, A. S. *World Development* (United Kingdom), Vol. 2 (March 1974), pp. 65–73.

192 *The Construction Industry in Communist China*
Chao, Kang. Edinburgh: Edinburgh University Press, 1968. 237 pp.

193 *"Computing in China: A Travel Report"*
Cheatham, Thomas E., Jr., *et al. Science,* Vol. 182, October 12, 1973, pp. 134–40. Report on July 1972 visit by six US experts.

194 *"Technological Change in the Chinese Textile Industry, 1950–1972"*
Chen, E. K. Y., and Hsia, R. *The Developing Economies* (Japan), Vol. 13 (March 1975), pp. 66–81.

195 *"Industrial Development in China"*
Chen, Nai-ruenn. *Asian Affairs,* Vol. 2 (May–June 1975), pp. 276–94.

196 *The Machine-Building Industry in Communist China, 1952–1966*
Cheng, Chu-yuan. Chicago: Aldine, 1971. 339 pp. For a shorter presentation of this subject, see the author's article in *China Quarterly* (United Kingdom), No. 41 (January–March 1970), pp. 26–57.

197 *The Development of China's Steel Industry and Soviet Technical Aid*
Clark, M. Gardner. Ithaca: Cornell University Press, 1973. 160 pp.

198 *"China's Steel: The Key Link"*
Clarke, William W. *US-China Business Review,* Vol. 2 (July–August 1975), pp. 26–40. Reprinted as China Sector Report No. 2. Washington, D.C.: National Council for US-China Trade, February 1976.

199 *"The Chinese Machine-Building Industry: A Reappraisal"*
Field, Robert Michael. *China Quarterly* (United Kingdom), No. 54 (April–June 1973), pp. 308–20.

200 *"Industrial Output by Province in China, 1949–1973"*
————, with Lardy, N. R. and Emerson, J. P. *China Quarterly* (United Kingdom), No. 63 (July–September 1975), pp. 409–34. Also published as US Department of Commerce, Foreign Economic Report, No. FER–7, 1975.

201 *The Process of Industrialization of China: Primary Elements of an Analytical Bibliography*
Ganiere, Nicole. Working Document No. CD/TI (74)9. Paris: Organisation for Economic Cooperation and Development, Development Centre, 1974. 137 pp. Annotated; chiefly English-language sources.

202 *China's Approach to Technology Acquisition*
Heymann, Hans, Jr. Docs. R–1573 and R–1575. Part I: Aircraft Industry; Part III: Summary Observations. Santa Monica, Calif.: Rand Corporation, 1975. Part II on the automotive industry has not been published.

203 *Industrial Development of Communist China*
Li, C. M., ed. New York: Praeger, 1973. 205 pp. Twelve contributors: Audrey Donnithorne (planning, industry), Charles Hoffmann (work incentives), William Hollister (capital formation), Fred C. Hung and Yuan-li Wu (measurement problems), Ronald Hsia (steel), L. T. C. Kuo (agricultural machinery), *et al.*

204 *"Report from China—The Shenyang Transformer Factory: A Profile"*
Meisner, Mitch. *China Quarterly* (United Kingdom), No. 52 (October–December 1972), pp. 717–37.

205 *Report of the Rural Small-Scale Industries Delegation*
National Academy of Sciences: see entry 188.

206. *"Measuring China's Industrial Performance, 1949–1975"*
Rawski, Thomas G. A paper presented at the Conference on Reconciling Quantitative Measures of China's Economic Output, January 17–18, 1975, sponsored by the Subcommittee on Research on the Chinese Economy, Joint Committee on Contemporary China of the Social Science Research Council and the American Council of Learned Societies. Mimeo. Published proceedings of this Conference forthcoming. This paper updates the author's earlier article. *"Chinese Industrial Production, 1952–1971", Review of Economics and Statistics* (United Kingdom), Vol. 15 (May 1973), pp. 169–81.

207 *"Problems of Technology Absorption in Chinese Industry"*
————. *American Economic Review,* Vol. 65 (May 1975), pp. 383–88.

208 *"A Firsthand Study of Marketing in Communist China"*
Richman, Barry. *Journal of Retailing,* Vol. 46 (Summer 1970), pp. 27–47, 59.

209 *"Ideology and Management: The Chinese Oscillation"*
————. *Columbia Journal of World Business,* Vol. 6 (January–February 1971), pp. 23–33.

210 *"Small Industry and the Chinese Model of Development"*
Riskin, Carl. *China Quarterly* (United Kingdom), No. 46 (April–June 1971), pp. 245–73.

211 *Balance in Coastal and Inland Industrial Development in the People's Republic of China*
Roll, Charles Robert, Jr., and Yeh, Kung-chia. Doc. No. P–5505. Santa Monica, Calif.: Rand Corporation, April 1975. 29 pp.

212 *Rural Industrialization in China*
Sigurdson, Jon. Cambridge, Mass.: Harvard University Press, 1977. 281 pp.

213 *"A Peasant-Built Ammonia Plant"*
     Simon, Eric. *Chemical Technology*, Vol. 5 (October 1975), pp. 582–84.
214 *"China's Computer Industry"*
     Szuprowicz, Bohdan O. *Datamation*, Vol. 21 (June 1975), pp. 83–88. The author earlier published an
     evaluation of the computer industry in China as *"Computers in Mao's China", New Scientist* (United
     Kingdom), March 15, 1973, pp. 598–600.
215 *"Electronics in China"*
     ————. *US-China Business Review*, Vol. 3 (May–June 1976), pp. 20–43.
216 *China: Role of Small Plants in Economic Development*
     US Central Intelligence Agency. Reference Aid Series, No. A (ER) 74–60, May 1974. 18 pp. Data on
     agricultural machinery, chemical fertilizers, cement, hydroelectric power, coal, iron and steel, etc.
     Available from Photoduplication Service, Library of Congress, Washington, D.C.
217 *Production of Machinery and Equipment in the People's Republic of China and Prices of Machinery and
     Equipment in the People's Republic of China*
     ————. Reference Aid Series, May 1975. Available from Photoduplication Service, Library of
     Congress, Washington, D.C.
218 *People's Republic of China: Chemical Fertilizer Supplies, 1949–1974*
     ————. Reference Aid Series, August 1975. Available from Photoduplication Service, Library of
     Congress, Washington, D.C.
219 *"China's Chemicals"*
     Yuan, Sy. *US-China Business Review*, Vol. 2 (November–December 1975), pp. 37–53. Reprinted as
     China Sector Report No. 3. Washington, D.C.: National Council for US–China Trade, March 1976.
220 *"China's Management Practices: A Firsthand View"*
     ————, *Hydrocarbon Process*, Vol. 53 (December 1974), pp. 101–4 *passim.*

II-D. ENERGY AND MINERALS

China still relies on coal as its basic source of energy. Water is becoming more important, however, and small hydroelectric works are increasingly evident in rural areas. The extent of China's petroleum resources and their potential for export are still matters of controversy. Nevertheless, the development of petroleum—now proceeding apace—will undoubtedly make oil and natural gas important parts of China's fuel balance in the future. As for China's mineral resources, they are varied and substantial; mineral exploitation is expanding rapidly, especially in western China.

The works cited below discuss China's fuel resources and energy balance from varying points of view. Petroleum has clearly excited the greatest interest among outside observers. Wang and Weintraub offer reports on the levels and kinds of minerals supplies in the People's Republic.

221 *The Taching Oilfield: A Maoist Model for Economic Development*
     Chan, Leslie W. Contemporary China Paper, No. 8. Canberra: Australian National University Press,
     1974. 28 pp.
222 *China's Petroleum Industry: Output, Growth and Export Potential*
     Chieng, Chu-yuon. New York: Praeger, 1976, 244 pp.
223 *"China's Petroleum Industry: An Enigma"*
     Connell, H. R. *American Petroleum Geologists Bulletin*, Vol. 58 (October 1974), pp. 2157–72.
224 *"Energy in the People's Republic of China"*
     Dean, Genevieve C. *Energy Policy* (United Kingdom), Vol. 2 (March 1974), pp. 33–54.
225 *China, Oil, and Asia: Conflict Ahead?*
     Harrison, Selig S. New York: Columbia University Press, 1977, pp. 317.
226 *"China's Coal Export Potential"*
     Ikonnikov, A. B. *Australian Outlook* (Australia), Vol. 27 (August 1973), pp. 179–90.
227 *"The Petroleum Industry in China"*
     Kambara, Tatsu. *China Quarterly* (United Kingdom), No. 60 (October–December 1974), pp.
     699–719. Revised and translated from Japanese.
228 *The Petroleum Industry of the People's Republic of China*
     Ling, H. C. Stanford: Hoover Institution, 1975. 264 pp. Includes full texts of relevant New China News
     Agency articles.

229 *China's Petroleum Industry*
National Council for US-China Trade. Special Report No. 16. Washington, D.C.: National Council for US-China Trade, June 1976. 122 pp.

230 *"Communist China's Oil Exports"*
Smil, Vaclav. *Issues and Studies* (Taiwan), Vol. 11 (March 1975), pp. 71–78.

231 *China's Energy Achievements, Problems, Prospects*
————. New York: Praeger, 1976. See also *China Quarterly* (United Kingdom), No. 65 (January–March 1976). pp. 54–82.

232 *"Exploiting China's Hydro Potential"*
————. *International Water Power and Dam Construction* (United Kingdom), Vol. 28 (March 1976), pp. 19–26. Emphasizes use of local materials, labour-intensive techniques.

233 *Energy Balance Projections for the People's Republic of China, 1975–1985*
US Central Intelligence Agency. Reference Aid Series, No. A (ER) 75–75, November 1975. 32 pp. Available from Photoduplication Service, Library of Congress, Washington, D.C. Reprinted as Special Report No. 15. Washington, D.C.: National Council for US-China Trade, 1975.

234 *Mineral Resources and Basic Industries in the People's Republic of China*
Wang, K. P. Boulder: Westview Press, 1977. 211 pp.

235 *"China's Minerals and Metals"*
Weintraub, Peter. *US-China Business Review*, Vol. 1 (November–December 1974), pp. 38–53. Reprinted as China Sector Report No. 1. Washington, D.C.: National Council for US-China Trade, February 1976.

II-E. SCIENCE AND TECHNOLOGY

In science as in other areas of Chinese development, the People's Republic has generally pursued a policy of "walking on two legs". On the one hand, there has been a strong push for participation of the masses in scientific and technological activities; on the other hand, the Chinese leadership has been well aware of the need to develop the modern industrial sector by importing or adapting advanced foreign technology. Like other development policies, however, policies toward science have fluctuated substantially over the past twenty-five years, depending on the weight given the "politics in command" principle at different periods of time.

Most of the information available to Westerners on the present status of science and technology is derived from the reports of scientists and engineers who have visited China in recent years—such as Yang's report on his visits to the Chinese academies of biochemistry, physiology, and nuclear physics. Dean's bibliographies provide an indication of what was (or was not) known about China's science and technology in the early 1970s. No recent substitute exists for the now outdated, field-by-field survey of Chinese science and technology done by the National Academy of Sciences in 1961.

Readers particularly interested in the process of technology selection in the People's Republic should also review the works, listed in section II-C on industry, which discuss the choice of industrial technology by specific sector.

236 *Science and Medicine in the People's Republic of China: Four Asia House Talks*
Asia (special issue), No. 26 (Summer 1972). 84 pp. Contributors include Tien-hsi Cheng (disease control), E. Grey Dimond (medical education), Victor Sidel (medical care), Chen-ning Yang (education and scientific research).

237 *China's Science through Visitors' Eyes*
Berner, Boel. Lund, Sweden: University of Lund Research Policy Programme, 1975, 58 pp. Analysis of questionnaire responses from about 200 Western scientists who have visited the People's Republic in recent years.

238 *"An Interview with Chinese Anthropologists"*
Cooper, Gene. *Current Anthropology*, Vol. 14 (October 1973), pp. 480–82.

239 *"A Note on the Sources of Technological Innovation in the People's Republic of China"*
Dean, Genevieve C. *Journal of Development Studies* (United Kingdom), Vol. 9 (October 1972), pp. 187–99. These themes are also discussed in her article in *Bulletin of the Institute of Development Studies*, Vol. 4, Nos. 2 and 3 (1972), pp. 39–48.

240 *"Science, Technology, and Development: China as a Case Study"*
————. *China Quarterly* (United Kingdom), No. 51 (July–September 1972), pp. 520–34.

241 *Technological Innovation in Chinese Industry: A Bibliography*
————. London: Mansell, 1972. Includes more than 3,000 references.

242 *Science and Technology in the Development of Modern China: An Annotated Bibliography*
————. Research Aids of the East Asian Institute. London: Mansell, 1974. 265 pp.

243 *"The Transfer of Technology to China"*
Dernberger, Robert F. *Asia Quarterly* (Belgium), No. 3 (1974), pp. 229–52.

244 *"The Tour of a Botanist in China"*
Hu, Shin-ying. *Arnoldia*, Vol. 35 (November–December 1975), pp. 264–95.

245 *"A Note on the Choice of Technology in China"*
Ishikawa, Shigeru. *Journal of Development Studies* (United Kingdom), Vol. 9 (October 1972), pp. 161–86.

246 *"Science and the Open-Doors Education Movement"*
Jen, C. K. *China Quarterly* (United Kingdom), No. 64 (October–December 1975), pp. 741–47.

247 *"Physics in China"*
Lubkin, Gloria B. *Physics Today*, Vol. 25 (December 1972), pp. 23–28. Interviews with seven recent visitors to China.

248 *"Research Institutes in the People's Republic of China"*
Nunn, Susan Swannack. *US-China Business Review*, Vol. 3 (March–April 1976), pp. 38–50.

249 *"How the Chinese Scientist Survives"*
Orleans, Leo A. *Science,* Vol. 177, September 8, 1972, pp. 864–66.

250 *"Marine Research in China"*
Ostrom, Bertil, *Nature,* Vol. 267 (June 1977), pp. 794–97.

251 *"Chinese Science Policy: A Comparative Analysis"*
Richter, Maurice N., Jr. *Bulletin of Atomic Scientists*, Vol. 32 (March 1976), pp. 13–16.

252 *"The Chinese Model for Science and Technology: Its Relevance for Other Developing Countries"*
Rifkin, Susan B. *Technological Forecasting and Social Change*, Vol. 7, No. 3 (1975), pp. 257–71.

253 *"Research and Development Policy in China after the Cultural Revolution"*
Schnarch, Alexander. *International Journal of Research Management*, Vol. 9 (January 1976), pp. 28–32.

254 *"Science and Technology in China"*
Shih, Joseph Anderson. *Asian Survey*, Vol. 12 (August 1972), pp. 662–75.

255 *"Technology and Employment in China"*
Sigurdson, Jon. *World Development* (United Kingdom), Vol. 2 (March 1974), pp.

255a *The Politics of Agricultural Mechanisation in China*
Stavis, Benedict. Ithoca, *New York:* Cornell University Press. 288 pp.

256 *Directory of Selected Scientific Institutions in Mainland China*
Surveys and Research Corporation. Stanford: Hoover Institution, 1970. 469 pp. Pre–1966 information on 490 research and development institutions in physical, biological, medical, and agricultural sciences, as well as engineering.

257 *Research and Revolution: Science Policy and Societal Change in China*
Suttmeier, Richard P. Lexington, Mass.: Lexington Books, 1974. 180 pp.

258 *"Recent Developments in the Politics of Chinese Science"*
————. *Asian Survey*, Vol. 17 (April 1977), pp. 264–95.

259 *"Biophysical Research in the People's Republic of China"*
Tien, H. Ti. *Biophysical Journal*, Vol. 15 (June 1975), pp. 621–30.

260 *"High Technology in China"*
Tsu, Raphael. *Scientific American*, Vol. 227 (December 1972), pp. 13–17.

261 *Annotated Bibliography on Science and Technology in China*
US House of Representatives, Committee on Science and Technology. Washington, D.C.: Government Printing Office, 1976. 52 pp.

262 *"Chinese Technology and Economic Capabilities: Is the People's Republic of China a Stabilizing or Destablizing Influence?"*
Wu, Yuan-li. *Orbis*, Vol. 17 (Fall 1973), pp. 880–94.

263 *The Organization and Support of Scientific Research and Development in Mainland China*
————, and Sheeks, Robert. New York: Praeger, 1970. 592 pp.

264 *"Education and Scientific Research in China"*
Yang, Chen-ning. *Asia*, No. 26 (Summer 1972), pp. 74–84.

II-F. EDUCATION

Education has long been a major political issue in the People's Republic, and many of the entries listed below analyze the elements of the "red v. expert" controversy that has raged ever since the Cultural Revolution of the late 1960s. Partly because the educational system has not been fully reestablished, no single publication provides a complete overview of the present situation in China, although several of the studies provide as broad a review as seems feasible. The Kessen volume is a current and useful source on early education and family life, while the special issue of the *Journal of General Education* focuses more on higher education. Ridley and his colleagues have analyzed texts used in secondary schools before the Cultural Revolution; Martin has done the same for elementary texts. (For the major changes in education policy instituted since the death of Mao Tse-tung, see Suzanne Pepper, entry 286. *Ed.*)

In addition to the studies cited in this section, see the studies by Jen (entry 246) and by Yang (264), which analyze problems associated with scientific and technical education, and those by Chen (64) and Prybyla (68), which discuss the effects of the rustication movement on the students sent out to the countryside. Munro's "Egalitarian Ideas and Educational Fact in Communist China", in the Lindbeck collection (349) is also pertinent and perceptive. The various symposia listed in section I-A on development strategy should also be consulted for relevant articles.

265 *The Educational Revolution in China*
     Barendsen, Robert D. Publication No. (OE)73–19102. Washington, D.C.: Department of Health, Education and Welfare, 1973. 52 pp.
266 *"Economic Necessity and Political Ideals in Educational Reform during the Cultural Revolution"*
     Bastid, Marianne. *China Quarterly* (United Kingdom), No. 42 (April–June 1970), pp. 16–45.
267 *Education in China: Tradition and Revolution*
     ————. Geneva: Graduate Institute of International Studies, 1973, 22 pp.
268 *"Impressions of the People's Republic of China: Engineering Education"*
     Bugliarello, G., and Rouse, H. *Mechanical Engineering*, Vol. 97 (April 1975), pp. 28–29.
269 *"Little Apple: How China's Kindergartners Grow"*
     Caldwell, B. *Education Digest*, Vol. 40 (October 1974), pp. 48–50.
270 *"Recent Developments in China's University Recruitment System"*
     Casella. A *China Quarterly* (United Kingdom), No. 62 (April–June 1975), pp. 297–301.
271 *"Politics and Educational Development in China: Patterns of Change and Continuity, 1949–1973"*
     Chen, Liu. *Asian Forum*, Vol. 5 (October–December 1973), pp. 21–33.
272 *Educational Theory in the People's Republic of China: Report of Ch'ien Chun-jui*
     Ch'ien Chun-jui. Honolulu: University of Hawaii Press, 1971. 122 pp. Commentary and translation by John N. Hawkins.
273 *"De-flowering the Cultural Revolution"*
     Cleverly, John, ed. *Change*, Vol. 9 (May 1977), pp. 32–37.
274 *"Chinese Education: Revolution and Development"*
     Fraser, Stewart E., and Hawkins, John N. *Phi Delta Kappan*, Vol. 53 (April 1972), pp. 487–500.
275 *China: The Cultural Revolution, Its Aftermath and Effects on Education and Society: A Bibliography*
     ————, and Hsu, Kuang-liang. Education Libraries Bulletin, Suppl. 16. London: University of London, Institute of Education, 1972. 102 pp. Partially annotated.
275a *Red and Expert: Education on the People's Republic of China*
     Gamberg, Ruth. New York: Schloken Books, 1978.
276 *China: Education since the Cultural Revolution: A Bibliography of English Translations*
     Gregory, Peter B., and Krenkel, Noele. Document No. 100. San Francisco: Evaluation and Research Analysts, 1972. Partially annotated.
277 *Toward a New World Outlook: A Documentary History of Education in the People's Republic of China*
     Hu, Shi Ming and Seitman, Eli. New York: AMS Press, 1977. 335 pp.
278 *Chinese Education under Communism*
     Hun, Chang-tu, ed. Classics in Education, No. 7. New York: Columbia University, Teachers College, 1974. 229 pp.

279 "Schools in the People's Republic of China"
     Joly, R. W. Education Digest, Vol. 39 (March 1974), pp. 2–6.
280 Education in China
     Journal of General Education (special issue), Vol. 26 (Fall 1974), pp. 179–266. Nine contributors.
281 Childhood in China: Report of the American Delegation on Early Childhood Development
     Kessen, William, ed. New Haven: Yale University Press, 1975. 241 pp.
282 Language and Linguistics in the People's Republic of China: An Account Based on the Visit of the
     Linguistics Delegation, October 16–November 13, 1974
     Lehman, Winfred P. Austin: University of Texas Press, 1975. 168 pp.
283 "The Socialization of Children in China and on Taiwan: An Analysis of Elementary School Textbooks"
     Martin, Roberta. China Quarterly (United Kingdom), No. 62 (April–June 1975), pp. 242–61.
284 Education in China
     Mauger, Peter, et al. Modern China Series, No. 5. London: Anglo-Chinese Educational Institute,
     January 1974. 81 pp. Contributors: Roland Berger (middle schools), Patrick Daly (universities), W. P.
     Edmonds (primary schools), Valerie Marrett (examinations), Peter Mauger (general), Sylvia Mauger
     (kindergartens).
285 "Educational Reform in China as a Readjusting Country"
     McDowell, S. Garrett. Asian Survey, Vol. 11 (March 1971), pp. 256–70.
286 "Education and Revolution: The Chinese Model Revisited"
     Pepper, Suzanne. Asian Survey, Vol. XVIII, No. 9 (September 1978), pp. 847–90.
287 "Continuity and Change in Chinese Education"
     Price, Ronald Francis. Asia Quarterly (Belgium), No. 2 (1975), pp. 127–52.
288 Education in Communist China
     ————. Boston: Routledge & Kegan Paul, 1970. 308 pp.
289 "Notes on Chinese Higher Education, 1974"
     Prybyla, Jan S. China Quarterly (United Kingdom), No. 62 (April–June 1975), pp. 271–96.
290 "Secondary Education In Communist China"
     ————. China Report (India), Vol. 10 (September–December 1974), pp. 114–22.
291 The Making of a Model Citizen in Communist China
     Ridley, Charles Price; Godwin, Paul H. B.; and Doolin, Dennis, Jr. Stanford: Hoover Institution, 1971.
     404 pp. An analysis of pre-Cultural Revolution textbooks.
292 Revolutionary Education in China: Documents and Commentary
     Seybolt, Peter J. White Plains, N.Y.: International Arts and Sciences Press, 1973. 408 pp.
293 "Education to the People: Higher Education in China"
     Shor, I. Social Policy, Vol. 5 (November 1974), pp. 30–37.
294 "Education and Science in China"
     Signer, Ethan, and Galston, Arthur. Science, Vol. 175, January 7, 1972, pp. 15–23.
295 "Industrial Education in China Today"
     To, C. Y. Education Digest, Vol. 39 (May 1974), pp. 13–15.
296 "Educational Reform and the Cultural Revolution: The Chinese Evaluation Process"
     Wang, Robert S. Asian Survey, Vol. 15 (August 1975), pp. 758–74.
297 "Big Red Schoolhouse"
     Yee, A. H. Today's Education, Vol. 63 (March 1974), pp. 46–50.

II-G. HEALTH

Improving the country's health conditions was one of the early priorities of the People's Republic. The multifarious approach pursued by the regime over the past decade can, perhaps, be summarized in three basic strategies: (1) major emphasis on preventive measures rather than curative medicine; (2) a continuing effort to integrate modern and traditional medicine, through full utilization of Chinese herbalists and their drugs; and (3) intensive training of paramedical personnel—the "barefoot doctors"—at varying levels of competence. This approach has succeeded in rapidly reducing the country's mortality rates; foreign visitors are almost unanimously impressed with the conditions of health and sanitation in China.

Perhaps the best overviews of China's medicine and health can be found in the the Quinn and Wegman collections and in the Sidels' book, *Serve the People*. The Kleinman collection includes papers on Malaysia, Thailand, and Taiwan as well as the People's Republic. The detailed and annotated bibliography by Akhta, which covers the period 1949–1974, is useful for those with interests in specific aspects of Chinese health care, including pediatrics, mental health, and medical education. A manual used by barefoot doctors has been translated and published—entry 306a.

298 *Health Care in the People's Republic of China: A Bibliography with Abstracts*
     Akhtar, Shahid. Ottawa: International Development Research Centre, 1975. 182 pp.
299 *"Nutritional Status of China's Children–An Overview"*
     Arena, Joy M. *Nutrition Review*, Vol. 3, No. 10 (October 1974), pp. 289–95.
300 *"Medical Training in China"*
     Berger, Roland. *Eastern Horizon* (Hong Kong), Vol. 12, No. 1 (1973), pp. 28–44.
301 *Acupuncture Anesthesia in the People's Republic of China*
     Chen, James Y. P. Washington, D.C.: National Institutes of Health, 1973. 106 pp.
302 *"Medicine in Modern China"*
     Cheng, T. O. *Journal of the American Geriatrics Society*, Vol. 21 (July 1973), pp. 289–313. A similar discussion of the issue may be found in his article in *Annals of Internal Medicine*, Vol. 78 (February 1973), pp. 285–90.
303 *"A Surgeon's Diary of His Visit to China"*
     de Bakey, Michael E. *Resident and Staff Physician*, Vol. 22 (March 1976), pp. 73–84.
304 *More than Herbs and Acupuncture*
     Dimond, E. Grey. New York: Norton, 1975. 223 pp.
305 *"Prevention and Treatment of Mental Illness in the People's Republic of China"*
     Ho, D. H. F. *American Journal of Orthopsychiatry*, Vol. 44 (July 1974), pp. 620–36.
306 *"Yesterday and Today: Dentistry in China"*
     Hudson, N. C. *Journal of the American Dental Association*, Vol. 84 (May 1972), pp. 985–93.
306a *A Barefoot Doctor's Manual*
     Human Revolutionary Health Committee, London: Routledge & Kegan Paul; and Philadelphia: Running Press. 372 pp.
307 *Medicine in Chinese Cultures: Comparative Studies of Health Care in Chinese and Other Societies*
     Kleinman, Arthur K.; Kunstadter, Peter; Alexander, E. Russell; and Gale, James L., eds. A publication of the Geographic Health Studies Project. Publication No. (NIH) 75–653. Washington, D.C.: Government Printing Office, 1975. 799 pp. Forty-nine contributors.
308 *"Herbal Pharmacology and Medical Therapy in the People's Republic of China"*
     Lasagna, Louis. *Annals of Internal Medicine*, Vol. 83 (December 1975), pp. 887–93.
309 *Chinese Herbal Medicine*
     Li, C. P. Publication No. (NIH) 75–732. Washington, D.C.: National Institutes of Health, 1974. 120 pp.
310 *"Politics and Health Care in China: The Barefoot Doctors"*
     Li, Victor H. *Stanford Law Review*, Vol. 27 (February 1975), pp. 827–40.
311 *Herbal Pharmacology in the People's Republic of China: A Trip Report of the American Herbal Pharmacology Delegation*
     National Academy of Sciences. Washington, D.C.: National Academy of Sciences, 1975. 269 pp.
312 *Report of the Medical Delegation to the People's Republic of China, 15 June–6 July 1973*
     ————. Washington, D.C.: National Academy of Sciences, 1973. 208 pp. Delegation leader: John Hogness. Contributors: M. Cherkasky (organization and policy), J. J. Ingle (dentistry), Ruth W. Lubic (maternity care, nursing), G. I. Lythcott (pediatrics), *et al.*
313 *Health Policies and Services in China, 1974*
     Orleans, Leo A. Washington, D.C.: Government Printing Office, 1974. 41 pp. Prepared for the US Senate, Committee on Labour and Public Welfare, Subcommittee on Health.
314 *"Barefoot Doctors in China: People, Politics, and Paramedicine"*
     Pickowicz, Paul G. *Eastern Horizon* (Hong Kong), Vol. 11, No. 5 (1972), pp. 25–38.
315 *Medicine and Public Health in the People's Republic of China*
     Quinn, J. R., ed. Publication No. (NIH) 73–67. Washington, D.C.: Department of Health, Education and Welfare, 1973. 333 pp. Contributors: Susan Rifkin (rural areas), Janet Salaff (family life), Victor Sidel (personnel and training), S. D. Yeh (nutrition), *et al.*
316 *Health Strategy and Development Planning: Lessons from the People's Republic of China*
     Rifkin, Susan B., and Kaplinsky, Raphael. Sussex, Eng.: University of Sussex, Science Policy Research Unit, 1973. 36 pp. Also published in *Journal of Development Studies* (United Kingdom), Vol. 9 (January 1973), pp. 213–32. Calls attention to factors which may prevent transfer of Chinese experience to other developing countries.

317 *"Role of Revolutionary Optimism in the Treatment of Mental Illness in the People's Republic of China"*
     Sidel, Ruth. *American Journal of Orthopsychiatry*, Vol. 43 (October 1973), pp. 732–36.

318 *Serve the People: Observations on Medicine in the People's Republic of China*
     Sidel, Victor W., and Sidel, Ruth. New York: Josiah Macy, Jr., Foundation, 1973. 317 pp. Shorter
     articles, by one or both of these authors, discussing the same theme can be found in *Scientific American*,
     Vol. 230 (April 1974), pp. 19–27; *Social Policy*, Vol. 2 (March–April 1972), pp. 25–34; *Asia*, No. 26
     (Summer 1972), pp. 3–30; and other journals.

319 *"Psychiatric Training and Practice in the People's Republic of China"*
     Walls, P.D.; Walls, L. H.; and Langsley, D. G. *American Journal of Psychiatry*, Vol. 132 (February
     1975), pp. 121–28.

320 *Public Health in the People's Republic of China*
     Wegman, M. E., ed. New York: Josiah Macy, Jr., Foundation, 1973. 354 pp. Contributors: Chu-yuan
     Cheng (manpower), A. Minkowski (maternal and child health), W. K. Ng (nutrition), Ruth and Victor
     Sidel (education and training), R. Worth (disease control), *et al.*

321 *Rural Nutrition in China*
     Whyte, R. O. Hong Kong: Oxford University Press, 1972. 54 pp.

322 *Medical Care Systems in Developing Countries and the Chinese Approach*
     Wilenski, P. S. Canberra: Australian National University Press, forthcoming.

323 *Health Care in China: An Introduction*
     World Council of Churches, Christian Medical Commission. Geneva: World Council of Churches,
     1974. 140 pp.

324 *"Medical and Health Work in Rural Areas"*
     Ying, Kuei-fang. *Issues and Studies* (Taiwan), Vol. 10 (September 1974), pp. 73–80.

325 *"Selected Bibliography on Recent Developments in Medicine and Public Health in the People's Republic
     of China"*
     Yu, L. C. *American Journal of Public Health*, Vol. 64 (April 1974), pp. 406–8.

II-H. POPULATION

The size and rate of growth of China's population continue to be mysteries outside
China and, most probably, inside China as well. The only census taken in the People's
Republic was in 1953, and the population of 582,600,000 reported for that year is still
the base for all projections. Current Western estimates range from 800,000,000 to
950,000,000 and estimates of the rate of population growth range from 1.5 per cent to
2.3 per cent.

Most of the entries in this section describe China's efforts to reduce the nation's
fertility—efforts which seem to be showing significant results. Other entries—especially
Orleans' *"China's Population: Can the Contradictions be Resolved?"*—discuss the
problems associated with estimating China's population and analyze some alternative
estimates.

In addition to the works cited below, the reader will find useful articles by John
Aird in the 1968 and the 1972 collections of the Joint Economic Committee of the US
Congress (entries 40 and 41).

326 *"China's Planned Birth Program and Its Transferability"*
     Chen, Pi-chao. *Studies in Family Planning*, Vol. 6 (October 1975), pp. 354–66.

327 *"China's Population Programme at the Grass-Roots Level"*
     ————. *Studies in Family Planning*, Vol. 4 (August 1973), pp. 219–27. Also included in *Population:
     Perspective 1973*, by Harrison Brown *et al.* San Francisco: Freeman, Cooper, 1973, pp. 79–95. Planned
     birth material from five training texts are summarized in an appendix.

328 *"Population and Health Policy in the P.R.C."*
     ————. Washington, D.C.: Smithsonian Institution Interdisciplinary Communications Programme,
     Occasional Monograph Series No. 9, 1976. 157 pp. Distributed by NEO Press, P.O. Box 32, Peaks
     Island, Maine 04108.

329 *"Observations on Current Fertility Control in China"*
     Djerassi, Carl. *China Quarterly* (United Kingdom), No. 57 (January–March 1974), pp. 40–59. Similar

articles appear in *New England Journal of Medicine*, Vol. 289, September 6, 1973, pp. 533–35, and in *Studies in Family Planning*, Vol. 5 (January 1974), pp. 13–30.

330 *"Health and Family Planning Services in the Chinese People's Republic"*
Faundes, A., and Luukkainen, T. *Studies in Family Planning*, Vol. 3 (July 1972), supplement, pp. 165–76.

331 *"China: Development of Population Policy"*
Fessler, Loren. In *Population: Perspective 1973*, by Harrison Brown *et al.* San Francisco: Freeman, Cooper, 1973, pp. 58–78. See also his *"How Many Hundred Million Chinese?"* (AUFS–EA18, No. 1, January 1972), *"Delayed Marriage and Planned Birth: Translation of a Chinese Birth Control Manual"* (AUFS–EA20, No. 1, January 1973), and *"People's Republic of China and Population Policy"* (AUFS–EA20, No. 3, May 1973). The AUFS Reports are published by American University Field Staff, Hanover, N.H.

332 *Report on the Family Panning Programme in the People's Republic of China*
Katagiri, T. Tokyo: International Planned Parenthood Federation, May 1972. 12 pp. Includes data from a people's commune, a factory workers' residential area, a factory, an urban residential area, and a hospital. A shorter discussion of the same theme is available in his article in *Studies in Family Planning*, Vol. 4 (August 1973), pp. 216–18.

333 *"Population Control in China: A Reinterpretation"*
Morrison, Raymond, and Salmon, Jack D. *Asian Survey*, Vol. 8 (September 1973), pp. 873–90.

334 *China's Experience in Population Control: The Elusive Model*
Orleans, Leo A. Washington, D.C.: Government Printing Office, September 1974. 45 pp. Prepared for the US House of Representatives, Committee on Foreign Affairs, by the Congressional Research Service, Library of Congress.

335 *"China's Population: Can the Contradictions be Resolved?"*
————. *Studies in Family Planning*, Vol. 7 (February 1976), pp. 52–57.

336 *Every Fifth Child: The Population of China*
————. Stanford: Stanford University Press, 1972. 191 pp.

337 *"Institutionalized Motivation for Fertility Limitation in China"*
Salaff, Janet W. *Population Studies* (United Kingdom), Vol. 26 (July 1972), pp. 233–62.

338 *China's Population Struggle: Demographic Decisions of the People's Republic, 1949–1969*
Tien, H. Yuan. Columbus: Ohio State University Press, 1973. 405 pp.

339 *"Fertility Decline via Marital Postponement in China"*
————. *Modern China*, Vol. 1 (October 1975), pp. 447–62.

III. POLITICAL AND SOCIAL CONDITIONS

III-A. POLITICAL INSTITUTIONS AND POWER

The special nature of Chinese politics and political thought suggests that the applicability of China's development experience to other developing countries may be limited. The following selection from the extensive literature available on politics in the People's Republic is not intended to be comprehensive, but rather to provide some useful background for readers primarily interested in development and to underline the specifically Chinese character of the evolving development strategy.

Relatively recent works by several of the best known China specialists are cited. Barnett's 1967 book offers a detailed look at how the People's Republic is administered at central, county, and commune levels. Other entries focus specifically on the People's Liberation Army (PLA), the Chinese Communist Party, and other political institutions. Gittings emphasizes the political and social roles of the PLA, while Whitson provides a comprehensive history of the military from 1927 to 1971. Essays in the Scalapino volume discuss elites on the national, urban, and provincial levels, as well as the roles of urban professors, the military, administrative cadres, and national minorities. Kau (entry 347) includes much material on the developmental role of the PLA.

For a detailed look at how one city has adapted to political change over two decades, see also Vogel's *Canton under Communism* (entry 77) in section I-C on urbanization.

340   *Cadres, Bureaucracy, and Political Power in Communist China*
      Barnett, A. Doak. New York: Columbia University Press, 1967. 563 pp.
341   *Uncertain Passage: China's Transition to the Post-Mao Era*
      —————. Washington, D.C.: Brookings, 1975. 387 pp.
342   *Chinese Communist Politics in Action*
      —————, ed. Seattle: University of Washington Press, 1969. 620 pp. Twelve contributors: R. J. Birrell
      (communes), Joyce Kallgren (social welfare), Ying-mao Kau (ruban elites), Michel Oksenberg (local-
      level leadership), Richard Soloman (Chairman Mao), James R. Townsend (youth), *et al.*
343   *"What do Commissars Do?"*
      Bhagwati, Jagdish N., *World Development* (United Kingdom), Vol. 3 (January–February 1975), pp.
      27–30.
344   *Power and Policy in China*
      Chang, Parris H. University Park: Pennsylvania State University Press, 1975. 276 pp.
345   *"County Administration in Fukien"*
      Falkenheim, Victor C. *China Quarterly* (United Kingdom), No. 59 (July–September 1974), pp.
      518–43.
346   *The Role of the Chinese Army*
      Gittings, John. Oxford: Oxford University Press, 1967. 331 pp. Includes pre-Cultural Revolution data
      on the army's economic contributions.
347   *The People's Liberation Army and China's Nationbuilding*
      Kau, Ying-mao. White Plains, N.Y.: International Arts and Sciences Press, 1973. 407 pp. Documents
      from the official organ of the PLA.
348   *Party Leadership and Revolutionary Power in China*
      Lewis, John Wilson, ed. Cambridge, Eng.: Cambridge University Press, 1970. 422 pp. Eleven con-
      tributors: John Gittings (military), Merle Goldman (party and society), Michel Oksenberg (party and
      society), Stuart Schram (power elites), Benjamin Schwarz (power elites), *et al.*
349   *China: Management of a Revolutionary Society*
      Lindbeck, John, ed. Seattle: University of Washington Press, 1971. 391 pp. Ten contributors: Ellis
      Joffe (military), Chalmers Johnson (authority), Victor Li (law), Donald Munro (education), Michel
      Oksenberg (political hierarchies), Lucien Pye (mass participation), Frederick Teiwes (provincial poli-
      tics), Peter Schran (economic management), *et al.*
350   *China: The Convulsive Society*
      Oksenberg, Michel. Headline Series, No. 203. New York: Foreign Policy Association, December 1970.
      78 pp.
351   *"The Exit Pattern from Chinese Politics and Its Implications"*
      —————. *China Quarterly* (United Kingdom), No. 67 (July–September 1976), pp. 501–18. Discusses
      changes in high-level Chinese leadership and how they have been accomplished.
352   *"Methods of Communication within the Chinese Bureaucracy"*
      —————. *China Quarterly* (United Kingdom), No. 67 (January–March 1974), pp. 1–39.
353   *"Soldiers in the Chinese Economy"*
      Powell, Ralph L. *Asian Survey*, Vol. 11 (August 1971), pp. 742–60.
354   *Elites in the People's Republic of China*
      Scalapino, Robert A., ed. Seattle: University of Washington Press, 1972. 669 pp. Fourteen con-
      tributors: June Dreyer (minorities), Victor Falkenheim (provincial elites), William Whitson (military),
      et al.
355   *The Chinese High Command: A History of Communist Military Politics, 1927–1971*
      Whitson, William. New York: Praeger, 1973. 650 pp.
356   *"Inequality and Stratification in China"*
      Whyte, Martin King. *China Quarterly* (United Kingdom), No. 64 (October–December 1975), pp.
      684–711.

III-B. IDEOLOGY AND THE ROLE OF LAW

Chinese development needs to be considered in the context of Chinese Communist doctrine, beginning with the philosophy of Mao Tse-tung. The works cited below offer a sampling of the rather extensive literature on Chinese ideology, including two collections of writings by Chairman Mao. The works by Schurmann and Schwartz continue to be of importance. More recent studies by MacFarquhar, Solomon, and others emphasize ideology in the context of the Cultural Revolution.

Other entries in this section focus on the role of law in a society dedicated to continuing change. Because law is seen as a function of class struggle, the Chinese have de-emphasized the elaboration of law as an independent set of rules; courts apparently were downgraded after the Cultural Revolution and, even more so, under the 1975 Constitution. Among Western observers, Cohen and Li have made the most thorough analyses, although Cohen's study of the Chinese criminal process is now somewhat dated. Brown and Ruge provide the most up-to-date information. Lubman is rare in paying attention to economic law, at least as it is related to foreign trade; also see his article on trade between the United States and China (entry 116), cited in section I-F on external economic relations.

357 *"Present-day Law in the People's Republic of China"*
     Brown, Richard P. *American Bar Association Journal*, Vol. 61 (April 1975), pp. 475–79.
358 *"Chinese Law: At the Crossroads"*
     Cohen, Jerome Alan. *China Quarterly* (United Kingdom), No. 53 (January–March 1973), pp. 139–143.
359 *The Criminal Process in the People's Republic of China, 1949–1963: An Introduction*
     ————. Cambridge, Mass.: Harvard University Press, 1968. 706 pp.
360 *Liu Shao-ch'i and the Chinese Cultural Revolution: The Politics of Mass Criticism*
     Dittmer, Lowell. Berkeley: University of California Press, 1974. 373 pp.
361 *"China's Quest for a Socialist Solution"*
     Dreyer, June Teufel. *Problems of Communism*, Vol. 24 (September–October 1975), pp. 49–62.
362 *Mao Tse-tung: An Anthology of His Writings*
     Freemantle, Anne, Ed. New York: New American Library, 1962. 297 pp.
363 *Ideology and Politics in Contemporary China*
     Johnson, Chalmers, ed. Berkeley: University of California Press, 1973. 390 pp. Ten contributors: Philip L. Bridgham (international impact), Rennselaer W. Lee (politics of technology), Richard Soloman (origins of ideology), *et al.*
364 *"The Role of Law in Communist China"*
     Li, Victor H. *China Quarterly* (United Kingdom), No. 44 (October–December 1970), pp. 66–111.
365 *"Mao and Mediation: Politics and Dispute Resolution in Communist China"*
     Lubman, Stanley. *California Law Review*, Vol. 55 (November 1967), pp. 1284–1359.
366 *"On Understanding Chinese Law and Legal Institutions"*
     ————. *American Bar Association Journal*, Vol. 62 (May 1976), pp. 597–99.
367 *The Origins of the Cultural Revolution: I, Contradictions Among the People, 1956–1957*
     MacFarquhar, Roderick. New York: Columbia University Press, 1974. 439 pp.
368 *"Ideology and Consciousness in China's Material Development"*
     Meisner, Mitch. *Politics and Society*, Vol. 5, No. 1 (1975), pp. 1–32.
368a *"Dazhai: The Mass Line in Practice"*
     ————. *Modern China*, Vol. 4, No. 1, January 1978, pp. 27–61.
369 *"An Interview with Chinese Legal Officials"*
     Ruge, Gerd. *China Quarterly* (United Kingdom), No. 61 (January–March 1975), pp. 118–26.
370 *Chairman Mao Talks to the People: Talks and Letters, 1956–1971*
     Schram, Stuart R., ed New York: Pantheon, 1974. 352 pp.
371 *Ideology and Organization in Communist China*
     Schurmann, Franz. 2nd. ed. Berkeley: University of California Press, 1968. 642 pp.
372 *Communism and China: Ideology in Flux*
     Schwartz, Benjamin A. Cambridge, Mass.: Harvard University Press, 1968. 254 pp.
373 *Mao's Revolution and the Chinese Political Culture*
     Solomon, Richard H. Berkeley: University of California Press, 1971. 604 pp.
374 *"Gemeinschaft, Gesellschaft, Mobilisation and Administration: The Future of Law in Communist China"*
     Tay, Alice Erh-soon. *Asia Quarterly* (Belgium), No. 3 (1971), pp. 257–304.

III-C. VALUES: CONTINUITY AND CHANGE

Of central interest in most selections in this section is consideration not only of changing values, but also of the continuity of values. Observers tend to emphasize either the newness of life in the People's Republic or the persistence of tradition, albeit in new guises. There is a range of sub-themes among these writers—including explicit efforts by Chinese authorities to eradicate or re-define traditional values; the viability of old values in a modern context; and the pre-People's Republic origin of some twentieth-century values.

A number of selections on family life have been included here, as are the few available reports that focus specifically on social work and social welfare. The work by Hsu-Balzer, Balzer, and Hsu provides an unusually intimate glimpse of everyday life in today's China, complete with photographs. Solomon is particularly concerned with the impact of politics on ordinary life. The studies of family life are, of course, also pertinent to those interested in the status of women, which is focused on more specifically in the next section.

The material on communes cited below complements that in section II-B on agriculture, some entries in section II-F on education, especially the Kessen and Lehman volumes (entries 281 and 282, respectively), are also relevant to changing values and lifestyles in China.

375   *China's Social Policy*
      Ascher, Isaac. Modern China Series, No. 3. London: Anglo-Chinese Educational Institute, revised edition forthcoming.
376   *"Social Work in China"*
      Bacon, M. H. *Social Work*, Vol. 20 (January 1975), pp. 68–69.
377   *"Transportation, Land Use, and Lifestyle in the People's Republic of China"*
      Chang, Chien. *Traffic Engineering*, Vol. 46 (January 1976), pp. 22–25.
378   *"The Chinese Language in Its New Social Context"*
      Fincher, Beverly Hong. *Journal of Chinese Linguistics*, Vol. 1, No. 1 (1973), pp. 163–69.
379   *China Day by Day*
      Hsu-Balzer, Eileen; Balzer, Richard; and Hsu, F. L. K. New Haven: Yale University Press, 1974. 114 pp.
380   *Heroes and Villains in Communist China: The Contemporary Chinese Novel as a Reflection of Life*
      Huang, Joe C. New York: Pica Press, 1974. 345 pp.
381   *"Continuity and Change in the Contemporary Chinese Family"*
      Jacobs, J. Bruce. *Asian Survey*, Vol. 15 (October 1975), pp. 882–91.
382   *"Secular Vision of a New Humanity in People's China"*
      MacInnis, Donald E. *Christian Century*, Vol. 92, March 12, 1975, pp. 249–53. A fuller discussion of this theme is available in his earlier work, *Religious Policy and Practice in Communist China*. New York: Macmillan, 1972.
383   *"The Malleability of Man in Chinese Marxism"*
      Munro, Donald J. *China Quarterly* (United Kingdom), No. 48 (October–December 1971), pp. 609–40.
384   *"Socialism and the Chinese Peasant Family"*
      Parish, William L., Jr. *Journal of Asian Studies*, Vol. 34 (May 1975), pp. 613–30.
385   *"Cinema and Revolution in China: Some Interpretive Themes"*
      Pickowicz, Paul G. *American Behavioral Scientist*, Vol. 17 (January 1974), pp. 328–59.
386   *"Report from a People's Commune"*
      Selden, Mark. *Eastern Horizon* (Hong Kong), Vol. 12, No. 2 (1973), pp. 37–50.
387   *"The Human Services in China"*
      Sidel, Ruth, and Sidel, Victor W. *Social Policy*, Vol. 2 (March–April 1972), pp. 25–34. A similar discussion of the issue is available in *Social Work*, Vol. 17 (November 1972), pp. 5–13.
388   *A Revolution is Not a Dinner Party: A Feast of Images of the Maoist Transformation of China*
      Solomon, Richard H. Garden City, N.Y.: Anchor, 1976. 199 pp.
389   *"Tenants in Revolution: The Tenacity of Traditional Morality"*
      Thaxton, Ralph. *Modern China*, Vol. 1 (July 1975), pp. 323–57.
390   *The Chinese: How They Live and Work*
      Tregear, Thomas R. London: C. Hurst, 1973. 164 pp.
391   *"Polarity and Equality in the Chinese People's Communes"*
      Wertheim, W. F. *Journal of Contemporary Asia* (United Kingdom), Vol. 4, No. 1 (1974), pp. 24–35.

III-D. STATUS OF WOMEN

The books and articles in this section deal primarily with the extensive changes in the status of women in China since 1949—with differing conclusions on their progress in assuming economic and political leadership roles. Davin's writings are of particular relevance to the status of women in other developing countries, as well as to the development process in China itself. Sidel's 1973 study includes her observations on the effects on Chinese women of the 1950 marriage law and of the establishment of day care centres. This and other works cited in this section overlap considerably with entries on the Chinese family listed in the previous section. Family planning and related topics are covered in section II-H on population. Readers with a more detailed interest in the situation of women in China should consult the Martin bibliography for further references.

392 *"Social Revolution and Woman's Emancipation: China During the Great Leap Forward"*
     Andors, Phyllis. *Bulletin of Concerned Asian Scholars*, Vol. 7 (January–March 1975), pp. 33–42.
392a *Women's Liberation in China*
     Broyelle, Claudie. London: Harvester Press, 1977. 174 pp.
393 *"The Role of Women in Chinese Communist Armed Units"*
     Ch'iu, Shih-tung. *Issues and Studies* (Taiwan), Vol. 10, No. 12 (1974), pp. 54–61.
394 *The Women's Movement in China: A Selection of Readings, 1949–1973*
     Croll, Elisabeth. Modern China Series, No. 6. London: Anglo-Chinese Educational Institute, 1974.
     115 pp.
394a *Feminism and Socialism in China*
     ————. London: Routledge & Kegan Paul, 1978. 360 pp.
395 *Women in China*
     Curtin, Kate. New York: Pathfinder, 1975. 95 pp.
396 *"The Implications of Some Aspects of C.C.P. [Chinese Communist Party] Policy toward Urban Women in the 1950s"*
     Davin, Delia. *Modern China*, Vol. 1 (October 1975), pp. 363–78.
397 *Woman-Work: Women and the Party in Revolutionary China*
     ————. Oxford: Oxford University Press, 1976. 244 pp.
398 *"Collectivization, Kinship, and the Status of Women in Rural China"*
     Diamond, Norma. *Bulletin of Concerned Asian Scholars*, Vol. 7 (January–March 1975), pp. 25–32.
399 *"For the Chinese Woman and Child: A New Lifestyle"*
     Johnson, W. O. *Smithsonian*, Vol. 5 (August 1974), pp. 38–47.
399a *About Chinese Women*
     Kristeva, Julie. London: Marion Boyar, 1977. 201 pp.
400 *"The Emancipation of Chinese Women"*
     Leader, Shelah Gilbert. *World Politics*, Vol. 26 (October 1973), pp. 55–79.
401 *Women in Development: An Annotated Bibliography on the Participation of Women in Chinese Society*
     Martin, Diana. Oxford: Commonwealth Bureau of Agricultural Economics, 1975. 208 entries.
402 *"Socialism and the Chinese Peasant Family"*
     Parish, P. *Journal of Asian Studies*, May 1975, pp. 613–30.
403 *Women and Child Care in China*
     Sidel, Ruth. New York: Penguin, 1973. 207 pp.
404 *Women in Modern China*
     Snow, Helen F. The Hague: Mouton, 1967. 264 pp. Profiles of ten "model" Chinese women.
405 *Comrade Chiang-ching: Mao's Wife Self-Revealed.*
     Witke, Roxanne. Boston: Little Brown, 1977. 549 pp.
406 *Women in Chinese Society*
     Wolf, Margery, and Witke, Roxanne, eds. Stanford: Stanford University Press, 1975. 315 pp.
407 *"The Current Women's Movement in the Chinese Mainland"*
     Ying, Kuei-fang. *Issues and Studies* (Taiwan), Vol. 10 (July 1974), pp. 50–63.
408 *Women in China: Studies in Social Change and Feminism*
     Young, Marilyn B. Papers in Chinese Studies, No. 15. Ann Arbor: University of Michigan Press, 1973.
     259 pp. Twelve papers by Delia Davin, Janet Salaff, Roxanne Witke, *et al.*

IV. BASIC SOURCES

IV-A. DOCUMENTS

Important documents of the People's Republic that are available in English include the new 1978 Constitution, the 1953–7 Five-Year Plan (the only one yet published), and the still incomplete collection of Mao Tse-tung's works. The Chai collection listed below supplies a miscellany of basic documents, including writings by Chairman Mao and various resolutions issued by the Chinese Communist Party. *Ten Great Years* is the only readily available, comprehensive collection of official statistics on the Chinese economy; these cover only the first decade of the existence of the People's Republic, but they are the starting point for almost all outside analyses of subsequent economic developments.

409   *Essential Works of Chinese Communism*
        Chai, Winberg, ed. New York: Bantam, 1972. 560 pp. Thirty-one basic documents.
410   *Selected Works of Mao Tse-tung*
        Mao Tse-tung. Peking: Foreign Languages Press, 1961–76. 5 Vols.
411   *Constitution of the People's Republic of China*, 1978.
        In *Documents of the First Session of the Fifth National People's Congress of the People's Republic of China*, Peking: Foreign Languages Press, 1978; and *Peking Review*, No. 11, 17 March 1978.
412   *The First Five-Year Plan for the Development of the National Economy of the People's Republic of China in 1953–1957*
        ————. Peking: Foreign Language Press, 1956. (See entry 417 for availability in the United States.)
413   *Ten Great Years: Statistics of the Economic and Cultural Achievements of the People's Republic of China*
        ————. Peking: Foreign Languages Press, 1956. (See entry 417 for availability in the United States.)

IV-B. TRANSLATION AND CURRENT ANALYSIS SERVICES

Translations and other materials based on People's Republic publications, news releases, and broadcasts are available from a number of sources. For the most part, these materials are probably more useful to the China scholar, with the background to extract significant details from a highly propagandistic and polemical context, than to the general development specialist. Some of these sources—notably China New Analysis and the US Consulate General's periodical, *Current Scene*—do include broad analyses, however.

414   *British Broadcasting Service*
        Broadcast House, London. Part 3 of the BBC's *Summary of World Broadcasts* (SWB) is the "Weekly Economic Report for the Far East"; it includes material from and about the People's Republic.
415   *China News Analysis*
        P.O. Box 13225, Hong Kong. Each issue of this weekly publication focuses on a specific subject. It draws heavily on People's Republic sources for its analyses and interpretations.
416   *International Arts and Sciences Press*
        901 North Broadway, White Plains, New York 10603. *Chinese Economic Studies*, a quarterly journal edited by George C. Wang, carries selections from Japanese sources as well as translations from People's Republic newspapers and magazines. Other translation series issued by the same publisher include *Chinese Education, Law and Government, Sociology and Anthropology, History*, and *Philosophy*, as well as the more general *China Review*.
417   *People's Republic of China, Foreign Languages Press*
        In addition to *ad hoc* books and monographs, the People's Republic publishes three magazines in English, containing translations and specially written material. In the United States, these publications are available from China Books and Periodicals, with branches at 2929–24th St., San Francisco, Calif.; 210 West Madison St., Chicago, Ill.; and 125 Fifth Avenue, New York, N.Y. *China Pictorial* is a popularly written monthly. *China Reconstructs* is an illustrated monthly. *Peking Review* is a weekly journal of political material.

418 *Union Research Institute*
Hong Kong. The Union Research Institute publishes *ad hoc* translations and reports on various topics.
419 *US Consulate General, Hong Kong*
The US Consulate General publishes a number of journals of translations, as well as an analytical journal. All are available from the National Technical Information Service, US Department of Commerce, Springfield, Virginia 22151. *Current Background* is a monthly; each issue focuses on translations relating to a single topic. *Current Scene* is now a monthly (bi-weekly prior to 1971); it contains analytical reports based on People's Republic sources. *Selections from People's Republic of China Magazines* (SPRCM) is a weekly collection of translations. *Survey of People's Republic of China Press* (SPRCP) is issued daily and carries translations from the *People's Daily* and other national newspapers.
420 *US Foreign Broadcast Information Service (FBIS)*
National Technical Information Service, US Department of Commerce, Springfield, Virginia 22151. Monitors broadcasts from the People's Republic. Its *Daily Report: The People's Republic of China* covers a wide range of topics.
421 *US Joint Publications Research Service (JPRS)*
National Technical Information Service, US Department of Commerce, Springfield, Virginia 22151. The JPRS SERIES, *People's Republic of China: Scientific Abstracts*, abstracts material from selected scientific and technical journals. In addition, JPRS publishes *ad hoc* monographs as well as translations of social science material from the People's Republic.

IV-C. BIBLIOGRAPHIES

The most comprehensive bibliography of secondary material on China is that by Skinner; it covers more than three centuries of writings and is elaborately annotated and cross-referenced. The Posner and de Keijzer resource and curriculum guide is particularly helpful for teachers planning courses on China, but its highly selective and annotated list of sources would be of interest to the general reader as well. A useful supplement to these works is the annual bibliography issued by the Association for Asian Studies, which includes an extensive section on China, with several sub-sections of developmental significance.

In addition to the sources cited below, readers should note that bibliographies relating wholly to specific aspects of Chinese development have been included in the appropriate other sections of this bibliography: II-C on industry, II-E on science and technology, II-F on education, II-G on health, and III-D on women. In addition, most of the longer works cited include bibliographic references.

422 *Bibliography of Asian Studies*
Ann Arbor, Michigan: Association of Asian Studies. Annual. Unannotated. Extensive section on China.
423 *A Bibliography of Secondary English Literature on Contemporary Chinese Politics*
Oksenberg, Michel, *et al.* New York: East Asian Institute, Columbia University, n.d.
424 *China: A Resource and Curriculum Guide*
Posner, Arlene, and de Keijzer, Arne J., eds. Chicago: University of Chicago Press, 1976. 2nd ed., rev. 317 pp. Includes a highly selective, annotated bibliography and extensive details on other source materials (films, visual aids, etc.), relating to the People's Republic. Also includes three essays on teaching about China.
425 *Doing Battle with Nature: Landscape Modification and Resource Utilization in the People's Republic of China, 1960–1972*
Salter, Christopher. Eugene, Oregon: University of Oregon, Asian Studies Committee, Occasional Paper No. 1. 95 pp. Covers English-language articles in Chinese and Western press on land-use, natural resources, environment, and development.
426 *Modern Chinese Society: An Analytical Bibliography*
Skinner, G. William, Ed. Stanford: Stanford University Press, 1975. 3 Vols. Entries begin in 1944 and run to the early 1970s. Materials referenced are in Chinese (Vol. 1), Japanese (Vol. 2), and major Western languages (Vol. 3). Comprehensively annotated and cross-referenced.

IV-D. ATLASES, GEOGRAPHIES AND BIOGRAPHIC DICTIONARIES

Shabad is the most comprehensive political and economic geography of China available. Of the atlases cited, Rand McNally is the most readily obtainable. Readers interested in maps of individual cities in China should also consult the CIA publication (entry 76) cited in section I-C on urbanization.

Two lengthy biographic dictionaries of Chinese leaders exist. Interested readers should note that the two-volume *Who's Who* actually covers more of the present Chinese leadership than does the Klein and Clark work published later, although the individual entries are more cursory than the well-researched entries in the later work.

426a *The Transformation of the Chinese Earth*
        Buchanan, Keith. New York: Praeger, 1970
427   *The Times Atlas of China*
        Geelan, P. J. M., and Twitchett, D. C. London: Times Books, 1974. 210 pp.
428   *Biographic Dictionary of Chinese Communism*
        Klein, Donald W., and Clark, Anne B. Cambridge, Mass.: Harvard University Press, 1971. 2 vols. 1196 pp. Includes 433 biographies and 96 outlines of Chinese governmental institutions and their staffs.
429   *An Illustrated Atlas of China*
        New York: Rand McNally, 1972. 80 pp. Based on a 1971 atlas compiled by the US Central Intelligence Agency; includes charts and descriptions.
430   *China's Changing Map: National and Regional Development, 1949–1971*
        Shabad, Theodore. New York: Praeger, 1972. 370 pp.
431   *Who's Who in Communist China*
        Union Research Institute. Kowloon: Union Research Institute, 1969 and 1970. 2 vols.
432   *People's Republic of China: Administrative Atlas*
        US Central Intelligence Agency. Reference Aid Series, March 1975. Available from Photoduplication Service, Library of Congress, Washington, D.C.

Author Index

The numbers refer to entries; those marked "a" are addenda

Champeau, Harold C., 152
Chan, Leslie W., 221
Chang, Chien, 377
Chang, Parris H., 2, 344
Chao, Kang, 26, 128, 153, 154, 155, 192
Cheatham, Thomas E., Jr., 193
Chen, C. S., 64
Chen, E. K. Y., 194
Chen, James Y. P., 301
Chen, Kuan-i, 3, 4, 8, 129
Chen, Liu, 271
Chen, Nai-ruenn, 5, 39, 39a, 130, 157, 195
Chen, Pi-chao, 65, 326, 327, 328
Cheng, Chu-yuan, 8, 46, 90, 196, 320
Cheng, Tien-hsi, 236
Cheng, Tsung O., 302
Cherkasky, Martin, 312
Ch'ien, Chun-jui, 272
Chieng, Chu-yuan, 222
China News Analysis, 415
Ch'iu, Shih-ting, 393
Clark, Anne B., 428
Clark, Colin, 6
Clark, M. Gardner, 197
Clarke, William W., 198
Cleverly, John, 273
Cohen, Jerome Alan, 358, 359
Committee of Concerned Asian Scholars, 7
Connell, H. R., 223
Cooper, Gene, 238
Copper, John Franklin, 104
Craig, Jack, 39
Crick, Bernard, 33
Croll, Elisabeth, 394, 394a
Crook, Frederick W., 159
Current History, 8
Curtin, Kate, 395

Daly, Patrick, 284
Davin, Delia, 396, 397, 408
Dean, Genevieve C., 224, 239, 240, 241, 242
de Bakey, Michael E., 303
de Keijzer, Arne J., 424
Denny, David L., 39, 105, 111
Dernberger, Robert F., 8a, 39a, 243
The Developing Economies, 9
Diamond, Norma, 398
Dimond, E. Grey, 236, 304
Dittmer, Lowell, 360
Djerassi, Carl, 329
Donnithorne, Audrey G., 10, 27, 96, 97, 106, 203
Doolin, Dennis, Jr., 291
Dowty, Stuart, 49
Dreyer, June Teufel, 345, 354, 361

Ecklund, George, 43
Eckstein, Alexander, 11, 12, 107, 108, 131
Edmonds, W. P., 284
Emerson, John Philip, 47, 200
Ensminger, Audrey, 13
Ensminger, M. E., 13
Erisman, Alva Lewis, 41
Etienne, Gilbert, 109, 160

F.A.O., 81, 158, 160a
Falkenheim, Victor C., 2, 345, 354
Far Eastern Economic Review, 132
Faundes, Anibal 330
Fessler, Loren, 331
Field, Robert Michael, 39, 41, 133, 181, 199, 200
Fincher, Beverly Hong, 378
Fletcher, M. D., 48
Fraser, Stewart E., 274, 275
Freemantle, Anne, 362
Fry, Richard, 110
Fung, K. K., 161

Galbraith, John Kenneth, 14
Gale, James L., 307
Galenson, Walter, 5
Galston, Arthur W., 294
Ganiere, Nicole, 201
Gamberg, Ruth, 275a
Gardner, John, 35
Garth, Bryant G., 111
Gayn, Mark, 162
Geelan, P. J. M., 426
Gittings, John, 346, 348
Godwin, Paul H. B., 291
Goldman, Merle, 348
Goldwasser, Janet, 49
Goodstadt, Leo, 15
Gray, Jack, 33, 35, 38
Gregory, Peter B., 276
Gurley, John W., 16

Harper, Paul F., 50
Harrison, Selig S., 225
Hawkins, John N, 274
Heine, Irwin Millard, 112
Heymann, Hans, Jr., 111, 202
Hinton, William, 163
Ho, D. H. F., 305
Hoffmann, Charles, 40, 51, 203
Hogness, John R., 312
Hollister, William H., 40, 203
Howe, Christopher, 16a, 33, 52, 53
Hsia, Ronald, 193, 194, 203
Hsiao, Katherine Huang, 98
Hsu, F. L. K., 379
Hsu, Kuang-liang, 275
Hsu-Balzer, Eileen, 379
Hu, Chang-tu, 278
Hu, Shi Ming, 277
Hu, Shiu-ying, 244
Huang, Joe C., 380
Hudson, N. C., 306
Hung, Fred C., 203

Ikonnikov, A. B., 226
Imfeld, Al, 17
Ingle, J. J., 312
International Arts and Sciences Press, 416
Ishikawa, Shigeru, 134, 245
Ivory, Paul, 66